CONTEMPORARY

American Civics and Government

Annotated Teacher's Edition

Matthew T. Downey

McGraw-Hill Wright Group

The McGraw-Hill Companies

Author
Matthew T. Downey received his Ph.D. in American History from Princeton University. He served as Director of the Clio Project in History-Social Science Education in the Graduate School of Education at the University of California, Berkeley. He also directed the U.C. Berkeley site of the California History-Social Science Project. He has taught at the University of Colorado, the University of California at Los Angeles, and at Louisiana State University. Currently, he directs the Social Science Program and the William E. Hewitt Institute for History and Social Science Education at the University of Northern Colorado.

Senior Editor: Mitch Rosin
Executive Editor: Linda Kwil

Reviewers and Consultants
Jeffrey J. Johll
K–12 District Social Studies Supervisor
Dubuque Community School District
Dubuque, Iowa

Jill DeLuccia
Social Studies Instructor
Atlanta, Georgia

Jill Smith-Mott
Social Studies Instructor
Giddings, Texas

Eleanor Nangle
Social Studies Instructor
Chicago, Illinois

Brian Silva
Social Studies Instructor and Technology Coordinator
Long Beach, California

About the Cover
The images on the cover include (from left to right): Thurgood Marshall, Cesar Chavez, Rosa Parks, Charles Sumner, Sandra Day O'Connor, and the United States Capitol.

Wright Group

ISBN: 0-07-704444-4 (Student Softcover Edition)
ISBN: 0-07-704443-6 (Student Softcover Edition with CD)
ISBN: 0-07-704523-8 (Student Hardcover Edition)
ISBN: 0-07-704524-6 (Student Hardcover Edition with CD)
ISBN: 0-07-704452-5 (Annotated Teacher's Edition)
ISBN: 0-07-704445-2 (Teacher's Resource Binder)

Send all inquiries to:
Wright Group/McGraw-Hill
P.O. Box 812960
Chicago, Illinois 60681

Printed in the United States of America.

2 3 4 5 6 7 8 9 10 QWD/QWD 11 10 09 08 07 06

The McGraw·Hill Companies

Contents

About the Student Edition

The Student Edition of *American Civics and Government* was created for those students who need extra help in reading and comprehension. The text is written at a fifth- to eighth-grade reading level, but it contains the key concepts and basic facts necessary for the study of civics and government at the high school level. Key support is given with pre-reading activities that guide students through a preview of the text and illustrations. These activities activate prior

Unit Opener
Units begin with a summary of the chapters included in the unit. Key concepts are identified and an overview of topics is introduced.

Opening Image
The illustration and text should be used to generate a discussion about the chapters and develop students' prior knowledge about the topics covered.

knowledge. Pre-reading questions and vocabulary focus the students' reading. Opportunity is given halfway through each lesson to stop and organize ideas, and again at the end of each lesson to summarize. Additional support is provided for remedial readers on the Student CD, and with Blackline Masters and Overhead Transparencies in the Teacher's Resource Binder. Extra help for English Language Learners is provided on the Student CD and on additional Blackline Masters on the Teacher's CD.

Chapter

5

CONGRESS

Getting Focused

Skim this chapter to predict what you will be learning.

- **Read the lesson titles and subheadings.**
- **Look at the illustrations and read the captions.**
- **Examine the maps and table.**
- **Review the vocabulary words and terms.**

What do you already know about Congress? Draw a table with three columns in your notebook. Label the first column "What I Know." Label the second column "What I Want to Learn." Label the third column "What I Learned."

Fill in column one before you examine this chapter. Then think about what the photographs and other illustrations show and what the subheadings say. In column two, write some questions you would like to answer as you read the chapter. After you study the chapter, complete column three.

On January 4, 2005, newly elected members of the 109th Congress took an oath of office in the House of Representatives.

Getting Focused

The Getting Focused section of each chapter should be used as a pre-reading activity. Students are directed to read the lesson titles and subheadings, look at illustrations and read captions; examine tables, charts, diagrams, and maps; and review vocabulary words. Then, students are asked to complete an activity in preparation for reading the chapter.

Chapter Opening Image

Each chapter begins with an image. These images are explained in the Annotated Teacher's Edition and represent topics discussed in the chapter. The images should be used to generate classroom discussion about the chapter topics. The images provide connections with key chapter concepts and help to further develop students' prior knowledge.

Thinking on Your Own

This section is a pre-reading activity. Students are encouraged to familiarize themselves with the Focus your Reading questions and the Words to Know words and terms. Some of these activities include working with a partner, doing a short writing assignment, or helping to organize students' reading of the lesson.

Focus Your Reading

Focus Your Reading questions should be read prior to reading the lesson. Students should be encouraged to use the questions as a guide as they read through the lesson text. The questions can also be used as a review after reading.

LESSON 1

The National Legislature

Thinking on Your Own

Suppose you wanted to run for election to the House of Representatives. What issue would you campaign on? Think of an important issue that faces the nation today. Make up a slogan to advertise your viewpoint on the issue.

focus your reading

What are the differences and similarities between representatives and senators?

What is the purpose of reapportionment?

Why is redistricting a political issue?

words to know

bicameral legislature
Senate
House of Representatives
term
recess
adjourn
constituents
incumbent
reapportionment
redistricting
gerrymandering

Congress is the lawmaking body of the national government. It is a **bicameral legislature**, which means that it has two houses. The upper house is the Senate. The lower house is the House of Representatives. The **Senate** is the smaller body, with 100 members. Membership in the **House of Representatives** was set at 435 in 1929. Until then, members were added as new states were admitted to the Union and the population grew.

Congress meets for **terms**, or periods of time. Each term is two years and is divided into two one-year sessions. A term begins on January 3 of odd-numbered years.

Usually Congress meets from January until November or December. There are **recesses**, or breaks, for holidays and vacations. Members of both houses must vote to **adjourn**, or take a break. If either house wants to adjourn for more than three days, the other house must approve. Article I and the Twentieth Amendment set out how Congress organizes itself.

New members of the Senate were sworn in on January 4, 2005.

Words to Know

Vocabulary words and terms are listed in a box at the beginning of each lesson. The words and terms appear in boldfaced print in the lessons. All the vocabulary words and terms are defined in the Glossary/Index at the end of the book. Many are defined in the context of the lesson.

the number of members of the House at 435. The law set up a process for **reapportionment**. Seats are reassigned after each ten-year census based on gains or losses in a state's population. The map on page 106 shows the gains and losses after the 2000 census.

stop and think

How are the House of Representatives and the Senate alike and different? Use information from the table on page 105 to create a Venn diagram in your notebook. Share your diagram with a partner. Discuss whether you have included all of the important facts.

Redistricting

When states gain or lose seats in the House of Representatives, they must redraw their districts. This is called **redistricting**. State legislatures draw new congressional districts. For example, after the 2000 census, California gained one representative for a total of 53 members in the House. The state legislature redrew its districts to add one more. Connecticut had the opposite problem. It had to collapse its six districts into five.

The political party in power in a state often tries to set up districts so that its members will win elections.

ideas to remember

Incumbents generally win reelection because

- it is easier for them to raise campaign funds.
- they are better known than challengers.
- their districts were drawn to favor their party.
- they help their constituents solve problems.

Congressional Apportionment

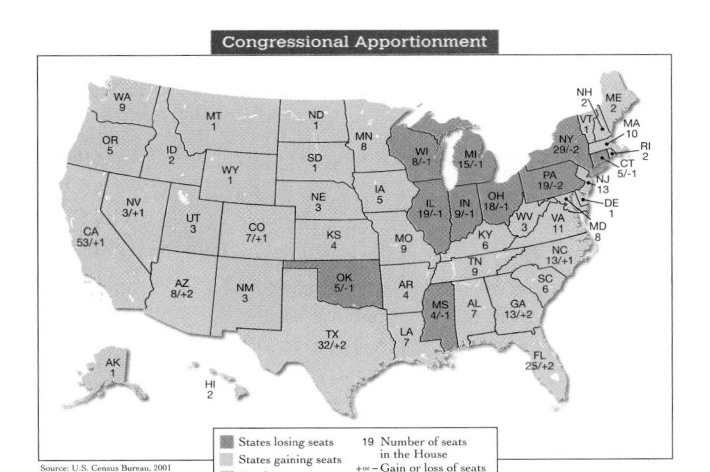

Stop and Think

Stop and Think activities are designed to help students organize and interact with the material they have just read so that it can be remembered. They are during-reading activities.The activity provides a stopping point midway through the lesson and encourages students to think about what they have read.

Ideas to Remember

Some chapters include an Ideas to Remember box. These are intended to help students remember critical points in the text and link them to prior knowledge.

Putting It All Together

At the end of each lesson is a Putting It All Together activity. These activities tie together the key concepts of the lessons. They often involve using a graphic organizer or creating a piece of written work. They frequently ask students to work together or discuss ideas with a partner to expand their viewpoint or understanding and serve as a post-reading activity. Students should be encouraged to incorporate key elements from each lesson into the Putting It All Together activities.

Redistricting Example: North Carolina Congressional Districts, 1992

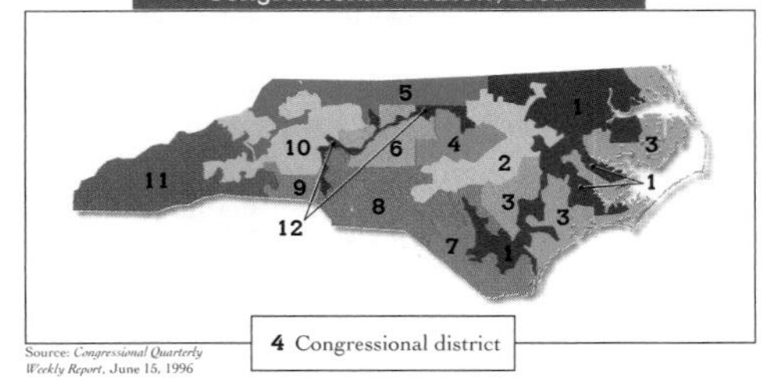

Source: Congressional Quarterly Weekly Report, June 15, 1996

As a result, the shape of congressional districts is sometimes very strange. Creating a district to favor one party over another is called **gerrymandering**.

There are two ways to gerrymander districts. One way is to push as many voters from the minority party as possible into a few districts. Then voters from the party in power become the majority in most of the districts. The second way is to divide the minority party's voters into many districts. The result is the same. The party in power is able to elect more of its candidates to office.

Landmark Supreme Court Cases: Redistricting

- ***Wesberry* v. *Sanders*** (Georgia, 1964): The difference in the number of voters in Georgia's new districts violated the Constitution. The Court ruled that the Framers intended that votes have equal value. This is the principle of "one person, one vote." As a result, congressional districts in all states now have about the same number of voters, 650,000.

- ***Shaw* v. *Reno*** (North Carolina, 1993): Race cannot be used as the major factor in redistricting. The purpose of creating districts with a majority of African Americans was to elect more African Americans to office. The Supreme Court ruled that these districts violated the Fourteenth Amendment rights of white voters. This ruling also applied to states that drew new districts with a majority of Latino voters.

Over the years, redistricting has resulted in several important Supreme Court decisions. Read the landmark cases on page 107 to learn about these decisions.

Remember, according to Article 1, no matter how few people a state has, it must have at least one representative.

Putting It All Together

Imagine that you are a member of Congress who wants to be reelected for another term. With a partner, discuss the things you can do to improve your chances of reelection. Write a paragraph in your notebook explaining what you have decided upon.

This 1812 political carto shows how political distri were redrawn the advantage Governor Eldridge Ge

Landmark Supreme Court Cases

Landmark Supreme Court cases are presented throughout the book. These can be used to extend the curriculum and provide a broader, national scope to the topic being discussed in the lesson.The Appendix also contains information about key Supreme Court cases.

Biography

Biographies are included in select chapters. The biographies draw attention to individuals pertaining to the issues covered in the chapter.

Chapter 2: James Madison (1751–1836)
Chapter 21: Ming Chin (1942–)
Chapter 22: Shirley Clarke Franklin (1945–)
Chapter 24: Wangari Maathai (1940–)

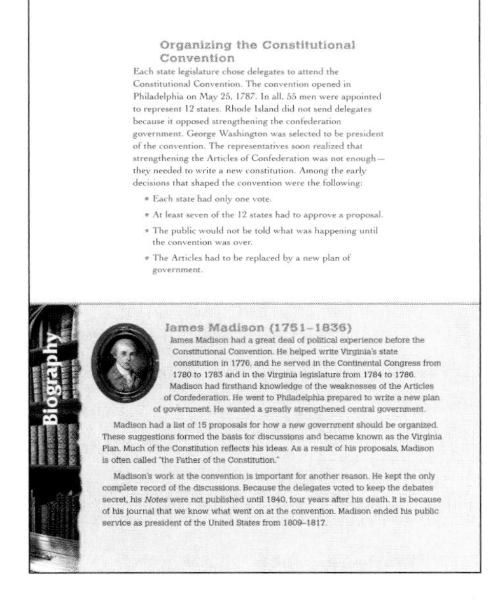

Organizing the Constitutional Convention

Each state legislature chose delegates to attend the Constitutional Convention. The convention opened in Philadelphia on May 25, 1787. In all, 55 men were appointed to represent 12 states. Rhode Island did not send delegates because it opposed strengthening the confederation government. George Washington was selected to be president of the convention. The representatives soon realized that strengthening the Articles of Confederation was not enough—they needed to write a new constitution. Among the early decisions that shaped the convention were the following:

- Each state had only one vote.
- At least seven of the 12 states had to approve a proposal.
- The public would not be told what was happening until the convention was over.
- The Articles had to be replaced by a new plan of government.

Biography

James Madison (1751–1836)

James Madison had a great deal of political experience before the Constitutional Convention. He helped write Virginia's state constitution in 1776, and he served in the Continental Congress from 1780 to 1783 and in the Virginia legislature from 1784 to 1786. Madison had firsthand knowledge of the weaknesses of the Articles of Confederation. He went to Philadelphia prepared to write a new plan of government. He wanted a greatly strengthened central government.

Madison had a list of 15 proposals for how a new government should be organized. These suggestions formed the basis for discussions and became known as the Virginia Plan. Much of the Constitution reflects his ideas. As a result of his proposals, Madison is often called "the Father of the Constitution."

Madison's work at the convention is important for another reason. He kept the only complete record of the discussions. Because the delegates voted to keep the debates secret, his *Notes* were not published until 1840, four years after his death. It is because of his journal that we know what went on at the convention. Madison ended his public service as president of the United States from 1809–1817.

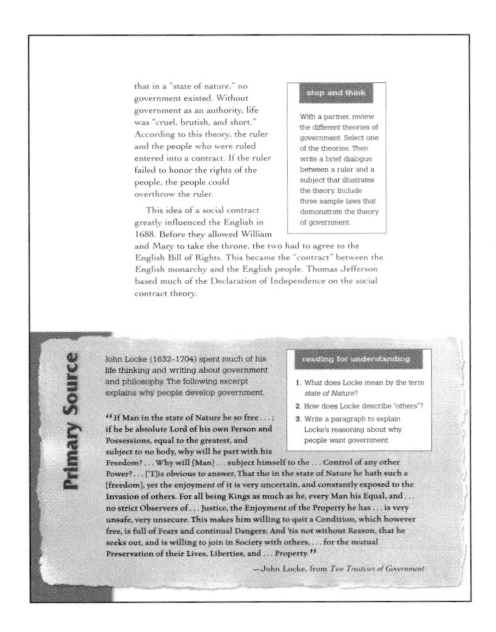

that in a "state of nature," no government existed. Without government as an authority, life was "cruel, brutish, and short." According to this theory, the ruler and the people who were ruled entered into a contract. If the ruler failed to honor the rights of the people, the people could overthrow the ruler.

This idea of a social contract greatly influenced the English in 1688. Before they allowed William and Mary to take the throne, the two had to agree to the English Bill of Rights. This became the "contract" between the English monarchy and the English people. Thomas Jefferson based much of the Declaration of Independence on the social contract theory.

stop and think

With a partner, review the different theories of government. Select one of the theories. Then write a brief dialogue between a ruler and a subject that illustrates the theory. Include three sample laws that demonstrate the theory of government.

Primary Source

John Locke (1632–1704) spent much of his life thinking and writing about government and philosophy. The following excerpt explains why people develop government.

"If Man in the state of Nature be so free . . . ; if he be absolute Lord of his own Person and Possessions, equal to the greatest, and subject to no body, why will he part with his Freedom? . . . Why will [Man] . . . subject himself to the . . . Control of any other Power? . . . [T]is obvious to answer, That tho in the state of Nature he hath such a [freedom], yet the enjoyment of it is very uncertain, and constantly exposed to the Invasion of others. For all being Kings as much as he, every Man his Equal, and . . . no strict Observers of . . . Justice, the Enjoyment of the Property he has . . . is very unsafe, very unsecure. This makes him willing to quit a Condition, which however free, is full of Fears and continual Dangers; And 'tis not without Reason, that he seeks out, and is willing to join in Society with others, . . . for the mutual Preservation of their Lives, Liberties, and . . . Property."

—John Locke, from *Two Treatises of Government*

reading for understanding

1. What does Locke mean by the term *state of Nature*?
2. How does Locke describe "others"?
3. Write a paragraph to explain Locke's reasoning about why people want government.

Primary Source

Select chapters include a Primary Source feature. The documents represent the issues covered in the chapter, and are often used to enhance the content of the chapter.

Chapter 1: John Locke's *Two Treatises of Government*
Chapter 10: The Pendleton Act (1883)
Chapter 12: The Influence of One Justice on Another
Chapter 14: Oath of Affirmation for New Citizens
Chapter 15: Passing Judgment on a Party's Policies
Chapter 17: What Polls Say About the Undecided Voter
Chapter 20: U.S. Agency for International Development

People in the News

Select chapters include a People in the News feature. These are used to enhance the content of the chapter.

Chapter 4: Candy Lightner and MADD
Chapter 5: Congress's Informal Networks—the Caucus
Chapter 9: President George W. Bush
Chapter 16: Antonio Gonzalez (1957–)
Chapter 23: Mohamed ElBaradei and the IAEA

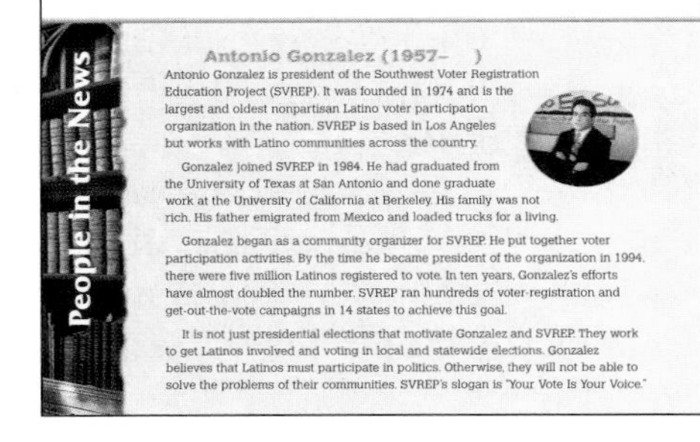

In all, there are 538 electoral votes. To become president, a candidate must get 270 votes. Sometimes, a candidate may win a huge number of electoral votes. For example, in 1980, Ronald Reagan defeated President Jimmy Carter by 489 votes to 49. Elections may also be much closer. In the 2000 election, George W. Bush won 271 votes to 266 for Al Gore. In the popular vote, Gore won 500,000 more votes. However, it is the electoral vote that counts in the election for president, not the popular vote.

Putting It All Together

How is a presidential election similar to and different from other elections? Discuss this question with a partner. Take notes as you talk. Then create a Venn diagram to show the differences and similarities. Refer to the notes you made in the Thinking on Your Own activity at the start of the lesson for ideas.

People in the News

Antonio Gonzalez (1957–)

Antonio Gonzalez is president of the Southwest Voter Registration Education Project (SVREP). It was founded in 1974 and is the largest and oldest nonpartisan Latino voter participation organization in the nation. SVREP is based in Los Angeles but works with Latino communities across the country.

Gonzalez joined SVREP in 1984. He had graduated from the University of Texas at San Antonio and done graduate work at the University of California at Berkeley. His family was not rich. His father emigrated from Mexico and loaded trucks for a living.

Gonzalez began as a community organizer for SVREP. He put together voter participation activities. By the time he became president of the organization in 1994, there were five million Latinos registered to vote. In ten years, Gonzalez's efforts have almost doubled the number. SVREP ran hundreds of voter-registration and get-out-the-vote campaigns in 14 states to achieve this goal.

It is not just presidential elections that motivate Gonzalez and SVREP. They work to get Latinos involved and voting in local and statewide elections. Gonzalez believes that Latinos must participate in politics. Otherwise, they will not be able to solve the problems of their communities. SVREP's slogan is "Your Vote Is Your Voice."

appeals involving patents and copyrights that were heard in a federal district court; and decisions made in some executive departments. Unlike the other federal appeals courts, the Court of Appeals for the Federal Circuit may take a case from any area of the country. Few cases ever go to the Supreme Court from this court. Like the 12 courts of appeals, there are no trials in the Court of Appeals for the Federal Circuit.

The Court of International Trade hears cases related to tariffs and other trade issues. A **tariff** is a tax on imports, or goods coming into the country for sale. The court sits in New York, but travels to other cities with major ports.

Legislative, or Special, Courts

Congress created the legislative courts to deal with particular issues. These issues are related to the power of Congress to carry out its legislative powers. Look at the diagram on page 206 to see where appeals from each court are heard.

The Government Printing Office

Need a copy of a Supreme Court decision? Want to read what your representative or senator said in Congress today? Looking for a committee's report on homeland security? The Government Printing Office (GPO) can provide each of these documents. The GPO prints the daily *Congressional Record* and the *Federal Register*. It also prints everything from Supreme Court decisions and executive department reports to consumer information and national park guides.

The mission of the GPO is "Keeping Americans Informed." Its Web site says that the GPO "is the federal government's primary centralized resource for gathering, cataloging, producing, providing, and preserving published information in all its forms." This means the GPO prints hard copies of government documents and also produces them in digital formats. The GPO's Web site provides 275,000 documents free to anyone with an Internet connection. Printed products such as booklets and full-length books are provided for the cost of printing.

For example, in 2004, the GPO provided the complete copy of *The 9-11 Commission Report* online at no cost.

Civics Today

Civics Today or Speaking of Government

Select chapters include a Civics Today or Speaking of Government. The topics featured represent the issues covered in the chapter, and are often used to enhance the content of the chapter.

Chapter 3: National Constitution Center
Chapter 6: Library of Congress
Chapter 7: Helping Constituents Across Maine
Chapter 8: Presidential Libraries
Chapter 11: The Government Printing Office
Chapter 13: Youth Court
Chapter 18: Making Money: The U.S. Mint and the Bureau of Engraving and Printing
Chapter 19: Consumer Protection

Participate in Government

The Participate in Government pages offer studentsspecific ways to become more involved in their community.

Chapter 1: Volunteer for Community Service
Chapter 2: Register to Vote
Chapter 3: Work for a Candidate
Chapter 4: Become an Informed Voter
Chapter 5: Ask Your Senators or Representative
Chapter 6: Contact a Government Agency
Chapter 7: Contribute to a Political Campaign
Chapter 8: Be a Poll Watcher
Chapter 9: Become a Candidate
Chapter 10: A Career in Government
Chapter 11: Serve on a Jury
Chapter 12: File a Civil Rights Complaint
Chapter 13: Apply for a Green Card
Chapter 14: Become a Naturalized Citizen
Chapter 15: Join a Political Party—or Not
Chapter 16: Join an Interest Group
Chapter 17: Analyze Public Opinion Polls
Chapter 18: File Your Income Tax
Chapter 19: The Census: Fill It Out and Be Counted
Chapter 20: Register for Selective Service
Chapter 21: Get a Driver's License
Chapter 22: Volunteer for a Local Government Commission
Chapter 23: Use Government Resources
Chapter 24: Apply for a Passport

Participate in Government

Be a Poll Watcher

A poll watcher is called a poll checker in some states. *Poll* is another word for ballot, or vote. Poll watchers monitor, or check, what goes on at the polling place. They are volunteers working for a political party. Their job is to make sure that anyone from their party who is registered to vote is allowed to vote. They also make sure that no one votes more than once.

Poll watchers sit near the check-in table with election workers. A voter comes to the table to sign in. An election worker calls out the voter's name. The poll checkers read down their lists. If the voter is a Republican, the Republican poll watcher checks off his or her name. If the voter is a Democrat, the Democratic poll watcher checks it off.

Suppose there is a problem. A voter is newly registered. By accident, his or her name is not yet in the registration book. The poll watcher watches to make sure that the voter is allowed to cast a provisional ballot.

Poll watchers may not wear any political buttons or signs. They may not talk about a candidate while on duty. However, they may carry signs and ask voters to vote for their candidate outside the polling place.

- Check the phone book for the number of your local or county political party committee. Call and ask what the qualifications are to be a poll watcher.
- Visit your local candidates' offices.

The Presidency 167

Skill Builder

Outline Information

An outline is an organized listing of information. Only the most important information about a topic is presented. The form for an outline is always a combination of Roman and Arabic numerals and capital and small letters.

I. Roman numerals for main ideas
  A. Capital letters for important details
    1. Arabic numerals for supporting details
      a. Small letters for less important details

Use Roman numerals for the biggest ideas—the main ideas. Use capital letters, Arabic numerals, and small letters as the information gets more detailed. If the information is not too detailed, you might need only capital letters or capital letters and Arabic numerals.

Outlines are useful for studying and for writing. Outlining a lesson or chapter helps to focus on just the important information to study. Outlining before writing an assignment helps to organize main ideas and supporting details.

A partial outline for Lesson 1 looks like this:

I. The Presidency
  A. Qualifications
    1. Native-born
    2. At least thirty-five years old
  B. Campaign chest
II. The Job of Vice President

Complete these activities.

1 Outline Lesson 2 to help you study the information.

2 Write an essay of at least three paragraphs to describe how cabinet members are chosen and what cabinet members do. Before you write, plan your writing by creating an outline. Use one Roman numeral for each paragraph. Add information with capital letters and Arabic numerals to help you fill out each paragraph.

168 Chapter 8

Skill Builder

Skill Builder pages address key skills necessary for successful mastery of social studies concepts. Skills include:

Chapter 1: Identifying Main Idea and Supporting Details
Chapter 2: Analyzing Timelines
Chapter 3: Reading a Diagram
Chapter 4: Participating in Discussions
Chapter 5: Read a Congressional District Map
Chapter 6: Summarizing and Paraphrasing
Chapter 7: Understand the Difference Between Percents and Actual Numbers
Chapter 8: Outline Information
Chapter 9: Analyze Primary and Secondary Sources
Chapter 10: Distinguish Fact from Opinion
Chapter 11: Draw Conclusions
Chapter 12: Understand Cause and Effect
Chapter 13: Identify Point of View
Chapter 14: Recognize Bias
Chapter 15: Recognize Propaganda
Chapter 16: Interpret Political Cartoons
Chapter 17: Analyze a Bar Graph
Chapter 18: Analyze a Pie Graph
Chapter 19: Analyze a Line Graph
Chapter 20: Problem-solving and Decision-making
Chapter 21: Read a State Legislative Map
Chapter 22: Writing or Speaking Persuasively
Chapter 23: Synthesize Information
Chapter 24: Make Comparisons and Contrasts

About the Student CD

The Student CD contains several instructional tools:

Student Book with Audio Files

The entire student edition is available on screen in PDF format. Next to each paragraph is an icon of a speaker. When the icon is clicked, the paragraph will be read aloud. Students with reading difficulties or English Language Learners will benefit from having the text read to them.

Spanish Introduction and Spanish Activity

Research has shown that English Language Learners benefit from generating prior knowledge verbally about a given topic in their first language before learning new concepts in English. Coupled with the generation of prior knowledge is a writing component. By writing about a concept in their first language, students increase comprehension and are better prepared for content acquisition in English. The last component is writing about acquired knowledge in English.

At the beginning of each chapter are two icons. The first icon is for a Spanish Introduction. This activity is designed to generate prior knowledge for Spanish speakers. It introduces the key concept of the chapter and presents lesson overviews. The second icon is for a Spanish Activity. This activity asks students to write about the key concept in Spanish. Students are instructed to revisit their Spanish paragraph after completing the chapter by completing an English writing activity that incorporates their prior knowledge with the new concepts learned. See pages xix—xxxv in this section for English translations of the Spanish Introductions and Activities.

Key Concepts Introduced in Spanish

Chapter 1: Citizenship
Chapter 2: Self-determination
Chapter 3: Constitutional Government
Chapter 4: Federalism
Chapter 5: Representation
Chapter 6: Legislation
Chapter 7: Compromise
Chapter 8: Executive
Chapter 9: Veto
Chapter 10: Civil Service
Chapter 11: Original Jurisdiction
Chapter 12: Unconstitutional and Constitutionality
Chapter 13: Civil Liberties
Chapter 14: Civil Rights
Chapter 15: Party System
Chapter 16: Voting Rights
Chapter 17: Public Influence
Chapter 18: Fiscal Policy
Chapter 19: Domestic Policy
Chapter 20: Diplomacy
Chapter 21: States' Rights
Chapter 22: Home Rule
Chapter 23: Ideology
Chapter 24: Globalization

Hot-linked Vocabulary Definitions

Vocabulary words and terms at the beginning of each lesson are hot-linked to provide Glossary definitions. To access the Glossary definition of each word or term, students should click on the vocabulary word or term. A dialogue box will then open that provides the Glossary definition.

Audio Captions

Captions for each photograph, painting, and cartoon are read aloud when the student clicks on the speaker icon.

Reading Comprehension and Vocabulary Reinforcement Activities

Each chapter is accompanied by four interactive games that reinforce reading comprehension and provide vocabulary reinforcement. They include: Fill in the Blank, Crossword Puzzle, eFlashcards, Multiple Choice, Text Identification, Concept Columns, Matching, and Vocabulary Concentration.

Voter's Handbook

The Voter's Handbook is designed to help students learn the voting process and to teach them how to become active voters. The handbook describes what citizens need to do to be able to use the right to vote.

Introduction

Frequently Asked Questions

- The BIG Questions
- Who Votes
- Qualifications for Voting
- Registering to Vote
- Voting
- Special Voting Conditions
- Preparing to Vote

Student Presentation Builder

The Student Presentation Builder utilizes PowerPoint technology and allows students to create presentations using images, tables, charts, diagrams, and maps from the chapters. An introductory lesson is included to teach students how to use this technology.

The Annotated Teacher's Edition

The Annotated Teacher's Edition provides answers to questions in the student text and extension activities to enhance the lessons. The extension activities are designed to help remedial students better understand the text material and to assist English Language Learners to develop a broader understanding of the text content.

Unit Objectives

Skills and concepts targeted in the chapters in each unit are identified at the beginning of each unit.

Getting Started

Getting Started provides teachers a method of introducing the unit to students. This section often includes an introduction to key vocabulary terms and concepts. Students are encouraged to read the Unit Introduction and generate prior knowledge.

Related Transparencies

The Related Transparency box lists the transparencies from the Teacher's Resource Binder that relate to the chapter.

Key Blacklines

Each chapter is accompanied by Blackline Masters from the Teacher's Resource Binder. These include: Biography, Primary Source, or Civics Today; Read for Understanding; Vocabulary; Map/Table/Graph/Chart Activity; Chapter Review; Chapter Activity; and Chapter Quiz. The topics of the Biography, Primary Source, Civics Today are indicated in the Key Blacklines box.

CD Extension

The CD Extension box is a reminder that students will benefit from the material presented on the CD.

Pre-Reading Discussion

The Pre-Reading Discussion is designed to provide questions and topics that generate prior knowledge among students. Often students are asked to review specific sections of text, images, or charts within the chapter.

Bio Extension

Some chapters of the Student Edition contain a biography. The Biography Extension includes additional background information about the person highlighted in the Student Edition. The material can be used to supplement class discussion and to provide additional material for student research.

Reading for Understanding

Each Primary Source feature contains reading comprehension questions to guide students through the text. Answers to the Reading for Understanding questions will vary, but suggestions of key facts are provided.

Lesson Summary

Summaries are provided at the beginning of each Lesson to help the teacher understand the overall themes and key concepts.

Lesson Objective

The Lesson Objective identifies the key goal for student learning.

Words to Know

Vocabulary words and terms are explained at the beginning of each lesson. Teachers are provided with techniques to introduce each vocabulary word and a method of linking the terms to a key concept of the lesson.

Putting It All Together

Answers and/or suggestions are provided for the Putting It All Together activities that end each lesson.

Picturing Government

The illustrations—photographs, cartoons, graphs and charts, tables, diagrams, and paintings—in *American Civics and Government* can be used to enhance student understanding of the topics covered and to generate classroom discussion. Most illustrations are identified in the Picturing Government boxes and additional information is presented about the illustrations.

Extension

Extension activities provide teachers with additional material and curriculum ideas to enhance the skills that are an important component of social studies instruction. These activities target key skills students must have to ensure academic achievement in the social studies.

Research Resources

At the end of each chapter is a list of books and Web resources that relate to the issues in the chapter.

Recommended Reading

At the end of each chapter is a list of supplemental reading materials for students. These books correlate to the concepts and topics of each chapter. The Thematic Strands of the National Council for the Social Studies are identified.

Classroom Discussion

The Classroom Discussion section provides teachers with questions to help wrap up the chapter. These questions incorporate key concepts from the chapter and guide students through making connections to related topics in American government.

The Teacher's Resource Binder

Blackline Masters

The Blackline Masters in the Teacher's Resource Binder are designed to enhance the curriculum provided in the Student Edition. Each chapter contains one Blackline Master for each of the following topics: Biography, Primary Source or Civics Today; Read for Understanding; Vocabulary; Map/Table/Graph/Chart Activity; Chapter Review; Chapter Activity; and Chapter Quiz. Included at the end of the Blackline Master section is an Answer Key.

Overhead Transparencies

There are 20 overhead transparencies in the Teacher's Resource Binder. They include key graphics that relate to the chapters, images that can be used to enhance classroom instruction, and graphic organizers: Three-Column Chart, Venn Diagram, and a Concept Web. Each overhead transparency is noted in the chapters where relevant, although many can be used repeatedly throughout the text.

Teacher's CD

Included with the Teacher's Resource Binder is a CD. The CD contains the entire Annotated Teacher's Edition in PDF format, so it is not necessary to carry around the Annotated Teacher's Edition. Also on the CD are additional PDF Blackline Masters that can be printed. Included are: Vocabulary Reinforcement pages designed for ELL instruction, Reading Comprehension pages designed for ELL instruction, Chapter Puzzles, Unit Assessments, and Book Assessments.

On-Line Book Assessment Correlated to State Standards

Final book assessments are available on the McGraw-Hill/Contemporary website: www.mhcontemporary.com. This 50-question test assesses skills outlined by the state standards.

Spanish Introductions and Activities

Each chapter on the Student CD is accompanied by an audio introduction to the chapter in Spanish and an audio activity in Spanish. The introductions are designed to generate prior knowledge in the English Language Learner's first language. The activities are designed to link prior knowledge with the chapter being studied. The English and Spanish versions of each chapter's Introduction and Activity are provided below. They can also be used to assist non-English Language Learners.

English	Spanish
Chapter 1 – Introduction	
The lessons in this chapter explain the relationship between government and the people. The key concept in this chapter is "citizenship." Citizenship refers to a person's legal status in a particular country as well as to the duties and responsibilities that are involved. In Lesson 1, you will read about the purposes of government. Lesson 2 describes various systems and forms of government.	Las lecciones en este capítulo explican la relación entre el gobierno y la gente. El concepto principal de este capítulo es la "ciudadanía." La ciudadanía refiere al estado legal de una persona en un país específico así como a los deberes y las responsabilidades que están implicadas. En la lección 1, vas a leer acerca de los propósitos del gobierno. La lección 2 describe varios sistemas y formas de gobierno.
Chapter 1 – Student Activity	
The legal status of immigrants in the United States is often a topic of public debate. Some people think undocumented immigrants take jobs away from U.S. citizens. Others feel they should not have access to health services. Some even think children of undocumented immigrants should not be allowed to go to public schools. With a partner, discuss in Spanish why these issues concern Americans. In Spanish, write a summary of your discussion. After reading the chapter, write a paragraph in English explaining how citizenship is connected to the four purposes of government.	El estado legal de los inmigrantes en los Estados Unidos es frecuentemente un tema de debate público. Algunos piensan que inmigrantes indocumentados les quitan trabajos a ciudadanos de los Estados Unidos. Otros piensan que no deben de tener acceso a los servicios médicos. Algunos incluso piensan que los niños de inmigrantes indocumentados no se les debe permitir que asistan a las escuelas públicas. Con un compañero, discute en español porqué estos temas preocupan a los norteamericanos. En español, escribe un resumen de la discusión. Después de leer el capítulo, escribe un párrafo en inglés explicando cómo la ciudadanía está relacionada a los cuatro propósitos del gobierno.

Chapter 2 – Introduction

This chapter is about how the United States government first began. The key concept is "self-determination." Self-determination refers to the freedom to choose without outside interference. Lesson 1 describes the foundations of the British government that ruled the colonies. Lesson 2 is about the events that led to the fight for independence from British rule. Lesson 3 is about the problems with the first attempt at a national government, which was known as a confederation. In Lesson 4, you will read about the Constitutional Convention and the writing of the U.S. Constitution.

Este capítulo es acerca de cómo el gobierno de los Estados Unidos comenzó. El concepto principal es la "autodeterminación." La autodeterminación refiere a la libertad de escoger sin intromisión externa. La lección 1 describe las bases del gobierno británico en las que se gobernaba a las colonias. La lección 2 es acerca de los eventos que llevaron a la guerra para la independencia del gobierno británico. La lección 3 es acerca de los problemas con el primer esfuerzo para un gobierno nacional que se reconocía como una confederación. En la lección 4, vas a leer acerca de la convención constitucional y la escritura de la Constitución de los Estados Unidos...

Chapter 2 – Student Activity

The idea of personal freedom is popular around the world. However, the need for some form of government also exists worldwide. Why do you think that is? With a partner, discuss this issue in Spanish. Write a paragraph in Spanish summarizing your discussion. After reading the chapter, write a paragraph in English explaining why the first American attempt at a national government failed.

La idea de libertad personal es popular alrededor del mundo. Sin embargo, la necesidad de alguna forma de gobierno también existe en todo el mundo. ¿Por qué piensas que es así? Con un compañero, discute esta cuestión en español. Escribe un párrafo en español dando un resumen de la discusión. Después de leer el capítulo, escribe un párrafo en inglés explicando porqué el primer esfuerzo americano para un gobierno nacional fracasó.

Chapter 3 – Introduction

The lessons in this chapter are about the Constitution of the United States. The key concept in this chapter is "constitutional government." Constitutional government refers to a government that is based on a formal constitution. Lesson 1 describes the foundation of the Constitution and how it was written. In Lesson 2, you will learn about the three branches of government. In Lesson 3, you will read how amendments to the Constitution are made. The text of the Constitution is in this chapter, also.

Las lecciones en este capítulo son acerca de la Constitución de los Estados Unidos. El concepto principal en este capítulo es el "gobierno constitucional." Gobierno constitucional se refiere a un gobierno basado en una constitución formal. La lección 1 describe la base de la Constitución y cómo fue escrita. En la lección 2, vas a aprender acerca de las tres ramas del gobierno. En la lección 3, vas a leer cómo se hacen las enmiendas a la Constitución. El texto de la Constitución también se encuentra en este capítulo.

Chapter 3 – Student Activity	
The Constitution is a document that outlines what the government can and cannot do. With a partner, discuss in Spanish why it was important to the Framers to have a document that stated what the government could and could not do. In Spanish, write a list of five reasons why the Framers believed government must be limited. (Hint: Think back to the American Revolution.) After reading the chapter, write a paragraph in English explaining why the Framers included a process for amending the Constitution.	La Constitución es un documento que expone a grandes rasgos lo que el gobierno puede y no puede hacer. Con un compañero, discute en español porqué era importante para los fundadores tener un documento que indicara lo que el gobierno podía y no podía hacer. En español, escribe una lista de cinco razones porqué los fundadores creían que se tenia que limitar al gobierno. (Pista: Piensa acerca de la revolución americana.) Después de leer el capítulo, escribe un párrafo en inglés explicando porqué los fundadores incluyeron un proceso para enmendar la Constitución.

Chapter 4 – Introduction	
This chapter is about the federal system of government. The key concept is "federalism." Federalism refers to the relationship between the states and the central government, with each having certain powers. Lesson 1 describes the division of powers between the states and the central government as outlined in the Constitution. In Lesson 2, you will learn how the Constitution defines the interaction between states. Lesson 3 describes how federalism has changed since the national government was first established.	Este capítulo es acerca del sistema de gobierno federal. El concepto principal es el "federalismo." El federalismo se refiere a la relación entre los estados y el gobierno central, donde cada uno tiene ciertos poderes. La lección 1 describe la división de los poderes entre los estados y el gobierno central como fue expuesto a grandes rasgos en la Constitución. En la lección 2, vas a aprender cómo la Constitución define las interacciones entre los estados. La lección 3 describe cómo el federalismo ha cambiado desde que el gobierno nacional se estableció.

Chapter 4 – Student Activity	
Why was it necessary to ensure equality among the states in the Constitution? How does this make federalism stronger? With a partner, discuss these questions in Spanish. Write a summary in Spanish about your discussion. After reading the chapter, write a paragraph in English explaining the following statement: "The Constitution is a living document."	¿Por qué fue necesario asegurar la igualdad entre los estados en la Constitución? ¿Cómo hace esto más fuerte el federalismo? Con un compañero, discute estas cuestiones en español. Escribe un resumen de la discusión en español. Después de leer el capítulo, escribe un párrafo en inglés explicando lo siguiente: "La Constitución es un documento viviente."

Chapter 5 – Introduction

This chapter is about the Congress of the United States, which consists of the Senate and the House of Representatives. The key concept in this chapter is "representation." As used in this chapter, representation refers to what the people who are elected to Congress do for those who elect them. Lesson 1 explains who the members of Congress are, what they do, and how decisions are made about the number of representatives from any given state. Lesson 2 describes how the House of Representatives works and what it does. In Lesson 3, you will learn about how the Senate works and what it does.

Este capítulo es acerca del Congreso de los Estados Unidos que consiste en el senado y la cámara de representantes. El concepto principal en este capítulo es la "representación." Como se usa en este capítulo, representación se refiere a lo que la gente que es elegida para el congreso hace para los que los eligieron. La lección 1 explica quienes son los miembros del congreso, lo que hacen, y cómo se decide el número de representantes de un estado. La lección 2 describe cómo trabaja la cámara de representantes y lo que hace. En la lección 3, vas a aprender acerca de cómo trabaja el senado y lo que hace.

Chapter 5 – Student Activity

In a democracy, every voter has the right to vote on every issue. The United States of America is a republican form of government, meaning that voters elect representatives to vote on issues for them. With a partner, discuss the advantages and disadvantages of a republic. Write a list in Spanish of three advantages and three disadvantages. After reading the chapter, think about this: What happens to a republican form of government when people do not vote? Write a brief radio announcement in English urging people to vote and explain why it's important.

En una democracia, cada votante tiene el derecho de votar en cada cuestión. Los Estados Unidos es una forma de gobierno republicana. Esto quiere decir que los votantes eligen a representantes que votan por ellos en cuestiones. Con un compañero, discute las ventajas y las desventajas de una república. Escribe una lista en español de tres ventajas y tres desventajas. Después de leer el capítulo, piensa en esto: ¿Qué ocurre en un gobierno republicano cuando la gente no vota? Escribe un breve anuncio de radio en inglés animando a la gente a que voten y explica por qué es importante..

Chapter 6 – Introduction

The lessons in this chapter are about the specific powers of Congress that are listed in the Constitution and the implied powers that have evolved over time. The key concept in this chapter is "legislation." Legislation refers to the laws passed by the legislature. In Lesson 1, you will read about the various powers of the Congress. Lesson 2 describes how congressional committees work and some of the jobs they perform. Lesson 3 is about some of the conflicts over power between the legislative and executive branches of the government as well as some of the causes of these conflicts.

Las lecciones en este capítulo son acerca de los poderes específicos del congreso que son enumerados en la Constitución y los poderes implícitos que se han desarrollado a través del tiempo. El concepto principal en este capitulo es la "legislación." La legislación se refiere a las leyes que la asamblea lesgislativa pasa. En la lección 1, vas a leer acerca de los varios poderes del congreso. La lección 2 describe cómo trabajan los comités del congreso y algunas de sus funciones. La lección 3 es acerca de los conflictos por el poder entre la rama ejecutiva y la rama legislativa del gobierno y también acerca de algunas de las causas de este conflicto.

Chapter 6 – Student Activity

We all live with rules about what we can and cannot do. Under the U.S. form of government, the people we elect make the rules. Sometimes they make rules we don't like. With a partner, discuss in Spanish what methods voters can use to express their discontent when a representative helps to make an unpopular rule. Write a summary of your discussion in Spanish. After reading the chapter, think about an issue that is important to you. Then, write a letter in English to your congressman expressing your views and the action(s) that you think should be taken.

Todos vivimos con reglas acerca de qué podemos y no podemos hacer. En el gobierno de los Estados Unidos, la gente que elegimos hace las reglas. Algunas veces se hacen reglas que no nos agradan. Con un compañero, discute en español que métodos pueden usar los votantes para expresar su descontento cuando un representante ayuda a hacer una regla impopular. Escribe un resumen de tu discusión en español. Después de leer el capítulo, piensa en un tema que es importante para ti. Entonces, escribe una carta en inglés a tu congresista expresando tus puntos de vista y las acciones que piensas que se deben tomar.

Chapter 7 – Introduction

This chapter is about how the work of Congress is done. The key concept in this chapter is "compromise." To compromise means to resolve an issue by agreeing that people on each side of the issue will give up something they want in order to reach a solution. Lesson 1 describes the various processes that bills must go through to become laws. In Lesson 2, you will learn about how members of Congress provide a variety of services to the people who elect them.

Este capítulo es acerca de cómo se hace el trabajo del congreso. El concepto principal en este capítulo es una "solución intermedia." Una solución intermedia se lleva a cabo cuando la gente en cada parte de una cuestión deja algo que quieren para llegar a una solución. La lección 1 describe los varios procesos por los que los proyectos de ley tienen que pasar para que lleguen a ser ley. En la lección 2, vas a aprender acerca de cómo los miembros del congreso proveen una variedad de servicios a la gente que los eligen.

Chapter 7 – Student Activity

The people who work together in Congress generally work together on many issues over a long period of time. With a partner, discuss in Spanish why compromise is a useful tool for a politician. Write a list in Spanish of five reasons why compromise can lead to better legislation. After reading the chapter, review your list. Write a paragraph in English explaining how compromise can be a tool to help get a controversial bill to a vote.

La gente que trabajan juntos en el congreso generalmente trabajan juntos en muchos asuntos en el transcurso del tiempo. Con un compañero, discute en español por qué las soluciones intermedias son instrumentos útiles para un político. Escribe una lista en español de cinco razones por las cuales las soluciones intermedias pueden llevar a una mejor legislación. Después de leer el capítulo, revisa tu lista. Escribe un párrafo en inglés explicando cómo las soluciones intermedias pueden ser instrumentos para ayudar a llevar al voto un proyecto de ley controversial.

Chapter 8 – Introduction

The lessons in this chapter are about the executive branch of the U.S. government. The key concept in this chapter is "executive." The executive branch of government is responsible for making sure that the laws of the country are carried out. The president is the chief executive. Lesson 1 describes the roles of the president and vice president and the qualifications for office. In Lesson 2, you will read about the various departments that make up the Cabinet and their roles in the government. Lesson 3 is about the Executive Office and the staff that provides direct support to the president.

Las lecciones en este capítulo son acerca de la rama ejecutiva del gobierno de los Estados Unidos. El concepto principal en este capítulo es "ejecutivo(a)." La rama ejecutiva del gobierno asegura que las leyes del país se lleven a cabo. El presidente es el director gerente o ejecutivo. La lección 1 describe los papeles del presidente y del vicepresidente y las capacidades necesarias para cada oficina. En la lección 2, vas a leer acerca de los varios departamentos que hacen el gabinete y sus papeles en el gobierno, La lección 3 es acerca de la oficina ejecutiva y el personal que provee apoyo directo al presidente.

Chapter 8 – Student Activity

With a partner, brainstorm a bulleted list of what you already know about the executive branch of government: the president's term of office, the people who work for him, his relationship to the other branches of government, and the other people who work in the executive branch. Write a summary of your discussion in Spanish. After reading the chapter, write a paragraph in English explaining why it is necessary for the president to have advisers.

Con un compañero, piensen en una lista de lo que ya saben acerca de la rama ejecutiva del gobierno: el mandato de la oficina del presidente, la gente quien trabaja para él, sus relaciones con las otras ramas del gobierno, y las otras gentes que trabajan en la rama ejecutiva. Escribe un resumen de su discusión en español. Después de leer el capítulo, escribe un párrafo en inglés explicando por qué es necesario que el presidente tenga consejeros.

Chapter 9 – Introduction

This chapter is about the powers and duties of the president. The key concept in this chapter is "veto." As used in this chapter, to veto refers to a president's refusal to sign a bill into law that has been passed by Congress and sent to him for his signature. In Lesson 1, you will learn about the various powers of the president and where they originate. Lesson 2 describes the specific official and unofficial roles and duties of the president. In Lesson 3, you will read about the qualities that make a president successful.

Este capítulo es acerca de los poderes y los deberes del presidente. El concepto principal en este capítulo es el "veto." En este capítulo, el veto se refiere a la negativa del presidente de firmar un proyecto que el congreso ha pasado y que le ha mandado al presidente para su firma para que se haga ley. En la lección 1, vas a aprender acerca de los varios poderes del presidente y de donde se originan. La lección 2 describe los papeles oficiales y extraoficiales específicos del presidente. En la lección 3, vas a leer acerca de las cualidades que hacen que un presidente tenga éxito.

Chapter 9 – Student Activity

People often refer to the "power of the presidency." What do you think this means? With a partner, discuss this in Spanish. Then, write a paragraph in Spanish of your discussion. After reading the chapter, review your Spanish paragraph and make changes if necessary. Then write a paragraph in English explaining how the president's veto power adds to the concept of checks and balances.	La gente a menudo se refiere al "poder de la presidencia." ¿Qué piensas que significa esto? Con un compañero, discute esto en español. Entonces, escribe un párrafo en español de tu discusión. Después de leer el capítulo, revisa tu párrafo en español y haz cambios si es necesario. Entonces, escribe un párrafo en inglés explicando cómo el poder del veto del presidente contribuye al concepto del equilibro de fuerzas.

Chapter 10 – Introduction

The lessons in this chapter are about the federal bureaucracy. The key concept in this chapter is "civil service." The civil service includes the civilian employees of the federal government. Lesson 1 describes the various departments, agencies, and commissions of the federal bureaucracy. In Lesson 2, you will learn how the civil service system began and how it works. Lesson 3 describes the various jobs of the federal bureaucracy.	Las lecciones en este capítulo son acerca de la burocracia federal. El concepto principal en este capítulo es la "administración pública." La administración pública incluye los empleos civiles del gobierno federal. La lección 1 describe los varios departamentos, agencias y comisiones de la burocracia federal. En la lección 2, vas a aprender cómo el sistema de la administración pública comenzó y cómo trabaja. La lección 3 describe las varias funciones de la burocracia federal.

Chapter 10 – Student Activity

Where in your neighborhood do you see employees of the federal government at work? With a partner, identify the federal workers that you have had contact with and discuss your experiences in Spanish. Select one category of federal worker and write a paragraph in Spanish describing your interaction with this person. After reading the chapter, write a paragraph in English explaining how the federal government contributes to the nation's welfare though its bureaucracy.	En tu vecindario, ¿dónde vez empleados del gobierno federal trabajando? Con un compañero, identifica los empleados federales con quien has tenido contacto y discute tus experiencias en español. Selecciona una categoría de trabajador federal y escribe un párrafo en español explicando tu interacción con esa persona. Después de leer el capítulo, escribe un párrafo en inglés explicando cómo el gobierno federal contribuye al bienestar de la nación por medio de la burocracia federal.

Chapter 11 – Introduction

The lessons in this chapter are about the various courts that make up the federal court system. The key concept in this chapter is "original jurisdiction." Original jurisdiction belongs to the original court that hears a particular case. Lesson 1 describes how the federal court system is organized and how it works. In Lesson 2, you will learn about the jurisdiction and power of the various federal courts.

Las lecciones en este capítulo son acerca de los varios tribunales que hacen el sistema del tribunal federal. El concepto principal en este capítulo es la "jurisdicción original." La jurisdicción original le pertenece al tribunal original que lleva un caso particular. La lección 1 describe cómo el sistema del tribunal federal está organizado y cómo trabaja. En la lección 2, vas a aprender acerca de la jurisdicción y el poder de los varios tribunales federales.

Chapter 11 – Student Activity

Imagine a country that has laws and law enforcement officials, but no judges to decide if someone has broken the law. Would this pose a danger to the citizens in any way? Discuss this with a partner in Spanish. Then write a summary of your discussion in Spanish. After reading the chapter, write a paragraph in English explaining why judicial review is important to maintaining the balance of powers among the three branches of government.

Imagina un país que tiene leyes y oficiales que las hagan cumplir, pero ningún juez para decidir si alguien ha violado la ley. ¿Supondría esto un peligro para los ciudadanos de alguna manera? Discute esto con un compañero en español. Entonces, escribe un resumen de tu discusión en español. Después de leer el capítulo, escribe un párrafo en inglés explicando por qué la revista judicial es importante para mantener el equilibrio de fuerzas entre las tres ramas del gobierno.

Chapter 12 – Introduction

This chapter is about the work of the Supreme Court. The key concepts in this chapter are "unconstitutional" and "constitutionality." The Supreme Court can decide that a law passed by Congress is unconstitutional if, in its opinion, that law is contrary to the Constitution. Constitutionality means that a given question brought before the Court is found to be in accord with the Constitution. Lesson 1 describes how the Supreme Court selects cases to review and how final decisions are made and communicated to the public. In Lesson 2, you will read about the influences on the justices of the Supreme Court. In Lesson 3, you will learn how the Supreme Court affects national policy.

Este capítulo es acerca del trabajo del Tribunal Supremo de Justicia. Los conceptos principales en este capítulo son "inconstitucional" y la "constitucionalidad." El Tribunal Supremo de Justicia puede decidir una ley que el congreso haya pasado como inconstitucional si, en su opinión, esa ley contradice la Constitución. Constitucionalidad quiere decir que un asunto que se presenta al tribunal está en concordancia con la Constitución. La lección 1 describe cómo el Tribunal Supremo de Justicia selecciona casos para revisarlos y cómo las decisiones finales se hacen y se comunican al público. En la lección 2, vas a leer acerca de las influencias en los jueces del Tribunal Supremo de Justicia. En la lección 3, vas a aprender cómo el Tribunal Supremo de Justicia afecta la política nacional.

Chapter 12 – Student Activity

With a partner, discuss in Spanish the benefits of the appeal process in the U.S. system of justice. Summarize your discussion in a few sentences in Spanish. After reading the chapter, consider this question: Why don't court cases go back to the lower courts after a decision has been made in the Supreme Court? Write a paragraph in English explaining your answer.

Con un compañero, discute en español los beneficios del proceso de apelación en el sistema de justicia de los Estados Unidos. Escribe un resumen breve de tu discusión en español. Después de leer el capítulo, considera esta pregunta: ¿Porqué los casos no regresan a los tribunales más bajos después de que se ha tomado una decisión en el Tribunal Supremo de Justicia? Escribe un párrafo en inglés explicando tu respuesta.

Chapter 13 – Introduction

The lessons in this chapter are about the civil liberties guaranteed in the Constitution. The key concept in this chapter is "civil liberties." Civil liberties are the freedoms guaranteed by the U.S. Constitution, without unnecessary restraint or interference by the government. In Lesson 1, you will read about how civil liberties for citizens and non-citizens are protected. Lesson 2 explains freedom of religion. Lesson 3 explains the freedom of speech and freedom of the press. In Lesson 4, you will learn about the freedom of assembly and petition. Lesson 5 explains the rights of persons accused of a crime.

Las lecciones en este capítulo son acerca de las libertades civiles garantizadas en la Constitución. El concepto principal en este capítulo es las "libertades civiles." Las libertades civiles son las libertades garantizadas por la Constitución de los Estados Unidos, sin restricciones innecesarias o la intromisión del gobierno. En la lección 1, vas a leer acerca de cómo las libertades civiles para los ciudadanos y para los que no son ciudadanos se protegen. La lección 2 explica la libertad de la religión. La lección 3 explica la libertad del habla y la libertad de la prensa. En la lección 4, vas a aprender acerca de la libertad de reunión y de petición. La lección 5 explica los derechos de las personas acusadas de un crimen.

Chapter 13 – Student Activity

Review the list of civil liberties from the Spanish Introduction. With a partner, select one to remove from the list. What difference would that make to our society? Discuss this question in Spanish. Then write a summary in Spanish of your discussion describing our society without this civil liberty. After reading the chapter, write a paragraph in English explaining why non-citizens in this country are provided with civil liberties.

Revisa la lista de libertades civiles en la introducción en español. Con un compañero, escoge una para quitarla de la lista. ¿Qué diferencia seria para nuestra sociedad? Discute esta cuestión en español. Entonces, escribe un resume en español de tu discusión describiendo nuestra sociedad sin esta libertad civil. Después de leer el capítulo, escribe un párrafo en inglés explicando por qué a los que no son ciudadanos en este país se les proveen libertades civiles.

Chapter 14 – Introduction

This chapter is about the rights and responsibilities of U.S. citizens and non-citizens. The key concept in this chapter is "civil rights." Civil rights are the rights of every individual to equal protection under the law. Lesson 1 explains what "equal protection under the law" means. In Lesson 2, you will read about some civil rights laws passed by Congress. Lesson 3 is about U.S. immigration policy worldwide.

Este capítulo es acerca de los derechos y las responsabilidades de los ciudadanos y de los que no son ciudadanos de los Estados Unidos. El concepto principal en este capítulo es los "derechos civiles." Los derechos civiles son los derechos de cada individuo a la protección de igualdad ante la ley. La lección 1 explica el significado de "la protección de igualdad ante la ley." En la lección 2, vas a leer acerca de algunas leyes de derechos civiles que el congreso pasó. La lección 3 es acerca de la política de los Estados Unidos acerca de la inmigración.

Chapter 14 – Student Activity

This chapter and the preceding chapter are about the "rights" of citizens and non-citizens. Are there any responsibilities that are associated with citizenship? With a partner, discuss this in Spanish. Then write a summary of your discussion in Spanish listing at least five responsibilities of citizenship. After reading the chapter, write a paragraph in English explaining the difference between "civil liberties" and "civil rights."

Este capítulo y el capítulo anterior son acerca de los "derechos" de los ciudadanos y de los que no son ciudadanos. ¿Hay algunas responsabilidades asociadas con la ciudadanía? Con un compañero, discute esto en español. Entonces, escribe un resumen de tu discusión dando por lo menos cinco responsabilidades de la ciudadanía. Después de leer el capítulo, escribe un párrafo en inglés explicando las diferencias entre las "libertades civiles" y los "derechos civiles."

Chapter 15 – Introduction

The lessons in this chapter are about the political organizations known as parties that control or want to control a government. The key concept in this chapter is the "party system." The party system refers to the methods used by groups that have opposing views about government to organize themselves. Lesson 1 describes the functions of political parties. In Lesson 2, you will learn how political parties got started in the United States and how they evolved over time. Lesson 3 is about how political parties are organized, from the national to the state and local levels.

Las lecciones en este capítulo son acerca de las organizaciones políticas que se conocen como partidos que controlan o desean controlar un gobierno. El concepto principal en este capítulo es el "sistema partidista." El sistema partidista refiere a los métodos de organización utilizados por los grupos cuyas con opiniones opuestas respecto al gobierno con. La lección 1 describe las funciones de los partidos políticos. En la lección 2, vas a aprender cómo los partidos políticos comenzaron en los Estados Unidos y cómo se han desarrollado a través del tiempo. La lección 3 es acerca de cómo los partidos políticos están organizados, del nivel nacional al nivel estatal y al nivel municipal.

Chapter 15 – Student Activity

Most students who run for an elected office in school run either as an individual or as part of a group. Suppose students began to organize themselves around a particular idea and formed parties to distinguish themselves from the ideas of other groups. How would this affect student elections? Discuss this in Spanish with a partner. Then, write a summary in Spanish of your discussion, listing three examples of how elections would change. After reading the chapter, write a paragraph in English explaining how independent parties make themselves powerful by being outside the two-party system.

La mayoría de los estudiantes que quieren ser elegidos para una oficina elegida en la escuela se presentan como individuos o como parte de un grupo. Supon que los estudiantes comenzaran a organizarse alrededor de una idea en particular y formaran partidos para distinguirse de las ideas de otros grupos. ¿Cómo afectará esto a las elecciones estudiantiles? Discute esto en español con un compañero. Entonces, escribe un resumen en español de tu discusión, dando tres ejemplos de cómo las elecciones cambiarán. Después de leer el capítulo, escribe un párrafo en inglés explicando cómo los partidos independientes se hacen poderosos estando fuera del sistema de dos partidos.

Chapter 16 – Introduction

This chapter is about the election process. The key concept in this chapter is "voting rights." Voting rights refer to the right to vote given to every citizen. In Lesson 1, you will learn how candidates for elected office get on the ballot. Lesson 2 explains how elections are financed and defines "hard" and "soft" money for political campaigns. In Lesson 3, you will learn about the history of voting rights and some of the ways these rights were denied to various groups of people. Lesson 4 describes how some people are influenced about how they vote and others are influenced not to vote.

Este capítulo es acerca del proceso de las elecciones. El concepto principal en este capítulo es los "derechos al voto." Los derechos al voto refieren al derecho al voto que se da a cada ciudadano. En la lección 1, vas a aprender cómo los candidatos para las oficinas elegidas son sometidos a votación. La lección 2 explica cómo las elecciones son financiadas y define el dinero "duro" y "suave" para las campañas políticas. En la lección 3, vas a aprender acerca de la historia de los derechos al voto y de algunas de las maneras que estos derechos fueron negados a varios grupos de personas. La lección 4 describe cómo algunas personas son influenciadas acerca de cómo votar y otras son influenciadas a no votar.

Chapter 16 – Student Activity

Imagine that one particular group at your high school—the varsity football team—wants to dominate school politics. With a partner, discuss how the varsity football team might control student elections to make certain that the team's candidates

Imagina que un grupo en particular en tu secundaria – el equipo de fútbol – desea dominar la política en la escuela. Con un compañero, discute cómo el equipo de fútbol podría controlar las elecciones estudiantiles para asegurar que los

Chapter 16 – Student Activity, continued

and ideas always win. Write a list in Spanish that includes five methods they could use. After reading the chapter, write a letter in English to the editor of your local newspaper explaining why every eligible citizen should vote. List at least five reasons.

candidatos del equipo siempre ganen. Escribe una lista en español que incluya cinco métodos que pudieran usar. Después de leer el capítulo, escribe una carta en inglés al director de tu periódico municipal explicando por qué cada ciudadano elegible debe votar. Por lo menos, da una lista de cinco razones.

Chapter 17 – Introduction

The lessons in this chapter are about how government policy is influenced by a variety of sources. The key concept in this chapter is "public influence." Public influence refers to the affect that organized groups of people who share a common interest or cause can have on elections and on government policy. Lesson 1 defines interest groups and describes how they function. In Lesson 2, you will read about the people who influence public policy, who they are, and what they do. Lesson 3 defines public opinion and describes some factors that influence pubic opinion. Lesson 4 is about the influence of the mass media on American politics.

Las lecciones en este capítulo son acerca de cómo la política del gobierno está influenciada por varias fuentes. El concepto principal en este capítulo es la "influencia pública." La influencia pública refiere al efecto que organizaciones de grupos de personas que tienen un interés o causa en común pueden tener en las elecciones y en la política del gobierno. La lección 1 define los grupos interesados y describe cómo funcionan. En la lección 2, vas a leer acerca de la gente que influye la política pública, quiénes son y qué hacen. La lección 3 define la opinión pública y describe algunos factores que influyen la opinión pública. La lección 4 es acerca de la influencia de los medios de comunicación masivos en la política americana.

Chapter 17 – Student Activity

With a partner, discuss the following situation: After the beginning of classes in September, a group of students proposes to change the date of the homecoming football game. Who are all the interest groups, both in the school and outside of the school, who would have to be consulted about changing the date? Write a paragraph in Spanish listing the interest groups and the reasons why they would have to be consulted. After reading the chapter, write a paragraph in English explaining how an interest group or the mass media can contribute to the "public opinion."

Con un compañero, discute la siguiente situación: Después del comienzo de clases en septiembre, un grupo de estudiantes propone cambiar la fecha del juego de regreso de fútbol. ¿Quiénes son todos los grupos interesados en la escuela y fuera de la escuela, a los que se tendría que consultar para cambiar la fecha? Escribe un párrafo en español dando una lista de los grupos interesados y las razones por las cuales se deberían de consultar. Después de leer el capítulo, escribe un párrafo en inglés explicando cómo un grupo interesado o los medios de comunicación masivos puede contribuir a la "opinión pública."

Chapter 18 – Introduction

This chapter is about where the money comes from that is used to pay for government programs. The key concept in this chapter is "fiscal policy." Fiscal policy refers to the decisions that the federal government makes about spending and taxation that are intended to affect employment and the economy. In Lesson 1, you will read about two sources of government funds—taxes and borrowing. In Lesson 2, you will learn how the president and Congress are involved in developing the federal budget. Lesson 3 describes how the nation's economy is managed.	Este capítulo es acerca de donde viene el dinero que se usa para pagar los programas del gobierno. El concepto principal en este capítulo es la "política fiscal." La política fiscal refiere a las decisiones que el gobierno hace acerca de gastos e impuestos que intentan afectar el empleo y la economía. En la lección 1, vas a leer acerca de dos fuentes de fondos para el gobierno – impuestos y prestamos. En la lección 2, vas a aprender cómo el presidente y el Congreso están involucrados en el desarrollo del presupuesto federal. La lección 3 describe cómo la economía de la nación se maneja.

Chapter 18 – Student Activity

State and federal taxes are used to provide many neighborhood services. With a partner, create a list in Spanish of five services in your neighborhood that are provided by state and federal taxes. Then, write a paragraph in Spanish explaining what would happen if state and federal funds were no longer available to pay for these services. After reading the chapter, write a paragraph in English explaining "entitlement programs" in your own words.	Los impuestos del estado y del gobierno federal se usan para proveer muchos servicios vecindarios. Con un compañero, hagan una lista en español de cinco servicios en tu vecindad que son proveídos con impuestos del estado y del gobierno federal. Entonces, escribe un párrafo en español explicando lo que pasaría si los fondos del estado y del gobierno federal no estuvieran disponibles para pagar estos servicios. Después de leer el capítulo, escribe un párrafo en inglés explicando los "programas de derecho" en tus propias palabras.

Chapter 19 – Introduction

The lessons in this chapter are about government policies that affect the health and welfare of the nation. The key concept in this chapter is "domestic policy." Domestic policy refers to the government's programs and regulations within the country. Lesson 1 describes how the government promotes and regulates both business and labor. In Lesson 2, you will learn about government policies related to agriculture, the environment, and energy sources. In Lesson 3, you will read about various government social welfare programs that are intended to help people in need. Lesson 4 describes the role of the federal government in education, housing, transportation, and security.	Las lecciones en este capítulo son acerca de las políticas del gobierno que afectan la salud y el bienestar de la nación. El concepto principal en este capítulo es la "política interior." La política interior refiere a los programas y los reglamentos del gobierno dentro del país. La lección 1 describe cómo el gobierno promueve y regula los negocios y la fuerza de trabajo. En la lección 2, vas a aprender acerca de las políticas del gobierno relacionadas con la agricultura, el ambiente, y las fuentes de energía. En la lección 3, vas a leer acerca de varios programas del gobierno acerca del bienestar social que intentan ayudar a la gente necesitada. La lección 4 describe el papel del gobierno en la educación, la vivienda, la transportación y seguridad.

Chapter 19 – Student Activity	
Government regulations affect how we drive, what we eat, and how we work. Do you think this is a good thing? Should the federal government be involved in our daily lives? With a partner, discuss this in Spanish. Then write a brief summary of your discussion in Spanish. After reading the chapter, think back to what you learned about public opinion in Chapter 17. Then write a paragraph in English explaining how public opinion influences the government's domestic policies.	Los reglamentos del gobierno afectan cómo manejamos un coche, lo que comemos, y cómo trabajamos. ¿Piensas que esto es algo bueno? ¿Debería el gobierno estar involucrado en nuestras vidas diarias? Con un compañero, discute esto en español. Entonces, escribe un resumen breve de tu discusión en español. Después de leer el capítulo, piensa en lo que aprendiste acerca de la opinión pública en el capítulo 17. Entonces, escribe un párrafo en inglés explicando cómo la opinión pública influye las políticas interiores del gobierno.

Chapter 20 – Introduction	
This chapter is about how the government of the United States interacts with other countries around the world to maintain good relations and ensure national security. The key concept in this chapter is "diplomacy." Diplomacy refers to the act of managing relationships between nations. Lesson 1 describes the goals of American foreign policy and explains how foreign policy has evolved over time. In Lesson 2, you will read about how foreign policy is influenced by both elected officials and public opinion. Lesson 3 is about how the United States achieves its foreign policy goals.	Este capítulo es acerca de cómo el gobierno de los Estados Unidos interactúa con otros países alrededor del mundo para mantener buenas relaciones y asegurar la seguridad nacional. El concepto principal en este capítulo es la "diplomacia." La diplomacia refiere al acto de manejar relaciones entre naciones. La lección 1 describe los objetivos de la política exterior americana y explica cómo la política exterior se ha desarrollado a través del tiempo. En la lección 2, vas a leer acerca de cómo la política exterior está influenciada por los oficiales elegidos y la opinión pública. La lección 3 es acerca de cómo los Estados Unidos logra sus objetivos de política exterior.

Chapter 20 – Student Activity

From time to time, some Americans argue that the United States should cut most of its ties with the rest of the world and concentrate only on American concerns. Based on what you've read so far, what effect would this have on the United States and on other nations around the world? Discuss this in Spanish with a partner. Then write a summary of your discussion in Spanish listing at least three effects. After reading the chapter, write a paragraph in English explaining how diplomacy works. List at least three tools that diplomats can use to promote our national security and avoid conflicts.

De vez en cuando, algunos americanos discuten que los Estados Unidos debería cortar sus lazos con el resto del mundo y concentrarse solamente en los asuntos del país. De acuerdo con lo que has leído hasta ahora, ¿qué efecto tendría esto en los Estados Unidos y en otras naciones alrededor del mundo? Discute esto en español con un compañero. Entonces, escribe un resumen de tu discusión dando por lo menos tres efectos. Después de leer el capítulo, escribe un párrafo en inglés explicando cómo la diplomacia trabaja. Enlista por lo menos tres herramientas que los diplomáticos pueden usar para promover nuestra seguridad nacional y evitar conflictos.

Chapter 21 – Introduction

The lessons in this chapter are about various aspects of state government. The key concept in this chapter is "states' rights." States' rights refers to those rights and powers that belong to the individual states, guaranteed under the Constitution of the United States. In Lesson 1, you will learn the basics of state constitutions. Lesson 2 describes the branches of government at the state level. In Lesson 3, you will read about state governments and public policy. Lesson 4 describes how state governments are financed.

Las lecciones en este capítulo son acerca de varios aspectos del gobierno estatal. El concepto principal en este capítulo es los "derechos estatales." Los derechos estatales refieren a los derechos y poderes que pertenecen a los estados individuales, garantizados bajo la Constitución de los Estados Unidos. En la lección 1, vas a aprender acerca de lo esencial de las constituciones estatales. La lección 2 describe las ramas del gobierno a nivel estatal. En la lección 3, vas a leer acerca de los gobiernos estatales y la política pública. La lección 4 describe cómo se financian los gobiernos estatales.

Chapter 21 – Student Activity

With such a strong federal government, why do we also need state governments? (Hint: Consider the differences between the state of California and the state of Maine.) Discuss this question in Spanish with a partner. Then write a brief summary of your discussion in Spanish. After reading the chapter, write a paragraph in English explaining why state taxes differ from state to state.

¿Con un gobierno federal tan fuerte, por qué necesitamos también gobiernos estatales? (Pista: Considera las diferencias entre el estado de California y el estado de Maine.) Discute esta pregunta en español con un compañero. Entonces, escribe un resumen breve en español de tu discusión. Después de leer el capítulo, escribe un párrafo en inglés explicando por qué los impuestos son distintos de un estado a otro.

Chapter 22 – Introduction

This chapter is about how government functions at the local level. The key concept in this chapter is "home rule." Home rule refers to local self-government. Lesson 1 describes various types of local government. In Lesson 2, you will read about various services provided by local governments. In Lesson 3, you will learn how local governments are funded.	Este capítulo es acerca de cómo el gobierno funciona a nivel municipal. El concepto principal en este capítulo es "autogobierno." Autogobierno se refiere al gobierno municipal. La lección 1 describe varias clases de gobiernos municipales. En la lección 2, vas a leer acerca de varios servicios que son provistos por los gobiernos municipales. En la lección 3, vas a aprender acerca de cómo se financian los gobiernos municipales.

Chapter 22 – Student Activity

How are local governments similar to or different from state governments and the federal government? Discuss this question with a partner in Spanish. Then write a list in Spanish of at least five similarities and five differences. After reading the chapter, find out who represents your neighborhood in local city or county government. Write that person a letter in English describing a neighborhood concern that you want to bring to their attention.	¿De que manera son los gobiernos municipales similares o distintos de los gobiernos estatales y del gobierno federal? Discute esta pregunta con un compañero en español. Entonces, escribe una lista en español de por lo menos cinco similitudes y cinco diferencias. Después de leer el capítulo, investiga quién representa tu vecindario en el gobierno municipal de la ciudad o el gobierno municipal del condado. Escribe una carta en inglés a esa persona acerca de un problema en tu vecindario del cual tu deseas informarle.

Chapter 23 – Introduction

The lessons in this chapter are about various forms of government around the world. The key concept in this chapter is "ideology." Ideology refers to a set of ideas or opinions about society or politics. Lesson 1 describes several examples of democratic forms of government, how they are organized, and how they function. In Lesson 2, you will read about authoritarian forms of government. Lesson 3 is about how global security has become a major issue for many world governments.	Las lecciones en este capítulo son acerca de las varias formas de gobierno alrededor del mundo. El concepto principal en este capítulo es la "ideología." La ideología refiere a un conjunto de ideas u opiniones acerca de la sociedad o de la política. La lección 1 describe varios ejemplos de formas de gobiernos democráticos y cómo están organizados, y como funcionan. En la lección 2, vas a leer acerca de formas de gobiernos autoritarios. La lección 3 es acerca de cómo la seguridad global se ha convertido en un tema de enorme importancia para muchos gobiernos en el mundo.

Chapter 23 – Student Activity

Is the world ready for a worldwide government? Yes or no? With a partner, discuss in Spanish reasons a worldwide government would work and why it would not. Write a summary of your discussion in Spanish listing at least five reasons it would or would not work. After reading the chapter, write a paragraph in English explaining how ideology might contribute to terrorism.

¿Está el mundo listo para un gobierno mundial? ¿Sí o no? Con un compañero, discute en español las razones por las cuales un gobierno mundial funcionaría o no. Escribe un resumen de tu discusión en español dando por lo menos cinco razones por las cuales funcionaría o no funcionaría. Después de leer el capítulo, escribe un párrafo en inglés explicando cómo la ideología podría contribuir al terrorismo.

Chapter 24 – Introduction

This chapter is about various economic systems around the world. The key concept in this chapter is "globalization." Globalization means the extension of something to the entire world. Lesson 1 describes capitalism and provides examples of mixed economies around the world. In Lesson 2, you will read about socialism and the economies of some developing nations. In Lesson 3, you will learn about communism and how it influences the economy of Communist nations. In Lesson 4, you will read about some of the economic issues facing the world today.

Este capítulo es acerca de varios sistemas económicos alrededor del mundo. El concepto principal en este capítulo es la "globalización." La globalización significa la extensión de algo en todo el mundo. La lección 1 describe el capitalismo y da ejemplos de economías variadas alrededor del mundo. En la lección 2, vas a leer acerca del socialismo y las economías de algunas naciones en vías del desarrollo. En la lección 3, vas a aprender acerca del comunismo y como influye la economía de paises comunistas. En la lección 4, vas a leer acerca de asuntos economicos con los que el mundo actual se enfrenta.

Chapter 24 – Student Activity

Ever wonder how the "global" economy affects you? With a partner, examine everything you have with you—your shoes, your clothes, your backpack, your books, and any electronic items. Look for labels that identify where these items were made. Create a list in Spanish of all the items you have identified and list the country where they were made or where they came from. After reading the chapter, write a paragraph in English explaining how a developing country might benefit economically by moving from communism or socialism to some form of capitalism.

¿Has pensado cómo la economía "global" te afecta? Con un compañero, examina todo lo que traes contigo – tus zapatos, tu ropa, tu mochila, tus libros, y cualquier cosa electrónica. Busca etiquetas que identifiquen en dónde fueron hechas estas cosas. Haz una lista en español de todas las cosas que haz identificado y escribe el nombre del país donde fueron hechas o de donde provienen. Después de leer el capítulo, escribe un párrafo en inglés explicando cómo un país en vías de desarrollo podría beneficiarse económicamente cambiando del comunismo o socialismo a alguna forma del capitalismo.

Unit Objectives

After studying this unit, students will be able to

- explain the British roots of American government
- describe the process by which the colonies became independent

Unit 1 focuses on the political and historical foundations of American government.

Chapter 1, Government and the People, examines political theories and principles, and systems and forms of government.

Chapter 2, Beginnings of U.S. Government, explains the history of the American quest for self-government.

Getting Started

Ask a volunteer to read aloud the title of the unit and the paragraphs that follow it on page 2. Then give students a series of laws or government responsibilities. Ask them to identify each as a task for local, state, or national government, or as a shared task.

CD Extension

Encourage students to use the reading comprehension, vocabulary reinforcement, and other activities on the student CD.

UNIT 1 FOUNDATIONS OF U.S. GOVERNMENT

When you vote for president of the United States, you are voting for the head of the federal government. When you vote for governor, you are voting for the head of your state government. When you vote for mayor, you are voting for the head of your local government.

The United States is a system of interlocking government units: federal, state, and local. How did the United States develop three sets of governments? This unit will help you answer that question. The rest of the book will answer the question "What do the three levels of government do?"

Picturing Government

The photograph on page 2 shows the west façade of the Capitol complex in Washington, D.C. The Capitol is located 88 feet above the Potomac River on a plateau. Prior to 1791, the national government had no permanent home; it met in eight different cities. The 1787 Constitution provided, in Article I, Section 8, for Congress to have governing authority over an area not more than ten square miles. The following year, Maryland ceded those ten miles to Congress. Virginia followed suit, but the land was not used and in 1846 was returned to Virginia. French engineer Pierre Charles L'Enfant, who had been influenced by the gardens of Versailles, designed the city of Washington. On the recommendation of Thomas Jefferson, the civil engineering design team for the new city included Benjamin Banneker, who was descended from slaves. He helped to decide the sites for the White House and the Treasury, as well as for the Capitol.

Chapter

1 GOVERNMENT AND THE PEOPLE

Getting Focused

Skim this chapter to predict what you will be learning.

- **Read the lesson titles and subheadings.**
- **Look at the illustrations and read the captions.**
- **Review the vocabulary words and terms.**

What do you think this chapter is about? Do the subheadings and pictures raise any questions for you? In your notebook, write at least five questions you want answered as you read this chapter.

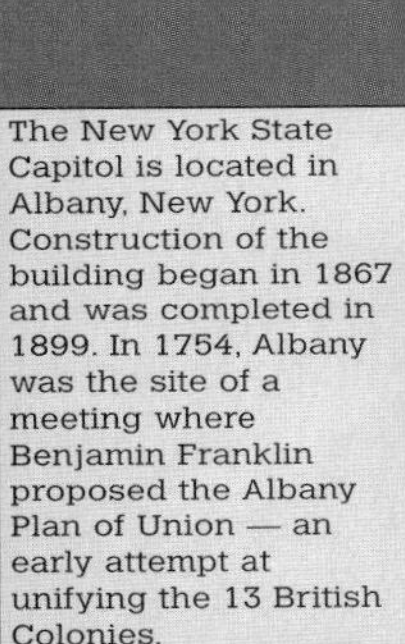

The New York State Capitol is located in Albany, New York. Construction of the building began in 1867 and was completed in 1899. In 1754, Albany was the site of a meeting where Benjamin Franklin proposed the Albany Plan of Union — an early attempt at unifying the 13 British Colonies.

Pre-Reading Discussion

1 Write the word *government* in the center of a word web on the board. Ask students to call out ideas about types and functions of government, adding these to the web. Refer and add to the web as you discuss the chapter content.

2 Elicit from students their ideas on ways in which a democracy differs from a monarchy or a dictatorship. Create a three-column chart on the board for students to copy in their notebooks, or distribute blank charts for them to use. Tell them that the charts will help them study for later quizzes or exams.

Related Transparencies

T-18 Three-Column Chart

T-20 Concept Web

Key Blacklines

Biography — Barbara Shaiman

Getting Focused

After students have written their questions, have them exchange lists with a partner. Ask each person to skim the chapter, looking for the answers to the questions. Then, have students note the page number on which the answer is located. Finally, have students return the papers to the original writers.

Picturing Government

New York State's capitol building in Albany, shown on page 3, took 30 years to build, from 1867–1897. Constructed in the manner of a French chateau, the capitol is located on one of the city's seven hills. It is famous for its Million Dollar Staircase, with more than 300 portraits carved in stone representing both famous New Yorkers and their families, and friends of the carvers. The Senate Staircase is sometimes called the Evolutionary Staircase because simple animals are carved into the bottom and, as the stairs rise, the creatures depicted are more complex.

Lesson Summary

Government serves as a tool of the political state. By means of government, a nation maintains order, offers public services, and enforces decisions over its citizens. There are four main theories about how government began and four major purposes of government. The theories include the evolutionary theory, the force theory, the divine right theory, and the social contract theory. The four main purposes of government are to provide a way that people can live in peace, to provide public services for the common good, to offer national security, and to make decisions that affect the economy.

Lesson Objective

Students will learn about the major theories and purposes of government.

Focus Your Reading Answers

1 A state is a group of people living in a defined territory who have a government with the power to make and enforce laws, without needing permission from a higher authority.

2 Four theories about how government began are the evolutionary theory, the force theory, the divine right theory, and the social contract theory.

3 The four main purposes of government are to provide a way that people can live in peace, to provide public services, to offer national security, and to make decisions affecting the economy and people in business.

LESSON 1

Principles of Government

Thinking on Your Own

What does the word *government* mean to you? Make a list of what you think government does. Then think about what your life would be like if there were no government. Write a paragraph to describe how your life would be different without government.

focus your reading

What is a state?

Describe the four theories about how government began.

Explain the four main purposes of government.

words to know

state

government

evolutionary theory

force theory

divine right theory

social contract theory

coercive

What exactly is government? We live under local, state, and federal governments, but what are they? How does each level of government affect us? How, in turn, do we affect each level of government?

To answer these questions, we first have to ask a more basic question: What is a state—not the 50 states of the United States, but the general idea, or concept, of state? A **state** is (1) a group of people (2) living in a definite territory who have (3) a government with the power to make and enforce laws (4) without having to ask permission from a higher authority.

Government, then, is a tool of the state. **Government** is the organization by which the state maintains order, provides public services, and enforces decisions over the people living in its territory. Another word for this meaning of *state* is *nation*.

The U.S. Senate

Words to Know

Introduce each of the following vocabulary terms to students.

Explain that in this context, a *state* is a group of people living in a defined territory who have a *government* with the power to make and enforce laws without needing permission from a higher authority. Another word for *state* is *nation*.

Government is the organization by which the *state* maintains order, provides public services, and enforces decisions over the people living in its territory. Scholars have studied the beginnings of *government* for many years.

The *evolutionary theory* of *government* says that *government* grew out of the structure of the father as head over a family. Those who believe in the *evolutionary theory* hold that this same kind of organization served as a model for clans or groups of families.

Theories of How Government Began

Scholars do not know how or when the first governments came about. Some scholars have developed theories, or ideas, about the origins of government.

One idea about the beginning of government is the **evolutionary theory**. According to this theory, the earliest government developed from the family. In most cultures, the father was the head of the family. He governed what the family did. Over time, groups living in an area grew in size to include many families. It was only natural that people set up the same kind of organization to govern these groups of families.

John Locke developed the social contract theory.

The **force theory** explains the beginning of government differently. Scholars who support the force theory claim that the first governments were established by the use of weapons. One man or a small group of men used force to bring others in an area under their control.

According to **divine right theory**, a ruler holds power because he or she is a god or was chosen by the gods to rule. The governments of many ancient civilizations were based on this theory. The Egyptians believed that their pharaoh was like a god and was chosen by the gods to rule. Divine right theory influenced Europeans in the 1600s. The rulers of France and Russia, for example, claimed that their authority was based on God's will. This claim gave the rulers absolute power over their subjects. To disobey the ruler was to disobey God.

ideas to remember

A state has four important characteristics
- population, or people
- territory, or land
- sovereignty, or authority
- government, or an organized way to maintain authority

By the late 1600s, however, some European philosophers were questioning the divine right theory. Thomas Hobbes helped to develop the **social contract theory**. Hobbes wrote

Words to Know, continued

According to the *force theory*, the earliest *governments* were established through weapons. Scholars who support the *force theory* think that one man or a small group of men brought others in the area under their control using force.

The *divine right theory* of *government* believes that a ruler has the right to rule from God or the gods. Ancient Egyptians held to the *divine right theory* of *government*.

The *social contract theory* suggests an agreement between the ruler and those ruled. Thomas Jefferson based his ideas in the Declaration of Independence on the *social contract theory*.

The power of *government* to make decisions and force the people to obey them is called *coercive*. This *coercive* power is what allows *governments* to function.

Picturing Government

Although known today primarily for his political philosophy, John Locke, shown on page 5, was a skilled physician. At thirty-five, he became personal physician and confidential secretary to Anthony Ashley Cooper, who was later the lord chancellor of England and the first Earl of Shaftesbury. This appointment led to problems for Locke when the earl was indicted for high treason. Though the earl was acquitted, Locke was suspected of disloyalty and fled to Holland, living there for five years, until the Glorious Revolution.

Ideas to Remember Extension

Review the ideas listed, further explaining difficult vocabulary words. Have students create graphic organizers in their notebooks to help them visualize the four major ideas.

Extension

Ask students to choose one of the four theories on the beginnings of government. Have them select a culture in world history that could exemplify the theory they choose. (Be prepared to suggest resources.) Then have them use library resources or the Internet to find out more about the civilization. Have them present their findings to the class by using the Student Presentation Builder on the student CD.

Picturing Government

The United States Senate, pictured on page 4, was originally designed to serve as a check on the House of Representatives, whose members were elected by popular vote. Until passage of the Seventeenth Amendment in 1913, state legislators elected senators. For a bill to become law, both houses of Congress must approve a bill with identical wording. While the number of representatives in Congress varies according to a state's population, the Senate has a constant two members from each state.

Stop and Think

Students' choices of theories of government will vary. Their dialogues should clearly illustrate the theory. In addition, they should include three laws that exemplify that theory.

Reading for Understanding Answers

1 By *state of Nature*, Locke means a person who lives alone and is not under the rule of any government.

2 "Others" can be those who would invade and spoil a person's freedom, as well as those to whom one might be joined in society for mutual protection of life, liberty, and property.

3 Students' paragraphs will vary but may express the idea that people want government to protect them from enemies and to preserve life, liberty, and property.

that in a "state of nature," no government existed. Without government as an authority, life was "cruel, brutish, and short." According to this theory, the ruler and the people who were ruled entered into a contract. If the ruler failed to honor the rights of the people, the people could overthrow the ruler.

This idea of a social contract greatly influenced the English in 1688. Before they allowed William and Mary to take the throne, the two had to agree to the English Bill of Rights. This became the "contract" between the English monarchy and the English people. Thomas Jefferson based much of the Declaration of Independence on the social contract theory.

stop and think

With a partner, review the different theories of government. Select one of the theories. Then write a brief dialogue between a ruler and a subject that illustrates the theory. Include three sample laws that demonstrate the theory of government.

Primary Source

John Locke (1632–1704) spent much of his life thinking and writing about government and philosophy. The following excerpt explains why people develop government.

"If Man in the state of Nature be so free . . . ; if he be absolute Lord of his own Person and Possessions, equal to the greatest, and subject to no body, why will he part with his Freedom? . . . Why will [Man] . . . subject himself to the . . . Control of any other Power? . . . ['T]is obvious to answer, That tho in the state of Nature he hath such a [freedom], yet the enjoyment of it is very uncertain, and constantly exposed to the Invasion of others. For all being Kings as much as he, every Man his Equal, and . . . no strict Observers of . . . Justice, the Enjoyment of the Property he has . . . is very unsafe, very unsecure. This makes him willing to quit a Condition, which however free, is full of Fears and continual Dangers; And 'tis not without Reason, that he seeks out, and is willing to join in Society with others, . . . for the mutual Preservation of their Lives, Liberties, and . . . Property."

—John Locke, from *Two Treatises of Government*

reading for understanding

1. What does Locke mean by the term *state of Nature*?
2. How does Locke describe "others"?
3. Write a paragraph to explain Locke's reasoning about why people want government.

Primary Source Extension

Locke was interested in many subjects, including psychology and education. He held to the belief that at birth the human mind was a *tabula rasa*, a blank slate, with ideas formed from sensory experiences. Further, Locke believed that education's task of forming character was more important than the teaching and learning of facts.

Extension

Have students interested in the social contract theory explore the work of another philosopher, Jean-Jacques Rousseau, who also influenced American ideas of liberty.

The Purposes of Government

As you have just read, the idea of government goes back to ancient civilizations. Governments have been around for thousands of years because they serve a purpose. In reality, they serve four main purposes.

First, government provides a way for people to live in peace. When people live together in groups, conflict often arises. Government sets up laws to handle conflict and to punish those who disobey the laws. For example, suppose a person steals money from another. The thief is arrested, tried, and sentenced to jail under the law.

Government is able to maintain law and order because its citizens have given it this power. Government has the authority to make decisions and to force its citizens to obey those decisions. This power is called **coercive**. It means that government can coerce, or force, people to obey it. The force is the fear of punishment if they do not obey. For example, many people might not willingly pay taxes. However, the fear of a fine and possible prison time forces people to pay their taxes.

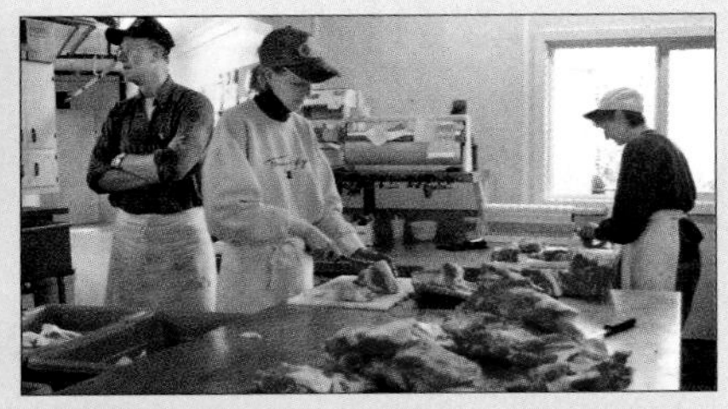

Each image represents one of the purposes of government. Work with a partner to determine which purpose of government is represented by each picture.

Picturing Government

The four photographs in the collage on page *7* illustrate the four purposes of government. Top left: In courtrooms, the law is upheld and those who break the law are punished. Top right: The government provides public services, such as regulating the safety of workplaces and of food supplies. Bottom left: The government makes economic decisions, such as those that govern farm policies. Bottom right: The government is in charge of national security and maintaining a military force.

Extension

Divide the class into four groups, assigning to each group one of the four purposes of government. Challenge them to monitor the news for a week using the Internet, a local newspaper, television news, or a weekly news magazine. Ask them each to keep a log of news stories that support their group's "purpose of government." Allow time for a class round table to discuss their findings.

Ideas to Remember Extension

Review the ideas listed, further explaining difficult vocabulary words. Have students create graphic organizers in their notebooks to help them visualize the four major ideas.

Extension

Have pairs of students choose one of the public services listed on pages 7 and 8 and investigate its impact locally. For example, with what regulations must fast-food restaurants comply? Have students imagine themselves as reporters on the local scene and write a brief article summarizing their findings.

Putting It All Together

Students' lists and laws will vary but should cover all four purposes of government. Students should include details from the lesson.

Second, government provides public services. In general, this means that government works to ensure the general welfare, or well-being, of the people. Government takes on tasks that individuals could not afford to do on their own, such as building schools, roads, and subways. Government also promotes the health and safety of its people. Some examples are federal food and drug laws to ensure the safety of the foods we eat and the medicines we take. The federal government also sets standards for airplane safety.

National security is the third purpose of government. Typically, the national government sets foreign policy and maintains the armed forces for national defense. It also directs the nation's response to external threats, like the war on terrorism.

Fourth, government makes decisions that affect the economy and economic activities of businesses and individuals. The power to tax is one way the government regulates economic activity. Government also uses direct payments and tax credits as other ways to influence economic activity. For example, some farmers are paid to limit the number of acres they plant of certain crops, such as corn. Surplus crops can drive down the price the farmer receives and hurt the economy. Government may pass laws that give tax credits to companies that provide job retraining to workers who would otherwise lose their jobs.

ideas to remember

Government has four main purposes

- to maintain social order, that is, to keep the peace
- to provide public services
- to provide national security
- to make economic decisions

Putting It All Together

With a partner, make a list of three laws that match each of the four purposes of government. Then develop a list of services the government provides. The government may be national, state, or local. Share your 12 laws and your list of services with the class.

Words to Know

Discuss each of the vocabulary terms on page 9 with students.

A *unitary government* gives all power to the national government. A *unitary government* is also called a centralized system of government. A *confederation government* is a loose union of states. The United States was originally a *confederation government*.

In a *federal system*, the national and state or provincial government divide the power. More than 20 modern nations have a *federal system* of government.

In an *autocracy*, one person rules. A monarchy is an example of an *autocracy*. *Absolute monarchs* are those who gained power through inheritance or force and kept that power. The Russian czars were *absolute monarchs*. Today, the *CIA World Factbook* does not list any examples of an absolute monarchy. *Constitutional monarchies* are those in which the government is in the hands of the legislature. Great Britain and Japan are *constitutional monarchies*.

LESSON 2

Systems and Forms of Government

Thinking on Your Own

Suppose you had to set up a government for a colony on the moon. What would you want your government to be like? Would you want it to be independent and free from interference from governments on Earth? Would you want citizens to vote for officials? Describe your ideas for a government in two or three paragraphs. Include what you have learned about the purposes of government in Lesson 1.

In Lesson 1, you learned about what government is and why people have set up governments since earliest times. This lesson discusses the systems and the forms, or types, that governments have taken over the years. There are three basic systems of government: unitary, confederation, and federal.

Knowing the system of government is different from knowing the type of government. Answering the question "Who governs?" tells you the type of government. A government may be an autocracy, an oligarchy, or a democracy.

focus your reading

What are the differences among unitary, confederation, and federal systems of government?

Compare and contrast autocracies and oligarchies.

What type of democracy is most common today?

words to know

unitary government
confederation government
federal system
autocracy
absolute monarchy
constitutional monarchy
dictator
oligarchy
democracy
direct democracy
representative democracy

The British Parliament holds all the power in the government but delegates powers to counties and local governments.

Lesson Summary

The three basic forms of government are unitary, confederation, and federal. Unitary systems of government grant all power to a centralized government. A confederation is a loose union of states. Federal systems divide power between a national and state or provincial government. The types of government are autocracy, oligarchy, and democracy. An autocracy consists of one person in power, such as a monarch. An oligarchy is a small group of people ruling.

Lesson Objective

Students will learn about the types and systems of governments.

Focus Your Reading Answers

1 Unitary systems of government give all power to the national government. A confederation is a loose union of states. Federal systems divide power between the national and state or provincial governments.

2 Autocracies and oligarchies are the same in that the people being governed have no voice. They are different in that an autocracy is rule by one person, such as a monarch, and an oligarchy is a small group of people ruling.

3 Today, the most common type of democracy is a representative democracy.

Words to Know, continued

A *dictator* is an example of a modern autocrat, controlling the government and ruling with absolute power. Adolf Hitler was a *dictator*. Today, the *CIA World Factbook* lists Libya as a military dictatorship.

An *oligarchy* is a small group of people ruling. Before and during World War II, Japan was ruled by an *oligarchy*. Today, the *CIA World Factbook* does not list any examples of an *oligarchy*.

A *democracy* is a form of government in which people rule. The United States Constitution established the government as a *democracy*.

A *direct democracy* is one in which the citizens vote on issues of government in a meeting of all citizens. A *direct democracy* is difficult to maintain except in small states.

In a *representative democracy*, people elect others to govern in their place. The United States is a *representative democracy*.

Unitary Government

Unitary government is one in which all government power is held by the national government. It uses its power to set up lesser governments, such as states and provinces. The national government gives these lesser levels of government the power to make and enforce laws. This is also called a centralized system of government. Modern European nations such as France, Italy, and Great Britain have unitary governments.

The 50 states of the United States also have unitary governments. They exercise their authority, or power, to set up local governments. These may take the form of counties, cities, towns, and villages.

ideas to remember

There are three basic systems of government

- unitary
- confederation
- federal

Confederation Government

A **confederation government** is a loose union of independent states. The difference between a unitary government and a confederation becomes clear if you think about how the United States was formed. In 1777, the original 13 British colonies set up a national government under the Articles of Confederation. The states gave up some of their power to set up the national government. The national government did not set up the states.

Federal System of Government

Note the word *loose* in the definition of a confederation government. The union among the states was so loose under the Articles of Confederation that it was unworkable. The writers of the Constitution agreed to a federal system of government in place of the confederation government.

Congress holds only certain powers, as noted in the Constitution.

Picturing Government

The British Parliament meets in the building shown in the photograph on page 9. Britain's monarch has the right to summon and dissolve Parliament. Each new session opens with a speech from the prime minister, who is the head of the government. The speech summarizes the goals of the government for that session. Parliament creates the laws and the monarch approves them, although that function is mostly a formality. The prime minister and a cabinet of about 20 members introduce new laws to Parliament. Defense, social security, overall economic policy, and foreign affairs are matters that Parliament handles for the entire United Kingdom.

Picturing Government

The United States Congress, seen in the photograph on page 10, was established by the 1789 Constitution. It is part of the system of checks and balances. Congress must convene jointly at least once annually, beginning on January 3. Joint sessions are also required to count Electoral College votes. In addition, when the president or a foreign dignitary addresses Congress, joint sessions occur.

Extension

Have interested students investigate the provisions of the Articles of Confederation. Ask them to explain to the class the reason the Articles did not work. Suggest that they use a radio or television broadcast format and answer the typical journalistic questions *who, what, why, where, when,* and *how* to explain the confederation government and what replaced it.

Ideas to Remember Extension

Review the ideas listed, further explaining difficult vocabulary words. Have students create graphic organizers in their notebooks to help them visualize the three basic systems of government.

A **federal system** divides government powers between the national government and state or provincial governments. The national government has certain powers, and the states have certain powers. Besides the United States, the nations of Australia, Germany, Mexico, India, and more than 20 other nations use the federal system of government.

stop and think

Reread the description of the imaginary government that you wrote for Thinking on Your Own. Does your government fit any of these three basic systems? If your imaginary government does not match any of them, rewrite your description to fit one. Then share your description with a partner. Ask your partner to identify your system of government.

Adolf Hitler

Autocracy and Oligarchy

Autocracy and oligarchy have a characteristic in common. The people who are governed do not have a voice in their government.

In an **autocracy**, a single person holds all power. This is probably the oldest type of government. Autocrats either inherit their role or use force to get and keep it. Monarchs in Europe from the 1400s to the 1700s and the czars in Russia were autocrats, also known as **absolute monarchs**. They inherited their positions and used force to keep them. Modern autocratic monarchies are rare. The king of Saudi Arabia is a modern absolute monarch.

Today, most monarchies, such as Great Britain's, are **constitutional monarchies**. The British monarch is mainly the ceremonial head of the British government. The position has little power. Real government power is in the hands of the British Parliament. Japan, Sweden, and Spain also have constitutional monarchies. Even though the heads of these governments are monarchs, the governments are democracies. The people vote for their representative leaders.

A **dictator** is a modern autocrat. A dictator controls the government and rules with absolute power. Adolf Hitler in Germany, Joseph Stalin in the Soviet Union, and Benito Mussolini in Italy were all twentieth-century dictators. Kim Jong-Il, the leader of North Korea, was one of the few remaining dictators at the beginning of the twenty-first century.

Picturing Government

Adolf Hitler, shown on page 11, has stood as the premier example of a dictator for more than half a century. Ironically, Hitler came to power on the same day that Franklin Roosevelt gave his first inaugural address, assuring America that "the only thing we have to fear is fear itself." In Germany, people were still angered by the perceived unfairness of the Treaty of Versailles and the huge reparations that led to Germany's financial collapse. They welcomed a strong leader and Hitler's belief that Germans were a master race.

Stop and Think

Students' descriptions and revisions will vary but should match one of the three basic systems of government: unitary, confederation, or federal.

Extension

Have interested students use library resources or the Internet to find out more about the dictators mentioned in the lesson. Allow time for them to share their findings with the class, comparing and contrasting the leaders. They may want to use the Student Presentation Builder on the student CD for their presentations.

Ideas to Remember Extension

Review the ideas listed, further explaining difficult vocabulary words. Have students create graphic organizers in their notebooks to help them visualize the three basic types of government.

Putting It All Together

Students' letters to the editor will vary but should support a position with details from the lesson.

An **oligarchy** is similar to an autocracy. The difference is that in an oligarchy, a small group of people, not just one person, rules with absolute power. Before and during World War II, Japan was run by an oligarchy of army officers and businessmen. Sometimes the group in power will hold elections. However, the only candidates up for election support the oligarchy, and voters must vote for them. This is the form of oligarchy in the People's Republic of China. The only political party is the Communist Party, and few dare to oppose it.

Democracy

Abraham Lincoln said that democracy is "government of the people, by the people, and for the people." The U.S. Constitution begins "We the people." In a **democracy**, the people rule.

There are two forms of democracy. One is direct democracy. In a **direct democracy**, individual citizens vote on issues of government in a meeting of all citizens. This was the form of democracy in ancient Athens. It is still used today in New England town meetings.

However, few places today are small enough to be governed efficiently by direct democracy. Instead, people practice **representative democracy**. They elect representatives who govern in their place. The voters give their representatives the power to make and enforce laws for the community, state, or nation.

ideas to remember

There are three basic types of government

- Autocracy
  - dictator
  - absolute monarchy
  - constitutional monarchy
- Oligarchy
- Democracy
  - direct
  - representative

Putting It All Together

Write a letter to the editor explaining why the United States should keep its federal system of government or change to a unitary or confederation government. What are the advantages of each? Also, take a position on whether the United States should have a more or less direct form of democracy.

Extensions

1 Encourage students to investigate the democracy of ancient Athens, using library resources or the Internet. Ask them to find out the limitations of that democracy, such as prohibiting women from voting.

2 Discuss with students the idea of *citizen*, noting how the word has changed in America. For example, in the nation's early days, *citizen* referred only to white men who owned land. Have students put together a timeline showing when African Americans, women, and Native Americans were declared citizens.

Participate in Government

Volunteer for Community Service

People contribute in many ways to the society in which they live. They take part in government by voting, paying taxes, and serving on juries. They contribute to community service through nongovernmental organizations (NGOs) and as volunteers. Doing volunteer service can be important and rewarding. You can be sixteen or eighty-six and be a volunteer.

There are many ways to volunteer your time and talents. The photo on this page shows one way. You can also volunteer your time to visit the elderly. You can work on clean-ups sponsored by your community, neighborhood, school, or local businesses. Another volunteer possibility for young adults is tutoring younger children.

Many communities offer classes in literacy or computer skills that are taught by trained volunteers.

Sometimes young adults are elected to serve on local community boards. Often, other local boards, such as the zoning commission, are appointed positions. Towns and small cities often have a volunteer fire department that will accept young volunteers.

To find volunteer opportunities in your community, ask your school guidance counselor. Also read your local newspaper for announcements by community groups that use volunteers.

Complete the following activity.

Locate a community organization that you are interested in learning more about. Develop a list of at least five questions to ask the coordinator of volunteers for the organization. You might ask more about what the organization does and what you would be doing as a volunteer.

Participate in Government

Students' questions will vary. Encourage students to set up an interview and pose their questions to the volunteer coordinator of their chosen organization. They may be able to do so using the Internet or by obtaining a copy of a brochure the organization offers. Compile the results into a "Handbook for Volunteers" and share it with the school library or media center as a resource for students engaging in community service programs.

Extension

Invite a representative from a local community organization that uses teen volunteers to speak to the class.

Research Resources

Below is a list of reference books and Web sites that relate to the issues covered in this chapter. Students may wish to use these to further their research on ideas in the preceding lessons. Web site addresses may change over time. Use keyword searching on a major search engine to locate sites.

Reference Books:

Donald C. Bacon, Roger H. Davidson, Morton Keller, eds. *The Encyclopedia of the United States Congress*. Simon & Schuster, 1995.

J. Denis Derbyshire. *Encyclopedia of World Political Systems*. Sharpe Reference, 2000.

Ellen Greenberg. *The House and Senate Explained: The People's Guide to Congress*. W.W. Norton, 1996.

Web Sites:

The Library of Congress maintains a site that is named for Thomas Jefferson. It offers access to information about legislation and all branches of government.

FirstGov is a search engine for all things related to the United States government.

Skill Builder

1 (a) The main idea of Lesson 1 is the theories and purposes of government.
(b) The main idea of Lesson 2 is the systems and types of government.

2 Paragraph 1: Government serves four main purposes.

Paragraph 2: Government provides a way for people to live in peace.

Paragraph 3: Governments rule by coercive power.

Paragraph 4: Government provides public services.

Paragraph 5: Government provides national security.

Paragraph 6: Government makes decisions on the economy. Main ideas are all stated.

Classroom Discussion

1 Discuss with students some of the broader topics covered in this chapter.

- How have types of governments evolved over the centuries?
- How can people gain a greater share of participation in government?
- What are the advantages of each form of government?

2 As a class, develop a chart of modern countries that follow different forms of government. Discuss the differences and similarities, as well as the differences within each classification, for example, the difference between a constitutional monarchy and a constitutional sultanate.

Skill Builder

Identifying Main Idea and Supporting Details

The **main idea** is the theme, or idea, that a piece of writing is mostly about. Your textbook can be a useful tool in helping you to identify main ideas. It is divided into chapters, which are divided into lessons, which are divided into sections. Each chapter has a main idea; so does each lesson and section.

The chapter title tells you the main idea of the chapter. The lesson title tells you the main idea of the lesson. For example, Lesson 1 in Chapter 1 explains the basic principles of government.

To find the main idea, ask yourself the following:

1. Is there a single sentence that states what the piece is about?

   If there is, then you have found the main idea. To be sure, restate the sentence in your own words. Does it still seem as if it is what the paragraph is mainly about?

2. If there is no single sentence, what does the piece seem to be about? What are the details describing or explaining?

   When you think you know, restate the main idea in your own words. This will help you to be sure you really figured out the main idea.

Complete the following activities.

1 What is the main idea of each of the following: (a) Lesson 1 in Chapter 1? (b) Lesson 2 in Chapter 1?

2 Read the section "The Purposes of Government," on pages 7–8. Identify the main idea in each paragraph. Decide whether it is stated or unstated.

Recommended Reading

Below is a list of books that relate to the issues covered in this chapter. The numbers in parentheses indicate the related Thematic Strands of the National Council for the Social Studies (NCSS).

Eileen Christelow. *Vote!* Clarion Books, 2003. (V, VI, X)

Lynn Curlee. *Capital.* Atheneum Books for Young Readers. (III, X)

Chapter

2 BEGINNINGS OF U.S. GOVERNMENT

Getting Focused

Skim this chapter to predict what you will be learning.

- Read the lesson titles and subheadings.
- Look at the illustrations and read the captions.
- Examine maps and charts.
- Review the vocabulary words and terms.

What do you already know about the British colonists' fight for independence? Make a list of at least ten facts about events that led up to the American Revolution.

Independence Hall in Philadelphia is often called the birthplace of our nation. It was in this building that the Declaration of Independence and the United States Constitution were signed. Philadelphia was the nation's capital from 1790 to 1800.

Pre-Reading Discussion

1 Ask students to list at least three qualifications they think a person should have in order to vote in local or national elections. When students have completed their lists, use them as a basis for discussion on voting rights criteria.

2 This chapter discusses both violent and nonviolent approaches to civil disobedience. Discuss with students the possible justifications for each approach.

CD Extension

Encourage students to use the reading comprehension, vocabulary reinforcement, and other activities on the student CD.

Related Transparencies

T-18 Three-Column Chart

T-19 Venn Diagram

T-20 Concept Web

Key Blacklines

Primary Source—Iraq Constitution

Getting Focused

After students have made their individual lists, put students in teams of four. Have the students combine their lists. See which student has the most facts, which has a fact no other student has, and so on. Then have teams combine their lists into a class list following the same steps. You may wish to make a combined master list and provide students with copies to use as study guides.

Picturing Government

Philadelphia's Independence Hall is pictured on page 15. Originally known as the State House, it was designed by Andrew Hamilton, a Philadelphia lawyer, and Edmund Woolley, a master carpenter. In 1735, the Pennsylvania Assembly first met in the building. The east wing was sometimes used to house Native Americans who were in town on business.

Lesson Summary

The colonists brought from England two ideas about their rights. These were limited government and representative government. Limited government was first expounded in the Magna Carta, which was signed in 1215. Further limits on the power of the monarchy included the Petition of Right, signed in 1628, and the Bill of Rights, signed in 1689. Parliament is an example of a representative government. The colonists developed written plans for government, including the Mayflower Compact and the Fundamental Orders of Connecticut. The first colonial legislature, the House of Burgesses, was established in Virginia in 1619.

Lesson Objective

Students will learn how the British colonies were governed.

Focus Your Reading Answers

1 Limited government and representative government were two basic principles of government that the English brought to the colonies.

2 The Magna Carta, the Petition of Right, and the English Bill of Rights are the three documents stating the basic rights of English people.

3 Colonial constitutions set up limited governments based on a rule of law. They also provided for representative government.

LESSON 1

Government of the British Colonies

Thinking on Your Own

Imagine you are deciding how laws will be passed in a new government. Describe your idea of the best way to set up a legislature, or lawmaking body. Consider qualifications for lawmakers and how people will become lawmakers.

focus your reading

Describe the two basic principles of government that the English brought to the colonies.

What three documents state the basic rights of the English people?

Explain how colonial constitutions and colonial legislatures relate to the two basic principles of English government.

words to know

limited government

representative government

Mayflower Compact

Fundamental Orders of Connecticut

Most of the people who settled in the British colonies came from England. They brought with them the rights that they had known as British citizens. These rights evolved over many centuries and were based largely on two ideas: limited government and representative government.

Foundations of English Government

Limited government is the idea that government is not all-powerful. People have certain rights that government cannot take away. This idea was first set down in the Magna Carta in England in 1215. This document was a first step toward limiting the power of the monarch and establishing certain rights, such as trial by jury.

King John was forced to sign the Magna Carta in 1215.

The Petition of Right, forced on King Charles I in 1628, also limited the monarch. It prohibited the monarch from levying taxes without the agreement of Parliament, forbade the housing of soldiers in private homes, and banned the jailing of people without just cause.

Words to Know

Introduce each of the following terms to students.

Explain that *limited government* is the idea that government is not all-powerful. *Limited government* was first set out in the Magna Carta. *Representative government* is based on people selecting others to govern for them. Parliament is an example of *representative government*.

The *Mayflower Compact* was the first written plan for colonial government. The Pilgrims created and signed the *Mayflower Compact* before going ashore in Plymouth in 1620.

The *Fundamental Orders of Connecticut* was the first formal constitution in the colonies. The *Fundamental Orders of Connecticut* set up a *representative government*.

The attempts to limit power in England did not end abuses by the government. The years between 1628 and 1688 were marked by civil war. Finally, in 1688, the leaders of Parliament overthrew King James II. They then invited his daughter Mary and her husband, William of Orange, to rule England. Before the two could be crowned, Parliament insisted they sign the Bill of Rights. Among the rights granted to the people were freedom from cruel and unusual punishment, the right to a fair and speedy trial, and freedom from excessive bail. The colonists brought these ideas about rights with them to North America.

William and Mary signed the English Bill of Rights in 1689.

The English colonists also brought with them the idea of **representative government**. The first meetings of Parliament took place in the 1200s. Parliament was, and still is, the legislative branch of English government. It is made up of an upper house, the House of Lords, and a lower house, the House of Commons. Members of the House of Lords hold office because they are part of the English nobility. Members of the House of Commons are elected by voters in their home districts. They represent the voters in Parliament. The process is similar to the way Americans vote for members of the U.S. House of Representatives.

ideas to remember

Three documents that describe the rights of the English are the

- Magna Carta
- Petition of Right
- English Bill of Rights

Written Plans of Government

England did not and does not have a written constitution. The collection of laws and documents such as the Magna Carta is considered England's unwritten constitution. The early English colonists, however, developed written plans for their colonial governments.

Picturing Government

William and Mary, shown in the engraving on page 17, were invited to assume power to prevent James II from establishing Roman Catholicism as the dominant religion in England. James had converted to Catholicism before his ascension to the throne in 1685. As king, he began showing preference to Roman Catholics in the appointments he made. His Declaration of Indulgence, issued in 1687, provided freedom of conscience for all denominations and may have been the last straw for an anti-Catholic nation. In 1689, as part of the Glorious Revolution, Parliament passed the Toleration Act. It granted freedom of worship to dissenting Protestants, but not to Roman Catholics or Unitarians. Dissenters were still forbidden from holding political office under the Toleration Act.

Picturing Government

The signing of the Magna Carta in 1215, pictured on page 16, was the cornerstone of English liberty. A group of barons took King John by force to the small island of Runnymede in the Thames River and forced him to sign the Magna Carta. It established the right to a trial by a jury of one's peers and to a writ of *habeas corpus*, and established that a person's own words could not be used against him or her in court.

Ideas to Remember Extension

Review the ideas listed, further explaining difficult vocabulary words. Have students create graphic organizers in their notebooks to help them visualize the three major documents.

Picturing Government

The signing of the Mayflower Compact is shown on page 18. Passengers on the *Mayflower* included both Pilgrims and "strangers," or adventurers. The Mayflower Compact came about because of difficulties between the two groups during the 66-day voyage. The document was created before the group disembarked in Plymouth.

Stop and Think

Students' lists of similarities will vary but may include no quartering of soldiers without consent, due process, speedy trial by a jury of peers, and no excessive bail or cruel and unusual punishment.

Extension

Help students build vocabulary by explaining the verbal connection of *magna*, on page 16. *Magna* means "great,"and relates to other English words such as *magnificent* and *magnanimous*. Present the Latin term *magna cum laude* as well.

The Pilgrims signed the Mayflower Compact in 1620.

The first such document was the **Mayflower Compact**. It was written and signed by the Pilgrims before they came ashore at Plymouth Rock in 1620. They agreed to form a government and to pass "just and equal laws" under that government.

The first formal constitution in the colonies was the **Fundamental Orders of Connecticut**, signed in 1639. Male property owners were granted the right to elect the governor and the representatives to the colonial legislature. As in Great Britain, all women, as well as any men who did not own property, were not allowed to vote. In time, each colony had a charter that set up a limited government based on rule by law. This means that government is always subject to, or under the control of, the law.

stop and think

The basic rights of the American people are found in the Bill of Rights—the first ten amendments to the United States Constitution. Find the Bill of Rights on page 66, and compare it to the rights of English people listed in this lesson. Work with a partner to list the similarities that you find.

Representative Government

The colonists set up their own versions of Parliament. The first colonial legislature met in the Virginia Colony in 1619. It was called the House of Burgesses.

Each of the other 12 colonies also established legislatures. Typically, they had two houses. The upper house was usually made up of wealthy landowners who were appointed by the governor. The lower house was elected. Among the issues that the legislators dealt with were laws regulating the ownership of land, relations with native groups, and taxation.

Putting It All Together

How were the governments of the colonies the same as and different from the government of England? With a partner, create a Venn diagram to compare and contrast the governments. Then write a paragraph explaining the similarities and differences.

Putting It All Together

Students' Venn diagrams and paragraphs will differ but may include the following points.

Similar: limited government; representative government; right to trial by jury of peers; freedom from cruel and unusual punishment; no taxation without representation; no jailing without just cause; no housing soldiers in private homes; Parliament and House of Burgesses

Different: colonies had written constitutions, but England did not

LESSON 2

Fighting for Independence

Thinking on Your Own

A compromise is the settlement of a disagreement in which each side gives up something. Parliament and King George on one side and the colonists on the other side would not compromise. Think of a disagreement you had with someone. What compromise did you or could you have proposed to settle it? Describe the compromise.

At the end of the French and Indian War in 1763, the colonists celebrated Britain's victory over France. They were proud to be citizens of the British Empire. By 1776, about one-third of the colonists were ready to declare independence from Great Britain. About one-third remained loyal to the monarchy, and the rest had no opinion. Many colonial leaders demanded independence from Britain. How did relations between the colonies and Great Britain get to this point?

focus your reading

Why did Parliament begin to place revenue taxes on the colonists?

What actions of the First Continental Congress brought the colonists closer to war with Great Britain?

What was the purpose of the Declaration of Independence?

words to know

revenue   boycott

Time Box

1754
Albany Plan of Union

1765
Stamp Act

1774
Intolerable Acts

1774
First Continental Congress

1775
Second Continental Congress

1776
Declaration of Independence

British Policies After 1763

The French and Indian War (1756–1763) in the colonies was part of a global conflict between Britain and France. The peace treaty gave Britain vast new territories in North America and India. To protect its huge empire, Britain had to keep thousands of troops stationed overseas. King George III refused to ask the people of England to pay all the costs.

Lesson Summary

Relationships between Britain and the colonies deteriorated after the French and Indian War. British revenue taxes angered the colonists to the point that a group of them dumped tea into Boston Harbor rather than pay tax on it. Parliament, in response, passed what the colonists called the four Intolerable Acts. The colonists formed Continental Congresses, which drafted documents, raised an army for defense, and began issuing money. Finally, the colonists issued a Declaration of Independence.

Lesson Objective

Students will learn about the American colonists' fight for independence.

Focus Your Reading Answers

1 Parliament placed revenue taxes on the American colonists to help pay for the cost of defending the colonies.

2 The First Continental Congress called for a boycott of British goods. It also would not recognize Britain's right to tax the colonies. It further maintained the colonists' rights to create their own laws and try anyone accused of a crime in American courts.

3 The Declaration of Independence was designed to explain why the colonists were rejecting British rule and forming their own government.

Words to Know

Discuss each of the terms with students.

A *revenue* tax is designed to raise income. The British had not levied any *revenue* taxes before the Stamp Act.

A *boycott* is a refusal to buy or sell goods. The First Continental Congress called for a *boycott* of British goods.

Time Box Extension

Have students re-create the Time Box as a timeline in their notebooks. Ask them to add illustrations and notes to help them remember the significance of each event.

Picturing Government

The Boston Tea Party, depicted on page 20, was the work of the Sons of Liberty, a group of colonists who favored independence. As many as 200 men and boys took part in the raid on the three British ships, which had been in Boston Harbor for more than two weeks. The participants worked efficiently, making sure that nothing except tea was damaged. Thousands of people watched from the wharf; the British admiral also watched the scene from an upstairs window of a friend's house as the contents of 342 chests of tea were dumped into the harbor.

Stop and Think

Students' journal entries will vary but should show that students understand the issues surrounding the Stamp Act.

Extension

Have interested students investigate the Quartering Act of 1765, which required American colonists to provide homes for the British soldiers stationed in America. (The colonists believed this was in violation of their rights as Englishmen, according to the Petition of Right. Within a few years, a disagreement with the soldiers would lead to the Boston Massacre.) Have the students present their findings to the class by using the Student Presentation Builder on the student CD.

They already had a large war debt to pay off. He asked Parliament to make the North American colonists help pay for their own defense.

A group of colonists dressed as Mohawk Native Americans dumped a cargo of tea in Boston Harbor.

Beginning in 1765, Parliament levied, or placed, new taxes on the colonies to raise **revenue**, or income. The first was the Stamp Act, which placed a tax on such items as newspapers, legal documents, and playing cards. Parliament had never collected a revenue tax from the colonists before. Colonists had always taxed themselves by sending representatives to their colonial assemblies. The colonists protested this as "taxation without representation," because they did not send representatives to Parliament. Parliament repealed the Stamp Act in 1766, after street protests and violence against royal tax collectors. British businesses were also suffering from the tax.

However, Parliament did not give up its right to tax the colonists. It claimed that it represented all British subjects, including the colonists. In 1773, Parliament passed the Tea Act. Among other things, it placed a tax on tea. In protest, some citizens of Boston dumped a load of imported British tea into the harbor. This is known as the Boston Tea Party. Parliament responded with the Intolerable Acts. The first of these acts closed the port of Boston until the colonists paid for the tea. The second act outlawed town meetings in Boston. The third act required the colony to pay the cost of food and housing for the British troops sent to enforce the acts. The fourth act allowed British officials accused of serious offenses while putting down riots to be sent to England for trial.

stop and think

Why would the colonists not want to send their tax money to Great Britain? Imagine you are a colonist in 1765. Write a journal entry explaining why you do not want to pay the Stamp Act. Share your writing with a partner and discuss your reasons.

Extension

The tea issue affected more than the American colonies. Early in 1773, the East India Company was nearing bankruptcy; the value of its stock on the London Exchange was down nearly fifty percent. Because of the connections among the British, their colony of India, and the East India Company, Parliament passed a bill offering complete remission of all British duties on teas sent to the American colonies. Only the import tax would remain. This allowed the company to undercut the prices of both the teas illegally imported from Holland and tea purchased through middlemen at higher prices. In September, the East India Company authorized shipment of half a million pounds of tea to Boston, New York, and Charleston Harbors. Although the tea sent to Charleston was unloaded, it sat in the warehouses until the revolutionary forces auctioned it off for funds to fight against the British.

Colonial Unity

The actions of King George III and Parliament created the opposite effect of what was expected to happen. Instead of forcing the colonists to obey, the Intolerable Acts pushed them toward independence. Twelve colonies sent representatives to a meeting in Philadelphia in September 1774. This meeting became known as the First Continental Congress.

The Congress rejected the Intolerable Acts and called for a **boycott** of British goods. This meant the colonists would neither sell nor buy British goods. The Congress also sent Parliament a "Declaration and Resolves" that defended the colonists' right to pass laws for themselves. The colonists claimed the right to make their own laws and to try those accused of crimes in their own courts, not in courts in England. The colonists also refused to accept Parliament's right to tax them.

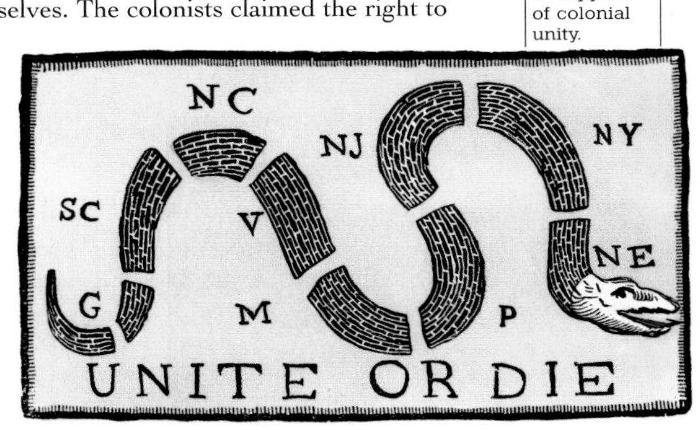

Benjamin Franklin published this drawing in support of colonial unity.

In May 1775, the Second Continental Congress met in Philadelphia. In April, colonists and British soldiers had fought the opening battles of the Revolutionary War at Lexington and Concord in the Massachusetts Bay Colony. Some members of Congress knew that declaring independence was only a matter of time. As a result, the new Congress acted to protect the colonies. It organized an army and chose George Washington as commander in chief. Congress also organized a navy and began to issue money.

Fighting between colonial and British forces continued in New England throughout 1775. Congress and King George traded petitions and proclamations. Congress's efforts at finding a peaceful solution ended with the Olive Branch Petition. It asked the king to protect the colonists from Parliament's unfair acts. The king refused to accept it and declared the colonists in rebellion.

Picturing Government

Benjamin Franklin created the cartoon on page 21 in 1754, promoting the ideas set forth at the Albany Conference. In 1775, the *Pennsylvania Journal* began using the drawing as part of its masthead.

Extension

Have students use library resources or the Internet to investigate modern efforts at preserving and displaying the Declaration of Independence and other important historical documents. Ask them to find out about the work of the National Archives and Records Administration.

Picturing Government

The engraving shown on page 22 shows members of the committee chosen to draft the Declaration of Independence: Benjamin Franklin, John Adams, and Thomas Jefferson. Robert Livingston and Roger Sherman were also members of the committee. Jefferson was chosen to write the draft, which he did in less than two weeks; Adams and Franklin then suggested changes. The document was sent to Congress on June 28, 1776. Congress made further changes to the draft's form and content on July 2 and 3, with final approval on July 4. Not until July 8 was the declaration proclaimed publicly, in Philadelphia; the following day it was read to Washington and his troops in New York City. That evening, some of New York's citizens pulled down a gilded statue depicting King George III riding a horse. Melted down, the metal of the statue yielded 42,000 bullets for the patriot cause.

Declaring Independence

In early 1776, support for independence from Great Britain grew rapidly. Thomas Paine's pamphlet, *Common Sense,* persuaded many colonists that the time for independence had come. He denounced King George III as a "royal brute" who could no longer be trusted to protect American rights. By spring, some colonial legislatures were telling their representatives to the Second Continental Congress to work toward independence. On June 7, Richard Henry Lee of Virginia introduced a resolution calling for independence.

Thomas Jefferson drafted the Declaration of Independence in 1776.

The representatives debated his resolution throughout June. In the meantime, Congress had named a committee to prepare a declaration of independence. The document would explain why the colonies were rejecting British rule and establishing their own national government. Thomas Jefferson was asked to write the document.

The Declaration of Independence was presented to Congress on June 28. On July 2, the Second Continental Congress passed Lee's Resolution. On July 4, the members of Congress signed the Declaration of Independence. There was no turning back. Congress then prepared to set up the new nation's government.

Putting It All Together

What steps led to the Declaration of Independence? With a partner, make a list of the actions taken by Parliament and King George III, on one side, and the colonists, on the other side, that led to the Declaration of Independence.

Putting It All Together

Students' lists of steps will vary. Possible responses:

Parliament and King George: levied revenue taxes, especially the Stamp Tax, which was later repealed, and the Tea Tax; Intolerable Acts; King George refused to read the Olive Branch Petition

Colonists: protested taxation without representation; Boston Tea Party; First and Second Continental Congresses; boycott of British goods; organized army; sent Olive Branch Petition; Thomas Paine published *Common Sense*; Declaration of Independence signed

The Declaration of Independence

Action of Second Continental Congress, July 4, 1776

The unanimous Declaration of the thirteen United States of America

WHEN in the Course of human Events, it becomes necessary for one People to dissolve the Political Bands which have connected them with another, and to assume among the Powers of the Earth, the separate and equal Station to which the Laws of Nature and of Nature's God entitle them, a decent Respect to the Opinions of Mankind requires that they should declare the causes which **impel** them to the Separation.

WE hold these Truths to be self-evident, that all Men are created equal, that they are **endowed** by their Creator with certain **unalienable** Rights, that among these are Life, Liberty and the Pursuit of Happiness — That to secure these Rights, Governments are instituted among Men, deriving their just Powers from the Consent of the Governed, that whenever any Form of Government becomes destructive of these Ends, it is the Right of the People to alter or to abolish it, and to institute new Government, laying its Foundation on such Principles, and organizing its Powers in such Form, as to them shall seem most likely to effect their Safety and Happiness. Prudence, indeed, will dictate that Governments long established should not be changed for light and **transient** Causes; and accordingly all Experience hath shewn, that Mankind are more disposed to suffer, while Evils are sufferable, than to right themselves by abolishing the Forms to which they are accustomed. But when a long Train of Abuses and **Usurpations**, pursuing invariably the same Object, evinces a Design to reduce them under **absolute Despotism**, it is their Right, it is their Duty, to throw off such Government, and to provide new Guards for their future Security. Such has been the patient Sufferance of these Colonies; and such is now the Necessity which constrains them to alter their former Systems of Government. The History of the present King of Great Britain is a History of repeated Injuries and Usurpations, all having in direct Object the Establishment of an absolute Tyranny over these States. To prove this, let Facts be submitted to a **candid** World.

Preamble

The Preamble, or first paragraph, states that the colonists have determined that it is necessary to break away from Great Britain. However, they respect the right of others to know why they have come to this decision. The Declaration is their explanation.

impel: force

Natural Rights

This section describes the political ideas behind the colonists' desire for independence. Thomas Jefferson borrowed ideas from the French philosopher Montesquieu and the English philosopher John Locke. People create governments in order to protect their natural rights. Natural rights are rights that belong to people because they are human beings. Jefferson lists the three basic rights as "life, liberty, and the pursuit of happiness." If government leaders do not protect these rights, then the people have the right to replace the leaders. However, Jefferson notes that governments should not be replaced for unimportant reasons. People should change a government only for the most serious reasons. People have a further duty to set up a new government that will safeguard their rights.

endowed: given
unalienable: cannot be taken away
transient: passing quickly
usurpations: unjust use of power
absolute despotism: complete control of government; same as absolute monarchy

candid: fair, sincere

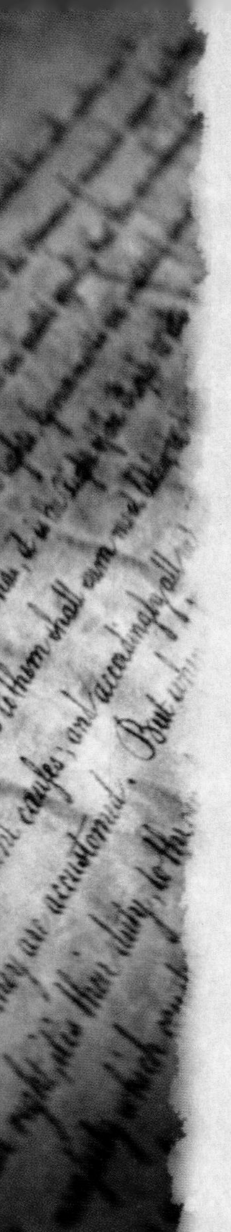

HE has refused his Assent to Laws, the most wholesome and necessary for the public Good.

HE has forbidden his Governors to pass Laws of immediate and pressing Importance, unless suspended in their Operation till his Assent should be obtained; and when so suspended, he has utterly neglected to attend to them.

HE has refused to pass other Laws for the Accommodation of large Districts of People, unless those People would **relinquish** the Right of Representation in the Legislature, a Right **inestimable** to them, and formidable to **Tyrants** only.

HE has called together Legislative Bodies at Places unusual, uncomfortable, and distant from the **Depository** of their public Records, for the sole Purpose of fatiguing them into Compliance with his Measures.

HE has dissolved Representative Houses repeatedly, for opposing with manly Firmness his Invasions on the Rights of the People.

HE has refused for a long Time, after such Dissolutions, to cause others to be elected; whereby the Legislative Powers, incapable of the **Annihilation**, have returned to the People at large for their exercise; the State remaining in the mean time exposed to all the Dangers of Invasion from without, and the **Convulsions** within.

HE has endeavoured to prevent the Population of these States; for that Purpose obstructing the Laws for Naturalization of Foreigners; refusing to pass others to encourage their Migrations hither, and raising the Conditions of new Appropriations of Lands.

HE has obstructed the Administration of Justice, by refusing his Assent to Laws for establishing Judiciary Powers.

HE has made Judges dependent on his Will alone, for the **Tenure** of their Offices, and the Amount and Payment of their Salaries.

HE has erected a Multitude of new Offices, and sent hither Swarms of Officers to harrass our People, and eat out their Substance.

HE has kept among us, in Times of Peace, Standing Armies, without the consent of our Legislatures.

HE has affected to render the Military independent of and superior to the Civil Power.

HE has combined with others to subject us to a **Jurisdiction** foreign to our Constitution, and unacknowledged by our Laws; giving his Assent to their Acts of pretended Legislation:

List of Charges Against King George III

Most of the Declaration lists the ways that George III had abused the rights of the colonists. Each paragraph lists an offense against the people. In truth, most members of Parliament had supported these actions. However, some members of Parliament had supported the colonists. Jefferson wanted to keep them on the colonists' side, so he made the monarch the target of the list.

relinquish: give up
inestimable: priceless
tyrant: dictator
depository: storehouse

annihilation: complete destruction

convulsions: violent disturbances

tenure: length of time in office

These are British troops stationed in the colonies after the French and Indian War.

This refers to the Quartering Act, one of the Intolerable Acts passed after the Boston Tea Party.

jurisdiction: authority, power

FOR quartering large Bodies of Armed Troops among us;

FOR protecting them, by a **mock** Trial, from Punishment for any Murders which they should commit on the Inhabitants of these States:

mock: imitation, not real

FOR cutting off our Trade with all Parts of the World:

FOR imposing Taxes on us without our Consent:

FOR depriving us, in many Cases, of the Benefits of Trial by Jury:

FOR transporting us beyond Seas to be tried for pretended Offences:

FOR abolishing the free System of English Laws in a neighbouring Province, establishing therein an **arbitrary** Government, and enlarging its Boundaries, so as to **render** it at once an Example and fit Instrument for introducing the same absolute Rules into these Colonies:

The Quebec Act allowed Canada to keep its French system of laws, which gave people fewer rights than English laws.

arbitrary: based on someone's idea rather than on laws or rules
render: make

FOR taking away our Charters, abolishing our most valuable Laws, and altering fundamentally the Forms of our Governments:

FOR suspending our own Legislatures, and declaring themselves invested with Power to legislate for us in all Cases whatsoever.

HE has **abdicated** Government here, by declaring us out of his Protection and waging War against us.

abdicated: given up

HE has plundered our Seas, ravaged our Coasts, burnt our Towns, and destroyed the Lives of our People.

HE is, at this Time, transporting large Armies of foreign Mercenaries to compleat the Works of Death, Desolation, and Tyranny, already begun with circumstances of Cruelty and **Perfidy**, scarcely paralleled in the most barbarous Ages, and totally unworthy the Head of a civilized Nation.

Not all the troops in the colonies were British soldiers. Parliament hired German mercenaries to patrol the colonies. Mercenaries are soldiers who work for foreign governments.

perfidy: disloyalty, breaking a trust

HE has constrained our fellow Citizens taken Captive on the high Seas to bear Arms against their Country, to become the Executioners of their Friends and Brethren, or to fall themselves by their Hands.

HE has excited domestic **Insurrections** amongst us, and has endeavoured to bring on the Inhabitants of our Frontiers, the merciless Indian Savages, whose known Rule of Warfare, is an undistinguished Destruction, of all Ages, Sexes and Conditions.

insurrections: rebellions

IN every stage of these Oppressions we have **Petitioned for Redress** in the most humble Terms: Our repeated Petitions have been answered only by repeated Injury. A Prince, whose Character is thus marked by every act which may define a Tyrant, is unfit to be the Ruler of a free People.

petitioned for redress: asked for a solution or remedy

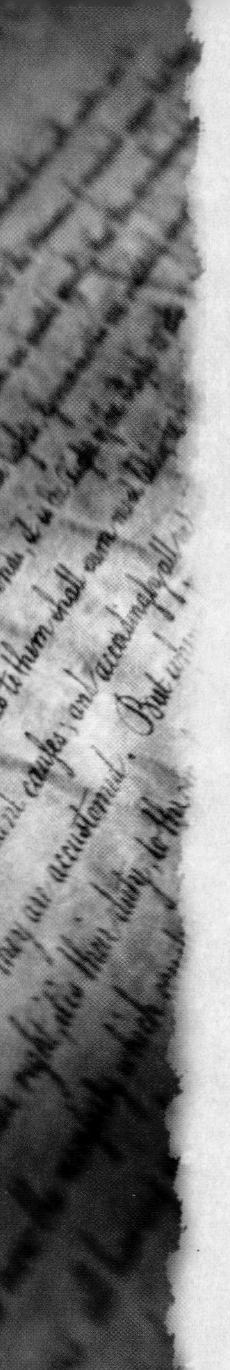

NOR have we been wanting in Attentions to our British Brethren. We have warned them from Time to Time of Attempts by their Legislature to extend an unwarrantable Jurisdiction over us. We have reminded them of the Circumstances of our Emigration and Settlement here. We have appealed to their native Justice and Magnanimity, and we have **conjured** them by the Ties of our common Kindred to disavow these Usurpations, which, would inevitably interrupt our Connections and Correspondence. They too have been deaf to the Voice of Justice and of **Consanguinity**. We must, therefore, acquiesce in the Necessity, which denounces our Separation, and hold them, as we hold the rest of Mankind, Enemies in War, in Peace, Friends.

conjured: asked for

consanguinity: blood relationship

WE, therefore, the Representatives of the UNITED STATES OF AMERICA, in GENERAL CONGRESS, Assembled, appealing to the Supreme Judge of the World for the **Rectitude** of our Intentions, do, in the Name, and by Authority of the good People of these Colonies, solemnly Publish and Declare, That these United Colonies are, and of Right ought to be, FREE AND INDEPENDENT STATES; that they are absolved from all Allegiance to the British Crown, and that all political Connection between them and the State of Great-Britain, is and ought to be totally dissolved; and that as FREE AND INDEPENDENT STATES, they have full Power to levy War, conclude Peace, contract Alliances, establish Commerce, and to do all other Acts and Things which INDEPENDENT STATES may of right do. And for the support of this Declaration, with a firm Reliance on the Protection of divine Providence, we mutually pledge to each other our Lives, our Fortunes, and our sacred Honor.

Resolution of Independence and Rights

The final section declares that the colonies are "free and independent states." It then lists the rights that the new nation has. Once this document was signed by the assembled representatives of the colonies, there was no turning back.

rectitude: correctness, rightness

John Hancock
Button Gwinnett
Lyman Hall
Geo Walton
Wm Hooper
Joseph Hewes
John Penn
Edward Rutledge
Thos Heyward Junr.
Thomas Lynch Junr.
Arthur Middleton
Samuel Chase
Wm. Paca
Thos. Stone

Charles Carroll Of Carrollton
George Wythe
Richard Henry Lee
Th Jefferson
Benja Harrison
Thos Nelson Jr.
Francis Lightfoot Lee
Carter Braxton
Robt Morris
Benjamin Rush
Benja. Franklin
John Morton
Geo Clymer
Jas. Smith

Geo. Taylor
James Wilson
Geo. Ross
Caesar Rodney
Geo Read
Tho M. Kean
Wm Floyd
Phil. Livingston
Frans. Lewis
Lewis Morris
Richd. Stockton
Jno Witherspoon
Fras. Hopkinson
John Hart
Abra Clark

Josiah Bartlett
Wm. Whipple
Saml Adams
John Adams
Robt Treat Paine
Elbridge Gerry
Step Hopkins
William Ellery
Roger Sherman
Samel Huntington
Wm. Williams
Oliver Wolcott
Matthew Thornton

LESSON 3

The Confederation Government

Thinking on Your Own

If you were going to draw up a new plan of government in 1776, how would you set up your government? How would your experience with Great Britain affect what you wanted in a government? Make a list of at least five things you would or would not want in your new government.

Once the Declaration was signed, the colonies were no longer colonies. Each became a state with the powers of a state.

States either quickly wrote new constitutions or used their colonial plans of government as their constitutions. The relationship between the states and the national government was not the same as it is today. The states were joined together in a loose union known as a confederation. The states kept most of their powers. They shared few powers with the national government.

focus your reading

Discuss why the new states set up a confederation form of government.

What did the confederation government accomplish?

Explain the weaknesses of the confederation government.

words to know

central government

ratify

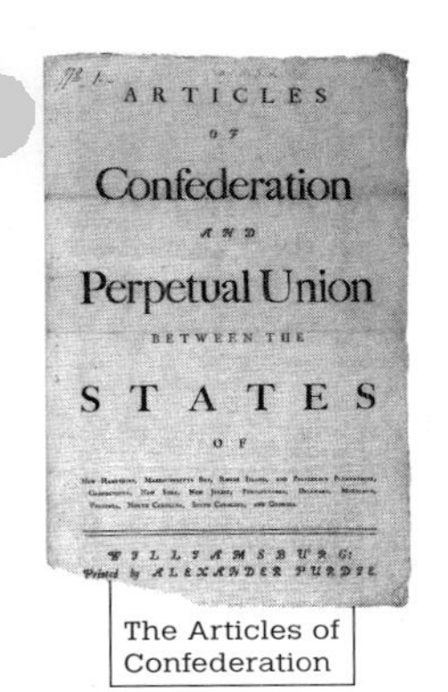
ARTICLES
OF
Confederation
AND
Perpetual Union
BETWEEN THE
STATES
OF

WILLIAMSBURG:
Printed by ALEXANDER PURDIE

The Articles of Confederation

The Confederation Government

It soon became clear that the new states needed some form of **central government**. For example, each state could not act alone in fighting Great Britain. As a result, in 1777, the Second Continental Congress agreed on the Articles of Confederation. By 1781, all the states had **ratified**, or approved, this new plan of government. It remained the government of the new nation until it was replaced by the United States Constitution in 1789.

Lesson Summary

The states formed a loose union under the Articles of Confederation. The document, ratified in 1781, provided for neither an executive nor a judicial branch. Congress did not have power to tax or to regulate trade. In spite of limitations, the confederation succeeded in negotiating a treaty with Britain and in devising a plan for western settlement. The weaknesses of the confederation led to problems with debt and economic hardships for many.

Lesson Objective

Students will learn about the first American government.

Focus Your Reading Answers

1 The states set up a confederation form of government so that there would be a central government to direct foreign affairs, coin money, and build a navy. However, fearing a central government as strong as Great Britain's, creators of the Articles of Confederation kept the central government weak, forbidding it power to regulate trade or collect taxes.

2 The confederation government negotiated the treaty with Great Britain following the end of the Revolutionary War. It also provided, through the Northwest Ordinance, a means of dividing, selling, and settling the newly acquired territory.

3 Weaknesses of the confederation government included lack of judicial and executive branches, inability to pass taxes or regulate trade, and the difficulty of creating new laws or changing the Articles.

Words to Know

Discuss each of the vocabulary terms with students.

A *central government* is one that acts for all the states. When the states realized they could not each fight Great Britain, the advantage of a *central government* became clear.

To approve a document is to *ratify* it. All the states needed to *ratify* the Articles of Confederation before they could take effect. You may wish to use the word *ratify* to discuss the way that word endings and suffixes change meaning and spelling of words.

In this text, students will shortly read the words *ratified* and *ratification*. Help them find the root word and expand its meaning.

Picturing Government

Between 1775 and 1789, when the new Constitution went into effect, 13 men served as presidents of the Continental Congress or during the Articles of Confederation. Most of them, such as Henry Laurens, pictured on this page, are no longer well known.

Stop and Think

Students' diagrams will vary but should accurately depict the confederation government's single branch and state delegates who composed it.

Extension

In addition to providing a framework for admitting new states to the union, the Northwest Ordinance also made provisions for funding public schools. Have students use library resources or the Internet to discover how the township division of the land helped education thrive.

Great Britain had a strong central government with a great deal of power over the colonies. The new states were determined to keep another strong central government from interfering with their newly won autonomy.

Henry Laurens was president of the Continental Congress from November 1777 to December 1778.

The Articles of Confederation created a weak central government. It consisted of a Congress similar to the earlier Continental Congresses. It had no separate executive branch or judicial branch. Congress had the power to coin money, direct foreign affairs, make war and peace, and build a navy. It could not collect taxes, enforce laws, or regulate trade. Those important powers were left to the states. State governments sent delegates to Congress, with each state having one vote in Congress.

stop and think

Draw a diagram to illustrate how the confederation government was set up. Ask a partner to review your diagram against the text to make sure it is accurate.

Accomplishments of the Confederation Government

The confederation government had two major accomplishments. The first was that the new nation negotiated a favorable treaty with Great Britain at the end of the Revolutionary War. As a result of the U.S. victory, Great Britain recognized the independence of its former colonies. In addition, all the land from the Great Lakes and Canada south to Florida, and from the Atlantic coast west to the Mississippi River, became U.S. territory.

The second major accomplishment related to a section of the newly acquired land called the Northwest Territory. Congress passed the Land Ordinance of 1785 to set up a system for dividing, selling, and settling the lands in this area. In time, the states of Ohio, Indiana, Illinois, Michigan, Wisconsin, and part of Minnesota were made from this region.

Extension

Resolving the issue of regulating trade between the states proved to be difficult. New York and New Jersey taxed imports from each other. In 1784, Maryland and Virginia nearly went to war over rights for oyster fishing in the Potomac River. Virginia was one of 11 states that had independent navies; with 72 ships, Virginia's navy was larger than the national navy. Boundary disputes were also common, especially among the states that had western borders and wanted to claim more territory.

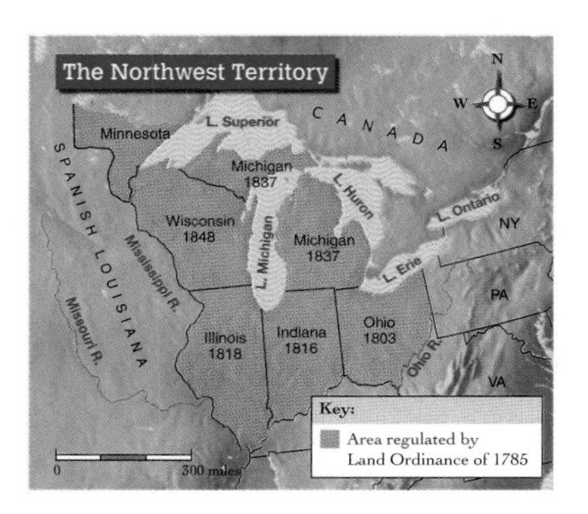

The Northwest Ordinance, which was passed in 1787, set up government for the area. The law divided the Northwest Territory into districts. Congress appointed a governor and three judges for each district. When a district had 5,000 free adult males, it could set up a legislature and elect lawmakers. When there were 60,000 people, a district could ask for statehood. The Northwest Ordinance was important for two reasons. First, it set up the system for adding new states to the United States. Second, it established the principle that old and new states had the same rights.

Weaknesses of the Articles

The Articles of Confederation had several weaknesses that made it difficult for the government to operate. First, Congress did not have the power to pass taxes. As a result, it depended on borrowing money or asking the states for money to support it. If a state refused, there was nothing Congress could do. This was the second problem with the Articles.

Third, Congress had no power to regulate trade. As a result, trade laws varied greatly from state to state and between the states and other nations. The different trade regulations hurt the economy of the new nation.

ideas to remember

The major weaknesses of the confederation government were:

- Congress could not pass taxes.
- Congress could not force states to obey its laws.
- Congress could not regulate, or manage, trade.
- Laws needed the approval of nine of the 13 states.
- All 13 states had to agree to changes in the Articles.
- There was no executive branch.
- There was no judicial branch.

Ideas to Remember Extension

Review the ideas listed, further explaining difficult vocabulary words. Have students create graphic organizers in their notebooks to help them visualize the weaknesses of the confederation government. Suggest that they group together ideas from three major areas: what the confederation government could not do, what it had to do, and what it did not include.

Picturing Government

The document shown on page 27 is the Articles of Confederation. Just two years after the document was finally ratified, the army chased the new government out of Philadelphia in anger over unpaid soldiers' salaries. However, without the power to tax, the central government was helpless to find the money needed for their pay.

Map Extension

Ask students to use the map on page 29 to answer the following questions.

- What was the western boundary of the territory? (Mississippi River)
- Which lakes formed the territory's northern border? (Superior, Michigan, Huron, and Erie)
- About how wide was the Northwest Territory from east to west? (750 miles)
- What states were eventually created out of the Northwest Territory? (Ohio, Indiana, Michigan, Illinois, Wisconsin, and part of Minnesota)

Fourth, representatives of nine of the 13 states had to approve a bill before it could become a law. However, representatives of all 13 states were rarely in Congress at the same time. Therefore, it was difficult to get laws passed.

Shays's Rebellion helped Congress realize the weaknesses of the Articles of Confederation.

Fifth, people realized over time that the Articles needed to be changed. However, the legislatures of all 13 states had to agree to changes in the Articles. No amendment was ever successful because all 13 states could never agree.

Sixth, there was no executive branch. As a result, the government could not enforce its own laws.

Seventh, there was no judicial branch. State courts heard lawsuits between the states and interpreted national laws. Interpretations could vary from court to court and state to state.

By the late 1780s, the new nation was in serious trouble. It owed millions of dollars in war loans. Economic problems were causing hardships among landowners and merchants. Small farmers suffered greatly. Many lost their land because they could not pay their debts. Something had to be done—and soon—about the confederation government.

Putting It All Together

The desire of the states to hold onto power shaped the way the Articles were written. With a partner, make a two-column table. In the left column, list the seven weaknesses of the Articles. In the right column, explain how each weakness resulted from the desire of the states not to give up power.

Picturing Government

Shays's Rebellion, depicted on page 30, was instrumental in demonstrating the wisdom of granting more power to a central government. Daniel Shays, who led the six-month rebellion, had been a captain during the Revolutionary War. The Massachusetts men closed the local courts so that they could not be condemned to debtors' prison. They later closed the state's supreme court as well to prevent being tried as traitors. Although the leaders were condemned for treason, they were later pardoned. Eventually, Shays received a war pension.

Putting It All Together

Students' tables should include the weaknesses listed on page 29. Their explanations will vary but should explain how the unwillingness of the states to relinquish power was at the root of the weakness.

Words to Know

Discuss each of the vocabulary terms on page 31 with students.

Tell them that *exports* are goods sold to other nations. Not taxing *exports* was one of the compromises made to ratify the Constitution.

Anti-Federalists were those who opposed the Constitution. The *Anti-Federalists* were strongest in Virginia and New York.

The *Federalists* supported ratifying the Constitution. Several *Federalists* wrote a series of essays to defend the need for a strong central government.

LESSON 4

The Constitutional Convention

Thinking on Your Own

If you were going to revise the Articles of Confederation, what would you change? Decide based on what you know about the federal government today and what you have learned about weaknesses of the confederation government. Compare your changes with those of a partner.

focus your reading

What six early decisions shaped the Constitutional Convention?

Describe the compromises made by the delegates.

What were the issues in the fight over ratification of the Constitution?

words to know

exports

Anti-Federalists

Federalists

By the mid-1780s, relations between Maryland and Virginia had become strained over trade issues. In 1785, George Washington asked the states to meet at Mount Vernon in Virginia to discuss the issues. The discussions went well enough that another meeting was called for the following year in Annapolis, Maryland. This time all the states were asked to attend. The purpose of the Annapolis Convention was to discuss trade issues. Only five states attended. After much discussion, the delegates called for a meeting in May 1787 to discuss ways to make the Articles of Confederation stronger.

The Constitutional Convention met in 1787 with the goal of revising the Articles of Confederation.

31

Picturing Government

The Constitutional Convention of 1787, shown on page 31, met in Philadelphia, the largest city in the nation at that time with 40,000 people. The city had more than 650 streetlights, water pumps to fight fires regularly spaced on each block, and some paved streets. The city boasted a university, a museum, 33 churches, two theaters, and ten newspapers. Directly across the street from the State House, where the 55 delegates met, was a jail that was a model for prison systems in Europe.

Lesson Summary

At a meeting in Annapolis, the delegates voted to strengthen the Articles of Confederation. That meeting, held in Philadelphia, led to the writing of a new constitution. Four major compromises were required: representation of states; population figures in Congress, including the counting of slaves; permitting slavery to continue in exchange for allowing the national government power to regulate trade; and having the Electoral College choose the president. The fight to ratify the Constitution focused on the need for a bill of rights and on the fear of a strong federal government.

Lesson Objective

Students will learn about the decisions and debates of the Constitutional Convention that led to a new and ratified Constitution.

Focus Your Reading Answers

1 Each state had only one vote; to approve a proposal required at least seven of the 12 states; the convention proceedings were secret; a new plan of government was needed to replace the Articles; both limited and representative government would be part of the new government; the federal government would have three branches: executive, legislative, and judicial.

2 The four major compromises were on representation, population in Congress, allowing slavery to continue if the national government had power to regulate trade, and the Electoral College as a means of electing the president.

3 The two major issues were the opposition to a strong central government and a desire for a bill of rights.

Organizing the Constitutional Convention

Each state legislature chose delegates to attend the Constitutional Convention. The convention opened in Philadelphia on May 25, 1787. In all, 55 men were appointed to represent 12 states. Rhode Island did not send delegates because it opposed strengthening the confederation government. George Washington was selected to be president of the convention. The representatives soon realized that strengthening the Articles of Confederation was not enough—they needed to write a new constitution. Among the early decisions that shaped the convention were the following:

- Each state had only one vote.
- At least seven of the 12 states had to approve a proposal.
- The public would not be told what was happening until the convention was over.
- The Articles had to be replaced by a new plan of government.

James Madison (1751–1836)

James Madison had a great deal of political experience before the Constitutional Convention. He helped write Virginia's state constitution in 1776, and he served in the Continental Congress from 1780 to 1783 and in the Virginia legislature from 1784 to 1786. Madison had firsthand knowledge of the weaknesses of the Articles of Confederation. He went to Philadelphia prepared to write a new plan of government. He wanted a greatly strengthened central government.

Madison had a list of 15 proposals for how a new government should be organized. These suggestions formed the basis for discussions and became known as the Virginia Plan. Much of the Constitution reflects his ideas. As a result of his proposals, Madison is often called "the Father of the Constitution."

Madison's work at the convention is important for another reason. He kept the only complete record of the discussions. Because the delegates voted to keep the debates secret, his *Notes* were not published until 1840, four years after his death. It is because of his journal that we know what went on at the convention. Madison ended his public service as president of the United States from 1809–1817.

Bio Facts

- Born March 16, 1751.
- Attended what is now Princeton University, graduating in two years.
- Married Dolley Dandridge Payne Todd, a widow, in 1794.
- Virginia representative to Congress, 1789–1797, where he introduced and shepherded the Bill of Rights to passage.
- Elected fourth president in 1808, succeeding his friend Thomas Jefferson; reelected in 1812.
- Died June 28, 1836.

Biography Extension

Madison suffered from several disadvantages. At 5 feet, 4 inches tall, he was the shortest president. From childhood, he experienced attacks of nerves similar to epileptic seizures, sometimes going to bed for days at a time. He was shy and didn't make small talk. In addition, he had a weak voice in an age of orators; the man who served as the Virginia legislature's recorder sometimes could not hear Madison.

Extension

Students may wish to use library resources or the Internet to find out more about Dolley Madison, one of the most popular of presidents' wives. She is often noted for her role in saving a famous portrait of George Washington during the War of 1812. She was also a noted hostess, not only for Madison but also for his close friend Thomas Jefferson. She worked with Benjamin Latrobe in remodeling the White House.

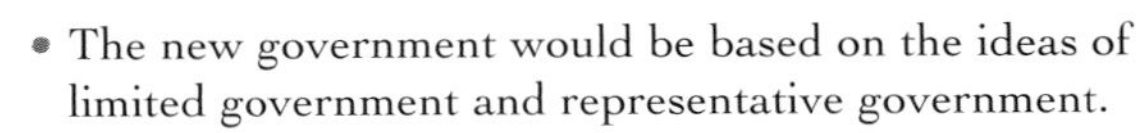

- The new government would be based on the ideas of limited government and representative government.

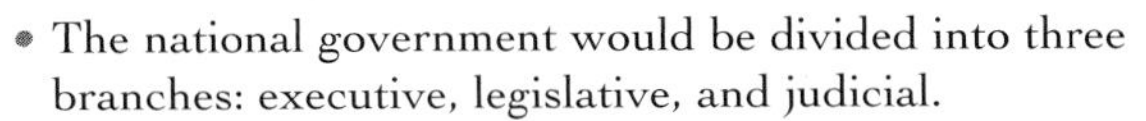

- The national government would be divided into three branches: executive, legislative, and judicial.

The Major Compromises

James Madison, a delegate from Virginia, arrived with a plan for a new national government. The Virginia Plan, as it was called, favored the large states, as it made a state's population the basis for representation. William Paterson of New Jersey offered a plan that favored the small states. Much of the convention was spent debating the two plans. After much debate, the convention almost broke up. It could not agree on either plan.

Finally, the Connecticut Compromise, also known as the Great Compromise, was proposed. The Connecticut Compromise was really a series of compromises that ended the deadlock. Analyze the table "Competing Plans and the Compromise Solutions" on page 34. It shows the differences between the plans and how compromise solved the problems.

stop and think

Compromise was an important part of the Constitutional Convention. With a partner, make a concept map of the four major compromises agreed to by the delegates. Draw lines and add circles to each compromise to show its most important details.

The delegates reached other important compromises. One dealt with how people would be counted to determine the number of representatives each state would have in the House of Representatives. Southern states wanted enslaved people counted. Northern states wanted only free people counted. The delegates approved the Three-Fifths Compromise to settle the disagreement. Three-fifths of the population of enslaved people would be counted in determining representation.

A third compromise also involved slavery—and trade in general. Southerners would not accept the Constitution if it banned the slave trade. They also would not accept the Constitution if it allowed the national government to tax **exports**, or goods being sold to other nations. As a result, the

Stop and Think

Students' concept maps will differ but should include the four major compromises and details about each.

Extension

Ask students to find out more about the function of the Electoral College using library resources or the Internet. Ask them to focus specifically on elections, most recently the 2000 election, in which the Electoral College vote and the popular vote differed.

Extensions

1 Roger Sherman suggested the Connecticut Compromise. Sherman, a former shoemaker who taught himself law, was the second-oldest man at the Convention, at sixty-six. He had signed both the Declaration of Independence and the Articles of Confederation. Sherman was well respected by his fellow delegates. Of him, Thomas Jefferson once said, "There is Mr. Sherman of Connecticut, who never said a foolish thing in his life." And John Adams called him "an old Puritan, honest as an angel."

2 The legislature was not the only branch on which delegates disagreed. Edmund Randolph wanted a committee of three men to act as the executive branch. Alexander Hamilton preferred an individual more like a monarch. To agree on a means of choosing the president, the delegates voted 60 times.

Extension

The Constitution does not justify or explain its contents. For example, students may wonder why senators are elected for six years and representatives for only two. The *Federalist Papers* do explain that difference, as well as other provisions, such as the separation of powers.

Chart Extension

Distribute four blank index cards to each student. Have them write a summary on each of the cards about the four issues debated in the fight for a new constitution. Tell students that the cards will be a handy way to review for a test or quiz.

delegates agreed not to tax exports. However, they agreed to give the national government the power to regulate trade between states and between states and foreign nations. In return, the national government did not ban the slave trade with foreign nations until 1808.

The fourth compromise involved how the president was elected. The delegates agreed on an Electoral College. The legislature in each state would choose electors who would meet after the national election by citizens. The electors would select the president based on the number of votes each candidate received.

Competing Plans and the Compromise Solutions

Issue	Virginia Plan	New Jersey Plan	U.S. Constitution
Representation	Based on population or wealth	Equal representation for each state	Upper house (Senate) made up of two delegates from each state; Lower house (House of Representatives) based on population
Executive Branch	Single executive chosen by Congress	Executive committee chosen by Congress	Single executive (president) chosen by the Electoral College; electors selected by individual states
Legislative Branch	Two houses: Upper house elected by the people; Lower house elected by the upper house	One house: appointed by state legislatures	Two houses: Upper house (Senate) selected by state legislatures*; Lower house (House of Representatives) elected by the people
Judicial Branch	National judiciary chosen by Congress	National judiciary appointed by executive committee	National judiciary: Supreme Court and lower courts; Supreme Court justices appointed by the president and confirmed by the Senate

*The Seventeenth Amendment in 1913 changed this. Senators are now elected by the people.

ideas to remember

The major compromises of the Constitutional Convention were

- Connecticut, or Great, Compromise that combined the Virginia Plan and the New Jersey Plan
- Three-Fifths Compromise on slavery
- compromise on commerce and the slave trade
- Electoral College compromise

Ratifying the Constitution

Nine of the 13 states had to ratify the Constitution before it could go into effect. However, its supporters knew that all 13 states had to approve it. Otherwise, the new nation would collapse.

Ratification, or approval, was not a sure thing. Opposition was centered on two issues. Some people did not want a strong central government. Others, like Thomas Jefferson, wanted a bill of rights included in the Constitution. They wanted the rights of individuals protected against government.

Anti-Federalists, those who opposed the Constitution, were especially strong in New York and Virginia.

The **Federalists** supported ratification. Several of them, including James Madison, John Jay, and Alexander Hamilton, wrote a series of essays defending the need for a strong government. The *Federalist Papers* won over the opposition in New York. A promise to include a bill of rights won over Virginians. The *Federalist Papers* and the promise of the bill of rights won over people in other states as well. By March 1789, only Rhode Island and North Carolina remained outside the new government. By May 1790, both states had ratified the Constitution.

Residents of New York City celebrate the ratification of the U.S. Constitution.

Putting It All Together

With a partner, brainstorm ideas for an ad to support ratification of the Constitution. List at least four ideas. Then choose one idea. Design an ad with text for your idea.

Ideas to Remember Extension

Review the ideas listed, further explaining difficult vocabulary words. Have students create graphic organizers in their notebooks to help them visualize the four key compromises.

Picturing Government

New Yorkers honored Alexander Hamilton, a delegate to the Philadelphia Convention and one of the leading Federalists. The float, shown in image on page 35, shows the nation as a ship. It was a comparison that many Americans used at the time. In what sense is a nation like an ocean-going ship? Who steers the ship?

Putting It All Together

Students' ads will vary, but the text should support ratifying the Constitution with at least one reason chosen from a list of four.

Recommended Reading

Below is a list of books that relate to the issues covered in this chapter. The numbers in parentheses indicate the related Thematic Strands of the National Council for the Social Studies (NCSS).

Candace Fleming. *Ben Franklin's Almanac: Being a True Account of the Good Gentleman's Life.* Anne Schwartz Books/Atheneum Books for Children, 2003. (I, IV, X)

Russell Freedman. *In Defense of Liberty: The Story of America's Bill of Rights,* 2003. (VI, X)

Ann Rinaldi. *Or Give Me Death: A Novel of Patrick Henry's Family.* Gulliver Books/Harcourt Children's Books, 2003. (I, IV, X)

Participate in Government

You may wish to divide the class into four groups. Assign each group a level of government: national, state, county, and local. Make each group responsible for the activities of the skill. When all the groups have gathered their material, have enough copies made for each member of the class. Allow time for each group to report on its findings and explain any forms.

Participate in Government

Register to Vote

The Twenty-sixth Amendment to the Constitution set the voting age at eighteen for all federal, state, and local elections. Before 1971, the voting age in some states had been twenty-one. Setting the qualifications for voting is still the responsibility of the states. Differences among the states usually involve how long a person must live in the state or the voting district in order to be able to vote. Typically, it is 15 to 30 days before an election.

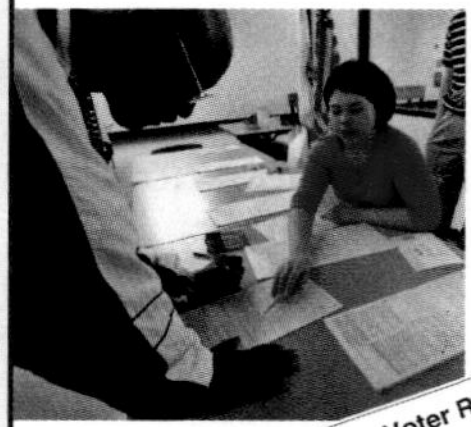

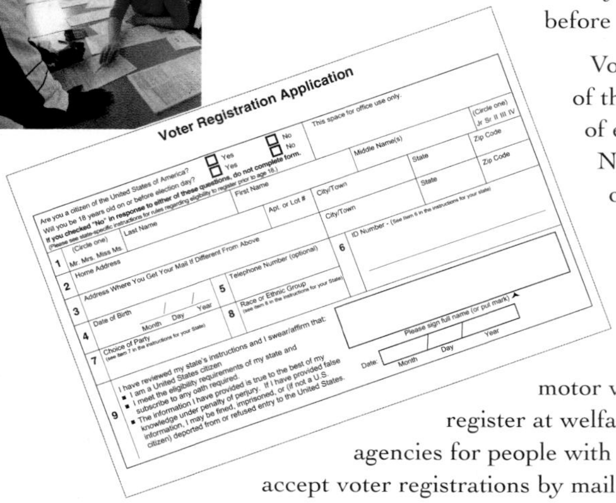
Voter Registration Application

Are you a citizen of the United States of America? Yes No
Will you be 18 years old on or before election day? Yes No
If you checked "No" in response to either of these questions, do not complete form.

1 (Circle one) Mr. Mrs. Miss Ms. | Last Name | First Name | Middle Name(s) | (Circle one) Jr Sr II III IV
2 Home Address | Apt. or Lot # | City/Town | State | Zip Code
3 Address Where You Get Your Mail If Different From Above | City/Town | State | Zip Code
4 Date of Birth Month Day Year | 5 Telephone Number (optional) | 6 ID Number
7 Choice of Party | 8 Race or Ethnic Group
9 I have reviewed my state's instructions and I swear/affirm that:
■ I am a United States citizen
■ I meet the eligibility requirements of my state and subscribe to any oath required.
■ The information I have provided is true to the best of my knowledge under penalty of perjury. If I have provided false information, I may be fined, imprisoned, or (if not a U.S. citizen) deported from or refused entry to the United States.
Please sign full name (or put mark)
Date: Month Day Year

Voters may register at the office of the county, city, or town board of elections where they live. The National Voter Registration Act of 1995 made it even easier to register. The law is sometimes called the "motor-voter act" because people can now register at their state's department of motor vehicles. Voters can also register at welfare offices and at government agencies for people with disabilities. States must also accept voter registrations by mail.

When you register to vote, you will be asked for your name, address, place and date of birth, gender, Social Security number, and political party. You may register as an independent, which means that you do not indicate a political party. This may limit whether you can vote in primary elections. You will also need to provide proof that you are a U.S. citizen.

To find out how to register in your state

- Check the government pages in your telephone directory or look online for the county, city, or town board of elections.
- Call to find out what you need to register and how or where to register.
- Gather the necessary documents.

Research Resources

Below is a list of reference books and Web sites that relate to the issues covered in this chapter. Students may wish to use these to further their research on ideas in the preceding lessons. Web site addresses may change over time. Use keyword searching on a major search engine to locate sites.

Reference Books:

Colonial America. Grolier Educational, 1998.

John Mack Faragher. *The Encyclopedia of Colonial and Revolutionary America.* Da Capo Press, 1996.

Bruce Frohnen. *The American Republic: Primary Sources*. Liberty Fund, 2002.

Web Sites:

The James Madison Center maintains the Madison archives as well as links to primary sources and commentary on national events during Madison's lifetime.

The United States National Archives and Records Administration offers access to the Declaration of Independence and other documents. An exhibit hall allows visitors to the site to view items of special interest, from founding documents to New Deal arts projects.

Skill Builder

Analyzing Timelines

Sequence is the order in which events happen. A timeline is a quick way to see the sequence of events. Dates and events on a timeline are arranged in chronological order. Chronological order is the same as time order. The first dates on a timeline are the earliest dates.

Being able to read a timeline is useful in understanding when certain events happened in relation to other events. For example, was the fighting at Lexington and Concord before or after approval of the Declaration of Independence? Knowing the time order of events can help you understand the causes of events. It can also tell you the effects of events. Lexington and Concord happened before the Declaration of Independence was written.

The timeline at the right uses dates and events from this chapter.

Time Box

- **1765** Stamp Act passed
- **1773** Boston Tea Party
- **1774** Intolerable Acts passed; First Continental Congress
- **1775** Battles of Lexington and Concord
- **1775–1781** Second Continental Congress
- **1776** Declaration of Independence
- **1777** Articles of Confederation written
- **1781–1789** Government under the Articles of Confederation
- **1785** Delegates from Virginia and Maryland met at Mount Vernon
- **1786** Annapolis Convention held
- **1786–1787** Shays's Rebellion
- **1787** Constitutional Convention
- **1788** U.S. Constitution ratified

Answer the following questions.

1. When did the Annapolis Convention take place?
2. How many years passed between the Annapolis Convention and the ratification of the U.S. Constitution?
3. Which took place first: passage of the Stamp Act or passage of the Intolerable Acts?
4. For how many years were the Articles of Confederation the basis of government for the United States?

Skill Builder

1. 1786
2. two
3. passage of the Stamp Act
4. eight

Classroom Discussion

Discuss with students some of the broader topics covered in this chapter.

- How do you see the advantages of a two-section Congress and a three-branch government playing out in current events?
- How can the experience of the United States in the early days of the republic help us understand the turmoil within nations currently trying to become more democratic?
- What are some recent national or local debates over taxes? How might the people of the early United States have responded to the debates?

Chapter 3

THE UNITED STATES CONSTITUTION

Getting Focused

Skim this chapter to predict what you will be learning.

- **Read the lesson titles and subheadings.**
- **Look at the illustrations and read the captions.**
- **Examine the charts and diagrams.**
- **Review the vocabulary words and terms.**

The Constitution provided a new form of government for the United States. Think about what you already know about the Constitution. Write five statements in your notebook about the kind of national government it created.

The United States Constitution was completed on September 17, 1787. The document became the "Law of the Land" when ratified on March 4, 1789.

Related Transparencies

T-1 Checks and Balances of the Federal Government and Proposing and Ratifying the Constitution

T-2 Amendments to the Constitution

T-18 Three-Column Chart

Key Blacklines

Primary Source—Iraqi Constitution 2005

Getting Focused

If students are having difficulty thinking of five things they know about the Constitution and the national government, you may wish to place them in small groups to work on the assignment together.

Picturing Government

The Preamble to the Constitution, shown on page 38, was the work of Gouverneur Morris. Morris, who was a delegate from Pennsylvania, spoke well and often at the Constitutional Convention. After the document was completed, it was given to Morris to polish. He created seven articles out of 23 resolutions. It was Morris who wrote "We the people," a phrase that angered Patrick Henry, who thought that the document should say "We the states."

Pre-Reading Discussion

1 Ask students for examples of division of labor from the world of sports. For example, football players generally play either offense or defense. How does specialization help the game and the team to work together? Tell students that in this chapter, they will learn about the ways in which the national government divides responsibilities and duties so that the government runs more smoothly.

2 Discuss with students the commonly given advice in business "Get it in writing." Ask them how writing something down can make it more binding. Have them suggest everyday examples in which it is wise to get something in writing. You may also want to share with them the idea that writing down goals is a good first step toward achieving them. How might the Declaration of Independence be considered a goal document and the Constitution the fulfillment of that goal?

LESSON 1

The Basic Principles

Thinking on Your Own

A representative government is one of the basic principles of the Constitution. Based on what you already know about the U.S. government, how did the writers include this principle in the Constitution? What clues do the vocabulary terms provide about the principles of government on which the Constitution was based? Discuss these questions with a partner. Then answer them in your notebook.

The U.S. Constitution is the basic law of the United States. It describes how the national government should be set up. It also describes the relationship between the national government and the states. No law—either national or state—is higher than the Constitution.

focus your reading

Explain how the Constitution is organized.

The Constitution is based on what six principles of government?

words to know

supremacy clause
amendments
Framers
popular sovereignty
federalism
separation of powers
checks and balances
judicial review

Organization of the Constitution

The Constitution is divided into three parts. The first part is called the Preamble. It explains why the document was written.

The second part of the Constitution is made up of seven articles. These articles lay out the plan of government for the United States.

- Article I describes the legislative branch (Congress), its duties and powers, and qualifications for its members.

George Washington with a copy of the U.S. Constitution in 1787

Lesson Summary

The lesson presents the overall organization of the Constitution and the six guiding principles that the Framers used to create it.

Lesson Objective

Students will learn how the Constitution is organized and the principles underlying the document.

Focus Your Reading Answers

1 There are three parts to the Constitution. The first is the Preamble, explaining why the document was written. The second section, which explains the plan of government, is made up of seven articles. The final section lists the amendments.

2 The Constitution is based on the principles of popular sovereignty, federalism, separation of powers, checks and balances, judicial review, and limited government.

Picturing Government

The meetings of the Constitutional Convention were secret. Despite the heat, the windows of the Pennsylvania State House were kept closed so that no one could listen in , so there were no eyewitness painters of the convention. The painting shown on page 39 was done later, with the artist using his imagination.

Words to Know

Introduce each of the following words and terms to students.

Explain that the *supremacy clause* states that the Constitution, acts of Congress, and treaties are the supreme law of the land. The *supremacy clause* is found in Article VI of the Constitution.

Point out to students that the term *amendment* includes the word *mend* within it. This offers a clue to the term's meaning. Ask if they have heard the term *make amends,* and be sure they know the meaning of that term as well. Invite examples of other uses for the word *amendment*. *Amendments* are additions to the Constitution. The first ten *amendments* are called the Bill of Rights.

The *Framers* were the writers of the Constitution. The delegates who attended the Constitutional Convention are all considered the *Framers*.

continued on page 40

Stop and Think

Students' ideas will vary but should be supported.

Extension

The vocabulary terms in this lesson offer a rich opportunity to help students build their knowledge of English by using prefixes and suffixes. You may wish to have students work in small groups, assigning each group a word part and challenging the group to use a dictionary to find the meaning. Then give the class several examples of the word part being used in other words. For example, the suffix *-tion* appears in both *constitution* and *ratification*.

Extension

Have students skim through Article I of the Constitution, noting the qualifications for senators and representatives. Have them make comparative charts of the minimum requirements for office. Then lead a discussion about those differences and why students think the Framers established them.

CD Extension

Encourage students to use the reading comprehension, vocabulary reinforcement, and other activities on the student CD.

- Article II describes the duties and powers of the executive branch and the qualifications for president and vice president. It also describes the process for electing the president and vice president.
- Article III creates the Supreme Court as head of the judicial branch.
- Article IV explains the relationship among the states and the states' relationship to the national government.
- Article V describes the process for amending, or changing, the Constitution.
- Article VI declares that the Constitution, acts of Congress, and treaties are the "supreme Law of the Land." This is known as the **supremacy clause**.
- Article VII sets out the process for ratifying, or formally approving, the Constitution.

The third part of the Constitution lists the **amendments**. The first ten are known as the Bill of Rights. These were written during the first session of Congress in 1789. They became laws when the Virginia legislature ratified them in 1791. Virginia was the ninth state to ratify them. In more than 200 years, only 17 additional amendments have been ratified.

stop and think

The first three articles of the Constitution describe the branches of the national government. The men who wrote the Constitution could have described them in a single section. Why do you think they gave each branch a separate article? Discuss your ideas with a partner and write your answer in a sentence or two in your notebook.

The Foundation of the Constitution

The delegates who attended the Constitutional Convention are known as the **Framers**, or writers, of the Constitution. They based the new government on six principles. These principles are: popular sovereignty, federalism, separation of powers, checks and balances, judicial review, and limited government.

The power of the U.S. government comes from the people of the nation. **Popular sovereignty** is the term that describes this. Government is able to govern as long as it has the consent, or approval, of the governed. As Abraham Lincoln described the government, it is "government of the people, by the people, [and] for the people."

Words to Know, continued

Popular sovereignty is the idea that people govern. *Popular sovereignty* was a new concept of government in the late 1700s.

Federalism is the relationship between the national government and the states. In *federalism*, both share duties and responsibilities.

The *separation of powers* means that each branch of government has its own responsibilities. Under the *separation of powers*, the legislative branch makes the laws but does not enforce them.

The system of *checks and balances* is a way that each branch has power to restrain the power of the others. Senate confirmation of presidential nominees is one example of *checks and balances*.

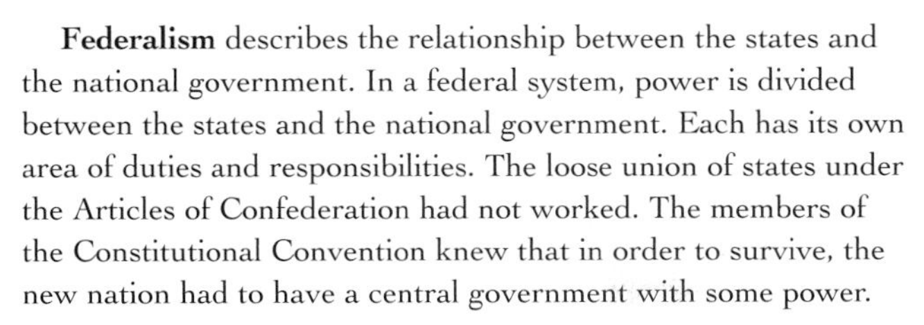

Federalism describes the relationship between the states and the national government. In a federal system, power is divided between the states and the national government. Each has its own area of duties and responsibilities. The loose union of states under the Articles of Confederation had not worked. The members of the Constitutional Convention knew that in order to survive, the new nation had to have a central government with some power.

The delegates set up three branches of government. Each branch was given its own duties and responsibilities. This division is based on the principle of **separation of powers**.

Checks and Balances of the Federal Government

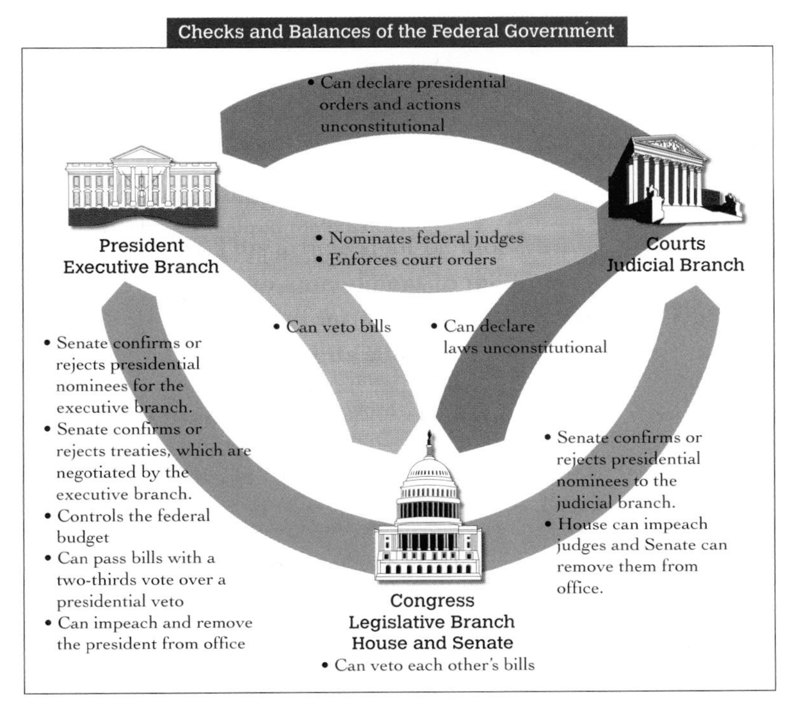

The writers of the Constitution built into the central government a system of **checks and balances**. Each branch has duties that check, or restrain, the power of the other two branches. For example, the president nominates federal judges. The Senate approves or rejects the president's candidates. The diagram "Checks and Balances of the Federal Government," above, explains how the system works.

Diagram Extension

Divide the class into three groups. Assign each group one of the three branches of government. Have the groups prepare graphic organizers for their branches, showing how they check and are checked by the other branches. Allow time for each group to present its information to the class. You may wish to photocopy the graphic organizers and distribute them to the class as a study aid.

Extension

The quotation by Abraham Lincoln at the bottom of page 40 is the conclusion of his Gettysburg Address. In his attempt to honor the dead of the Civil War, particularly those who had died at Gettysburg, Lincoln tried to assure his listeners that those deaths had not been in vain, but would ensure that the government of, by, and for the people would not perish. The speech, which Lincoln delivered in about three minutes, was notable for its brevity. Lincoln followed a great orator of the day, Edward Everett, who spoke for two hours.

Words to Know, continued

Judicial review is the ability of courts to rule on whether a law or action of government is constitutional. The power of *judicial review* is not stated in the Constitution.

Limited government restricts the power of government to do some things. The Bill of Rights expresses the idea of *limited government* by listing rights that the government cannot take away.

Picturing Government

The Supreme Court, shown in the photograph at the left of the collage on page 42, did not have its own building until 1935. No provision was made for a building; Congress loaned the Court space in the Capitol. Not until 1929 did Chief Justice and former president William Howard Taft call for the construction of a separate building. The architect was Cass Gilbert; the building was constructed between 1932 and 1935.

An Irish-born architect, James Hoban, designed the White House, shown at the center. Of nine proposals, his won the competition to design the President's House, as it was then known. Although Washington helped to oversee the construction, John Adams was the first president to live in the White House. It remains the only private home of a head of state that is open to the public without fees. It takes 570 gallons of paint to cover the exterior of the White House.

In 1792, advertisements appeared in American newspapers for a design for the Capitol building, pictured at the right. The Commissioners of the District of Columbia, along with Washington and Jefferson, were the judges. They were disappointed at the entries they received. Most of the competitors used architectural styles from the Renaissance, which in turn drew from classical Roman and Greek architecture. This became the dominant architectural style of the new capital city.

The buildings represent the three branches of the United States government. These branches provide checks and balances on each other.

ideas to remember

The Constitution is based on the following principles

- popular sovereignty
- federalism
- separation of powers
- checks and balances
- judicial review
- limited government

The principle of **judicial review** gives power to the courts. The courts can rule on the constitutionality of a law or action of local, state, or the national government. *Constitutionality* means whether a law or action violates the U.S. Constitution. The lower courts have the power of judicial review. But the U.S. Supreme Court has the final decision on what is or is not constitutional. This power is not stated as such in the Constitution. It has developed since 1803, when Chief Justice John Marshall wrote the opinion in *Marbury* v. *Madison*. He declared unconstitutional a law that Congress had passed.

Limited government limits, or restricts, the power of government to do certain things and not others. The Bill of Rights, for example, lists those freedoms that people have and that government may not take away.

Putting It All Together

Write a definition for each of the six principles that form the basis of the Constitution. Then play "Which Principle?" with a partner. Take turns reading your definitions and asking each other to identify the principle.

Extension

Ask students to track the news for two weeks, using the Internet, a newspaper, or a newsweekly. Ask them to keep logs (or copies of the articles if possible, without cutting up a source they do not own) of examples of checks and balances in action.

Ideas to Remember Extension

Review the ideas listed, further explaining difficult vocabulary words. Have students create graphic organizers in their notebooks to help them visualize the six major principles.

Putting It All Together

Students' definitions will vary but should be based on paraphrases of the definitions in the text.

LESSON 2

The Branches of Government

Thinking on Your Own

The Framers of the Constitution wrote a plan of government they hoped would last for centuries. The government that they created had to be able to solve problems in the future. With a partner, make a list of at least five issues that the U.S. government must deal with today that the Framers could not have predicted. Write these in your notebook.

focus your reading

Describe the expressed and enumerated powers of Congress.

What powers does the executive branch have?

What is the major duty of the judicial branch?

words to know

veto

expressed powers

enumerate

naturalization

elastic clause

jurisdiction

appeal

Most of the articles of the Constitution lay out the separate powers of each branch of the national government. However, the Constitution also lists powers that the branches share. For example, the executive and legislative branches must cooperate on passing the annual budget for the federal government. Declaring war and agreeing on legislation are two other areas of cooperation between the two branches.

Congress—the Legislative Branch

Article I of the U.S. Constitution deals with Congress, the lawmaking body of the national government. Section 1 establishes Congress. Sections 2 and 3 describe the House of Representatives and the Senate.

Section 4 states how elections to the House and Senate should be held and when Congress should meet. Section 5 sets out the organization and rules of procedure for both houses. Section 6 makes the federal government responsible for paying the salaries of members of Congress.

Lesson Summary
This lesson discusses the powers and duties of each branch of federal government.

Lesson Objective
Students will learn about the legislative, executive, and judicial branches of the national government.

Focus Your Reading Answers

1 The expressed and enumerated powers of Congress are those specifically stated in Article I, Section 8, Clauses 1–18, of the Constitution.

2 The powers of the executive branch include those listed in Article II, Section 2. The president is commander in chief of the armed forces, appoints department heads, negotiates treaties with other countries, and can pardon prisoners convicted of federal crimes.

3 The major duty of the judicial branch, as stated in Article III, is to hear cases involving other nations' officials and those between states.

Words to Know
Discuss each of the vocabulary terms with students.

To *veto* is to refuse to approve. When the president refuses to sign a bill that Congress passes, he is using *veto* power.

The *expressed powers* of Congress are those that are specifically stated in the Constitution. Section 8 of Article I lists the *expressed powers*. To *enumerate* is to number. The Framers of the Constitution decided to *enumerate* the powers of Congress.

The process by which people from other nations become United States citizens is called *naturalization*. Determining the *naturalization* process is one of the enumerated powers of Congress.

The *elastic clause* allows Congress to stretch its powers to meet future challenges that might arise. The *elastic clause* is listed in Article I, Section 8, Clause 18.

The *jurisdiction* of a court is the area of law over which it can hear cases. The Supreme Court's *jurisdiction* is often over an interpretation of the Constitution. An *appeal* is a request for a further hearing of a case.

According to Section 7, all bills related to taxation must come from the House. Section 7 also describes how a bill becomes a law and what happens if the president refuses to sign a bill. This is known as the president's **veto**. Section 7 gives Congress the power to override the president's veto by a two-thirds vote of both houses. The legislative branch is discussed in detail in Chapter 5.

The Framers of the Constitution listed specific powers for Congress. These are known as the **expressed powers** because they are stated. Section 8, Clauses 1 to 18, lists most of these powers. They are also called the enumerated powers. The word **enumerated** means "numbered."

- The first six expressed powers deal with the economy. Among these are the power to levy taxes, to regulate bankruptcies, to coin money, and to punish counterfeiters. Clause 4 also gives Congress the power to determine the **naturalization** process for people of other nations to become United States citizens. Clause 7 gives Congress the power to set up post offices.
- Clause 8 deals with copyrights and patents. Congress may pass laws to protect people's writings and inventions.
- Clause 9 gives Congress the power to set up the federal court system below the level of the U.S. Supreme Court.
- Clauses 10 through 16 give Congress powers related to defending the nation. These include the powers to set up an army and navy, and to declare war.
- Clause 17 gives Congress the power to pass laws to govern the District of Columbia.
- Clause 18 gives Congress the power to make all laws that are "necessary and proper" in order to exercise its other 17 powers. Clause 18 is also known as the **elastic clause**, because it allows Congress to stretch the use of its powers.

The "necessary and proper," or elastic, clause is one of the most important and controversial powers of Congress. The Framers were thoughtful men and realized that the nation would change over time. However, they had no way of knowing what

Extension

You may wish to use the vocabulary list in this lesson to present strategies for students to search for word meanings within the structure of the new words. For example, *enumerate* contains the same base as *numeral* or *number*; *jurisdiction* has the root of *jury* embedded in it. Suggest to students that they look for a familiar word within new words to help them figure out meanings. Challenge students to skim the lesson and look for other words that have familiar terms as their roots. (for example: qualifications, qualify; procedure, process; solution, solve)

Extension

Divide the class into five groups. Have groups use library resources or the Internet to find out what bills the five most recent presidents have vetoed. Then have each group choose one bill. Ask them to locate any explanation of why the veto was used. Challenge students to find out about the use of pocket vetoes as well. Have them present their findings to the class by using the Student Presentation Builder on the student CD.

Extensions

1 You may wish to invite a speaker from the local immigration office to discuss the naturalization process with your students. Ask the speaker to cover any changes Congress has made over time and to discuss past efforts to limit particular groups, such as the Chinese exclusion acts of the nineteenth and twentieth centuries.

2 The issues of legal rights to music, film, computer software, or Web content can be confusing. Invite interested students to use library resources or the Internet to find out more about copyright laws concerning music or Internet content.

those changes would be. But they intended the Constitution to last for centuries. The elastic clause was one solution for governing the nation in the unknowable future.

Section 9 lists powers that Congress does not have. For example, Congress may not create a system of nobles like British dukes and counts. Many of the powers denied to Congress have their basis in powers that Parliament or the monarchy had over the colonists.

Section 10 lists powers denied to the states. For example, the states may not conduct business with foreign nations or wage war on other nations. There was a reason for removing the states from areas that involved other nations or other states. It meant they were less likely to come into conflict with the federal government.

stop and think

Write a paragraph to explain how the Framers of the Constitution provided for change. Use the ideas that you wrote in Thinking on Your Own as examples in your paragraph. Share and discuss your paragraph with a partner.

The Executive Branch

Article II creates the executive branch headed by the president. This branch has the power to enforce laws. The executive branch is more than the president and vice president. Since 1789, it has evolved into 15 departments, 33 independent agencies, and 12 offices. Today more than 2.6 million employees work for the executive branch of the federal government in the United States and throughout the world.

Article II has only four sections. Section 1 states the term of office of the president and vice president, the method of election for these offices, qualifications, their salaries, and the oath of office that the president must take.

The powers of the presidency listed in the Constitution are somewhat broad and vague. Over time, presidents have used these powers to increase the duties and responsibilities of the presidency. For example, Congress determines the annual budget for the federal government. However, the discussion begins with a budget prepared by the executive branch. Congress makes the laws, but the president often suggests what those laws should be. The executive branch of the U.S. government is discussed in detail in Chapter 8.

President George W. Bush was sworn in as president for a second term on January 20, 2005.

Stop and Think

Students' paragraphs will vary but should explain the amendment process the Framers provided.

Picturing Government

The photograph on page 45 shows the Second Inauguration of George W. Bush in January 2005. Beside him is his wife, Laura. While presidential spouses have become more active since the twentieth century, Laura Bush made history in 2001, during her husband's first term of office, by becoming the first spouse of a president to deliver the weekly radio address. At that time, she focused on the difficulties for women suffering under the Taliban regime in Afghanistan. In March 2005, Laura Bush went to Afghanistan to see the results of the first democratically elected Afghan government. Under the Taliban, girls were forbidden to attend school. Mrs. Bush went to Kabul and visited the Women's Teacher Training Institute, a clear sign of progress in women's rights in Afghanistan.

Extensions

1 Divide the class into 15 small groups, assigning each one of the departments within the president's cabinet. Have students use library resources or the Internet to find out what each department does, its history, and the current secretary of the department.

2 Some states, such as California, would rank in the top ten world economies if they were independent nations. Ask students to imagine what could happen if the Constitution in Article I, Section 10, did **not** forbid individual states from conducting business with other nations.

Section 2 lists the powers of the president. The president

- is commander in chief of the nation's armed forces including state militias, now known as the National Guard.
- appoints the heads of the departments within the executive branch, ambassadors to foreign nations, federal judges, and other top officials in the executive branch. The Senate approves these appointments. This is part of the system of checks and balances.
- may pardon, set free, or reduce a prison sentence or fine of a person convicted of a federal crime.
- negotiates treaties with other nations. The Senate approves the treaties. This is part of the system of checks and balances.

Section 3 lists the duties of the president. The president

- delivers an annual State of the Union address to Congress.
- may call Congress into special session as needed.
- represents the United States with other nations.
- commissions, or approves for service, every officer in the armed forces.
- enforces all the laws that Congress passes.

Section 4 lists the reasons why the president and vice president may be impeached and removed from office. Those reasons are "treason, bribery, or other high crimes and misdemeanors." A misdemeanor is misbehavior of some kind. The Constitution leaves it to Congress to decide what a high crime or misdemeanor may be.

The Judicial Branch

The United States has two separate judicial systems. One is the judiciary of the 50 states. Each state constitution empowers its state government to set up a court system. Local communities also have courts, such as criminal court and traffic court. These courts get their power to hear cases from the state. The judicial branch of the government is discussed in detail in Chapter 11.

Article III of the U.S. Constitution creates the federal judicial branch. However, the only court mentioned by name is the

Extensions

1 President Gerald Ford, who took office after the resignation of Richard Nixon following the Watergate scandal, extended the executive privilege of pardon. Believing that placing a former president on trial would be bad for the nation, a month after taking office, Ford pardoned Nixon of any crimes Nixon *may* have committed during his tenure of office. Some citizens were angry, noting that Nixon was pardoned, but those who had resisted being drafted during the Vietnam conflict were not. Some suspected that a deal had been made prior to Nixon's resignation.

2 Andrew Johnson and Bill Clinton are the only two presidents who have been impeached. Ask interested students to use library resources or the Internet to find out more about these men and their trials. Have them present their findings to the class, including their own opinions as to the validity of the accusations and trials.

3 The use of the Electoral College to determine the outcome of presidential elections has come under increasing fire since the 2000 election. Have students use library resources or the Internet to investigate the history of the Electoral College and the most recent controversies. You may wish to hold a debate on the issue after students have done their research.

Picturing Government

The 2005 Supreme Court is pictured on page 47. Point out to students that although Clarence Thomas is currently the only African American on the Court, he is not the first. That honor was given to Thurgood Marshall, appointed by Lyndon Johnson in 1967. The first woman on the Court, Sandra Day O'Connor, who was appointed by President Reagan in 1981, was joined in 1993 by Ruth Bader Ginsburg after President Clinton nominated her. Sandra Day O'Connor retired at the end of the 2005 session. John Roberts was sworn in as 17th Chief Justice of the United States Supreme Court on September 29, 2005.

Supreme Court. The article does not say anything about the levels of federal courts that may be set up below the Supreme Court. Section 1 only states:

> The judicial Power of the United States, shall be vested [placed] in one supreme Court, and in such inferior [lower level] Courts as the Congress may from time to time ordain [create] and establish.

Section 2 describes the **jurisdiction**, or area of the law that the federal courts may hear cases about. Most cases are challenges to laws passed by Congress and cases involving the Constitution. Federal courts also hear cases related to ships and shipping on rivers, lakes, and canals within the United States.

The justices of the United States Supreme Court

The U.S. Supreme Court alone may hear cases involving officials of other nations and cases involving the states. This is called the Supreme Court's original jurisdiction. However, most cases come to the Supreme Court on **appeal** from a lower court. This happens when one party to the lawsuit requests a further hearing. This is known as the Supreme Court's appellate jurisdiction.

Section 2 also grants accused persons the right to a trial by jury. Section 3 defines the crime of treason and states the punishment for it.

Neither the executive nor the legislative branch may throw out a ruling of the Supreme Court. However, there are actions that these branches can take. One is to rewrite the law that the Court found unconstitutional. Congress and the president hope that by rewriting it, they can remove the reasons the Court found it unconstitutional. A second action is to turn the rejected law into an amendment to the Constitution. Congress then passes and sends the amendment to the states for ratification.

Putting It All Together

In your notebook, make a three-column chart with the columns labeled "Legislative," "Executive," and "Judicial." List the major powers of each branch of the national government. Share these with a partner.

Extension

Marbury v. *Madison* established the right of the Supreme Court to review the constitutionality of any law. William Marbury was one of John Adams's "midnight judge" appointments, signed the night before Adams left office in his attempt to ensure a continuation of Federalist power. Many appointments were not delivered when James Madison, the secretary of state under Jefferson, took office. Under the Judiciary Act of 1789, Marbury asked the Supreme Court for a writ to have the papers delivered. Chief Justice John Marshall agreed that Marbury had a right to receive his judicial commission and that Madison broke the law in not delivering it. However, Marshall also determined that Congress did not have the power to grant to the Supreme Court the right to hear the case. Thus, Marbury never served as a judge.

Putting It All Together

Students' charts will vary but should list the three branches of government and their major powers.

Extension

George Wythe was Thomas Jefferson's mentor and lectured on law in Williamsburg, Virginia, where John Marshall studied with him for about six weeks at the College of William and Mary. It was from Wythe that Marshall got the idea for judicial review. Marshall was elected to Congress in 1799, named secretary of state under John Adams in 1800, and became Chief Justice in 1801. Interestingly, he and Thomas Jefferson were cousins, and each disliked the other. Jefferson also disliked the idea of judicial review.

The pages that follow contain the original text of the United States Constitution. Sections that are no longer enforced have been crossed out. The spelling and punctuation of the document remain in their original format. The headings are not part of the original Constitution.

The United States Constitution

We the People of the United States, in Order to form a more perfect Union, establish Justice, insure domestic Tranquility, provide for the common defence, promote the general Welfare, and secure the Blessings of Liberty to ourselves and our Posterity, do ordain and establish this Constitution for the United States of America.

Preamble

The first section of the Constitution is the Preamble. It states the purposes for which the Constitution was written. These purposes are to ensure (1) greater cooperation among the states, (2) equal justice for all, (3) peace within the nation, (4) defense against other nations, (5) the general well-being of the people, and (6) liberty now and in the future. The phrase "We the People" is based on the ideas of popular sovereignty and representative government. The phrase means that the power of the government comes from the people.

Article I Legislative Branch

Article I. Legislative Branch

Article I describes the legislative branch of the national government.

Section 1 Congress

All legislative Powers herein granted shall be vested in a Congress of the United States, which shall consist of a Senate and House of Representatives.

Section 1. Congress

The legislative branch is called Congress and is made up of two houses. It is the only lawmaking body for the federal government. The lower house, called the House of Representatives, is elected directly by the people in their home districts. House members represent the interests of their particular voters. As written, members of the Senate were to be elected by state legislatures and represent the overall interests of their state. The election of senators was changed by the 17th Amendment, ratified in 1912. Senators continue to represent the overall interests of their state, but they are elected directly by voters.

Section 2 House of Representatives

Clause 1: The House of Representatives shall be composed of Members chosen every second Year by the People of the several States, and the Electors in each State shall have the Qualifications requisite for Electors of the most numerous Branch of the State Legislature.

Section 2. House of Representatives

1. Election and Term of Office. *Electors* means "voters". Members of the House are elected every two years. Anyone who can vote for a candidate to a state legislature may vote for a House member. States may determine who may vote. However, Amendments 15, 19, 24, and 26 place limits on the rights of states to decide who may or may not vote.

Clause 2: No Person shall be a Representative who shall not have attained to the Age of twenty five Years, and been seven Years a Citizen of the United States, and who shall not, when elected, be an Inhabitant of that State in which he shall be chosen.

2. Qualifications. Representatives must be at least twenty-five years old and have been a U.S. citizen for seven years. Representatives must also live in the state that they wish to represent in the House. The Constitution does not say that a House member must live in the district that he or she represents. However, custom has made this a qualification for a candidate.

Clause 3: Representatives and direct Taxes shall be apportioned among the several States which may be included within this Union, according to their respective Numbers, ~~which shall be determined by adding to the whole Number of free Persons, including those bound to Service for a Term of Years, and excluding Indians not taxed, three fifths of all other Persons~~.

The actual Enumeration shall be made within three Years after the first Meeting of the Congress of the United States, and within every subsequent Term of ten Years, in such Manner as they shall by Law direct.

The Number of Representatives shall not exceed one for every thirty Thousand, but each State shall have at Least one Representative~~; and until such enumeration shall be made, the State of New Hampshire shall be entitled to chuse three, Massachusetts eight, Rhode-Island and Providence Plantations one, Connecticut five, New-York six, New Jersey four, Pennsylvania eight, Delaware one, Maryland six, Virginia ten, North Carolina five, South Carolina five, and Georgia three.~~

3. Division of Representatives Among the States. The number of representatives that a state has is based on population. Each state must have at least one representative.

The nation counts its citizens every ten years in a census. This clause gives the government the authority to conduct a census. The first census was taken in 1790. The final sentence in Section 2, Clause 3, lists the number of representatives that each of the first 13 states had until the first census was taken.

The first House had 65 members. As the nation grew, the House added seats. In 1929, Congress limited the number of members in the House to 435. Instead of adding members to the House as the population of some states grows, states with declining populations lose representatives. In the beginning, there was one representative for about every 30,000 citizens in a state. Today, there is one member for about every 650,000 citizens in a state.

"Three-fifths of a person" refers to the Three-Fifths Compromise worked out by the Framers. Three-fifths of a state's enslaved population was counted to determine representation. The 13th Amendment replaced this clause in 1865.

Native Americans were not counted. When the Constitution was written, they were considered members of foreign nations. Since 1924, Native Americans have been U.S. citizens and included when determining representation in the House.

Clause 4: When vacancies happen in the Representation from any State, the Executive Authority thereof shall issue Writs of Election to fill such Vacancies.

4. Vacancies. A member of the House may die in office or leave office for some reason before his or her term is over. Then the governor of the state calls a special election to fill the vacancy. The phrase *executive authority* refers to the governor.

Clause 5: The House of Representatives shall chuse their Speaker and other Officers; and shall have the sole Power of Impeachment.

5. Officers. The House has the power to choose its own officers, including the Speaker. This person calls House sessions to order and runs the business of the House. Typically, the Speaker is from the majority party in the House.

The House has the power to impeach, or bring charges against, federal officials, including the president and vice president. See Section 3, Clause 6, for the Senate's role in the impeachment process.

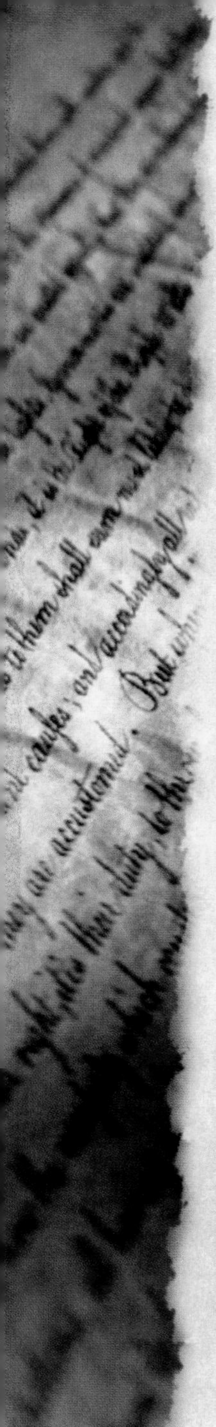

Section 3 Senate

Clause 1: The Senate of the United States shall be composed of two Senators from each State, chosen ~~by the Legislature thereof,~~ for six Years; and each Senator shall have one Vote.

Clause 2: Immediately after they shall be assembled in Consequence of the first Election, they shall be divided as equally as may be into three Classes. The Seats of the Senators of the first Class shall be vacated at the Expiration of the second Year, of the second Class at the Expiration of the fourth Year, and of the third Class at the Expiration of the sixth Year, so that one third may be chosen every second Year; ~~and if Vacancies happen by Resignation, or otherwise, during the Recess of the Legislature of any State, the Executive thereof may make temporary Appointments until the next Meeting of the Legislature, which shall then fill such Vacancies.~~

Clause 3: No Person shall be a Senator who shall not have attained to the Age of thirty Years, and been nine Years a Citizen of the United States, and who shall not, when elected, be an Inhabitant of that State for which he shall be chosen.

Clause 4: The Vice President of the United States shall be President of the Senate, but shall have no Vote, unless they be equally divided.

Clause 5: The Senate shall chuse their other Officers, and also a President pro tempore, in the Absence of the Vice President, or when he shall exercise the Office of President of the United States.

Clause 6: The Senate shall have the sole Power to try all Impeachments. When sitting for that Purpose, they shall be on Oath or Affirmation. When the President of the United States is tried, the Chief Justice shall preside: And no Person shall be convicted without the Concurrence of two thirds of the Members present.

Clause 7: Judgment in Cases of Impeachment shall not extend further than to removal from Office, and disqualification to hold and enjoy any Office of honor, Trust or Profit under the United States: but the Party convicted shall nevertheless be liable and subject to Indictment, Trial, Judgment and Punishment, according to Law.

Section 3. Senate

1. Number of Members, Terms, and Voting. Since the admission of Hawaii in 1959, the Senate has had 100 members.

2. Staggered Elections and Vacancies. The first part of this clause relates to the election of 1788. The division of senators into three groups staggered the terms of office of the first 26 senators. In this way, the Senate was able to set up a system in which one-third of all Senate seats are up for election every two years.

The second part of the clause was replaced by the 17th Amendment. A state governor may fill a vacant Senate seat by calling a special election. Depending on state law, the governor may also appoint a person to fill the vacant seat.

3. Qualifications. A senator must be thirty years old and have been a U.S. citizen for at least nine years. A senator must also live in the state that he or she represents.

4. President of the Senate. The vice president presides over, or runs, the meetings of the Senate. If a vote results in a tie, the vice president votes to break the tie. Otherwise, the vice president may not vote. Presiding over the Senate is the only duty assigned to the vice president by the Constitution.

5. Other Officers. The Senate chooses its own officers, including a president pro tempore. *Pro tempore* means "for a time." The president pro tempore presides over Senate sessions when the vice president is absent or when he has become president. For example, when President John Kennedy was assassinated in 1963, Vice President Lyndon Johnson became president. He no longer could preside over the Senate.

6. Impeachment. The House impeaches a federal official, which means that it finds enough evidence of wrongdoing to bring the official to trial. The trial is held in the Senate.

If the official being tried is the president of the United States, the Chief Justice of the Supreme Court presides over the Senate. Otherwise, the vice president presides.

Two-thirds of the members of the Senate must vote to convict or the official is found not guilty.

7. Penalty If Convicted. If a person is convicted in an impeachment case, he or she is removed from office. The Senate may also bar the person from holding any other federal office. These are the only two punishments that the Senate may hand down. However, a convicted official may be tried in a regular court for any crime committed as part of the impeachment case.

Section 4 Elections and Meetings

Clause 1: The Times, Places and Manner of holding Elections for Senators and Representatives, shall be prescribed in each State by the Legislature thereof; but the Congress may at any time by Law make or alter such Regulations, ~~except as to the Places of chusing Senators.~~

Clause 2: The Congress shall assemble at least once in every Year, ~~and such Meeting shall be on the first Monday in December, unless they shall by Law appoint a different Day.~~

Section 5 Rules of Procedure

Clause 1: Each House shall be the Judge of the Elections, Returns and Qualifications of its own Members, and a Majority of each shall constitute a Quorum to do Business; but a smaller Number may adjourn from day to day, and may be authorized to compel the Attendance of absent Members, in such Manner, and under such Penalties as each House may provide.

Clause 2: Each House may determine the Rules of its Proceedings, punish its Members for disorderly Behaviour, and, with the Concurrence of two thirds, expel a Member.

Clause 3: Each House shall keep a Journal of its Proceedings, and from time to time publish the same, excepting such Parts as may in their Judgment require Secrecy; and the Yeas and Nays of the Members of either House on any question shall, at the Desire of one fifth of those Present, be entered on the Journal.

Clause 4: Neither House, during the Session of Congress, shall, without the Consent of the other, adjourn for more than three days, nor to any other Place than that in which the two Houses shall be sitting.

Section 4. Elections and Meetings

1. Elections. As written, the Constitution gives state legislatures the right to schedule elections for U.S. representatives and senators. In 1842, Congress changed part of this. It passed a law requiring that representatives be elected on the first Tuesday after the first Monday in November in even-numbered years. In 1914, Congress passed a law setting the same date for the election of senators.

2. Sessions. Congress must meet at least once every year.

Section 5. Rules of Procedure

1. Organization. As written, the Constitution gives each house the right to judge the qualifications of those elected to serve in it. However, in 1969, the Supreme Court modified this power. It ruled that Congress cannot legally exclude anyone who meets all the qualifications as stated in Article I, Section 2, Clause 2.

A quorum must be present for either house to conduct business. A quorum is half the total number plus one. In the House, a quorum is 218 of its 435 members. In the Senate, it is 51 of its 100 members.

2. Rules. The House and the Senate each have rules to guide how they conduct business. Each has methods for punishing members for unacceptable behavior. Expelling a member requires a two-thirds (287 and 66) vote of its members.

3. Record. Each house must keep a record of its daily business. The *Congressional Record* publishes a complete and official record of the daily sessions of both houses of Congress. Members' votes are included, as well as everything that is said or done during the daily session. With constant media coverage, the daily meetings of both houses are no longer secret.

4. Adjournment. Once Congress opens a session, neither house can adjourn, or stop meeting, for more than three days unless the other house agrees. For example, the House cannot decide to suspend meeting for three days without asking the Senate if it is all right. Both houses must always meet in the same place.

Section 6 Privileges and Restrictions

Clause 1: The Senators and Representatives shall receive a Compensation for their Services, to be ascertained by Law, and paid out of the Treasury of the United States. They shall in all Cases, except Treason, Felony and Breach of the Peace, be privileged from Arrest during their Attendance at the Session of their respective Houses, and in going to and returning from the same; and for any Speech or Debate in either House, they shall not be questioned in any other Place.

Clause 2: No Senator or Representative shall, during the Time for which he was elected, be appointed to any civil Office under the Authority of the United States, which shall have been created, or the Emoluments whereof shall have been encreased during such time; and no Person holding any Office under the United States, shall be a Member of either House during his Continuance in Office.

Section 7 How Bills Become Laws

Clause 1: All Bills for raising Revenue shall originate in the House of Representatives; but the Senate may propose or concur with Amendments as on other Bills.

Section 6. Privileges and Restrictions

1. Salary and Immunity. Members of the Confederation Congress were paid by their state legislatures. The Framers of the Constitution saw a problem with this arrangement. Members could be influenced by their state legislature because it paid them. As a result, Congress is paid by the U.S. government.

The last sentence in this clause sets up what is called "legislative immunity." *Immunity* means "exception or freedom from." Members of Congress may not be arrested on their way to or from a session of Congress or during a session. However, if they are accused of treason, felony, or breach of the peace, they may be arrested. A felony is any major crime, such as robbery. Breach of the peace is any lesser crime. Members may not be arrested for what they say in Congress.

2. Limits. *Emolument* means "salary." Members of Congress are barred from taking jobs in the executive or judicial branch if they were in Congress when the job was created. They also may not take the job if they were in Congress when the salary for the job was raised. This clause is meant to keep members of Congress from enriching themselves by their votes.

A person may not serve in Congress and the judicial or executive branch at the same time. This is one example of the Framers' efforts to reinforce the separation of powers among the branches of government.

Section 7. How Bills Become Laws

1. Revenue Bills. Revenue is income, and most government income comes from taxes. All bills that raise income must begin in the House of Representatives. This means that all tax bills begin in the House. The Senate, however, has the right to amend, or change, revenue bills that it receives from the House. The Framers gave the House the responsibility for taxation for two reasons. Originally, only its members were elected directly by the people. Second, House elections are held every two years. Therefore, members of the House are more easily accountable to the voters for their actions.

Clause 2: Every Bill which shall have passed the House of Representatives and the Senate, shall, before it become a Law, be presented to the President of the United States; If he approve he shall sign it, but if not he shall return it, with his Objections to that House in which it shall have originated, who shall enter the Objections at large on their Journal, and proceed to reconsider it. If after such Reconsideration two thirds of that House shall agree to pass the Bill, it shall be sent, together with the Objections, to the other House, by which it shall likewise be reconsidered, and if approved by two thirds of that House, it shall become a Law. But in all such Cases the Votes of both Houses shall be determined by yeas and Nays, and the Names of the Persons voting for and against the Bill shall be entered on the Journal of each House respectively.

If any Bill shall not be returned by the President within ten Days (Sundays excepted) after it shall have been presented to him, the Same shall be a Law, in like Manner as if he had signed it, unless the Congress by their Adjournment prevent its Return, in which Case it shall not be a Law.

Clause 3: Every Order, Resolution, or Vote to which the Concurrence of the Senate and House of Representatives may be necessary (except on a question of Adjournment) shall be presented to the President of the United States; and before the Same shall take Effect, shall be approved by him, or being disapproved by him, shall be repassed by two thirds of the Senate and House of Representatives, according to the Rules and Limitations prescribed in the Case of a Bill.

Section 8 Powers of Congress

Clause 1: The Congress shall have Power To lay and collect Taxes, Duties, Imposts and Excises, to pay the Debts and provide for the common Defence and general Welfare of the United States; but all Duties, Imposts and Excises shall be uniform throughout the United States;

Clause 2: To borrow Money on the credit of the United States;

Clause 3: To regulate Commerce with foreign Nations, and among the several States, and with the Indian Tribes;

2. Passing Bills and the Presidential Veto. A bill is a proposed law. A bill becomes law if both houses of Congress pass it and the president signs it. However, the president does not have to sign a bill. If the president disapproves of a bill, he has three choices. (1) He can veto the bill and send it back to Congress, explaining why he vetoed it. (2) He can allow the bill to become law. This happens if the president does not act on the bill within ten days (not counting Sundays) of receiving it from Congress. In other words, he neither signs nor vetoes the bill. (3) If the president receives the bill at the end of a session of Congress, he can use the pocket veto. To do this, the president does not act on the bill within ten days of receiving it and Congress adjourns during those ten days. As a result of adjourning, Congress cannot vote on the bill again. To pass a law over a presidential veto, two-thirds of both houses have to pass the bill.

3. Presidential Approval or Veto. Every vote that Congress takes must be sent to the president for approval or veto. The exception is a vote to adjourn. The Framers included this clause to keep Congress from passing joint resolutions. A joint resolution is an expression of opinion on an issue. A joint resolution would not need to be sent to the president for an approval or veto. The Framers wanted to prevent Congress from going around the president's authority and weakening the system of checks and balances.

Section 8. Powers of Congress

Section 8 lists 27 of the expressed powers granted in the Constitution to Congress.

1. Revenue. Congress has the power to levy and collect certain types of taxes. Duties and imposts are taxes on goods brought into the country. Excises are taxes paid on goods made and sold within the country. The purpose of raising money is to fund government operations, including the armed forces. Tax rates must be the same throughout the country.

2. Borrowing. The government, through Congress's actions, may borrow money. Generally, the money is borrowed by selling government bonds to investors. Investors receive interest on their bonds. Note that the clause does not say how much the government may borrow.

3. Commerce. This is known as the Commerce Clause. It grants Congress the power to regulate interstate and foreign trade. Over time, Congress has enlarged and extended the meaning of commerce and thus enlarged its own power. For example, Congress has passed laws regulating interstate transportation and banking based on the Commerce Clause.

Clause 4: To establish an uniform Rule of Naturalization, and uniform Laws on the subject of Bankruptcies throughout the United States;

4. Naturalization and Bankruptcy. Naturalization is the process by which a citizen of another nation becomes a U.S. citizen. Congress passes bankruptcy laws for the nation.

Clause 5: To coin Money, regulate the Value thereof, and of foreign Coin, and fix the Standard of Weights and Measures;

5. Currency. Congress has the power to issue money for the nation. It also has the power to set national standards for weights and measures. Measures include time, distance, weight, volume, and area.

Clause 6: To provide for the Punishment of counterfeiting the Securities and current Coin of the United States;

6. Counterfeiting. Counterfeiting is the making of fake money. Congress has the responsibility for setting the punishment for counterfeiters.

Clause 7: To establish Post Offices and post Roads;

7. Postal Service. Congress has the power to set up post offices and post roads. These are the routes over which mail is carried. Until 1970, the Post Office was one of the departments in the executive branch. In 1970, Congress created the United States Postal Service and made it a government-owned corporation. Congress can veto increases in postal rates but cannot set rates.

Clause 8: To promote the Progress of Science and useful Arts, by securing for limited Times to Authors and Inventors the exclusive Right to their respective Writings and Discoveries;

8. Copyrights and Patents. The Framers wanted to encourage the arts, science, and industry. As a result, they granted Congress the power to make laws regulating copyrights and patents. Copyrights protect the rights of writers, artists, and composers to their works for a period of time. During that time, others cannot use their works without their permission. Patents enable inventors to control how their inventions are manufactured and sold.

Clause 9: To constitute Tribunals inferior to the supreme Court;

9. Lower Courts. Article III creates the U.S. Supreme Court. However, Congress has the power to set up the federal court system below the Supreme Court. *Inferior* means "lower in rank."

Clause 10: To define and punish Piracies and Felonies committed on the high Seas, and Offences against the Law of Nations;

10. Piracy and Other Crimes Against Nations. Piracy is the robbing of ships on the high seas, or oceans. Congress has the power to decide what actions should be considered federal crimes committed outside the United States. Congress also has the power to decide on the punishment for these crimes.

Congress has the same power to define and set the punishment for crimes committed within the United States against another nation. Blowing up a foreign embassy in the United States is an example.

Clause 11: To declare War, grant Letters of Marque and Reprisal, and make Rules concerning Captures on Land and Water;

11. Declare War. According to the Constitution, only Congress has the power to declare war. However, presidents, as commander in chief, have sent U.S. troops into battle without a formal declaration of war. This has caused much controversy at times in the nation's history.

Letters of marque and reprisal authorize private citizens to capture and destroy enemy ships during wartime. In 1856, this practice was outlawed by international law.

Congress has the right to make rules about people and property captured in war.

Clause 12: To raise and support Armies, but no Appropriation of Money to that Use shall be for a longer Term than two Years;

12. Army. Congress has the power to set up an army. However, bills to finance the army may not request money for more than two years at a time. The purpose of this clause is to keep the control of the army in the hands of the civilian Congress.

Clause 13: To provide and maintain a Navy;

13. Navy. Congress also has the power to set up and finance a navy.

Clause 14: To make Rules for the Government and Regulation of the land and naval Forces;

14. Rules for the Armed Forces. Congress has the power to make rules for the army and navy. These rules were collected into the Uniform Code of Military Justice in 1950.

Clause 15: To provide for calling forth the Militia to execute the Laws of the Union, suppress Insurrections and repel Invasions;

15. Militia. State militias were first organized in 1792. They became the National Guard in 1916. Guard members take an oath of loyalty to their state and to the federal government. Federal laws authorize the use of Guard members for three reasons. The Guard may be asked to uphold the laws of the nation, to put down rebellions, and to fight off invasions. For example, in 1957, the Arkansas National Guard protected African-American students who were integrating Little Rock Central High School in Arkansas. In 2001, Guard members provided security at airports and train stations after the events of September 11, 2001.

Clause 16: To provide for organizing, arming, and disciplining, the Militia, and for governing such Part of them as may be employed in the Service of the United States, reserving to the States respectively, the Appointment of the Officers, and the Authority of training the Militia according to the discipline prescribed by Congress;

16. National Guard. The states are responsible for appointing National Guard officers and training the Guard. However, Congress provides the funding to equip the Guard. Congress also has the power to make rules for the Guard when members are called into federal service.

Clause 17: To exercise exclusive Legislation in all Cases whatsoever, over such District (not exceeding ten Miles square) as may, by Cession of particular States, and the Acceptance of Congress, become the Seat of the Government of the United States, and to exercise like Authority over all Places purchased by the Consent of the Legislature of the State in which the Same shall be, for the Erection of Forts, Magazines, Arsenals, dock-Yards, and other needful Buildings;--And

17. Nation's Capital. Virginia and Maryland donated land for the nation's capital, Washington, D.C. This was one of the compromises to win ratification of the Constitution. Virginia's land was never used and was returned in 1846.

Congress has the power to make laws for the District of Columbia. Among the laws are ones setting up a city government for the District and allowing residents to vote in presidential elections (23rd Amendment).

Clause 18: To make all Laws which shall be necessary and proper for carrying into Execution the foregoing Powers, and all other Powers vested by this Constitution in the Government of the United States, or in any Department or Officer thereof.

18. Elastic Clause. This is also known as the "necessary and proper" clause. Congress is granted the power to make whatever laws are needed to carry out its other powers. Congress has used this clause to enlarge and extend its authority. This clause is the basis for the implied powers of Congress.

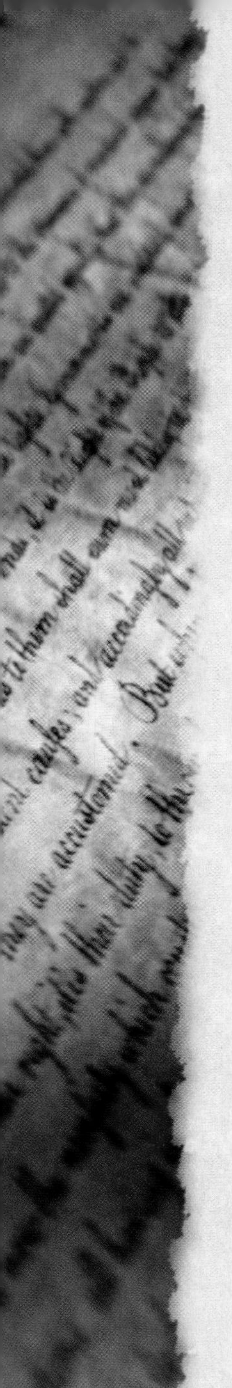

Section 9 Powers Denied to the Federal Government

Clause 1: ~~The Migration or Importation of such Persons as any of the States now existing shall think proper to admit, shall not be prohibited by the Congress prior to the Year one thousand eight hundred and eight, but a Tax or duty may be imposed on such Importation, not exceeding ten dollars for each Person.~~

Clause 2: The Privilege of the Writ of Habeas Corpus shall not be suspended, unless when in Cases of Rebellion or Invasion the public Safety may require it.

Clause 3: No Bill of Attainder or ex post facto Law shall be passed.

Clause 4: No Capitation, or other direct, Tax shall be laid, unless in Proportion to the Census or Enumeration herein before directed to be taken.

Clause 5: No Tax or Duty shall be laid on Articles exported from any State.

Clause 6: No Preference shall be given by any Regulation of Commerce or Revenue to the Ports of one State over those of another: nor shall Vessels bound to, or from, one State, be obliged to enter, clear, or pay Duties in another.

Clause 7: No Money shall be drawn from the Treasury, but in Consequence of Appropriations made by Law; and a regular Statement and Account of the Receipts and Expenditures of all public Money shall be published from time to time.

Clause 8: No Title of Nobility shall be granted by the United States: And no Person holding any Office of Profit or Trust under them, shall, without the Consent of the Congress, accept of any present, Emolument, Office, or Title, of any kind whatever, from any King, Prince, or foreign State.

Section 9. Powers Denied to the Federal Government

1. Slave Trade. This is the Commerce Compromise reached by the Framers. In return for Southern support, the Framers agreed not to ban the foreign slave trade for 20 years. In 1808, Congress outlawed the importing, or bringing into the United States, of enslaved persons. However, the trade in slaves within the United States was allowed to continue.

2. Habeas Corpus. The writ, or order, of habeas corpus is one of the basic rights of English citizens. *Habeas corpus* is Latin, meaning "you have the body." A judge issues a writ of habeas corpus to a law official. The writ directs the official to bring a prisoner to a court hearing in order to find out if the person is being held legally. The writ may be suspended only during a rebellion or an invasion.

3. Bill of Attainder. A bill of attainder punishes a person without a trial. *Ex post facto* means "something done after the fact." An ex post facto law makes an action a crime after the action has been done. Congress may pass neither type of law.

4. Taxes. A capitation tax is a "head" tax, a tax on each person. Direct taxes are ones paid by taxpayers directly to the government. Income tax is a direct tax. The federal tax on gasoline is an indirect tax. Motorists pay it to the gasoline company, which then pays it to the government. The 16th Amendment changed part of this clause. The amendment allows Congress to levy an income tax directly on taxpayers.

5. Tax on Exports. Congress may not tax goods that are exported, or sent out of the country. This was part of the Commerce Compromise reached by the Framers. Congress may tax imports, or goods brought into the country.

6. Single System of Treatment. All ports (and states) must be treated the same. Congress may not pass laws that favor one port (or state) over another. Goods shipped by water from one state to another may not be taxed.

7. Appropriations Law. An appropriation is money set aside for a particular use. Congress must pass a law to authorize the spending of any federal money. The government must regularly publish a record of all the money it receives and spends.

8. Nobility. Congress may not set up a system of nobles such as princes and duchesses. No public official may accept a present, salary, job, or title of nobility from another government. The purpose was to keep other governments from trying to bribe, or buy the support of, U.S. officials.

Section 10 Powers Denied to the States

Clause 1: No State shall enter into any Treaty, Alliance, or Confederation; grant Letters of Marque and Reprisal; coin Money; emit Bills of Credit; make any Thing but gold and silver Coin a Tender in Payment of Debts; pass any Bill of Attainder, ex post facto Law, or Law impairing the Obligation of Contracts, or grant any Title of Nobility.

Clause 2: No State shall, without the Consent of the Congress, lay any Imposts or Duties on Imports or Exports, except what may be absolutely necessary for executing it's inspection Laws: and the net Produce of all Duties and Imposts, laid by any State on Imports or Exports, shall be for the Use of the Treasury of the United States; and all such Laws shall be subject to the Revision and Controul of the Congress.

Clause 3: No State shall, without the Consent of Congress, lay any Duty of Tonnage, keep Troops, or Ships of War in time of Peace, enter into any Agreement or Compact with another State, or with a foreign Power, or engage in War, unless actually invaded, or in such imminent Danger as will not admit of delay.

Section 10. Powers Denied to the States

1. Limits on Power. This clause lists nine powers that the states do not have. The first part of the clause forbids states from conducting relations with other nations. The purpose of most of this clause is to prevent conflicts between the national government and state governments. Both levels of government could not conduct foreign policy with other nations, for example, or have two sets of money.

State governments may not grant letters of marque and reprisal. This power was reserved for the national government. See Article I, Section 8, Clause 11.

States may not issue their own money or use anything but national currency. They may not issue bills of credit, or notes promising to pay debts.

Like the national government, state governments may not pass bills of attainder and ex post facto laws. Article I, Section 9, Clause 3, prohibits Congress from passing these kinds of laws.

State governments may not interfere with contracts between individuals.

State governments also may not give anyone a title such as duke or princess.

2. Taxes on Exports and Imports. Imposts are taxes on imports, goods brought into a country. Only Congress may levy taxes on imports. However, states may charge a small fee for inspecting goods.

Neither the national government nor the states may tax exports. The ban on the national government is stated in Article I, Section 9, Clause 5.

3. Taxes, Armed Forces, War. A duty of tonnage is a tax on ships based on how much cargo they can carry. States may not levy this kind of tax.

States may not keep an army or navy. However, Congress recognizes their right to set up militias. The National Guard is the modern form of the state militia.

States may enter into compacts, or written agreements, with other states if Congress agrees. However, based on this clause, Congress does not permit states to enter into agreements with foreign nations.

A state may not go to war on its own unless it is attacked or it is about to be attacked and cannot wait for Congress to act. This clause expressly denies certain powers to the states that the Constitution grants to the national government.

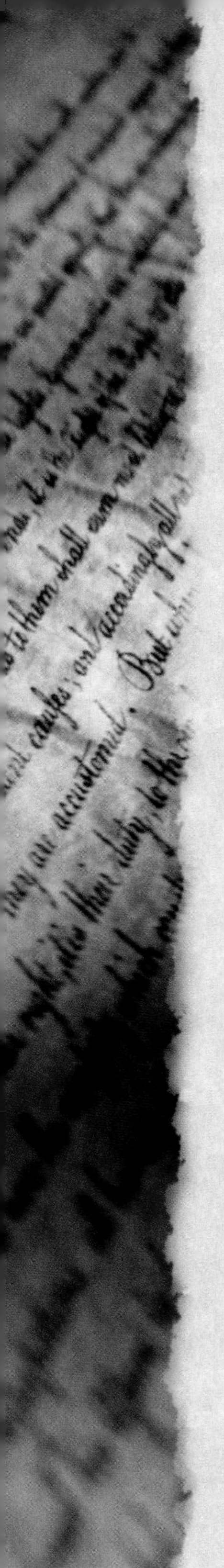

Article II Executive Branch

Section 1 President and Vice-President

Clause 1: The executive Power shall be vested in a President of the United States of America. He shall hold his Office during the Term of four Years, and, together with the Vice President, chosen for the same Term, be elected, as follows

Clause 2: Each State shall appoint, in such Manner as the Legislature thereof may direct, a Number of Electors, equal to the whole Number of Senators and Representatives to which the State may be entitled in the Congress: but no Senator or Representative, or Person holding an Office of Trust or Profit under the United States, shall be appointed an Elector.

Clause 3: ~~The Electors shall meet in their respective States, and vote by Ballot for two Persons, of whom one at least shall not be an Inhabitant of the same State with themselves. And they shall make a List of all the Persons voted for, and of the Number of Votes for each; which List they shall sign and certify, and transmit sealed to the Seat of the Government of the United States, directed to the President of the Senate. The President of the Senate shall, in the Presence of the Senate and House of Representatives, open all the Certificates, and the Votes shall then be counted. The Person having the greatest Number of Votes shall be the President, if such Number be a Majority of the whole Number of Electors appointed; and if there be more than one who have such Majority, and have an equal Number of Votes, then the House of Representatives shall immediately chuse by Ballot one of them for President; and if no Person have a Majority, then from the five highest on the List the said House shall in like Manner chuse the President. But in chusing the President, the Votes shall be taken by States, the Representation from each State having one Vote; A quorum for this Purpose shall consist of a Member or Members from two thirds of the States, and a Majority of all the States shall be necessary to a Choice. In every Case, after the Choice of the President, the Person having the greatest Number of Votes of the Electors shall be the Vice President. But if there should remain two or more who have equal Votes, the Senate shall chuse from them by Ballot the Vice President.~~

Article II. Executive Branch

Section 1. President and Vice President

1. Term of Office. The "executive power" gives the president the power to enforce the laws passed by Congress and to run the executive branch of government. The president and vice president are elected for four-year terms. See also the 22nd Amendment, which sets limits on how long a person may serve as president.

2. Election Process. The Framers set up an Electoral College to elect the president and vice president. Candidates are not elected directly by the voters. Instead, voters elect each state's electors, who meet in December to cast their ballots for president and vice president. The number of electors for each state is based on the state's combined number of senators and members of the House. Political parties nominate the electors. State law determines the election process for electors. No U.S. senator, representative, or official may be an elector.

3. Former Method of Electing the President and Vice President. This clause was replaced by the 12th Amendment in 1804. The amendment was approved and ratified as a result of the election of 1800. Before the 12th Amendment, ballots did not indicate which person was a candidate for president and which was a candidate for vice president. In the election of 1800, the top two candidates received the same number of votes. The election had to be decided in the House of Representatives.

Clause 4: The Congress may determine the Time of chusing the Electors, and the Day on which they shall give their Votes; which Day shall be the same throughout the United States.

Clause 5: No Person except a natural born Citizen, or a Citizen of the United States, at the time of the Adoption of this Constitution, shall be eligible to the Office of President; neither shall any Person be eligible to that Office who shall not have attained to the Age of thirty five Years, and been fourteen Years a Resident within the United States.

4. Date of Election. Congress has set the date for presidential elections as the first Tuesday after the first Monday in November. Electors vote on the Monday after the second Wednesday in December.

5. Qualifications. To be president, a person must have been born a citizen of the United States and have lived in the United States for at least 14 years. The person must also be at least thirty-five years old. The 22nd Amendment also sets limits on how long a person may serve as president.

Clause 6: ~~In Case of the Removal of the President from Office, or of his Death, Resignation, or Inability to discharge the Powers and Duties of the said Office, the Same shall devolve on the Vice President,~~ and the Congress may by Law provide for the Case of Removal, Death, Resignation or Inability, both of the President and Vice President, declaring what Officer shall then act as President, and such Officer shall act accordingly, until the Disability be removed, or a President shall be elected.

6. Vacancies. If the president is removed, dies, resigns, or is unable to carry out his duties, the vice president becomes president. The 25th Amendment states the process for deciding whether the president is unable to fulfill his duties. The process for filling the vice presidency, if it becomes vacant, is also described by this amendment.

Clause 7: The President shall, at stated Times, receive for his Services, a Compensation, which shall neither be encreased nor diminished during the Period for which he shall have been elected, and he shall not receive within that Period any other Emolument from the United States, or any of them.

7. Salary. Since 1999, the president receives $400,000 in salary and $50,000 as a taxable expense account. In addition, the president receives $100,000, which is nontaxable, for travel and entertainment.

Salary and benefits may not change while a president is in office. A president may not receive other income from the national government or state while in office.

Clause 8: Before he enter on the Execution of his Office, he shall take the following Oath or Affirmation:—"I do solemnly swear (or affirm) that I will faithfully execute the Office of President of the United States, and will to the best of my Ability, preserve, protect and defend the Constitution of the United States."

8. Oath of Office. The president takes this oath when being sworn into office. Typically, the Chief Justice of the U.S. Supreme Court administers the oath. However, any judicial official may administer it.

Section 2 Powers of the President

Clause 1: The President shall be Commander in Chief of the Army and Navy of the United States, and of the Militia of the several States, when called into the actual Service of the United States; he may require the Opinion, in writing, of the principal Officer in each of the executive Departments, upon any Subject relating to the Duties of their respective Offices, and he shall have Power to grant Reprieves and Pardons for Offences against the United States, except in Cases of Impeachment.

Section 2. Powers of the President

1. Military, the Cabinet, and Pardons. The Framers made the president the head of the armed forces. This ensures that the military is under civilian control.

This clause is also the basis for the cabinet. The cabinet is made up of the heads of the executive departments and advises the president.

The president may grant reprieves and pardons for federal crimes only. The exception is impeachment. A reprieve is the postponement of punishment and a pardon is forgiveness of punishment.

Clause 2: He shall have Power, by and with the Advice and Consent of the Senate, to make Treaties, provided two thirds of the Senators present concur; and he shall nominate, and by and with the Advice and Consent of the Senate, shall appoint Ambassadors, other public Ministers and Consuls, Judges of the supreme Court, and all other Officers of the United States, whose Appointments are not herein otherwise provided for, and which shall be established by Law: but the Congress may by Law vest the Appointment of such inferior Officers, as they think proper, in the President alone, in the Courts of Law, or in the Heads of Departments.

2. Treaties and Appointments. The president has the responsibility for deciding on and conducting foreign policy. Negotiating treaties is one part of this responsibility. However, as a check on presidential power, two-thirds of the Senate must ratify any treaties. Over time, presidents have used executive agreements as a way to avoid Senate debate and possible vetoes of treaties.

The president also has the power to appoint ambassadors to other nations and to the United Nations, justices to the Supreme Court, and other officials of the executive branch. Again, the Senate must approve each appointment. Only the highest-level officials are appointed in this manner. Most government workers receive their jobs through the civil service system. This is covered by the last part of the clause.

Clause 3: The President shall have Power to fill up all Vacancies that may happen during the Recess of the Senate, by granting Commissions which shall expire at the End of their next Session.

3. Vacancies in Federal Offices. The president may fill any vacancy that occurs when the Senate is in recess. The appointment is called a "recess appointment" and is temporary.

Section 3 Duties of the President

He shall from time to time give to the Congress Information of the State of the Union, and recommend to their Consideration such Measures as he shall judge necessary and expedient; he may, on extraordinary Occasions, convene both Houses, or either of them, and in Case of Disagreement between them, with Respect to the Time of Adjournment, he may adjourn them to such Time as he shall think proper; he shall receive Ambassadors and other public Ministers; he shall take Care that the Laws be faithfully executed, and shall Commission all the Officers of the United States.

Section 3. Duties of the President

The president must deliver to both the House and the Senate information about how the nation is doing. This information is to be accompanied by suggestions about possible laws. The president's annual State of the Union address fulfills this section. The president addresses a joint session of Congress each year at the beginning of the first session of Congress. The speech is given in the evening and is televised so the public can see it. Within a few weeks, the executive branch also delivers the president's annual budget request to Congress. In addition, the president may send special messages to Congress on matters that he considers important.

This section gives the president the power to call special sessions of one or both houses of Congress. The president may also adjourn Congress if the two houses cannot agree on a date.

In his role as maker of foreign policy, the president receives ambassadors from other nations.

The president also sees that the nation's laws are enforced.

The president also approves the promotion of all officers in the armed forces.

Section 4 Impeachment

The President, Vice President and all civil Officers of the United States, shall be removed from Office on Impeachment for, and Conviction of, Treason, Bribery, or other high Crimes and Misdemeanors.

Section 4. Impeachment

This section lists the reasons for which the president and vice president may be impeached and removed from office. The causes are treason, bribery, and "other high crimes and misdemeanors." The Framers left it to Congress to decide what makes actions high crimes and misdemeanors. Article I, Section 2, Clause 5, and Section 3, Clauses 6 and 7, set out the process for impeachment.

Article III Judicial Branch

Section 1 Federal Courts

The judicial Power of the United States, shall be vested in one supreme Court, and in such inferior Courts as the Congress may from time to time ordain and establish. The Judges, both of the supreme and inferior Courts, shall hold their Offices during good Behaviour, and shall, at stated Times, receive for their Services, a Compensation, which shall not be diminished during their Continuance in Office.

Section 2 Extent of Judicial Powers

Clause 1: The judicial Power shall extend to all Cases, in Law and Equity, arising under this Constitution, the Laws of the United States, and Treaties made, or which shall be made, under their Authority;—to all Cases affecting Ambassadors, other public Ministers and Consuls;—to all Cases of admiralty and maritime Jurisdiction;—to Controversies to which the United States shall be a Party;—to Controversies between two or more States;—between a State and Citizens of another State; —between Citizens of different States, —between Citizens of the same State claiming Lands under Grants of different States, and between a State, or the Citizens thereof, and foreign States, Citizens or Subjects.

Clause 2: In all Cases affecting Ambassadors, other public Ministers and Consuls, and those in which a State shall be Party, the supreme Court shall have original Jurisdiction. In all the other Cases before mentioned, the supreme Court shall have appellate Jurisdiction, both as to Law and Fact, with such Exceptions, and under such Regulations as the Congress shall make.

Article III. Judicial Branch

Section 1. Federal Courts

This section sets up the federal court system and empowers it to hear cases. The only court that is mentioned by name is the Supreme Court. However, this section states that Congress may set up lower federal courts as needed. Congress has used this power to establish federal district courts and, above them, federal courts of appeal.

Federal judges may keep their positions "during good behavior." For the most part, this means until they die or retire.

The salary of judges may not be decreased while they serve.

Section 2. Extent of Judicial Powers

1. General Jurisdiction. Jurisdiction is an area of the law where a court has authority to act. This section lists the areas of the law where the federal courts have jurisdiction, or authority. For the most part, federal courts deal with cases involving the Constitution, laws passed by Congress, and treaties.

Lawsuits involving ambassadors, public officials, and consuls—those who also deal with foreign nations—are heard in federal courts.

Federal courts hear cases involving ships and shipping on the oceans, and within the nation on rivers, lakes, and canals.

Any lawsuit against the United States is heard in federal court.

Lawsuits brought by a state or states against another state, lawsuits between citizens of different states, and lawsuits between citizens of the same state who claim land in different states come within the jurisdiction of federal courts.

The 11th Amendment changed the court system in which citizens of foreign nations could bring lawsuits against a state. The amendment sent these lawsuits to state courts.

2. The Supreme Court Jurisdiction. Original jurisdiction gives a court the right to hear a case in the first place. Appellate jurisdiction means the court may hear the case only if it is appealed from a lower court. An appeal is a request to rehear the case.

The Supreme Court has original jurisdiction in all cases involving ambassadors, public officials, and consuls, as well as any case in which a state is involved.

The Supreme Court has appellate jurisdiction in all other cases. Most cases come to the Supreme Court on appeal from federal appeals courts and state supreme courts.

Clause 3: The Trial of all Crimes, except in Cases of Impeachment, shall be by Jury; and such Trial shall be held in the State where the said Crimes shall have been committed; but when not committed within any State, the Trial shall be at such Place or Places as the Congress may by Law have directed.

3. Jury Trials. Those who are accused of a federal crime have the right to a trial by jury in a federal court. The trial must take place in a federal court in the state where the crime was committed. The exception is anyone who is impeached. That person's trial is held in the Senate.

Various amendments further spell out the rights of the accused in court. The 5th and 7th Amendments deal with the federal courts. The 14th Amendment provides guarantees for accused persons in state courts. The 6th Amendment applies to both.

Section 3 Treason

Clause 1: Treason against the United States, shall consist only in levying War against them, or in adhering to their Enemies, giving them Aid and Comfort. No Person shall be convicted of Treason unless on the Testimony of two Witnesses to the same overt Act, or on Confession in open Court.

Clause 2: The Congress shall have Power to declare the Punishment of Treason, but no Attainder of Treason shall work Corruption of Blood, or Forfeiture except during the Life of the Person attainted.

Section 3. Treason

1. Definition. Treason is defined as making war against the United States or supporting the nation's enemies. Two people must witness the act of treason and testify against the accused. The only other way a person can be convicted is to confess. The Framers defined treason carefully for a reason. They wanted to prevent government officials from charging opponents of the government with treason.

2. Punishment. Deciding on the punishment for treason is the duty of Congress. Sentencing guidelines list a prison term of from five years to life in prison. A person may also be fined $10,000. According to this section, the children of a person convicted of treason may not be punished. Also, the property of a convicted person may not be taken from his or her children.

Article IV The States

Section 1 Recognition of Each Other's Acts

Full Faith and Credit shall be given in each State to the public Acts, Records, and judicial Proceedings of every other State. And the Congress may by general Laws prescribe the Manner in which such Acts, Records and Proceedings shall be proved, and the Effect thereof.

Section 2 Citizens' Rights in Other States

Clause 1: The Citizens of each State shall be entitled to all Privileges and Immunities of Citizens in the several States.

Article IV. The States

Section 1. Recognition of One Another's Acts

This section is known by the name "full faith and credit." It requires that each state recognizes the laws, public records, and court rulings of every other state. This section is limited to civil actions and laws. States cannot enforce one another's criminal laws.

Section 2. Mutual Duties of States

1. Privileges and Immunities. Privileges and immunities are rights and freedoms. States may not discriminate against residents of other states. However, they may consider some reasonable differences between their residents and nonresidents. For example, they may charge nonresidents higher fees for fishing licenses. States may also require new residents to live in the state for a period of time before being able to vote.

Clause 2: A Person charged in any State with Treason, Felony, or other Crime, who shall flee from Justice, and be found in another State, shall on Demand of the executive Authority of the State from which he fled, be delivered up, to be removed to the State having Jurisdiction of the Crime.

2. Extradition. Extradition is the returning of a person wanted for a crime to the state where he or she is wanted. The purpose is to prevent people from escaping justice by fleeing from state to state.

Clause 3: ~~No Person held to Service or Labour in one State, under the Laws thereof, escaping into another, shall, in Consequence of any Law or Regulation therein, be discharged from such Service or Labour, but shall be delivered up on Claim of the Party to whom such Service or Labour may be due.~~

3. Fugitive-Slave Clause. Enslaved persons could not escape into free states and become free. This clause was in force from 1788 until the end of the Civil War. In 1865, the 13th Amendment was ratified and slavery was abolished.

Section 3 New States and Territories

Clause 1: New States may be admitted by the Congress into this Union; but no new State shall be formed or erected within the Jurisdiction of any other State; nor any State be formed by the Junction of two or more States, or Parts of States, without the Consent of the Legislatures of the States concerned as well as of the Congress.

Section 3. New States and Territories

1. New States. The power to admit new states to the Union is given to Congress. New states may not be created from land belonging to another state unless the state legislature and Congress agree. Maine was created in this way. It had been part of Massachusetts. The exception is West Virginia, which was created from Virginia. It occurred during the Civil War, and Virginia was considered in rebellion against the United States.

Clause 2: The Congress shall have Power to dispose of and make all needful Rules and Regulations respecting the Territory or other Property belonging to the United States; and nothing in this Constitution shall be so construed as to Prejudice any Claims of the United States, or of any particular State.

2. Territories and Property. This clause empowers Congress to manage territories, lands, and other property that belong to the federal government. Although the United States has acquired territory over the years, there is nothing in the Constitution that says that it can.

Section 4 Guarantees to the States

The United States shall guarantee to every State in this Union a Republican Form of Government, and shall protect each of them against Invasion; and on Application of the Legislature, or of the Executive (when the Legislature cannot be convened) against domestic Violence.

Section 4. Guarantees to the States

This section lists the three obligations of the national government to the states. The national government must guarantee representative government to each state. The national government must also protect states from attacks and from riots and civil disorder. If a state's legislature or governor requests help, the federal government may send federal troops to restore law and order. However, over time, presidents have sent federal troops to uphold the law and the Constitution without a request.

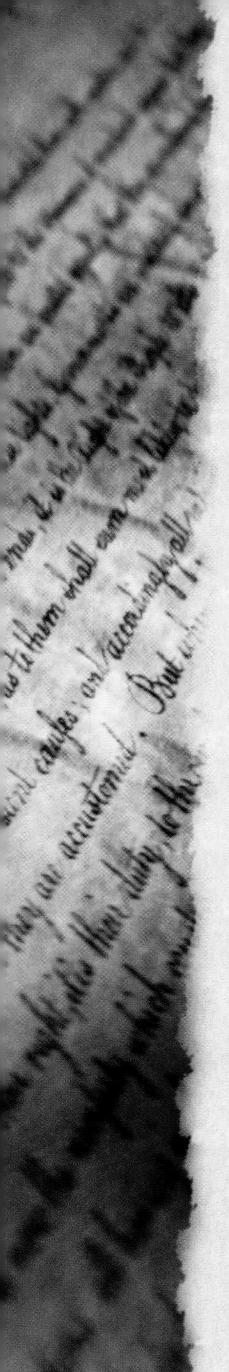

Article V Amending the Constitution

The Congress, whenever two thirds of both Houses shall deem it necessary, shall propose Amendments to this Constitution, or, on the Application of the Legislatures of two thirds of the several States, shall call a Convention for proposing Amendments, which, in either Case, shall be valid to all Intents and Purposes, as Part of this Constitution, when ratified by the Legislatures of three fourths of the several States, or by Conventions in three fourths thereof, as the one or the other Mode of Ratification may be proposed by the Congress; ~~Provided that no Amendment which may be made prior to the Year One thousand eight hundred and eight shall in any Manner affect the first and fourth Clauses in the Ninth Section of the first Article; and~~ that no State, without its Consent, shall be deprived of its equal Suffrage in the Senate.

Article V. Amending the Constitution

The Framers wanted the Constitution to be flexible and adaptable to changing times. However, they did not want to make it too easy to amend the Constitution. The result is a two-step process: first, proposing an amendment and, second, ratifying an amendment.

Amendments may be proposed by a two-thirds vote of both houses of Congress.

Amendments may also be proposed by a national constitutional convention called by Congress. However, two-thirds of the state legislatures must request a constitutional convention. So far, no constitutional convention has been held to propose an amendment.

Amendments may be ratified by three-fourths of the state legislatures or by three-fourths of special conventions called by the states to consider the amendment. Congress decides which method to use. Only the 21st Amendment has been ratified by special state conventions.

The part that is no longer in force deals with an amendment to outlaw the international slave trade. The slave trade with other nations was banned in 1808.

Article VI National Supremacy

Clause 1: All Debts contracted and Engagements entered into, before the Adoption of this Constitution, shall be as valid against the United States under this Constitution, as under the Confederation.

Clause 2: This Constitution, and the Laws of the United States which shall be made in Pursuance thereof; and all Treaties made, or which shall be made, under the Authority of the United States, shall be the supreme Law of the Land; and the Judges in every State shall be bound thereby, any Thing in the Constitution or Laws of any State to the Contrary notwithstanding.

Clause 3: The Senators and Representatives before mentioned, and the Members of the several State Legislatures, and all executive and judicial Officers, both of the United States and of the several States, shall be bound by Oath or Affirmation, to support this Constitution; but no religious Test shall ever be required as a Qualification to any Office or public Trust under the United States.

Article VI. National Supremacy

1. Public Debts and Treaties. The Framers promised to repay all debts that were run up during the Revolution and under the confederation government.

2. The Supreme Law. This clause is known as the Supremacy Clause. It declares that the Constitution, federal laws, and treaties are the supreme law of the new nation. They are superior, or more important, than any state or local government law. State and local governments may not pass laws that conflict with federal law. The decision in *McCulloch* v. *Maryland* was based on this clause. The 14th Amendment reinforced the supremacy of national law over state law.

3. Oaths of Office. Members of national and state executive, legislative, and judicial branches must take an oath to support the Constitution. This clause reaffirms the Supremacy Clause.

No religious qualifications can be required to determine a person's fitness for office. The 1st Amendment reinforces and enlarges on the separation of church and state.

Article VII Ratification

The Ratification of the Conventions of nine States, shall be sufficient for the Establishment of this Constitution between the States so ratifying the Same. Done in Convention by the Unanimous Consent of the States present the Seventeenth Day of September in the Year of our Lord one thousand seven hundred and Eighty seven and of the Independence of the United States of America the Twelfth In witness whereof We have hereunto subscribed our Names,

Article VII. Ratification
Only nine of the 13 states were needed to ratify the Constitution. Of the 55 delegates present, 39 signed the Constitution. When the ninth state, New Hampshire, ratified the Constitution in June 1788, it went into effect.

George Washington, President and Deputy from Virginia

Delaware
George Read
Gunning Bedford, Junior
John Dickinson
Richard Bassett
Jacob Broom

Maryland
James McHenry
Daniel of St. Thomas Jenifer
Daniel Carroll

Virginia
John Blair
James Madison, Junior

North Carolina
William Blount
Richard Dobbs Spaight
Hugh Williamson

South Carolina
John Rutledge
Charles Cotesworth Pinckney
Charles Pinckney
Pierce Butler

Georgia
William Few
Abraham Baldwin

New Hampshire
John Langdon
Nicholas Gilman

Massachusetts
Nathaniel Gorham
Rufus King

Connecticut
William Samuel Johnson
Roger Sherman

New York
Alexander Hamilton

New Jersey
William Livingston
David Brearley
William Paterson
Jonathan Dayton

Pennsylvania
Benjamin Franklin
Thomas Mifflin
Robert Morris
George Clymer
Thomas FitzSimons
Jared Ingersoll
James Wilson
Gouverneur Morris
Attest: William Jackson, Secretary

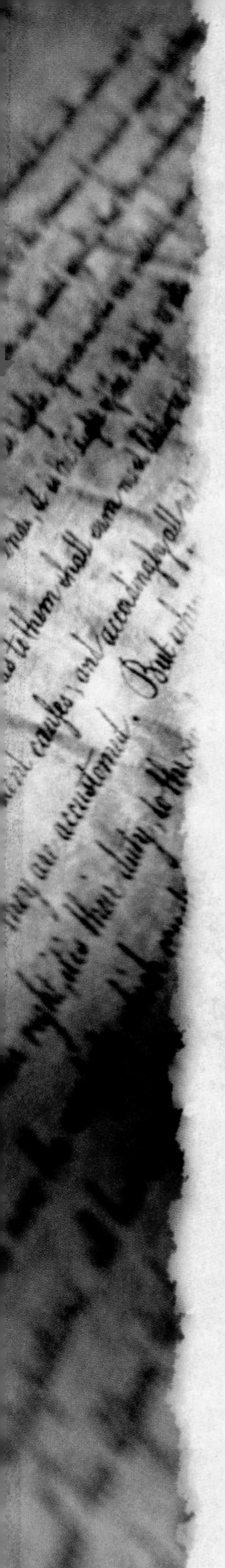

The pages that follow contain the original text of the amendments to the United States Constitution. Sections that are no longer enforced have been crossed out. The spelling and punctuation of the document remain in their original format. The headings are not part of the original amendments.

Amendments to the Constitution

Amendment 1 (1791) Religious and Political Freedom

Congress shall make no law respecting an establishment of religion, or prohibiting the free exercise thereof; or abridging the freedom of speech, or of the press; or the right of the people peaceably to assemble, and to petition the Government for a redress of grievances.

Amendment 2 (1791) Right to Bear Arms

A well regulated Militia, being necessary to the security of a free State, the right of the people to keep and bear Arms, shall not be infringed.

Amendment 3 (1791) Quartering of Soldiers

No Soldier shall, in time of peace be quartered in any house, without the consent of the Owner, nor in time of war, but in a manner to be prescribed by law.

Amendments to the Constitution

The first ten amendments are known as the Bill of Rights. Supporters of the Constitution agreed to propose these amendments in order to win ratification of the Constitution. When first adopted, the Bill of Rights applied only to actions of the national government. However, the Supreme Court has enlarged these guarantees. Many of these same rights safeguard citizens against mistreatment by the states.

Amendment 1. Religious and Political Freedom (1791)

The 1st Amendment safeguards civil liberties. Civil liberties are those protections that citizens have against abuse, or mistreatment, by the government. The 1st Amendment, however, does not mean that these freedoms are unlimited. People may use these rights as long as they do not interfere with the rights of others.

The 1st Amendment protects the right of people to practice their religion. It also sets up separation between church and state.

Freedoms of speech and press guarantee people the right to speak, publish, and express their opinions.

The right to assemble means that people may gather together in a public meeting. It also protects their right to join political parties, public interest groups, and other organizations.

The right to petition guarantees the right to ask the government to correct injustices. In other words, it guarantees the right of the people to influence public policy.

Amendment 2. Right to Bear Arms (1791)

States may set up militias for their protection. Over time, the state militias have developed into the National Guard. This amendment guarantees the right of people to have weapons. However, the national and state governments may regulate the possession, or ownership, of guns.

Amendment 3. Quartering of Soldiers (1791)

Quartering means "housing." This amendment was passed to safeguard people's privacy. During the colonial period, the British government housed troops in private homes. This amendment forbids that action.

Amendment 4 **(1791) Search and Seizure**

The right of the people to be secure in their persons, houses, papers, and effects, against unreasonable searches and seizures, shall not be violated, and no Warrants shall issue, but upon probable cause, supported by Oath or affirmation, and particularly describing the place to be searched, and the persons or things to be seized.

Amendment 4. Search and Seizure (1791)

Besides taking property, *seizure* refers to arresting a person. In order to conduct a search, police must have a search warrant, or order, from a judge. The judge gives the order only if the police can show "probable cause." The police must give reasons why they think someone has done something illegal or has goods that are illegal or stolen.

The Supreme Court has enlarged the protections of this amendment. Court rulings have developed the Exclusionary Principle. Goods seized without a search warrant may not be used as evidence in a trial. This amendment is now applied to state as well as federal courts.

Amendment 5 **(1791) Life, Liberty, and Property**

No person shall be held to answer for a capital, or otherwise infamous crime, unless on a presentment or indictment of a Grand Jury, except in cases arising in the land or naval forces, or in the Militia, when in actual service in time of War or public danger; nor shall any person be subject for the same offence to be twice put in jeopardy of life or limb; nor shall be compelled in any criminal case to be a witness against himself, nor be deprived of life, liberty, or property, without due process of law; nor shall private property be taken for public use, without just compensation.

Amendment 5. Rights of the Accused (1791)

A presentment, or indictment, is a formal charge of wrongdoing. A federal grand jury must determine if there is enough evidence to bring an accused person to trial. Only then can a person be brought to trial for a federal crime.

The exception is members of the armed forces and the militia, or National Guard. They are tried under military law.

A person may not be tried twice in federal court for the same crime. This is known as double jeopardy. However, if a trial ends without a verdict, a person may be tried again.

A person cannot be forced to testify against himself or herself.

The government may take private property for public use. This is called the Right of Eminent Domain. However, the government must pay the owner for the loss of the property.

The Due Process of Law Clause is very important and the basis of many rights of the accused. Due process means that the government may not act in an unfair or unreasonable way. The 14th Amendment extends due process to people's dealings with the states.

Amendment 6 **(1791) Rights of the Accused**

In all criminal prosecutions, the accused shall enjoy the right to a speedy and public trial, by an impartial jury of the State and district wherein the crime shall have been committed, which district shall have been previously ascertained by law, and to be informed of the nature and cause of the accusation; to be confronted with the witnesses against him; to have compulsory process for obtaining witnesses in his favor, and to have the Assistance of Counsel for his defence.

Amendment 6. Right to a Speedy and Fair Trial by Jury (1791)

An accused person has the right to a (1) speedy trial (2) in public (3) before a jury. Holding a person for a long time before trial is punishing someone without the benefit of a trial. Holding the trial in public is one way to ensure that it is fair.

The trial must be held where the crime was committed. This ensures that witnesses will be available.

The accused must be told what he or she is charged with.

The accused must also be allowed to question witnesses against him or her.

The accused must be allowed to have his or her own witnesses testify.

The accused must be allowed a lawyer. In 1963, the Supreme Court ruled that a lawyer must be provided for a defendant who is too poor to hire one.

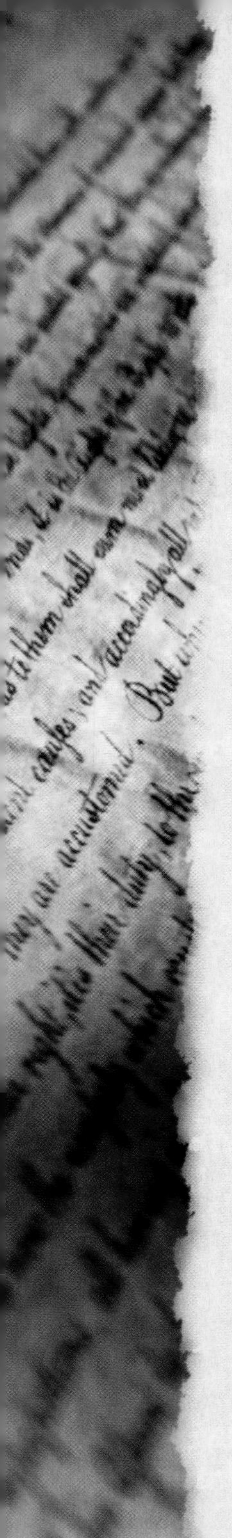

Amendment 7 **(1791) Right to Trial by Jury**

In Suits at common law, where the value in controversy shall exceed twenty dollars, the right of trial by jury shall be preserved, and no fact tried by a jury, shall be otherwise re-examined in any Court of the United States, than according to the rules of the common law.

Amendment 7. Civil Lawsuits (1791)

This amendment applies only to civil lawsuits in federal court. A civil lawsuit is between two private parties or between the government and a private party. *Party* means "a person or group of persons, or a business or group of businesses." Civil lawsuits often involve money or property. There is no crime involved.

If the money involved is more than $20, the 7th Amendment guarantees a jury trial. In practice, federal courts hear civil suits only if much larger amounts of money are involved. Also, the parties to the lawsuit may agree to have the case heard just by a judge.

Common law is not a law passed by legislatures. It is law that has developed from court decisions and custom. It has the force of laws passed by legislatures.

Amendment 8 **(1791) Bail and Punishment**

Excessive bail shall not be required, nor excessive fines imposed, nor cruel and unusual punishments inflicted.

Amendment 8. Bail and Punishment (1791)

Bail is money that a person must give the court as a guarantee that he or she will appear for trial. In place of being sentenced to prison or in addition to a prison sentence, a convicted person may have to pay a fine. Neither bail nor fines can be out of proportion to the crime. A serious crime requires a higher bail and/or fine.

"Cruel and unusual punishment" safeguards convicted persons from unreasonable punishment, such as whipping.

Amendment 9 **(1791) All Other Rights**

The enumeration in the Constitution, of certain rights, shall not be construed to deny or disparage others retained by the people.

Amendment 9. Powers Reserved to the People (1791)

Amendment 9 declares that the people have more civil rights than those listed in the Constitution and its amendments.

Amendment 10 **(1791) Rights of States and the People**

The powers not delegated to the United States by the Constitution, nor prohibited by it to the States, are reserved to the States respectively, or to the people.

Amendment 10. Powers Reserved to the States (1791)

The Constitution lists certain powers that belong to the national government. Certain other powers are denied the people and the states. The 10th Amendment declares that all other powers belong to the people or to the states. The purpose of this amendment is to safeguard the rights of the people and the states. The fear was that the national government would become too powerful.

Amendment 11 (1795) Suits Against a State

The Judicial power of the United States shall not be construed to extend to any suit in law or equity, commenced or prosecuted against one of the United States by Citizens of another State, or by Citizens or Subjects of any Foreign State.

Amendment 12 (1804) Election of President

The Electors shall meet in their respective states, and vote by ballot for President and Vice-President, one of whom, at least, shall not be an inhabitant of the same state with themselves; they shall name in their ballots the person voted for as President, and in distinct ballots the person voted for as Vice-President, and they shall make distinct lists of all persons voted for as President, and of all persons voted for as Vice-President, and of the number of votes for each, which lists they shall sign and certify, and transmit sealed to the seat of the government of the United States, directed to the President of the Senate;

The President of the Senate shall, in the presence of the Senate and House of Representatives, open all the certificates and the votes shall then be counted;

The person having the greatest number of votes for President, shall be the President, if such number be a majority of the whole number of Electors appointed; and if no person have such majority, then from the persons having the highest numbers not exceeding three on the list of those voted for as President, the House of Representatives shall choose immediately, by ballot, the President. But in choosing the President, the votes shall be taken by states, the representation from each state having one vote; a quorum for this purpose shall consist of a member or members from two-thirds of the states, and a majority of all the states shall be necessary to a choice.

~~And if the House of Representatives shall not choose a President whenever the right of choice shall devolve upon them, before the fourth day of March next following, then the Vice-President shall act as President, as in the case of the death or other constitutional disability of the President.~~

The person having the greatest number of votes as Vice-President, shall be the Vice-President, if such number be a majority of the whole number of Electors appointed, and if no person have a majority, then from the two highest numbers on the list, the Senate shall choose the Vice-President; a quorum for the purpose shall consist of two-thirds of the whole number of Senators, and a majority of the whole number shall be necessary to a choice. But no person constitutionally ineligible to the office of President shall be eligible to that of Vice-President of the United States.

Amendment 11. Lawsuits Against the States (1795)

The 11th Amendment repeals part of Article III, Section 2, Clause 1. A resident of a state or of a foreign nation must bring a lawsuit against a state in state court. Such lawsuits may not be heard in federal court.

The Supreme Court has enlarged the meaning of this amendment. It has ruled that a foreign nation may not sue a state in federal court. Also, a resident of a state may not sue that state in federal court.

Amendment 12. Election of the President and Vice President (1804)

This amendment changes Article II, Section 1, Clause 3. It was added because of the election of 1800. Until the ratification of the 12th Amendment, ballots were not marked "president" and "vice president." In the election of 1800, two candidates tied for president. The House of Representatives had to decide the election. The 12th Amendment states that separate ballots are to be cast for president and vice president.

Electors may not vote for two candidates from their home state for president and vice president.

The amendment sets up a process if no single candidate for president receives a majority of Electoral College votes. All but the top three vote-getting candidates are eliminated, and House members vote for president among these three.

The Senate chooses the vice president if no candidate receives a majority in the Electoral College. The Senate chooses from the two highest vote-getting candidates.

The deleted section was changed by the 20th Amendment.

The vice president must have the same qualifications as the president. This enlarges on Article II, Section 1, Clause 5.

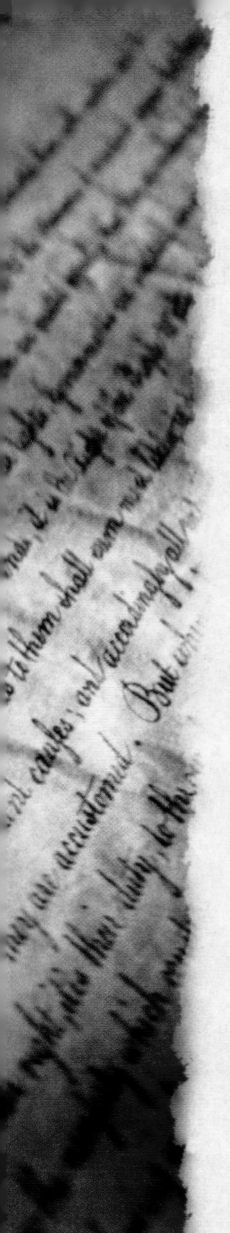

Amendment 13 (1865) Abolition of Slavery

Section 1 Neither slavery nor involuntary servitude, except as a punishment for crime whereof the party shall have been duly convicted, shall exist within the United States, or any place subject to their jurisdiction.

Section 2 Congress shall have power to enforce this article by appropriate legislation.

Amendment 13. Abolition of Slavery (1865)

This amendment ended slavery in the United States and in territory under U.S. control. In addition to enslavement of African Americans, it ended the enslavement of persons to repay debts.

Section 2. Enforcement. Congress may make all laws that are needed to ensure that the amendment is carried out.

Amendment 14 (1868) Civil Rights in the States

Section 1 All persons born or naturalized in the United States, and subject to the jurisdiction thereof, are citizens of the United States and of the State wherein they reside. No State shall make or enforce any law which shall abridge the privileges or immunities of citizens of the United States; nor shall any State deprive any person of life, liberty, or property, without due process of law; nor deny to any person within its jurisdiction the equal protection of the laws.

Amendment 14. Rights of Citizens (1868)

Section 1. Definition of Citizenship. This amendment grants U.S. citizenship to everyone born within the United States and to all naturalized persons. As a result, all former enslaved African Americans became citizens.

States are forbidden to pass any laws that would interfere with the "privileges or immunities" of citizens.

States may not take "life, liberty, or property" from someone without "due process of law." The 12th Amendment extends the Due Process Clause of the 5th Amendment to dealings between states and individuals.

All citizens are entitled to equal protection under the law. The Supreme Court used the Equal Protection Principle to overturn segregation in *Brown* v. *Board of Education.*

Section 2 Representatives shall be apportioned among the several States according to their respective numbers, counting the whole number of persons in each State, excluding Indians not taxed. But when the right to vote at any election for the choice of electors for President and Vice President of the United States, Representatives in Congress, the Executive and Judicial officers of a State, or the members of the Legislature thereof, is denied to any of the male inhabitants of such State, being twenty-one years of age, *(See Note 15)* and citizens of the United States, or in any way abridged, except for participation in rebellion, or other crime, the basis of representation therein shall be reduced in the proportion which the number of such male citizens shall bear to the whole number of male citizens twenty-one years of age in such State.

Section 2. Representation in Congress. The Three-Fifths Clause, Article I, Section 2, Clause 3, counted enslaved African Americans as three-fifths of the population in deciding the number of representatives for each states in the House of Representatives. Section 2 of the 14th Amendment did away with this clause. Native Americans were not considered citizens and were not counted.

There was a penalty if a state refused to allow African Americans to vote. The number of representatives that the state had in the House would be reduced. This section was never enforced. African Americans' voting rights were guaranteed by the 24th Amendment and other civil rights laws.

Section 3 No person shall be a Senator or Representative in Congress, or elector of President and Vice President, or hold any office, civil or military, under the United States, or under any State, who, having previously taken an oath, as a member of Congress, or as an officer of the United States, or as a member of any State legislature, or as an executive or judicial officer of any State, to support the Constitution of the United States, shall have engaged in insurrection or rebellion against the same, or given aid or comfort to the enemies thereof. But Congress may by a vote of two-thirds of each House, remove such disability.

Section 3. Punishment for Rebellion. The section is aimed at officials and military officers who joined the confederacy. Anyone who once swore to uphold the Constitution and then rebelled against the United States may not hold a job in federal or state government. Congress is empowered by a vote of two-thirds of both houses to remove this ban. By the end of the 1870s, almost all former Confederate officials had been allowed to hold public office again.

Section 4 The validity of the public debt of the United States, authorized by law, including debts incurred for payment of pensions and bounties for services in suppressing insurrection or rebellion, shall not be questioned. But neither the United States nor any State shall assume or pay any debt or obligation incurred in aid of insurrection or rebellion against the United States, or any claim for the loss or emancipation of any slave; but all such debts, obligations and claims shall be held illegal and void.

Section 5 The Congress shall have power to enforce, by appropriate legislation, the provisions of this article.

Section 4. Public Debt. Both the Union and the Confederacy piled up huge debts in the Civil War. This section states that the Union debt was valid, or legal. However, the Confederate debt was declared invalid, or illegal. It would not be repaid.

In addition, former slaveholders were not to be paid for the loss of their enslaved persons.

Section 5. Enforcement. Congress may make all laws that are needed to ensure that this amendment is carried out.

Amendment 15 (1870) Black Suffrage

Section 1 The right of citizens of the United States to vote shall not be denied or abridged by the United States or by any State on account of race, color, or previous condition of servitude.

Section 2 The Congress shall have power to enforce this article by appropriate legislation.

Amendment 15. The Right to Vote (1870)

Section 1. African-American Voting Rights. This amendment bars the states from discriminating against anyone "on account of race, color, or previous conditions of servitude." *Servitude* refers to slavery.

Section 2. Enforcement. Congress may make all laws that are needed to ensure that the amendment is carried out.

Amendment 16 (1913) Income Tax

The Congress shall have power to lay and collect taxes on incomes, from whatever source derived, without apportionment among the several States, and without regard to any census or enumeration.

Amendment 16. Income Tax (1913)

Congress is given the power to levy a tax on income. This is a direct tax and changes Article I, Section 9, Clause 4, which bars Congress from collecting direct taxes.

Amendment 17 (1913) Direct Election of Senators

Section 1 The Senate of the United States shall be composed of two Senators from each State, elected by the people thereof, for six years; and each Senator shall have one vote. The electors in each State shall have the qualifications requisite for electors of the most numerous branch of the State legislatures.

Section 2 When vacancies happen in the representation of any State in the Senate, the executive authority of such State shall issue writs of election to fill such vacancies: Provided, That the legislature of any State may empower the executive thereof to make temporary appointments until the people fill the vacancies by election as the legislature may direct.

Section 3 This amendment shall not be so construed as to affect the election or term of any Senator chosen before it becomes valid as part of the Constitution.

Amendment 17. Direct Election of Senators (1913)

Section 1. Election Process. Section 1 changes the process for the election of senators described in Article I, Section 3, Clause 1. Voters in each state now vote for senators. This is known as direct election of senators. Before this amendment, state legislators elected U.S. senators.

Senators still serve for six years and still have one vote each in the Senate.

Electors mean "voters." Anyone who is eligible to vote for state legislators is eligible to vote for U.S. senators.

Section 2. Vacancies. Section 2 changes the process for filling a Senate vacancy described in Article I, Section 3, Clause 1. The governor must call a special election to fill the opening. If the state legislature authorizes it, the governor may appoint someone as senator until the election is held.

Section 3. Timing. The amendment must be ratified before it can go into effect. Until then, no election or temporary appointment of a senator will be affected.

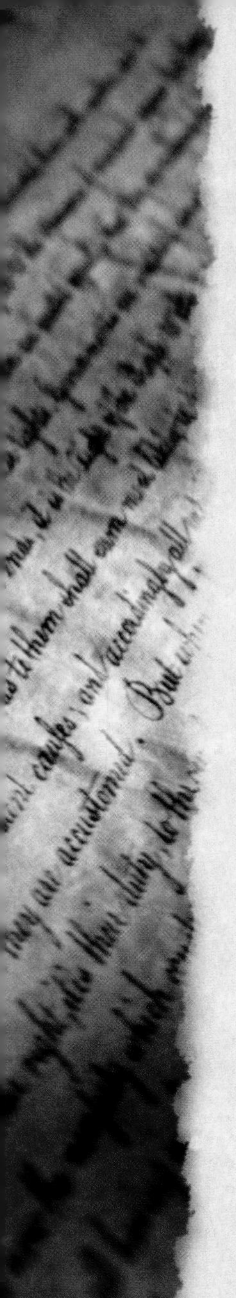

Amendment 18 (1919) National Prohibition

~~Section 1 After one year from the ratification of this article the manufacture, sale, or transportation of intoxicating liquors within, the importation thereof into, or the exportation thereof from the United States and all territory subject to the jurisdiction thereof for beverage purposes is hereby prohibited.~~

~~Section 2 The Congress and the several States shall have concurrent power to enforce this article by appropriate legislation.~~

~~Section 3 This article shall be inoperative unless it shall have been ratified as an amendment to the Constitution by the legislatures of the several States, as provided in the Constitution, within seven years from the date of the submission hereof to the States by the Congress.~~

Amendment 19 (1920) Women's Suffrage

The right of citizens of the United States to vote shall not be denied or abridged by the United States or by any State on account of sex.

Congress shall have power to enforce this article by appropriate legislation.

Amendment 20 (1933) "Lame-Duck" Amendment

Section 1 The terms of the President and Vice President shall end at noon on the 20th day of January, and the terms of Senators and Representatives at noon on the 3d day of January, of the years in which such terms would have ended if this article had not been ratified; and the terms of their successors shall then begin.

Section 2 The Congress shall assemble at least once in every year, and such meeting shall begin at noon on the 3d day of January, unless they shall by law appoint a different day.

Section 3 If, at the time fixed for the beginning of the term of the President, the President elect shall have died, the Vice President elect shall become President. If a President shall not have been chosen before the time fixed for the beginning of his term, or if the President elect shall have failed to qualify, then the Vice President elect shall act as President until a President shall have qualified; and the Congress may by law provide for the case wherein neither a President elect nor a Vice President elect shall have qualified, declaring who shall then act as President, or the manner in which one who is to act shall be selected, and such person shall act accordingly until a President or Vice President shall have qualified.

Amendment 18. National Prohibition (1919)

The 18th Amendment outlaws the making, selling, or transporting of alcoholic beverages in the United States. Over time, many Americans openly disobeyed the law. The 21st Amendment repealed Prohibition in 1933.

Amendment 19. Women's Suffrage (1920)

Women may not be denied the right to vote in federal and state elections. This is extended to local elections.

Congress may make all laws that are needed to ensure that the amendment is carried out.

Amendment 20. "Lame-Duck" Amendment and Succession (1933)

A lame duck is someone who is defeated or not eligible for reelection but serves out his or her term.

Section 1. New Starting Dates for Terms of Office. The Framers set the inauguration of the president and vice president for March 4. This was four months after the election. In the late 1700s, it could take months for the presidential and vice presidential candidates to make their way to the capital and prepare to take office. However, by the 1930s, travel was much easier and there was no need for so much time. As a result, inauguration day was changed to January 20. This shortened the time that a defeated or retiring president remained in office.

Section 2. Meeting Time for Congress. Every two years, Congress had a lame-duck session. At least some senators and members of the House were retiring or were defeated. Like the president and vice president, they served until March. The 20th Amendment moved the opening of the new Congress to January 3 of the year after the election.

Section 3. Succession of the President and Vice President. Article II and the 12th Amendment also deal with presidential selection. A president-elect is a person who has been elected president by the Electoral College but who has not yet been inaugurated.

If the president-elect dies before taking office, the vice president-elect becomes president.

If there is no president-elect, the vice president-elect may become president temporarily.

Congress is empowered to choose a temporary president if no one qualifies as either president or vice president.

The purpose of the section is to try to cover all possibilities in which no president or vice president is elected or able to serve.

Section 4 The Congress may by law provide for the case of the death of any of the persons from whom the House of Representatives may choose a President whenever the right of choice shall have devolved upon them, and for the case of the death of any of the persons from whom the Senate may choose a Vice President whenever the right of choice shall have devolved upon them.

Section 4. Filling a Presidential Vacancy. This section deals with several "if's." The Electoral College votes for the president and vice-president. If one presidential candidate does not get a majority of electoral votes, then the election is sent to the House of Representatives. If a presidential candidate dies before the House chooses a president, the House has to figure out what to do. It has to pass a law to solve the problem. If no vice-presidential candidate wins a majority in the Electoral College, then the Senate has to choose the vice president. If a vice-presidential candidate dies while the Senate is deciding on the vice president, the Senate must decide what to do.

Section 5 Sections 1 and 2 shall take effect on the 15th day of October following the ratification of this article.

Section 5. Using the New Starting Dates. This section states when the new starting dates in Sections 1 and 2 will go into effect. The president elected in November 1936 was the first president to take office on January 20. The members of Congress elected in 1934 were the first group to take their seats on January 3.

Section 6 This article shall be inoperative unless it shall have been ratified as an amendment to the Constitution by the legislatures of three-fourths of the several States within seven years from the date of its submission.

Section 6. Time Limit on Ratification. Three-fourths of the state legislatures must ratify the 20th Amendment within seven years from March 2, 1932. This was the date that Congress proposed the amendment. The states took less than a year to ratify the amendment.

Amendment 21 (1933) Repeal of Prohibition

Section 1 The eighteenth article of amendment to the Constitution of the United States is hereby repealed.

Section 2 The transportation or importation into any State, Territory, or possession of the United States for delivery or use therein of intoxicating liquors, in violation of the laws thereof, is hereby prohibited.

Section 3 This article shall be inoperative unless it shall have been ratified as an amendment to the Constitution by conventions in the several States, as provided in the Constitution, within seven years from the date of the submission hereof to the States by the Congress.

Amendment 21. Repeal of Prohibition (1933)

Section 1. Ending Prohibition. *Repeal* means "to cancel or end." The 21st Amendment repealed the 18th Amendment and ended Prohibition.

Section 2. Limit. States and territories could continue to ban the shipping of alcoholic beverages across their borders. Any state or territory that wished to make it a crime would have to pass its own laws against the transportation of alcoholic beverages.

Section 3. Time Limit on Ratification. This amendment also contains a clause putting a seven-year time limit on ratification. Congress proposed the amendment in February 1933, and special state conventions ratified it by the end of December 1933.

Amendment 22 (1951) Presidential Term of Office

Section 1 No person shall be elected to the office of the President more than twice, and no person who has held the office of President, or acted as President, for more than two years of a term to which some other person was elected President shall be elected to the office of the President more than once. But this article shall not apply to any person holding the office of President when this article was proposed by the Congress, and shall not prevent any person who may be holding the office of President, or acting as President, during the term within which this article becomes operative from holding the office of President or acting as President during the remainder of such term.

Amendment 22. Presidential Term of Office Limits (1951)

Section 1. Term Limits. This amendment limits presidents to two elected terms in office.

A vice president can become president if the president dies in office or resigns. If the vice president serves more than two years of the previous president's term, he or she may be elected only once. If the vice president serves less than two years, then the vice president may be elected for two terms (eight years) of his or her own.

This section states that the amendment does not cover anyone who is president when the amendment is proposed or until the amendment goes into effect.

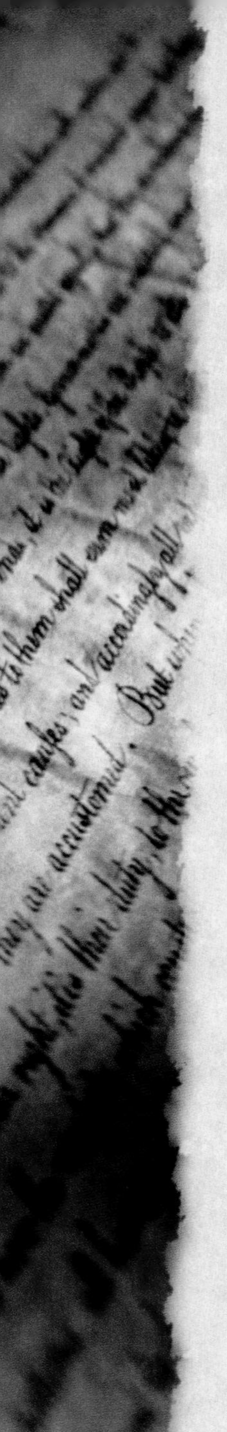

Section 2 This article shall be inoperative unless it shall have been ratified as an amendment to the Constitution by the legislatures of three-fourths of the several states within seven years from the date of its submission to the states by the Congress.

Section 2. Time Limit on Ratification. Congress set a seven-year time limit on ratification. Congress proposed the amendment in March 1947, and it was not ratified until 1951.

Amendment 23 (1961) Voting in the District of Columbia

Section 1 The District constituting the seat of government of the United States shall appoint in such manner as the Congress may direct:

A number of electors of President and Vice President equal to the whole number of Senators and Representatives in Congress to which the District would be entitled if it were a state, but in no event more than the least populous state; they shall be in addition to those appointed by the states, but they shall be considered, for the purposes of the election of President and Vice President, to be electors appointed by a state; and they shall meet in the District and perform such duties as provided by the twelfth article of amendment.

Section 2 The Congress shall have power to enforce this article by appropriate legislation.

Amendment 23. Voting in the District of Columbia (1961)

Section 1. Voting Rights. Residents of the District of Columbia could not vote in presidential elections until this amendment was passed. The District now has three electors. This is equal to the number of senators and representatives it would have if it were a state. However, the District is not represented in Congress, although Congress supervises its government.

Section 2. Enforcement. Congress may make all laws that are needed to ensure that the amendment is carried out.

Amendment 24 (1964) Abolition of Poll Taxes

Section 1 The right of citizens of the United States to vote in any primary or other election for President or Vice President, for electors for President or Vice President, or for Senator or Representative in Congress, shall not be denied or abridged by the United States or any state by reason of failure to pay any poll tax or other tax.

Section 2 The Congress shall have power to enforce this article by appropriate legislation.

Amendment 24. Abolition of Poll Taxes (1964)

Section 1. Some southern states used the poll tax to discriminate against African Americans. In order to vote, people had to pay this tax. The 24th Amendment banned the payment of any tax in order to vote in a primary or regular election for federal offices. A federal office includes president, vice president, and members of Congress. In 1966, the Supreme Court extended the ruling to include state elections.

Section 2. Enforcement. Congress may make all laws that are needed to ensure that the amendment is carried out.

Amendment 25 (1967) Presidential Disability and Succession

Section 1 In case of the removal of the President from office or of his death or resignation, the Vice President shall become President.

Section 2 Whenever there is a vacancy in the office of the Vice President, the President shall nominate a Vice President who shall take office upon confirmation by a majority vote of both Houses of Congress.

Section 3 Whenever the President transmits to the President pro tempore of the Senate and the Speaker of the House of Representatives his written declaration that he is unable to discharge the powers and duties of his office, and until he transmits to them a written declaration to the contrary, such powers and duties shall be discharged by the Vice President as Acting President.

Amendment 25. Presidential Disability and Succession (1967)

Section 1. Filling a Presidential Vacancy. This section spells out what happens if the president dies, resigns, or is removed from office. The vice president becomes president. This section makes clear what Article II, Section 1, Clause 6, implies.

Section 2. Filling a Vice-Presidential Vacancy. If a vice president dies, resigns, or is removed from office, the president selects a replacement. The nominee must be approved by a majority of members of both the Senate and the House.

Section 3. Replacing the President with His Agreement. From time to time, a president may be unable to carry out his duties. Usually, the reason is a health problem. The president must notify the president pro tempore of the Senate and the Speaker of the House of the problem in writing. The vice president then becomes acting president. When the president is able to resume his duties, he again notifies the president pro tempore of the Senate and the Speaker of the House in writing. The vice president then gives up his duties as acting president.

Section 4 Whenever the Vice President and a majority of either the principal officers of the executive departments or of such other body as Congress may by law provide, transmit to the President pro tempore of the Senate and the Speaker of the House of Representatives their written declaration that the President is unable to discharge the powers and duties of his office, the Vice President shall immediately assume the powers and duties of the office as Acting President.

Thereafter, when the President transmits to the President pro tempore of the Senate and the Speaker of the House of Representatives his written declaration that no inability exists, he shall resume the powers and duties of his office unless the Vice President and a majority of either the principal officers of the executive department or of such other body as Congress may by law provide, transmit within four days to the President pro tempore of the Senate and the Speaker of the House of Representatives their written declaration that the President is unable to discharge the powers and duties of his office. Thereupon Congress shall decide the issue, assembling within forty-eight hours for that purpose if not in session. If the Congress, within twenty-one days after receipt of the latter written declaration, or, if Congress is not in session, within twenty-one days after Congress is required to assemble, determines by two-thirds vote of both Houses that the President is unable to discharge the powers and duties of his office, the Vice President shall continue to discharge the same as Acting President; otherwise, the President shall resume the powers and duties of his office.

Section 4. Replacing the President Without His Agreement. A president's health problem may be so severe that he is unable to send a message to Congress. That happened when President Ronald Reagan was shot in 1981. Section 4 gives the job of notifying the president pro tempore and the Speaker to others. The vice president and either a majority of the heads of the executive departments or a majority of Congress must send a written message stating that the president is unable to carry out his duties.

When the president sends a written message that he is no longer disabled, he once again assumes his duties. However, the vice president and a majority of department heads or members of Congress may disagree. They then have four days to notify the president pro tempore and the Speaker. Congress then must decide by a two-thirds vote of both houses if the president is capable. If not, the vice president continues as acting president.

Amendment 26 (1971) Eighteen-Year-Old Vote

Section 1 The right of citizens of the United States, who are 18 years of age or older, to vote, shall not be denied or abridged by the United States or any state on account of age.

Section 2 The Congress shall have the power to enforce this article by appropriate legislation.

Amendment 26. Eighteen-Year-Old Vote (1971)

Section 1. Voting Age. Because of this amendment, eighteen-year-olds have the right to vote in all federal, state, and local elections. Before this amendment, twenty-one had been the minimum voting age.

Section 2. Enforcement. Congress may make all laws that are needed to ensure that the amendment is carried out.

Amendment 27 (1992) Congressional Salaries

No law varying the compensation for the services of the Senators and Representatives shall take effect until an election of Representatives shall have intervened.

Amendment 27. Congressional Salaries (1992)

This amendment changed Article I, Section 6, Clause 1. When the members of Congress approve a raise for themselves, the raise may not go into effect until after the next election for Congress. The purpose is to keep members from enriching themselves at the taxpayers' expense.

Lesson Summary

The Constitution can be amended by formal or informal means. Formally, the amendment is introduced in Congress. If two-thirds of the members of both the House of Representatives and the Senate approve it, it may then be ratified by three-fourths of the state legislatures. If two-thirds of the states request a constitutional convention, the amendment may be approved there. It then goes to be ratified by three-fourths of the state constitutional conventions. Informally, the Constitution is amended by legislation, practices, presidential actions, court decisions, and custom and usage.

Lesson Objective

Students will learn about formal and informal ways to change the Constitution.

Focus Your Reading Answers

1 The formal way to amend the Constitution is to propose and then ratify an amendment.

2 Informal ways to change the Constitution include legislation, practice, presidential actions, and court decisions. Customs and usage are other ways to change the Constitution informally.

LESSON 3

Amending the Constitution

Thinking on Your Own

Does your school have a set of rules or policies for students? Would you like to see any of the rules amended by having the present rules changed? List at least four rules that you would like to amend. Write the rules as they are now. Then rewrite them your way. Share these with a partner.

focus your reading

Describe the formal process for adding amendments to the U.S. Constitution.

What are the informal ways to change the Constitution?

words to know

executive agreements

judicial restraint

The Framers understood the need to make the Constitution adaptable. As a result, they built into the document a way to amend, or change, the Constitution. This is the formal amendment process. However, informal ways of changing the Constitution have also developed since 1789.

Formal Methods for Amending the Constitution

The chart on page 78 lists the 27 amendments to the Constitution. The first 10 are called the Bill of Rights. As you remember, supporters of the Constitution agreed to add them in order to win ratification of the Constitution. The other 17 amendments were added as the nation and the role of government changed over time.

Adding an amendment to the Constitution requires two steps: (1) proposing an amendment and (2) ratifying the proposed amendment.

There are two ways to propose an amendment. First, the amendment may be introduced into the House of Representatives and the Senate. Two-thirds of the members of both the House (287) and the Senate (67) must approve the proposed amendment. Under the second method, two-thirds of

Words to Know

Discuss each of the vocabulary terms with students.

Executive agreements are informal agreements that presidents make. The use of *executive agreements* allows presidents to bypass the need for Senate approval of treaties.

The idea that the Supreme Court should not take the initiative on political and social questions is known as *judicial restraint*. Those who favor *judicial restraint* believe that the Court should allow others to make national policy.

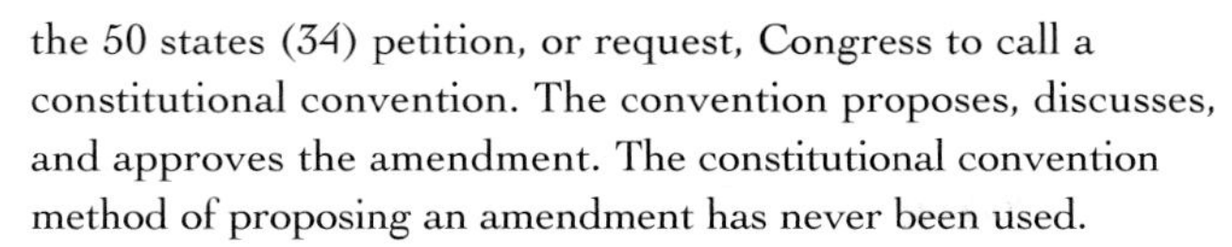

the 50 states (34) petition, or request, Congress to call a constitutional convention. The convention proposes, discusses, and approves the amendment. The constitutional convention method of proposing an amendment has never been used.

Once an amendment is approved, there are two ways it may be ratified. According to the first way, three-fourths (38) of the state legislatures of all 50 states must ratify it. For the second method, Congress asks the states to call special constitutional conventions to ratify the proposed amendment. If that method is used, then three-fourths (38) of all 50 state constitutional conventions must ratify it.

Congress determines which method of ratification to use. Since 1789, special constitutional conventions have been called only once to ratify an amendment. The Twenty-first Amendment was ratified in this way in 1933. The other 26 amendments were proposed by Congress and ratified by state legislatures.

Informal Changes to the Constitution

The Constitution leaves the day-to-day operation of the government to the people who run it. When the Constitution was first written, there were a few million people living in 13 states. Today, the nation has grown to more than 280 million people and 50 states. Yet the Constitution still works as the plan of government for the nation.

One reason is that the Framers left many details to be filled in later. As you have just read, amendments are one way that the Constitution changes with the times. There are also informal ways. Informal changes do not revise the wording of the Constitution. Instead, they develop as Congress, presidents, and the courts go about the daily business of running the government.

The first source of informal change is legislation. Congress passes laws that explain and enlarge on the powers given to Congress in Article I. For example, the Framers gave Congress the power to levy taxes. However, the questions of what kinds of taxes, on whom, and how much, were left to Congress to answer.

Extensions

1 Discuss with students why the Twenty-first Amendment might have used special constitutional conventions. Ask them to draw on their general knowledge of history and economics to form ideas.

2 The Twenty-seventh Amendment, which prohibits midterm pay raises for Congress, was adopted in 1992 after being ratified by three-fourths of the states. James Madison first proposed it 202 years earlier! Congress now generally includes time limits for amendments, most often seven years. There was no limit placed on this amendment, however.

The United States Constitution 77

Chart Extension

Have students count off, and assign each the corresponding amendment. Ask students to use library resources or the Internet to find out more about the amendment's history and at least one current application of it. Have students take turns presenting their amendment to the class.

Amendments to the Constitution

Amendment	Year	Subject
First	1791	Guarantees freedom of religion, speech, assembly, press, and petition
Second	1791	Protects the right of states to have militias and the right of citizens to carry guns
Third	1791	Limits how and when soldiers may be housed in private homes
Fourth	1791	Protects against "unreasonable searches and seizures"
Fifth	1791	Guarantees the right to a speedy and fair trial by a jury
Sixth	1791	Guarantees the right of "due process" under the law
Seventh	1791	Guarantees the right to a jury trial
Eighth	1791	Protects against high bail and "cruel and unusual punishment"
Ninth	1791	States that people's rights are not limited to those listed in amendments 1 through 8
Tenth	1791	States that powers not granted to the federal government and not forbidden to the states belong to the states and the people
Eleventh	1795	Forbids certain kinds of lawsuits against the states
Twelfth	1804	Changes how the Electoral College votes for president and vice president
Thirteenth	1865	Abolishes slavery
Fourteenth	1868	Defines citizenship and states the rights of citizens to due process and equal protection of the laws
Fifteenth	1870	Guarantees the right to vote regardless of race, color, or previous enslavement
Sixteenth	1913	Grants Congress the power to tax incomes
Seventeenth	1913	Provides for the election of senators by the people
Eighteenth	1919	Sets up Prohibition, which forbids the sale and manufacture of alcohol
Nineteenth	1920	Grants women the right to vote
Twentieth	1933	Changes the beginning dates for presidential and congressional terms of office
Twenty-first	1933	Repeals, or ends, Prohibition
Twenty-second	1951	Places a limit on the number of terms a president may serve
Twenty-third	1961	Grants citizens in the District of Columbia the right to vote in presidential elections
Twenty-fourth	1964	Prohibits the poll tax, a tax that voters had to pay in order to vote
Twenty-fifth	1967	Sets policies for presidential succession, filling a vice presidential vacancy, and presidential illness
Twenty-sixth	1971	Lowers the voting age to eighteen
Twenty-seventh	1992	Places limits on raises for members of Congress

Extension

Students may not easily see the application of the Constitution or its amendments to their lives. Point out the Eighth Amendment and tell students that it had a direct bearing on the 2005 Supreme Court case *Roper* v. *Simmons*. By a 5–4 decision, the Court ruled that the death penalty might not be invoked for those under age eighteen, because the majority regarded execution as cruel and unusual punishment for a minor.

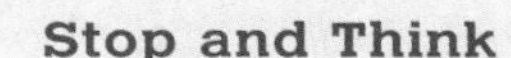

The second source of informal change is practice, or how things are done. For example, the Constitution gives the House the power to impeach a federal official. However, the Framers did not define "high crimes and misdemeanors" in Article II, Section 4. They left it to members of the House of Representatives to decide.

Presidential actions are a third source of informal change. Beginning with Theodore Roosevelt (1901–1909) and Woodrow Wilson (1913–1921), presidents in the twentieth century began asserting their power with Congress. The Framers gave Congress the power to make laws. However, since Theodore Roosevelt, presidents have been more assertive. They regularly send proposed legislation to Congress and threaten to veto bills that they do not want passed.

stop and think

Read through the 27 amendments to the Constitution. Choose five that you think are the most important. For each amendment, explain in a sentence or two why you think it is important. Share your essay with a partner. Try to reach agreement on what the two of you think are the most important amendments.

Another example of presidential action is the power to declare war. The Framers gave Congress this power but made the president the commander in chief of the armed forces. This is part of the system of checks and balances. However, presidents have sent United States troops into battle many times without asking Congress for a declaration of war. Modern presidents also get around Congress's power to approve treaties. They make **executive agreements**. These are informal documents with other nations, rather than treaties. The Senate must approve treaties, but the Constitution does not mention executive agreements.

Using the military for humanitarian missions is one of the powers of the presidency.

The fourth method of informal change is court decisions. The principle of judicial review developed from Supreme Court decisions. By hearing cases and handing down decisions, the federal judiciary interprets the Constitution and laws passed by Congress. Some critics of the judiciary claim that it reads into the Constitution things that the Framers never meant. These

Stop and Think

Students' choices of most important amendments will vary but should be supported with a sentence or two.

Picturing Government

The United States military created the Office of Reconstruction and Humanitarian Assistance (ORHA), headed by retired general Jay Garner, to assist in aid delivery. The war budget included funding for aid. Civilian groups, including those from the United Nations, work alongside military personnel, which are shown in the photograph on page 79.

Extension

Have interested students use library resources or the Internet to learn more about Congress's power to tax, using the Sixteenth Amendment as a guideline. Some of the students may already have part-time jobs; ask them to notice the percentage of their paychecks taken for taxes. Have them find out how the national, state, and local taxes are used.

ideas to remember

The United States Constitution is changed
- by the formal amendment process
- by informal means
  - legislation
  - practices
  - presidential actions
  - court decisions
  - customs and usage

critics believe in **judicial restraint**. However, others believe that the Court should be involved in how the government makes and enforces laws. These people support judicial activism.

Customs and usage also result in informal change. For example, the Constitution says nothing about political parties. However, political parties began to take shape as early as George Washington's first term. Since the early 1800s, elections have been based on party differences. Congress is organized according to party membership.

Putting It All Together

With a partner, create a table to list the formal and informal ways that the Constitution changes over time. Your table should have three columns and a title. In the first column, list the methods for change. In the second column, explain the method. In the third column, list an example.

National Constitution Center

One of the most important government documents ever written is the U.S. Constitution. But how do you honor a document? How do you make a document come to life? Visit the National Constitution Center in Philadelphia. If you cannot visit in person, then visit online. Millions of people have taken a virtual tour of the center since it opened in September 2003. One million people visit the actual building every year. The goal of the center is to increase "public understanding of, and appreciation for, the Constitution, its history, and its contemporary relevance."

The National Constitution Center is just two blocks from Independence Hall, where the Constitution was written. One exhibit has life-sized statues of each delegate to the Constitutional Convention. You can walk among the delegates and look eye to eye with Benjamin Franklin and James Madison.

Visit the interactive center and learn about the Constitution's effect on Americans' rights. Type in a description for yourself, such as an enslaved person in 1860, or a woman in 1880 who wants to vote. Then learn if the Constitution granted you any rights. If not, continue with your search to find out when you did gain your rights.

Ideas to Remember Extension

Review the ideas listed, further explaining difficult vocabulary words. Have students write definitions for each in their notebooks.

Civics Today Extension

In 1988, Congress passed and President Ronald Reagan signed the Constitution Heritage Act. This legislation was the basis for the National Constitution Center. The center broke ground exactly 213 years after the Constitution was signed. The groundbreaking ceremonies, over which President Bill Clinton presided, included naturalizing 75 new citizens and announcing a gift from the Annenberg Foundation. In honor of that $10 million gift, the Annenberg Center for Education and Outreach was named. The center opened on July 4, 2003. An estimated one million visitors come there annually to view more than 100 multimedia and interactive exhibits, along with text, sculpture, photographs, artifacts, and film. To honor National Constitution Week (September 17–23), the center has developed programs such as "I Signed the Constitution."

Putting It All Together

Students' tables should list the methods of changing the Constitution, along with an explanation and an example for each.

Participate in Government

Work for a Candidate

Political campaigns are a good way to become involved in politics. Candidates, especially in local elections, need volunteers. You do not have to be old enough to vote in order to volunteer.

Volunteers do all kinds of jobs to get the message about their candidate out to voters. Volunteers stuff envelopes with campaign literature. They also canvass neighborhoods for votes. They go door-to-door, handing out campaign information and talking about their candidate. On election day, volunteers may drive voters to the polls or call voters to remind them to vote.

To Find Out More About Volunteering:

- Decide which candidate you support in the election.
- Check the phone book or the Internet for the phone number of the political party of this candidate. Call the party to find the local campaign office for the candidate.
- Look at an ad for the candidate or at campaign literature you receive.
- Call for information or visit the campaign office to sign up as a volunteer.

Participate in Government

Divide the class into three groups. Assign each group one of the two major political parties, and a third party of your choice. Have each group find the party's local office, call or visit there, and obtain literature on volunteering. Give each group time to present its findings to the class.

Research Resources

Below is a list of reference books and Web sites that relate to the issues covered in this chapter. Students may wish to use these to further their research on ideas in the preceding lessons. Web site addresses may change over time. Use keyword searching on a major search engine to locate sites.

Reference Books:

CQ . . . Almanac Plus. Congressional Quarterly Inc., 2002.

Bruce Wetterau. *Congressional Quarterly's Desk Reference on the Presidency*. CQ Press, 2000.

Web Sites:

The National Constitution Center maintains an interactive Web site. This site is a virtual tour of the museum dedicated to the Constitution. It includes special sections for students and children.

The Supreme Court has a Web site. At this site, students can track recent Court decisions and opinions, as well as read oral arguments and briefs.

Skill Builder

1 A constitutional convention called by Congress on petition of two-thirds of the states has never been used.

2 two

3 a two-thirds vote of both houses of Congress, with three-fourths of states ratifying

4 three-fourths of the fifty states

Recommended Reading

Below is a list of books that relate to the issues covered in this chapter. The numbers in parentheses indicate the related Thematic Strands of the National Council for the Social Studies (NCSS).

Linda R. Monk. *The Bill of Rights: A User's Guide*. Close Up Publishing, 2004. (VI, X)

Amy Pastan. *First Ladies*. Dorling Kindersley Publishing, Inc., 2001. (V, VI, X)

David Ruble. *Scholastic Encyclopedia of the Presidents and Their Times*. Scholastic, Inc., 2001. (V, VI, X)

Skill Builder

Reading a Diagram

A diagram presents information by using pictures and symbols. For example, in Lesson 3, you read about the steps in proposing and ratifying an amendment to the Constitution. Instead of using text, the author might have used a diagram like the one below. A diagram is especially useful in presenting information that includes steps or a sequence. It can make it easier to remember information.

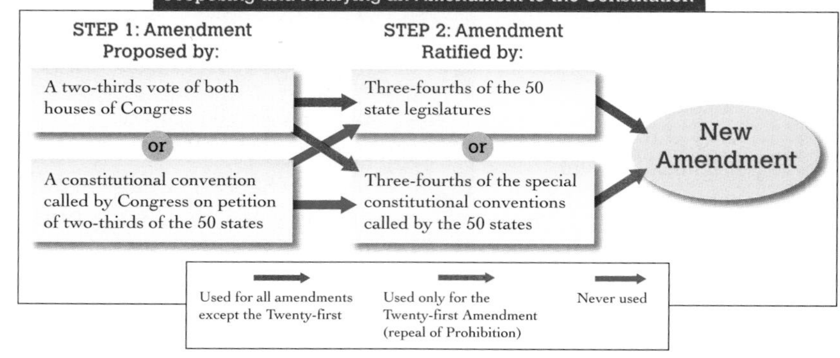

To read a diagram:

1. Read the title first to find out what the diagram is about.
2. Read the legend to identify symbols and colors.
3. Read all the labels and check them against symbols or pictures to understand the diagram.
4. Locate any arrows or numbers to identify the sequence or movement within the information shown.
5. Summarize for yourself what the diagram shows.

Answer the following questions about the diagram on this page.

1 What method of ratification has never been used?

2 Adding an amendment requires how many steps?

3 What method of proposing an amendment has been used most often?

4 How many of the 50 states must ratify an amendment for it to become law?

Classroom Discussion

Discuss with students some of the broader topics covered in this chapter.

- Should the Supreme Court's membership include more people? Should there be a mandatory retirement age for Supreme Court justices?
- How can the process of amending the Constitution be made more simple and fair?
- Are there other basic rights you would add to the Bill of Rights?
- In what ways might limiting a president to two terms be unwise?

Chapter 4 THE FEDERAL SYSTEM

Getting Focused

Skim this chapter to predict what you will be learning.

- Read the lesson titles and subheadings.
- Look at the illustrations and read the captions.
- Examine the chart and diagram.
- Review the vocabulary words and terms.

Federalism requires cooperation between the national government and the states. Think of a time when you and another person or group cooperated to get something done. Write a paragraph in your notebook describing what you had to do and how everyone cooperated to get it done.

Federal funds are used for many projects, including the construction of the nation's highway system.

Pre-Reading Discussion

1 Invite students to share examples they already know of cooperation among different levels of government in the community. If necessary, offer suggestions, such as airports or elections, and ask students to explain the cooperation.

2 Ask students how schools have changed in the short time they have been attending them. Invite them to suggest different sources, such as technology, funding levels, or population growth, for the changes. Tell them that in this chapter, they will be learning about ways that the government changes to respond to the changing needs of citizens.

Related Transparencies

T-3 Division of National and State Powers and Balance of Power

T-20 Concept Map

Key Blacklines

Biography— John Calhoun

Getting Focused

Allow students time to share their ideas with the class. You may wish to extend the activity to include examples from different areas of students' lives, such as clubs, service projects, or sports.

Picturing Government

The United States Department of Transportation maintains a National Highway System. It includes about 160,000 miles of roads that are important to the country's defense, economy, and mobility. While the interstate highways are part of the system, it also includes rural and urban highways that connect to airports, ports, or other transportation sites. In addition, highways between major military installations are part of what is known as the Strategic Highway Network (STRAHNET).

Lesson Summary

The federal system depends on the division of powers between the national and state governments. The national government has several responsibilities toward the states, including guaranteeing a representative form of government, protecting from foreign invasion, and guaranteeing territorial integrity. States are responsible for running national elections.

Lesson Objective

Students will learn about the division of powers in the federal system.

Focus Your Reading Answers

1 Expressed powers are those directly stated in the Constitution. Implied powers are those that can be assumed or suggested from the expressed powers. Inherent powers are those that belong to the national government because it *is* the national government.

2 Power is given to the states in the Tenth Amendment, which says that states have any powers that are not already part of the national government or denied to the states.

3 The responsibilities of the national government toward the states include guaranteeing a representative government and protecting the states from both invasion and domestic disorder. It also guarantees the borders of the states. The states have the duty of enforcing laws and keeping order. They also run the national elections and pay for them.

4 One role of the Supreme Court is to try state actions and laws to determine if they are constitutional.

LESSON 1

Division of Powers

Thinking on Your Own

This lesson focuses on powers of the national and state governments. Title a page in your notebook "Powers of Government" and create a two-column chart. In the left-hand column, include the powers listed in the Words to Know box. In the right-hand column, add the definition of each kind of power as you read about it. Be sure to leave space between each power to provide room for a full-sentence definition.

As you read in earlier chapters, the Constitution is based on six principles. One of those principles is federalism. In a federal system, power is divided between the states and the national government. This is known as the **division of powers**. Both the national government and the state governments have their own duties and responsibilities. These are described in the Constitution. However, these duties and responsibilities have shifted and changed over the years as the nation has grown and changed.

focus your reading

Explain the differences among expressed, implied, and inherent powers of the national government.

How is power distributed to the states?

What guarantees and obligations exist between the national and state governments?

Describe the role of the U.S. Supreme Court in the division of powers.

words to know

division of powers
delegated powers
expressed powers
implied powers
inherent powers
denied powers
reserved powers
concurrent powers

Powers of the National Government

The Constitution delegates, or gives, the national government three types of powers. Together, these are known as the **delegated powers**. They are expressed powers, implied powers, and inherent powers.

Expressed powers are expressed, or stated directly, in the Constitution. Articles I, II, and III contain most of these powers. For example, Article I, Section 8, Clauses 1 to 18, lists 27 powers delegated to Congress. Among them are the power to tax and to set up an army and navy.

Words to Know

Introduce each of the following vocabulary terms to students.

The *division of powers* is the sharing of power between the states and the national government. As the nation has grown, the *division of powers* has changed.

Delegated powers are those given to the national government. *Delegated powers* include three different types of powers. The *expressed powers* are those stated directly in the Constitution. The power to tax is one of the *expressed powers*. The *implied powers* can be assumed by the *expressed powers*. Having *implied powers* allows the government to meet the changing needs of the times. The *inherent powers* are those that belong to the national government, simply because it *is* the national government. One of the *inherent powers* is the power to make treaties with other nations.

Implied powers are those not stated directly in the Constitution. However, they can be reasonably assumed, or suggested, by the expressed powers. Clause 18 of Article I, Section 8, is the basis for the implied powers. This is the "necessary and proper" clause. It gives Congress the power to make laws that are needed for the government to function. The implied powers enable the government to meet the needs of changing times. For example, the modern Congress funds a national railroad system, regulates the nuclear power industry, and sets laws about environmental pollution. All these are based on Congress's implied powers. None of these topics would have been known in 1787.

Congress has the power to set up an army and navy.

Inherent powers are not directly stated in the Constitution. They belong to the national government. To act as the government of a nation, the government must have and use certain powers. For example, the national government must have the power to regulate immigration. It must also deal with other nations.

The Constitution also denies certain powers to the national government. **Denied powers** include the right to tax exports. Exports are goods sent out of the country for sale. Powers expressly denied Congress, for example, are stated in Article I, Section 9. The first ten amendments to the Constitution also deny the national government certain powers. For example, the national government may not limit freedom of speech or of religion.

In addition, any power that is not an expressed, implied, or inherent power is denied the national government. For example, the national government cannot set up a national system of public schools. There is nothing in the Constitution that gives the national government that right. The Tenth Amendment gives powers to the states that are not given to the federal government.

Extensions

1 There are occasionally calls for a reinstating of the military draft, which was ended after the Vietnam War. Ask students to investigate the issues of the debate, using library resources or the Internet. Have them present their findings to the class by using the Student Presentation Builder on the student CD.

2 Work with the vocabulary terms from this lesson to show students how the past tense of a verb becomes an adjective. *Delegate*, *express*, *imply*, *deny*, and *reserve* are all examples to use.

3 Funding for Amtrak, the national railroad system, has been in jeopardy. Have students interested in transportation and city planning issues use library resources or the Internet to find out the current state of Amtrak and other rail systems, such as high-speed bullet trains, subways, and elevated trains. Ask them to find out the issues in subsidizing routes that lose money.

Words to Know, continued

The *denied powers* are those specifically forbidden by the Constitution. Article I, Section 9, lists some of the *denied powers* of Congress.

Powers that belong to the states alone are called *reserved powers*. Creating public school systems is one of the *reserved powers* of the states.

Concurrent powers are those that both the national and state governments exercise. The power to levy taxes is one of the *concurrent powers*.

CD Extension

Encourage students to use the reading comprehension, vocabulary reinforcement, and other activities on the student CD.

Stop and Think
Students' lists of powers and examples will vary but should be based on the school's student government association.

People in the News Extension

The national law establishes an age not for drinking alcohol but for purchasing or publicly possessing it. The states have the right to regulate the sale and distribution of alcohol. These laws deal with purchasing, selling to minors, possession, consumption, or misrepresentation of age to buy alcohol. Have students find out the local laws related to this issue.

Picturing Government

In the photograph on page 85, members of the U.S. military are taking a pledge. Point out to students that both women and men serve in the military.

In 2002, the military (including the army, navy, Marine Corps, and air force) had more than one million members on active duty. The army is the largest branch, with more than three times the personnel of the next largest group, the navy.

Powers of the States

Like the national government, the 50 states have certain powers that belong to them alone. These are called **reserved powers.** There are also certain powers denied to the states. The states and the national government exercise some of the same powers. These are known as **concurrent powers.**

The powers reserved, or set aside, for the states are not listed in the Constitution. The Tenth Amendment, however, provides guidance on state powers. It declares that those powers belong to the states that are neither given to the national government nor forbidden to the states. For example, only states may set up local governments such as counties and cities. Only states may create public school systems and license teachers.

stop and think

Your school probably has a student government. With a partner, think of an expressed, implied, and inherent power that your student government probably has. Also, think of a denied power. In your notebook, write a sentence describing each power. For example, the constitution for the student government denies it the power to develop cafeteria menus.

People in the News

Candy Lightner and MADD

The National Minimum Purchase Act was announced in 1983.

What do you do if you want all 50 states to pass a particular law? If you are Candy Lightner, you lobby, or push your case, in Congress. Lightner's thirteen-year-old daughter was killed by a drunk teenage driver. In 1980, Lightner founded Mother Against Drunk Driving (MADD) to educate the public about the problem of underage drinking. MADD set up chapters in all 50 states. They campaigned to get laws passed to raise the minimum drinking age to twenty-one. Of the 50 states, 31 allowed people under age twenty-one to drink alcohol in 1980.

Lightner and MADD decided that there was a quicker way than approaching every state legislature. They wanted Congress to pass the law setting the minimum drinking ag at twenty-one. There was one problem. Congress did not have the power to pass a minimum drinking age law. That power rested with the states.

Lightner and her supporters in Congress, as well as Secretary of Transportation Elizabeth Dole, found a way. They used the federal power to fund highways as a tool. Under their National Minimum Purchase Act, if a state did not raise its minimum legal drinking age to twenty-one by 1988, the federal government would withhold ten percent of the state's federal highway funds. The bill passed and was signed into law in 1984.

Extensions

1 Since 1975, an estimated 18,220 lives have been saved through the minimum drinking age laws, according to the National Highway Traffic Safety Administration. A higher number of eighteen-to twenty-year-olds die in alcohol-related crashes than any other age group. Even in crashes involving a low blood alcohol count (between .01 and .09), a higher number of eighteen-year-olds die than any other age.

2 Have students find out about local chapters of Students Against Drunk Drivers (SADD) and their activities. You may also wish to invite a speaker from MADD or SADD to the class to talk about the importance of not drinking and driving.

Division of National and State Powers

NATIONAL GOVERNMENT

(Expressed, Implied, and Inherent Powers)

- Regulate foreign and interstate commerce
- Coin money
- Provide an army and navy
- Declare war
- Establish federal courts below the Supreme Courts
- Conduct foreign relations
- Exercise powers implied from the expressed powers

NATIONAL and STATE GOVERNMENTS

(Concurrent Powers)

- Levy taxes
- Borrow money
- Spend for general welfare
- Establish courts
- Enact and enforce laws

STATE GOVERNMENTS

(Reserved Powers)

- Regulate intrastate commerce
- Establish local government systems
- Administer elections
- Protect the public's health, welfare, and morals

Article I, Section 10, lists powers expressly denied to the states. For example, states may not negotiate treaties with foreign nations. States also may not grant titles of nobility. The Bill of Rights and the Thirteenth, Fourteenth, Fifteenth, Nineteenth, Twenty-fourth, and Twenty-sixth Amendments place the same limits on the states as they do on the national government. For example, the states may not allow slavery or keep women from voting in elections.

President Eisenhower signed the proclamation making Hawaii a state on August 21, 1959. Admitting a state is the responsibility of Congress; however, the president has the power of veto. Once admitted, all states are treated equally.

Concurrent powers are those that the national and state governments both have. For example, both levels of government have the power to levy taxes. The national government and state governments also have the power to create their own court systems.

Chart Extension

Divide the class into three groups, assigning each group one of the sections of the Venn diagram. Ask group members to take one of the bulleted points and become the group expert on that idea. Then rearrange the composition of the groups, and have students teach one another the point on which they have become an expert. You may wish to continue rotating the groups several times.

Picturing Government

The process of becoming a state can be lengthy and arduous. Hawaii began petitioning for statehood in 1903, repeating the request at least 17 times. Alaska, also admitted in 1959, first introduced a bill for statehood in 1916. The pro–civil rights stance of both states helped cause the delay in Congress. The photograph on this page shows the president signing the proclamation for Hawaii.

Extensions

1 The United States budget for military expenses is more than six times the next highest amount, spent by Russia. Have students select nine other nations, then use library resources or the Internet to find out how much each of these nations spends on military resources. Ask them to create graphs to show the differences.

2 Invite interested students to use library resources or the Internet to learn about times prior to the passage of the amendments discussed in the first paragraph on page 87, when states *did* permit slavery and prevented women from voting. Ask students to focus on one particular example, such as the imprisonment of twentieth-century suffragettes, and share it with the class.

Guarantees and Obligations

Article IV, Sections 3 and 4, lists the responsibilities of the national government toward the states. First, the national government must guarantee each state "a republican form of government." This means making sure that each state has a representative government. Congress enforced this guarantee after the Civil War. It refused to seat senators and House members from Southern states that had not ratified the Thirteenth, Fourteenth, and Fifteenth Amendments. These amendments ended slavery and recognized the rights of African Americans.

ideas to remember

The national government
- has certain delegated powers, which are expressed, implied, or inherent.
- is denied certain powers.
- shares concurrent powers with the states.

Second, the national government guarantees to protect the states from invasion and from domestic disorder, such as riots or rebellion. If a foreign nation invades one state, it is considered an attack on the nation itself.

Federal troops were called in to enforce desegregation at Little Rock Central High School in 1957.

The states have the primary duty of enforcing laws and keeping order within their borders. However, there are times when state forces are overwhelmed by violence, and the governor asks for help. There is also the issue of upholding federal law when state or local officials will not. For example, in 1957, President Dwight Eisenhower sent federal troops to enforce integration at Little Rock Central High School. This was the result of the governor trying to prevent the desegregation of schools.

Ideas to Remember Extension

Review the ideas listed, further explaining difficult vocabulary words. Have students create graphic organizers in their notebooks to help them visualize the three points on the powers of the national government.

Picturing Government

Three years after *Brown* v. *Board of Education*, public schools in the Deep South had not followed the ruling to desegregate with "all deliberate speed." A federal judge ruled that Little Rock's schools must be integrated. Orval Faubus, the Arkansas governor, threatened to bring in National Guard troops to keep Central High from being integrated. The nine African-American students faced a mob. As shown in the photograph on page 88, President Eisenhower finally sent in federal troops, stating, "Mob rule cannot be allowed to override the decisions of our courts."

Extensions

1 Ask interested students to use library resources or the Internet to learn the history of the decision to desegregate public schools. Have them focus specifically on the Supreme Court's ruling in the 1954 case *Brown* v. *Board of Education*. Invite them to find out the history of the case and the legal defense team involved.

2 Have interested students use library resources or the Internet to find out more about the Little Rock Nine and what happened to them. Use this research as a springboard for a discussion about the difference one person, or a small group of people, can make.

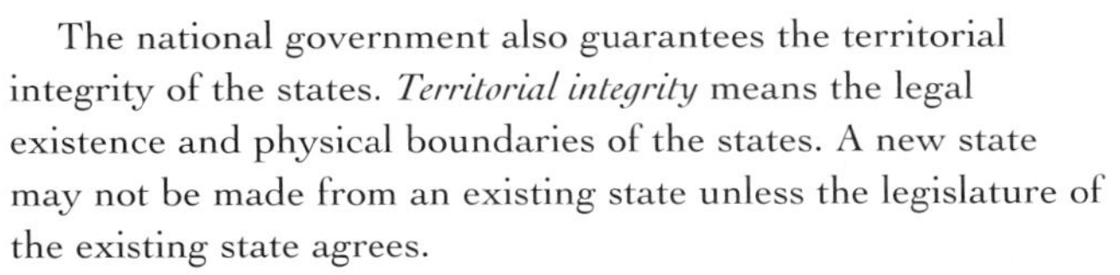

The national government also guarantees the territorial integrity of the states. *Territorial integrity* means the legal existence and physical boundaries of the states. A new state may not be made from an existing state unless the legislature of the existing state agrees.

In turn, the states have certain obligations toward the national government. The states are responsible for national elections. These are the elections for president and vice president, senators, and members of the House of Representatives. The states run the elections and pay for them.

The Supreme Court often acts as umpire in disputes between states and the federal government.

The Role of the Federal Courts

The Framers realized the possibility of conflicts between the national government and the states. As a result, the Framers included Article VI, Clause 2, known as the Supremacy Clause. It states that the Constitution, all laws made by the United States, and United States treaties are the "supreme Law of the Land." In other words, state constitutions and state laws must agree with the U.S. Constitution and national laws.

When conflicts arise, lawsuits are brought in the federal court system. Federal courts determine whether the state action or law is constitutional or not. This is known as the power of judicial review. As you have read, this power developed from court decisions. The first time it was applied to conflicts between states and the national government was in *McCulloch* v. *Maryland*. In that 1819 ruling, the Supreme Court denied states the right to tax a national bank established by Congress.

Putting It All Together

Review the list of powers and their definitions that you have been keeping in your notebook. Quiz a partner to see if she or he knows the definitions. Then ask your partner to quiz you.

Cartoon Extension

Ask students to use newspapers or newsmagazines to find a case in which the courts sided against the federal government. Ask them to explain the issue and the rationale the judges gave for their decision.

Extension

Direct students to the discussion of the *McCulloch* v. *Maryland* case on page 89.

Putting It All Together

You may wish to walk around the room during the time of paired quizzing. Check notebooks to be sure that students have correctly written the definitions for the different powers.

Lesson Summary

The Constitution's Full Faith and Credit Clause requires the states to recognize every other state's public acts, records, and judicial proceedings. Citizens also have privileges and immunities, such as being able to travel freely. States can treat those from out of state differently, however, in matters such as tuition at state-supported universities. States are also required to extradite fugitives. Subject to congressional approval, states may enter into interstate compacts. The Supreme Court settles disagreements between the states.

Lesson Objective

Students will learn about the relationships among the individual states.

Focus Your Reading Answers

1 The Full Faith and Credit Clause allows the public acts, records, and court decisions of one state to be recognized as valid by another state.

2 The Privileges and Immunities Clause protects citizens of different states from discrimination in another state.

3 The Extradition Clause makes sure that criminals or suspected criminals cannot escape justice merely by going to another state. The states are required to return fugitives to the original state of jurisdiction.

4 States may bring lawsuits against each other. These cases go to the Supreme Court.

LESSON 2

State-to-State Relations

Thinking on Your Own

The United States is one of only 11 nations in the world that has a federal system. The others have unitary governments. That is, they have one national authority but no state or provincial governments. Federal systems face special problems. They have to keep each state from going its separate way. What would happen if your state refused to enforce a neighboring state's laws, loan contracts, or jail sentences? Write a paragraph to describe life without state governments.

focus your reading

What is the effect of the Full Faith and Credit Clause?

Discuss how the Privileges and Immunities Clause protects citizens of different states.

What is the purpose of the Extradition Clause?

Explain how states resolve conflicts among themselves.

words to know

privileges

immunities

extradition

interstate compacts

The unwillingness of the states to give up power was a major reason why the Articles of Confederation had been so weak. The Framers of the Constitution were determined not to have this happen again. They strengthened the powers of the national government. They also laid out rules for how the states are to deal with one another. Article IV, Sections 1 and 2, states the mutual duties of the states.

Full Faith and Credit Clause

Article IV, Section 1, is known as the Full Faith and Credit Clause. It requires that every state recognize, or accept, the "public Acts, Records, and judicial Proceedings of every other State." For example, every state must accept the legality of the birth certificates of every other state.

Public acts are laws passed by state legislatures that relate to civil matters, not criminal ones. The Full Faith and Credit Clause refers to civil actions and laws only. One state's criminal laws cannot be enforced by another state.

Words to Know

Discuss each of the vocabulary terms with students.

Tell them that *privileges* are freedoms or special rights. A citizen of one state keeps certain *privileges* when traveling to another state.

Immunities are protections. Just as people can have *immunities* from diseases, they can also have *immunities* from illegal treatment in other states.

Returning a fugitive to the state where he or she is wanted is called *extradition*. Governors usually respond to requests for *extradition*.

Agreements between the states are known as *interstate compacts*. The Supreme Court enforces *interstate compacts*.

Records are documents such as mortgages, deeds, leases, and wills. For example, a will signed in one state will be valid in all 50 states.

Judicial proceedings under Article IV refer to court decisions in civil lawsuits only. A civil court ruling in one state must be recognized and enforced in the other 49 states. For example, a person cannot move from New Jersey to California to avoid paying damages in a lawsuit he or she lost. The person who won the case could bring a suit in California. The courts there would have to enforce the New Jersey decision.

All authority within a state comes from the state government. States create local governments, including counties, cities, towns, villages, and boroughs. Each local unit of government gets its authority to act from the state. Like the states, local governments may not pass laws that conflict with the Constitution.

Privileges and Immunities

Article IV, Section 2, Clause 1, states that "the Citizens of each State shall be entitled to all Privileges and Immunities" of citizens of every other state. Because of this clause, a state may not discriminate against residents of other states. **Privileges** and **immunities** refer to freedoms, or rights.

There is no complete list of privileges and immunities. However, over time, the courts have recognized certain rights. For example, people may travel freely from one state to another. People may freely change residence from state to state. People are also free to buy, sell, and own property in any state or enter into contracts to do business in any state.

However, the courts have recognized the right of states to make "reasonable distinctions" between their own residents and residents of other states. For example, states may charge out-of-state students more to attend state-funded universities. States may also require that voters live in the state for a period of time before being allowed to vote. States may also have residency requirements before a person may become a public official in the state.

Picturing Government

A city council meeting in progress is shown on page 91. Tell students that city governments generally follow one of two formats: commission or council-manager form. Tell them that they will study these formats in a subsequent chapter.

Extensions

1 Invite students to write brief skits to perform about the likely consequences if there were no Full Faith and Credit Clause. You may wish to suggest what would happen if documents such as adoption or naturalization papers were not accepted from state to state.

2 The right to travel freely from state to state was tested during the civil rights movement. Have interested students use library resources or the Internet to investigate the court cases that led to the 1961 Freedom Rides. Ask them to find out how and why the Interstate Commerce Commission got involved.

Picturing Government

The photograph on page 92 shows college students in a lecture hall. Non-residents, who do not pay taxes to support the state university system, can be charged higher fees. Many states are experiencing significant tuition increases, prompting actions from both the national and state governments that would lock in tuition rates.

Stop and Think

Students' letters and explanations will vary but should reflect an understanding of the Constitution.

Ideas to Remember Extension

Review the ideas listed, further explaining difficult vocabulary words. Have students create graphic organizers in their notebooks to help them visualize the three ways that states must cooperate with one another.

States have the right to set different tuition rates. Students may be charged more money to attend a state university if they are not from that state.

stop and think

Imagine that a neighboring state has just passed a set of laws refusing to let citizens of your state buy property, attend schools, and collect debts there. In your notebook, write a letter to the governor of that state explaining why these laws are unconstitutional.

Extradition

Article IV, Section 2, Clause 2, deals with extradition. When a person is wanted for a crime, or is convicted and flees before he or she can be jailed, the person is known as a fugitive. **Extradition** means the returning of a fugitive to the state where he or she is wanted. The purpose of the clause is to make sure that criminals and suspected criminals do not escape justice by fleeing from state to state. The governor of the state where the fugitive is found is responsible for having the person sent back.

Governors have usually responded to requests for a fugitive by turning the person over. However, sometimes a governor has refused. Finally, Congress made the issue a federal matter. Crossing state borders to avoid prosecution for a felony became a federal crime. In 1987, the Supreme Court declared that federal courts are empowered to order governors to turn over fugitives.

ideas to remember

The Constitution lists three ways that the states must cooperate with one another

- give "full faith and credit" to the laws, court decisions, and records of other states
- extend the "immunities and privileges" of their citizens to citizens of all states
- extradite fugitives

Extension

Have students check the tuition rates at several colleges. Ask them to select their examples from a range of in-state public universities and private colleges, as well as community colleges, out-of-state schools, and Ivy League schools. Ask them to create graphs or tables that illustrate the differences among the various categories. Lead a discussion about ways they can pay for rising college costs.

Interstate Compacts

What if states disagree about an issue? How can they settle the disagreement? Article I, Section 10, Clause 3, declares that states may enter into compacts, or agreements, with one another. However, Congress must agree to the terms of these **interstate compacts**. Once a compact is signed, state governments may not change their minds. The U.S. Supreme Court enforces compacts.

The National Governors Association is a bipartisan group that helps governors in developing state policies and in lobbying the national government for policies that aid the states.

Compacts are rare. Congress has agreed to and states have signed about 200 interstate compacts. Early ones dealt mainly with disagreements over state borders. Modern ones often deal with regional issues such as air and water pollution, use of water resources, and prevention of forest fires.

When states cannot agree on a solution, they may bring lawsuits against one another. More than 220 such lawsuits have been filed since the beginning of the nation. The U.S. Supreme Court hears these cases. It is the only court authorized to hear lawsuits filed by states against states.

Putting It All Together

With a partner, create a concept map about interstate relations. Draw a large circle and label it "Interstate Relations." Then add smaller circles connected by lines to the large circle. Label these with the three ways that the states must cooperate. Add the two ways states have of settling conflicts among themselves.

Picturing Government

Members of the National Governors Association (NGA), pictured on page 93, meet to discuss issues of importance to all state governments. The chairman of the group focuses attention on his or her initiatives each year. To help governors look at and create policy and address key issues, four standing committees exist: Health and Human Services; Economic Development and Commerce; Natural Resources; and Education, Early Childhood, and Workforce.

Extension

The NGA also has a Center for Best Practices. Divide the class into small groups, allowing each to choose a field of interest that would affect all states, such as air quality, the arts, or information technology. Have the groups check the NGA Web site and other sources to see what is being done across the nation in various states. Allow time for the groups to report their findings to the class.

Extension

Divide the class into five small groups. Give each group one of the following five categories: voter registration, drivers' licenses, drinking age, income or sales tax, or education. Ask each group to use library resources or the Internet to find the requirements of the states bordering their own. Have students decide which state compares most favorably. Then present data about the state in which they live and compare those statistics. In which area would a business be likely to open a new branch?

Putting It All Together

Students' concept maps will vary. Possible answers include the three areas of cooperation listed on page 92 and the two ways of settling interstate conflicts: compacts and courts.

Lesson Summary

Federalism develops over time. The balance of power between the national and state governments has been a source of disagreement. Arguments are put forth for states' rights and nationalist positions. The states' rights debate was a factor in the Civil War. During the New Deal, Franklin Roosevelt advanced the nationalist position. However, the Supreme Court appears to favor the states at the beginning of the twenty-first century. The power of the federal government has increased due to three powers: war power, commerce power, and power to tax. The federal government also gains power through its grants of federal aid to the states. These grants come with guidelines that must be heeded. Federalism influences public policy, political parties, and political participation.

Lesson Objective

Students will learn about changes in the ways that the federal government and the states affect one another.

LESSON 3

Federalism: The Ongoing Process

Thinking on Your Own

One way the federal government relates to states is by providing money for special programs. Federal money might pay for more police officers or new highways. Make a list in your notebook of problems in your community that more federal money could help solve.

focus your reading

What is the difference between states' rights and nationalist positions?

What powers has the national government used to expand its reach?

How has federal aid to the states expanded the power of the national government?

How does the political process affect federalism?

words to know

states' rights position

nationalist position

war power

commerce power

power to tax

guidelines

public policy

Federalism is defined as the division of powers between the national government and the states. What powers are involved? How are they divided? As you have learned, the Constitution lists many of the powers that are divided, shared, or denied the national government and the states.

The Framers could not have planned for federal aid to fund school lunches. Public education did not exist in 1787.

However, the nation has changed and grown since the document was written. Laws, court decisions, and practice have added duties and responsibilities to both the national and state governments. With these changes, the relationship between the national government and the states has shifted. In other words, federalism continues to develop over time. It is not the same as it was in 1787.

Focus Your Reading Answers

1 The states' rights position holds that the states created the national government, which acts for and in place of the states. States better understand the needs of their people. Believing in a strict interpretation of the Constitution, they base their ideas on the Tenth Amendment.

Nationalists believe that the people created the national and state governments. The national government represents all people and is not subordinate to the states.

Their ideas are based on the "necessary and proper" clause in Article I. They believe in a loose interpretation of the Constitution.

2 The powers are war power, commerce power, and power to tax.

3 States rely on federal aid for about one-fourth of their budgets. The federal government gives aid with guidelines attached that must be obeyed.

4 The political process affects federalism through a strong political party system.

Balance Between the States and the National Government

One area of disagreement over the years has been the balance of power between the states and the national government. What is the right balance?

The **states' rights position** is that the state and local governments should deal with social, economic, and other problems. The **nationalist position** is that the national government is better suited to act for all the people in dealing with these problems. The chart below shows the arguments that each side uses to support its viewpoint.

Balance of Power

States' Rights Viewpoint	Nationalist Viewpoint
1. The national government was created by the states, which gave it only limited powers.	1. The people created the states and the national government.
2. The national government only acts for, or in place of, the states.	2. The national government is not subordinate to the states.
3. States are closer to the people and better understand what the people want and need.	3. The national government represents all the people, not just the people of one state.
4. States' rightists base their view on the Tenth Amendment. Part of the Bill of Rights, it states that powers not delegated to the national government are reserved to the state or the people.	4. Nationalists base their view on the "necessary and proper clause" (Article I, Section 8, Clause 18). It states that the government of the United States will make all laws "necessary and proper for carrying out the foregoing Powers and all other Powers" placed in that government. Powers reserved to the states or the people do not limit how the national government may act or what it should do.
5. States' rights advocates usually insist on a narrow, or strict, interpretation of the Constitution.	5. Nationalists usually favor a broad, or loose, interpretation of the Constitution.

Picturing Government

The photograph on page 94 shows children eating meals provided by the government. In 2001–2002, some 16 million children were cared for under the National School Lunch Program, at a cost of more than $6 million in federal funds. Lunches may be free or served at reduced prices to certain students. The federal government also funds school breakfasts. In 2002–2003, more than 8 million children participated in the program.

Chart Extensions

1 Divide the class into two groups, assigning each group one of the positions on page 95. Have the groups debate their positions, keeping careful notes as they do so. Then have the groups switch sides and argue, using points made during the debate by the opposing team.

2 Have students create flash cards with the information from the chart on page 95. Pair students and have them quiz each other to be sure they correctly identify the viewpoint of each statement.

Words to Know

Discuss each of the vocabulary terms with students.

The *states' rights position* is that state and local governments should deal with the area's social, economic, and other problems. Those who believe in the *states' rights position* feel that the states created the national government but gave it very limited powers.

The *nationalist position* is that the national government is better suited to deal with problems. The followers of the *nationalist position* believe that the people created the Constitution.

War power is the right given to the national government to wage war. *Commerce power* is the power over most areas of making, selling, buying, and transporting goods. Congress has *commerce power*. The *power to tax* is the ability to assess personal and corporate income tax. The government uses the *power to tax* to raise money to run the government.

Rules are also known as *guidelines*. Federal *guidelines* note how states can spend federal money they receive. The goals that government sets for itself to solve problems are known as *public policy*. Federalism affects how *public policy* is made.

Picturing Government

Prior to the 1930s, the Tennessee River, shown in the photograph on page 96, flooded and washed away the fertile soil during heavy rains, then dried to nearly a trickle during the dry seasons. In 1933, the federal government created the Tennessee Valley Authority. While the TVA's chief purpose was to control the river, the project also allowed electricity to be brought to the seven-state region. Prior to the electrification project, only 3 percent of all farms in the Tennessee Valley had access to electricity. The TVA, which serves almost three million customers in all of Tennessee and parts of Kentucky, Virginia, North Carolina, Alabama, Georgia, and Mississippi, is the largest U.S. utility company. It maintains 51 dams on the Tennessee River and its tributaries.

Stop and Think

Students' lists will vary but should include reasons for the national government to expand or not to expand its powers.

The issue of states' rights was a major cause of the Civil War. Southern states believed the states should regulate slavery. Today, many states' rightists think states should control all school spending. Nationalists believe the U.S. government should control federal grants to schools for education.

The New Deal allowed construction of power plants under the direction of the Tennessee Valley Authority.

A good example of the nationalist argument is Franklin Roosevelt's New Deal. The New Deal was created to provide employment during the Depression. These programs greatly expanded the role of the national government. The Supreme Court's first rulings found them unconstitutional. Later, they upheld them.

In the late 1990s, the Supreme Court appeared to be moving toward the states again. In cases involving gun control laws and the Americans with Disabilities Act, the Court ruled that Congress was overreaching its powers.

stop and think

Make a list in your notebook of the reasons why you think the national government should or should not be allowed to expand its powers. Add to this list as you continue reading this lesson.

Expansion of the National Government

When the Framers met in Philadelphia in 1789, the new United States was a nation of farms. In the late 1800s, the nation shifted from farming to industry as its major business. The modern United States is moving from selling manufactured goods to selling services and information. The national government has expanded its powers to meet the changes in society as well as in the economy. Much of this expansion is based on three constitutional powers.

- **War power**: The Constitution gives the national government the power to wage war. Modern war is more than protecting the nation from attack. A great amount of time and energy of the executive and legislative branches is taken up with foreign affairs and the resources of the nation.

Waging war may involve building coalitions, or partnerships, with other nations. It may mean going to war to fulfill our obligations to foreign partners. The impact of war on the economy has to be considered. What effect will spending

Extensions

1 Have students use library resources or the Internet to learn about the Tennessee-Tombigbee Waterway. In 1984, the Army Corps of Engineers completed the extension of the Tennessee River route. Ask them to find out how the waterway has improved transportation in the region and why the Army Corps of Engineers, rather than the TVA, constructed it.

2 Invite students interested in conservation and environmental issues to use library resources or the Internet to find out about the TVA's record on reforestation and water and air pollution.

billions of dollars on defense have on programs at home, such as worker training and health care? Decisions about defense impact all parts of the economy and society.

- **Commerce power**: Congress has the power to regulate commerce. Over time, Congress has broadened this power to include more than buying and selling goods across state borders and with other nations. Commerce has come to mean almost everything involved in the making, selling, buying, and transporting of goods.

U.S. troops served in Kosovo as part of a NATO force during the 1990s.

Congress used this expanded power as the basis for its civil rights legislation in the 1960s. It banned racial discrimination in interstate travel, based on the commerce clause. Various Supreme Court rulings have confirmed Congress's expanded definition of its commerce power.

ideas to remember

The national government has expanded its reach based on three constitutional powers:

- war power
- commerce power
- power to tax

- **Power to tax**: The major purpose of taxes is to raise revenue, or money, for the government. About half of the national government's revenue comes from personal and corporate income taxes. No state can match this amount of revenue. It gives the national government huge resources to spend on national, state, and local programs.

Federal Aid to States

Another way that the national government has expanded its power is through grants to states. The federal government collects taxes in order to fund programs. Some of the money for programs such as Social Security and unemployment payments goes directly to citizens. Some pays for services for older Americans such as Medicare. Other funds go directly to the state and local governments.

These federal grants enable the national government to expand into areas that are not delegated to it by the Constitution. For example, the national government offers grants to fund low-income housing. Once a state or local

Picturing Government

NATO armed forces in Kosovo, shown on page 97 were part of a 78-day bombing campaign that bypassed the United Nations after attempts at brokering peace between the Serbs and Albanians failed. Eventually, in 1999, Slobodan Milosevic, president of Yugoslavia, withdrew his troops from Kosovo. The United Nations then began to administer the government in the war-torn region.

Ideas to Remember Extension

Review the ideas listed, further explaining difficult vocabulary words. Have students create graphic organizers in their notebooks to help them visualize the three ways that the national government has expanded its reach.

Extension

For a historical example of the effect of defense spending on domestic programs, have interested students use library resources or the Internet to find out more about the Great Society. Lyndon Johnson's dream to end poverty in America did some notable good, introducing programs such as Head Start and Medicare that continue to benefit millions. However, the costs of the Vietnam War slowed LBJ's agenda. Allow time for students to present their findings to the class.

Picturing Government

The Conference of Mayors grew out of the desperate situation the nation faced during the Great Depression. For the first time in history, Congress created a $300 million federal assistance program for cities. Thomas Menino, the mayor of Boston for more than 12 years, is shown on page 98 addressing the U.S. Conference of Mayors during his presidency of that body in 2002–2003. His emphasis in that group was in housing availability and homeland security. He joined three other previous Boston mayors who have held the position. Menino was serving his third term as Boston's mayor, having first been elected in 1993. He was Boston's first Italian-American mayor.

government accepts grant money, it must obey federal **guidelines**, or rules, for using the money. Federal money means federal control. For this reason, not everyone likes the idea of grants from the national government.

The Influence of Federalism

Federalism has a far-reaching influence on the political life of the nation. For example, it affects how and by whom public policy is made. **Public policy** is the goals that a government sets for itself in order to solve problems.

The national government sets public policy for the nation as a whole. However, state and local governments also set public policy. At times, their solutions have been adopted by the national government or by other state and local governments. For example, Florida's Government-in-the-Sunshine Law became a model for other states. The law prohibits public officials from closing their meetings to the public.

Federalism also affects political parties and political participation. A strong political party system is one result. Because there are many government units, one party may lose control of the presidency and Congress, but remain strong in state and local politics. This happened to the Democratic Party after the Civil War and to the Republican Party during the Great Depression.

Because the United States has a federal system, citizens benefit from having thousands of governments—state and local—trying out public policy solutions. Citizens also have many opportunities to become active in politics. A person might become involved to protect local parkland or to oppose a new highway. As a person becomes more involved in politics and government, he or she has a greater chance of influencing public policy.

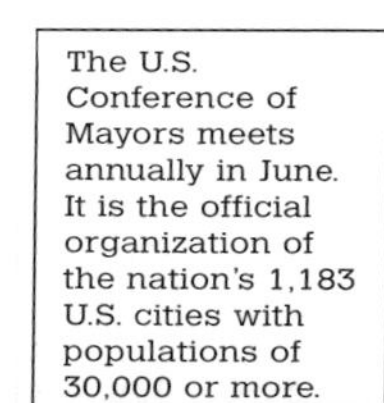

The U.S. Conference of Mayors meets annually in June. It is the official organization of the nation's 1,183 U.S. cities with populations of 30,000 or more.

Putting It All Together

Is federalism a good thing for the nation or not? Discuss the question with a partner. When you reach a conclusion, write a sentence stating your conclusion. Use the sentence as the introduction to a paragraph answering the question. Use at least five examples from the lesson to support your answer.

Putting It All Together

Students' conclusions and paragraphs will vary but should include at least five examples to support those conclusions.

Participate in Government

Become an Informed Voter

The right to vote comes with a responsibility. That responsibility is to be an informed voter. There are many ways that voters can learn about candidates and issues.

Candidates and political parties pay for and distribute all kinds of campaign information. They

- hand out brochures.
- pay for ads on television, cable, and radio.
- put up Web sites.
- sponsor campaign rallies and meet-the-candidate question-and-answer sessions.
- appear on cable and television talk shows. and talk radio programs.
- host town hall meetings.
- participate in political debates.

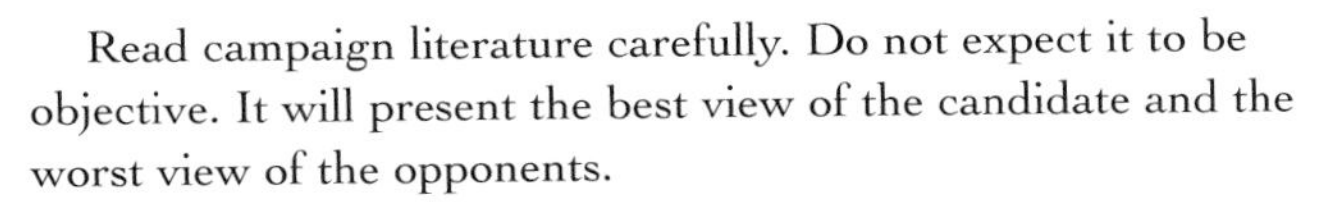

Read campaign literature carefully. Do not expect it to be objective. It will present the best view of the candidate and the worst view of the opponents.

A better way to find out about candidates and issues is to read news stories and interviews with candidates. Even when listening to candidates, pay attention to the accuracy of what they say. Does their record agree with what they say? Are they exaggerating their own record or their opponents' records? Do not believe everything you hear, see, or read. Investigate, analyze, and make informed voting decisions.

Find Out More:

Check the phone book to see if your community has a local branch of the League of Women Voters. This is a nonpartisan group that monitors elections. Contact your local branch for information about the candidates running in upcoming elections.

Participate in Government

Invite students to create a classroom display of election materials that they have gathered. Use the brochures and other print material to analyze the persuasive techniques each candidate uses. Do they find the materials persuasive? Consider holding a mock election to make use of the materials.

Research Resources

Below is a list of reference books and Web sites that relate to the issues covered in this chapter. Students may wish to use these to further their research on ideas in the preceding lessons. Web site addresses may change over time. Use keyword searching on a major search engine to locate sites.

Reference Books:

S. L. Alexander. *Media and American Courts: A Reference Handbook*. ABC-CLIO, 2004.

Peggy Garvin. *The United States Government Internet Manual*. Bernan Press, 2004. (revised annually)

Kathleen Thompson Hill and Gerald N. Hill. *Encyclopedia of Federal Agencies and Commissions*. Facts on File, 2004.

Web Sites:

A site is maintained for each branch of the U.S. military.

The U.S. Conference of Mayors and the National Governors Association maintain Web sites that provide information on issues.

Skill Builder

1 Students' paragraphs and explanations will vary.

2 Students' ideas and discussions will vary.

Recommended Reading

Below is a list of books that relate to the issues covered in this chapter. The numbers in parentheses indicate the related Thematic Strands of the National Council for the Social Studies (NCSS).

Ted Gottfried. *Homeland Security* vs. *Constitutional Rights*. 21st Century, 2003. (VI, X)

Carol Rust Nash. *The Fight for Women's Right to Vote in American History (In American History)*. Enslow Publishers, 1998. (V, VI, X)

A. Thomas, J. D. Jacobs, Jay E. Johnson. *What Are My Rights?: 95 Questions and Answers About Teens and the Law*. Free Spirit Publishing, 1997. (V, VI, X)

Joyce Carol Thomas. *Linda Brown, You Are Not Alone: The* Brown *v.* Board of Education *Decision*. Jump at the Sun/Hyperion Books for Children, 2003. (V, VI, X)

Skill Builder

Participating in Discussions

Does this ever happen to you? You are having a discussion with someone and the other person cuts you off in the middle of a sentence. Do you ever do this to others? Being a courteous listener and speaker are important skills. You want your ideas to be heard. You have to let others have their say. The following tips will help you be a good participant in a discussion.

1. Be willing to listen to other people's ideas. This means not cutting them off when they are speaking.
2. Be willing to share your ideas and opinions. Do not just say someone else is wrong. Explain your reasons.
3. Be clear when you explain your ideas. If someone does not understand, restate your idea in a different way.
4. Restate what the other person said to be sure you understand.
5. Respect what others have to say. Everyone has the right to an opinion. Do not laugh at someone else's ideas.
6. Do not make disagreements personal. You can disagree with someone's ideas without disagreeing with the person.
7. Speak calmly.
8. Most important, if you are having a discussion in class, be sure you are prepared. Read your assignment.

Complete the following activities.

1 Choose the two tips from this list that you think would be the most helpful in your discussions with friends, teachers, or parents. Then write a paragraph explaining how the tips you chose might help your conversation or listening skills.

2 Discuss the following question with a partner: How does federalism affect relations between the states? Use the tips for discussion as a guide.

Classroom Discussion

Discuss with students some of the broader topics covered in this chapter.

- How would the nation be different if the Constitution began with the words "We the states"?
- What are some interstate compacts that you could suggest for your state and a neighboring state? In other words, what mutual concerns might you address better by working together?
- In what ways might those who hold states' rights views and those who hold nationalist views both compromise to prevent legislative gridlock?

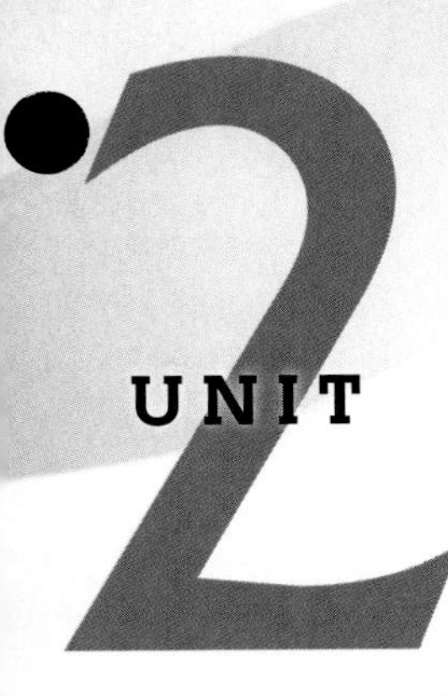

UNIT

THE LEGISLATIVE BRANCH

- The National Legislature
- Congress
- The House of Representatives
- The Senate

What do these terms mean? Who are our national legislators? What do they do? How are they chosen? In writing the Constitution, the Framers gave Congress a great deal of power. How do members of Congress use this power? How do their actions affect our daily lives? This unit will help you answer these questions.

Picturing Government

The photograph on page 101 shows the exterior of the Capitol Building in Washington, D.C. The familiar dome is made of cast iron, a late crowning touch to the building, added in 1866. The west front terraces were completed in 1892 and the east front extension in 1962. On the first floor of the Senate wing are the Brumidi Corridors, named for the Italian artist Constantino Brumidi, who spent the last quarter-century of his life decorating the rooms with murals. In the House wing, the Hall of Columns showcases 28 fluted white marble columns lining the high-ceilinged hall, which is more than 100 feet long.

Unit Objectives

After studying this unit, students will be able to

- compare and contrast the work of the two houses of Congress
- explain the powers of Congress and their applications
- describe the work of Congress nationally and locally

Unit 2 focuses on the legislative branch of the government.

Chapter 5, Congress, examines the House of Representatives and the Senate.

Chapter 6, Powers of Congress, explores the varied powers of Congress.

Chapter 7, Congress at Work, summarizes the tasks of Congress nationally and among their local constituencies.

Getting Started

Have a student read aloud the title of the unit and the bulleted list and paragraph that follow it on page 101. Ask students to record their preliminary answers to the questions in their notebooks. They might also jot down any further questions they have about the content of this unit. Encourage them to add answers to those questions as they read Unit 2.

Related Transparencies

T-18 Three-Column Chart

T-19 Venn Diagram

T-20 Concept Map

Key Blacklines

Biography—Three Firsts in Congress

Getting Focused

You may wish to allow students to work in pairs when completing the second column of the assignment. The partners can help each other decode the photographs and textual clues. After studying the chapter, have the pairs re-form to complete the third column. At this stage, the partners can assist each other in recalling what has been learned.

CD Extension

Encourage students to use the reading comprehension, vocabulary reinforcement, and other activities on the student CD.

Picturing Government

The photograph on page 102 shows a swearing-in ceremony of the House of Representatives. New members are assigned to work on one of more than 20 committees that do the real legislative work.

Chapter 5 CONGRESS

Getting Focused

Skim this chapter to predict what you will be learning.

- **Read the lesson titles and subheadings.**
- **Look at the illustrations and read the captions.**
- **Examine the maps and table.**
- **Review the vocabulary words and terms.**

What do you already know about Congress? Draw a table with three columns in your notebook. Label the first column "What I Know." Label the second column "What I Want to Learn." Label the third column "What I Learned."

Fill in column one before you examine this chapter. Then think about what the photographs and other illustrations show and what the subheadings say. In column two, write some questions you would like to answer as you read the chapter. After you study the chapter, complete column three.

On January 4, 2005, newly elected members of the 109th Congress took an oath of office in the House of Representatives.

Pre-Reading Discussion

1 Discuss with students a law that is currently in the news, one that is either under discussion or was recently passed by Congress. Ask them how the law will affect their community. Tell them that in this chapter, they will learn about the legislative branch of government.

2 Show students a map of your state with the congressional districts clearly marked. Have them note any oddities in the configuration of districts and suggest political reasons for the shapes. Explain that in this chapter, they will read about the reasons for the way districts are formed.

LESSON 1

The National Legislature

Thinking on Your Own

Suppose you wanted to run for election to the House of Representatives. What issue would you campaign on? Think of an important issue that faces the nation today. Make up a slogan to advertise your viewpoint on the issue.

focus your reading

What are the differences and similarities between representatives and senators?

What is the purpose of reapportionment?

Why is redistricting a political issue?

words to know

bicameral legislature
Senate
House of Representatives
term
recess
adjourn
constituents
incumbent
reapportionment
redistricting
gerrymandering

Congress is the lawmaking body of the national government. It is a **bicameral legislature**, which means that it has two houses. The upper house is the Senate. The lower house is the House of Representatives. The **Senate** is the smaller body, with 100 members. Membership in the **House of Representatives** was set at 435 in 1929. Until then, members were added as new states were admitted to the Union and the population grew.

Congress meets for **terms**, or periods of time. Each term is two years and is divided into two one-year sessions. A term begins on January 3 of odd-numbered years.

Usually Congress meets from January until November or December. There are **recesses**, or breaks, for holidays and vacations. Members of both houses must vote to **adjourn**, or take a break. If either house wants to adjourn for more than three days, the other house must approve. Article I and the Twentieth Amendment set out how Congress organizes itself.

New members of the Senate were sworn in on January 4, 2005.

Lesson Summary

Congress is a bicameral legislature, composed of the Senate and the House of Representatives. Congress meets in two-year terms divided into sessions. Congress's duties are to pass laws, represent and aid constituents, and oversee the federal government. Requirements for the two houses differ, but salaries and privileges are the same. Reapportioning seats in the House occurs after each census, as does congressional redistricting.

Lesson Objective

Students will learn about the composition and workings of Congress.

Focus Your Reading Answers

1 The differences between representatives and senators include age and citizenship requirements, as well as length of term. The House proposes tax laws. The Senate confirms or rejects treaties and presidential nominees. The similarities between representatives and senators are salaries and benefits, as well as the need to serve on committees and assist constituents.

2 The purpose of reapportionment is to reassign the number of representatives each state has, based on the national census.

3 Redistricting is a political issue because parties in power can gerrymander to ensure that they remain in power.

Words to Know

Introduce each of the following vocabulary terms to students.

Explain that a *bicameral legislature* is a lawmaking body with two houses. The U.S. Congress, like the British Parliament, is a *bicameral legislature*. The upper house of Congress is known as the *Senate*. The *House of Representatives* is the lower house.

Congress's *terms* are periods of time. Each *term* is two years long. Congressional breaks are known as *recesses*. Holidays and vacations make up the *recesses*. To take a break is to *adjourn*. Both houses must agree to *adjourn* if the break will be three days or longer.

Constituents are the people that a member of Congress represents. An *incumbent* is a person who already holds office. Seats in the *House of Representatives* are determined after each census by *reapportionment*. Gains or losses in a state's population determine the amount of *reapportionment*. When states gain or lose seats in the House, they are redrawing, or *redistricting*. *Gerrymandering* is creating a district to favor one political party over another. The goal of *gerrymandering* is to give the party in power more votes.

Members of Congress and Their Jobs

Who are the members of Congress? The average member of Congress is a white male in his fifties. However, this average does not reflect the growing gender and ethnic diversity in Congress. In a recent congressional term, there were 63 women in the House of Representatives and 14 in the Senate. The same congressional term had 39 African Americans, 23 Latinos, 5 Asian Americans, and 3 Native Americans.

The major duties of members of Congress are to (1) pass laws, (2) represent what they think is best for their constituents, (3) oversee the workings of the federal government, and (4) help their constituents solve problems with the federal government. **Constituents** are the people back home in the member's state or district. The table on page 105 shows some of the differences and the many similarities between the two houses of Congress.

Reelecting Incumbents

Once a person is elected to office, it is easier for him or her to be reelected. In other words, anyone who challenges an incumbent has a difficult time being elected. An **incumbent** is a person who already holds the office. For example, about 90 percent of all incumbents in Congress were reelected between 1945 and 1990. Sometimes an incumbent does not even face a challenger. Opponents feel they have little chance to defeat an incumbent.

There are four major reasons why incumbents are difficult to beat. First, raising campaign funds is easier for incumbents. People know them and what they have done in office. Being better known than challengers is the second reason. Third, the district may have been set up so that the majority of voters belong to the incumbent's political party. Party members tend to vote for their party's candidates. Fourth, incumbents do favors and solve problems for their constituents. This develops loyalty among voters.

Incumbent Congresswoman Loretta Sanchez (D-California) wins reelection, while her sister Linda Sanchez (left) also wins a seat in the House.

Picturing Government

The photograph on page 103 shows new senators being sworn into office in 2005. Visible in the front row, second from left, is Barack Obama, senator from Illinois, who is biracial. The first African American to serve in the Senate was Hiram R. Revels, from Mississippi, who took the oath of office in 1870. Carol Moseley Braun, from Illinois, became the first African-American woman in the Senate in 1993. In the back row, barely visible, is Hillary Rodham Clinton (New York), who made history in 2000 as the first First Lady to be elected to the Senate.

Extension

Students interested in math may wish to study one of the gender or ethnicity categories and create graphs demonstrating the changes over time. Have them explain their findings to the class.

Picturing Government

Linda and Loretta Sanchez, shown in the photograph on page 104, made history by becoming the first sisters elected to Congress. Loretta, who was first elected in 1996, defeated an incumbent to earn her seat in the 47th Congressional District of California. Her background is in business. She is the ranking woman on the House Armed Services Committee, as well as a past member of the Committee on Education and the Workforce. Democratic Leader Nancy Pelosi chose her to serve on the House Committee on Homeland Security as the second-ranking Democrat. Linda, who entered the House in 2003, serves the 39th Congressional District of California, which was created to be a Hispanic district. Linda earned a law degree and was a civil rights attorney and labor leader before running for office. She is on the Judiciary Committee, the Small Business Committee, and the Committee on Government Reform. Both women, from a family of seven, credit their mother, a Mexican immigrant, for their interest in education and politics.

Differences and Similarities Between the House of Representatives and the Senate

Categories	House of Representatives	Senate
Qualifications	• Be twenty-five years of age • Be a citizen for at least seven years • Live in the state from which he or she is elected	• Be thirty years of age • Be a citizen for at least 14 years • Live in the state from which he or she is elected
Term of Office	• Two years	• Six years
Salary	• Representatives: $158,000 • Speaker: $193,600 • Majority and minority leaders: $172,900	• Senators: $158,000 • President pro tempore: $193,600 • Majority and minority leaders: $172,900
Privileges and Benefits	• Tax deduction because they keep homes in their districts and in Washington, D.C. • Free postage for all official business • Free printing of speeches, newsletters • Pension plan • Low-cost health and life insurance	• Tax deduction because they keep homes in their states and in Washington, D.C. • Free postage for all official business • Free printing of speeches, newsletters • Pension plan • Low-cost health and life insurance
Some Duties of Members	• Serve on committees • Help constituents in dealing with the federal government	• Serve on committees • Help constituents in dealing with the federal government
Some Duties of Each House	• Propose revenue, or tax, laws • Elect president in the event of a tie	• Confirm or reject presidential nominees • Confirm or reject treaties with other nations

Reapportionment

The Framers were divided about how to choose members of Congress. They worked out the Great Compromise to solve the problem. It provided for electing members of the House of Representatives based on population. However, population can change over time. Some states gain people, whereas other states lose people.

Until 1929, Congress just added representatives as territories became states. However, the Reapportionment Act of 1929 set

Table Extension

Use the six categories as general headings for a game of What House of Congress Am I. Have students identify whether the items within the category apply to the Senate, the House, or both.

Extensions

1 Have interested students use library resources or the Internet to investigate the Supreme Court decision in *Baker* v. *Carr*, a 1964 reapportionment case. Have them present their findings to the class.

2 Have students research the most recent local election to see if any incumbents were defeated in their reelection bid. You may also wish to apply this to presidential elections and have students examine the history of reelections. Have them present their findings to the class by using the Student Presentation Builder on the student CD.

Stop and Think

Students' Venn diagrams may suggest that the differences between senators and representatives include age and citizenship requirements, as well as length of term. The House proposes tax laws. The Senate confirms or rejects treaties and presidential nominees. The similarities between senators and representatives are their salaries and benefits and their serving on committees and assisting constituents.

Ideas to Remember Extension

Review the ideas listed, further explaining difficult vocabulary words. Have students create graphic organizers in their notebooks to help them visualize the four reasons why incumbents usually win elections.

the number of members of the House at 435. The law set up a process for **reapportionment**. Seats are reassigned after each ten-year census based on gains or losses in a state's population. The map on page 106 shows the gains and losses after the 2000 census.

ideas to remember

Incumbents generally win reelection because

- it is easier for them to raise campaign funds.
- they are better known than challengers.
- their districts were drawn to favor their party.
- they help their constituents solve problems.

stop and think

How are the House of Representatives and the Senate alike and different? Use information from the table on page 105 to create a Venn diagram in your notebook. Share your diagram with a partner. Discuss whether you have included all of the important facts.

Redistricting

When states gain or lose seats in the House of Representatives, they must redraw their districts. This is called **redistricting**. State legislatures draw new congressional districts. For example, after the 2000 census, California gained one representative for a total of 53 members in the House. The state legislature redrew its districts to add one more. Connecticut had the opposite problem. It had to collapse its six districts into five.

The political party in power in a state often tries to set up districts so that its members will win elections.

Congressional Apportionment

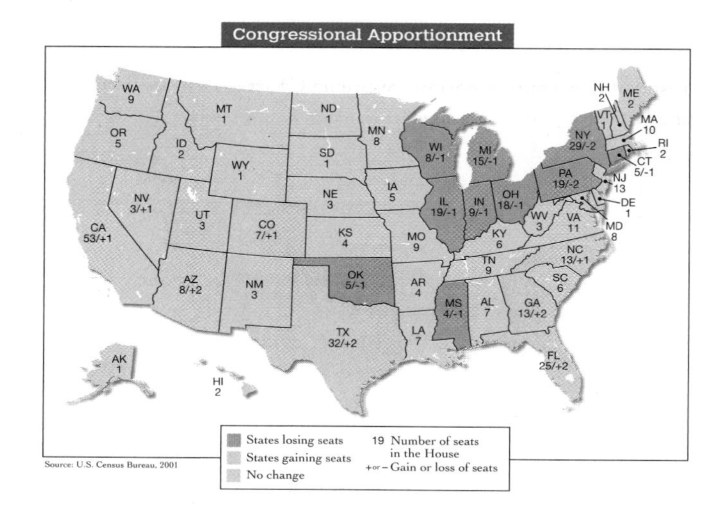

Source: U.S. Census Bureau, 2001

Map Extensions

1 Ask students to use the map on page 106 to answer the following questions.

- What general statement can you make about the change of seats? (Most states didn't gain or lose seats; losses were primarily in the East and upper Midwest; gains were in the South and West.
- Which areas of the country gained seats after the 2000 census? (the West and South)
- Which states lost the most seats? (New York and Pennsylvania)

2 Ask students to use the map on page 107 to answer the following questions.

- How many congressional districts did North Carolina have in 1992? (12)

Redistricting Example: North Carolina Congressional Districts, 1992

4 Congressional district

Source: *Congressional Quarterly Weekly Report*, June 15, 1996

As a result, the shape of congressional districts is sometimes very strange. Creating a district to favor one party over another is called **gerrymandering**.

There are two ways to gerrymander districts. One way is to push as many voters from the minority party as possible into a few districts. Then voters from the party in power become the majority in most of the districts. The second way is to divide the minority party's voters into many districts. The result is the same. The party in power is able to elect more of its candidates to office.

Landmark Supreme Court Cases: Redistricting

- ***Wesberry* v. *Sanders*** (Georgia, 1964): The difference in the number of voters in Georgia's new districts violated the Constitution. The Court ruled that the Framers intended that votes have equal value. This is the principle of "one person, one vote." As a result, congressional districts in all states now have about the same number of voters, 650,000.

- ***Shaw* v. *Reno*** (North Carolina, 1993): Race cannot be used as the major factor in redistricting. The purpose of creating districts with a majority of African Americans was to elect more African Americans to office. The Supreme Court ruled that these districts violated the Fourteenth Amendment rights of white voters. This ruling also applied to states that drew new districts with a majority of Latino voters.

Over the years, redistricting has resulted in several important Supreme Court decisions. Read the landmark cases on page 107 to learn about these decisions.

Remember, according to Article I, no matter how few people a state has, it must have at least one representative.

Putting It All Together

Imagine that you are a member of Congress who wants to be reelected for another term. With a partner, discuss the things you can do to improve your chances of reelection. Write a paragraph in your notebook explaining what you have decided upon.

This 1812 political cartoon shows how political districts were redrawn to the advantage of Governor Eldridge Gerry.

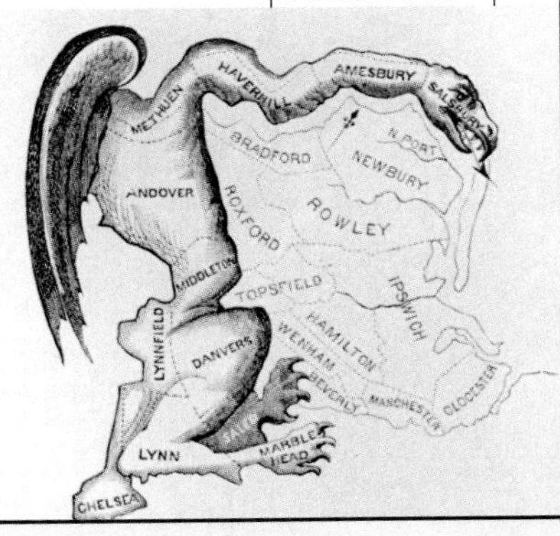

Supreme Court Case Extension

In 2004, the Supreme Court again ruled on a case about redistricting. Have students use library resources or the Internet to find out about the ruling in *Vieth* v. *Jubelirer*.

Putting It All Together

Students' paragraphs and their ideas to improve the chance of reelection will vary.

Extension

The word *gerrymandering* comes from Eldridge Gerry, a signer of the Declaration of Independence, a member of Congress, and vice president during Madison's second term. In 1810, Gerry was elected as governor of Massachusetts. When he divided electoral districts for political advantage, the new district was shaped somewhat like a salamander. Cartoonists of the day drew Gerry's head on the reptile.

Map Extensions, continued

- Which districts are shaped to indicate gerrymandering? (the 1st, 3rd, and 12th)
- What do you think might have happened after the 2000 census? (Student predictions will vary.)

Cartoon Extension

Help students identify the state in the cartoon on page 107. (Massachusetts) Then ask what the cartoonist was trying to convey. Ask students to analyze whether the cartoon is effective and why.

Lesson Summary

Because the United States has a two-party system, the House and the Senate are arranged into majority and minority parties. They may not be the same in both houses. House leadership is under the Speaker of the House, who belongs to the majority party and is selected by a caucus. The majority leader, majority whip, and deputy majority whips assist the Speaker in passing legislation. The minority party also has a leader, whips, and deputies. The majority and minority leaders and whips are not official positions, but political ones. Committees do most of the work of the House, which is to pass laws. The Rules Committee decides whether a bill will go to the floor and how quickly it will move. It can also limit the debate and the number of amendments added to it.

Lesson Objective

Students will learn about the work of the House of Representatives.

Focus Your Reading Answers

1 The leadership roles in the House of Representatives are Speaker of the House, majority and minority leaders, majority and minority whips, and deputy whips.

2 The duties of the House Rules Committee include determining if a bill will reach the floor and setting the time limits of the debate and the number of amendments the bill can carry.

LESSON 2

The House of Representatives

Thinking on Your Own

There are 435 members of the House of Representatives. Imagine that you are one of 60 new members who are called "freshmen members." How would you go about meeting other freshmen and learning how the House is run? List four things you could do to learn about your fellow members and about the House.

focus your reading

Describe the leadership roles in the House of Representatives.

What are the duties of the House Rules Committee?

words to know

majority party

minority party

caucus

majority leader

majority whip

minority leader

minority whip

committees

The United States has a two-party system. Most people think of themselves as either Democrats or Republicans and vote that way. As a result, both the House and the Senate are organized along political party lines. The **majority party** is the party that has the most members in the Senate or the House during a term. A term lasts for two years.

The elephant is the symbol of the Republican Party, and the donkey is the symbol of the Democratic Party.

The majority party in the House during a term may be different from or the same as the majority party in the Senate. For example, from 2001 to 2003, the Republicans were the majority party in the House, whereas the Democrats were the majority party in the Senate. The party with fewer seats is called the **minority party**.

Leadership in the House of Representatives

The majority political party manages the business of each house. The Speaker of the House belongs to the majority party. The Speaker is the most important and powerful member of the House. He or she is chosen by

Words to Know

Discuss each of the vocabulary terms with students.

The *majority party* is the party that has the most members in the Senate or the House during a term. The *minority party* is the party with fewer seats. The Republican Party was the *majority party* in the House and the *minority party* in the Senate during the 2001–2003 term.

A *causus* is a closed meeting when the *majority party* picks the Speaker of the House.

The *majority leader* of the House assists the Speaker and is the party's main spokesperson in the House. The *minority leader* of the House is the head of the party with the fewer number of seats. The *minority leader* decides how the party will respond to the programs suggested by the *majority party*. The *majority whip* and *minority whip* make sure that party members vote as the leadership wants them to.

Small groups of representatives that work out the details of bills are called *committees*.

a **caucus**, or closed meeting, of the majority party. The full House, however, must vote to approve the choice.

The jobs of the Speaker of the House include keeping order in the House as presiding officer; leading the majority party in the House; appointing members to certain committees; scheduling bills for votes in the House; and sending bills to the proper committees. The Speaker is also next in line to become president after the vice president.

U.S. House of Representatives Speaker Dennis Hastert (R-Illinois) is sworn in at the start of the 109th Congress.

The **majority leader** is the second-most powerful member of the House. First, he or she helps the Speaker and other party leaders plan the party's legislative agenda, or program. Together, they decide what bills the House will work on during the session. Second, the majority leader guides the party's agenda through the House. He or she pushes committees to complete their work on bills and then schedules bills for votes. Third, the majority leader is the main spokesperson for his or her party in the House.

The majority leader has assistants, known as the **majority whip** and deputy majority whips. The job of the whips is to see that party members vote as the leadership wants them to. First, whips talk to party members before votes to see how they plan to vote. Second, whips try to convince members to vote with the party leaders. Third, whips make sure that party members are present when it is time to vote. Fourth, whips report to party leaders what party members think about issues.

stop and think

With a partner, create a table to list the duties of the majority leader and whips and the minority leader and whips. Be sure to give your table a title.

The minority party in the House also has a **minority leader**, **minority whip**, and deputy minority whips. Their duties are similar to the majority party's leader and whips. In addition, the minority leader determines how his or her party will react to the majority party's programs. He or she takes the lead in criticizing the majority party's programs. The minority leader delivers this criticism through news conferences, interviews, and press releases.

House minority leader Nancy Pelosi (D-California) in 2005

The floor leaders and whips are political jobs. They are not official positions in the House.

Stop and Think

Students' tables listing duties should include the information on page 109.

Picturing Government

Speaker of the House Dennis Hastert, shown in the photograph at the top on page 109, took that position in 1999. He served as Chief Deputy Majority Whip for five years prior to being elected Speaker. Hastert is known for setting clear, achievable goals and emphasizing team-building.

Extension

Invite interested students to use library resources or the Internet to learn more about influential Speakers in recent history, such as Sam Rayburn, Thomas P. O'Neill, and Newt Gingrich.

Picturing Government

Shown in the photograph at the bottom on page 109 is Nancy Pelosi, elected as Democratic Leader of the House of Representatives in 2002. She is the first woman to lead a major party in Congress. She holds the record for the longest continuous period of service on the House Permanent Select Committee on Intelligence (10 years). Pelosi has focused on the environment, health care, and human rights.

Picturing Government

The symbols for the Democratic and Republican Parties, shown at the left on page 108, came into widespread use during the late nineteenth century. The donkey was first used to symbolize the Democrats during Andrew Jackson's presidency. Thomas Nast, the famous political cartoonist, did so in 1870. Four years later, Nast drew a cartoon that showed an elephant labeled "The Republican Vote." Democrats use the donkey image (which they view as smart, courageous, humble, and lovable), but have not adopted it as an official symbol. However, Republicans have adopted the elephant as their official symbol, seeing it as intelligent, strong, and dignified. Students interested in drawing may wish to learn more about Thomas Nast.

Picturing Government

The photograph at the top of page 110 shows a representative putting a bill into the hopper, or box. Bills in the House can be submitted in this way.

Picturing Government

Discussion on a bill in the House of Representatives, shown in the photograph in the center of page 110, may involve "crossing the aisle" to promote a bipartisan agenda. Following the British model used in Parliament, each major party sits on one side of the center aisle.

Extension

Invite interested students to use library resources or the Internet to find out about the work of one of the committees of the House. Have them present their findings to the class by using the Student Presentation Builder on the student CD.

The Business of the House of Representatives

The chief business of the House of Representatives is to pass laws for the nation. Most of the work of the House is done in **committees**. These are small groups of representatives who work out the details of bills. All laws begin as bills. The chairperson of each committee belongs to the majority party. The majority of the members on a committee will always be from the majority party. Committees review and discuss the bills. Chapter 7 describes in detail how a proposed bill moves through Congress.

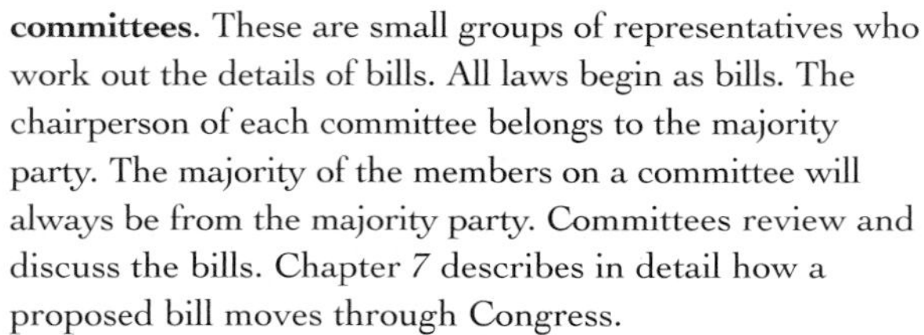

A bill is dropped in the hopper in the House chamber.

Each year, between 10 and 20 percent of bills—a few hundred bills—are "reported out of committee." This means that a committee votes to send the bill to the full House for a vote. First, however, the bill goes to the powerful Rules Committee. The Rules Committee is called the "traffic cop" of the House. It must issue an order called a "rule" before a bill can be sent to the House. The Rules Committee decides how quickly or slowly a bill will be voted on. Its members may also decide to keep a bill from reaching the House floor at all.

The House requires a quorum of 218 members before a vote can be taken.

The Rules Committee sometimes limits how long the House can debate a bill. It may also limit the number of amendments that can be added to a bill. When a bill is finally sent to the House, it is placed on the calendar for debate and a vote. You will learn more about how a bill becomes a law in Chapter 7.

Putting It All Together

With a partner, create a concept map to illustrate the business of the House of Representatives. Make "Business of the House" the label for your central circle. Then draw lines out from the circle to connect smaller circles that list supporting details.

110 Chapter 5

Putting It All Together

Students' concept maps will vary but may include committee work, debating a bill, and passing legislation.

Picturing Government

The Senate's president pro tem, Ted Stevens, is shown in the photograph on page 111. The senator from Alaska has been in Congress since 1968. He is thus the most senior Republican and the fourth-most senior member overall. A World War II veteran, Stevens moved to Alaska while it was still a territory and worked for its admission as a state. He reminds colleagues frequently that Alaska has half of the nation's coastline and is one-fifth the size of the entire United States. His motto, therefore, is "Do what's best for Alaska."

LESSON 3

The Senate

Thinking on Your Own

Over the years, the House has developed a system for managing its members. Would you use the same system to organize the Senate, which is a much smaller group? Why or why not? Explain your reasons in a paragraph in your notebook.

focus your reading

What are the leadership roles in the Senate?

How is a bill scheduled for a vote in the Senate?

Explain the purpose of a filibuster.

words to know

president pro tempore

filibuster

cloture

The organization of the Senate is similar to that of the House of Representatives. The members are organized along party lines, and most work is done in committees. However, the Senate is less formal than the House. The rules about how the Senate works are more flexible. This is done on purpose. The goal is to allow senators time to discuss a bill, think about the issues, and discuss the bill again—and again. The debate on a bill may run for weeks before a vote is ever taken on it. During that time, any senator who wants to express his or her views on the issues may do so.

Leadership in the Senate

According to Article II of the Constitution, the vice president is the presiding officer of the Senate. The vice president may not vote except to break a tie. Generally, the vice president has other duties and rarely chairs the daily sessions.

In place of the vice president, the **president pro tempore** chairs daily sessions. The title means "president for a time" and is usually shortened to president pro tem. Generally, the president pro tem is the senior member of the majority party. The whole Senate elects the president pro tem. Like the Speaker of the House, the president pro tem manages the daily sessions and keeps order. The position, however, lacks the power of the Speaker of the House.

Senator Ted Stevens (R-Alaska), president pro tem of the Senate, in 2005

Lesson Summary

The Senate, although similar in function to the House, is a smaller body and less formal. The vice president heads the Senate; in his or her absence, the president pro tempore, an elected official, acts as chair. The Senate also has majority and minority leaders, whips, and deputy whips. In addition to making laws, the Senate confirms or rejects treaties and votes on nominees for federal judgeships and other high government positions. The Senate has no Rules Committee to schedule votes. Nor does the Senate set a time limit for discussing a bill. To block legislation, senators use a filibuster.

Lesson Objective

Students will learn about the function of the Senate.

Focus Your Reading Answers

1 The leadership roles in the Senate include president pro tempore, majority and minority leaders, and whips.

2 The majority and minority leaders decide when to schedule a bill for a vote in the Senate. Then the bill is put on the calendar.

3 The purpose of a filibuster is to talk until the sponsor of the nomination or bill agrees to modify or withdraw it.

Words to Know

Discuss each of the vocabulary terms with students.

The senatorial title *president pro tempore* means "president for a time." The *president pro tempore* takes the place of the vice president in chairing the Senate. He or she is usually called the president pro tem.

A *filibuster* is nonstop talking. A *filibuster* is used to influence the opposition to change or withdraw a bill or nomination.

Cloture limits the time for debate on a bill. After approving *cloture,* senators can debate for only 30 more hours.

Picturing Government

Senator Bill Frist, shown at left in the photograph on page 112, became the majority leader of the Senate in 2002, having served fewer total years (six) in Congress than any previous leader. A graduate of both Princeton and Harvard, and a heart and lung surgeon, he is the first practicing physician in the Senate since 1928. Frist has an interest in the global AIDS epidemic and has traveled to Africa on medical mission trips. He became one of two congressional representatives to the United Nations General Assembly in 2001.

Extension

Have students use library resources or the Internet to find out more about the senators from their state. Divide the class into two groups, assigning each group one of the senators. Then challenge the groups to create and answer ten basic questions about the senator's experience and areas of interest, as well as his or her educational background. Have each group report to the class.

Senate majority leader Bill Frist (R-Tennessee) (left) and Senator Mitch McConnell (R-Kentucky) in 2003

Like the House of Representatives, the Senate has majority and minority leaders. It also has majority and minority whips and assistant majority and minority whips. They are elected by their party. All these positions are political.

Like the majority leader in the House, the Senate majority leader, with other party leaders, sets the agenda for the Senate. The majority leader guides bills through the Senate. The minority leader develops his or her party's position on bills. The minority leader then makes sure that party members support their party's views. Both the majority and minority leaders are the main spokespeople for their party in the Senate.

The whips work with the leaders to see that members are present for votes. Like the House whips, they find out before a vote how their party's senators plan to vote. They try to persuade their party's members to vote with the party leaders. The whips also let party leaders know what members are thinking about the issues.

stop and think

With a partner, create a Venn diagram to compare and contrast the organization of the House of Representatives with that of the Senate. Then write a paragraph to explain how the organization of the two houses is similar and how it is different.

The Business of the Senate

Like the House of Representatives, the major job of the Senate is to pass laws. However, the Senate also votes on nominees for federal judgeships and some high-level government positions. The Senate also confirms or rejects treaties.

Any member of the Senate may introduce a bill. However, there is no Speaker to decide which committee to send it to. There is no Rules Committee to decide when or if a bill will be voted on. Instead, the majority leader has the power to decide what happens to the bill.

Stop and Think

Students' Venn diagrams and paragraphs will vary but should compare and contrast the organization of the two houses of Congress.

The system of reviewing and discussing bills in the Senate is similar to the system in the House. Committees review bills, call witnesses, and discuss the issues. A bill may or may not be reported out of committee. If a bill is sent to the Senate for a vote, it is put on the calendar. The majority leader consults with the minority leader to decide when to schedule a debate and a vote. However, the majority leader has the final say. He or she may delay the debate and a vote until he or she has enough votes to pass the bill. The majority leader can also kill a bill by never bringing it to a vote.

Senators prepare to vote on the Homeland Security bill in 2002.

The Senate does not set time limits for discussing bills. Usually, however, the majority and minority leaders agree ahead of time when the debate will end. At that point, the Senate calls unanimously for a vote. However, if even one senator disagrees, the vote cannot be taken. Debate goes on. The Senate prides itself on being open to unlimited debate. The purpose is to make sure that all sides of an issue are heard.

Discussion on the Senate floor, shown in the photograph on page 113, allows senators time to solve differences over bills.

Congress's Informal Networks—the Caucus

You learned that each political party holds a caucus to set up its organization for the session. However, there is another kind of caucus in Congress. This caucus is a group of members of Congress who share an interest or characteristic.

Three of the best-known caucuses are the Congressional Black Caucus, the Congressional Hispanic Caucus, and the Congressional Women's Caucus. Each caucus includes members of both the House of Representatives and the Senate.

The Congressional Black Caucus (CBC) was founded in 1970 to be "the voice of the voiceless." Its members work for universal health care for all Americans, equal educational opportunities for all children, and strong enforcement of civil rights.

The Congressional Hispanic Caucus (CHC) was formed in 1976. Members support laws that will aid Hispanic Americans, including greater educational and economic opportunities.

The Congressional Women's Caucus first met in 1977. The Women's Caucus focuses on issues important to women and families.

People in the News Extensions

The House Administration Committee has a list of more than 240 caucuses that members of Congress have formed. These may focus on a region of the nation or world, an age group, a health issue, or the environment. The Senate has only one caucus, on International Narcotics Control.

1 Divide the class into three groups, assigning each group one of the caucuses mentioned in the feature. Have them use library resources or the Internet to find out more about the caucus's most recent activities.

2 Have students choose an area in which they are interested and locate a caucus that deals with that area or a similar topic. Ask students to prepare a sound bite to tell the class the 5 *W*'s and *H* (who, what, where, why, when, and how) of a news story.

Picturing Government

The photograph on page 114 shows cots being set up in Senate offices. The cots were used by senators who were required to remain at the Capitol overnight. Until 1917, unlimited debate was allowed in the Senate. At that time, President Woodrow Wilson encouraged the Senate to adopt a rule that allowed a two-thirds vote (or 67 members) to end a filibuster. In 1975, the requirement was reduced to three-fifths (or 60 members). The first modern filibuster occurred in 1919 when a filibuster in the Senate prevented a vote on the Treaty of Versailles. Two of the most famous filibusters were completed by Senator Huey Long in 1932 and Senator Strom Thurmond in 1957. Senator Long once spent 15 hours speaking about such things as recipes for cooking oysters. His purpose was to protest against legislation and policies he opposed. Senator Thurmond holds the record for the longest filibuster. In 1957, he spoke against civil rights legislation for 24 hours.

The Filibuster

Suppose a group of senators does not want a bill to pass or a presidential nominee to be approved. Suppose they also know that there are not enough votes to kill the bill or the nomination. They may use a **filibuster** to talk until the sponsor of the bill or nomination agrees to modify or withdraw the bill. Senators talk and talk for hours, days, and even weeks in an effort to wear down the opposition. The filibustering senators hope to force the opposition to give up on the bill or to change the parts they object to.

In May 2005, cots were set up in Senate offices to accommodate staff during an all-night debate over the use of the filibuster.

The Senate can end filibusters. Three-fifths of the senators, or 60 members, must vote for cloture. **Cloture** limits the time for debate. Once cloture has been approved, the Senate may spend only 30 more hours discussing the bill. Then the Senate must vote on the bill. It is not easy to reach cloture, however. Senators fear that their opponents could turn around one day and use cloture against them.

Filibusters used to close down all business in the Senate. However, the Senate changed its rules. It now conducts regular business for a period of time each day during a filibuster.

Putting It All Together

How does a bill go from introduction to a vote in the Senate? Create a flowchart to answer this question. Share your flowchart with a partner. Ask your partner to check to make sure you included all of the most important supporting details.

Extensions

1 *Filibuster* comes from the Spanish word *filibustero*, meaning "freebooter." It originally referred to people from the United States who, in the mid-1800s, tried to start revolutions in the countries of Latin America. Ask students to explain how they think this term came to refer to lengthy speeches in the Senate to delay votes.

2 Have students use library resources or the Internet to find out about the 2005 case for and against limiting filibusters in the case of a judicial nominee.

Putting It All Together

Students' flowcharts should include the following stages: bill is introduced, put on the calendar, discussed and debated, and voted on. The bill can be subject to filibuster.

Participate in Government

Ask Your Senators or Representative

You might contact a member of your congressional delegation when

- you want to tell your senators what you think about an upcoming bill.
- your family is going to visit Washington, D.C., and would like to tour the White House.
- you think you might like to go into government service and would like an internship to find out.
- your school district wants to fund an after-school program, and the superintendent needs information on possible funding.

These are just some of the items that senators and representatives can help their constituents with.

Each member of Congress has his or her own home page within either the House or the Senate's main Web site. The home pages list what are known as Constituent Services. These are services that members of Congress offer their constituents. Members of Congress also help with problems related to veterans' benefits, visa issues, and similar federal programs.

To Contact Your Senators or Representative:

- Check your local phone book for the address and phone number of the office nearest you.
- Find your senators and representative by visiting the House and the Senate's Web sites.
- Send him or her an e-mail. Click on the "contact" link button on the home page of your senators and representatives.

Participate in Government

You may wish to have students work in small groups to develop a list of questions or comments to send to their members of Congress. Extend the lesson by having students use library resources or the Internet to find current bills before each chamber. Then, in light of what they find, select the most useful questions or comments to be sent.

Research Resources

Below is a list of reference books and Web sites that relate to the issues covered in this chapter. Students may wish to use these to further their research on ideas in the preceding lessons. Web site addresses may change over time. Use keyword searching on a major search engine to locate sites.

Reference Book:

Donald A. Ritchie. *The Congress of the United States: A Student Companion (Oxford Student Companions to American Government)*. Oxford University Press, 2002.

Web Sites:

The Senate site includes committees and information about the Senate.

The House site summarizes the bills on the floor of the House of Representatives.

A site by the Architect of the Capitol, a position appointed by the president, has links to information about the nation's Capitol, including its art, gardens, architecture, and functions.

Skill Builder

1 district 10

2 district 2

3 central

Classroom Discussion

Discuss with students some of the broader topics covered in this chapter.

- Should the Senate abolish or limit the technique of filibustering?
- How can the practice of redistricting be made more fair?
- In what ways would imposing term limits for members of Congress be an advantage or a disadvantage?

Skill Builder

Read a Congressional District Map

A state's congressional district map shows its election districts for the U.S. House of Representatives. Each district represents one member of the House. The state legislature draws the boundaries for the districts. Each district has to have 650,000 people.

However, some districts cover much larger areas of land than others. Districts that are smaller in size mean that they are more densely, or heavily, populated. Small-sized districts have more large cities than districts with more land area. Because of the "one-person, one vote" principle, every district has the same number of people.

To read a congressional district map or any map:

- Read the title of the map first. What is the map about?
- Read the map key. What do the symbols stand for?
- Examine the map. Look at the placement of symbols carefully.

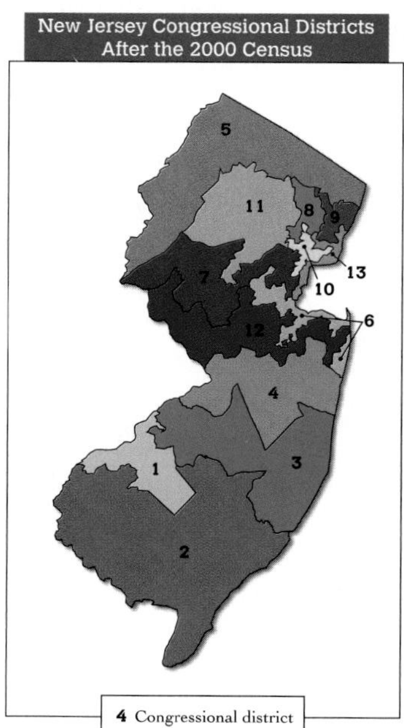

Use the map above to answer the following questions:

1 Which district has the smallest area?

2 Which district has the largest area?

3 Which part of the state probably has more cities—north, south, or central?

Recommended Reading

Below is a list of books that relate to the issues covered in this chapter. The numbers in parentheses indicate the related Thematic Strands of the National Council for the Social Studies (NCSS).

Barbara Silberdick Feinberg. *Term Limits for Congress (Inside Government)*. 21st Century, 1997. (VI, X)

Ruth Tenzer Feldman. *How Congress Works: A Look at the Legislative Branch (How Government Works)*. Lerner Publishing Group, 2003. (VI, X)

Veda Boyd Jones, Arthur Meier Schlesinger. *The Senate (Your Government: How It Works)*. Chelsea House Publications, 2000. (VI, X)

Daniel Partner. *The House of Representatives (Your Government: How It Works)*. Chelsea House Publications, 2000. (VI, X)

Chapter

6 POWERS OF CONGRESS

Getting Focused

Skim this chapter to predict what you will be learning.

- Read the lesson titles and subheadings.
- Look at the illustrations and read the captions.
- Examine the tables.
- Review the vocabulary words and terms.

The federal government makes laws that affect many areas of daily life. Think of at least four activities that are regulated by federal law. For example, airport security is under the authority of the federal government.

The Transportation Security Administration (TSA) was created in response to the terrorist attacks of September 11, 2001. It is part of the Aviation and Transportation Security Act signed into law by President George W. Bush on November 19, 2001. The TSA became part of the Department of Homeland Security in March 2003.

Pre-Reading Discussion

1 Discuss with students some groups, clubs, or sports teams in which they participate. Diagram the organization of these groups on the board as students explain them. Tell students that in this chapter, they will learn more about how the organization of Congress helps the legislative branch function.

2 Explain to students the phrases "the letter of the law" and "the spirit of the law." Use illustrations from their own lives. For example, if they are told to come home directly after school and they do so, they are obeying the letter of the law. If they detour to the public library to get research materials before heading home, they may be obeying the spirit of the law, which is intended to keep them out of dangerous or difficult situations, since they did not just hang out with friends at the mall. Tell them that the Constitution can also be interpreted in the letter or the spirit of the law, and that they will learn more about it in this chapter.

Related Transparencies

T-4 Powers of Congress

T-5 Permanent Committees of the House and Senate

T-18 Three-Column Chart

Key Blacklines

Primary Source – Speaker Dennis Hastert's Remarks to Open the 109th Congress

CD Extension

Encourage students to use the reading comprehension, vocabulary reinforcement, and other activities on the student CD.

Picturing Government

Airport security, as shown in the photograph on page 117, is only one aspect of the work of the Transportation Security Administration (TSA). The Explosives Detection Canine Team Program, previously under the control of the Federal Aviation Administration, is another segment of the TSA's work.

Getting Focused

Have students work in pairs to develop lists of activities that the federal government regulates. When they have finished, conduct a class discussion. Students may suggest federal highways and school lunch programs.

Lesson Summary

The powers of Congress depend on the interpretation of the Constitution. A strict constructionist wants to interpret the document narrowly, rarely permitting the use of implied powers. A loose constructionist interprets the Constitution more broadly. Congress has four broad powers: money powers, commerce powers, military and foreign powers, and the enumerated powers in Article I, Section 8, of the Constitution. The two branches of Congress have other powers as well, such as the Senate's power to ratify treaties and confirm presidential appointments.

Lesson Objective

Students will learn about the powers given to Congress by the Constitution.

Focus Your Reading Answers

1 Strict constructionists interpret the Constitution narrowly. Loose constructionists interpret the Constitution, particularly the implied powers, more broadly.

2 Legislative powers of Congress include money powers, commerce powers, military and foreign powers, and the enumerated powers in Article I, Section 8, of the Constitution.

3 Nonlegislative powers of Congress include power to select the president and vice president, to remove federal officials from office, to confirm federal nominees, to ratify treaties, and to propose amendments to the Constitution.

LESSON 1

Constitutional Powers

Thinking on Your Own

In your notebook, write three facts that you already know about the powers of Congress. As you read the lesson, add at least two new facts.

Congress receives its powers to act from the Constitution. Article I sets up Congress and lists its duties and responsibilities. The major job of Congress is to pass legislation. However, it also has nonlegislative duties and responsibilities.

focus your reading

What is the difference in viewpoint between strict constructionists and loose constructionists?

What are some legislative powers of Congress?

Describe nonlegislative powers of Congress.

words to know

strict constructionist

loose constructionist

tax-and-spend

appropriations bill

commerce

copyright

patent

Conflict Over Congress's Power

Since 1789, Congress has enlarged its powers and, therefore, the powers of the national government. Americans have argued ever since about how powerful the national government should become. The argument centers on the interpretation of the Constitution.

Strict constructionists believe the Constitution should be interpreted narrowly. The result would be a government with limited powers. The national government could use the expressed powers as much as it wanted, because the Constitution lists those powers. However, the government could use

Congress has the power to impose taxes on many items, including gasoline.

Words to Know

Introduce each of the following vocabulary terms to students.

Explain that *strict constructionists* are people who interpret the Constitution narrowly. *Strict constructionists* want the national government to use the expressed powers and reserve the implied powers for situations in which they are necessary. *Loose constructionists* interpret the Constitution broadly. *Loose constructionists* have enlarged the powers of the national government.

The power to *tax-and-spend* is one of the powers granted to Congress. *Appropriations bills* are used to pay for the programs Congress authorizes. *Appropriations bills* often begin with the president's budget requests.

The buying and selling of goods and services is known as *commerce*. Congress has the power to regulate *commerce* between the states.

A *copyright* protects an artist's control over his or her work. A *patent* allows inventors to control the manufacture and sale of their inventions. *Patents* must be registered in Washington, D.C., at the Patent Office.

ideas to remember

Congress

- has **expressed powers**—or those directly stated.
- has **implied powers** that are reasonably assumed based on the "necessary and proper" clause.
- is denied certain powers based on Article I, Section 9.

implied powers only when they were absolutely necessary to fulfill expressed powers.

Loose constructionists interpret the Constitution more broadly. They claim the Constitution is a living document that gives the government whatever powers it needs to grow and change with the changing nation. Generally, loose constructionists have had more influence in Congress, in the presidency, and on the Supreme Court. They have succeeded in expanding the powers of the national government.

Landmark Supreme Court Case: Implied Powers of Congress

***McCulloch* v. *Maryland* (1819):** Congress set up a national bank in 1816. Strict constructionists did not believe the Constitution gave Congress this power. The Court ruled that Congress had an implied power to set up the bank. The implied power was based on the "necessary and proper" clause. The national bank aided Congress in fulfilling its duties to tax, borrow money, create money, and regulate commerce, or business.

McCulloch v. *Maryland* was also important because the Court ruled that federal law took priority over state law.

Legislative Powers

The legislative powers of Congress can be grouped into four categories. They are money powers, commerce powers, military and foreign policy powers, and other powers stated in Article I, Section 8, Clauses 1–17. These are known as the enumerated powers.

Row two of the table on page 120 lists the expressed powers of Congress. Implied powers often come from the expressed powers. Row three lists some of the implied powers that Congress has found in the expressed powers. Remember that the "necessary and proper" clause, Clause 18, justifies the principle of implied powers.

Congress has the power to authorize the creation of money.

Extension

The Second Bank of the United States ended during the presidency of Andrew Jackson. A westerner, Jackson disliked banks, feeling that they tightened credit and slowed economic development in the West. He went through two treasury secretaries before finding a third who would withdraw federal assets from the Second Bank and instead put them into state banks. When this was done, state banks began loaning money at low rates, leading to land speculation in the West.

Ideas to Remember Extension

Review the ideas listed, further explaining difficult vocabulary words. Have students create graphic organizers in their notebooks to help them visualize the expressed, implied, and denied powers of Congress.

Supreme Court Case Extension

McCulloch v. *Maryland* is one of Supreme Court Chief Justice John Marshall's most important rulings. After the War of 1812, finances were disorganized. State banks used popular feeling against the Second Bank of the United States to change its operations. Maryland passed a law saying that all banks other than those created by the state had to comply with state rules or pay a tax of $15,000 per year. James W. McCulloch, the cashier of the national bank's Baltimore branch, ignored these rules and the state sued him. Daniel Webster was one of the lawyers who represented the bank. Marshall based his opinion on Alexander Hamilton's loose construction of the Constitution in setting forth the constitutionality of the First Bank of the United States. The ruling caused many states to issue declarations against the loss of state power, which Marshall answered with anonymously published articles.

Table Extension

Divide the class into four groups, assigning each group a type of power listed in the table. Challenge the groups to create a way to remember the various expressed and implied powers. Suggest they make up rap songs, acrostics, or graphics that incorporate the information. Then have each group present its ideas to the class.

Picturing Government

The congressional power to tax, as illustrated in the photograph on page 118, has led to the national income tax, which is under fire in some places. Republican representative John Lindner has proposed a national sales tax. Proponents of the plan say it would give the poor more money to spend and would also do away with the Internal Revenue Service. Critics, however, say that a national tax would have to be anywhere from 23 to 50 percent. Have interested students find out about the proposed legislation and then present their findings to the class by using the Student Presentation Builder on the student CD.

Powers of Congress

Type of Power	Money Power	Commerce Power	Military and National Defense Power	Other Legislative Powers
Expressed Powers	• To tax (Clause 1) • To borrow money (Clause 2) • To regulate bankruptcies (Clause 4) • To print and coin money (Clause 5) • To punish counterfeiters (Clause 6)	• To regulate business between states and business with other nations (Clause 3)	• To punish crimes at sea (Clause 10) • To declare war (Clause 11) • To set up, fund, and regulate the armed forces (Clauses 12, 13, and 14) • To provide for, regulate, and call into service a militia (the National Guard) (Clauses 15 and 16)	• To establish laws for naturalization (Clause 4) • To set up post offices (Clause 7) • To grant copyrights and patents (Clause 8) • To set up a system of federal courts beneath the Supreme Court (Clause 9) • To govern Washington, D.C. (Clause 17) • To make all laws necessary and proper for carrying out the other powers (Clause 18)
Some Implied Powers	• To punish those who do not pay their taxes • To use tax revenue to support programs such as education and public housing	• To outlaw discrimination in movie theaters, restaurants, hotels, and similar places • To set a minimum wage • To protect those with disabilities	• To draft Americans into the armed forces	• To limit and regulate immigration

The money powers give Congress the power to tax and appropriate, or authorize the spending of, the income from taxes. Because of its **tax-and-spend** powers, Congress has a great deal of control over the nation's policies. Congress must approve all funding for every program that the federal government sets up.

All bills that raise money for the government begin in the House. The Framers set up this system on purpose. Representatives are elected every two years. As a result, the Framers thought they would be more careful to follow the wishes of voters.

Picturing Government

The power to print money is depicted in the photograph on page 119. The Bureau of Engraving and Printing was established in 1862. Now, the United States has more than 2,500 employees working in facilities in Washington, D.C., and Fort Worth, Texas. In the past, the bureau has also printed currency for the Philippines, the Republic of Cuba, Siam, and Korea. The bureau prints postage stamps as well as currency.

Landmark Supreme Court Case: Interstate Commerce

Heart of Atlanta Motel v. *United States* (1964): Congress passed the Civil Rights Act of 1964 to ban discrimination in restaurants, hotels, motels, and jobs. The owner of the Heart of Atlanta Motel sued to have the law declared unconstitutional. The owner claimed that it was a local business. However, the motel advertised on interstate highways and attracted travelers from out of state. The Supreme Court ruled that the motel was part of interstate commerce. The Civil Rights Act was declared constitutional.

In order to pay for programs, Congress passes **appropriations bills.** Requests to fund programs usually come from the president. Each year, the president sends a budget proposal to Congress. Both houses review the proposed budget. Committees hold hearings to determine how much they think the executive departments need.

Commerce is the buying and selling of goods and services. The Constitution gives Congress the power to regulate commerce between states and with other nations. However, over the years, Congress has enlarged the meaning of commerce. Today, *commerce* means "any business that crosses state lines." For example, Congress regulates banking, television and cable, clean air, and working conditions.

Congress and the president share military and national defense powers. The president is commander in chief of the armed forces. However, he must ask Congress to declare war. Congress has declared war five times in U.S. history. Yet, U.S. troops have fought in more than 200 undeclared wars. In 1973, Congress attempted to get back its power to declare war. It passed the War Powers Act. A president must notify Congress within 48 hours if he sends U.S. troops into battle. Congress must approve the use of troops in a war zone for more than 60 days.

The Constitution gives Congress six other legislative powers. Clause 18 is the all-important "necessary and proper" clause. The other five expressed powers deal with particular topics. **Copyrights** protect the rights to their works of writers, artists, and composers for a period of time. **Patents** enable inventors to control how their inventions are manufactured and sold. Congress was given the power to set up all federal courts under the Supreme Court in Clause 9. Clause 7 allows Congress to set up the post offices, Clause 4 to set laws for citizenship, and Clause 17 to govern Washington, D.C.

stop and think

What are implied powers? Write a paragraph to explain implied powers. Be sure to include at least two examples. Ask a partner to check your paragraph to see if it is clear and complete. Revise it based on your partner's suggestions.

Supreme Court Case Extension

The owner of the Heart of Atlanta Motel filed suit as soon as the Civil Rights Act of 1964 was passed. His 216-unit motel was advertised in national magazines; nearly three-fourths of his clients were from out of state. The Supreme Court judges unanimously declared that the Civil Rights Act was constitutional. In delivering the opinion of the Court, Justice Tom C. Clark quoted from Justice John Marshall's *Gibbons* v. *Ogden* decision from 140 years earlier.

Stop and Think

Students' paragraphs will vary but should explain implied powers and give two examples.

Extensions

1 Ask students interested in the environment to use library resources or the Internet to find out more about the interstate regulations of clean air and water. Have them find creative solutions to pollution that businesses have used. For example, a power company based in Ohio has created a 30,000-acre recreation area, the largest such outdoor area in that state, from land reclaimed after being surface-mined.

2 Students interested in military science may wish to use library resources or the Internet to find out more about the five wars Congress declared. Ask them to create charts showing the dates of the wars, the allies and enemies, key battles, and the outcomes of the wars.

President Andrew Johnson was tried and acquitted by the U.S. Senate in 1868.

Nonlegislative Powers

The House and the Senate have certain nonlegislative powers. These are powers that are not related to the passing of laws. In most cases, the House and the Senate have separate duties in fulfilling these powers. The table on page 123 lists the powers and then explains the duties of each house.

The House has only had to choose a president twice. In 1800, they chose Thomas Jefferson, and in 1824, they chose John Quincy Adams.

In 1973, Congress confirmed Gerald Ford as vice president. He succeeded Spiro Agnew, who had resigned. Then, in 1974, Congress confirmed Nelson Rockefeller as vice president. He replaced Ford, who had become president when Richard Nixon resigned the presidency.

In 2005, the Senate held confirmation hearings for the appointment of Alberto Gonzales as Attorney General.

Since 1789, the House has impeached 17 federal judges, and the Senate has convicted seven. Congress has also impeached and tried two presidents, Andrew Johnson in 1868 and Bill Clinton in 1998. Both were acquitted.

Confirmation power over presidential appointees belongs to the Senate alone. The Secretary of State and the Attorney General of the United States are examples of the heads of executive departments who are appointed. The Senate's confirmation duties also include approving justices to the U.S. Supreme Court, some diplomats, and some top-level military positions.

The executive branch has the responsibility to make treaties. The Senate alone has the power to ratify, or approve, treaties. This is part of the system of checks and balances.

Putting It All Together

Make a T-chart in your notebook. On one side, list four expressed powers of Congress that affect you. On the other, list four implied powers that affect you. Discuss your selections with a partner, and make any changes to which you both agree.

Picturing Government

Andrew Johnson's impeachment trial, shown at the top of page 122, marked the first time the Senate issued gallery passes to its proceedings, a practice that continues to this day. Johnson, who had been a loyal senator from Tennessee, was chosen to run with Lincoln in 1864 to gain support of the border states. Political rivalries led to Johnson's impeachment after he vetoed Reconstruction legislation and fired Edwin Stanton, secretary of war. Johnson missed being impeached by one vote on each of the two votes taken. Although not renominated in 1868 for the presidency, he returned to the Senate in 1875, which was also the year he died.

Picturing Government

Alberto Gonzales, shown in the photograph at the bottom of page 122, is the first Hispanic Attorney General of the United States. His connection with President George W. Bush began in Texas, when Bush was governor of the state and Gonzales served as secretary of state and on the Texas Supreme Court. As Texas secretary of state, he served as the chief liaison on Mexico and border issues. For three years prior to being secretary of state, he was Bush's General Counsel.

Extension

Have students use library resources or the Internet to find out about the impeachment trial of Bill Clinton. What were the real issues and what defense did Clinton offer? How did the trial affect his presidency?

Putting It All Together

Students' T-charts will vary but should include four expressed and four implied powers that affect them.

Nonlegislative Powers of Congress

Power	Source of Power	House of Representatives	Senate
Power to appoint the president and vice president	• Twelfth Amendment • Twentieth Amendment, Sections 3 and 4 • Twenty-fifth Amendment, Section 2	Twelfth Amendment • A joint session of Congress counts the Electoral College votes. • If no presidential candidate has a majority, House selects from top three candidates. Twentieth Amendment • House and Senate together pass legislation to deal with the death of a presidential or vice presidential candidate if the person died before taking office. Twenty-fifth Amendment • A majority vote of House and Senate must approve a nominee to replace a vice president who died or resigned.	Twelfth Amendment • A joint session of Congress counts the Electoral College votes. • If no vice presidential candidate has a majority, Senate selects from top two candidates. Twentieth Amendment • House and Senate together pass legislation to deal with the death of a presidential or vice presidential candidate if the person died before taking office. Twenty-fifth Amendment • A majority vote of House and Senate must approve a nominee to replace a vice president who died or resigned.
Power to remove a federal official from office, including federal judges	• Article II, Section 2, Clause 5: the House • Article I, Section 3, Clause 6: the Senate	The House impeaches a federal official. This means the House finds enough evidence of wrongdoing to turn the official over to the Senate for trial.	The Senate tries the impeached official. If found guilty, the person is removed from office.
Power to confirm federal nominees	• Article II, Section 2, Clause 2	No responsibilities	Senate must confirm presidential nominees for the • heads of executive departments and their highest level of assistants. • heads of regulatory agencies. • federal judges. • major diplomatic positions. • major military positions.
Power to ratify treaties	• Article II, Section 2, Clause 2	No responsibilities	• Senate must approve any treaty with another nation by a two-thirds vote.
Power to propose amendments to the Constitution	• Article V	• This power is shared with the Senate. • The House must propose an amendment by a two-thirds vote.	• This power is shared with the House. • The Senate must propose an amendment by a two-thirds vote.

Table Extension

The power to appoint a president and vice president is represented by three different amendments. Divide the class into three groups, assigning one amendment to each group. Have students use library resources or the Internet to find out the historical background of these amendments and when they were used. Have groups present their findings to the class by using the Student Presentation Builder on the student CD.

Extension

Have students use library resources or the Internet to find out if any amendments to the Constitution are currently being proposed in Congress. Ask students to find out who sponsored them and why. Also have students take a position on whether the proposal should be ratified.

Lesson Summary

Congress has expressed, implied, and inherent powers. Two of the inherent powers of Congress are the power to investigate and the power of legislative oversight. Most of Congress's work is done through committees and subcommittees. Both the House and the Senate have permanent, or standing, committees. Party leadership chooses the members of the committees, usually from the majority party in either house. Each committee has a chair, usually based on seniority. Monday is kept free for committee work. Select committees are temporary, set up to study a topic or issue and report on it. Joint committees are from both houses. Conference committees are temporary. They work out differences in bills created by the House and the Senate. Congressional committees can also hold investigations. Witnesses who have been subpoenaed testify; if they lie under oath, they can be charged with perjury. Witnesses may be granted immunity if they have valuable information. Refusing to testify leads to being charged with contempt, which is a crime. Legislative oversight of the federal bureaucracy occurs through committees. Departments are required to send annual reports to committees. The General Accounting Office checks the budgets of the departments. Committees exercise the power of the purse and hold annual hearings on the budget.

Lesson Objective

Students will learn about the work of congressional committees.

LESSON 2

The Work of Committees

Thinking on Your Own

Have you ever been on a sports team or served on a committee or group that made decisions? What was the hardest part of working as a team? What was the most enjoyable part? If you have never been part of a team or committee, think about a time when you had to work with someone else to get something done. Answer each question with two or three sentences in your notebook.

focus your reading

Describe the committee system in Congress.

How does Congress use its investigative power?

What is Congress's legislative oversight?

words to know

inherent power
legislative oversight
standing committee
subcommittee
seniority system
select committee
joint committee
conference committee
subpoena
perjury
immunity
contempt
federal bureaucracy
power of the purse

As you just read, the Constitution gives Congress expressed powers and implied powers. Congress also has inherent powers. **Inherent powers** are not directly stated in the Constitution. These powers belong to the government because it is the government. The government must have and use certain powers in order to carry out its duties.

Two of these inherent powers belong to Congress. One is the power to investigate issues and topics that are viewed as important. The other is the power to oversee how laws are carried out. This is known as **legislative oversight**.

Congress usually works through committees and subcommittees when it uses its investigative and oversight powers. Most of Congress's work is done through committees. By serving on committees in both the House of Representatives and in the Senate, members of Congress become experts in specific topics.

Words to Know

Discuss each of the vocabulary terms with students.

Certain powers belong to the government because it must have those powers in order to govern. These are called *inherent powers*. The power to oversee how laws are being carried out is called *legislative oversight*. *Legislative oversight* is one of the *inherent powers* of Congress.

Standing committees are permanent committees. The Senate has 18 *standing committees*. *Subcommittees* are smaller working groups within a committee. *Select committees* are also called special committees. The work of *select committees* is temporary. Committees with members from both houses are called *joint committees*. Most *joint committees* are permanent. *Conference committees* are permanent and are made up of members from both houses. *Conference committees* work out differences in Senate and House versions of a bill.

The *seniority system* bases chairmanship of the committee on the person from the majority party who has been on the committee the longest. The *seniority system* rewards people for remaining dedicated to a task.

The Committee System

Both the Senate and the House have their own committees. The Senate has 18 permanent committees, or **standing committees.** The House has 19 standing committees.

Each committee is divided into several subcommittees. **Subcommittees** are small working groups of members of the standing committees. Each subcommittee deals with a piece of the larger committee's work. For example, the House Committee on Veterans' Affairs has four subcommittees. Its Subcommittee on Disability Assistance and Memorial Affairs handles all issues related to salaries and pensions of the armed forces. The Senate has about 70 subcommittees, and the House has about 80. These numbers change as the responsibilities of committees change.

Senator Diane Feinstein (D-California), shown here at the 2004 Democratic National Convention, serves on the Senate Judiciary Committee.

The members of committees are chosen by the party leaders in the House and the Senate. Senators and representatives request committees based on how they can best serve their constituents. For example, a representative from New Jersey might ask to be assigned to the Homeland Security Committee. This would be useful because New Jersey is home to Newark Airport, an airport that serves the New York metropolitan area.

The majority of members on committees are from the majority party in the House and the Senate. For the 109th Congress (2005–2007), for example, the Republican Party won more seats in Congress than the Democrats. As a result, the majority on every committee was made up of Republicans.

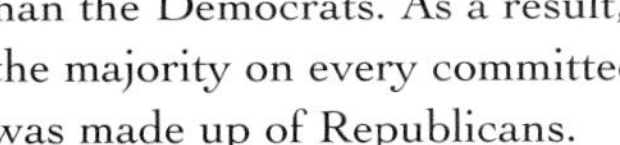

Each committee has a chairperson. The chair of every committee for the 109th congress was also a Republican.The chair is usually the person from the majority party who has been on the committee the longest. This is known as the **seniority system**.

ideas to remember

The committee system in Congress is made up of

- standing committees.
- subcommittees.
- select committees.
- joint committees.
- conference committees.

Ideas to Remember Extension

Review the ideas listed, further explaining difficult vocabulary words. Have students create graphic organizers in their notebooks to help them visualize the congressional committee system.

Focus Your Reading Answers

1 The committee system is the division of both the Senate and the House into smaller groups, which are in turn divided into subcommittees. Each house has close to 20 standing committees, whose members are selected by party leadership. Most members are from the majority party. Each committee has a chair, usually based on seniority.

2 Committees are involved in the investigative power of Congress. Witnesses are subpoenaed to testify. They can be charged with perjury, granted immunity, or charged with contempt if they refuse to testify. Investigative committees determine if a law is needed, gather information to write a better bill, educate the public, or look into alleged wrongdoing of members of Congress or others.

3 Legislative oversight is Congress's power to see how the departments of the executive branch are doing their work. Departments must send reports yearly. Congress controls the budget appropriations as well, so it can pressure the executive branch to follow the will of the committee members.

Words to Know, continued

To *subpoena* a witness is to give someone legal notice to appear before a committee. All congressional committees have the power to *subpoena* witnesses.

Perjury is lying under oath. *Perjury* is a crime, whether it is done before a court of law or a congressional committee.

Committees can refuse to charge someone with a crime, or grant *immunity*. Witnesses usually gain *immunity* because they have valuable information about a crime.

To be charged with *contempt*, a person must refuse to testify before a committee. *Contempt* is a crime.

The federal government's many departments make up one example of *federal bureaucracy*. It is difficult to review all of the workings of the *federal bureaucracy*.

The *power of the purse* is the control of money. Committees exercise the *power of the purse* by cutting or ending funding for some programs or by adding it to other programs.

Picturing Government

Diane Feinstein, shown in the photograph on page 125, was elected to the U.S. Senate in 1992. Senator Feinstein (D-California) serves on the Judiciary Committee, where she is the ranking member of the Terrorism, Technology, and Homeland Security Subcommittee; the Appropriations Committee, where she is the ranking member of the Military Construction and Veterans Affairs Subcommittee; the Energy and Natural Resources Committee; the Select Committee on Intelligence; the Homeland Security Subcommittee of Appropriations; and the Rules and Administration Committee. Encourage interested students to further explore Senator Feinstein's career or the various committees and subcommittees on which she serves.

Extension

Ask students to use library resources or the Internet to find out what conference committees are currently working on bills before Congress. Have them track the progress of the bill in the news media as you complete this unit.

Stop and Think

Students' choices and reasons will vary but should include three committees from the list on page 127.

Hillary Rodham (Clinton) served on the Watergate Committee in 1974, officially known as the Select Committee on Presidential Campaign Activities.

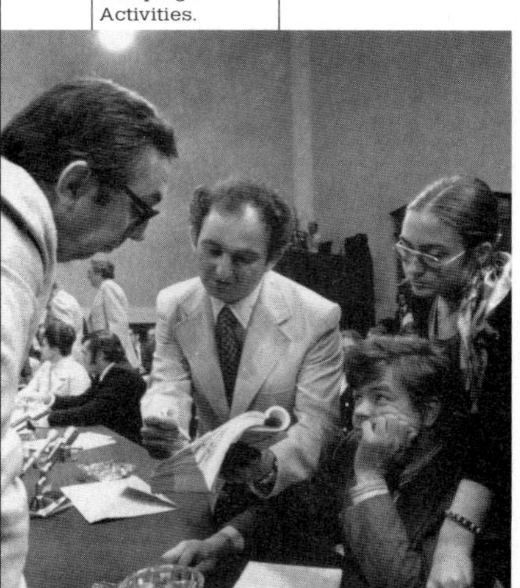

Each senator sits on three or four standing committees and several subcommittees. Representatives generally sit on one or two committees and several subcommittees. Much of the senators and representatives' time is spent on committee work. That is why the House and the Senate do not hold sessions on Monday or before noon on other days.

There are three other types of committees in Congress. **Select committees**, also known as special committees, are temporary. They are set up to study one topic or issue and report on it to the House or the Senate. Both the House and the Senate have their own select committees. The Senate committee that investigated the Watergate break-in and the involvement of President Richard Nixon in the cover-up was a select committee.

Joint committees are made up of members of both houses. Joint committees may be permanent or temporary. Most joint committees are permanent, however. For example, the Joint Committee on Printing oversees the printing of all government publications.

Conference committees are temporary and made up of members of both houses. Their job is to work out differences in House and Senate versions of a bill. As you will learn, a bill must pass both houses before it goes to the president. The two versions must be exactly the same. The members of conference committees come from the House and the Senate committees that proposed the bills. However, the majority party in each house has more members on a conference committee.

stop and think

Read the committees listed in the table on page 127. If you were a member of Congress, on which three committees would you want to serve? Discuss your choices with a partner. Write three reasons for each of your choices.

Picturing Government

Sam Ervin began his Senate career during the Eugene McCarthy era, in 1954. He retired 20 years later, four months after Richard Nixon resigned the presidency. Ironically, in 1954, it was Vice President Nixon who appointed Ervin to a committee charged with determining whether Senator McCarthy should be censured. The Senate majority leader, Mike Mansfield, chose Ervin, a strict constructionist, to lead the Watergate Committee, stating that he was "the only man [sic] in the Senate who had the respect of the entire body." Hillary Rodham (Clinton), shown at the right in the photograph on page 126, was one of the counsels to the committee.

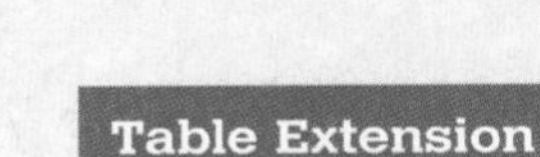

Permanent Committees of the House and the Senate

House Standing Committees	Senate Standing Committees	Joint Committees
Agriculture	Agriculture, Nutrition, and Forestry	Economic
Appropriations	Appropriations	Printing
Armed Services Budget	Armed Services	Taxation
Education and the Workplace	Banking, Housing, and Urban Affairs	
Energy and Commerce	Budget	
Financial Services	Commerce, Science, and Transportation	
Government Reform	Energy and Natural Resources	
Homeland Security	Environment and Public Works	
House Administration	Finance	
International Relations	Foreign Relations	
Judiciary	Health, Education, Labor, and Pensions	
Resources	Homeland Security and Governmental Affairs	
Rules	Indian Affairs	
Science	Judiciary	
Small Business	Rules and Administration	
Standards of Official Conduct	Small Business and Entrepreneurship	
Transportation and Infrastructure	Veterans Affairs	
Veterans' Affairs		
Ways and Means		

House Select, or Special, Committees	Senate Select, or Special, Committees
Permanent Select Committee on Intelligence	Select Committee on Ethics
	Special Committee on Aging
	Select Committee on Intelligence

Power to Investigate

Standing committees, subcommittees, and select committees conduct investigations. Investigations take the form of hearings, in which witnesses testify. Congressional committees have the power to **subpoena** witnesses. Witnesses are served with a legal order to appear before the committee. Witnesses do not always testify under oath. If a witness is caught lying under oath, however, he or she can be charged with **perjury**. As in a regular court of law, a witness before a committee can be prosecuted for perjury.

Table Extension

Divide the class into pairs, and assign each pair one of the standing committees. Be sure to have an equal number of House and Senate committees represented. Ask the pairs to use library resources or the Internet to find the current issues that their committee is working on. Allow time for students to report their findings to the class. Consider using a bulletin board or other display to highlight the issues.

Extension

Have students debate the merits and limits of the seniority system. Tell them about the career of the longest-serving senator, Strom Thurmond, who served in the Senate for 47 years and 5 months, retiring a month after his 100th birthday. At what point do they think he may not have been the best person to chair a committee, despite the seniority system? What additional criteria do they think might be applied?

Extension

The Constitution also denies certain powers to Congress in Article I, Section 9. Invite interested students to use library resources or the Internet to find out about writ of habeus corpus, bills of attainder, and ex post facto laws. Allow time for them to report their findings to the class.

Picturing Government

Enron, whose executives are shown in the photograph at the top of page 128, was involved in one of several corporate scandals that broke during the early years of the twenty-first century. Students who are interested in business may wish to use library resources or the Internet to find out more about white-collar crimes at Enron, WorldCom, Tyco International, HealthSouth, or Adelphia Communications.

Picturing Government

Major General Antonio Taguba, shown in the photograph at the bottom of page 128, was the army's second-highest-ranking Filipino-American officer when he authored a report on the abuses at Iraq's Abu Ghraib prison in 2004. The abuses, which were perpetrated by members of the U.S. Army, created both embarrassment and a call for reform.

Executives from Enron Corporation testified before the Senate in the early 2000s about corruption and the eventual financial failure of the corporation.

Sometimes a committee will grant a witness **immunity**. The person will not be charged with any crime that he or she testifies about committing. A committee grants immunity for one reason. The witness has information about others involved in the crime and the committee wants that information. If a person refuses to testify, he or she can be charged with **contempt**. This is a crime.

Congressional investigations have several purposes. First, investigations may be conducted to determine whether a law is needed. Second, a committee may hold hearings to gather information to help it write a better bill. Third, some investigations look into possible wrongdoing by members of Congress or others. Fourth, hearings may be held to educate the public on issues of importance.

Major General Antonio Taguba testified before the Senate Armed Services Committee in 2004.

Power of Legislative Oversight

Legislative oversight, or review, is an important part of the system of checks and balances. Congress makes the laws, and the executive branch carries them out. Through legislative oversight, Congress checks on what the departments of the executive branch are doing and how they are doing it.

Extension

One of the most famous investigations in U.S. history took place in the 1950s, when Senator Joseph McCarthy of Wisconsin chaired the Senate Permanent Subcommittee on Investigations. Turning the committee's attention from investigating waste in the executive branch to hunting Communists everywhere, he conducted both public and closed sessions, calling hundreds of witnesses. Democrats resigned from the committee over disputes of staff hirings; Republicans stopped attending because hearings were called on short notice or held away from the Capitol. For three months in 1954, the Army-McCarthy hearings were televised after McCarthy brought charges of lax security at a top-secret army post. Boston lawyer Joseph Welch, arguing for the army, finally broke McCarthy's hold on the nation after McCarthy charged that one of Welch's attorneys was a Communist. "Have you no sense of decency?" Welch demanded, as viewers across the nation watched. Three years later, McCarthy died, at age forty-eight. Students interested in drama may wish to read Arthur Miller's drama *The Crucible*, written about the Salem witchcraft trials, but full of allusions to the Communist hysteria gripping the nation at the time.

Congress exercises its legislative oversight through its committees. However, committees do not have the time or staff to review the daily workings of the huge departments that make up the federal bureaucracy. The **federal bureaucracy** includes everyone who works for the government, including nonelected employees. Departments are run smoothly and efficiently for the most part. What the public hears about are the cases where problems arise. This is when Congress's oversight power is important.

Congress has several ways to use this power. Committees can and do require departments to send yearly reports about their activities. Congress has a support agency called the General Accounting Office (GAO). Committees can request that the GAO investigate how departments are using their budgets.

Luis V. Gutierrez (D-Illinois) is a member of the House Committee on Veterans Affairs.

Committees hold hearings each year on the budget requests of each department. Committee members often lecture members of the executive departments on how they should do their jobs and what their departments should or should not be doing. Committees hold what is called the **power of the purse**. They use it by adding money for certain programs, cutting spending on others, or ending funding for some programs completely. In these ways, committees can pressure the executive branch to do what their committee members want.

Putting It All Together

For the Stop and Think activity, you selected the committees you would want to serve on if elected to Congress. Research what one of those committees might investigate. Select an issue or problem that you might investigate as a member of the committee. In your notebook, list three people or kinds of people whom you would ask your committee to subpoena as witnesses. Write three questions you would like to ask them.

Picturing Government

Luis Gutierrez, shown in the photograph on page 129, was the first Latino elected to Congress from the Midwest. He chairs the Congressional Hispanic Caucus's Task Force on Naturalization and Citizenship. His workshops to help prospective citizens have aided more than 25,000 people to begin the process of applying for citizenship. Other members of the Congressional Hispanic Caucus have used his model in their own districts.

Extension

The House Committee on Veterans Affairs began in 1946. The committee has oversight responsibility to monitor and evaluate the work of the Department of Veterans Affairs. Areas of legislative concern for veterans include life insurance, pension, national cemeteries, veterans' hospitals and medical care, and other issues related to veterans.

Putting It All Together

Students' choices of a committee, witnesses, and questions will vary.

Lesson Summary

The president influences the actions of Congress, usually through veto power and pushing a legislative agenda. Conflicts occur, especially if different parties control the two branches. Five major sources of conflict exist: party politics, the rules and policies of Congress, the different priorities that come from representing a region or a nation, checks and balances, and different timetables for action. Congress has used four strategies to gain power: additional staff members, the War Powers Act of 1973, the National Emergencies Act, and the budget. Presidents once responded to conflict by impounding funds, but this is no longer possible. The Congressional Budget Office reviews the president's budget requests and provides data.

Lesson Objective

Students will learn about the conflicts that may occur between Congress and the president.

Focus Your Reading Answers

1 Conflicts may come from five major sources: party politics, the rules and policies of Congress, the different priorities that come from representing a region or a nation, checks and balances, and different timetables for action.

2 Congress has tried to limit presidential power by adding staff members and by passing several bills—the War Powers Act of 1973, the National Emergencies Act, and the Budget Impoundment and Control Act of 1974.

LESSON 3

Congressional Power and Presidential Power

Thinking on Your Own

Think of a time when you worked with a group to complete a project or to play a sport. What kinds of conflicts came up? How did the group settle those conflicts? Write a paragraph in your notebook to describe a conflict and how it was settled.

focus your reading

Explain why conflicts develop between Congress and the president.

How has Congress tried to limit presidential power?

words to know

staff members

impoundment

The president comes to Congress once a year—to give the annual State of the Union address. However, the president's influence is felt in Congress every day. This has not always been the case.

Some presidents have taken a more active role in shaping national policy than others. Andrew Jackson used his veto power to keep Congress in check. Both Theodore Roosevelt and Franklin D. Roosevelt pushed legislation they wanted through Congress. Active presidents often have conflicts with Congress. This is especially true when the two branches are controlled by different political parties.

President George W. Bush delivered the State of the Union address on February 2, 2005.

Conflict Between Congress and the President

Party politics can be a major reason for conflict between Congress and the president. When the president and the majority of both houses belong to the same political party, there are few conflicts.

Words to Know

Discuss each of the vocabulary terms with students.

Staff members are those who assist Congress in getting information and writing reports. The work of *staff members* frees legislators to work on committees and subcommittees.

A president refusing to spend money that Congress has designated for a program is called *impoundment*. Through the use of *impoundment*, a president could force the government to do what he or she wanted.

For example, the Republicans controlled the House of Representatives and the Senate for most of George W. Bush's presidency. Many of his legislative proposals became law. During Bill Clinton's first term, the Democrats lost the majority in both houses in the 1994 election. President Clinton was less successful in getting his proposals passed.

Second, the rules and organization of Congress can also cause conflicts. The filibuster, for example, means that the opposite party can talk until a bill fails in the Senate. Even members of the president's own party may not support his proposals. For example, southern Democrats used the filibuster to try to stop President Lyndon Johnson's civil rights legislation in the 1960s.

President Ronald Reagan met with congressional leaders of both parties in the Oval Office in February 1981.

As you just read, both houses are organized into committees to work on legislation. Committees review and rework the president's proposals. The resulting bill may be greatly changed from what the president wanted. Committees may also delay a bill from one session to another or kill it by not bringing it out of committee.

Third, the president represents the nation as a whole. Members of Congress represent their districts or states. Different parts of the country may have different concerns about issues. For example, western landowners want to develop their lands, but environmentalists want to save western forests. The president sends a proposal to Congress to set aside thousands of acres as national forests in western states. Senators and representatives from those states put the interests of their constituents first. They fight the proposed law. This occurred during Clinton's presidency. In the end, President Clinton issued an executive order to set aside the land. An executive order is a rule issued by the president that has the force of law. When President George W. Bush came into office, the executive order was overruled.

A fourth reason for conflict between Congress and the presidency is the system of checks and balances. The Framers meant it as a way to balance the power of the branches of government. However, the system sets Congress against the

Picturing Government

President Reagan, shown meeting with congressional leaders in the photograph on page 131, was the first actor to become president. Known as the Great Communicator for his charming, folksy style, he won over both Congress and voters. Reagan, who was a Republican, won the 1980 election in a landslide—489 Electoral College votes to incumbent Jimmy Carter's 49. During 1981, his inaugural year, Reagan worked with a Republican Senate and a Democratic House. During his first 100 days in office, sometimes called the "honeymoon period," Reagan won 31 Senate votes and two House votes on bills that were important to him. Reagan was especially successful with the Democratic House during 1981.

Picturing Government

The State of the Union address, being delivered by George W. Bush in the photograph on page 130, has become an annual event. The Constitution states in Article II, Section 3, that "the President shall from time to time give to Congress information of the State of the Union. . . ." George Washington delivered the first such address in person to a joint session of Congress in 1790. Thomas Jefferson, however, thought that a public address was too formal, and sent his speech in writing to each house of Congress. The speech was then reprinted in newspapers. That action set a precedent that lasted for 112 years, until Woodrow Wilson returned to Washington's method in 1913. Ten years later, Calvin Coolidge became the first president to deliver his address on the radio. In 1947, Harry Truman's speech was the first to be televised.

Cartoon Extension

Be certain that students understand the allusion to the story of the Dutch boy who held back the sea by placing his finger in a dike (retaining wall). The story became well known through a novel written more than a century ago by Mary Mapes Dodge, *Hans Brinker, or The Silver Skates*. Also point out the symbol of the donkey, and review with students which party it represents.

Stop and Think

Students' T-charts should contain the five reasons for conflict between Congress and the presidency: party politics, the rules and policies of Congress, the differences between representing a district or state and representing a nation, the system of checks and balances, and differing political timetables. Examples of each may vary.

president if he vetoes or threatens to veto a bill. The threat of a veto forces members of Congress to try to change the bill enough so that the president will sign it. If the president actually vetoes a bill, then supporters must try to get enough votes to override, or overturn, the veto. Since President George Washington, presidents have used their veto power 2,552 times. Congress has overridden only 107 of these vetoes.

Social Security was a source of tension between the president and Congress in 2005.

Fifth, presidents and members of Congress have different political timetables. A president has four years, or perhaps eight, to see his proposals become laws. Members of Congress may be reelected as many times as they are willing to run. Members of Congress may believe that their constituents are not yet ready for certain policies. As a result, they may not be willing to support the president. This is true even when the president is from their own party. This appeared to be the case when President George W. Bush proposed a major change to Social Security. After Republicans listened to constituents' concerns, they were not willing to make the changes that the president wanted.

stop and think

With a partner, make a T-chart to show the five reasons why conflicts develop between Congress and the presidency. Label the left column "Reasons for Conflicts." Label the second column "Examples."

Acting to Limit Presidential Power

By the 1970s, Congress began to take back some of the power it had lost. First, it added people to help committees and subcommittees. **Staff members** do much of the work gathering and reviewing information and writing reports for committee members.

Extensions

1 Have students interested in politics use library resources or the Internet to track the first 100 days of recent administrations. Suggest that they create graphs depicting the amount of legislation passed or the success/failure rate of president-sponsored bills.

2 Invite students to use library resources or the Internet to find out more about the controversies surrounding Social Security since its inception under the New Deal. Allow time for a debate in class over current proposals to revise Social Security.

3 One of the most dramatic conflicts between the executive and legislative branches occurred in late 1995, when the federal government shut down for a record-setting 22 days. President Clinton, a Democrat, and the Republican Congress could not work out a budget deal or reach a compromise. Early in January, Clinton finally agreed to the seven-year balanced budget plan that Congress had demanded. Clinton accused Congress of holding "needed government services and hard-working government employees hostages in a political battle." About 760,000 federal workers were affected by the shutdown.

As you read in Lesson 1, Congress passed the War Powers Act in 1973. It requires the president to tell Congress if troops are sent into a battle area. President Richard Nixon vetoed the bill. Congress overrode the veto. In 2002, Congress gave up some of its recently gained power. It passed a resolution to give President George W. Bush the power to take any steps "necessary and appropriate" in the face of threats by Saddam Hussein in Iraq. The result was the invasion of Iraq in 2003.

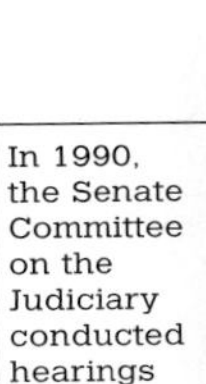

In 1990, the Senate Committee on the Judiciary conducted hearings about the War Powers Act.

A third limit on presidential power was passage of the National Emergencies Act in 1976. Congress has voted to give presidents emergency powers in times of war and other troubles. These emergency powers include the power to declare martial law and take over the transportation system. In 1943, Congress voted to declare a state of national emergency because of World War II. After the war, the state of emergency was never lifted. Later presidents used it to deal with problems without asking Congress for the power to do so. Congress ended the nation's state of emergency in 1978. The National Emergencies Act requires presidents to tell Congress if they are going to declare a national emergency. The state of emergency may last for one year. Congress may end it at any time by passing a law.

A fourth area where Congress has tried to limit presidential power is the budget. Two efforts, the legislative veto and the line-item veto, were declared unconstitutional. The Budget

Picturing Government

The Senate holds investigative hearings on important issues, as shown in the photograph on page 133. Students may wish to use library resources or the Internet to find out more about some of the major investigations, including one in 1912 on the sinking of the *Titanic,* or the 2002 inquiry into the September 11, 2001, terrorist attacks.

Extension

The War Powers Act of 1973 was not the first such legislation passed. After the attack on Pearl Harbor in 1941, Congress passed the First and Second War Powers Acts. These gave Franklin Roosevelt authority over wages, prices, farming, transportation, labor, manufacturing, and the allotment of raw materials. Roosevelt created a number of departments and boards to deal with the situation, setting up war agencies as needed.

Impoundment and Control Act of 1974 was more successful. **Impoundment** is the refusal of the president to spend money that Congress has set aside for a program. This was one way that a president could force the government to do or not do what he wanted. The Budget Impoundment Act ended this practice. Presidents must spend the money for programs unless Congress agrees that the money will not be spent.

The 1974 act also set up standing Budget Committees for both the Senate and the House. It also created the Congressional Budget Office (CBO). The staff of the CBO reviews the annual budget requests of the executive branch and provides Congress with economic data and analyses.

Putting It All Together

Write a two-line newspaper headline about three of the tensions between Congress and the presidency. Then write a two-line headline about each of the ways Congress has tried to limit the president's power. Work with a partner to decide which ideas to write about. Then write the headlines together.

Library of Congress

What houses 29 million books and other print materials, 2.7 million recordings, 12 million photographs, 4.8 million maps, and 58 million manuscripts—on 530 miles of bookshelves in three buildings? The Library of Congress!

The Library of Congress was set up in 1800 as a place for members of Congress to do research. Today, the Library is a rich resource for anyone with a computer. Many of the Library's materials, including recordings, are available online.

The Library has so many books, maps, sheet music, photographs, and recordings (records, tapes, CDs, and DVDs) because the Library also handles copyrights. Anyone who wishes copyright protection for his or her work applies to the Library's division of copyrights. Two copies of each work to be copyrighted are sent to the Library with an application form.

The first Library of Congress was housed in the Capitol. It was burned when the British set fire to Washington, D.C., during the War of 1812. President Thomas Jefferson offered to sell his own collection of books to the government to replace it. Congress agreed and paid him $23,950. His 6,487 books were shipped to the Capitol in 1815. Over time, the Library outgrew its space. The current building opened in 1897. As the collections grew, two more buildings were added.

Civics Today Extensions

1 One reason that the Library of Congress rapidly outgrew its space was the Copyright Law of 1870, sponsored by Ainsworth Rand Spofford, then Librarian of Congress. The law called for two copies of all copyrighted works—not only books, but also maps, prints, music, pamphlets, and photographs—to be sent to the Library. Created in 1800, the Joint Committee on the Library has been a standing committee since 1811.

2 Between 1950 and 1992, the size of both the staff and the collections tripled. In the same time period, the appropriations grew from $9 million to more than $330 million. The collections include materials in more than 450 languages, covering a huge variety of subjects, as was Jefferson's intent. Appropriately, the building opened in 1897 is known as the Jefferson Building. In 1939, the Adams Building opened, followed in 1980 by the Madison Building. More than 5,000 staffers in these spaces welcome the 2 million tourists, scholars, and researchers who visit annually.

Putting It All Together

Students' headlines will vary but should be concerned with three tensions between Congress and the presidency and about the ways Congress has tried to limit presidential power.

Recommended Reading

Below is a list of books that relate to the issues covered in this chapter. The numbers in parentheses indicate the related Thematic Strands of the National Council for the Social Studies (NCSS).

Joan Axelrod-Contrada. *Career Opportunities in Politics, Government, and Activism (Career Opportunities)*. Facts on File, 2003. (VI, X)

Barbara Silberdick Feinberg. *Term Limits for Congress (Inside Government)*. 21st Century, 1997. (VI, X)

Participate in Government

Contact a Government Agency

Do you need to find the nearest state motor vehicle office? Are you looking for the phone number of the state's office of student loans? Do you have a question about the local services available for an elderly relative?

Two sources of information will help you find addresses and phone numbers for local, state, and federal government departments and agencies. One source is the telephone book and the other is the Internet.

To Contact a Government Agency:

- Use your phone book. Phone books have a section called "The Blue Pages of Government Listings." The pages are edged in blue so you can find them easily. These Blue Pages are divided into listings for local, state, and federal government departments and agencies. You will find phone numbers and addresses. Some agencies have toll-free 800 numbers. The listings in each section are in alphabetical order.
- Use the Internet. Every state and some local communities have their own Web sites. The Web sites are set up so that you can link to pages for state, county, or local departments, agencies, and services. You can find addresses and phone numbers as well as the names of people to contact. Many times, you can e-mail a message to the person you are looking for and ask your question that way.

Participate in Government

1 You may wish to use this exercise with the phone book as an opportunity to help students who are just gaining basic life skills in English. Show them the organization of the phone book and the use of guide words at the top of each page's listings, similar to a dictionary's guide words. Point out the need for using synonyms; for example, they may not find anything under the heading "Drugstores," but they might find a listing under "Pharmacies."

2 If your school has a computer lab, schedule time for students to work together in pairs or small groups. Ask each group to find local, county, state, and national Web sites.

Research Resources

Below is a list of reference books and Web sites that relate to the issues covered in this chapter. Students may wish to use these to further their research on ideas in the preceding lessons. Web site addresses may change over time. Use keyword searching on a major search engine to locate sites.

Reference Books:

Donald A. Ritchie. *The Young Oxford Companion to the Congress of the United States.* Oxford University Press, 1993.

David R. Tarr, Ann O'Connor, editors. *Congress A to Z.* 4th ed. CQ Press, 2003.

Web Sites:

The Library of Congress Web site includes documents and images, as well as oral histories. It is also home to Thomas, a source of current Internet legislative information, with access to legislation, the *Congressional Record,* and committee information.

Ben's Guide to U.S. Government for Kids, a division of the Government Printing Office, contains informative materials on all branches of government, at different levels of ability, along with games and puzzles.

Powers of Congress 135

Skill Builder

Students' answers will vary. Possible responses are given.

1 The Senate and the House each have committees and subcommittees. Party leadership selects members of the committees. Most members on committees are from the majority party. Members of Congress sit on several committees or subcommittees. Select committees are temporary. Joint committees have members from both houses. Conference committees are temporary and have members from both houses.

2 Various committees conduct investigations. Witnesses are subpoenaed to testify at hearings. A committee may grant a witness immunity. A person who refuses to testify is charged with contempt. Congressional investigations have four purposes: to see if a law is needed, to help gather information to write bills, to look into possible wrongdoing by members of Congress, and to educate the public.

3 Conflict between the president and Congress can result from party politics. The rules of Congress can also cause conflict. Third, the president represents the nation as a whole while members of congress represent states or districts. Therefore, they may have different priorities. The system of checks and balances is a fourth reason for conflict, especially with the president's veto power. Lastly, members of Congress and the president are elected for different terms of office, so their timetables for making laws are often different.

Skill Builder

Summarizing and Paraphrasing

A **summary** is a brief retelling of something longer. It may be something that you have read, heard, or seen. For example, when you retell the story of a movie, you are giving a summary of the movie. You are briefly describing the main idea and giving only the most important details.

Be sure to leave out minor details, descriptions, and examples. They can confuse your audience and get in the way of their understanding of the basic information you want to tell. Minor details, descriptions, and examples also add length to your summary. Remember, a summary should be brief.

In writing reports, you often need to **paraphrase** what you have read. When you paraphrase, be careful not to write word for word what you have read. Use your own words and keep the important details as well as the main idea. A paraphrase may be about the same length as the original.

To write a summary, remember to

- state the main idea
- use only the most important details
- make the summary short

To paraphrase, remember to

- state the main idea
- include all important details
- make it as long as needed

Complete the following activities:

1 Reread the section under the subheading "The Committee System," on pages 125–126. Find the main idea of each paragraph.

2 Paraphrase the section "Power to Investigate," on page 127.

3 Write a summary of the section "Conflict Between Congress and the President," pages 130–132.

Classroom Discussion

Discuss with students some of the broader topics covered in this chapter.

- How do strict constructionists help limit the power of government?
- How can Congress best use the power to declare war to prevent more of the 200 undeclared wars that presidents have waged?
- What are some possible congressional committees that students feel could be helpful?
- In what ways could the system of committees and subcommittees be changed to make government more efficient?

Chapter

7 CONGRESS AT WORK

Getting Focused

Skim this chapter to predict what you will be learning.

- Read the lesson titles and subheadings.
- Look at the illustrations and read the captions.
- Examine the diagram.
- Review the vocabulary words and terms.

You have learned that the main job of Congress is to pass laws. You have also learned that most of the work of Congress is done in committees. This chapter is titled "Congress at Work." Make a list of at least three things that you think Congress does.

When you have finished studying the chapter, review your list. Check how accurate your predictions were. Write an essay of three or four paragraphs to explain what the chapter was about.

Vol. 150 WASHINGTON, MONDAY, OCTOBER 11, 2004 No. 13

Congressional Record

The *Congressional Record* is the official record of the proceedings and debates of the United States Congress. It is published daily when Congress is in session.

Related Transparencies

T-6 How a Bill Becomes a Law

Key Blacklines

Primary Source—Handing Out the Pork

CD Extension

Encourage students to use the reading comprehension, vocabulary reinforcement, and other activities on the student CD.

Picturing Government

The image on page 137 is from the online edition of the *Congressional Record*. It has four sections: a Daily Digest, a section for the House, a section for the Senate, and the Extension of Remarks. The Daily Digest is both the table of contents and a summary of the day's floor and committee activity. It is located at the back of each issue. The *Congressional Record* has been continuously published since 1873. Copies of it can be read online; it is usually updated each day by 11 A.M.

Pre-Reading Discussion

1 Show students a map of their congressional district, and help them relate to its boundaries. Then ask students what current civic issues their representative in Congress should address.

2 Ask students how they think a member of Congress could best divide his or her time between Washington, D.C., and the district or state he or she represents. What possible dangers do students see if either place claims too much of the member's time?

Getting Focused

Students' lists and final essays about congressional work will vary. After students have completed their lists, you may wish to take a class poll and make a master list of possible activities. If students suggest an item that belongs to another branch of government, review with the class the three branches and their overall responsibilities.

Lesson Summary

Congress passes both public bills, which apply to the entire country, and private bills, which apply to certain individuals or groups. All bills except revenue bills, which must begin in the House, can begin in either house. Bills can be presented only by members of Congress, even though the idea for a bill can come from private citizens, interest groups, or the president. Bills can be co-sponsored or sponsored by members of both political parties. When each house has passed its version of a bill, the bill goes to a conference committee, where members shape it through compromise. Once that bill passes both houses, it goes to the president. It becomes law when signed or if the president holds the bill for ten days, unless Congress adjourns during that time. The president may also veto a bill and send it back to Congress. To override a president's veto requires a two-thirds majority vote in both houses.

Lesson Objective

Students will learn about the process of introducing, shaping, and passing a bill in Congress.

LESSON 1

How a Bill Becomes a Law

Thinking on Your Own

You want Congress to pass a law that will provide summer jobs for teenagers. You e-mail your representative in Congress to urge him or her to introduce such a bill. Which of the vocabulary words would help you explain what you hope to accomplish?

Each year, members of Congress propose thousands of bills. However, less than ten percent actually become laws. The 108th Congress (1999–2001), for example, introduced more than 8,000 bills. Only 504 became laws.

There are several reasons why so few proposals become laws. First, the process for passing bills is very long. As you can see from the diagram on page 140, many steps are involved. A bill can be delayed or killed several times during the process.

Second, a bill's sponsors may delay a bill on purpose. **Sponsors** are the senators or representatives who introduce a bill. They delay it because they know there are not enough votes to pass it.

Third, a bill may be killed because powerful members of Congress, the president, or special interest groups oppose it. Interest groups may also oppose a bill or work on members of Congress to kill it.

focus your reading

Summarize the different types of bills and resolutions.

What is the first step in getting a bill through Congress?

Explain what happens once a bill is reported out of committee.

What is the final step in how a bill becomes a law?

words to know

sponsor
public bill
private bill
rider
simple resolution
joint resolution
concurrent resolution
interest group
bipartisan
pigeonhole
quorum
compromise bill
pocket veto
override

Words to Know

Introduce each of the following vocabulary terms to students.

A *sponsor* is a senator or representative who introduces a bill. A bill's *sponsor* may delay a bill on purpose to gain support.

A *public bill* is of interest to the entire country. The Clean Air Act of 1990 is a *public bill.* A *private bill* is one of interest only to some people or places. A bill about immigration is an example of a *private bill.* An amendment to a bill that has nothing to do with the bill is called a *rider.* A *rider* is sometimes added to keep a bill from being passed.

A *simple resolution* is one that concerns only one of the houses of Congress. An example of a *simple resolution* is a rule about how bills will be introduced in the Senate. A *joint resolution* deals with a special case and must be passed by both houses of Congress. After September 11, 2001, Congress passed a *joint resolution.* A *concurrent resolution* is one submitted by both the House and the Senate at the same time. A *concurrent resolution* isn't signed by the president and doesn't become law.

Bills and Resolutions

Congress considers two kinds of bills. One is the **public bill**. It deals with an issue of general interest that applies to the entire nation. An example is the Clean Air Act of 1990. A **private bill** deals with an issue of interest only to certain people and places. An example is a bill to allow an immigrant to enter the United States without waiting until his or her turn comes up on the list of applicants for visas. Both kinds of bills become laws when both houses pass them and the president signs them.

According to Article I, Section 7, Clause 1, all revenue bills must begin in the House of Representatives. All other kinds of bills may begin in either the House or the Senate. The House Ways and Means Committee deals with most tax legislation. However, the Senate also has a role in setting tax policy. Article I, Section 7, Clause 1, goes on to state that the Senate may propose amendments to tax bills. The Senate Committee on Finance works on tax policy.

After being printed, proposed legislation and the federal budget are distributed to members of Congress.

As it passes through Congress, a bill may have a series of riders added to it. A **rider** is an amendment to a bill that does not have anything to do with the subject of the bill. For example, a rider was added to a budget bill in 2001 to allow drilling for oil in the Arctic National Wildlife Refuge in Alaska.

Congress also considers several types of resolutions. A **simple resolution** is a decision that concerns only the Senate or the House. A new rule about how bills are introduced in the Senate would be a simple resolution. It is not a law and the president does not sign it.

Joint resolutions and concurrent resolutions are passed by both houses of Congress. **Joint resolutions** deal with some special cases. The two houses passed a joint resolution after the terrorist attacks of September 11, 2001. It gave the president the power to use whatever force necessary to pursue those responsible for the disaster. The president must sign a joint resolution for it to become a law. A **concurrent resolution** is not signed by the president and is not a law. Setting the date for Congress's adjournment for vacation requires a concurrent resolution.

Picturing Government

President Bush proposed a federal budget of $2.57 trillion for 2006. The proposed budget, as shown on page 139, is printed by the government for review by members of Congress and the public.

Focus Your Reading Answers

1 Public bills apply to the entire nation. Private bills apply only to certain individuals or groups. A simple resolution concerns only one house. It doesn't become law. Both houses pass a joint resolution, which becomes law when the president signs it. A concurrent resolution comes from both houses but is not signed by the president and does not become law.

2 The first step in getting a bill through Congress is to have it written, introduced, and read.

3 Bills reported out of committee are sent to the House or the Senate for debate.

4 To become law, the president must sign the bill, or each house must override the president's veto with a two-thirds majority vote.

Words to Know, continued

An *interest group* is made up of people who share ideas and try to influence government policy. *Interest groups* sometimes write the bills presented to Congress. *Bipartisan* means two-party. A *bipartisan* bill signals that both parties favor it.

To *pigeonhole* a bill means that the committee doesn't act on it. A bill does not progress out of committee if it is *pigeonholed*.

A *quorum* is a majority. To vote on a bill requires a *quorum*.

A *compromise bill* is one that has been through the work of a conference committee. A *compromise bill* must return to both houses for a vote.

A *pocket veto* occurs if Congress adjourns during the ten days after the president receives a bill. Members of Congress generally try to avoid a *pocket veto*.

To *override* a veto is to reverse it. A two-thirds majority vote in both houses is needed to *override* a veto.

Table Extensions

1 For the benefit of students who are kinetic learners, select students to represent the progress of a bill in both the House and the Senate. Set up stations in the classroom, and have students proceed through the stages of getting a bill passed. You may also wish to have some students holding signs they made to represent the different stages. Question or assist students as they move around the room—for example: *Would you go to Keisha or to Josh next?*

2 Students who are interested in computer languages may wish to create alternative flowcharts of the information presented in the table. Allow time for them to present and explain their flowcharts to the class.

How a Bill Becomes Law

Action	House	Senate
Introduction of a Bill	1. A representative introduces a bill. 2. The bill is given a House number and title. 3. The bill is sent to a House committee.	1. A senator introduces a bill. 2. The bill is given a Senate number and title. 3. The bill is sent to a Senate committee.
Committee Action	1. The committee may pigeonhole the bill, kill it, or send it to a subcommittee. 2. The subcommittee holds hearings on the bill. 3. The subcommittee marks up the bill. 4. If the subcommittee votes to approve the marked-up bill, it is sent back to the standing committee. 5. The standing committee reviews the marked-up bill. 6. The standing committee may pigeonhole the bill, kill it, or report it out to the House for debate.	1. The committee may pigeonhole the bill, kill it, or send it to a subcommittee. 2. The subcommittee holds hearings on the bill. 3. The subcommittee marks up the bill. 4. If the subcommittee votes to approve the marked-up bill, it is sent back to the standing committee. 5. The standing committee reviews the marked-up bill. 6. The standing committee may pigeonhole the bill, kill it, or report it out to the Senate for debate.
Floor Action	1. The Rules Committee decides on a time limit for debate and whether amendments may be added. 2. The House debates the bill and votes. Amendments may be added. 3. The bill passes and is sent to the Senate for approval; **OR** If the House version is different from the Senate version, it is sent to a conference committee.	1. The Senate debates the bill and votes. There is no time limit on debate in the Senate. Amendments may be added. 2. The bill passes and is sent to the House for approval; **OR** If the Senate version is different from the House version, it is sent to a conference committee.

Conference Committee

Members of both the House and the Senate meet to work out differences between the two bills. A compromise bill is sent back to both houses to vote on.

Floor Action	The House votes and passes the bill.	The Senate votes and passes the bill.

Presidential Action

The president takes one of four actions:

1. Signs the bill. 2. Keeps the bill for ten days without taking any action.	3. Vetoes the bill and sends it back to Congress. 4. Uses a pocket veto. This happens if Congress adjourns during the ten days the president has the bill.	The bill becomes a law.	**Congressional Action** Congress attempts to override the veto by a two-thirds majority vote in both houses. If both houses vote to override the veto, the bill becomes a law. If one house does not have a two-thirds majority, the bill is killed, or stopped.

Extensions

1 All bills or resolutions are numbered when they are introduced. The number identifies the body that originated it. S. 1 indicates a Senate bill; H.R. 1 identifies a bill from the House of Representatives.

2 No limits are placed on the number of members of Congress who can sponsor a bill. In the 109th Congress, for example, H.R. 810, a bill on human embryonic stem cell research, had 202 sponsors, including members from both major parties and an independent.

3 Joint resolutions cover a wide range of topics. The 108th Congress, for example, suggested several constitutional amendments, honored several individuals, and recognized special places, as well as planning events such as the 60th anniversary of the landing at Normandy during World War II.

The First Steps

Ideas for bills can come from anyone. In Chapter 4, you read how Candy Lightner wanted the legal drinking age raised through federal action. Often, a bill comes from the president. However, bills are also written by members of Congress and by interest groups. **Interest groups** are made up of people who share common ideas and come together to influence government policy.

Even if a bill comes from the president, only a senator or representative may introduce it in Congress. Often, several members of the House or the Senate will co-sponsor a bill. At times, members of both parties will sponsor a bill. This **bipartisan**, or two-party, effort shows that the bill has support from members of both parties.

After a bill is introduced, it receives its first reading. This involves the clerk of the House or the Senate numbering the bill and giving it a title. The bill is printed in the daily *Congressional Record* and the daily *Journal* of the house in which it was introduced.

Representative Charles Rangel (D-New York), at center, discusses Social Security privatization in 2005.

Next, the bill is sent to the standing committee that has responsibility for the topic of the bill. For example, a Senate bill asking for more pollution controls on cars would be sent to the Senate Commerce, Science, and Transportation Committee. Once a bill goes to the committee chair, any of the following may occur. (1) The bill can be **pigeonholed**. The committee does not act on the bill, so it does not progress. This is what happens to most bills that are introduced in Congress. (2) The committee can vote to kill the bill. (3) The committee chair can send the bill to a subcommittee to deal with. (4) The committee or subcommittee can act on the bill.

If a subcommittee decides to consider a bill, the next step is to hold hearings. As you learned in Chapter 6, committees and subcommittees can call witnesses to testify. These witnesses have some special knowledge of or interest in the bill. They may be government officials or outside experts. Witnesses may also be private citizens, businesspeople, or members of public interest groups.

Picturing Government

Charles B. Rangel, New York's representative from the 15th Congressional District, is shown in the photograph on page 141. In 2005, Rangel was the ranking member of the House Committee on Ways and Means. The committee has a subcommittee on Social Security to which the Committee on Ways and Means refers matters related to the federal fund. During the impeachment hearings for Richard Nixon, Rangel was a member of the House Judiciary Committee. He is also a founding member of the Congressional Black Caucus.

Extension

Old-fashioned desks were made with several compartments, known as pigeonholes, for stashing letters or bills. (Pigeons build their nests in small holes or recesses.) The bits of paper would sometimes be forgotten or lost in the large desk. So to *pigeonhole* something came to mean to tuck it away and forget about it.

Extension

Invite students to form small groups based on a common area of interest, such as the environment. Have them use library resources or the Internet to locate an interest group that represents their area of interest. Ask them to find out more about the interest group and explain to the class what it does, along with any current efforts related to pending legislation. Have them present their findings to the class by using the Student Presentation Builder on the student CD.

Stop and Think

Six steps are mentioned in this section. Students' lists of vocabulary words will vary.

Extension

The Civil Rights Act of 1964 included Title VII, which prohibits discrimination in the workplace. Michigan's representative Martha Griffiths, who served in Congress for nearly 20 years, pushed for the addition of the word *sex* to the list of criteria (race, religion, or national origin) in the act. Virginia representative Howard Smith added it at the last minute. Some believe his action was an attempt to defeat the entire bill. The bill passed, however, and Senator Margaret Chase Smith then guided the bill through the Senate.

stop and think

This section is titled "The First Steps." How many steps are discussed in this section? Look again at the list of vocabulary words that you made for the Thinking on Your Own activity. Work with a partner to add words to your vocabulary list.

Once the hearings are over, the subcommittee meets to "mark up" the bill. The members go through the bill and make changes to it. A majority of members must agree to every change.

Once the changes are made, the subcommittee has several choices. It may pigeonhole the bill or vote to kill it outright. Members may also vote to send the revised bill back to the standing committee. The standing committee can also kill the bill or report the bill out of committee. If the bill is reported, it is sent to the House or the Senate for debate.

Floor Action

In the House of Representatives, the Rules Committee sets a time limit for floor debate. The committee also decides whether amendments may be added to the bill during debate. The Senate does not ban amendments or have time limits.

The clerk of the House or the Senate reads the bill for the second time. Amendments may be proposed after each section is read. A majority of members must approve an amendment before it can be added. Amendments are proposed for several reasons. Sometimes members believe that the changes are truly important and needed. At other times, opponents of a bill add amendments as a way to kill the bill.

Once the bill is read and all the amendments have been added, the bill is read again. After this third reading, a vote is taken. A **quorum**, or majority, of senators or representatives is needed for a vote to take place. If a quorum is not present, no vote can be taken. To pass a bill, a majority of the members present must vote to approve it.

The House uses voice votes, standing votes, and electronic voting. In a voice vote, members call out either "aye" or "no." In a standing vote, members stand to show whether they are for or against a bill. In 1973, the House introduced electronic voting. Members push buttons at their seats to vote yes or no. Each member's vote appears on a large panel behind the Speaker.

The Senate also uses voice and standing votes. It uses a roll-call vote instead of electronic voting. Each senator calls out his or her vote.

Final Steps

Usually, House and Senate bills on the same topic are different. Their subcommittees may have included different issues. When the bills reach floor debate, senators and representatives may have raised new concerns. One house may have added amendments that the other house did not. To become a law, House and Senate versions of a bill must be exactly the same.

Once the two versions of a bill have passed their houses, the bills go to a conference committee. The committee is made up of members from both houses and both parties. The committee works out the differences between the two bills. The **compromise bill** is then sent back to the two houses for a vote.

A public hearing of the Joint Congressional Intelligence Committee in 2002

If the compromise bill is passed in both houses, it is sent to the president. The president may sign the bill and it becomes a law. The president may also choose not to take action. If the president holds the bill for ten days, it becomes a law. There is one exception. If Congress adjourns during those ten days, then the bill is vetoed. This is called a **pocket veto**. The president may also veto a bill outright. Then he sends the bill back to Congress with an explanation of why he vetoed it.

President George W. Bush signed the Garrett Lee Smith Memorial Act on October 21, 2004.

Congress may choose to rework the bill and try to pass a new version. However, Congress may also try to **override** the president's veto. To do this, both houses must repass the bill with a two-thirds majority vote. If either house fails to get a two-thirds majority vote, the bill dies.

Putting It All Together

Write a one-paragraph summary explaining how a bill becomes a law. Refer to the information in this lesson, and use as many vocabulary words as you can.

Picturing Government

The photograph at the top of page 143 shows questioning at a public hearing. The Senate Select Committee on Intelligence and the House Permanent Select Committee on Intelligence formed a joint committee to study the activities of the intelligence community with regard to the events of September 11, 2001. Establishing the joint committee was an unusual venture to attempt to prevent further attacks by fixing any systemic problems.

Picturing Government

Oregon's senator Gordon Smith's son committed suicide in 2003 at the age of twenty-one. The senator proposed the first teen suicide prevention act in memory of his son. The act provided funding for three years for teen suicide prevention programs, including voluntary screening programs. In the photograph at the bottom of page 143, President George W. Bush is signing the act. The federal Substance Abuse and Mental Health Services Administration (SAMHSA) implemented the law. Encourage interested students to use library resources or the Internet to find out about the programs and successes of the law.

Putting It All Together

Students' paragraphs will vary but should match the information given in the table on page 140 and include several vocabulary terms.

Lesson Summary

Members of Congress help their constituents by solving problems with federal agencies and by attracting money and jobs to the district or state. Staff members assist with casework. Casework is important because it helps members of Congress to be reelected, aids them in legislative oversight, and provides needed services for constituents. Members of Congress bring jobs and funding to their states or districts in three major ways: funding public works projects, which may be simply pork-barrel legislation; getting federal grants and contracts; and keeping federal grants and contracts.

Lesson Objective

Students will learn about the ways in which members of Congress serve their constituents back home.

Focus Your Reading Answers

1 Members of Congress help individual constituents by solving their problems with federal agencies.

2 Members of Congress aid their districts and states by bringing jobs and funding.

3 Constituents can reelect a member of Congress. The concerns of the constituents must influence any member of Congress. The complaints of constituents also influence members of Congress in their role of legislative oversight.

LESSON 2

Working for the Folks Back Home

Thinking on Your Own

Your congressional representative has just visited your U.S. government class. Her parting words were "If I can be of help in any way, please contact my office." List at least three ways that she might be able to help you or your school.

focus your reading

Explain how members of Congress help individual constituents.

How do members of Congress help their districts and states?

Describe how constituents influence members of Congress.

words to know

casework

pork-barrel legislation

logrolling

The "folks back home" are a Congress member's constituents. Everyone in a representative's district or a senator's state is a constituent. There are two main ways that members of Congress aid their constituents. One is to help them solve problems with federal agencies. The second is to bring money and jobs to their state or district.

Handling Casework

Citizens often turn to their senator or representative to help them with problems such as:

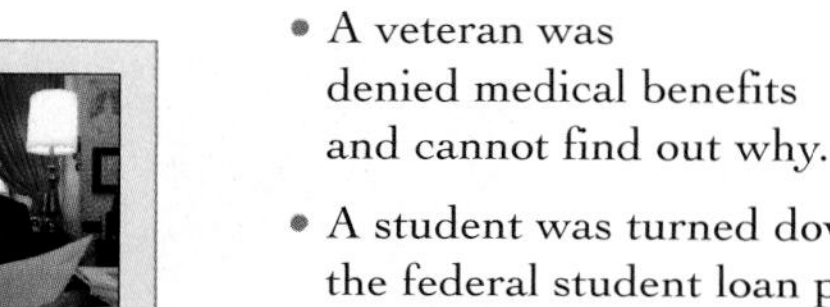

- A veteran was denied medical benefits and cannot find out why.

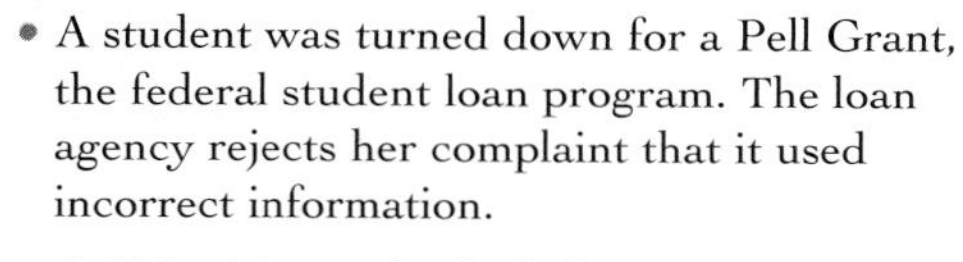

- A student was turned down for a Pell Grant, the federal student loan program. The loan agency rejects her complaint that it used incorrect information.
- A U.S. citizen asks for help in getting his German-born wife back into the United States. She went to Germany for a visit. The U.S. immigration service says her visa has expired. She cannot return to the United States.

Representative Rush Holt (D-New Jersey) at work in the Capitol and at home at a rally

Words to Know

Discuss each of the vocabulary terms with students.

Casework is made up of the requests of the people the member of Congress serves. Staff members assist with *casework*.

Money or jobs that benefit the constituency of only one member of Congress are known as *pork-barrel legislation*. While many members of Congress have complained about *pork-barrel legislation*, nothing has been done to stop it. *Logrolling* occurs when members of Congress promise to support one another's pork-barrel bills. *Logrolling* may keep things moving but wastes federal money.

Every member of Congress hires staff members to handle **casework.** A caseworker's job is to help constituents solve problems with federal agencies. On his Web site in 2005, Senator Richard Lugar (R-Indiana) lists 11 categories of "common needs and concerns with which my constituent services team" can help Indiana residents. Other representatives and senators offer similar help.

Casework Services from Senator Richard Lugar's Office

Military and Veterans' Issues
- Enlistments and discharges
- Veterans' benefits
- Awards and medals

Labor
- Pensions and benefits
- Unemployment insurance
- Workers' compensation

Education
- Student loans, grants, and scholarships
- Vocational rehabilitation
- Job training programs

Social Security
- Retirement benefits
- Disability applications
- Medicare

Over the years, casework has become an important part of the work of members of Congress. First, helping constituents can help senators and representatives win reelection. Casework shows that a congressional member is interested in the needs and concerns of constituents. People talk about their problems and the help they get to solve them. At election time, this kind of free word-of-mouth advertising is priceless.

Senator Barack Obama (D-Illinois) greets constituents after being elected in 2004

stop and think

Look at the list you wrote before you began this lesson. Pick one of the items and write a letter to your congressional representative asking for help in solving one of the problems.

Second, casework helps members of Congress with legislative oversight. By listening to constituents' problems, members of Congress get an idea of how certain federal agencies and departments are working. They can tell how well the executive branch is carrying out programs.

Picturing Government

The photograph on page 145 shows Senator Barack Obama greeting constituents the day after his election. Elected in 2004, Obama was only the third African American elected to the Senate since Reconstruction. He was also the first African-American president of the *Harvard Law Review*. After earning his law degree at Harvard, he chose not to pursue a lucrative job in law or business. He returned to Chicago, where he'd cut his political teeth after college, working with a church-based group to help residents of the South Side cope with industrial plant closings. Even before Obama won his seat in the Senate, this Illinois state senator was recognized as a rising star. Party leadership invited him to address the 2004 Democratic National Convention in Boston.

Stop and Think

Letters will vary, but should have reasonable requests.

Picturing Government

The photographs on page 144 show two aspects of the work of a member of Congress, New Jersey representative Rush Holt. Before entering politics in 1998, Holt served as an arms control expert at the State Department, as well as the Assistant Director of the Plasma Physics Laboratory at Princeton University. Holt is the only scientist to sit on the House Permanent Select Committee on Intelligence. Holt's father was the youngest person, at age twenty-nine, ever to be elected to the Senate; his mother was the first woman to serve as secretary of state in West Virginia.

Table Extension

Have students use library resources or the Internet to find the casework services that senators from your state offer. Invite students to create tables organizing the services as the box on page 145 does.

Third, casework truly provides a service for constituents. The federal government is a huge bureaucracy run by rules and systems. It can be overwhelming for a person to try to deal with. The caseworker can cut through all of this to the heart of the problem to get an answer.

Bringing Home Jobs and Money

Members of Congress also serve their constituents by bringing jobs and federal funds to their state or district. There are three ways that members of Congress do this.

The first is through public works projects. Many of these projects are very much needed. For example, a rapidly growing region needs a rail system to ease traffic jams. There is general agreement among members of Congress that this is a good use of federal money.

However, a number of projects every year are known as **pork-barrel legislation**. For example, a senator sponsors a bill to spend $50 million to build a road to a town with 200 people. The only value is to the senator's constituents. It will make travel easier into and out of the town. The project will also bring jobs to the area.

Metrolink, the mass transit system in Los Angeles, is an example of a federally funded public works project.

Over time, a number of members of Congress have criticized pork-barrel legislation. However, the practice is difficult to stop. What is one senator's "pork" is another senator's aid to constituents. As a result, little is done to stop passage of pork-barrel legislation. In fact, senators or representatives at times promise to support one another's pork-barrel bills. This is known as **logrolling**.

Picturing Government

The photograph on page 146 shows Metrolink, which connects Southern California cities. Experts estimate that Metrolink eliminates more than 25,000 automobile trips each week. About 65 percent of weekday commuters formerly drove alone or carpooled. Los Angeles Union Station is the destination for more than 60 percent of the work trips taken each week.

Picturing Government

The photograph on page 147 shows the building of a Humvee, a High Mobility Multi-Purpose Wheeled Vehicle. In 1979, the U.S. Army called for a new tactical vehicle that would replace some of its light civilian trucks, most of which were ten to twenty years old. Delivery of the vehicles, designed to support both combat and non-combat roles, began six years later. The company that won the contract designed 11 different prototypes — five utility vehicles and six weapons carriers. Humvees were tested over more than 600,000 miles that simulated various environments, such as Arctic cold, desert heat, deep sand, water up to five feet deep, and rocky hills. Over a span of five years, the company produced the required 55,000 Humvees, the majority of which went to the army, while the other branches of service shared the rest. More than 175,000 Humvee.

Extension

Identify students interested in military science. Assign a different branch of the military to each student. Ask them to find out where U.S. military bases are located, and have them use flags or other devices to note them on a map. Lead a discussion on current Base Realignment and Closing (BRAC) recommendations.

146 Chapter 7

ideas to remember

Members of Congress help constituents by

- solving their problems with federal agencies.
- bringing jobs and money to their state or district through
  - pork-barrel projects.
  - federal grants and contracts.
  - keeping federal projects in the state or district.

The second way a member of Congress brings home money and jobs is through federal contracts and grants. The federal government spends billions of dollars every year. Much of it goes out in contracts and grants. For example, the federal government awarded billions of dollars in contracts to fight the war in Iraq. The money bought supplies such as uniforms, weapons, and food as well as services such as security for U.S. officials in Iraq.

Federal grants are awards of money given for many different kinds of activities. A grant might be $100,000 to improve the downtown area of a small city. A grant might also be millions of dollars to a major university for research. Federal grants and contracts bring money and jobs into an area.

Humvees are fortified with armor at a Fairfield, Ohio, facility.

This leads to the third way that federal lawmakers aid their states and districts. Once they get federal contracts or grants, members of Congress work hard to keep them. For example, the closing of military bases is often contested by local cities and towns. In recent years, the Defense Department closed bases across the nation. A base closing can badly hurt the economy of a district and state. Senators and representatives worked with state and local officials and others to argue against closing their base.

Putting It All Together

Imagine that you want a summer job with one of your state's U.S. senators. Imagine that he or she has an office in your community. Write a letter explaining why you want the job and why the senator should hire you. Use information from this lesson to support your request. Share your letter with a partner. Ask your partner to help you make your letter more convincing.

Extensions

1 The colorful language of politics is rooted in American history. While logrolling is currently a sport, at one time, neighbors clearing land helped each other roll felled tree logs into piles for burning.

2 Pork-barrel legislation takes its name from a custom from the South prior to the Civil War. On occasion, slaveholders placed salt pork in large barrels at a particular time and day. Slaves were permitted to rush to the barrels and take what they could. The custom first influenced political slang in the 1870s.

3 The group Citizens Against Government Waste monitors pork-barrel legislation. According to CAGW, pork-barrel spending has increased from $10 billion in 1995 to $27.3 billion in 2005. The number of pork-barrel projects during that same time period increased from fewer than 2,000 to 14,000. Have students interested in finance check the CAGW Web site to find out more.

Putting It All Together

Students' letters will vary but should request a summer job from a senator. Letters should include the motive for seeking employment and the student's qualifications.

Extension

You may wish to invite a colleague from the language arts or English department to review with students the proper form for a business letter. Help students use grammar handbooks or the Internet to find the correct forms of address in writing to a member of Congress.

Ideas to Remember Extension

Review the ideas listed, further explaining difficult vocabulary words. Have students create graphic organizers in their notebooks to help them visualize the ways that members of Congress help their constituents.

Reading for Understanding

1 Dealing with various parts of the government can be frustrating for people.

2 They have the expertise to investigate and resolve problems, and they understand the concerns of the local areas in which they work, which is also where they live.

3 Their purpose is to serve the people of Maine.

Speaking of Government

Helping Constituents Across Maine — Senator Susan M. Collins (R-Maine)

The following was written by Senator Susan M. Collins, a Republican senator from Maine. The column appeared in a local Maine newspaper.

"What do you do when the Social Security Administration insists . . . that you're dead? . . .

"It's as simple as the old phrase: you write (or phone, or fax, or e-mail) your representatives in Congress. And in each case, Maine citizens were helped by the dedicated staff in one of the six offices I maintain in the various parts of our state. . . . I'm very proud of the personal assistance my staff have given to Mainers in need. It can be frustrating for people to try to navigate the often muddy waters of federal regulations. . . .

"[M]y state office staff . . . acts as an important liaison between federal agencies and the people of our state. They understand the cares and concerns of the local areas in which they work because that's where they come from, and they have the expertise to investigate and resolve problems. . . .

"[Y]ou are always welcome just to walk into any of my state offices where my staff will be glad to greet you. . . . It may seem strange to think of asking one arm of the government to help clear up a problem with another, but it's important to remember why we're here—to serve the people of Maine."

—Senator Susan M. Collins,
Magic City Morning Star, January 9, 2004

reading for understanding

1. What reason does Senator Collins give to explain why people ask her office for help?
2. Why are the staff in Senator Collins's offices so good at helping Mainers?
3. According to Senator Collins, what is her and her staff's purpose?

Picturing Government

Susan Collins, shown in the photograph on page 148, was first elected to the Senate in 1996. Two years before, she had become the first woman in Maine's history to win a major party nomination. She lost that election for governor, leaving her free to run for the Senate. There she co-authored the 1998 Higher Education Act, as well as the Collins-Lieberman bill, which became the National Intelligence Reform Act of 2004. The latter makes the most major changes to the United States intelligence system in half a century, incorporating many of the suggestions of the 9-11 Commission. One of Senator Collins's committee assignments is the Committee on Armed Services. Within that committee, she serves on three subcommittees: Emerging Threat and Capabilities, Personnel, and Sea Power. In addition to her work as Chair of the Committee on Homeland Security and Governmental Affairs, Collins also serves on the Senate Special Committee on Aging.

Participate in Government

Contribute to a Political Campaign

Running political campaigns is very expensive. Presidential campaigns cost more than $200 million. A state governor's race may cost as much as $40 million. Even a mayor's race in a big city can cost millions. Where does the money to fund campaigns come from?

Federal campaign finance laws regulate large contributions, as you will learn in Chapter 16. However, much of the money to fund campaigns comes in small amounts. Ordinary citizens who want to support causes and candidates give what they can.

The Democratic National Committee and the Republican National Committee regularly mail out fund-raising letters. They go to registered party members and anyone who has given in the past. The two national committees also have Web sites where contributions are accepted by credit card.

State and local candidates and political parties may also have their own Web sites. They, too, mail out fund-raising letters and hold fund-raisers.

A fund-raiser may be a $25,000-a-plate dinner at a fancy restaurant for a Senate candidate. In this case, the speaker would be an important national political figure, such as the president. A fund-raiser for a city council member may be a $25 coffee-and-bagels get-together at a supporter's home.

To Find Out More About Contributing to a Political Campaign:

- Check the candidate's or party's Web site to see if it accepts contributions online.
- Call the county office of the political party you want to support.
- Call the campaign office of the state or local candidate you want to support.

Research Resources

Below is a list of reference books and Web sites that relate to the issues covered in this chapter. Students may wish to use these to further their research on ideas in the preceding lessons. Web site addresses may change over time. Use keyword searching on a major search engine to locate sites.

Reference Books:

C. B. Brownson, ed. *Congressional Staff Directory.* Congressional Quarterly, Inc., updated annually.

Washington Information Directory. Congressional Quarterly, Inc., updated annually.

Web Sites:

The United States Government Printing Office Web site allows access to texts of laws, as well as the *Congressional Record*, the daily record of the proceedings in both houses.

Recommended Reading

Below is a list of books that relate to the issues covered in this chapter. The numbers in parentheses indicate the related Thematic Strands of the National Council for the Social Studies (NCSS).

Geoffrey M. Horn. *Congress (World Almanac Library of American Government)*. World Almanac Library, 2002. (VI, X)

Suzanne Levert. *Congress.* Franklin Watts, 2005. (VI, X)

Skill Builder

Understand the Difference Between Percents and Actual Numbers

Understanding percents is important in analyzing information. Percents do not represent actual numbers. For this reason they can sometimes be misleading. People might make decisions based on a very small number, but think it is larger because it is a percent.

For instance, suppose a newspaper reports that 75 percent of people surveyed believe that veteran's should receive more benefits. Seventy five percent represents a significant number of people who share this belief. However, you need to know the actual number to make better sense of this percent. If only four people were surveyed, then three people represent the 75 percent. But, if 10,000 people were surveyed, then 7,500 represent the 75 percent. These numbers might have an impact on how you would vote or feel about increasing benefits.

Newspapers often report information as percentages rather than actual numbers. This information often comes from polls or surveys. By reading closely you can find out how many people were surveyed.

WASHINGTON, JULY 7—A national study shows that the number of births to immigrants in Broward County almost doubled between 1990 and 2002. In that time, births to immigrant mothers went from 22.7 percent to 43.2 percent.

Births went from 22.7 percent to 43.2 percent. What does this information mean? What is the number of children who were born to immigrant mothers in 2002? You cannot answer this question because the news story only gives you a percentage. To answer the question, you need to know the **actual number**. The actual number is the number represented by the percentage.

150 Chapter 7

Classroom Discussion

Discuss with students some of the broader topics covered in this chapter.

- Should the process for a bill to become law be made simpler? What are the advantages of a more complex process?
- How can government spending in pork-barrel legislation be reduced?
- What are some of the projects that members of Congress have brought to your state or area? Were they worthwhile?

Sometimes the actual number is given along with the percentage. Sometimes, however, you have to do some work with the information. Suppose the article went on to say that the total number of births in Broward County was 22,134 children. Then you could find the actual number of children born to immigrant mothers. You would multiply the total number of children by the percentage born to immigrant mothers.

$22{,}134 \times 0.432 = 9{,}562$ children born to immigrant mothers

Why is it important to know an actual number instead of just a percentage? The actual number could be anything from 1 to 1 million. A person who is against immigration could read the article and be alarmed. On the other hand, percentage does not give a supporter of immigration any facts to help his or her arguments. Actual numbers help people form opinions based on facts.

Read the following news article and answer the questions.

> **WASHINGTON, JULY 28—The Transportation Security Administration unfolded a new plan for airport screening. Kennedy International Airport will lose nearly ten percent of its 1,844 screeners, or 184. Newark Airport will go from 1,319 to 1,281 screeners, or about three percent fewer people.**

1. How many screeners will Kennedy International Airport lose?
2. How do you know this number?
3. What percentage of Kennedy's screeners is this?
4. How many screeners will Newark Airport lose?
5. How did you find this number?
6. Why is the information in this article easier to understand than the information than in the first article?

Skill Builder

1. 184
2. This number is given in the article.
3. nearly 10 percent
4. 38
5. $1{,}319 - 1{,}281 = 38$
6. The information in this article is easier to understand because actual numbers are provided, rather than only percents.

Congress at Work 151

Unit Objectives
After studying this unit, students will be able to

- describe the positions within the executive branch
- summarize the constitutional and informal powers of the presidency
- explain the workings of the federal bureaucracy

Unit 3 focuses on the executive branch of the federal government.

Chapter 8, The Presidency, examines the role of the president and others within the executive branch.

Chapter 9, The Powers of the Presidency, discusses the powers, roles, and duties of the president.

Chapter 10, The Federal Bureaucracy, explores the work of the various departments, agencies, and commissions of the executive branch.

Getting Started

Have a student read aloud the title of the unit and the two paragraphs that follow it on page 152. Write the words *execute*, *executor*, and *executive* on the board. Use each word in a sample sentence without relying on the words' political meanings, and ask students to define the words in context. Then have students extend the meaning of the words to the executive branch. Remind students of the three branches of the U.S. government and their distinct duties.

UNIT 3 THE EXECUTIVE BRANCH

When you think of the executive branch, you may think only of the president—and maybe the cabinet. In reality, more than 2.7 million people are employed in the executive branch. That does not count the 1.4 million men and women on active duty in the armed forces.

How did the federal government get to be so big? Over the years, the federal government has developed thousands of programs. What do all those federal employees do? They work for you.

Picturing Government

Since 1800, every president has lived in the White House, shown on page 152. Only George Washington did not, but he chose the location and approved the design. Since 1800, when John and Abigail Adams moved in, presidents have improved the residence, adding indoor plumbing, electricity, telephones, a movie theater, and a bowling alley. The White House has 132 rooms on four main levels, with two basement floors. Before September 11, 2001, more than 1 million people visited annually, without being charged an admission fee.

Chapter

8 THE PRESIDENCY

Getting Focused

Skim this chapter to predict what you will be learning.

- **Read the lesson titles and subheadings.**
- **Look at the illustrations and read the captions.**
- **Examine the tables.**
- **Review the vocabulary words and terms.**

What do you already know about the job of president? Think about what you have read or heard about what the current president is doing. Think, too, about what you have learned already about the powers of the president. Make a list of at least five things you already know about the job of president.

When you finish studying this chapter, add to your list. Write at least five new things that you learned about the presidency.

In 2005, there were four living former presidents: Jimmy Carter, George H. W. Bush, Bill Clinton, and Gerald Ford.

Pre-Reading Discussion

1 In recent years, some people have called for a revision of the requirement that the president be native born. Ask students to give arguments for and against changing the policy.

2 The office of the president has been called the most powerful office in the world. Ask students to brainstorm some of the problems and difficulties that a president would face, despite the power.

Related Transparencies

T-7 Cabinet-Level Officers

T-18 Three-Column Chart

T-20 Concept Web

Key Blacklines

Primary Source—President Harry Truman on Being President

CD Extension

Encourage students to use the reading comprehension, vocabulary reinforcement, and other activities on the student CD.

Getting Focused

Students' lists about the president's job will vary. When students have completed their lists, you may want to invite their responses and make a master list for the class. Invite students who enjoy art to make a poster with the known facts and illustrate it with line drawings or photos clipped from magazines, such as newsweeklies.

Picturing Government

The photograph on page 153 was taken during Bill Clinton's first term of office. With him are three living former presidents: Jimmy Carter, George H. W. Bush, and Gerald Ford. At the time the photograph was taken, Ronald Reagan was still alive, but unable to attend.

Lesson Summary

The roles of the president include head of the country, commander in chief of the armed forces, and chief official of the executive branch of government. To become president or vice president, a person must meet certain constitutional criteria. In addition, experience in government is helpful. Wealth is also a factor in winning elections. Vice presidents are often selected to balance the ticket, usually geographically, to attract the most voters. Only nine vice presidents have been called on to serve as president. The Twenty-fifth Amendment, ratified in 1967, clearly spells out the succession of the presidency.

Lesson Objective

Students will learn about the qualifications for and duties of the president and vice president.

Focus Your Reading Answers

1 The official qualifications for the presidency include being a natural-born citizen, at least thirty-five, and a resident of the country for at least 14 years before taking office. The unofficial qualifications for the presidency include having government experience and enough money to run a campaign.

2 The job of the vice president is to preside over the Senate and to fill in if the president is disabled or serve if he or she is killed.

3 If the president resigns or dies in office, the vice president becomes the chief executive.

LESSON 1

The President and Vice President

Thinking on Your Own

What qualities do you want in your president? Write a list in your notebook of personal or political characteristics that you expect in a president. Then use your list as the basis for an essay. Title your essay "What I Want in My President."

focus your reading

What are the official and unofficial qualifications for the presidency?

What is the job of the vice president?

What happens if the president resigns or dies in office?

words to know

liberal

conservative

moderate

balance the ticket

Like the legislative and judicial branches, the executive branch has grown and changed. In some ways, the modern presidency is similar to the presidency of George Washington. The constitutional duties are the same. However, the size of the federal government is much larger. The nation's importance in the world is vastly greater. When George Washington was president, the nation was just trying to survive. Today, the United States is the most powerful nation in the world.

The Presidency

The presidency includes many roles. The president is the chief official of the executive branch, the head of the nation, and the commander in chief of the armed forces. He or she represents the nation to the rest of the world. You will learn about duties of the presidency in Chapter 9.

The table on page 155 lists the basic qualifications, term, salary, and other privileges of the president. Any vice-presidential candidate must meet the same qualifications.

Geraldine Ferraro was the first female candidate for executive office. She ran as Walter Mondale's running mate in 1984.

The official qualifications tell only part of the story. Anyone running for president must also meet some unofficial qualifications. First, the person probably will have had some experience in government. Being either

Words to Know

Introduce each of the following vocabulary terms to students.

Explain that a *liberal* is one who believes that the federal government should expand its role through actively promoting social programs. Franklin D. Roosevelt is an example of a *liberal*.

A *conservative* believes in a limited governmental role in social and economic programs. A *conservative* tends to feel that private individuals should fund social programs.

The views of a *moderate* lie between those of a *liberal* and a *conservative*. A *moderate* may hold traditional values but want government regulation of business.

To *balance the ticket* is to strengthen a presidential candidate by choosing the vice president based on geographic considerations. Presidential candidates may also *balance the ticket* in terms of religion, gender, or ethnicity.

a U.S. senator or a state governor has been the usual road to the presidency. Holding past elective office shows that the person can be elected. He or she can win votes. It also means that the person has built up a network of political allies who will offer support.

Second, a candidate must have a large "campaign chest." This means that the person must be able to raise millions of dollars to run for the presidency.

Third, a candidate must hold views that attract the majority of voters. Moderates tend to be elected over very liberal or very conservative candidates. A **liberal** believes that the federal government should expand its role by actively promoting programs such as health care and equal opportunity. A **conservative** believes that the federal government should limit its role in social and economic programs. A **moderate's** views are somewhere in between.

Qualifications, Term, and Salary of President

Categories	President
Qualifications	• Be a native-born citizen of the United States • Be at least thirty-five years old • Have lived in the United States for at least 14 years
Term of Office	• Possible two terms of four years each • A vice president who steps into the presidency and serves two years or less of the president's term may be elected for two full terms of four years each. (Twenty-second Amendment)
Salary and Benefits	• $400,000 in salary • $100,000 travel allowance • $50,000 expense allowance • Free health care • Living rent-free in the White House • Retirement pension
Privileges	• Use of *Air Force One* (the presidential airplane) • Use of Camp David (the presidential retreat) • Use of other aircraft, including helicopters, and land vehicles

stop and think

With a partner, create a table with two columns. Label the columns "Qualifications" and "Why Important." Label the rows "Formal Qualifications" and "Informal Qualifications." Fill in the qualifications for president. Then discuss with a partner why each of the qualifications is important. In the second column, write a sentence to explain your reasons.

Picturing Government

Democrat Geraldine Ferraro, shown in the photograph on page 154, was the first woman nominated by a major party as a vice-presidential candidate. Ferraro, former vice president Walter Mondale's running mate, capitalized on both her record in the House of Representatives as an advocate for women and on her status as the daughter of an Italian immigrant.

Table Extension

Have students use library resources or the Internet to find out the average salary and benefits of CEOs at major corporations. Ask them how it compares to the president's salary and benefits.

Stop and Think

Students' tables should contain information from the text and from the table. Ideas about the relative importance of each qualification and the explanations will vary.

Extensions

1 A few women have chosen to run for president, two of them before women even had the right to vote. Assign interested students one of the following women: Victoria Woodhull, Belva Ann Lockwood, Margaret Chase Smith, Shirley Chisholm, or Patricia Schroeder. Ask them to use library resources or the Internet to find out about the political careers and presidential candidacies of these women. Have them present their findings to the class by using the Student Presentation Builder on the student CD.

2 The first modern female head of state became the president of Mongolia in 1953. In each decade since, the number of women presidents and prime ministers has increased, covering every major region of the globe. About 20 percent of these women have been a relative of a prominent political figure. Invite students to use library resources or the Internet to find out about these modern heads of state. You may wish to suggest more familiar names such as Margaret Thatcher, Golda Meir, or Corazon Aquino. Challenge students to find a modern woman head of state for each continent.

Picturing Government

The photograph at the top left of page 156 shows the home of the vice president at the Naval Observatory. Built in 1893 as the residence for the superintendent of the Naval Observatory, it was used by the chief of naval operations from 1929 until 1974. In that year, Congress made it the official residence of the vice president. However, three years passed before Walter Mondale became the first vice president to occupy the home.

Picturing Government

In the 1973 photograph at the bottom of page 156, Gerald Ford is shown being sworn in as vice president, while his wife, Speaker of the House Carl Albert, President Pro Tempore James O. Eastland, and President Richard Nixon look on. Less than a year later, Ford would become president in the wake of Nixon's resignation.

The vice president lives at the Naval Observatory in Washington, D.C.

The Job of Vice President

People often wonder what the vice president does. The answer depends on the president. The Constitution lists only two duties for the vice president. According to Article I, Section 3, Clause 4, the vice president presides over the Senate and votes only when needed to break a tie. The Twenty-fifth Amendment also defines another role for the vice president, described on page 157.

Until the presidency of Dwight Eisenhower in the 1950s, vice presidents had few responsibilities. Their role was to **balance the ticket** at election time. Suppose a presidential candidate was from a Northeastern industrial state. A running mate from a Midwestern farm state may have been selected.

Since the 1950s, however, vice presidents have been given more duties. For example, Vice President Al Gore was given the job by President Bill Clinton of reducing the number of federal employees. President George W. Bush asked Vice President Dick Cheney to put together a new energy policy. Both vice presidents served as trusted advisers to their presidents.

Presidential Succession

Representative Gerald Ford was sworn in as vice president in December 1973, after the resignation of Spiro Agnew.

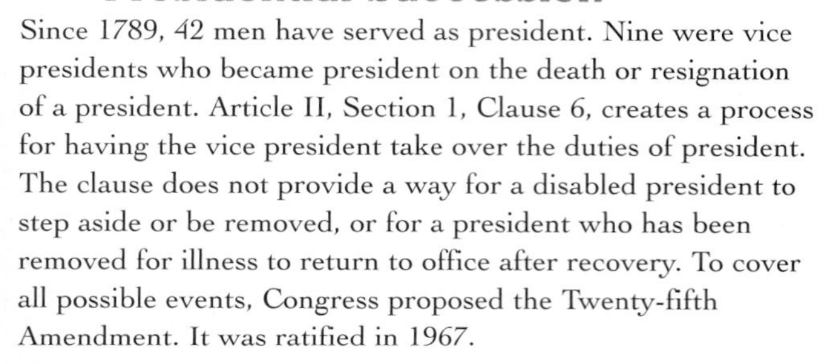

Since 1789, 42 men have served as president. Nine were vice presidents who became president on the death or resignation of a president. Article II, Section 1, Clause 6, creates a process for having the vice president take over the duties of president. The clause does not provide a way for a disabled president to step aside or be removed, or for a president who has been removed for illness to return to office after recovery. To cover all possible events, Congress proposed the Twenty-fifth Amendment. It was ratified in 1967.

First, the amendment clears up the language of Article II. The amendment clearly states what happens if the president dies, resigns, or is removed from office. The vice president becomes president.

Second, the amendment also states what happens if a vice president dies, resigns, or is removed from office. The president selects a replacement. A majority of both the Senate and the House of Representatives must approve the person.

Extension

A number of Hollywood films have dealt with the challenges of the presidency, some seriously, some humorously. Have students interested in film choose two films, one from each perspective, and watch them both. Then have them act as a reviewer to explain to the class what seemed truthful and what stretched the facts.

In 1973, President Richard Nixon had to replace his vice president, Spiro Agnew, who had resigned because of criminal charges. Nixon nominated Gerald Ford, and Congress approved him. In 1974, President Ford had to replace himself. He had become president when President Nixon resigned because of the Watergate scandal. President Ford nominated Nelson Rockefeller, and Congress approved him. This was the only time in U.S. history that neither the president nor vice president was elected to office.

Vice President George H. W. Bush temporarily assumed the responsibilities of president after the failed assassination attempt on President Ronald Reagan in 1981.

Third, the Twenty-fifth Amendment deals with replacing a president who is unable to carry out presidential duties. The president must notify the president pro tempore of the Senate and the Speaker of the House in writing. The vice president then becomes acting president. When the president is again able to carry out the duties of the office, notification must be sent to the president pro tem and the Speaker in writing. The vice president then gives up the duties as acting president.

The amendment also states what happens if the president is unable to notify Congress. The vice president and either a majority of the heads of the executive departments or a majority of Congress must notify Congress in writing. The president once again takes up the duties of the office when a written message is sent indicating that the disability is no longer an issue.

If both the president and vice president are unable to carry out their duties, then the Succession Act of 1947 applies. The Speaker of the House is next in line to become president. If the Speaker is unable, the president pro tem of the Senate takes over. The table on page 159 lists the further order of presidential succession.

Putting It All Together

Imagine that a public figure whom you admire has just been nominated to run for president. In your notebook, write him or her an e-mail that lists the qualifications of the person he or she should look for in a vice-presidential running mate. Explain why each qualification is important.

Picturing Government

The photograph on page 157 was taken at the scene of the 1981 assassination attempt on Ronald Reagan in Washington, D.C. Reagan's life was saved due to quick action by the Secret Service and prompt medical attention. He joked with hospital staff, "If I had had this much attention in Hollywood, I'd have stayed there."

Putting It All Together

Students' lists of vice-presidential qualifications will vary but may mention the need to balance the ticket.

Lesson Summary
George Washington began the practice of consulting a cabinet of advisers composed of heads of various departments. In appointing heads of these departments, who must be approved by Congress, the president considers urban/rural, gender, and ethnic balances; experience in the area; and executive background; as well as the desires of various interest groups. Cabinet members run the departments they head and advise the president. The inner cabinet is made up of four main departments: Defense, State, Treasury, and Justice.

Lesson Objective
Students will learn about the advisory function of the cabinet.

Focus Your Reading Answers

1 The president's cabinet is made up of the vice president, the heads of the executive departments, and top officials representing various departments within the Executive Office of the President.

2 Heads of executive departments must be confirmed by the Senate. They should be experienced in the work of the department. They should also have experience managing a large organization. They must also be responsive to the associated interest groups.

3 The roles of the cabinet are to run the departments they head and to advise the president.

LESSON 2

The Cabinet as Advisers

Thinking on Your Own

Suppose you have just been elected president. One of your first jobs is to name people to run the executive departments. What qualifications would you want in your department heads? Discuss this question with a partner. Together, come up with two or three qualifications and list them in your notebook.

focus your reading

Who makes up the president's cabinet?

What qualifications do heads of executive departments need to have?

What are the roles of the cabinet?

words to know

cabinet — inner cabinet

Voters elect a president to lead the nation and manage the federal government. However, he or she does not do these jobs alone. Once a candidate is elected, people are appointed to run the executive departments. The Constitution has only one mention of the relationship between the president and the heads of executive departments. Article II, Section 2, Clause 1, states that the president

> . . . may require the opinion, in writing, of the principal officer in each of the executive departments, upon any subject relating to the duties of the respective offices . . .

However, the heads of executive departments play an active role in government decision-making.

Frances Perkins, the first female member of a president's cabinet, served as secretary of labor from 1933–1945.

The Cabinet

Since George Washington, every president has had a **cabinet**. These people advise the president and help set policy for the nation. In Washington's time, the heads of the executive departments made up his cabinet. In modern times, the president's cabinet also includes the vice president and several other top officials. These other officials are part of the Executive Office of the President, which you will read about in Lesson 3.

Words to Know
Discuss each of the vocabulary terms with students.

The *cabinet* is a group of departments to advise the president and help set national policy. George Washington began the practice of having a *cabinet*. The *inner cabinet* is made up of four major departments: Defense, State, Treasury, and Justice. Members of the *inner cabinet* meet with the president regularly.

Being named to head an executive department is a great honor. However, not everyone accepts. These jobs are very stressful and not very high-paying. If a person accepts, he or she must be confirmed by the Senate.

The person must appear before the Senate committee that deals with the department the person will run. Usually, the hearing is friendly, and the committee sends the nominee's name to the full Senate for approval. However, sometimes a person's past actions may raise issues among committee members. Questioning may become heated. However, in the end, committees usually send the person's name to the full Senate.

Selecting the Heads of Departments

The president weighs a number of factors in deciding whom to appoint to lead executive departments. First, the person should have experience with the work of the department. For example, the head of the agriculture department should have firsthand knowledge of the issues involved in modern farming. Second, the person should have experience managing large organizations. The executive departments have thousands of workers and budgets in the billions of dollars. For this reason, presidents often choose successful business executives.

Cabinet-Level Officials

Heads of Executive Departments
Secretary of State
Secretary of the Treasury
Secretary of Defense
Attorney General (Justice Department)
Secretary of the Interior
Secretary of Agriculture
Secretary of Commerce
Secretary of Labor
Secretary of Health and Human Services
Secretary of Transportation
Secretary of Energy
Secretary of Housing and Urban Development
Secretary of Education
Secretary of Veterans Affairs
Secretary of Homeland Security

Other Cabinet Members
Vice President
White House Chief of Staff
Director, Office of Management and Budget
Director, Environmental Protection Agency
United States Trade Representative
Director, Office of National Drug Control Policy

The order shown here is the order of succession named in the Twenty-fifth Amendment.

Table Extension

Challenge students to identify the jurisdiction of each of the departments. You may wish to pose questions to students, using various situations that would apply to the departments. For example, to the answer "Regulates shipping trucks that cross state lines," a student would correctly respond, "What is the Department of Commerce?"

Extension

Ask students to use library resources or the Internet to find out about recent Senate challenges to presidential appointments. What objections did senators raise? What was the outcome of the challenges?

Picturing Government

The photograph on page 158 shows the first female cabinet member, Frances Perkins. Franklin D. Roosevelt appointed her secretary of labor in 1933; she served one of the longest terms of any of his appointees, from 1933 until two months after his death in 1945. As governor of New York, Roosevelt had appointed her state industrial commissioner in 1929. Perkins helped to draft the Social Security Act and pushed for unemployment compensation, a limit to labor by children under sixteen, a maximum hourly work week, minimum wage, and the creation of the Civilian Conservation Corps.

Picturing Government

Pictured on page 160 are four people who broke new ground in the cabinet. Robert C. Weaver led the newly created Department of Housing and Urban Development when it began in 1966. He was the first African American appointed to a cabinet post. In 1997, Madeline K. Albright became the first female secretary of state. Formerly, she had been a representative to the United Nations and a member of President Clinton's National Security Council. Secretary of Labor Elaine L. Chao took office in 2001 as the first Asian-American cabinet member. Chao and her family immigrated to the United States when she was eight. Chao formerly served as director of the Peace Corps and president of United Way. The first Hispanic cabinet member was Lauro F. Cavazos, who was secretary of education under Ronald Reagan. Cavazos, a sixth-generation Texan, was recognized as an expert in both education and medicine.

Robert Weaver (left), the first African-American member of a president's cabinet, served as secretary of housing and urban development in the administration of President Lyndon Johnson. Madeline K. Albright (second from left), the first woman to serve as secretary of state, was appointed by President Bill Clinton. Elaine Chao (second from right), secretary of labor during the George W. Bush administration, is the first Asian American to serve in a president's cabinet. President Ronald Reagan appointed Lauro F. Cavazos (right) as secretary of education, the first Hispanic to serve in a president's cabinet.

Third, the president has to consider interest groups. Interest groups often play important roles in electing candidates to office. They expect their candidates, once elected, to be responsive to their interests. Suppose the airline industry has helped to elect the president. They then expect the president to appoint someone to the Department of Commerce who will help the airlines.

Fourth, the president also tries to balance the members of the cabinet. He tries to select people from different parts of the country and from urban and rural backgrounds. Geographic balance helps ensure that the concerns of all regions are heard.

Gender and ethnic balance are also important. Since the 1960s, presidents have become more aware of balancing ethnic backgrounds and gender.

The Role of the Cabinet

Cabinet members who are heads of executive departments have two duties. One is to run the departments they head. The other is to act as adviser to the president. However, presidents have not always called on their cabinets for advice.

Very strong presidents have tended to tell their cabinets what to do. Abraham Lincoln and Lyndon Johnson, for example, set national policy and expected their cabinets to carry it out.

Later presidents have used the experience of their cabinets to help shape policy. Both George H. W. Bush and Bill Clinton consulted their cabinets regularly. These two presidents would put ideas on the table and ask for cabinet members' opinions.

Extension

Ask students to use library resources or the Internet to find out the current balance of gender and ethnicities in the cabinet.

stop and think

Review the paragraph that you wrote in Thinking on Your Own. How do your ideas match what actual presidents look for in department heads? Discuss the similarities and differences with a partner. Revise your paragraph to include at least two qualifications that an actual president considers. If your ideas match, then revise your paragraph to add another qualification from the president's list.

Even when presidents rarely consult their full cabinets, they do listen to certain cabinet members. These are generally the heads of the four main departments: Defense, State, Treasury, and Justice. They make up what is called the **inner cabinet**. These department heads meet regularly one-on-one with the president. The secretaries of other departments tend to meet with the president only in large cabinet meetings. Some presidents call full cabinet meetings weekly, and some rarely call them at all.

A president wants a department head who will be loyal. Once they take office, however, department heads may find this difficult. Members of their own departments, members of Congress, and special interest groups compete for their loyalty. All three groups have their own ideas about what the secretary should do. Their ideas may not be the same as the president's. This can set up tension between the secretary and the president.

The White House staff and members of the Executive Office of the President may also become close advisers to presidents. They usually are intensely loyal to the chief executives they serve. The president may find them more trustworthy than a cabinet member who is trying to advance his or her own interests. Most presidents place a high value on loyalty and trust.

Putting It All Together

Work with a partner. Draw a small circle inside a larger circle. Then draw a bigger circle around these two. Label the smallest circle "President." In the middle circle, write the names of the executive departments that make up the president's inner cabinet. Also in the middle circle, include the offices in the cabinet that are not heads of executive departments. In the outer circle, write the names of the other executive departments.

Stop and Think

Students' paragraphs and revisions will vary but should include at least two qualifications that a president would consider in appointing a department head.

Putting It All Together

Students' drawings should show three circles, with the president in the smallest one. The next circle should show the inner cabinet: departments of Defense, State, Treasury, and Justice. The outermost circle should contain the names of the other executive departments, as listed in the table on page 159.

Lesson Summary

Presidents may also seek advice from members of the Executive Office of the President (EOP) or White House Office staffs. These people advise the president, implement the president's ideas, and help run the executive branch. In 1939, Congress created the EOP, which has grown and changed to meet the needs of the changing nation. The Council of Economic Advisers, the Office of Management and Budget (OMB), and the National Security Council are three of the most important agencies in the EOP. The White House Office includes the president's personal advisers and key staff members. These jobs are presidential appointments that the Senate doesn't need to confirm. Three of the most important members of the White House staff are the press secretary, the chief of staff, and the White House counsel.

Lesson Objective

Students will learn about the work of the Executive Office of the President and White House Office.

Focus Your Reading Answers

1 The purpose of the Executive Office of the President is to help the president oversee the executive branch and to coordinate efforts to address issues.

2 The Executive Office of the President is made up of councils, boards, and offices. The White House Office includes the president's key staff and personal advisers. People in the White House Office are appointed by the president and do not need Senate confirmation.

LESSON 3

The Executive Office and the White House Staff

Thinking on Your Own

What personal qualities do you think an adviser to the president should have? Discuss this question with a partner and list at least three personal qualities in your notebook.

focus your reading

What is the purpose of the Executive Office of the President?

What is the difference between the Executive Office of the President and the White House Office?

words to know

Executive Office of the President

White House Office

briefings

The main constitutional job of the president is to oversee the executive branch. Today, this is an enormous task. The executive branch has over 2.7 million civilian employees in 15 departments and other agencies and commissions. Two offices have evolved to help the president with this job. They are the **Executive Office of the President** (EOP) and the **White House Office**.

In general, the people who work in the EOP and the White House Office have three main goals. First, they offer

The West Wing houses the offices of the executive branch.

Words to Know

Discuss each of the vocabulary terms with students.

The *Executive Office of the President* is made up of agencies and individuals who directly assist the president. Congress created the *Executive Office of the President* in 1939. The *White House Office* is a group of trusted advisers the president selects.

Briefings are the short reports given to members of the press. During a crisis, the press secretary may issue hourly *briefings*.

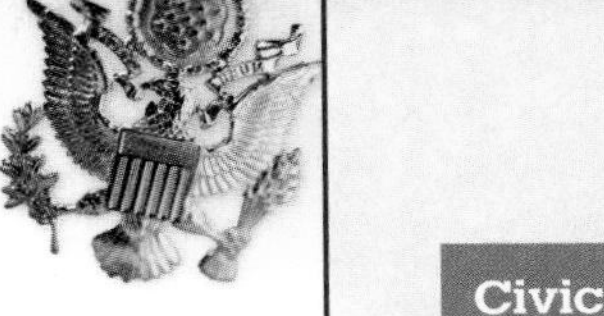

advice and information to help the president make decisions. They usually have special expertise in the areas they work in. For example, the people in the Office of Management and Budget (OMB) have financial and budgeting experience.

Second, members of the EOP and White House Office help carry out the president's ideas. For example, offices such as that of the U.S. Trade Representative may write bills for Congress to consider. An office such as the Environmental Protection Agency may actually carry out laws. EOP and White House staff members also push members of Congress to act on the president's proposals.

Third, the EOP and White House Office help the president to manage the executive branch. The president's advisers and staff members keep in touch with the executive departments, agencies, and commissions. They pass information back and forth. In this way, the president knows what is going on and the executive branch knows what the president expects.

Civics Today Extension

The top left photograph on page 163 shows the interior of the Hoover National Historic Site. The bottom left photograph is the exterior of the William Jefferson Clinton Presidential Library. The presidential libraries began in 1939 during Franklin D. Roosevelt's presidency. Concerned that many papers and records from previous administrations had been lost, ruined due to poor storage, or sold at a profit, Roosevelt established a public depository for preserving presidential records. In 1955, Congress passed the Presidential Libraries Act, making FDR's decision official. The Presidential Records Act of 1978 establishes that the documents that record the ceremonial, constitutional, or statutory duties of the president are United States government property. The archivist of the United States assumes custody of those documents when the president leaves office.

Presidential Libraries

Every president since Herbert Hoover has built a library to house his presidential papers. Actually, the 12 presidential libraries and the Nixon Presidential Materials Project maintain much more than documents. Each building is both a museum and a library.

The interior of President Herbert Hoover's Presidential Library (top) and President Bill Clinton's Presidential Library (bottom)

Together, they store 400 million pages in print or electronic form. There are also close to 10 million photographs; 15 million feet of movie film; nearly 100,000 hours of material on discs, audiotapes, and videotapes; and about 500,000 objects. Among the objects are presidential family photos as well as gifts given to presidents by leaders of other nations.

The documents of each administration, however, are the most valuable part of each library. They provide historians with firsthand accounts of the thinking behind policy decisions.

Each library is built with private contributions. Each library must also set up a fund to help maintain the library. The rest of the money comes from the federal government.

Extensions

1 Presidential libraries are located throughout the nation. Challenge students to find out where each library is located and to pinpoint them on a United States map.

2 Obtain a copy of the current budget from your library to show students the size of the document. Explore the various subcategories of the budget; invite students to make comparisons to a personal budget.

Table Extension

Have students work in pairs and choose one office to research. After pairs have completed their research, have them use posters to present their findings to the class.

Some Offices Within the Executive Office of the President

Office	Responsibility
Council of Economic Advisers	• Helps the president decide on economic policy for the nation • Is the president's major source of information on the health of the economy • Predicts future economic growth • Suggests solutions to economic problems such as high unemployment • Helps write the annual *Economic Report of the President*
Council on Environmental Quality	• Advises the president on environmental issues • Works with the Environmental Protection Agency and the Interior, Energy, and Agriculture Departments to ensure that environmental policies are carried out
Domestic Policy Council	• Aids the president in developing and carrying out long-range policies in all areas that are not concerned with foreign affairs; for example, an energy policy for the nation
National Economic Council	• Helps carry out long-range economic policies
National Security Council	• Advises the president on foreign policy issues that affect the nation's security • Chaired by the president • Includes the vice president and Secretaries of State and Defense, as well as other advisers • Managed by the National Security Adviser
Office of Administration	• Handles the day-to-day needs of the other EOP groups such as clerical help and library services
Office of Faith-Based and Community Initiatives	• Oversees efforts to expand the work of religious and other private groups working to fight drug abuse, illiteracy, and similar problems of society
Office of Management and Budget	• Reviews budgets submitted by each executive department and other agencies and commissions • Recommends to the president changes in the budgets of executive departments, agencies, and commissions • Uses information from all departments, agencies, and commissions and prepares the federal budget that the president sends to Congress each year • Reviews how the funds in the approved budget are used during the year • Reviews all bills proposed by executive departments before they are sent to Congress to ensure they agree with the president's policies
Office of National AIDS Policy	• Develops and advises on the nation's policy and programs for the prevention and potential cure of HIV-AIDS
Office of National Drug Control Policy	• Develops long-range policies on the control of illegal drugs
Office of Science and Technology Policy	• Advises the president on scientific, engineering, and technology issues
Office of the United States Trade Representative	• Negotiates trade agreements with other nations
President's Critical Infrastructure Protection Board	• Advises the president on security issues related to cyberspace
President's Foreign Intelligence Advisory Board	• Advises the president on how effective the intelligence, or spy, agencies are in collecting information to keep the nation secure from enemies

Executive Office of the President

Congress created the Executive Office of the President (EOP) in 1939 to provide the president the staff needed to oversee the executive branch. It has grown over time, as every president adds offices, councils, and boards. A president changes the EOP to meet changes in the nation and to provide information necessary to perform the duties of president. For example, before the late 1980s there was no reason to have an Office on National AIDS Policy. AIDS was not an issue.

As the nation has grown, its problems have become more complex. Presidents must make decisions about how to deal with these very complex issues. As a result, the president must be able to ask the advice of people who have experience with these issues. For example, the growth of the World Wide Web resulted in the creation of the President's Critical Infrastructure Protection Board. This board deals with dangers to the nation's security from cyberspace.

stop and think

For which group within the EOP would you like to work? Why? List at least four reasons why you want to work for that group. Share your list with a partner. Ask your partner how you could make your ideas clearer.

Offices within the EOP coordinate federal efforts to address issues. For example, the nation's anti-drug program is managed by 50 agencies. The Office of National Drug Control Policy was created to oversee the activities of these agencies. The office is supposed to make sure that there are no overlaps among the agencies' programs.

Three of the most important agencies in the EOP are the Council of Economic Advisers, the National Security Council, and the Office of Management and Budget (OMB). The OMB is the largest group within the EOP.

With each new president, offices, councils, boards, and agencies within the EOP may change. Even during a president's term, he or she may add or do away with a group within the EOP.

The White House Office

The White House Office is part of the Executive Office of the President. It includes the president's key staff and personal advisers. They have a great deal of influence in shaping policies for the nation. They decide who sees the president. They also decide which of the thousands of reports that come from the executive departments to send to the president.

Stop and Think

Students' reasons and lists will vary but should indicate four reasons for choosing one of the groups in the EOP.

Picturing Government

The photograph on page 166 shows the Oval Office. The rug with the presidential seal was new to the George W. Bush White House, arriving in December 2001. Have students use library resources or the Internet to find out about the various attempts to redecorate or otherwise beautify the White House or its grounds.

Extension

Some students may be interested in finding out what size of staff is required to keep the White House clean and its grounds cared for, given the number of daily visitors. Work with the class to create a list of domestic tasks that would have to be done, then challenge students to find out who does them at the White House. Is there, for example, a White House window washer? How many gardeners care for the grounds?

The Oval Office is the official office of the president of the United States.

The president appoints the main members of the White House Office. Unlike the heads of departments and some EOP members, none of the White House staff need to be confirmed by the Senate. Many of the top White House staff have worked with the president for years in previous jobs or as friends and unpaid advisers.

Among the most important positions are the chief of staff, White House counsel, and the press secretary. The chief of staff manages the White House Office. The White House counsel provides legal advice to the president on policy. The press secretary handles daily, and sometimes hourly, **briefings** to the reporters who follow the actions of the president.

Putting It All Together

With a partner, write a summary of this lesson. Be sure to include only the most important ideas. Do not include your own opinions.

Putting It All Together

Students' summaries will vary but should include major points from the lesson. See the summary at the beginning of the TE chapter on page 154 for a sample.

Research Resources

Below is a list of reference books and Web sites that relate to the issues covered in this chapter. Students may wish to use these to further their research on ideas in the preceding lessons. Web site addresses may change over time. Use keyword searching on a major search engine to locate sites.

Reference Books:

William Degregorio. *Complete Book of U.S. Presidents: From George Washington to George W. Bush*. 5th edition. Gramercy, 1997.

Michael Nelson. *The Presidency A to Z*. CQ Press, 2003.

David Rubel. *Scholastic Encyclopedia of the Presidents and Their Times*. Scholastic, 2005.

Participate in Government

Be a Poll Watcher

A poll watcher is called a poll checker in some states. *Poll* is another word for ballot, or vote. Poll watchers monitor, or check, what goes on at the polling place. They are volunteers working for a political party. Their job is to make sure that anyone from their party who is registered to vote is allowed to vote. They also make sure that no one votes more than once.

Poll watchers sit near the check-in table with election workers. A voter comes to the table to sign in. An election worker calls out the voter's name. The poll checkers read down their lists. If the voter is a Republican, the Republican poll watcher checks off his or her name. If the voter is a Democrat, the Democratic poll watcher checks it off.

Suppose there is a problem. A voter is newly registered. By accident, his or her name is not yet in the registration book. The poll watcher watches to make sure that the voter is allowed to cast a provisional ballot.

Poll watchers may not wear any political buttons or signs. They may not talk about a candidate while on duty. However, they may carry signs and ask voters to vote for their candidate outside the polling place.

- Check the phone book for the number of your local or county political party committee. Call and ask what the qualifications are to be a poll watcher.
- Visit your local candidates' offices.

Picturing Government

The photograph on page 167 depicts a woman at the polls on Election Day, 2004, showing a sample ballot while another woman fills out a voter form.

Participate in Government

1 Have interested students use library resources or the Internet to find out more about the role of poll watchers in the 2004 presidential election. Allow time for them to report their findings to the class.

2 You may wish to invite someone from the local branch of the League of Women Voters or a related organization to discuss the local use of poll watchers.

Research Resources, continued

Web Sites:

The White House has its own searchable site. It includes a video tour of the Oval Office and videos of press briefings, as well as information about the current cabinet and past presidents. Also included are special pages on everything from baseball and the executive pastry chef to holidays and inaugural outfits.

The American Presidents site features life portraits of American presidents to 1999, as a companion to a C-SPAN video program, which won a Peabody Award. It includes links to birthplaces, gravesites, and inaugural addresses, as well as highlights of the administration and little-known facts. There are also links to further biographical information and to quotations and documents.

Skill Builder

1 I. The Cabinet as Advisers
   A. The Cabinet
      1. Includes heads of departments, the vice president, and other officials
      2. Senate approval required
   B. Selecting the Heads of Departments
      1. Needs experience in the field and in running large organizations
      2. Needs to be responsive to interest groups
   C. The Role of the Cabinet
      1. Two roles are head departments and advise president
      2. Inner cabinet consists of heads of four main departments

2 Students' outlines and final essays will vary, but outlines should follow the correct form given.

Classroom Discussion

Discuss with students some of the broader topics covered in this chapter.

- How could the experience of recent vice presidents enlarge the impact of that office on the nation?
- Are all roles of the president equally valuable? Which do students view as most important and why?
- Should the Senate be allowed to refuse or filibuster the president's nominees for important posts?

Skill Builder

Outline Information

An outline is an organized listing of information. Only the most important information about a topic is presented. The form for an outline is always a combination of Roman and Arabic numerals and capital and small letters.

I. Roman numerals for main ideas
   A. Capital letters for important details
      1. Arabic numerals for supporting details
         a. Small letters for less important details

Use Roman numerals for the biggest ideas—the main ideas. Use capital letters, Arabic numerals, and small letters as the information gets more detailed. If the information is not too detailed, you might need only capital letters or capital letters and Arabic numerals.

Outlines are useful for studying and for writing. Outlining a lesson or chapter helps to focus on just the important information to study. Outlining before writing an assignment helps to organize main ideas and supporting details.

A partial outline for Lesson 1 looks like this:

I. The Presidency
   A. Qualifications
      1. Native-born
      2. At least thirty-five years old
   B. Campaign chest
II. The Job of Vice President

Complete these activities.

1 Outline Lesson 2 to help you study the information.

2 Write an essay of at least three paragraphs to describe how cabinet members are chosen and what cabinet members do. Before you write, plan your writing by creating an outline. Use one Roman numeral for each paragraph. Add information with capital letters and Arabic numerals to help you fill out each paragraph.

Research Resources

Below is a list of books that relate to the issues covered in this chapter. The numbers in parentheses indicate the related Thematic Strands of the National Council for the Social Studies (NCSS).

Ilene Cooper. *Jack: The Early Years of John F. Kennedy*. Dutton Children's Books, 2003. (IV, VI, X)

Betsey Harvey Kraft. *Theodore Roosevelt: Champion of the American Spirit*. Clarion Books, 2003. (IV, VI, X)

Chapter

9 THE POWERS OF THE PRESIDENCY

Getting Focused

Skim this chapter to predict what you will be learning.

- **Read the lesson titles and subheadings.**
- **Look at the illustrations and read the captions.**
- **Examine the table.**
- **Review the vocabulary words and terms.**

As you learned from skimming this chapter, the president has many responsibilities. In your notebook, list the five duties of a president that you consider to be the most important.

President George W. Bush with Secretary of State Condoleezza Rice, in the oval office.

Pre-Reading Discussion

1 Discuss with students, based on their general knowledge, how the current president differs from what they know of earlier famous presidents, such as George Washington, Abraham Lincoln, or Franklin Roosevelt. Do they think that the presidency has become more or less powerful?

2 Ask students to form small groups and discuss some of the potential difficulties and dangers a president and the First Family might face.

Related Transparencies

T-7 Presidential Influence

T-18 Three-Column Chart

T-20 Concept Web

Key Blacklines

Primary Source—The President as Commander in Chief

CD Extension

Encourage students to use the reading comprehension, vocabulary reinforcement, and other activities on the student CD.

Getting Focused

Students' choices of important duties will vary. After students have made their lists, you may wish to hold a classroom vote on the most important duties or allow students to debate their answers.

Picturing Government

The photograph on page 169 shows President George W. Bush making a call to Prime Minister Jose Maria Aznar of Spain to discuss a United Nations vote on Iraq. Shown at the right is Condoleezza Rice, then national security adviser and later secretary of state.

Lesson Summary

According to the Constitution, the president has legislative, military, diplomatic, judicial, and executive powers. Informal sources of presidential power include control over the federal government, times of national crises, and mandates for or against policies. Congress, the federal courts, the federal bureaucracy, and public opinion each limit the president's power.

Lesson Objective

Students will learn about the powers of the president and limits to those powers.

Focus Your Reading Answers

1 The Constitution grants the president legislative, military, diplomatic, judicial, and executive powers.

2 Informal sources of presidential power include exercising control over the federal government. In the process, presidents expand the role through the use of inherent power. National crises are another time when presidents gain more power. A mandate from the people is a third source of informal presidential power.

3 The president's power is limited through Congress, the federal courts, the federal bureaucracy, and public opinion.

LESSON 1

Executive Powers

Thinking on Your Own

Name two or three U.S. presidents who are remembered as powerful chief executives. What did they do to expand the powers of the presidency? List as many facts as you can in your notebook about each president.

focus your reading

What powers does the Constitution give the president?

What are the informal sources of presidential power?

How is the president's power limited?

words to know

execute

recess appointment

mandate

The Framers could not have imagined the many issues that a modern president deals with, such as terrorism, the Internet, and relations with more than 190 other nations. However, the Framers were very wise. Their idea for the presidency allows for growth and change as the nation grows and changes.

Constitutional Source of Power

Article II of the U.S. Constitution creates the executive branch and the office of president. The first job of the president is to run the executive department. This is part of the oath of office that the president takes at his inauguration. He promises to "faithfully execute the office of president." **Execute** in this context means to carry out, or perform, the duties of president.

Section 2 of Article II lists the powers of the president. Power comes with duties, and Section 3 lists the president's duties. The president's powers and duties can be grouped as executive, military, diplomatic, legislative, and judicial. That is, the president appoints department heads, ambassadors, and federal judges; is commander in chief; and issues pardons. The president's powers and duties are discussed in Chapter 3.

President Nixon's 1972 visit to China represents the foreign policy powers of the presidency.

Words to Know

Introduce each of the following vocabulary terms to students.

To *execute* is to perform or to carry out. The president promises to *execute* the duties of the office.

If the president appoints someone to office when the Senate is not in session, it is a *recess appointment*. A *recess appointment* lasts only until the end of the next session of Congress.

Strong support from the people is called a *mandate*. A *mandate* is a source of presidential power.

The checks and balances written into the Constitution limit the president's powers. For example, his power to appoint federal judges and department heads is checked by the Senate. The Senate has the power to approve or reject his appointments. Presidents can ignore the Senate by making **recess appointments** when that body is not in session. These appointments last only until the end of Congress's next session. The Senate still has the last word.

Informal Sources of Power

Despite the limited powers granted by the Constitution, presidents have found ways to increase the powers of the office. They have expanded its inherent, or informal, powers. As a result, the presidency is more powerful today than it was in the days of George Washington.

One reason for this increase in power is the way presidents do their job. Strong presidents exercise firm control over the federal government. In exercising control, they expand what the presidency can do. For example, Thomas Jefferson agreed to buy the Louisiana Territory from France. The Constitution does not state that the president—or the nation—has the power to add territory.

However, Jefferson and his advisers found an inherent power in the Constitution. Inherent power is power that the president has because he is the president. Using inherent power, Jefferson bought the Louisiana Territory. Once Jefferson set the pattern, later presidents acquired more territory. They added the rest of the continental United States and also Alaska, Hawaii, Puerto Rico, Guam, and other territories.

Presidents have also gained power during times of national crises. In 1861, the federal government was not prepared for the Civil War. President Abraham Lincoln took it upon himself to expand the army and navy. He later asked Congress to approve his actions by passing the necessary laws. Franklin D. Roosevelt strengthened the presidency by taking bold action during the Great Depression.

stop and think

Create a concept map to show the sources of the president's powers. Draw a large circle in the center and label it "Sources of Power." Then add smaller circles as needed. Work with a partner. When you have finished your concept map, write a statement to explain the sources of the president's powers.

Stop and Think

Students' concept maps and statements will vary but should express the sources of presidential power. Possible answers include the Constitution, national crises, and popular mandates.

Extensions

1 During 2005, President George W. Bush used the Senate's August recess to appoint controversial nominee John Bolton to the position of ambassador to the United Nations. Have students use library resources or the Internet to find out the result of Bolton's appointment to the U.N.

2 Invite students to investigate the history of adding territory through the use of inherent powers. Ask them to work together in groups, with each group focusing on one of the locations mentioned in the text. Have them present their findings to the class by using the Student Presentation Builder on the student CD.

Picturing Government

President and Mrs. Nixon are shown in the photograph on page 170 during their trip to China in 1972. They are standing in front of the Great Wall of China with the Chinese premier at the time, Zhou Enlai. Nixon was the first U.S. president to visit China. Relations between the two nations had gradually begun to thaw after the Cold War. The game of table tennis (ping-pong) aided China's openness; the U.S. ping-pong team visited China before Nixon announced his mission to seek normalization of relations between the two countries.

Picturing Government

The 1981 photograph on page 172 shows then-president Ronald Reagan and his vice president, George H. W. Bush. After Reagan's two terms, Bush became president in 1988 but was defeated in his bid for reelection in 1992. He later became only the second president to see his son in the same office. (John Adams and John Quincy Adams were the other father-son pair.)

President Ronald Reagan and Vice President George H. W. Bush.

His White House staff wrote many of the bills that Congress passed to put people back to work.

The mandate of the people is the third, and probably the greatest, source of presidential power. A **mandate** is strong support from the people. In 1980, Ronald Reagan won 489 electoral votes, representing 44 states and 50 percent of the vote. He claimed a mandate from the people to put his ideas into practice.

Presidents use a variety of ways to get their ideas across to the public. They use televised speeches and interviews. They also give interviews to newspaper and magazine reporters. Presidents also send out the heads of executive departments to talk about presidential policies. The goal of all these actions is to keep up public support for the president's policies.

Limits on Presidential Powers

Congress, the federal courts, the federal bureaucracy, and public opinion all limit a president's power. The Senate has the power of "advice and consent" over presidential nominees. In fact, few nominees are ever rejected. It is a courtesy to allow the president to choose his own cabinet members. However, nominees for federal judgeships are sometimes rejected. This includes nominees for the Supreme Court.

As you read in Chapter 7, Congress may override a presidential veto and has the power of the purse. Congress decides on the federal budget each year. It may or may not fund programs at the amount that the president asks. Congress also has impeachment power over the president.

Federal courts have the power to rule on the constitutionality of presidential actions. The Landmark Case on page 173 describes an example.

Extension

Have students use library resources or the Internet to investigate controversial nominees of the Supreme Court, including Robert Bork in 1987 and Clarence Thomas in 1991. Allow time for students to report their findings to the class.

Public opinion can give the president a mandate to act, but it can also turn against a president. If people do not like a president's policies, it shows up in opinion polls. If presidents lose public support, getting Congress to pass their proposals can be difficult.

Landmark Supreme Court Case: Presidential Authority

***Youngstown Sheet and Tube Company* v. *Sawyer* (1952):** During the Korean War, steelworkers were threatening to strike. President Harry Truman believed a steel strike would harm the war effort. The president took over most of the nation's steel mills and had the military run them. He said the inherent powers of the presidency allowed him to act. The Supreme Court ruled against him.

Public opinion played a large role during the Vietnam war and influenced President Johnson's decision not to seek reelection.

Putting It All Together

Outline this lesson. Review outlining on page 168 if necessary. Share your outline with a partner. Ask your partner to check it for completeness. If you missed important information, revise your outline.

Supreme Court Case Extension

Truman could have used the Taft-Hartley Act to impose an 80-day cooling off period before a strike. However, Truman had opposed the passage of the act and refused to invoke it in 1952. The subsequent lawsuit was based not on the premise that the government had no right to seize property, but that the wrong branch of government had intervened. The steel company sued, for all practical purposes, on behalf of Congress, arguing that Truman had violated the doctrine of the separation of powers. The power of the presidency had greatly expanded during Franklin Roosevelt's four terms in office; this case was a means of restoring balance.

Picturing Government

The photograph on page 173, taken during a 1967 protest in Washington, D.C., highlights the unpopularity of United States involvement in Vietnam. Protesters angry over the escalating number of deaths in that country regularly greeted President Johnson with the chant "Hey, hey, LBJ, how many kids did you kill today?" Johnson's commitment to the war led to an approval rating of only 26 percent and ultimately led him not to seek reelection.

Putting It All Together

Students' outlines will vary. A sample is shown below.

I. Executive Powers
- A. Constitutional Source of Power
  1. Article II, Section 2
  2. Article II, Section 3
- B. Informal Sources of Power
  1. Use of inherent power
  2. National crises
  3. Mandate of the people
- C. Limits on Presidential Powers
  1. Congress
  2. Federal courts
  3. Federal bureaucracy
  4. Public opinion

LESSON 2

Roles and Duties of the President

Lesson Summary

The Constitution grants the president five roles: head of state, chief executive, chief legislator, chief diplomat, and commander in chief. In addition, the president is the nation's chief economic planner and the unofficial leader of his or her political party.

Lesson Objective

Students will learn about the official and unofficial roles and duties of the president.

Focus Your Reading Answers

1 The official constitutional duties of the president include serving as head of state, chief executive, chief legislator, chief diplomat, and commander in chief.

2 The two unofficial duties of the president are economic planner and head of his or her political party while in office.

Picturing Government

The photograph on page 174 portrays one of the president's ceremonial duties. From left to right, First Lady Laura and President George W. Bush, former presidents Bush and Clinton, and Secretary of State Condoleezza Rice pay their respects at a viewing of Pope John Paul II, who died in April 2005. Bush was the first U.S. president to attend the funeral of a pope.

Thinking on Your Own

Read the Ideas to Remember in this lesson. It lists the roles of the president. Create a table in your notebook with two columns. In the left column, write the seven roles of the president. As you study this lesson, fill in the right column. Write at least one fact about each role of the president, and name a president who was a model for that role.

focus your reading

What are the official constitutional duties of the president?

What are the unofficial duties of the president?

words to know

ceremonial duties

diplomat

executive order

partisan

Article II, Sections 1 and 2, of the U.S. Constitution describe the powers and duties of the president. He or she has five roles, or responsibilities, based on these powers and duties. They are: head of state, chief executive, chief legislator, chief diplomat, and commander in chief.

Anyone who has ever watched a presidential nominating convention knows that the president has a sixth role. He is the leader of his political party. Also, since Franklin Roosevelt, the president has been the chief economic planner for the nation. These two roles are not part of the president's constitutional powers and duties. They developed over time.

President George W. Bush and former Presidents Bush and Clinton attend the funeral of Pope John Paul II in 2005.

Constitutional Roles

Head of state: The president as the head of state represents the United States to the world and to the nation and performs certain **ceremonial duties**.

Words to Know

Discuss each of the following vocabulary terms with students.

Ceremonial duties are those that involve public appearances or hospitality to visiting dignitaries. One of the president's *ceremonial duties* is to lay a wreath at the tomb of the Unknown Soldier at Arlington National Cemetery on Veterans Day.

A *diplomat* is someone who represents the country in its dealings with other countries. The president is the chief *diplomat*.

An *executive order* is a regulation about how laws are to be carried out. To set up affirmative action programs, President Lyndon Johnson used an *executive order*.

Anyone who takes sides is *partisan*. Presidents must be cautious about *partisan* politics.

For example, on Veterans Day, the president lays a wreath at the tomb of the Unknown Soldier in Arlington National Cemetery. Welcoming leaders from other nations to the White House is another ceremonial duty.

Chief executive: The president is also the chief executive of the United States. It is the president's job to see that the government carries out the laws that Congress passes. The president must also see that decisions of the federal courts are put into effect.

Chief legislator: The president is also the chief legislator. In this role, the president proposes the annual budget and other legislation to Congress. The executive departments and the EOP actually write proposed laws. These are then sent to Congress, as described in Chapter 7.

Chief diplomat: A **diplomat** is a person who represents the nation in dealings with governments of other nations.

The Constitution gives the president the power to make treaties, or formal agreements, with other nations. However, the Senate has the power to approve or reject them. The president also has the power to make executive agreements. These are agreements between the president and the heads of other nations. However, the Senate does not have to approve them. This is one way that presidents get around a Senate that does not agree with their foreign policies.

The president as chief diplomat also has the power to recognize other nations. To recognize means to accept the legal existence of another nation. For example, Communists defeated the non-Communist government of China in 1949. They set up a new government and declared it the People's Republic of China (PRC). However, it was not until 1972 that President Nixon recognized the PRC as China's government.

Commander in chief: The president is commander in chief of the armed forces. This role allows the president to use the military to support foreign policy goals. For example, President George W. Bush believed that Saddam Hussein had a program to build weapons of mass destruction (WMD) in Iraq. To rid Iraq of the WMD and Hussein, he took the United States into war.

As chief legislator, President Johnson met with congressional officials (top). In his role as chief diplomat, President Clinton welcomed South African President Nelson Mandela to the White House (middle). President George W. Bush greeted the troops as commander in chief.

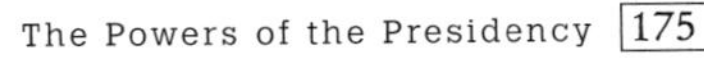

Picturing Government

The photographs on page 175 show various roles and duties of the president. The top photograph shows President Lyndon Johnson meeting with members of a "peace panel" he set up to advise him in 1964. The center photograph is of President Clinton and former president of South Africa Nelson Mandela. In the bottom photograph, President George W. Bush as commander in chief greets military personnel returning from war in Iraq at Fort Campbell.

Extension

Invite students to use library resources or the Internet to find out more about recent executive agreements that the current president has made with other nations.

Extension

President Harry Truman used executive orders to establish equality within the armed forces after Congress failed to include a ban against discrimination in the Selective Service Act of 1948. Truman set up the President's Committee on Equality of Treatment and Opportunity in the Armed Services. Their report, issued in 1947, coupled with the need for personnel in the Korean War, helped to end segregation and discrimination in the service. Through an executive order in 1948, Truman also banned discrimination in the hiring of federal employees.

Table Extension

Divide the class into five groups, assigning each group one of the areas of influence listed in the left column of the table. Ask each group to use library resources or the Internet to find examples, other than those given, of that influence at work in the current or recent administrations. Allow time for class presentations.

The president decides when and if the nation should go to war. The president also approves or rejects requests from the armed forces for funding. However, Congress also has a role. It alone has the power to declare war. Congress also must approve all funding requests. However, as you read in Chapter 6, presidents have involved the nation in undeclared wars many times. As a result, Congress passed the War Powers Act in 1973.

Presidential Influence

Influence in the Role of Chief Executive	
Executive Orders	• **Executive orders** are regulations about how laws are to be carried out. For example, President Lyndon Johnson used an executive order to set up affirmative action. The order spelled out how the federal government is to award contracts for federal building projects. An executive order has the "force of law." This means it must be obeyed the same way a law must be obeyed.
Appointment of Officials	• Presidents appoint executive department heads and another 2,200 top-level officials. A president chooses men and women who agree with his policies and will work to carry them out. • Presidents also appoint federal judges, including Supreme Court justices. This is an area where a president's views can greatly affect government policy. Modern Republican presidents tend to appoint judges with more conservative views. Some of the justices on the Supreme Court are strict constructionists, which you read about in Chapter 6. Democratic presidents tend to appoint judges with more liberal views.
Removal of Officials	• Executive department heads, top-level officials, and members of the EOP and the White House Office serve "at the pleasure of the president." This means that if they oppose the president, they may find themselves out of a job. President George W. Bush fired his first secretary of the treasury for opposing his tax cuts.
Influence in the Role of Chief Legislator	
Granting Political Favors	• Presidents use political favors to gain congressional support for their policies. For example, the president might agree to campaign for a senator in return for his or her vote on a program.
Veto Power	• Presidents can always use the veto against a bill they do not want to become law. However, the threat of a veto can work as well. Congress will delay a bill or revise it rather than have it vetoed. Overriding a president's veto is difficult.

stop and think

Which constitutional role of the president do you think is the most important? Review the table that you created. Review what you have read up to this point. Select four roles and list one reason why each role is important. Discuss your ideas with a partner.

Presidents have another kind of power besides the powers given to them by the Constitution. They have the power of influence. They can use favors and try to persuade, pressure, and encourage Congress and others to do what they want. The table on page 176 lists the kinds of influence that presidents have.

Unofficial Roles

The five roles that you just read about are based on the Constitution. Over time, the presidency has expanded to include two more roles.

The role of economic planner became important during Franklin Roosevelt's terms in office. The nation was deep in the Depression. President Roosevelt took control of economic planning to pull the nation out of the Depression. The president sends a report on the state of the economy to Congress each year. In addition, the president sends the annual federal budget to Congress.

ideas to remember

Official, constitutional duties and roles of the president

- head of state
- chief executive
- chief legislator
- chief diplomat
- commander in chief

Unofficial duties and roles of the president

- economic planner
- political party leader

The president is also the head of his political party while he is in office. As party leader, he appears at fund-raisers for the party and for candidates. He also campaigns for his party's candidates for public office.

A president has to walk a fine line between partisan politics and public policy. **Partisan** means "following a certain party." Presidents are supposed to represent all Americans, not just those who belong to their political party.

Putting It All Together

Play "What Role Am I?" with a partner. Write a definition of each of the president's seven roles. End each definition with the question "What role am I?" Take turns with your partner asking and answering questions. Use the information from your table to write questions.

Stop and Think

Students' views on the importance of executive roles and the reasons for their opinions will vary but should be supported.

Ideas to Remember Extension

Review the ideas listed, further explaining difficult vocabulary words. Have students create graphic organizers in their notebooks to help them visualize the duties and roles of the president.

Putting It All Together

Students' questions and answers may vary but should be based on the seven roles discussed on page 177.

Lesson Summary

Presidential leadership involves six qualities: an understanding of the American public's hopes and fears, an ability to communicate ideas and policies to the public, an understanding of the correct time to act, a willingness to accept new ideas and change plans, a willingness to compromise, and political courage. Presidents face the danger of isolation, because the president is surrounded by a small group of trusted advisers who may not give an accurate picture of public opinion.

Lesson Objective

Students will learn about the qualities and problems of presidential leadership.

Focus Your Reading Answers

1 Six qualities of presidential leadership are an understanding of the hopes and fears of the public, an ability to communicate ideas and policies to the public, an understanding of whether the time to act is right, a willingness to accept new ideas and change plans if needed, a willingness to compromise, and political courage.

2 Isolation is a problem for presidents because the president's advisers may limit contact with others to gain even more personal influence. A president may not hear conflicting points of view.

LESSON 3

Presidential Leadership

Thinking on Your Own

What does the word *leadership* mean to you? Think of someone you know who is a leader. What qualities, or characteristics, do you think make a good leader? List at least three qualities of a good leader in your notebook. Add to your list as you read the lesson.

focus your reading

What are the six qualities of presidential leadership?

Why is isolation a problem for presidents?

words to know

political scientists

landslide

political courage

What makes a good president? Political scientists have debated this question for years. **Political scientists** study the principles and organization of government. They take opinion polls to find out what Americans think of their presidents. They also examine the records of past presidents to learn the effects of their actions. They have found that successful presidents share a number of qualities. Not all presidents have every quality. However, successful presidents have several of them.

The Qualities of Presidential Leadership

Successful presidents understand the hopes and fears of the American public. This understanding helps presidents gain public support. With public support, a president is better able to convince Congress to pass his or her proposals.

A good example is the 1932 election. President Herbert Hoover was a strong believer in limited action by the federal government. However, the American public wanted help in dealing with the Depression. Because of his ideas about limited government, Hoover could not address their needs. Franklin D. Roosevelt was more flexible. He promised that

Words to Know

Discuss each of the vocabulary terms with students.

People who study the principles and organization of government are called *political scientists*. *Political scientists* have debated the qualities of an effective president.

A *landslide* is a victory with a large number of votes. Franklin Roosevelt was able to push his ideas through Congress because he'd won the election in a *landslide*.

Political courage is the courage to do what a person believes is right, even if one's own party and the voters disagree. Exercising *political courage* sometimes costs a person the presidency.

the federal government would take forceful action to end the Depression. As a result, voters elected him president over President Hoover. Because he won in a landslide, Roosevelt was able to push his policies through Congress. A **landslide** is a victory with a huge number of votes.

The ability to communicate policies to the public is another important leadership quality. President Ronald Reagan, a former movie actor, was known as the "Great Communicator." He was very good at explaining his policies to the public and gaining support. President Reagan was in his seventies and a Republican. However, two-thirds of Americans in their twenties and early thirties believed the Republican Party had more new ideas and energy than the Democratic Party did.

Third, presidents need a sense of timing. They need to know whether or not the time is right to act. This may mean introducing a new program or changing an existing one. One of President Bill Clinton's greatest accomplishments was reforming the welfare system. He sensed that the rising costs of the program made the public ready to accept change.

People in the News

reading for understanding

1. What is the subject of the president's speech?
2. What is the question that the president is trying to answer?
3. What is his answer?

A president needs leadership skills in difficult times. One of the most difficult is wartime. For example, the United States and its allies invaded Iraq in 2003. By mid-2005, many Americans wondered if the war was worth the monetary cost and the cost in lives. President George W. Bush went on television on June 28, 2005, to boost the nation's spirits. The following is part of that speech.

"Our mission in Iraq is clear. . . . We are helping Iraqis build a free nation that is an ally in the war on terror. We are advancing freedom in the broader Middle East. We are removing a source of violence and instability and laying the foundation of peace for our children and our grandchildren.

"The work in Iraq is difficult and it is dangerous. Like most Americans, I see the images of violence and bloodshed. Every picture is horrifying—and the suffering is real. Amid all this violence, I know Americans ask the question: Is the sacrifice worth it? It is worth it, and it is vital to the future security of our country."

—George W. Bush, *Address to the Nation*, June 28, 2005

Reading for Understanding

1 The subject of the president's speech is the need for continued work in Iraq.

2 The president is trying to answer the question of whether the sacrifice of American lives is worth it.

3 He believes that the sacrifices are worth it and that the war in Iraq is vital to the nation's security.

People in the News Extension

The government of Iraq met its August 2005 deadline for drafting a constitution. However, some members of the Iraqi Congress continued to object to the presence of American troops with no firm commitment to a pullout date. President Bush continued to back his secretary of defense, Donald Rumsfeld. Have students find out the result of the conflict of opinions.

Extensions

1 President Clinton did act forcefully in reforming the welfare system. However, his proposals for revising the health care system were not enacted. Have interested students use library resources or the Internet to contrast the two results. Have them speculate with the class as to why it was the right time for reforming welfare but not for reforming health care.

2 Invite interested students to use library resources or the Internet to find out more about Herbert Hoover and Franklin Roosevelt. Have them contrast the two men's leadership styles and theories of government. Allow time for students to present their findings to the class.

Ideas to Remember Extension

Review the ideas listed, further explaining difficult vocabulary words. Have students create graphic organizers in their notebooks to help them visualize the qualities of successful presidents.

Stop and Think

Students' choices of the two most important qualities of a president will vary but should be supported by reasons.

Picturing Government

The photograph on page 180 shows Bill Clinton campaigning for the presidency in Missouri in 1992. Clinton was one of the people who knew from an early age that he wanted to be president and charted a path to the White House.

ideas to remember

Among the qualities that successful presidents have are

- an understanding of the hopes and fears of the American public
- an ability to communicate ideas and policies to the public
- an understanding of whether the time is right to act
- a willingness to accept new ideas and change plans as a result of new thinking
- a willingness to compromise
- political courage

Fourth, presidents should be flexible in their thinking. They need to be willing to listen to and accept new ideas. One way they do this is by encouraging their advisers to voice differing opinions in discussions. Both Presidents George H. W. Bush and Bill Clinton welcomed debate among their advisers.

Fifth, a president should be willing to compromise. Compromise is an important part of the interaction between opposing views. Democrats and Republicans have many differences. However, they also have many common interests. A successful president works with the opposite party and with those within his own party who disagree with him. President Bill Clinton compromised with the Republican-controlled Congress to get a series of proposals passed in 1996. In compromising, he angered some of his own party members. His supporters said that the president showed political courage, another leadership quality.

stop and think

Not all presidents show all six leadership qualities. Which two qualities do you think are most important in a president? With a partner, write a list of reasons why each quality is important.

Political courage is the courage to do what a person thinks is right even though the person's own party and voters disagree. Sometimes a president is proven right and sometimes not. For example, in 1968, much of the nation turned against the Vietnam War. However, President Lyndon Johnson continued to send troops to Vietnam. He had to pull out of the presidential election because of lack of support from his own party and from the American public.

President Clinton is often credited as having political courage.

Extension

Have students use library resources or the Internet to find other examples they think show a president's political courage. You may also wish to extend the task to include those who have run for president but have not ultimately received their party's endorsement or who have run as independents. Allow time for students to share their findings with the class. Discuss the difference between political courage and arrogance or reliance on privilege.

The Isolation of Presidents

The president has many advisers in the cabinet, the EOP, and the White House Office. These people work for the president. Within this larger circle, there is often a small group of advisers. This inner circle is perhaps ten or fewer people. The president sees them on a daily basis. Usually, many of them have been with the president for a long time. They may have worked for him in other jobs. They may also have helped him win election to the presidency. He trusts them completely.

President Richard Nixon in 1969

This small inner circle of advisers represents a potential danger. Sometimes staff members limit others' access, or contact, with the president on purpose. They may do this to enlarge their own influence on the president. They may also do it because they truly believe the president is already too busy. If the president hears only from the same people, he or she can become isolated. The president may hear only praise for the various policies that are in place and never hear conflicting points of view.

Different presidents have reacted to presidential isolation in different ways. President Richard Nixon did not want people around him who disagreed with him. As the Watergate scandal unfolded, he closed himself off more and more from outside opinions. President George H. W. Bush, on the other hand, enlarged his circle of trusted advisers. He included many members of his cabinet in it. He did not rely on just an inner circle.

Putting It All Together

Review the list of leadership qualities that you wrote in Thinking on Your Own. In your notebook, list three qualities that you would add after having read this lesson. Identify at least one quality that would help prevent a president from becoming isolated. Then exchange your list with a partner and decide if your partner could make his or her list clearer. Suggest how your partner could revise the topics on the list.

Picturing Government

The photograph on page 181 shows Richard Nixon alone in his office, preparing for a trip to Europe in 1969. Nixon distrusted others and had an "enemies list" not only of political adversaries, but also of movie stars, such as Jane Fonda, and athletes, such as Joe Namath. Nixon also issued orders to have the phones of his enemies wiretapped, stating that it was for "national security concerns."

Extension

Have students use library resources or the Internet to investigate the cabinets of the earliest presidents. Were they composed of those who agreed with one another, or those with varied opinions? Have students debate the pros and cons of each approach.

Putting It All Together

Students' lists of leadership qualities and their choices of the one that would keep a president from being isolated will vary but should show thought based on the lesson content.

Participate in Government

1 Discuss students' experiences in running for office in school or other organizations, or in helping a friend do so. What techniques have they used that could apply to local or national elections?

2 Brainstorm ideas for local offices that students may run for and ways to fund the campaign. What strategies for publicity would they use? For example, would they select print, radio, or television ads? Or would they set up a Web site to marshal grass-roots efforts, as Howard Dean did so effectively in the 2004 presidential campaign?

Participate in Government

Become a Candidate

Do you want to have a say in school board decisions? Are you interested in improving public services such as garbage collection in your community? Do you think your county should spend more on road repair? Do you want your state legislature to repeal the state income tax?

Steve Allen, nineteen, was elected to the Riverside Town Council in Riverside, AL, in 2004.

These are some of the reasons that prompt people to run for public office. Being elected to public office gives a person a direct say in government. Age is not always a problem. High school students have been elected to school boards and to town councils. State legislators are sometimes in their twenties.

Age, length of residency, and other requirements vary from state to state. The process for becoming a candidate also varies. This is true for local as well as statewide elections. Usually, a person who wants to run for office must

- obtain an official petition from the state or local elections board.
- gather the required number of signatures from registered voters.
- file the petition with the elections board by the deadline.

Running for office costs money. Candidates need to pay for newspaper, television, cable, and radio ads. They also need to pay for printing brochures and mailing them to voters. A major expense is telephones. Volunteers use them to call voters to talk about the candidate and ask for support. No candidate can be successful without excited volunteers.

Research Resources

Below is a list of reference books and Web sites that relate to the issues covered in this chapter. Students may wish to use these to further their research on ideas in the preceding lessons. Web site addresses may change over time. Use keyword searching on a major search engine to locate sites.

Reference Books:

Michael A. Genovese. *Encyclopedia of the American Presidency.* Facts on File, 2004.

Leonard W. Levy and Louis Fisher, eds. *Encyclopedia of the American Presidency.* Simon and Schuster, 1994.

Web Sites:

The Smithsonian Web site, subtitled "A Glorious Burden," offers artifacts from the museum's collection as well as teacher resources.

The American Presidency Project is located at University of California, Santa Barbara. It contains public papers and public addresses of modern presidents, along with more than 50,000 documents for studying the presidency.

Skill Builder

Analyze Primary and Secondary Sources

A primary source describes an event or idea firsthand. It may be a speech, letter, memo, report, autobiography, photograph, painting, cartoon, poem, or song. The creator may have been part of the event or an eyewitness to it. A primary source may also be a person's explanation of his or her ideas. President Bush's speech on page 179 is a primary source.

A secondary source is not an eyewitness account. The creator pulls together information from others to create the work. Government reports are secondary sources. Newspaper articles may also be secondary sources if they summarize information.

The following is an excerpt from a newspaper article that was published before the president's speech:

> WASHINGTON (AP)—President George W. Bush is using the first anniversary of Iraq's sovereignty to try to ease Americans' doubts about the mission. . . .
>
> In a prime-time address from Fort Bragg, N.C., home of the Army's elite 82nd Airborne Division, Bush was to argue that there is no need to change course in Iraq despite the upsetting images produced by daily insurgent attacks. . . .
>
> Secretary of State Condoleezza Rice said today that Bush will stress the need for patience. . . .
>
> Tapping into Americans' emotions over terrorists' attacks, White House Press Secretary Scott McClellan said Bush will talk about insurgents killing innocent people and how stopping the violence "will be a major blow to the ambitions of the terrorists."
>
> —*Columbia Daily Tribune*, June 28, 2005

Answer the following questions.

1. What is the news article about?
2. Does it reprint the president's speech or summarize it?
3. What information does the news article give that the speech does not?

Recommended Reading

Below is a list of books that relate to the issues covered in this chapter. The numbers in parentheses indicate the related Thematic Strands of the National Council for the Social Studies (NCSS).

Kevin J. McNamara. *The Presidency*. Chelsea House, 2000. (X)

Kristen Woronoff. *American Inaugurals: The Speeches, the Presidents and Their Times.* Blackbirch Press, 2002. (X)

Skill Builder

1. It is about the efforts of the Bush administration to allay the public's concerns over the war in Iraq.
2. It summarizes the speech.
3. It includes the mention of Americans' doubts and emotions.

Classroom Discussion

Discuss with students some of the broader topics covered in this chapter.

- Are there presidential powers that students think should be added or removed?
- How can presidents best remain in touch with the electorate rather than becoming isolated?
- What are appropriate ways to use executive orders?

Related Transparencies

T-8 The Executive Departments—Part 1

T-9 The Executive Departments—Part 2

Key Blacklines

Primary Source—Report on the National Performance Review

CD Extension

Encourage students to use the reading comprehension, vocabulary reinforcement, and other activities on the student CD.

Getting Focused

Invite students to volunteer an explanation for each of the agencies listed. Have students add to the list as they read through this chapter and subsequent chapters.

Picturing Government

The Coast Guard vessel shown on page 184 is patrolling the San Diego harbor. Part of the Coast Guard's mission is to protect the nation's coastlines from intruding vessels or attack by rogue nuclear weapons.

Chapter 10 THE FEDERAL BUREAUCRACY

Getting Focused

Skim this chapter to predict what you will be learning.

- **Read the lesson titles and subheadings.**
- **Look at the illustrations and read the captions.**
- **Examine the tables.**
- **Review the vocabulary words and terms.**

What do you already know about the federal agencies and commissions listed below? Write a sentence to explain what each of the following does. Answer as many as you can.

- **Internal Revenue Service**
- **Federal Bureau of Investigation**
- **Secret Service**
- **Amtrak**
- **Food and Drug Administration**
- **Coast Guard**
- **United States Postal Service**

The United States Coast Guard, along with dozens of other agencies, represents part of the vast federal bureaucracy.

Pre-Reading Discussion

1 Discuss with students their ideas about what qualifies a person to work for the government. For example, should tests, background checks, or family connections be required? Tell students that in this chapter, they will learn about the process of gaining employment in the federal government.

2 Ask students to name the underlying things that make the community work, such as roads, plumbing and sewage systems, and water treatment plants. Tell them that this is called an infrastructure. Then extend the idea of an infrastructure to people. Tell students that this chapter will introduce the federal infrastructure.

LESSON 1

Departments, Agencies, and Commissions

Thinking on Your Own

Turn each subheading in this lesson into a question in your notebook before you read. After you read the lesson, answer each question that you wrote.

focus your reading

What areas of government do executive departments manage?

Explain the role that independent agencies play in the federal government.

What is the purpose of regulatory commissions?

words to know

independent agency

government corporation

independent regulatory commission

deregulation

The first Congress created three executive departments—foreign affairs, war, and treasury—and the position of attorney general. Today, there are 15 executive departments to deal with the issues facing the nation in the twenty-first century. The executive branch also has independent agencies, corporations, boards, and commissions. In 1801, the federal government had 2,120 civilian employees. Today, 2.7 million civilian employees work for the federal government.

The Executive Departments

In Chapter 8, you read that the heads of the executive departments make up the president's cabinet. Their main role, however, is to manage the departments of the executive branch. The table on pages 186–187 describes the main responsibilities of each department.

Each department is further divided into agencies. These are smaller groups that have particular duties within the larger executive department. For example, the National Park Service (NPS) is part of the Department of the Interior. The NPS takes care of all national parks, national seashore areas, national battlefields, and national monuments.

Lesson Summary

Nearly three million civilian employees work for the federal government in executive departments, independent agencies, corporations, boards, and commissions. Fifteen executive departments deal with the issues facing the country in the twenty-first century. Each department is further divided into agencies. Congress has also set up independent agencies that are part of the executive branch and report to the president. Ten independent regulatory commissions set rules to govern the operations of businesses and industries. They are independent of any branch of government. A board of commissioners, whose members must be approved by the Senate, directs each one. As a result of opposition to regulation, many businesses have been deregulated.

Lesson Objective

Students will learn about departments, agencies, and commissions that comprise the executive branch.

Focus Your Reading Answers

1 Executive departments manage 15 different areas of government, including state, defense, treasury, justice, interior, commerce, agriculture, and so on.

2 Independent agencies take on work not done by any executive department. They were also intended to be free from political pressure.

3 Regulatory commissions make rules that govern the way businesses and industries operate. They have both legislative and judicial powers.

Words to Know

Introduce each of the following vocabulary terms to students.

Independent agencies are not part of executive departments. *Independent agencies* are free from political interference. *Government corporations* are also *independent agencies* set up to be run as businesses. The federal government has more than 50 *government corporations*.

The *independent regulatory commissions* set rules to govern the operation of businesses and industry. Ten *independent regulatory commissions*, such as the Federal Trade Commission, are part of the federal government.

Reducing the regulations on business is called *deregulation*. Congress and the presidents have practiced *deregulation* since the 1970s.

Table Extension

Each of the executive departments has a Web site. Invite students to select one of the departments listed and browse the site to find out what information is given that may be immediately useful to them. For example, the Department of Education maintains a site, Federal Resources for Educational Excellence, offering links for homework help in all subjects. Have them present their findings to the class by using the Student Presentation Builder on the student CD.

The Executive Departments

Executive Department	Main Responsibilities and Important Agencies
State, 1789 (originally Foreign Affairs)	• Advises the president on foreign affairs • Protects the rights of U.S. citizens traveling in other nations • Represents the United States at the United Nations and in other global organizations • Maintains embassies and other agencies in foreign countries
Treasury, 1789	• Prints paper money and makes coins • Collects taxes through the Internal Revenue Service • Borrows money for the federal government • Regulates the production and sale of alcohol, tobacco, and firearms
Defense, 1789 (originally War)	• Maintains the armed forces to protect the nation
Interior, 1849	• Protects and manages public lands such as national parks and national historic sites • Oversees the use of natural resources • Provides aid to Native Americans living on reservations
Justice, 1870 (attorney general became head of the department)	• Advises the president on legal issues • Investigates and prosecutes anyone accused of a federal crime • Enforces federal laws such as civil rights laws • Operates federal prisons
Agriculture, 1889	• Develops and administers soil and water conservation programs • Provides financial aid to farmers and ranchers through loans and subsidies, or interest-free payments • Manages the national forests • Oversees food stamp and school lunch programs
Commerce, 1903	• Takes the national census, which means it counts the nation's population every ten years • Issues patents for inventions and registers copyrights for creative works such as books • Sets standards, or values, for weights and measurements; for example, a pound is always 16 ounces • Encourages the nation's economic growth by supporting business and technological development
Labor, 1913	• Enforces federal laws on working conditions, the minimum wage, and pension benefits • Manages unemployment insurance and worker compensation programs • Develops and runs job-training programs • Encourages cooperation between business and labor

Extension

George Washington felt keenly the responsibility of being the nation's first president. He chose the ablest men he knew for assistance in governing. Alexander Hamilton, who had been important at the Constitutional Convention and had written some of the *Federalist Papers*, was secretary of the treasury. His political rival Thomas Jefferson, author of the Declaration of Independence, was the first secretary of state. The secretary of war was Henry Knox, who had been the general in charge of artillery during the Revolution. The Department of Justice wasn't officially created until 1870. However, from the time of Washington on, the attorney general joined the cabinet meetings, becoming head of the Department of Justice when it began. The first attorney general was Edmund Randolph, governor of Virginia.

The Executive Departments, continued

Executive Department	Main Responsibilities and Important Agencies
Housing and Urban Development, 1965	• Enforces federal fair-housing laws • Works to preserve and renew cities and neighborhoods • Manages home mortgage, rent subsidy, and public housing programs
Transportation, 1966	• Regulates the nation's transportation systems • Regulates oil and gas pipelines
Energy, 1977	• Develops the nation's energy policy • Conducts research on and develops new energy technologies such as solar, or sun, power • Encourages energy conservation • Conducts research on nuclear weapons
Health and Human Services, 1979	• Manages Medicare and Medicaid • Funds medical research • Approves new drugs for sale • Runs disease prevention and control programs through the Center for Disease Control • Enforces pure food and drug laws
Education, 1979	• Enforces federal education laws such as Individuals with Disabilities Education Act (IDEA) and No Child Left Behind (NCLB) • Oversees federal funding programs for public and private schools • Oversees federal loan programs for students
Veterans Affairs, 1989	• Operates veterans' hospitals • Manages educational training, pension, and medical benefits programs for veterans • Operates military cemeteries
Homeland Security, 2002	• Oversees the security of the nation's borders, transportation systems, oil and gas pipelines, electric power sources, and similar resources • Enforces immigration laws • Manages emergency preparedness and the response to emergencies • Protects the president, vice president, and other top-level officials through the Secret Service

In 2002, Congress created the Department of Homeland Security to deal with terrorism. Many of the executive departments had to give up some of their agencies. These were agencies that dealt with the nation's borders, transportation security, and response to emergencies.

Extensions

1 Challenge students to work in teams creating questions based on the executive departments for a class-wide game. Use the questions as a way to begin the class or to review before a quiz or test.

2 Have the class create a timeline showing the dates for each of the departments. Have them use library resources or the Internet to find out world events around the same time and add them to the timeline. Encourage them to theorize how current national or world events may have affected the creation of new departments, as the text points out terrorism as the cause for creation of the Department of Homeland Security. Post the timeline in the classroom as a reference for the study of this chapter.

Stop and Think

Students' choices and sentences will vary but should relate to one of the executive departments.

Table Extension

Divide the class into seven small groups. Assign each group one of the corporations. Have the groups use library resources or the Internet to find more about their assigned government corporation. Allow time for a panel discussion on the work of these corporations.

Picturing Government

After national threat levels were raised in May 2003, San Francisco's Golden Gate Bridge was closely monitored through vehicle inspection. In the photograph on page 188, a National Park Ranger guards the road leading to Fort Point under the bridge.

The National Park Service monitors the Golden Gate Bridge during a heightened security alert.

Independent Agencies

As you just read, each executive department is made up of agencies. In addition, the executive branch has close to 150 **independent agencies.** These are not part of any executive department. Some, like the Social Security Administration, are as large as, or larger than, executive departments.

stop and think

Reread the table on executive departments on pages 186–187. Make a list of the departments that affect your life in some way. Next to each department, write a sentence to explain how it affects your life. Share your list with a partner and compare your experiences.

Some Government Corporations

Government Corporation	Area of Business
Corporation for Public Broadcasting	• Oversees public-supported radio and television stations • Provides some funding for developing programs
Federal Deposit Insurance Corporation (FDIC)	• Insures bank accounts up to a certain limit. If a bank fails, its depositors will get their money up to that limit.
Federal Election Commission (FEC)	• Enforces federal laws dealing with campaign funding
National Railroad Passenger Corporation (Amtrak)	• Operates the nation's passenger railroad service
Pension Guaranty Corporation	• Protects employees pension plans when companies go bankrupt
Tennessee Valley Authority (TVA)	• Operates electric power plants in eight southeastern states
United States Postal Service (USPS)	• Runs the nation's mail service

188 Chapter 10

Congress creates independent agencies for two main reasons. First, some agencies do not match the work of any executive department. For example, the General Services Administration (GSA) is responsible for all federal buildings. It is the federal government's housekeeper. The GSA oversees the construction of all federal buildings and their upkeep after they are built. No executive department has similar duties.

Second, Congress sets up some independent agencies that need to be free from political pressure. The Government Accountability Office (GAO), for example, investigates how executive departments and other agencies use government resources. It needs to be free from interference to do its job.

The federal government also runs more than 50 **government corporations**. These, too, are considered independent agencies. Congress sets up these corporations to be run as businesses. Executives and a board of directors head them. Any profits go back into the business. The federal government covers losses. As you can see by the table on page 188, government corporations run many kinds of businesses.

U.S. Consumer Product Safety Commission Chairman Hal Stratton shows a product that was recalled due to safety concerns.

ideas to remember

The federal bureaucracy is made up of

- executive departments
- independent agencies
- government corporations
- regulatory commissions

It is important to remember that independent agencies and government corporations are not independent of the government. They are part of the executive branch. Although established by Congress, they report to the president. The president appoints their chief executives, boards, and often other top officials.

Picturing Government

The photograph on page 189 shows the chairman of the U.S. Consumer Product Safety Commission, Hal Stratton. As part of a warning before the holiday gift-buying season, Stratton was pointing out a toy that had been recalled for unsafe operation.

Ideas to Remember Extension

Review the ideas listed, further explaining difficult vocabulary words. Have students create graphic organizers in their notebooks to help them visualize the parts of the federal bureaucracy.

Extension

The Government Accountability Office has been called a congressional watchdog, because it tracks how the federal government uses tax income. Each year, the GAO issues more than 1,000 reports. The Comptroller General, who is appointed to serve a 15-year term, heads this agency. This longer term of office creates a continuity of leadership that's rare in government. The GAO was created in 1921 in response to the financial situation following World War I. Initially an auditing operation with about 1,700 employees, by the end of World War II, the GAO had more than 14,000 staff members.

Table Extension

Have students work in teams to create flash cards for the commissions and their major duties. Then have students use the flash cards to help each other review the material before a quiz or test.

Independent Regulatory Commissions

Independent regulatory commissions make rules that govern how industries and businesses operate. There are ten independent regulatory commissions. The table on page 190 lists them.

Independent Regulatory Commissions

Independent Regulatory Commission	Major Duties
Consumer Product Safety Commission (CPSC)	• Creates and enforces safety standards for products • Oversees recalls of unsafe products
Commodity Futures Trading Commission (CFTC)	• Regulates the commodities markets, which buy and sell goods, such as farm products, and metals, like aluminum
Federal Communications Commission (FCC)	• Regulates television, cable, radio, and satellite businesses
Federal Energy Regulatory Commission (FERC)	• Sets rates for and regulates the oil, natural gas, and electricity industries
Federal Maritime Commission (FMC)	• Regulates the shipping industry
Federal Reserve System (the Fed)	• Oversees the banking system • Regulates the money supply
Federal Trade Commission (FTC)	• Enforces laws against unfair business activities
National Labor Relations Board (NLRB)	• Enforces labor-management laws
Nuclear Regulatory Commission (NRC)	• Regulates all uses of nuclear materials by civilians
Securities and Exchange Commission (SEC)	• Regulates investment companies, stock and bond brokers, and stock and bond exchanges • Enforces laws against dishonest investment activities

Extension

Alan Greenspan served as head of the Federal Reserve system for 20 years. Originally taking the office in 1987 to fill an unexpired term on the board, he was appointed chairman by presidents Reagan, George H. W. Bush, Clinton, and George W. Bush. His fifth term ended in January 2006. In 2003, he was the first to receive the Gerald R. Ford Medal for Distinguished Public Service.

Independent regulatory commissions are different from independent agencies and government corporations in several ways. Independent regulatory commissions do not report to the president. They are independent of both the executive and legislative branches. Congress set them up in this way so political pressure would not affect their decisions.

A board of commissioners directs each independent regulatory commission. A commission has from 5 to 11 members. They serve from 4 to 14 years, depending on the commission. This means that many members will serve longer than the president who appointed them. No more than half the members, plus one, may belong to any single political party. The Senate must approve all nominees. Presidents cannot fire commissioners once they are appointed.

Independent regulatory commissions have both legislative and judicial powers. Commissions make rules for the industries they oversee. For example, the FCC decides how many television and cable stations a company may own in an area of the country. When commissions investigate supposed wrongdoing in an industry, they use their judicial powers. In the early 2000s, the SEC investigated fraud by various corporations. When the SEC found wrongdoing, it fined the corporations heavily.

For years, critics charged that business was too heavily regulated. Since the 1970s, Congress and both Democratic and Republican presidents have worked to lessen regulations. Regulations in the airline, trucking, and railroad industries were greatly reduced. This is known as **deregulation**.

Putting It All Together

Create a three-column chart. Write "Executive Departments," "Independent Agencies," and "Regulatory Commissions" at the top of the columns. In each column, explain in one or two sentences how that type of government agency is different from the other two.

Extension

Agencies sometimes clash with Congress. For example, in 2003, the Senate passed a joint resolution opposing the ruling on media ownership that the Federal Communications Commission had issued. Have students find out what happened in the controversy about what percentage of media outlets one firm should be able to control.

Putting It All Together

Students' explanations will differ. Possible response:

Executive departments are made up of agencies and headed by secretaries that make up the cabinet.

Independent agencies are not part of any department but are free from governmental pressure.

Regulatory commissions are independent and make rules for how businesses and industries operate.

Lesson Summary

The civil service system began as a reaction against the spoils system, which had unofficially been government policy from the time of Andrew Jackson until a disappointed office seeker assassinated James A. Garfield. The Pendleton Act of 1883 imposed a fair way to hire, promote, and fire federal employees. The Office of Personnel Management, an independent agency, now handles federal employment. In an attempt to protect federal employees from political pressure, Congress passed the Hatch Act in 1939 and the Federal Employees Political Activities Act 50 years later.

Lesson Objective

Students will learn about the process of gaining employment in the federal bureaucracy.

Focus Your Reading Answers

1 Congress created the civil service system as a result of the assassination of James A. Garfield. The civil service system is intended to be a more fair way to gain employment than the patronage system.

2 People get jobs in the federal government by applying to the Office of Personnel Management, which posts jobs on its Web site, in newspapers, and on bulletin boards.

3 Some jobs in the federal government go to political appointees because the president wants to employ people he or she knows and trusts and to reward loyalty.

4 Government workers may not participate in political activities because the party in power might try to force employees to campaign.

LESSON 2

The Civil Service System

Thinking on Your Own

Review the information about departments, agencies, and commissions in Lesson 1. Choose one that you might like to work for. List three reasons for your choice in your notebook. How would you apply for this job? Write a paragraph, using the vocabulary words, stating your choice and explaining your reasons.

focus your reading

Explain why Congress created the civil service system.

Describe how ordinary people get jobs in the federal government today.

Why are political appointees given jobs in the federal government?

Why are government workers not allowed to participate in political activities?

words to know

civil service system

civil servant

patronage

spoils system

political appointee

career civil servant

Who works in the federal bureaucracy? Who gets these jobs? What are the qualifications for working for the federal government? How are people hired for these jobs?

The Beginning of the Civil Service System

The **civil service system** is the process the federal government uses to hire, employ, and promote workers. Federal government workers are called **civil servants**. To be hired, a person must have the required education and skills. He or she may also have to pass a competitive exam.

From the beginning of the nation, presidents appointed supporters to government jobs. It was a way to thank them. Government jobs were called **patronage**. Appointing supporters to public offices became known as the **spoils system**. After he took office, President Andrew Jackson, for example, fired about 1,000 federal employees. Their jobs went to his supporters. Many politicians, not just

"Keep her head straight for Civil Service reform" is the original caption of this cartoon of President Grover Cleveland at the helm of a ship in stormy weather.

Words to Know

Discuss each of the vocabulary terms with students.

The *civil service system* is the process that the federal government uses to hire, employ, and promote workers. The Pendleton Act created the current *civil service system*.

Civil servants are those who work for the federal government. *Civil servants* may have to pass an exam to get a job.

Patronage is a government job given as a thank-you. Presidents practiced *patronage* from the beginning of the nation.

The system of giving government jobs to supporters is known as the *spoils system*. The *spoils system* was in effect at all levels of government.

presidents, gave government jobs to supporters. Big-city politicians and state leaders created their own spoils systems.

As early as the 1850s, people were calling for reform of government employment. However, little was done until 1883. In that year, Congress passed the Pendleton Act. It created the present civil service system. Congress acted after President James A. Garfield was killed in 1881. A man who had been turned down for a government job shot him.

About 2,200 jobs in the executive department are not part of the civil service system. The president names people to these jobs. Those who get them are called **political appointees**. Congress must approve some of the appointees. These include the heads of executive departments and ambassadors.

U.S. Ambassador to Great Britain Robert H. Tuttle, a political appointee, signs a guest book in London after the terror attacks in July 2005.

These high-level jobs go to political supporters of the president. They may not have experience with the issues in the particular group they run. They hold their jobs only as long as the president is in office. Because of this, career civil servants run the departments, agencies, and commissions on a day-to-day basis. They also create much of the policy that each department, agency, and commission carries out. A **career civil servant** is a not a political appointee. It is a person who expects to work for the government for many years.

The Modern Civil Service

The Office of Personnel Management (OPM) handles employment for the federal government. The OPM is an independent agency in the executive branch. The president appoints the director. The Senate must approve the person.

Scientists at the National Institutes of Health (left) are part of the civil service system. U.S. Ambassador to Pakistan John K. Bauman (right) is a political appointee.

Words to Know, continued

Political appointees are people whom the president names to jobs in the executive department. Some *political appointees* require congressional approval.

Career civil servants are those who expect to work for the government for many years. *Career civil servants* run the agencies, commissions, and departments on a daily basis.

Picturing Government

The photograph at the top of page 193 shows Robert H. Tuttle, the U.S. ambassador to Great Britain, and his wife, Maria, signing a book of condolence after the London terrorist attacks in 2005. It was one of the first duties Tuttle performed as the new ambassador.

Picturing Government

The photograph at the bottom, far left, on page 193 depicts a medical researcher, Wen Hua Zheng, at the National Institutes of Health. The photograph at the right shows John K. Bauman, the U.S. ambassador to Pakistan, talking to local police officers after a shooting outside the consulate in 2003.

Extension

The OPM manages a national network of nearly 1,000 testing administrators as well as a central test storage and distribution center. Since 1976, it has offered ongoing testing services to the Department of Defense Recruitment Command. Other federal agencies that use the service range from the National Park Service to the U.S. Patent and Trademark Office.

Stop and Think
Students' ideas and paragraphs will vary but may mention that employment became based on ability and merit, rather than on a political spoils system.

Picturing Government

The Web site shown on page 194 discusses the provisions of the Hatch Act for federal employees. The act was passed in response to alleged political malpractices in Kentucky, Tennessee, and Maryland. The Supreme Court upheld the constitutionality of the act in both 1947 and 1974.

The OPM is the main recruiter for federal employees. Job openings are advertised on bulletin boards in post offices and in newspapers. They are also posted on the OPM's Web site. The OPM gives the civil service exams for clerical and secretarial jobs. It also keeps lists of the people who pass. The top three candidates are sent to an agency when a job opens for which they qualify. The OPM also recruits professionals such as lawyers, doctors, accountants, and social workers.

stop and think

How did the civil service system change the way employees were hired and fired for government jobs? Discuss this question with a partner. Make notes. Then, write a paragraph to answer the question. Share your paragraphs.

One reason for creation of the civil service system was to protect workers' jobs. Government employees, however, can be fired. A manager who wants to fire an employee must have serious reasons. He or she must go through a number of hearings to prove that the person should be let go.

Political Activities

In the past, many people feared that political parties would take advantage of government workers. The party in power might try to force workers to campaign for it or to contribute money to it. Workers who refused might be fired or overlooked for promotions. To make sure this did not happen, Congress passed the Hatch Act in 1939. The Hatch Act allowed federal government workers to vote. However, they could not take part in any other political activities. In more recent times, federal employees claimed the act violated their right to free speech.

The U.S. Office of Special Counsel is responsible for enforcing the Hatch Act and the Federal Employees Political Activities Act.

Extension

Invite students to use library resources or the Internet to find out about the civil service system in other nations. Ask them to investigate particularly the history of civil service in China.

In 1993, Congress passed the Federal Employees Political Activities Act. A federal employee now has many more political rights. For example, federal employees may register new voters. They may make contributions to political parties and candidates and take part in political campaigns. However, there are still limits on federal employees' actions. They may not run for political office. They may not do any political party work while on the job or on government property. This includes wearing a campaign button or displaying campaign literature. Federal employees may not collect political contributions from those they manage or from the general public. Some states have adopted similar rules for their government employees.

Putting It All Together

The way people get jobs with the federal government has changed over time. So have the limits on political activities in which federal employees can participate. In your notebook, list five or six ways that these changes have impacted federal employees. Share your list with a partner. Revise your list if necessary.

Reading for Understanding

1 practical, related to the matters that will test the person's ability to do the job

2 from among the highest test scores

Primary Source

The Pendleton Act (1883)

The Pendleton Act was passed in 1883 to create a fair way to hire, promote, and fire federal employees. The following is an excerpt from the law:

"... [R]ules shall provide ... as follows:

"First, for open, competitive examinations for testing the fitness of applicants for the public service ... Such examinations shall be practical ... and ... shall relate to those matters which will fairly test the ... capacity and fitness of the persons examined to discharge the duties ...

"Second, that all offices, places, and employments ... shall be filled ... from among those graded highest as the results of competitive examinations."

—from U.S. Information Service,
based on U.S. Statutes at large 22 (1883): 403

reading for understanding

1. What kinds of tests should the civil service system give to people applying for jobs?
2. According to the law, how are jobs to be filled?

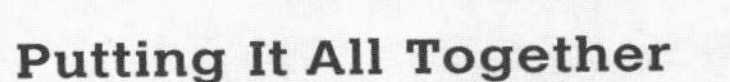
Putting It All Together

Students' lists will vary but may include the need to prepare for civil service exams and the inability to rely on political or family connections for government jobs.

Lesson Summary

Bureaucrats both make and enforce national policy. Although Congress passes laws, the federal bureaucrats must determine how to carry out the law. Some bureaucrats also write laws and send them as proposals to Congress. The influence of the bureaucracy has grown because the country has grown, as well as because of technology and economic problems. Expanding client groups and international crises, such as terrorism, have increased the bureaucracy as well. Client groups, congressional committees, and a federal commission, agency, or department make up an iron triangle, with each of the three requiring the help of the other two.

Lesson Objective

Students will learn about the bureaucracy's many tasks.

Focus Your Reading Answers

1 Duties of the federal bureaucracy include carrying out the laws of the United States, writing regulations, offering expert opinions, writing proposed laws, interpreting laws, and gathering data.

2 The bureaucracy is able to make policy decisions because Congress writes the laws but does not fill in the details.

3 Congress and client groups and their lobbyists influence bureaucratic decisions.

LESSON 3

The Many Jobs of the Bureaucracy

Thinking on Your Own

The federal bureaucracy grew from 2,120 people in 1801 to about 2.7 million in 2001. Why do you think this happened? List at least two reasons. To help you, think about how the U.S. has changed during the past 200 years.

focus your reading

Describe the different duties of the federal bureaucracy.

Why is the bureaucracy able to make decisions about policy?

Who influences bureaucratic decisions?

words to know

bureaucrat

client group

intelligence gathering

lobbyist

iron triangle

The federal government has 2.7 million civilian employees. What do they do? How do they interact with ordinary citizens? What is their relationship with the legislative and judicial branches? Only about 300,000 federal employees work in the Washington, D.C., area. Some represent the United States in other nations. Most, however, live and work in cities and towns throughout the United States. Your postal carrier is a federal employee. The person who helps a retiree fill out forms at the local office of the Social Security Administration is also a federal employee.

The Work of the Bureaucracy

Federal employees are called **bureaucrats**. Their main job is to carry out the laws of the United States. In reality, the job of the bureaucracy is much more than that. Bureaucrats not only carry out the nation's policy, they make national policy.

Writing regulations is one way that the bureaucracy influences national policy. Congress writes and passes laws. But they do not state the details—the who, what, where, when, and how a law will be enforced.

Words to Know

Discuss each of the vocabulary terms with students.

Bureaucrats are federal employees. *Bureaucrats* both make national policy and carry it out.

Client groups are the people and groups most affected by the decisions of any given department. Each agency, department, and commission has its own set of *client groups*.

Finding out about other nations is the work of *intelligence gathering*. A new federal office to oversee *intelligence gathering* was set up in 2005.

Lobbyists are people in Washington, D.C., who represent *client groups*. *Lobbyists* try to influence members of Congress as they write and vote on legislation.

A federal agency, commission, or department may join with congressional committees and *client groups* to form an *iron triangle*. The three groups that make up an *iron triangle* work together to develop programs and policies.

Title IX of the Education Act of 1972 is a good example. It bars gender discrimination in any education program or activity that receives federal funding. Section 844 of the law states:

> The Secretary . . . shall prepare and publish . . . proposed regulations implementing the provisions of Title IX relating to prohibition of sex discrimination in Federally assisted educational programs which shall include . . . intercollegiate athletic activities.

Congress gives the executive department the duty to write the rules and regulations describing the law. The bureaucrats in the Department of Health, Education, and Welfare (now the Department of Education) had to figure out what the Title IX law meant and how to carry it out.

Bureaucrats also influence laws while they are being written. As you read in Chapter 7, congressional committees hold hearings on proposed laws. They call expert witnesses to testify. Often, these witnesses are from the federal government's own bureaucracy. They have information that the lawmakers need in order to make reasonable decisions. Lawmakers also know that they will need the cooperation of bureaucrats in a particular department, agency, or commission to carry out the law.

Often, bureaucrats actually write a proposed law and pass it to Congress to review and debate. This is one way that bills are introduced into Congress. Medicare, for example, began as a proposal from the old Department of Health, Education, and Welfare, and from labor unions and hospitals.

President Johnson signs Medicare into law in 1965, as former President Truman looks on.

Independent agencies like the Social Security Administration and the regulatory commissions have judicial powers. They settle arguments and claims in their area of authority. In settling disagreements, they interpret what rules and regulations mean. These decisions determine national policy. For example, the SSA makes decisions about who may or may not receive disability benefits. These decisions are interpretations of its regulations. They give others guidance

Picturing Government

The photograph on page 197 is of President Lyndon Johnson flipping the pages of the 1965 Medicare Bill to show to former president Harry Truman, as their wives and Vice President Hubert Humphrey look on. Truman had proposed the legislation nearly two decades before. Johnson flew to Truman's home state of Missouri to sign the bill in front of him.

Extension

Title IX has come under attack in the early years of the twenty-first century. Have students use library resources or the Internet to investigate the challenges to the provisions. Ask them to find instances of how the federal bureaucracy and client groups have been involved. Allow time for students to present their findings to the class.

Ideas to Remember Extension

Review the ideas listed, further explaining difficult vocabulary words. Have students create graphic organizers in their notebooks to help them visualize how bureaucrats influence federal policy.

Picturing Government

The photograph on this page shows President Bill Clinton and Vice President Al Gore announcing a proposal for government reform in September 1993.

ideas to remember

Bureaucrats influence national policy in the following ways:

- by writing rules and regulations to carry out laws
- by helping Congress write proposed laws
- by settling arguments over what regulations mean
- by advising Congress and other decision-makers

on whether or not they will qualify for the same benefits. Once laws are passed, bureaucrats also provide information and advice. One of the most important duties of the federal bureaucracy is to gather data about the nation: its people, resources, and economy. Bureaucrats share this data with members of Congress and the political appointees in top positions in each department, agency, and commission. This information helps officials make decisions about whether current policy is or is not achieving its goals.

The Growing Influence of Bureaucrats

In the early 1800s, and even through the beginning of the 1900s, bureaucrats did not have so much influence. What changed?

The first reason for the change is the growth of the nation. In 1801, the United States extended west only to the Mississippi River. Today, the nation has 50 states, a number of territories, and more than 280 million people.

President Clinton posed in front of the White House with thousands of government documents as he launched an initiative to reduce the number of reports required annually.

Second, technology has become more complex and widespread. When Franklin Roosevelt was president, television was just beginning. Since the 1980s, cable television, computers, cell phones, and the Internet have been developed. Each new technological development has raised issues. Congress has created agencies to deal with these issues or given responsibility for them to existing agencies.

Third, economic problems have also increased the size of the federal bureaucracy.

Fourth, Congress has created executive departments and other agencies to deal with the needs of certain groups. Executive departments, agencies, and commissions have their own sets of **client groups**.

198 Chapter 10

Fifth, international crises have added to the bureaucracy. After World War II, the nation was involved in the Cold War with the Soviet Union. To ensure that the nation's military was strong, Congress added workers and responsibilities to the Department of Defense. Aid was increased to other nations to ensure they became U.S. allies.

The terrorist attacks in 2001 focused attention on the nation's security preparedness. How well was the nation able to deal with terrorism? President George W. Bush asked Congress to create the Department of Homeland Security. Twenty-two existing agencies were placed within the department. In 2005, the Office of the Director of National Intelligence was set up to oversee **intelligence gathering**. New counterterrorism agencies were added in the Justice Department as well.

ideas to remember

The federal bureaucracy has grown in importance for the following reasons:

- the growth of the nation
- the growth of technology
- economic problems
- the pressure of client groups
- years of international problems

Influence on Bureaucrats

Others influence the decisions that bureaucrats make. For example, Congress uses its powers to influence the bureaucracy. It can pass laws that overrule, or change, regulations that a department, agency, or commission has written. Congress can also cut or threaten to cut funding for a program.

However, client groups are the biggest influence on bureaucratic decisions. Each department has its own set of client groups. For example, labor unions are a major client group for the Labor Department. Client groups often hire lobbyists to represent them in Washington, D.C. A **lobbyist's** job is to attempt to influence members of Congress as they prepare and vote on bills. Client groups, congressional committees, and a federal department, agency, or commission may form an **iron triangle**. The three groups depend on one another and work closely to develop policies and programs. Each side of the triangle has something that the other two need.

Ideas to Remember Extension

Review the ideas listed, further explaining difficult vocabulary words. Have students create graphic organizers in their notebooks to help them visualize the reasons for the growth of the federal bureaucracy.

Stop and Think
Students' lists will vary.

Graphic Extension

Invite volunteers to work in pairs or small groups. Ask them to use library resources or the Internet to provide examples of the iron triangle at work in a current political situation.

The Defense Department is a good example. When the budgets are passed, the department needs the support of the congressional committees on defense. Members see that the department's budget requests are filled. Members of the congressional committees need information from the department to help them write laws.

stop and think

Review the list of reasons you wrote for Thinking on Your Own. How does your list match the reasons described in the lesson for the growth of the bureaucracy? Share your list with a partner. Discuss the similarities and differences between your lists and the text.

The department also needs the goods that the defense contractors make. These goods include weapons systems, military ships and planes, and similar equipment. The contractors need the billions of dollars that the department gives out each year. In return, the defense contractors support the department's budget requests.

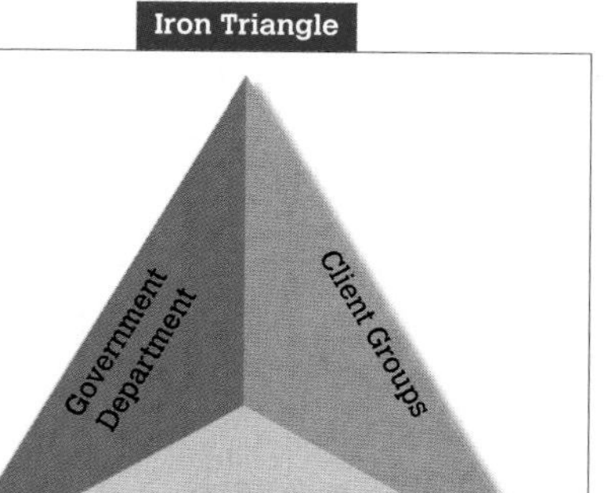

When they write bills, the congressional committees on defense need the experience of the defense contractors. In return, defense contractors provide political support for committee members. They make campaign contributions and work for their reelection. In return, the congressional committees write legislation that favors the client group.

Putting It All Together

Imagine that you have been asked to debate the following proposition: "Resolved, that bureaucrats have too much influence over the federal government." Using information from this lesson, make an outline in your notebook of the reasons you would use to support or oppose this proposition. Review or revise the list after discussing your reasons with a partner.

Putting It All Together
Students' lists of reasons supporting or opposing the resolution on bureaucratic influence will vary but should be supported with material from the lesson.

200 Chapter 10

Participate in Government

A Career in Government

Are you interested in a job in the federal government? You do not have to move to Washington, D.C., to work for the government. You can stay in your home community or you can move to Antarctica. The government runs a research base in Antarctica staffed with government scientists.

The Office of Personnel Management is the official recruiter of workers for the federal government. Visit its Web site to find out the kinds of jobs that federal employees do. The home page also has links to information on salaries, wages, and benefits. On the link to student jobs, you can search for information on different kinds of jobs and create your resumé.

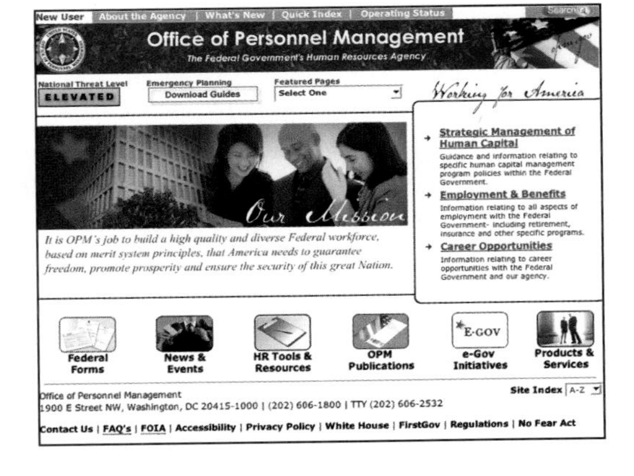

You can also find out about scholarship opportunities. In addition to student jobs, summer jobs and internships are available for qualified students. Some departments have co-op and mentoring programs. In a co-op, or cooperative job, students get to work on real-world projects that use what they are learning in school. The goal of all these student programs is to attract future full-time employees to government work.

To learn more about job opportunities in the federal government:

- Click on the OPM Web site.
- Use the buttons to find out more.
- Download information and talk to your guidance counselor.

Participate in Government

If possible, use a computer and projector to access the OPM Web site as a class activity before sending students to navigate the site. Show them the most likely places to find information about a career, including information geared for students.

Invite students to imagine their dream location: perhaps a major metropolitan area or a city near an ocean or the mountains. Then have them use the OPM Web site to find jobs in that area.

Research Resources

Below is a list of reference books and Web sites that relate to the issues covered in this chapter. Students may wish to use these to further their research on ideas in the preceding lessons. Web site addresses may change over time. Use keyword searching on a major search engine to locate sites.

Reference Books:

Federal Regulatory Directory. Congressional Quarterly, Inc., annual.

Kathleen Hill. *Encyclopedia of Federal Agencies and Commissions.* Facts on File, 2004.

Kelle S. Sisung. *Federal Agency Profiles for Students.* Gale Group, 1998.

United States Government Manual. Office of the Federal Register, annual.

Web Sites:

The Federal Statistics site offers statistical data that has been collected by more than 100 federal agencies, which are listed by subject as well as alphabetically. It also includes press releases from the individual agencies.

The Federal Bureaucracy 201

Skill Builder

Students' explanations will vary.

1 fact

2 opinion

3 opinion

4 fact

5 opinion

Recommended Reading

Below is a list of books that relate to the issues covered in this chapter. The numbers in parentheses indicate the related Thematic Strands of the National Council for the Social Studies (NCSS).

Geoffrey M. Horn. *The Cabinet and Federal Agencies.* Gareth Stevens Audio, 2003. (X)

Michael Kronenwetter. *The FBI and Law Enforcement Agencies of the United States.* Enslow Publishers, 1997. (X)

Skill Builder

Distinguish Fact from Opinion

A fact is a statement
- of specific information.
- that can be proven true or false.

An opinion
- is what a person thinks or feels.
- cannot be proven true or false.

> Client groups, congressional committees, and executive departments form iron triangles.

This sentence states a fact. It gives specific information that could be proven true or false through additional research.

> Iron triangles are bad for the taxpayer.

This sentence states the author's personal belief about iron triangles. The author provides no evidence to support the statement.

Look for signal words and phrases to help you decide if a statement is a fact or an opinion. Opinion statements often use

- words such as *none, no one, every, always, never, perhaps, probably, maybe, excellent, greatest, best, worst, bad, good,* or *poor.*
- phrases such as *I think, I believe, in my opinion, in my judgment,* or *as far as I am concerned.*

Decide whether each of the following is a statement of fact or of opinion. Explain how you decided.

1 Article I of the Constitution creates the legislative branch.

2 I think Franklin Roosevelt was the greatest president.

3 The civil service system was a much-needed reform.

4 The executive branch has 15 departments, and their heads are part of the president's cabinet.

5 The growth of technology is probably the greatest cause of the increase in the bureaucracy.

Classroom Discussion

Discuss with students some of the broader topics covered in this chapter.

- How can presidential administrations strike a balance between rewarding loyalty and the need for civil service exams?
- Should there be restrictions on the political involvement of federal employees?
- In what ways should the power of client groups be limited?

THE JUDICIAL BRANCH

Article III of the U.S. Constitution created the Supreme Court. The Framers left it to Congress to decide what inferior, or lower, courts were needed. Over the years, Congress has filled in the federal court system. Today, there are 113 courts that hear cases concerning the Constitution, federal laws, federal officials, the states, and foreign governments.

The U.S. Supreme Court has only nine justices. The Court hears cases for only part of the year. It accepts only a few of the many cases sent to it for review. However, the decisions of the U.S. Supreme Court greatly affect national policy. That is why a decision by the Court, or an appointment of a justice, creates so much national interest.

Unit Objectives

After studying this unit, students will be able to

- summarize the organization and jurisdiction of federal courts
- describe the workings of the Supreme Court

Unit 4 explains the workings of the federal judicial branch.

Chapter 11, The Federal Court System, examines how federal courts are organized and notes their various jurisdictions.

Chapter 12, The Supreme Court at Work, outlines the Court's processes, influences, and effect on national policy.

Getting Started

Ask a volunteer to read aloud the title of the unit and the two paragraphs that follow it on page 203. Ask students to preview the unit by skimming titles of chapters and lessons and scanning photographs, diagrams, tables, and charts. Then have them make K-W-L charts. Encourage them to add answers to the charts as they read Unit 4.

Picturing Government

The photograph on page 203 shows the United States Supreme Court Building in Washington, D.C. The main west entrance to the building has 16 marble columns. At the top of the entrance, the phrase "Equal Justice Under Law" is inscribed in stone. The statue grouping at the top is *Liberty Enthroned Guarded by Order and Authority*. Robert Aitken created the sculpture. At the east entrance, the words "Justice the Guardian of Liberty" are inscribed. That sculpture group, by Herman A. McNeil, represents the great lawgivers: Moses, Confucius, and Solon. Surrounding them are groups symbolizing "Means of Enforcing the Law," "Tempering Justice with Mercy," "Carrying on Civilization," and "Settlement of Disputes Between States."

Related Transparencies

T-10 The Federal Court System and Decision-making on the Supreme Court

T-18 Three-Column Chart

Key Blacklines

Biography—John Marshall

CD Extension

Encourage students to use the reading comprehension, vocabulary reinforcement, and other activities on the student CD.

Getting Focused

Invite students to incorporate what they already know about the judicial system into a K-W-L chart. They can add to the chart as they read through the chapter and use it as a study guide for tests or quizzes.

Chapter 11 THE FEDERAL COURT SYSTEM

Getting Focused

Skim this chapter to predict what you will be learning.

- **Read the lesson titles and subheadings.**
- **Look at the illustrations and read the captions.**
- **Examine the map, tables, and diagram.**
- **Review the vocabulary words and terms.**

What do you know about what goes on in a courtroom? Think about television shows or movies that take place in courtrooms. Write down five things in your notebook that you have learned about courtrooms from watching these shows or movies.

The John Joseph Moakley United States Courthouse in Boston, MA, was completed in 1998. It serves as headquarters for the United States Court of Appeals for the First Circuit and the United States District Court for the District of Massachusetts. The building has two courtrooms for the Court of Appeals and 25 courtrooms for the District Court. It also has 40 judges' chambers, a Circuit law library, the office of a United States congressman, and offices for the United States attorney.

Picturing Government

U.S. federal courthouses, such as the one in the photograph on page 204, provide office space for many federal officials. The office of the U.S. attorney is in this building. A total of 93 U.S. attorneys, who are appointed by the president and approved by the Senate, serve throughout the U.S. and its territories. They have three responsibilities: to prosecute criminal cases brought by the federal government, to prosecute and defend civil cases in which the United States is a party, and to collect debts owed to the federal government.

Pre-Reading Discussion

1 Ask students to share their ideas from the Getting Focused exercise. Correct any misinformation that they may have learned from the media.

2 Have students share their ideas about how people become judges. What are the requirements? What are the dangers or difficulties?

LESSON 1

Organization of the Federal Courts

Thinking on Your Own

Look through the lesson. Read the subheadings, diagram, map, and table. What questions about the information come to mind? Write at least three questions in your notebook that you would like answered by the end of the lesson.

focus your reading

Explain the organization of the federal court system.

What kinds of cases do federal courts hear?

How are federal judges appointed?

words to know

constitutional court

legislative court

civil case

tariff

Article III of the Constitution mentions only setting up a Supreme Court. Congress has created the lower levels of federal courts as needed. For example, the latest lower court was set up in 1988 to deal with veterans' claims.

It is important to remember that the federal courts deal with cases involving the Constitution, federal laws, and certain other issues. Each state has its own system of courts and laws. State and local courts cannot hear cases involving federal laws or the Constitution.

The Lower Federal Courts

The diagram on page 206 shows the levels of courts and the types of courts in the federal court system. The courts shown in blue on the diagram are known as **constitutional courts**. Congress set up these 108 courts under the authority of Article III of the Constitution. These courts hear both criminal and civil cases related to federal laws.

The other six federal courts are special courts, also known as **legislative courts**. Congress created these courts to hear particular kinds of cases. The cases are related to Congress's power to govern under Article I. For example, Congress has the power to tax. It set up the Tax Court to hear cases involving federal tax law.

Federal District Judge Sonia Sotomayer of New York issued a ruling that ended the Major League Baseball strike during the 1995–1996 season.

Lesson Summary

Congress can set up lower types of federal courts as needed. Congress sets up constitutional courts in the federal court system. There are also five special legislative courts to hear certain kinds of cases. Constitutional courts include federal district courts, federal courts of appeals, the U.S. Court of Appeals for the Federal Circuit, and the U.S. Court of International Trade. Federal district courts hear civil cases. Federal courts of appeals try cases appealed from the federal district courts. Judges issue rulings after hearing lawyers present evidence. The U.S. Court of Appeals for the Federal Circuit hears only certain types of civil cases but may take a case from any part of the nation. Legislative courts deal with special issues such as the armed forces or taxes. Federal judges are appointed by the president and approved by the Senate. They serve for 15 years or for life, depending on the court.

Lesson Objective

Students will learn how the federal court system is organized.

Words to Know

Introduce each of the following vocabulary terms to students.

Explain that *constitutional courts* are those set up under Article III of the Constitution. There are 108 *constitutional courts*. *Legislative courts* are special courts that hear particular sorts of cases. One of the *legislative courts* hears appeals for veterans claims. A *civil case* involves a disagreement between two or more organizations or people. No crime has been committed in a *civil case*.

The taxes placed on imported goods coming to be sold in this country are called *tariffs*. The U.S. Court of International Trade hears cases about *tariffs*.

Focus Your Reading Answers

1 The federal court system is organized into constitutional courts and legislative courts.

2 Federal courts hear civil and criminal cases and appeals.

3 Federal judges are appointed by the president and confirmed by the Senate.

Diagram Extension

Ask students to use the diagram on page 206 to answer the following questions.

- What color represents constitutional courts? (blue)
- Which kind of court is the U.S. Court of Appeals for the Armed Forces? (legislative, or special, court)
- Which court hears cases appealed from the U.S. Court of International Trade? (the U.S. Court of Appeals for the Federal Circuit)

Picturing Government

The photograph on page 205 is of Federal District Judge Sonia Sotomayer of New York.

The courts shown in green on the diagram are not part of the federal system. However, appeals of decisions in these courts are sent to federal courts. Appeals of decisions in regulatory commissions such as the Federal Communications Commission are also appealed in federal court.

Constitutional Courts

The constitutional courts are the (1) federal district courts, (2) federal courts of appeals, (3) U.S. Court of Appeals for the Federal Circuit, and (4) U.S. Court of International Trade. The map on page 207 shows that the United States is divided into 94 districts and 12 circuits. Each state has at least one district court. Circuits cross state boundaries. The courts of appeals are divided into circuits.

The Federal Court System

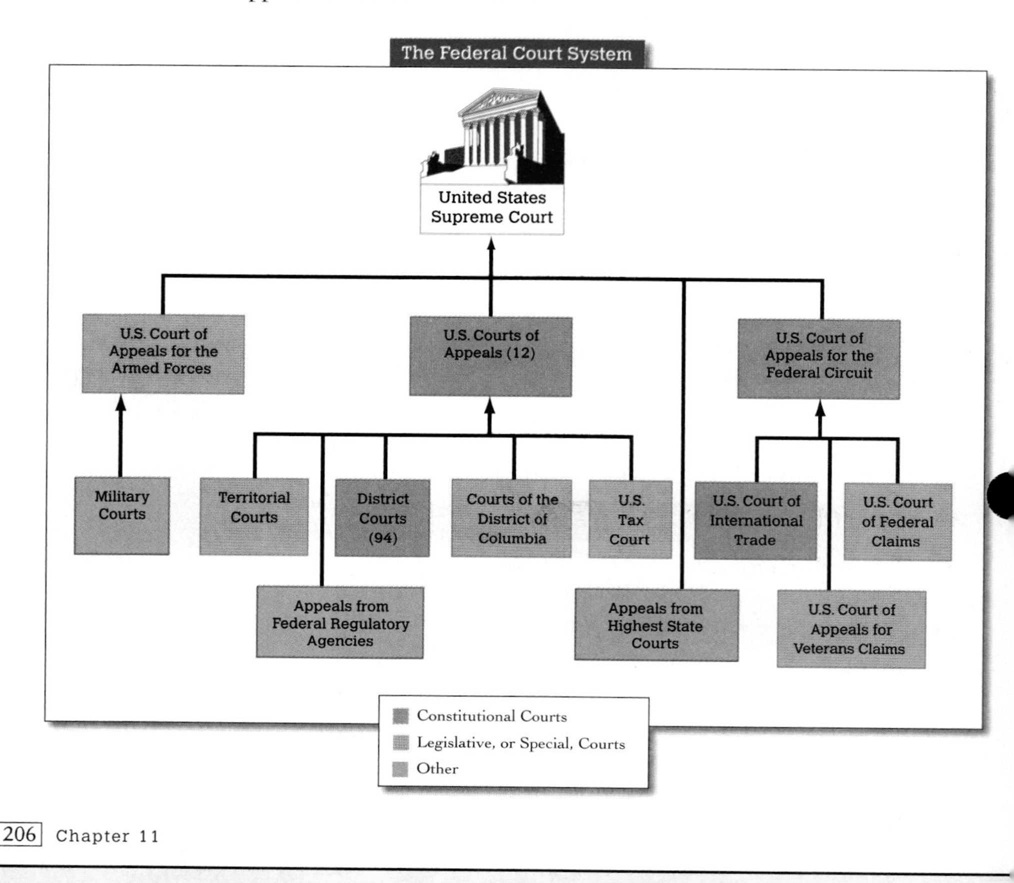

Extension

Ask students to choose one of the courts in the federal system and further research its history and responsibility. Ask them to find at least one case to illustrate how the court works. Have them present their findings to the class by using the Student Presentation Builder on the student CD.

Federal Court Districts and Circuits

(12) Federal Courts

-------- Boundaries for Federal District Courts

The 94 federal district courts are trial courts. They hear both civil and criminal cases. A **civil case** involves a disagreement between two or more persons or organizations. There is no crime involved. Federal district courts hear 80 percent of all cases brought to federal courts in a year. This totals hundreds of thousands of lawsuits.

The 12 courts of appeals hear appeals of decisions by the federal district courts. Most cases end in the district courts. However, about 55,000 cases a year are appealed to the next level, the courts of appeals. These courts do not have trials. Judges rule based on arguments and documents that are presented by lawyers.

stop and think

Create a table in your notebook of the types of federal courts to help you organize the information in the first two subheadings. Work with a partner to make sure that you include all the important information.

Map Extension

Ask students to use the map on page 207 to answer the following questions.

- In which federal court district is your state located?
- The Virgin Islands is in the same district as some states located where? (along the northeastern continental United States)
- Why do you think there are so few states in district 2? (New York, which is in that district, is one of the most populous states.)

Stop and Think

Students' tables will vary but should reflect lesson content on the types of federal courts.

Extension

Congress has attempted through legislation, including the Speedy Trial Act of 1974, to ensure that every district court has a plan to prevent long delays in bringing cases to trial. A goal is to have each civil case come to trial within 18 months of its being filed. However, with each district court judge dealing with an average of more than 400 new cases annually, this goal is not always reached.

Picturing Government

Thurgood Marshall, shown in the photo feature on page 208, was a lively boy who sometimes got into trouble at school. When he did so, the principal of the school sent him to the basement to memorize sections of the U.S. Constitution. This memorization served Marshall well when he argued cases; he won 29 of the 32 major cases he argued as director of the Legal Defense and Education Fund of the National Association for the Advancement of Colored People (NAACP). Lyndon Johnson was a personal friend. The two men had joked about Johnson appointing Marshall to the Supreme Court. Johnson had originally said he wouldn't do it, because their friendship would have to end. But he changed his mind in 1967. Marshall served until 1991 and was once called the "conscience of the Court."

Sandra Day O'Connor, (center photograph) stunned the world by announcing her retirement in 2005, ending an 11-year stretch without openings on the Supreme Court. She served for 24 terms and was noted as a swing voter on key issues such as the death penalty and abortion. O'Connor ended the 191-year reign of males only on the Supreme Court alone until 1993, when President Clinton appointed Ruth Bader Ginsburg.

Thurgood Marshall, appointed to the Supreme Court by President Lyndon Johnson in 1967, was the first African American on the Court. President Ronald Reagan appointed Sandra Day O'Connor, the first female justice on the Court, in 1981. Louis Brandeis, the first Jewish member of the Court, was appointed by President Woodrow Wilson in 1916.

The Court of Appeals for the Federal Circuit hears appeals for only certain types of civil cases. It takes appeals from the Court of International Trade, the U.S. Court of Federal Claims, and the U.S. Court of Appeals for Veterans Claims;

Federal Court System and Judges

Court	Number of Courts	Number of Judges	Term of Appointment
Supreme Court	1	9	Life
District Courts	94	642	Life
Court of Appeals	12	179	Life
Court of Appeals for the Federal Circuit	1	12	Life
Trade Court	1	9	Life
Court of Appeals for the Armed Forces	1	5	15 years
Tax Court	1	19	15 years
Court of Federal Claims	1	16	15 years
Court of Appeals for Veterans Claims	1	7	15 years

Picturing Government, continued

Louis Brandeis (photograph on the right) was confirmed to the Supreme Court despite the opposition of both anti-Semites and business interests. In his private practice in Boston, Brandeis had attacked monopolies and aided the passage of the Clayton Anti-Trust Act and the Federal Trade Commission Act. Although Brandeis supported much of the New Deal legislation, he did not do so unthinkingly. For example, he agreed with the majority opinion that the National Industrial Recovery Act of 1933 was unconstitutional.

208 Chapter 11

appeals involving patents and copyrights that were heard in a federal district court; and decisions made in some executive departments. Unlike the other federal appeals courts, the Court of Appeals for the Federal Circuit may take a case from any area of the country. Few cases ever go to the Supreme Court from this court. Like the 12 courts of appeals, there are no trials in the Court of Appeals for the Federal Circuit.

The Court of International Trade hears cases related to tariffs and other trade issues. A **tariff** is a tax on imports, or goods coming into the country for sale. The court sits in New York, but travels to other cities with major ports.

Legislative, or Special, Courts

Congress created the legislative courts to deal with particular issues. These issues are related to the power of Congress to carry out its legislative powers. Look at the diagram on page 206 to see where appeals from each court are heard.

Civics Today

The Government Printing Office

Need a copy of a Supreme Court decision? Want to read what your representative or senator said in Congress today? Looking for a committee's report on homeland security? The Government Printing Office (GPO) can provide each of these documents. The GPO prints the daily *Congressional Record* and the *Federal Register*. It also prints everything from Supreme Court decisions and executive department reports to consumer information and national park guides.

The mission of the GPO is "Keeping Americans Informed." Its Web site says that the GPO "is the federal government's primary centralized resource for gathering, cataloging, producing, providing, and preserving published information in all its forms." This means the GPO prints hard copies of government documents and also produces them in digital formats. The GPO's Web site provides 275,000 documents free to anyone with an Internet connection. Printed products such as booklets and full-length books are provided for the cost of printing.

For example, in 2004, the GPO provided the complete copy of *The 9-11 Commission Report* online at no cost.

Civics Today Extension

The Government Printing Office (GPO) began in 1813 through a congressional mandate. Located in Washington, D.C., the GPO's main plant is, at 1.5 million square feet, the world's largest information processing, printing, and distribution center. In contrast to most federal agencies, the GPO operates as businesses do; customers pay for the publications. The GPO also receives two appropriations annually to cover costs of congressional printing and the Federal Depository Library Program.

Extension

Have interested students use library resources or the Internet to find out about the Federal Depository Library Program, which partners with the GPO to distribute government information to 1,250 libraries across the nation. Allow time for students to share their findings with the class.

Table Extension

Ask students to use the table on page 208 to answer the following questions.

- Which of the federal courts has the greatest number of judges? (district courts)
- What are the two possible terms of appointment for a judgeship? (15 years or life)
- How many courts of appeals are there? (12)

Extension

Divide the class into nine small groups. Assign each group one of the current Supreme Court justices. Ask them to present information on that person's life and his or her influence on the Court.

Extension

Have students choose one of the special courts. Ask them to use library resources or the Internet to find out more about what the court does, as well as a current example of a case before the court.

Putting It All Together

Students' summaries will vary but should be based on information from the table on page 208.

The Tax court hears trials related to tax disputes between taxpayers and the IRS or the Treasury Department. It is a national court.

Territorial courts were created by Congress in Guam, the Virgin Islands, and the Northern Mariana Islands. These are territories governed by the United States. Each court system hears criminal and civil trials.

The Court of Appeals for Veterans Claims hears appeals of rulings by the Board of Veterans' Appeals in the Department of Veterans Affairs. Individuals appeal if they believe the board has denied them their lawful veterans' benefits.

The Court of Federal Claims is a national court. It hears cases asking for damages from the federal government. *Damages* refer to the payment of money for loss or injury.

The Court of Appeals for the Armed Forces hears appeals of verdicts in military court cases. Military courts are not part of the federal court system.

Appointing Federal Judges and Supreme Court Justices

Federal judges are appointed by the president and approved by the Senate. Most federal judges serve "during good behavior." Generally, this means they serve until they choose to retire or resign. Judges in the special courts serve 15-year terms. The reason for the long terms is judicial independence. Judges do not have to worry about their jobs. As a result, political pressure to rule one way or the other has little effect on them.

In choosing candidates for federal judgeships, presidents tend to look for two things. Usually, they choose people from their own party and people who share their views on issues likely to come before the court.

This is especially true of appointments to the Supreme Court. As you will read in Chapter 12, the Supreme Court's rulings can have a great impact on national policy.

Putting It All Together

Using the table of the Federal Court System and Judges on page 208, write a one-paragraph summary of the federal court system.

Picturing Government

The photograph on page 211 shows a lawyer arguing a case. Note that the evidence is presented to jurors on computer screens.

LESSON 2

Judicial Jurisdiction and Power

Thinking on Your Own

Suppose a friend of yours disagrees with a brother or sister or another friend over the ownership of a CD. They have asked you to settle the disagreement. Describe in a paragraph in your notebook what you could do to help your friend.

focus your reading

Explain the types of jurisdiction held by federal courts.

How did the power of judicial review develop?

words to know

jurisdiction

original jurisdiction

appellate jurisdiction

The job of the federal court system is the same as that of state and local courts. Courts apply the law to cases that come before them. For federal courts, the cases may be civil, criminal, or constitutional. Federal courts get their power to hear cases and hand down decisions from the Constitution.

Jurisdiction of Federal Courts

Federal courts cannot hear just any type of law case. Federal courts have the authority to hear only certain types of cases. This authority is called a court's **jurisdiction**. Article III, Section 2, Clause 1, of the Constitution lists the types of cases that federal courts can hear. They are classified by the topic of the case and by the parties involved. The table on page 212 gives the jurisdiction of federal courts.

How does jurisdiction work in reality? For many years, the states of New Jersey and New York argued over ownership of Ellis Island in New York Harbor. The case was finally decided in the federal courts. Ellis Island was given to the state of New Jersey. Suppose a citizen of California sues a citizen of Nevada for damages from a car accident. The case is heard in federal district court. If the Nevada resident loses, the person may appeal to the U.S. Court of Appeals.

Trials are heard in federal district courts.

Lesson Summary

Federal courts may try civil, criminal, or constitutional cases. Different courts have different jurisdiction. The federal district courts have only original jurisdictions. The federal courts of appeals have only appellate jurisdiction. The Supreme Court has both original and appellate jurisdiction. The Judiciary Act of 1789 gave the Supreme Court power to review state constitutions and laws. Chief Justice John Marshall added to the Court's power by reviewing acts of Congress, known as the power of judicial review, a power that has never been challenged.

Lesson Objective

Students will learn about the jurisdiction of federal courts and the power of judicial review.

Focus Your Reading Answers

1 Federal courts have both original and appellate jurisdiction. Federal district courts have only original jurisdiction. The federal courts of appeals have only appellate jurisdiction. The Supreme Court has both.

2 The power of judicial review began when John Marshall was Chief Justice of the Supreme Court. The Court took it upon itself to review a law in the case of *Marbury* v. *Madison*.

Words to Know

Discuss each of the vocabulary terms with students.

The authority to hear a particular type of case is called *jurisdiction*. The Constitution lists the *jurisdiction* of federal courts. The first court to hear a case has *original jurisdiction*. The 94 federal courts have the only *original jurisdiction* in cases. Courts that hear appeals have *appellate jurisdiction*. The federal courts of appeal have only *appellate jurisdiction*.

Table Extension

Invite interested students to use library resources or the Internet to find an example of at least one of the types of cases over which federal courts have jurisdiction. Have them outline the case for the class and explain the ruling.

Federal Court Jurisdiction

Cases by Topic	Cases by Parties Involved
• U.S. Constitution	• Representatives of foreign governments, such as ambassadors
• Federal laws, including federal bankruptcy laws	• Governments of two or more of the 50 states
• Treaties	• Federal government or one of its officials or departments
• Admiralty law (laws relating to activities on the oceans, and on U.S. rivers, lakes, and canals)	• A state or one of its citizens and a foreign country or one of its citizens
• Maritime law (laws relating to shipping activities)	• Citizens of different states
	• A state and a citizen of a different state
	• Citizens of the same state who claim land under grants from different states

The 94 federal district courts have only **original jurisdiction** in cases. They are the first, or original, court to hear a case. The federal courts of appeal have only **appellate jurisdiction**. They hear only appeals.

The Supreme Court has both original and appellate jurisdiction. However, the Court's original jurisdiction is limited. The case must involve a representative of a foreign government or be a certain type of case involving a state. The total number of such cases usually amounts to fewer than five a year.

The U.S. Supreme Court's main work is hearing appeals from lower federal courts of appeals. The Supreme Court also hears cases appealed from state supreme courts. However, the case must be related to the Constitution or to federal law. The U.S. Supreme Court is able to rule only on the federal issue in the case. For example, the Supreme Court will not decide if a convicted murderer is innocent or guilty. The Court can only decide whether the person received a fair trial.

Extension

Federal judges are appointed for life. However, Congress can impeach them for "treason, bribery, or other high crimes and misdemeanors." Salaries cannot be reduced during a term of a federal judge, thus removing the possibility of political influence. In these two ways, the Constitution promotes judicial independence.

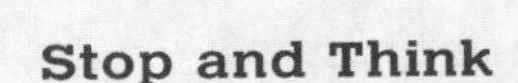

stop and think

In your notebook, summarize in one paragraph the table on page 212. Share your summary with a partner, and make any necessary changes.

Power of Judicial Review

Of the three branches of government, the Framers had the least to say about the judicial branch. Article III, Section 1, Clause 1, states simply that the "judicial power of the United States, shall be vested [held] in one Supreme Court, and in such inferior Courts as the Congress may . . . establish." What exactly does this mean?

Congress began to spell out the power of the federal judiciary by passing the Judiciary Act of 1789. This act created the first of the lower federal courts. It also gave the Supreme Court the power to review state constitutions and state laws. If they disagreed with the U.S. Constitution, the Court had the power to declare them unconstitutional.

John Marshall added to the power of the federal judiciary. He served as Chief Justice of the Supreme Court from 1801 to 1835. In Marbury v. Madison, the Court declared a part of a federal law unconstitutional. In doing this, the Court took for itself the power to review acts of Congress. This is known as the power of judicial review. Since then, neither Congress nor any president has ever argued that the Supreme Court does not have this power.

Chief Justice John Marshall

Landmark Supreme Court Case: Judicial Review

***Marbury* v. *Madison* (1803):** Democrat Thomas Jefferson had won the election of 1800. John Adams was the outgoing president and a Federalist. He wanted to appoint as many Federalists as possible to office. He appointed 42 judges in the District of Columbia. By the time Adams left office, several men had not received their appointment papers. The new secretary of state, James Madison, refused to deliver them. William Marbury sued Madison for his papers. The Supreme Court heard the case because it involved an official of the federal government. The Court decided that the Constitution did not grant the power to rule on this case. It ruled that part of the Judiciary Act of 1789 was unconstitutional.

Putting It All Together

Review what you wrote in Thinking on Your Own. Suppose your friend did not like the way you settled the disagreement. How could your friend appeal your decision? Who might serve as an appellate court in this case?

Stop and Think

Students' summaries will vary but should reflect the information in the table on page 212.

Picturing Government

John Marshall, shown on page 213, was the fourth Supreme Court Chief Justice. During his 35 years on the court, he shaped American jurisprudence. Oddly, prior to accepting the appointment, he had rejected several other offers of federal employment: President Washington asked him to be United States attorney for Virginia and attorney general; John Adams offered him a Supreme Court position. Marshall finally accepted Adams's offer to become the secretary of state, and then Chief Justice.

Putting It All Together

Students' answers will vary.

Supreme Court Case Extension

In *Marbury* v. *Madison*, Chief Justice John Marshall defined the relationship of the Supreme Court to the other branches of government. Although the practice of judicial review has become widely accepted, both President Jefferson and President Jackson disagreed with it. Through passing the Eleventh, Fourteenth, Sixteenth, and Twenty-sixth Amendments to the Constitution, the public has expressed disapproval of several Supreme Court decisions.

Participate in Government

1 You may wish to take your students to watch a local trial. Contact the clerk of courts to see what trials are open to the public and the schedule for the trial.

2 Have students research reasons people are excused from jury duty, such as serious illness. Have them report to the class on these few, and often temporary, exceptions to the responsibility of serving on a jury.

Recommended Reading

Below is a list of books that relate to the issues covered in this chapter. The numbers in parentheses indicate the related Thematic Strands of the National Council for the Social Studies (NCSS).

Lisa Aldred. *Thurgood Marshall: Supreme Court Justice.* Chelsea House Publishers, 2005. (III, IV, VI, X)

Geoffrey M. Horn. *The Supreme Court.* Gareth Stevens Audio, 2003. (VI, X)

Brendan January. *The Supreme Court.* Watts Franklin, 2005. (VI, X)

Participate in Government

Serve on a Jury

Jury duty is one of the few responsibilities that citizens have. To serve on a jury, you must

- be a U.S. citizen
- be at least eighteen years of age
- understand English
- never have been convicted of a serious crime

Serving on a jury is one of the civic responsibilities of citizenship.

People are chosen for jury duty at random. Names are drawn from lists of registered voters or those holding driver's licenses. When you are called to jury duty, you receive a jury summons in the mail. It will tell you when and where to report. Ignoring a jury summons is a serious offense. If you do not report, you can be charged with a crime.

At the courthouse, you will not be assigned to a jury right away. Potential jurors go into a jury pool. First, you will be asked to fill out some forms. Then you will be given a number and sent to a room with other possible jurors. You may be asked to answer a list of questions.

When your number is called, you will be taken to a courtroom. The case could be either criminal or civil. Lawyers for both sides will ask you questions. The judge may also question you. They want to see what or who you know that could affect your decision as a juror. For example, the case involves a hit-and-run. The person charged with the crime was found drunk nearby. A possible juror has been the victim of a drunk driver. The juror would probably be excused from hearing that case.

If you are not called to serve on a jury the first day, you usually do not have to come to the jury room again. You may only have to call in each day to see if your number has been called. Whether you serve or not, you are doing your duty and supporting the rule of law.

Skill Builder

Draw Conclusions

A conclusion is the result of thinking. In order to reach a conclusion, you have to gather and analyze, or think about, information. Then you have to decide what it means.

You draw conclusions every day without noticing what you are doing. You consider buying one of three shirts. You look at the prices and the colors. You think about what you can wear with each shirt. Then you put all these ideas together to find out which shirt best meets your needs. Perhaps you want to buy a computer. You analyze the features on four computers and compare them to your needs. Then you reach a conclusion about which computer is best for you.

Juries are asked to draw conclusions when they decide verdicts in trials. They base their conclusions on the evidence and the law. Appellate judges also draw conclusions based on the evidence and the law.

To Draw a Conclusion:

- Gather information about the topic.
- List any other facts you already know about the topic.
- Put all your information together.
- Analyze the information and decide what it means.

Answer the following questions by drawing conclusions.

1 Where would a case involving federal drug charges first be heard? Explain how you reached your conclusion.

2 Where would a lawsuit brought by a Native-American nation against the federal government first be heard? Explain how you reached your conclusion.

Skill Builder

1 A case involving federal drug charges would first be heard in federal district court, because it is a federal offense. Students' explanations of how they reached their conclusion will vary.

2 A lawsuit brought by a Native-American nation against the federal government would first be heard in federal district court. Students' explanations of how they reached their conclusion will vary.

Classroom Discussion

Discuss with students some of the broader topics covered in this chapter.

- How can court loads be reduced so that cases come up rapidly for trial?
- Is the federal court system adequate as it is currently structured? Are there other types of courts that would be helpful?
- In what ways could frivolous lawsuits be discouraged?

Research Resources

Below is a list of reference books and Web sites that relate to the issues covered in this chapter. Students may wish to use these to further their research on ideas in the preceding lessons. Web site addresses may change over time. Use keyword searching on a major search engine to locate sites.

Reference Books:

Kermit Hall, ed. *The Oxford Companion to the Supreme Court of the United States.* 2nd edition, 2005.

Gary R. Hartman. *Landmark Supreme Court Cases*, 2004.

David G. Savage. *Guide to the U.S. Supreme Court.* 4th edition, 2004.

Web Sites:

The Supreme Court's site includes recent decisions, as well as general information about the Court and oral arguments.

Information about the courts of appeals, district courts, and bankruptcy courts, along with the Supreme Court, can be found on court sites.

Chapter

12 THE SUPREME COURT AT WORK

Getting Focused

Skim this chapter to predict what you will be learning.

- **Read the lesson titles and subheadings.**
- **Look at the illustrations and read the captions.**
- **Examine the diagram.**
- **Review the vocabulary words and terms.**

After skimming the chapter, write at least five things in your notebook that you already know about the U.S. Supreme Court.

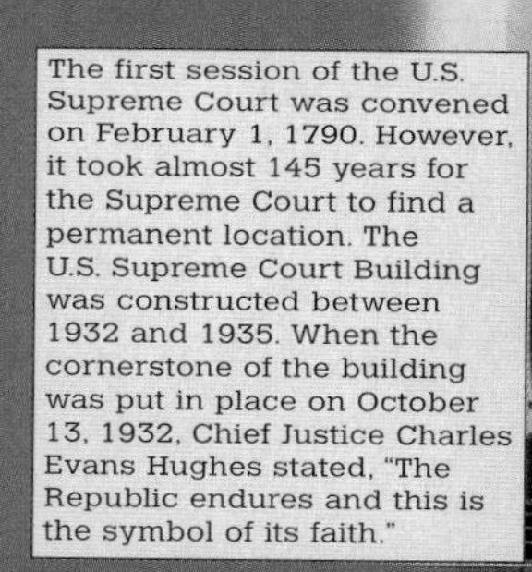

The first session of the U.S. Supreme Court was convened on February 1, 1790. However, it took almost 145 years for the Supreme Court to find a permanent location. The U.S. Supreme Court Building was constructed between 1932 and 1935. When the cornerstone of the building was put in place on October 13, 1932, Chief Justice Charles Evans Hughes stated, "The Republic endures and this is the symbol of its faith."

Words to Know

Introduce each of the following vocabulary terms to students.

Explain that *oral arguments* are presentations that lawyers give before the Supreme Court justices. The Court hears *oral arguments* on Mondays through Wednesdays and sometimes on Thursdays.

A *conference* is a time for the justices to discuss cases among themselves. The justices generally meet for a *conference* on Wednesday afternoons and Friday mornings.

A *law clerk* does research for a justice. A *law clerk* may help shape a justice's opinion on a case.

The writ of certiorari, which asks the justices to hear a case, is known as a *cert*. A *cert* is the way most cases arrive at the Court.

The *rule of four* is the need for four of the Supreme Court justices to agree to take a case. Because of the *rule of four*, most cases never reach the Supreme Court for trial. A government policy related to women and minorities is called *affirmative action*. The goal of *affirmative action* is to make up for past discrimination.

Related Transparencies

T-10 The Federal Court System and Decision-making on the Supreme Court

T-20 Concept Web

Key Blacklines

Biography—Byron White

CD Extension

Encourage students to use the reading comprehension, vocabulary reinforcement, and other activities on the student CD.

Getting Focused

After students have written their lists, place the students in small groups to see how many facts each group can tally by combining their lists. Be sure to correct any misunderstandings about the work of the Court when groups share their master lists in the follow-up discussion.

Pre-Reading Discussion

1 Review with students the duties of the judicial branch.

2 Using current examples, discuss with students the professional and personal qualifications that a Supreme Court justice must possess.

LESSON 1

How the Court Process Works

Thinking on Your Own

Everyone is entitled to his or her opinion. Every year, the U.S. Supreme Court issues dozens of opinions. Write a paragraph in your notebook about why a Court opinion would outweigh yours.

The Supreme Court's term begins in October. The nine justices hear cases from the first week in October until early May. The term is named for the year in which it begins. For example, the term that begins in October 2007 is the 2007 term.

During the term, justices hear oral arguments for two weeks each month. **Oral arguments** are the presentations that lawyers make before the justices. Remember that the Supreme Court acts as a court of appeals. These courts decide whether to uphold or reverse a lower court's decision or send the case back for a retrial.

The Court hears arguments from Monday through Wednesday and sometimes on Thursdays. The justices meet among themselves on most Wednesday afternoons and Friday mornings. In these **conferences**, the justices discuss the cases before them for rulings. They also discuss which new cases to take.

focus your reading

Why do cases reach the Supreme Court?

Explain the process the Supreme Court uses for hearing and deciding on cases.

words to know

oral arguments
conference
law clerk
rule of four
cert
affirmative action
brief
precedent
amicus curiae brief
swing vote
opinion

William Rehnquist was sworn in as Chief Justice of the U.S. Supreme Court on September 26, 1986.

Words to Know, continued

A *brief* is a document that offers legal arguments. The *brief* usually includes legal *precedents* and facts about the case.

An example from a case already decided is a *precedent*. Justices will be guided by a *precedent* in the cases they decide.

An *amicus curiae brief* is one filed by government bodies, lobbyists, or interested parties as a "friend of the court." An *amicus curiae brief* will provide additional information supporting one side or the other.

The *swing vote* is the one that breaks the tie if four justices each hold opposite *opinions*. The *swing vote* is important because at least five justices are needed for a majority.

An *opinion* is the document expressing the legal reasoning behind a decision. A justice who disagrees with the majority may write a dissenting *opinion*.

Lesson Summary

The Supreme Court's annual term begins in October and ends in May. Each month, the justices spend half their time listening to oral arguments. They spend the rest of their time meeting in conference and doing legal research. Cases come through a writ of certiorari, which requests a review of the case. Four judges must agree to take a case. A case that is accepted is placed on the Court's calendar, and lawyers begin preparing briefs, which include facts of the case and precedents. People and groups submit amicus curiae briefs. Lawyers are permitted to give oral arguments for only 30 minutes. In their private meetings, the Chief Justice summarizes the case, and the justices vote and then write opinions on the case.

Lesson Objective

Students will learn about the process that the Supreme Court follows.

Focus Your Reading Answers

1 Cases reach the Supreme Court through an appeals process and are considered if they address legal or constitutional questions.

2 A case that is accepted is scheduled; lawyers prepare and file briefs. People and groups submit amicus curiae briefs. Lawyers are permitted to give oral arguments for only 30 minutes. In the justices' private meetings, the Chief Justice summarizes the case, and the justices vote and then write opinions on the case. There are majority, concurrent, and dissenting opinions, which are reviewed, finalized, and eventually published.

In 2000, the Supreme Court heard arguments regarding the presidential election between Al Gore and George W. Bush. Theodore Olson, an attorney for George W. Bush, spoke to reporters on the steps of the Supreme Court Building after making his argument to the Court.

During the rest of the time, the justices read, work on decisions, and meet with their law clerks. Clerking for a Supreme Court justice is an important job. The **law clerks** do most of the legal research for each justice. They are young men and women who graduated near the top of their classes from the nation's best law schools. Justices value their ideas. Law clerks can help shape a justice's opinion about a case.

Getting on the Court's Calendar

How do cases get to the Supreme Court? As you read in Chapter 11, a few cases come under the original jurisdiction of the Court.

Most cases arrive at the Court by writ of certiorari. The writ is called cert for short. The cert is issued as the result of a petition, or legal request, by a party—person or group—involved in a case. The petition asks the Court to review the case. Four justices must agree to take the case. This is known as the **rule of four**. Decisions are made during the justices' weekly conferences. If at least four justices vote "yes," the Court issues the writ of certiorari. The **cert** directs the lower court to send up the records of the case. The case is then scheduled for a hearing. If the Court refuses to take a case, the decision of the lower court is final.

The issue of affirmative action received national attention when the Supreme Court heard a case involving the University of Michigan.

About 8,000 requests for review are sent to the Supreme Court each year. Fewer than 100 are heard in open court and receive full written opinions.

Why do justices take some cases and not others? Typically, the justices take a case for only two reasons: it must raise either an important constitutional or legal question. For example, in the 2003 term, the Court dealt with two cases on affirmative action in education. **Affirmative action** is a government policy related to women and minority groups. Its

"Do you ever have one of those days when nothing seems constitutional?"

Picturing Government

The photograph at the top left of page 218 shows Theodore Olson, who was the lawyer for George W. Bush during the 2000 Supreme Court case *Bush* v. *Gore*. The Court heard arguments and made a decision the following day, holding that the Florida manual recount of presidential election ballots was unfair in practice, even if it was fair in theory.

Cartoon Extension

In the cartoon at the right of page 218, the justices are all reading over briefs. Remind students that the role of the Court is to determine a law's constitutionality.

Extension

Have interested students use library resources or the Internet to find out more about law clerking for any branch of government. What are the minimum requirements? How does a person apply for such a job? Have them present their findings to the class by using the Student Presentation Builder on the student CD.

Picturing Government

The interior of the Supreme Court is shown in the photograph on page 216. Cass Gilbert, the architect, also designed the Minnesota State Capitol, the United States Custom House, and the Woolworth Building, which was the world's tallest building at that time. Chosen to design the first building for the Supreme Court, he died before its completion. The Court had previously met in various buildings in New York, Philadelphia, and Washington, D.C. Former president William Howard Taft, who became Chief Justice from 1921–1930, lobbied for a separate building. When the cornerstone was laid in 1932, Chief Justice Charles Evans Hughes said, "The Republic endures and this is the symbol of its faith." Discuss that quotation with students; do they agree with Hughes? What symbols of faith in the Republic do they hold?

stop and think

Make an outline in your notebook of the most important information that you read in this lesson so far. Compare your outline with that of a partner. Add to it as you continue reading.

goal is to make up for past discrimination against these groups. The 2003 cases involved admissions policies at the University of Michigan law school and undergraduate school. The cases raised the issue of whether affirmative action was itself discriminatory.

The Decision-making Process

The first step once a cert is issued is scheduling the case on the Court's calendar.

The attorneys take the next step. Each side submits a **brief**. This document describes the legal arguments in favor of the lawyer's side. It also includes facts and legal precedents. A **precedent** is an example from a similar case that has already been decided. Typically, the Supreme Court uses precedents as a guide in deciding cases. The justices usually rule in the same way in similar cases.

Sometimes people who are not directly involved in a case file briefs, too. These are called **amicus curiae briefs**. The phrase means "friend of the court." Their purpose is to provide additional information to support one side or the other in the case. Government departments, agencies, and commissions, as well as individuals and lobbying groups, submit amicus curiae briefs. For example, both pro-gun and anti-gun lobbyists would submit briefs in a gun control case.

Law clerks, such as those who work with Justice Clarence Thomas, play a key role at the Supreme Court.

The next step is oral arguments. Each lawyer is given 30 minutes to present the case for his or her side. The lawyer summarizes the brief and highlights the major legal points. During the presentations, justices often question the lawyers. They may challenge the lawyer's argument or ask questions that help to draw out the lawyer's points. At the end of the half hour, the lawyer's time is up—even if the lawyer is mid-sentence.

The next step is the justices' conferences on Wednesdays and Fridays. The room is empty except for the nine justices—and 20 or more carts. These contain petitions for writ of certiorari, as well as briefs and paperwork related to the cases the justices are

Stop and Think

Students' outlines will vary but should cover content from the lesson so far.

Picturing Government

The photograph on page 219 shows Clarence Thomas, far right, with three of his law clerks in 2002. Nominated to the Supreme Court in 1991 when Thurgood Marshall retired, Thomas survived stormy Senate judiciary hearings that were eventually broadcast nationally after accusations of sexual misconduct surfaced. The Senate confirmed Thomas, who is known as a conservative, by a vote of 52 to 48.

Picturing Government

The 1986 photograph on page 217 shows William Rehnquist being sworn in as Chief Justice of the Supreme Court. At far right is then-president Ronald Reagan. At left is Justice Antonin Scalia. Richard Nixon had appointed Rehnquist, who was then an assistant attorney general, to the Supreme Court in 1972, in the wake of two vacancies on the Court. Rehnquist, who presided over the Court's shift to a more conservative tone, is also noted for improving the Court's efficiency and limiting the number of cases heard. He died of thyroid cancer in September 2005.

Extension

Have students work in small groups to review the Supreme Court decisions of the past year. Encourage them to use online resources to help them summarize the arguments and decisions. You may wish to preview these sites (some of them are suggested at the end of this chapter and at the end of Chapter 11) and assign individual cases to each group.

Picturing Government

The photograph at the bottom left of page 218 captures a University of Michigan protest concerning a case on affirmative action. The case, *Grutter* v. *Bollinger*, was first filed in a district court in 2001, then appealed in 2002 before reaching the Supreme Court for oral arguments in April 2003. The Court ruled that the University of Michigan could use race as a consideration in admitting students to the law school.

Picturing Government

At the top of page 220, Justice David H. Souter is shown in a photograph taken in front of a painting of Chief Justice Charles Evans Hughes. Souter was relatively unknown outside New Hampshire, where he was on the state's supreme court, when he was appointed to the U.S. Court of Appeals in 1990. Just five months later, President George H. W. Bush nominated him to the Court when William J. Brennan retired. The Senate confirmed Souter without controversy. Souter has settled firmly into the Court's moderate camp, voting in accord with centrist Sandra Day O'Connor 24 times.

Chart Extension

Have pairs of students write each of the steps toward a published ruling on individual index cards. Then have them shuffle the cards and take turns putting the steps in order until both have mastered it. You may wish to use a similar exercise with the entire class to review before a quiz or test.

Putting It All Together

Students' summaries will vary but should cover lesson content. See the Lesson Summary on page 217 for an example.

Justice David H. Souter

hearing. The Chief Justice runs the conferences. Any petitions for cert are discussed and decided. Then the justices discuss the cases they have heard in the past two weeks. The Chief Justice begins by summarizing the case. He or she also explains what he or she thinks about it. Each justice in turn expresses his or her opinion. The Chief Justice then takes a vote.

The vote may be unanimous—meaning that all the justices agree—or there may be majority and minority views. At least five justices must agree on one point of view to make a majority. About one-third of the votes are unanimous. When the vote is tied, four to four, the fifth and deciding vote is called the **swing vote**.

Decision-making at the Supreme Court

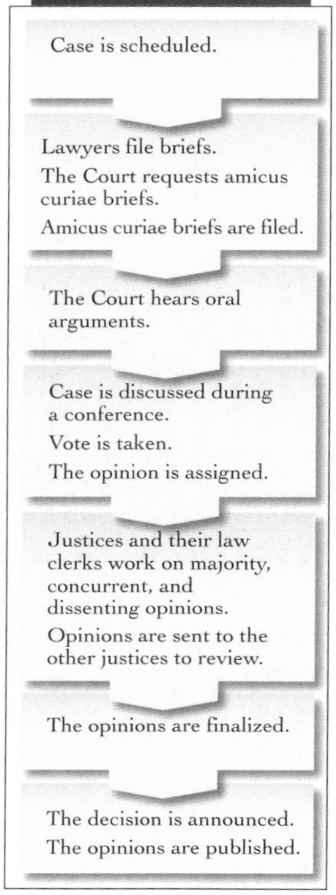

- Case is scheduled.
- Lawyers file briefs. The Court requests amicus curiae briefs. Amicus curiae briefs are filed.
- The Court hears oral arguments.
- Case is discussed during a conference. Vote is taken. The opinion is assigned.
- Justices and their law clerks work on majority, concurrent, and dissenting opinions. Opinions are sent to the other justices to review.
- The opinions are finalized.
- The decision is announced. The opinions are published.

Once the vote is taken, the justices have to turn their decision into a written opinion. The **opinion** is a document stating the legal reasoning behind the decision. If the decision is unanimous, then the opinion is a unanimous opinion. If the vote is split, one of the justices on the majority side will write the majority opinion. Sometimes a justice will agree with the final decision but arrive at the conclusion differently. Then the justice may write a concurring opinion. Often, a justice who disagrees will write a dissenting opinion.

After the conference, the justices and their law clerks go to work to write the opinions. The opinions are sent around for the other justices to review. This step in the process can go on for months. At some point during the term, however, the decision is announced and the opinion, or decision, is published.

Putting It All Together

Write a summary of this lesson. Use the outline you made in the Stop and Think activity for information. If necessary, review the Skill Builder on page 136.

LESSON 2

Influences on the Supreme Court

Thinking on Your Own

Do other people ever influence what you do? Think of something that you did or bought because someone else told you it was a good idea. Write two sentences in your notebook that describe the situation.

focus your reading

Describe the role of the Constitution and laws in the decisions of the Supreme Court.

Why does a justice's views and interaction with other justices affect his or her decisions?

Explain how public opinion may affect Supreme Court decisions.

List how the executive and legislative branches influence the Supreme Court.

words to know

view

court packing

nominee

Supreme Court justices do not decide cases in isolation. The nine men and women on the Court are the products of their backgrounds and education. The interaction among justices also influences decisions. Public opinion plays a role as well. Remember, too, that the Court is one branch among three. As a result, the system of checks and balances also impacts the Court. However, the Constitution and federal law are the basic guides to decision-making for the justices.

The seal of the United States Supreme Court

The Basic Guides

Why are there dissenting opinions in Supreme Court cases? How can three justices agree on the reasoning behind a decision and a fourth justice disagree on the reasoning? Yet that fourth justice agrees with the end result of the

The scales of justice appear in front of the Albert V. Bryan United States Courthouse in Alexandria, VA.

Lesson Summary

The Supreme Court is influenced by a number of factors. These include the justices' personal views and experiences as citizens, their interaction and discussion, public opinion, and the other branches of government.

Lesson Objective

Students will learn about the various influences on Supreme Court decisions.

Focus Your Reading Answers

1 The principles of the Constitution and the laws guide the justices in making decisions.

2 The individual justices may be moderates or strict or loose constructionists, which influences their interpretation of the law. As the justices talk about a case, they discuss ideas, which can affect their decisions.

3 Justices consider how most Americans feel about an issue. They are also shaped by living in the society themselves and by reading and watching what others do.

4 The executive branch has an effect because of the power of appointment. The legislative branch influences the Court by limiting the rulings with laws or amendments to the Constitution. Also, the Senate approves justices appointed to the Court.

Words to Know

Discuss each of the vocabulary terms with students.

The *views* of the justices are their philosophies. A justice's *views* may be changed through talking with another member of the Court.

Court packing is adding justices to support a particular agenda. Franklin Roosevelt's attempt at *court packing* failed.

A *nominee* is someone selected to fill a vacant position. The Senate must approve the *nominee*.

Cartoon Extension

Review with students the provisions of the First Amendment. What is the cartoon on page 222 suggesting that people will lose if the amendment is repealed? Have them explain the idea of legislating from the bench.

Picturing Government

In the photograph at the bottom of page 222, Justices Ruth Bader Ginsburg (left) and Sandra Day O'Connor (right) talk with Chief Justice Rehnquist during a 1993 recess. After O'Connor resigned in 2005, Ginsburg became the only woman on the Court.

Picturing Government

The front of the seal of the United States is shown on the left of page 221. It depicts the bald eagle shielded by the flag with 13 stripes. In his talons, the eagle holds arrows, signifying military power, and an olive branch, the symbol of peace. The Latin motto *e pluribus unum* (meaning "from many, one") appears on a ribbon that the eagle has in its beak. Charles Thomson, who designed the final seal, said the stars in the cloud above the eagle's head should appear as "a glory, breaking through a cloud." The seal appears on dollar bills.

"Call it 'legislating from the bench,' if you will, but on this occasion I should like to repeal the First Amendment."

others' thinking. A fifth justice may disagree with both sets of ideas but agree with the end result. The other three justices disagree with the reasoning and the vote. Is the law not the law?

The principles of the Constitution remain the same. However, the Framers described general principles in the Constitution. They left it to later people to apply these principles. For example, the Constitution gave Congress the power to regulate commerce. It did not spell out the meaning of that term. Differences in how justices interpret such powers can result in different Supreme Court opinions.

The Justices

The **views**, or philosophies, of the justices and their relationships with one another also influence decisions. As you read in Chapter 4, there are two very different views of the Constitution. One view is strict constructionist and the other is loose constructionist. Strict constructionists are considered conservatives, and loose constructionists are considered liberals. Those in between are considered moderates. Since the 1970s, Republican presidents have tended to name more conservative justices. President Bill Clinton, a Democrat, appointed justices in the 1990s who were more moderate.

Differences in views influence how justices look at and interpret the Constitution and the law. Conservative justices stay as close as possible to what they think the Framers meant. Liberal justices tend to be more flexible about what the Constitution permits. For example, in the 2003 term, the majority of justices upheld affirmative action in two education cases. The two justices who are the most conservative disagreed strongly with this opinion.

Chief Justice William Rehnquist confers with Justices O'Connor and Ginsburg.

Replacing a justice can become a huge political issue. This occurred twice in 2005 when President George W. Bush had to replace Justice Sandra Day O'Connor, who retired, and Chief Justice William Rehnquist, who passed away.

Picturing Government

At the bottom of page 221 is a photograph of the statue of Justice, based on the Roman idea of the goddess Justitia, blindfolded and balancing scales. In Greek myth, she is called Themis and, because of her gift for prophecy, is not blindfolded. The origin of the goddess goes back to the Egyptian goddess Ma'at, who aided Osiris in judging the dead by weighing their hearts.

stop and think

Make a heading in your notebook entitled "Why Justices Disagree." List the reasons you have already read about. Add to the list as you continue reading.

Conservative Republicans wanted conservative replacements. Democrats and moderate Republicans wanted more moderate justices. John Roberts was confirmed as Chief Justice, to replace Rehnquist in September 2005.

The Chief Justice can also influence the Court's decisions. He or she makes up the list of what will be discussed in each weekly conference. He or she summarizes each case and presents his or her viewpoint before the other justices speak. The Chief Justice can also keep conflicts among justices from getting out of hand. This results in a better working relationship among justices.

United States Society

The justices are members of U.S. society. They read and hear the same news every day as other Americans. Their values and beliefs are shaped by living and working in this country. As a result, their viewpoints reflect the values and beliefs of other Americans.

Primary Source

reading for understanding

1. What did Justice Marshall force his fellow justices to consider?
2. How does this excerpt show how justices influence one another?

The Influence of One Justice on Another

Thurgood Marshall was the first African American named to the U.S. Supreme Court. He had been a justice for 14 years before Sandra Day O'Connor joined the Court in 1981. The following is from an article she wrote when Justice Marshall retired in 1992.

"Although all of us come to the Court with our own personal histories and experiences, Justice Marshall brought a special perspective. His was the eye of a lawyer who saw the deepest wounds . . . in the social fabric and used law to help heal them. . . . His was the mouth of a man who knew the anguish of the silenced and gave them a voice.

"At oral arguments and conference meetings, in opinions and dissents, Justice Marshall imparted not only his legal acumen but also his life experiences, constantly pushing and prodding us to respond not only to the persuasiveness of legal arguments but also to the power of moral truth."

—Justice Sandra Day O'Connor, "A Tribute to Justice Thurgood Marshall" (44 Stan L. Rev. 1217), *Stanford Law Review*, June 1992

Stop and Think
Students' lists will vary but may include personal views, constitutional interpretations, the opinions of the Chief Justice, and U.S. society.

Reading for Understanding

1 Marshall made the other justices aware of deep wounds in the social fabric and of the anguish of the silenced.

2 The speech mentions oral arguments, conference meetings, and opinion as ways justices influence each other.

Extension

Have students use library resources or the Internet to track the Supreme Court appointments in their lifetimes. Are the newest justices noted for being strict or loose constructionists? Are they moderate, conservative, or liberal? Have students make graphic organizers to explain their findings.

Extension

Have students investigate the ideas of the current members of the Court. Ask them to speculate on which issues they might disagree and what their opinions might be.

Cartoon Extension

Ask students to recall from their general knowledge of history when the historical "Era of Good Feelings" took place. (James Monroe's presidency, 1816–1824) Help students understand that the Roosevelt "era of good feelings" was a time of cooperation within the government that ended with Roosevelt's court-packing scheme. In the cartoon on page 224, point out the dove flying off and dropping the olive branch symbolizing peace.

In deciding which cases to take, justices tend to weigh public opinion. What do most Americans think about the issue? How strongly do they hold those views? Is the nation ready to take a step beyond those views? Justices look at the same questions when making their rulings.

A good example is the University of Michigan admissions cases in 2003, discussed in Lesson 1. Justice Sandra Day O'Connor wrote the majority opinion. She stated that in 25 years, affirmative action policies might no longer be necessary. However, there is evidence to show the need for them now.

The Executive and Legislative Branches

As you remember, the Framers set up a system of checks and balances among the three branches of government. The purpose was to make sure that no branch had too much power. As a result, the other two branches also influence the Court's decisions.

This 1937 political cartoon addresses the issue of court packing by President Roosevelt.

The most important way that presidents affect the Court is by the power of appointment. The president fills openings on the Court. As you read on page 210, presidents usually appoint judges who share their philosophies. However, presidents inherit Courts that were named by earlier presidents. These justices may not share the new president's views. Even a justice whom a president appoints may be a surprise. A justice may also turn out not to hold exactly the same views as the president who named him or her.

President Franklin Roosevelt was faced with such a Court. The justices declared unconstitutional a number of Roosevelt's New Deal programs. In 1937, he tried to add six members to the Court. He wanted more justices who would support the New Deal. Republicans accused Roosevelt of trying to fill the Court with justices who would support his beliefs. In Congress, conservative Democrats joined with Republicans to defeat the measure. They thought **court packing** would upset the system of checks and balances created by the Constitution.

Extension

Have students use library resources or the Internet to investigate examples of major disagreements over presidential nominees to the Supreme Court. Ask them to discover what about the nominee the Senate objected to, as well as the outcome of the disagreement.

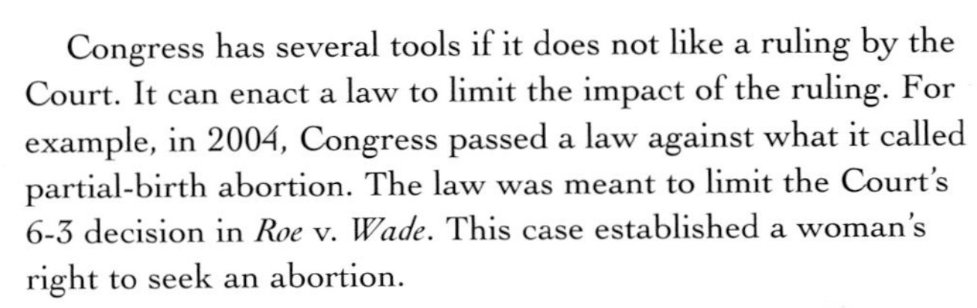

Congress has several tools if it does not like a ruling by the Court. It can enact a law to limit the impact of the ruling. For example, in 2004, Congress passed a law against what it called partial-birth abortion. The law was meant to limit the Court's 6-3 decision in *Roe* v. *Wade*. This case established a woman's right to seek an abortion.

Congress can also use constitutional amendments to get around a Court ruling. This is not done often. However, the Sixteenth Amendment came about as the result of a Court ruling. In 1895, the Court declared unconstitutional a federal income tax law. Congress then proposed and approved the Sixteenth Amendment, which created a federal income tax. The amendment was ratified by the states.

The president appoints the justices, but the Senate must approve them. The Senate Judiciary Committee questions nominees very carefully. Committee members want to know what the nominees' judicial philosophies are. They review how nominees have decided certain issues in the past. The most heated constitutional issues in the late twentieth and early twenty-first centuries tend to deal with social policies. These include affirmative action, abortion, and gay marriage.

The Senate can and has refused to approve nominees. **Nominees** are people who have been selected to fill a vacant position. It can also threaten to reject nominees with certain views on issues. As a result of its consent power, the Senate can greatly influence how the Court will rule on certain cases in the future.

ideas to remember

Five factors help shape Supreme Court decisions:

- the Constitution and federal law
- the justices' own backgrounds and views
- the interaction among justices
- U.S. society
- the executive and legislative branches

Putting It All Together

Create a concept map that shows the influences on Supreme Court decisions. Draw a large circle and label it "Influences on the Supreme Court." Then draw smaller circles for each influence. Connect each smaller circle with a line to the large circle. Label each smaller circle. Share your concept map with a partner.

Ideas to Remember Extension

Review the ideas listed, further explaining difficult vocabulary words. Have students create graphic organizers in their notebooks to help them visualize the five factors that help shape Supreme Court decisions.

Putting It All Together

Students' concept maps will vary but should include the five factors listed in the Ideas to Remember box on page 225.

Lesson Summary

The Supreme Court sets national policy by the cases it takes on or refuses, as well as by the opinions it gives. The Court may strike down federal, state, or local laws. On rare occasions, it will reverse a previous Court decision. Limits on cases accepted include the following factors: the case must make a difference, involve real harm, and apply to many people. The Court is also limited by its inability to enforce its rulings.

Lesson Objective

Students will learn about the ways in which the Supreme Court affects national policy.

Focus Your Reading Answers

1 The Supreme Court affects national policy by the cases it chooses and the decisions it hands down.

2 The Court usually limits itself to cases involving civil liberties or economic issues. It tries to only take cases that make a difference, could cause harm, and affect a large number of people. It is also limited by the inability to enforce its rulings.

LESSON 3

The Supreme Court and National Policy

Thinking on Your Own

Have you ever made a decision and then changed your mind? What happened to make you change your mind? Write a paragraph in your notebook to describe your decision, and then explain why you changed it.

focus your reading

In what ways does the Supreme Court affect national policy?

Name some limits on the power of the Supreme Court.

words to know

struck down

reverse

civil liberties

As you just read, the Supreme Court hears cases and hands down decisions. However, the Court does more than just decide individual cases. By the cases it chooses and the opinions it delivers, the Court sets government policy. It sets policy just as much as the executive and legislative branches do. This is why appointing a justice to the Supreme Court is so important.

Judicial Review and Interpreting the Law

The Supreme Court has three tools to shape national policy. The first is its power of judicial review. The Court declared this power in *Marbury* v. *Madison*. In the 200 years since, the Court has **struck down**—declared unconstitutional—about 150 federal laws and over 1,000 state and local laws.

Judicial review affects public policy in two ways. First, once a law is struck down, legislators tend not to pass similar laws. Second, a Court decision can greatly affect how the nation deals with an issue. For example, the decision in *Miranda* v. *Arizona* changed the way law officers are allowed to question suspects. They must inform them of their rights. These include the right to remain silent and the right to have an attorney, or lawyer, present during questioning.

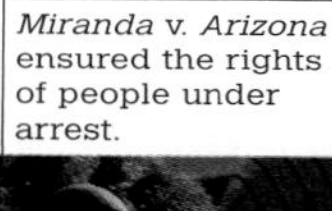
Miranda v. *Arizona* ensured the rights of people under arrest.

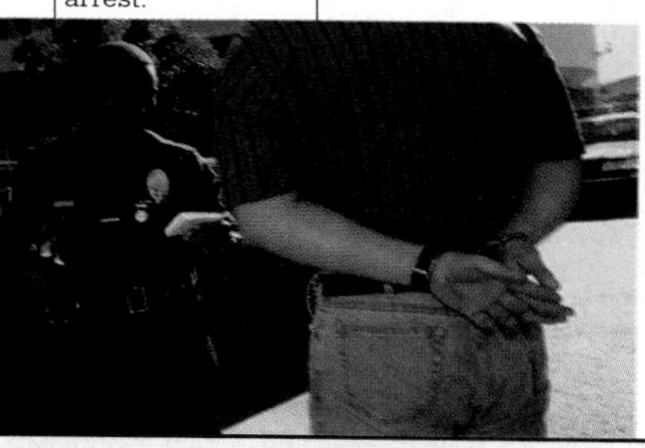

Words to Know

Discuss each of the vocabulary terms with students.

When a law is declared unconstitutional, it is *struck down*. The Court has *struck down* more than 1,000 state and local laws.

To *reverse* a decision is to overturn it. The Court will rarely *reverse* a previous decision.

Protections against abuse by the government are *civil liberties*. The majority of Supreme Court cases involve violation of *civil liberties*.

Picturing Government

A Los Angeles police officer, shown in the photograph on page 226, is reading a suspect his Miranda Rights. Miranda Rights were upheld in the 2000 Supreme Court case *Dickerson* v. *United States*, which had requested that the decision in *Miranda* v. *Arizona* be overturned. Justices Scalia and Thomas filed dissenting opinions.

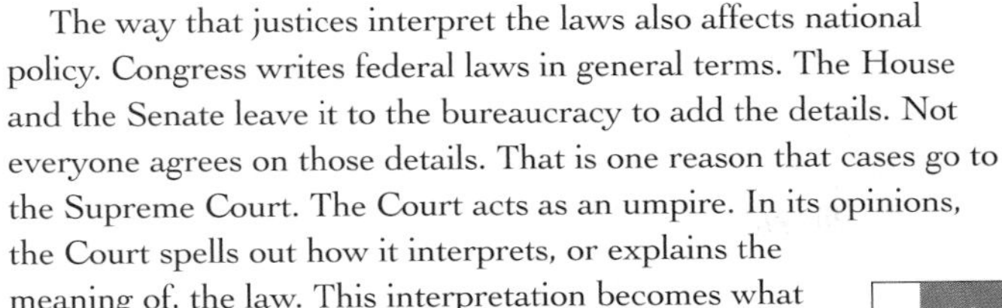

The way that justices interpret the laws also affects national policy. Congress writes federal laws in general terms. The House and the Senate leave it to the bureaucracy to add the details. Not everyone agrees on those details. That is one reason that cases go to the Supreme Court. The Court acts as an umpire. In its opinions, the Court spells out how it interprets, or explains the meaning of, the law. This interpretation becomes what people must obey.

For example, in 1990, Congress passed the Americans with Disabilities Act. The law required employers and public places such as office buildings to make "reasonable accommodations" for people with disabilities. Entrances with ramps and automatic doors are two outcomes of the law. Another goal was to end employment discrimination against people with disabilities.

ideas to remember

The Supreme Court shapes national policies

- by its use of judicial review
- by the way it interprets laws
- by overturning earlier decisions

What disabilities does the law cover? Some people believed it covered those with HIV. Not all employers agreed. A lawsuit, *Bragdon* v. *Abbott*, was filed. The case reached the Supreme Court, and it agreed to hear the appeal. In 1998, the Court ruled that the law included people who were HIV-positive. As a result of this ruling, people with HIV and AIDS are protected against discrimination in the workplace.

Landmark Supreme Court Case: Separate but Equal

***Plessy* v. *Ferguson* (1896):** By the 1890s, African Americans and whites were separated by law in the South. For example, African Americans were barred from eating in the same restaurants as whites. They could not use the same drinking fountains. African Americans were forced to sit in their own sections in theaters, railroad trains, and other public places.

Homer Plessy, an African American, tested a Louisiana segregation law. The law required separate but equal accommodations, or facilities, for African Americans and whites. Plessy sat down in a whites-only railroad car and refused to leave. He was arrested. A court convicted him of breaking the state law. Plessy appealed.

The Supreme Court upheld Plessy's conviction. The justices said the state law was constitutional. It did not violate the equal protection clause of the Fourteenth Amendment. The clause (Section 1) guarantees that all citizens will be treated alike under the law. The justices ruled that the law was constitutional because it said that the separate accommodations had to be equal. This principle of "separate but equal" lasted for more than 50 years. It was used both by the courts and legislators to continue segregating society.

Ideas to Remember Extension

Review the ideas listed, further explaining difficult vocabulary words. Have students create graphic organizers in their notebooks to help them visualize the three ways in which the Supreme Court shapes national policies.

Supreme Court Case Extension

In 1896, Homer Plessy was a willing part of a deliberate case. In his family, everyone was of European descent except his great-grandmother. Plessy appeared to be white, but he was deemed legally black. His friends in New Orleans wanted to show how absurd the notion of racial categories was. They had to tell the railroad conductor that white-skinned Plessy was black, at which point Plessy was arrested and jailed. New Orleans Judge John Ferguson said that the "separate but equal" law was constitutional, a decision with which the Supreme Court agreed. Justice John Harlan wrote the only dissenting opinion, stating that the "Constitution is colorblind, and neither knows nor tolerates classes among citizens."

Extension

Have students use library resources or the Internet to find examples of decisions that the Court has overturned. Allow time for them to present their findings to the class, explaining the original ruling and the decision to overturn it.

The Supreme Court at Work 227

Picturing Government

Linda Brown Smith is shown on page 228 in a 1964 photograph taken in front of the Topeka, Kansas, school that had refused her as a student. Brown was only seven when her father, Reverend Oliver Brown, decided that it was not right that she had to walk across railroad tracks and ride a bus to school when a better school was only five blocks from their home. Although the case was named for them, it also represented four other suits against school segregation from South Carolina, Virginia, Delaware, and Washington, D.C.

Supreme Court Case Extension

Thurgood Marshall, a lawyer with the National Association for the Advancement of Colored People, argued the case before the Supreme Court. He had already won 13 of the 15 cases argued before the Court. He practiced arguments for the case on the faculty and students of Howard Law School, a historically black college in Washington, D.C.

Stop and Think

Students' lessons will vary but may include the following:

- The Supreme Court can reverse decisions.
- The Court considers the public's mood.
- New justices have new ideas.

Linda Brown in 1964

Landmark Supreme Court Case: Separate but Unequal

***Brown* v. *Board of Education of Topeka* (1954):** By the 1950s, racial ideas in the United States outside the South were changing. A growing number of Americans began to question segregation. How could the United States fight World War II to defend democracy in Europe and Asia while denying rights to African Americans at home? In reality, facilities for African Americans were not equal. Segregated schools did deprive African-American children of equal opportunities. That was well established in a legal brief presented to the Supreme Court in the case of *Brown* v. *Board of Education of Topeka* (1954). The brief was prepared by the National Association for the Advancement of Colored People (NAACP). Thurgood Marshall, the lawyer who argued the case, later became the first African American to be appointed to the Supreme Court.

In 1954, the Supreme Court used *Brown* v. *Board of Education of Topeka* to overturn *Plessy*. The case involved Linda Brown, who could not attend the school closest to her. It was an all-white school. Instead, she had to go to an all-black school across town. The justices reversed the precedent, or ruling, in *Plessy*. They declared that separate was not equal and that segregation violated the equal protection clause of the Fourteenth Amendment. States were ordered to end segregation. Different times, along with different justices, resulted in a different decision.

Reversing Past Decisions

Very rarely, the Court **reverses**, or overturns, a previous court decision. This is another way the Court influences national policy. For example, at one point in time, a Court decision represents the justices' thinking on an issue. However, those justices retire over a period of years. New justices are appointed. They may have different philosophies than the justices who decided the original case. A shift in public opinion may also have taken place during these years. When a similar case comes before the new justices, they decide it differently.

stop and think

Write the following heading in your notebook: *"Brown* v. *Board of Education."* Under it, list three "lessons" that we can learn from this case about the United States Supreme Court. Review what you have read and keep this assignment in mind as you continue reading.

This proves the truth of what you learned in Lesson 2. In many ways, Supreme Court justices represent the same attitudes as the general public. Over time, the nation's attitudes about certain issues change. The Supreme Court's views change along with them. Two important civil rights cases stand out as an example of a change in judicial viewpoints.

As you read in Lesson 1, the rulings of the Supreme Court set precedents. However, there are decisions such as the one in *Plessy* that later justices no longer believe are correct.

Extension

The seats for interested members of the public were filled, and 400 people were turned away, when arguments in *Brown* v. *Board of Education of Topeka* began in the Supreme Court. Former California governor Earl Warren became Chief Justice as the case was debated. He used his influence with the justices to bring about a unanimous decision. Still, enforcing the decision remained difficult. Prince Edward County in Virginia, the site of one of the cluster cases, closed all public schools for five years rather than integrate them.

Limits on the Supreme Court

The majority of Supreme Court cases involve **civil liberties.** These are a person's protection against abuse by the government. For example, in 1963, Clarence Gideon petitioned the Court because he said he did not get a fair trial. He was too poor to hire a lawyer to represent him. In *Gideon* v. *Wainwright*, the Court declared that courts must appoint an attorney for anyone too poor to hire one.

The Supreme Court also takes cases related to economic issues. These may involve environmental protection regulations or anti-trust laws. Other cases involve suits against federal officials or between the national government and the states.

In deciding which cases to take, the Court looks at what is involved. First, the case must make a difference in some way. *Gideon* v. *Wainwright*, expanded the civil liberties of the poor. Second, there must be real harm involved. Without a lawyer, Clarence Gideon was sent to jail. Third, the case must apply to a large number of people. Gideon was not the only poor person to go through a trial without a lawyer.

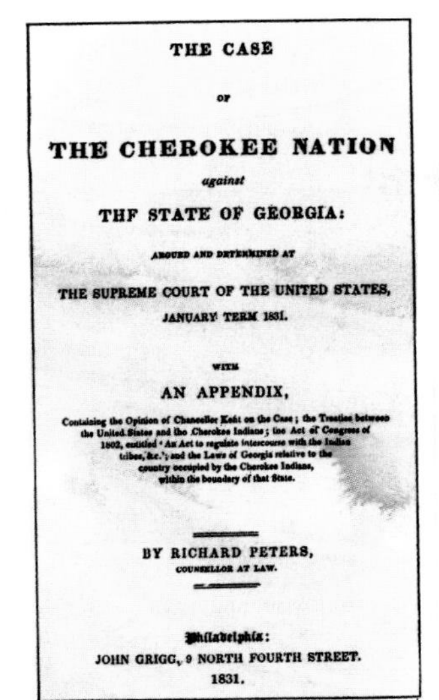

THE CASE

OF

THE CHEROKEE NATION

against

THF STATE OF GEORGIA:

ARGUED AND DETERMINED AT

THE SUPREME COURT OF THE UNITED STATES,

JANUARY TERM 1831.

WITH

AN APPENDIX,

Containing the Opinion of Chancellor Kent on the Case; the Treaties between the United States and the Cherokee Indians; the Act of Congress of 1802, entitled 'An Act to regulate intercourse with the Indian tribes, &c.'; and the Laws of Georgia relative to the country occupied by the Cherokee Indians, within the boundary of that State.

BY RICHARD PETERS,

COUNSELLOR AT LAW.

Philadelphia:

JOHN GRIGG, 9 NORTH FOURTH STREET.

1831.

The Supreme Court sided with the Cherokee Nation in a land dispute during the 1830s.

ideas to remember

Limits on the Supreme Court include

- the issues it chooses to consider
- the types of cases it chooses to hear
- lack of control over when cases are sent to it
- no power of enforcement

A fourth limit on the Court's influence is its lack of enforcement power. The Framers gave the executive branch the power to carry out laws and to enforce the Court's rulings. In the 1832 case *Worcester* v. *Georgia*, the Court ruled that the state of Georgia had no authority in Cherokee land. President Andrew Jackson said, "John Marshall has made his decision. Now let him enforce it." In other words, Jackson ignored the Court and the Cherokee were forced to move to Indian Territory.

Putting It All Together

Write three paragraphs summarizing the following topics: 1) The Supreme Court works slowly and carefully. 2) Court decisions are influenced by society. 3) The Supreme Court has an impact on American life.

Picturing Government

At the right of page 229 is a copy of the Supreme Court record of the *Worcester* v. *Georgia* case. Georgia was the largest of the 27 states in 1832, and the Cherokee occupied land prime for development. Samuel Worcester was a Christian missionary who was jailed for residing on Cherokee land. He and others who supported the Cherokee refused to abandon their missions. He moved to North Carolina, but when he returned to his family in Georgia after his youngest child died, he was arrested again and sentenced to four years hard labor.

Ideas to Remember Extension

Review the ideas listed, further explaining difficult vocabulary words. Have students create graphic organizers in their notebooks to help them visualize the four limits on the Supreme Court.

Putting It All Together

Students' summaries will vary but should begin with the three topic sentences presented and reflect lesson content.

Participate in Government

1 Suggest that students use library resources or the Internet to find out more about local issues that could lead to civil rights complaints. These issues might include predatory lending, unequal pay, age discrimination, and so on.

2 Have students download the booklet "Getting Uncle Sam to Enforce Your Civil Rights." Then assign different sections of the booklet to small groups to read and then explain to the rest of the class.

Recommended Reading

Below is a list of books that relate to the issues covered in this chapter. The numbers in parentheses indicate the related Thematic Strands of the National Council for the Social Studies (NCSS).

John J. Patrick. *Supreme Court of the United States: A Student Companion.* 2nd ed. Oxford University Press, 2002. (VI, X)

Mark Rowh. *Thurgood Marshall: Civil Rights Attorney and Supreme Court Justice.* Enslow Publishers, Inc., 2002. (VI, X)

Participate in Government

File a Civil Rights Complaint

Unfortunately, discrimination on the basis of race, gender, religion, ethnic background, and disability still occurs. People face discrimination in education, credit, employment, housing, law enforcement, voting, and public services. Public services include restaurants, movies, hotels, and public transportation.

Everyone has the right to file a civil rights complaint when discrimination occurs.

If a person believes that he or she has been discriminated against, that person can take action. A civil rights complaint can be filed. The U.S. Commission on Civil Rights offers a booklet entitled *Getting Uncle Sam to Enforce Your Civil Rights.* It is available online from the commission. The commission does not investigate complaints but can help you find the right agency to contact.

Usually, complaints need to be filed within 180 days of the alleged discrimination. The commission sets out the following guidelines for filing a complaint. The complaint must

- be typed or printed neatly, dated, and signed.
- include your name, address, and telephone number.
- state the name and address of the person or place of business that discriminated against you.
- explain the act or acts of discrimination. The date, place of the action, and the basis for the discrimination need to be identified and explained. For example, was it because of your skin color?
- include the names, addresses, and telephone numbers of any witnesses or others who have information about your complaint.

When your complaint is investigated, you may also need to offer proof. This can be receipts, contracts, or any other records that support your complaint.

230 Chapter 12

Classroom Discussion

Discuss with students some of the broader topics covered in this chapter.

- How can the impact of poor decisions by the Supreme Court be lessened?
- How can the Court retain a balance of viewpoints?
- What are some issues that students feel should be argued before the Court?

Skill Builder

Understand Cause and Effect

A cause is what makes something happen. An effect is the result or the outcome of the cause. For example:

Identifying the cause and the effect in this sentence is easy. The verb *caused* signals the relationship between the backlog and the Court's taking fewer cases. A flowchart is one way to determine cause-and-effect relationships.

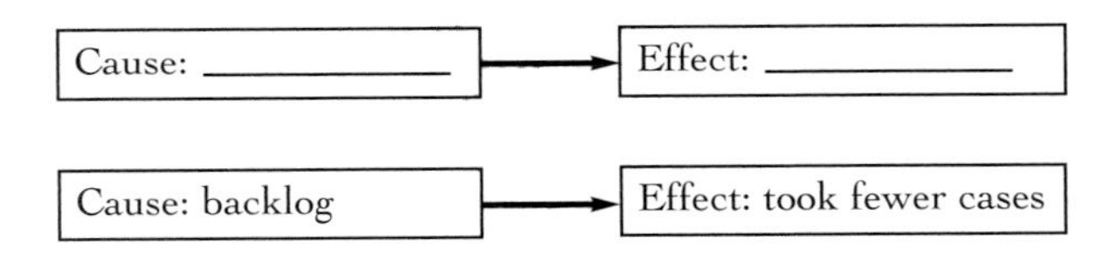

Sometimes the effect of one event is the cause of another. Then your flowchart would look like this:

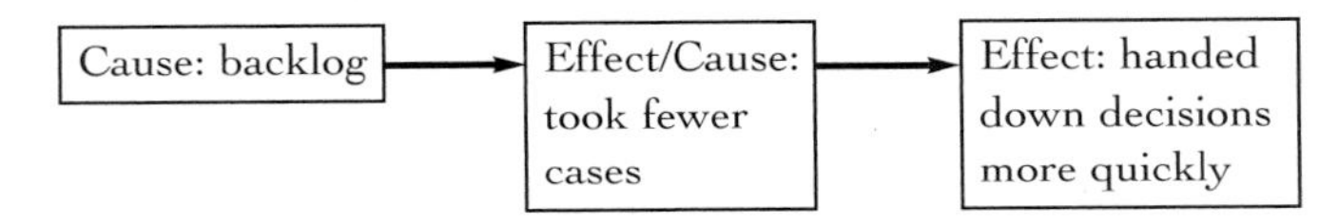

Use the information from Chapter 12 to complete these activities.

1. Create a cause-and-effect flowchart to describe why the Sixteenth Amendment was passed, page 225.
2. Create a cause-and-effect flowchart to describe how the Court ruled in *Plessy* and *Brown*, pages 227 and 228.
3. Use a cause-and-effect flowchart to write a summary of the influences on the Supreme Court.

Skill Builder

1. Students' cause-and-effect flowcharts will vary. Possible answer:

   Cause: The Supreme Court declared a federal income tax law unconstitutional.

   Effect: Congress proposed and approved the Sixteenth Amendment, creating a federal income tax.

2. Students' cause-and-effect flowcharts will vary. Possible answer:

   Cause: The Supreme Court decided that the state law was constitutional.

   Effect: "Separate but equal" became the rule for more than 50 years.

3. Students' cause-and-effect flowcharts and summaries will vary. Possible answer:

   Cause: The Supreme Court is influenced by the events of American society.

   Effect: Justices weigh public opinion when deciding the outcome of cases.

Research Resources

Below is a list of reference books and Web sites that relate to the issues covered in this chapter. Students may wish to use these to further their research on ideas in the preceding lessons. Web site addresses may change over time. Use keyword searching on a major search engine to locate sites.

Reference Books:

Clare Cushman, ed. *Supreme Court Decisions and Women's Rights: Milestones to Equality.* CQ Press, 2001.

Thomas T. Lewis and Richard L. Wilson, eds. *Encyclopedia of the U.S. Supreme Court.* Salem Press, 2001.

The Supreme Court Yearbook. Congressional Quarterly, annual.

Web Sites:

A site is available to find out about the history of the Supreme Court. This site was developed to expand the public's awareness of the Supreme Court's history and heritage. It includes information about the Chief Justices.

Unit Objectives

After studying this unit, students will be able to

- explain the civil liberties and freedoms that the Constitution guarantees
- describe the struggles of various groups to achieve full civil rights

Unit 5 distinguishes between civil rights and civil liberties.

Chapter 13, Civil Liberties: Constitutional Freedoms, examines provisions of the Bill of Rights and other key amendments.

Chapter 14, Civil Rights: Equal Justice, discusses the ways that different groups fought for equality.

Getting Started

Have a student read aloud the title of the unit and the two paragraphs that follow it on page 232. Ask students to brainstorm and list in their notebooks all the rights they believe they have as residents of the United States. As you study the unit together, have them add to that list.

CIVIL LIBERTIES AND CIVIL RIGHTS

Do you want to start a petition to ask the mayor and council to fix up the local basketball court? Do you want to organize a march to city hall to present the petition? In some nations, you would be arrested and sent to jail for these actions. In the United States, these actions are expressions of a person's civil liberties. The U.S. Constitution guarantees civil liberties. It also guarantees civil rights.

This unit will explain the differences between civil liberties and civil rights. You will also learn how these liberties and rights have been expanded over time.

Civil liberties and civil rights are often taken for granted by Americans. However, it took almost 200 years before these were guaranteed by law to all Americans. In the photograph at the right, A. Philip Randolph, march director (right); Roy Wilkins, Executive Secretary of the National Association for the Advancement of Colored People (second from right); and the Rev. Martin Luther King, Jr., (seventh from right) led the March on Washington on August 28, 1963. On that day, thousands of people walked along Constitution Avenue in Washington, D.C.

Picturing Government

The photograph on page 232 shows the 1963 March on Washington. At center (seventh from right) is Dr. Martin Luther King, Jr. At the far right is the organizer of the march, A. Philip Randolph. Randolph had been a union organizer, beginning in 1925 when he formed the Brotherhood of Sleeping Car Porters to protect the Pullman train workers. Although for years, Pullman executives fought the union and fired more than 500 active participants, by 1937 they had to agree to negotiate with the union. In 1941, in response to the segregation and poor treatment of African Americans serving in the military, Randolph threatened a march on Washington, D.C. To prevent this march, Franklin Roosevelt met with African American leaders and issued Executive Order 8802, which banned job discrimination in the defense industries and instituted a Fair Employment Practices committee. Not until 1948, with Harry Truman's Executive Order 9981, were the armed forces integrated. However, by 1963, Randolph saw the need for a true march on Washington and organized it. More than a quarter of a million people took part.

Chapter

13 CIVIL LIBERTIES: CONSTITUTIONAL FREEDOMS

Getting Focused

Skim this chapter to predict what you will be learning.

- Read the lesson titles and subheadings.
- Look at the illustrations and read the captions.
- Examine the table.
- Review the vocabulary words and terms.

What rights does the Bill of Rights guarantee? List as many rights as you can remember. Check your list against the Constitution. Add to or revise your list as needed.

Freedom of religion is one of the liberties guaranteed by the U.S. Constitution. Judaism, Islam, Catholicism, and Protestantism are four of the main religions in the United States.

Pre-Reading Discussion

1 Ask students to review their lists of rights guaranteed in the Bill of Rights. Propose that any one of them, such as the right to a fair and speedy trial, be taken away. Have them discuss how their lives would change without that right.

2 Have students discuss whether the power of the national government should be able to supersede the powers of the state governments. Should a state be able to suspend any of the rights in the Bill of Rights during a time of emergency?

Related Transparencies

T-18 Three-Column Chart

T-19 Venn Diagram

Key Blacklines

Primary Source—John G. Roberts at His Confirmation Hearings

CD Extension

Encourage students to use the reading comprehension, vocabulary reinforcement, and other activities on the student CD.

Getting Focused

After students have identified all the rights in the Bill of Rights, have them count off from one to ten. Tell them that they are to become the class experts on whichever number amendment matches their number. Ask them to work together in pairs or small groups to prepare additional material on their amendment as the class discusses it.

Lesson Summary

The United States Constitution, particularly the Bill of Rights, guarantees civil liberties such as the freedom of religion, press, assembly, and speech. Civil rights guarantee equal protection under the laws to all, regardless of religion, race, gender, or ethnicity. The Bill of Rights protects both citizens and aliens, although aliens are limited in some of their rights to travel freely, vote, or serve on juries. The Fourteenth Amendment, passed in 1868, incorporates the state and local governments in offering equal rights to all people. The Ninth Amendment prohibits governments from allowing people *only* the rights expressed in the Constitution.

Lesson Objective

Students will learn about rights guaranteed by the Constitution, particularly the First through the Tenth Amendments and the Fourteenth Amendment.

Focus Your Reading Answers

1 The Bill of Rights guarantees civil liberties such as the freedom of speech, press, assembly, and religion. It also lists the right to bear arms, to be safe from unwarranted search and seizure, and rights to and during a trial.

2 The principle of incorporation affects civil liberties by extending their guarantees to state and local governments.

3 The Ninth Amendment is important because it prevents the government from denying liberties not enumerated in the Bill of Rights.

LESSON 1

Constitutional Rights

Thinking on Your Own

What do you know about the Fourteenth and Ninth Amendments? Create a four-column chart in your notebook. Label the first column "What I Know About the Fourteenth Amendment." Label the third column "What I Know About the Ninth Amendment." Fill in those two columns with what you already know. Label the second and fourth columns "What I Learned." Fill in those columns after you study the lesson.

focus your reading

What civil liberties are guaranteed by the Bill of Rights?

How does the principle of incorporation affect civil liberties?

Explain why the Ninth Amendment is important.

words to know

civil liberties

civil rights

alien

incorporation

Civil liberties are the freedoms guaranteed by the U.S. Constitution. The Bill of Rights, the first ten amendments to the Constitution, lists many of these civil liberties. Among them are freedom of speech, religion, and assembly.

Civil rights are the rights of everyone to equal protection under the law. No one can be discriminated against on the basis of race, religion, gender, or ethnic origin. The Fifth and Fourteenth Amendments protect us from discrimination by the government or by any other group or individual.

The right to vote is a civil liberty.

Some states would not ratify the Constitution until 1788 when the Bill of Rights was added. However, it took almost 200 years for the nation to recognize the civil rights of women, African Americans, and other groups.

Words to Know

Introduce each of the following vocabulary terms to students.

Explain that *civil liberties* are the freedoms that the U.S. Constitution guarantees. The Bill of Rights lists many of the *civil liberties*. The rights of everyone to equal protection under the laws are known as *civil rights*. Recognizing the *civil rights* of some ethnic groups and women took nearly 200 years after the Constitution went into effect. Persons living in the United States who are not citizens are *aliens*. The Bill of Rights applies not only to citizens but also to *aliens*.

Interpreting the law to include state and local government is called *incorporation*. One example of *incorporation* is the extension of the Fifth Amendment protections into state courts.

The Bill of Rights

The first ten amendments to the Constitution make up the Bill of Rights. Review the table on page 78, which lists what each amendment guarantees. Both citizens and aliens are guaranteed these rights.

Aliens are non–U.S. citizens in the United States. In a number of cases, the Supreme Court has ruled that they have the same basic rights as citizens. The Bill of Rights applies to them as well as to citizens. They also have the same guarantees of due process that you will read about in Lesson 5. However, aliens may not vote or serve on juries.

Incorporation of Rights

The first members of Congress who proposed the Bill of Rights meant for these amendments to apply only to the national government. Remember that they had just won their independence from Great Britain. They did not fear the power of their own state governments. The British government had tried to limit people's rights, and members of Congress feared the national government might do the same. In 1868, the Fourteenth Amendment was added to the Constitution. It states that citizens are citizens of both the United States and their state. No state may pass any laws that violate the rights of citizens of the United States. In addition, no state may "deprive any person of life, liberty, or property without due process of law." Beginning in 1925, the Supreme Court interpreted the Fourteenth Amendment to include people's dealings with both state and local governments. This is known as **incorporation**.

The U.S. Constitution guarantees the right to an attorney in a criminal trial.

The Court began by expanding the rights guaranteed under the First Amendment. Since the 1960s, the Court has expanded the "due process" guarantee to include other amendments in the Bill of Rights. For example, the decision in *Malloy* v. *Hogan* extended the protection of the Fifth Amendment into state courts. A defendant in state court has the right to remain silent and not incriminate himself or herself. This is the same right that someone tried in federal court has. By the end of the twentieth century, almost all the

Picturing Government

The photograph on page 234 shows a polling station in Columbus, Ohio, on Election Day, 2004. People waited for as long as two hours to vote at this station. The right to vote is one of the civil liberties.

Picturing Government

The photograph on page 235 shows a lawyer and client conferring during a trial. The Sixth Amendment guarantees the right to a public and speedy trial, as well as to counsel.

Extension

Many people in the United States were upset to learn that hundreds of terrorist suspects were being held as prisoners at a U.S. military base in Guantanamo Bay, Cuba, without official charges or trial. Have students find out more about the U.S. government's dealing with terrorist suspects following the events of 9/11. Have them present their findings to the class by using the Student Presentation Builder on the student CD.

Picturing Government

The photo collage on page 233 shows the interiors of a Jewish synagogue (top left), an Islamic mosque (bottom left), a Roman Catholic cathedral (top right), and a Protestant church (bottom right). Through the First Amendment, the United States government guarantees freedom of religion. All major world religions, as well as several other groups, have established houses of worship in the nation. The United States has more houses of worship per person than any other nation; more than 60 percent of all charitable donations are given to religious institutions.

Stop and Think

Students' explanations will vary but should focus on how the Ninth and Fourteenth Amendments and the Court's rulings on incorporation protect civil liberties.

Extension

Have students use the information in the case section at the end of the book to learn more about *Escobedo* v. *Illinois* and *Gideon* v. *Wainwright*. Suggest that they make a graphic organizer, such as a Venn diagram or a two-column chart, to summarize their findings.

Putting It All Together

Students' lists of rights and their protections will vary.

guarantees of the Bill of Rights had been incorporated. Why is incorporation important? State constitutions also guarantee civil liberties. However, states have not always used those guarantees to protect their people. Almost 100 years of discrimination against African Americans is an unfortunate example of state government abuse. Expansion of the guarantees of the U.S. Constitution offers protection to all people in all states.

stop and think

In your notebook, explain how the Fourteenth Amendment and the Court's rulings on incorporation have helped protect your civil liberties. Work with a partner to explain how the Ninth Amendment adds to that protection.

Ninth Amendment

The Constitution lists many rights of Americans. However, neither the Constitution nor the amendments list all of them. This would have been an impossible task because the nation, society, and the world keep changing. Instead, the Framers included the Ninth Amendment. The amendment says:

> The enumeration in the Constitution, of certain rights, shall not be construed to deny or disparage others retained by the people.

In other words, just because a right is not listed in the Constitution does not mean that the people do not have it. The Ninth Amendment places a limit on government power. Government may not claim that the people have only the rights listed in the Constitution.

Many Supreme Court decisions have dealt with these additional rights. For example, in *Escobedo* v. *Illinois*, the Supreme Court determined that accused persons have the right to remain silent during questioning. In *Gideon* v. *Wainwright*, the justices ruled that accused persons have the right to be represented by an attorney.

Putting It All Together

The Bill of Rights protects many of the basic freedoms we enjoy as Americans. However, we have other rights not protected by it. In your notebook, list some of these rights and how they are protected.

LESSON 2

Freedom of Religion

Thinking on Your Own

Freedom of religion is very important in a society that includes many different religious beliefs. What problems could arise if the government favored one religion over others?

Many colonists and later immigrants came to America to have greater freedom to practice their religion. Many colonists and later immigrants came to these shores to escape religious persecution. The first two clauses of the First Amendment to the Constitution deal with religion.

focus your reading

Why was the Establishment Clause added to the Constitution?

Explain the issues involving religion and education.

Describe what the Free Exercise Clause guarantees.

words to know

Establishment Clause

Free Exercise Clause

The Establishment Clause

The First Amendment begins: "Congress shall make no law respecting an establishment of religion." This is known as the **Establishment Clause**. Great Britain had established, or made, the Church of England its official religion. Many citizens of the new United States wanted to make sure this did not happen here. They did not want the government to support any one religion. Thomas Jefferson said the Establishment Clause set up "a wall of separation between church and state."

The Supreme Court has heard many cases involving the place of religion in American life. Most of these cases involved the separation of church and state. For example, should religious symbols be placed on government property?

In 2005, the Court handed down two important decisions. Hanging copies of the Ten Commandments in county courthouses in Kentucky was declared unconstitutional. However, a monument of the Ten Commandments on the grounds of the Texas state capitol was not unconstitutional. The monument was in a 17-acre park along with other monuments.

Lesson Summary

The First Amendment begins with the Establishment Clause, prohibiting a national religion and separating church and state. The Supreme Court has ruled on several issues relating to religion and education. Four issues most often surface in lawsuits: aid to parochial schools, release time, school prayer and Bible reading, and student religious groups. The case *Lemon* v. *Kurtzman*, which set precedent for later decisions, was especially important. The First Amendment also includes the Free Exercise Clause, which allows people to believe what they wish, although they may not practice anything that goes against the public order or social duties.

Lesson Objective

Students will learn about the First Amendment as it relates to religious freedom.

Focus Your Reading Answers

1 The Establishment Clause was added to the Constitution because people did not want the government to establish a religion, as had been the case in England. They wanted what Thomas Jefferson called "a wall of separation between church and state."

2 Some of the issues that deal with religion and education include aid to parochial schools, release time, school prayer and Bible reading, and student religious groups.

3 The Free Exercise Clause guarantees that the government will not limit what people believe.

Words to Know

Discuss each of the vocabulary terms with students.

The *Establishment Clause* was written to make sure that the federal government did not establish an official religion for the new nation. The *Establishment Clause* is at the beginning of the First Amendment.

The *Free Exercise Clause* is a guarantee that the government will not limit what a person is allowed to believe. The *Free Exercise Clause* does not, however, extend to what actions are permitted.

Extension

Invite interested students to use library resources or the Internet to find out more about Thomas Jefferson's ideas about religion and government.

Picturing Government

The photograph on page 238 shows students at a parochial school working on computers. Parochial schools often require students to wear uniforms, which can help to create a climate for study. The Supreme Court has ruled in many cases that affect private education.

Supreme Court Case Extension

Lemon v. *Kurtzman* has been called the most-cited case in the history of the Supreme Court. Alton T. Lemon of Philadelphia began attending monthly meetings of the American Civil Liberties Union (ACLU) after spending time in the army thinking about the First Amendment's Establishment Clause. It was at an ACLU meeting that the idea was first proposed to sue over new laws, in both Pennsylvania and Rhode Island, that allowed the use of public tax monies to reimburse parochial schools. The Lemon test was used in Pennsylvania in 2002 to order the removal of a plaque of the Ten Commandments in the West Chester courthouse. The case was also cited in the 2005 Supreme Court case *McCreary County, Kentucky, et al.* v. *American Civil Liberties Union of Kentucky, et al.*, which concerned posting the Ten Commandments in county courthouses.

Religion and Education

Not everyone favors separation of church and state or the Supreme Court's interpretation of the Establishment Clause. The biggest area of disagreement involves education. Most lawsuits have dealt with (1) aid to parochial schools, (2) release time, (3) school prayer and Bible reading, and (4) student religious groups.

Parochial schools are those run by religious organizations.

Parochial schools are schools run by religious or church groups. The kind of aid that governments can give to parochial schools has been the subject of several cases decided by the Supreme Court. The Court's decision in *Lemon* v. *Kurtzman* was especially important. This case laid the basis for the Court's decisions in later lawsuits about aid to parochial schools. The Court ruled in *Lemon*, first, that the aid must have a nonreligious purpose. Second, it must be neutral toward religion. The aid cannot be used to promote religion or harm it. Third, there cannot be an "excessive entanglement" of religion and government. These three factors are known as the "Lemon test." The justices use this test in ruling on new parochial aid cases.

Landmark Supreme Court Case: Aid to Parochial Schools

Lemon **v. *Kurtzman*** **(1971):** Private schools in Pennsylvania were repaid from government funds for teachers' salaries, books, and other classroom materials.

The Court decided that the law allowing the payments was unconstitutional. The payments directly helped the schools by reducing their costs. This, in turn, helped the religious groups that ran the schools. The state closely monitored the program. This violated the third factor of the Lemon test. The monitoring involved the government in the business of the religious groups.

The Court has not struck down all laws involving state aid to parochial schools. Among the laws upheld were

- state payments to parochial schools to administer standardized tests required by the state
- lending of some materials and equipment, such as projectors, computers, and software, to parochial schools for nonreligious uses

Extension

The majority of Supreme Court justices in 2003 disagreed with the ruling of *Lemon* v. *Kurtzman*. Ask students to use library resources or the Internet to find out the opinion of the justices currently sitting on the Court, as well as any recent rulings in church-state matters applying to religion and education.

- a Minnesota law that allows parents to deduct certain costs to send their children to parochial schools. The Court said that the tax deduction was available to all families. If parents send their children to public schools, they do not pay for tuition, textbooks, or transportation directly. Allowing parents of parochial schoolchildren to deduct these costs from their taxes makes the system equal.
- an Ohio law that allows parents in Cleveland to use school voucher payments to send their children to private schools. The Court ruled that the goal of the law was to aid low-income children. Otherwise, the children would remain in low-performing schools. The justices said that the goal of the vouchers was to aid the children, not the schools.

The second area of disagreement about religion and education has been release time. Students in public school are "released" from class to attend religious instruction. In 1948, the Court held that teaching religion courses in public school classrooms was unconstitutional. In 1952, the Court heard another release time case. This time, the Court ruled that students could be released from class to attend religious instruction. However, the courses had to be given in some place other than in the public school.

One of the most heavily debated issues is school prayer and Bible reading. The Supreme Court has ruled seven times since 1962 against prayer and Bible reading in schools. School buildings are public—government—buildings, and teachers are paid by the government. Allowing teachers to say prayers or read from the Bible in school buildings amounts to support of religion.

The Supreme Court has, however, upheld the use of public schools for student-led religious groups. In 1984, Congress passed the Equal Access Act. Most public high schools receive some kind of federal funding. According to the 1984 law, these schools must allow student-run religious groups to meet in the school. In 1990, the Court declared the law constitutional. The Court said that the schools may not lead such groups. However, the schools must allow religious groups the same freedom to use the school as any other student club, such as the school newspaper or debate team.

Extension

Although the 1984 Equal Access Act originally focused on permitting religious clubs to form, the law is now being applied in other controversial areas. Courts have now sided with gay-straight clubs, which attempt to provide a forum for discussion of hostile situations that gay students may face in school. In 2003, a federal judge in Kentucky ruled in favor of the Boyd County High School Gay-Straight Alliance's right to an after-school club.

Extension

Divide the class into two groups. Ask them to select one of the major issues of religion and education and stage a debate. Challenge students to use library resources or the Internet to find Supreme Court cases that have influenced the outcome of the issue.

Civil Liberties: Constitutional Freedoms 239

Stop and Think

Students' summary sentences will vary but should cover each of the four areas relating to religion and education. Possible answer: Aid to parochial schools is subject to the Lemon test: it must have a nonreligious purpose, be neutral toward religion, and cannot promote or harm religion. Students may be released from class to attend religious instruction, but it must be offered away from the school. School prayer and Bible reading are not permitted in public schools, since the government pays for the building and teachers, and saying prayers or reading from the Bible is considered supporting religion. Student-run religious groups can use public school facilities for their meetings, just as any club can use them, although the schools may not lead the groups.

Picturing Government

The students pictured in the photograph on page 240 are saluting the American flag. However, the Supreme Court has ruled that students cannot be forced to recite the Pledge of Allegiance if doing so violates their religious beliefs. During the patriotic fervor of World War II, about 2,000 Jehovah's Witness children were expelled from schools across the nation because they wouldn't salute the flag. In 1943, the Supreme Court reversed a ruling just three years old. The new decision made saluting the flag optional if it conflicted with religious beliefs.

Free Exercise of Religion

The First Amendment has a second clause about religion. It states that Congress shall not pass any law "prohibiting the free exercise" of religion. This is known as the **Free Exercise Clause**.

stop and think

The Supreme Court's rulings about religion and education have set precedents in each area. With a partner, write a sentence to explain the reasoning in each of the four areas related to religion and education.

Under the Free Exercise Clause, government may not limit what people believe. However, the Supreme Court has upheld government limits on what people practice as religion. For example, in 1879, the Court upheld the conviction of a Mormon for having two wives. Federal law bans polygamy—having more than one spouse at a time. The man claimed that the law violated the Free Exercise Clause. The Supreme Court disagreed. It ruled that Congress may pass laws that uphold social duties and public order.

In other rulings, the Court has found that

- parents must allow children to be vaccinated even if vaccination is against their religion.
- an Orthodox Jew on active duty in the air force may not wear his yarmulke.
- a person can be denied state unemployment benefits if fired for taking drugs as part of a religious ceremony.

Students may choose not to salute the American flag based on religious beliefs.

However, the Court has upheld the right of Jehovah's Witnesses not to salute the U.S. flag. Saluting the flag violates their religious beliefs. The Court declared that the flag is a patriotic symbol. People do not have to go against their religious beliefs to show patriotism. There are other ways to develop and express patriotism.

Putting It All Together

Is separation of church and state helpful or harmful to the nation? With a partner, make a T-chart. On one side, list reasons why you think it is helpful. On the other side, list reasons why you think it is harmful. Then decide on an answer to the question. Write a paragraph to state and explain your answer.

Putting It All Together

Students' T-charts and paragraphs will vary but should take a position on the separation of church and state and support that position with reasons.

LESSON 3

Freedom of Speech and the Press

Thinking on Your Own

What do you think "freedom of speech" and "freedom of the press" mean? Discuss these terms with a partner. Then write a definition of each freedom in your notebook.

focus your reading

Summarize why speech is regulated.

When may prior restraint be used?

Discuss the major issues for freedom of the press.

words to know

mass media
pure speech
symbolic speech
seditious speech
defamation
slander
libel
fighting words
student speech
prior restraint
shield laws
commercial speech

The First Amendment guarantees freedom of speech and freedom of the press. Speech is the spoken word. When the Constitution was written, "the press" meant the printed word: newspapers, books, and pamphlets. Today, the press is just one part of the **mass media**. Freedom of the press now extends to movies, radio, television, cable, and the Internet. Does freedom of the press extend to blogs and podcasts? The Supreme Court has yet to hear any cases involving these uses of the Internet.

Why are freedom of speech and freedom of the press important? After all, ideas do not need to be protected when most people agree with them. A democracy works best when all ideas—even unpopular ones—are discussed and thought about. For example, protests against the Vietnam War were very unpopular in the mid-1960s. By the late 1960s, the nation had turned against the war. The protests had forced many Americans to think about the war in new ways.

Lesson Summary

The First Amendment guarantees freedom of the press and freedom of speech. The expansion of mass media forms presents new challenges to free speech. Government may limit seditious speech, defamation, slander, libel, student speech, and fighting words. The Supreme Court has upheld the right to desecrate the flag, but not to burn a draft card. Freedom of the press promises no prior restraint, which is censorship, on what can be published, except for obscenity and during times of war. The Court doesn't protect a journalist's right to confidentiality of sources, but states may pass shield laws. Advertising is a form of commercial speech. Certain ads may be banned for reasons of public health and safety.

Lesson Objective

Students will learn about the freedoms of speech and the press.

Focus Your Reading Answers

1 Speech is regulated to protect people from violence or other harm.

2 Prior restraint may be used during wartime or when the communication urges violence or is obscene. Student speech is also regulated by prior restraint.

3 Major issues for freedom of the press include confidentiality of sources and indecency.

Words to Know

Discuss each of the vocabulary terms with students.

Mass media includes the printed word, movies, radio, television, cable, and the Internet. The Court has yet to hear any *mass media* cases about Web blogs or podcasts.

Pure speech is just words alone. *Pure speech* is one of the two types of speech. Combining actions and symbols creates *symbolic speech*. Not all forms of *symbolic speech* are protected. Any speech that encourages overthrowing the government or disrupting it is *seditious speech*. In cases related to *seditious speech*, the Court uses the "clear and present danger" rule.

Using false words that damage a person's good name, character, or reputation is *defamation*. Acts of *defamation* are not protected by the First Amendment. Spoken defamatory speech is *slander*. Freedom of speech does not extend to *slander*. To write defamatory speech is to *libel*. Cases of *libel* may relate to some tabloid publications.

Picturing Government

In the 1967 photograph at the right of page 242, a University of Wisconsin student burns his draft card. During the unpopular Vietnam War, burning draft cards was a common act of protest, indicating a young man's unwillingness to enter the armed forces. It was not, however, protected speech. Compulsory draft registration (which the Supreme Court upheld as being for young men but not for young women) ended in 1975, but funding for it was reauthorized in 1980. Prior to the 2004 presidential election, many people believed that compulsory military service would be reinstated to provide soldiers for the war in Iraq. The House of Representatives voted down a bill proposing compulsory military or civil service in October 2004.

Picturing Government

The 1936 photograph at the left of page 242 shows a soapbox orator (foreground, left) speaking at the Los Angeles Plaza during a meeting of striking orange grove workers. By 1932, farm income had fallen to one-third of what it had been before the Great Depression began. Since many farmers lost their land, they took to the roads, looking for work. One million people were wandering the country by 1932. Without any relief four years later, people were calling for Socialist or Communist governments.

Freedom of Speech

According to Supreme Court decisions, there are two types of speech. **Pure speech** is the spoken word. Pure speech may be a conversation between two people or a speech delivered to a crowd of 2,000.

The U.S. Supreme Court ruled that burning a draft card as a form of protest against the Vietnam War was not protected by the U.S. Constitution as symbolic speech.

Symbolic speech combines actions and symbols—with or without words—to express ideas. The Supreme Court has held that burning the U.S. flag to protest the Vietnam War was symbolic speech. As such, it was protected under the First Amendment. The Court also struck down a later federal law that made it a crime to burn the flag. The ruling was very clear. Congress may not pass a law to limit the expression of an idea just because society does not like the idea.

Limits on Free Speech

Free speech is important to a free nation. However, government has the right to limit speech that is harmful. One type of speech that is limited is **seditious speech**. This is any speech that encourages the overthrow of the government or attempts to disrupt it.

Seditious speech is not allowed if it promotes violent action.

The "clear and present danger" rule is the test for these cases. According to this rule, a person can be punished for using words that promote criminal acts. The Supreme Court has used this rule to test cases brought under the Smith Act of 1940. This sedition law was passed just before World War II. It has three major parts: it is a crime to encourage the overthrow of the government, to hand out material promoting the overthrow, or to belong to a group that promotes the overthrow. In its rulings, the Court has noted a difference between asking people to believe in something and encouraging them to act on that belief. Speech is protected when it only encourages people to believe something. However, speech is not protected when it encourages violent actions.

Words to Know, continued

Words that incite another person to hit are called *fighting words*. The First Amendment doesn't protect *fighting words*.

Speeches in school publications or productions are *student speech*. Indecent or vulgar speech in a school is also called *student speech*.

Freedom of the press guarantees no *prior restraint* on what is published. A list of ideas that cannot be expressed is an example of *prior restraint*. *Censorship* is a synonym for *prior restraint*. Censorship can be applied to *student speech*, however. Laws that protect a journalist's sources are known as *shield laws*. Individual states must pass *shield laws*.

Speech for business purposes is called *commercial speech*. Since 1975, *commercial speech* has been regarded as protected speech.

Landmark Supreme Court Case: "Clear and Present Danger" Rule

***Schenck* v. *United States* (1919):** During World War I, Congress passed the Espionage Act of 1917. It forbade the speaking, writing, printing, or publishing of anything against the government. Charles Schenck was the general secretary of the Socialist Party. He was convicted of printing and mailing leaflets to 15,000 draftees. The leaflet urged them to refuse to report for military service. Schenck claimed that he was protected by the First Amendment.

The Supreme Court ruled against him. The Court agreed that in peacetime, Schenck would be protected. However, in wartime, his "speech" represented a "clear and present danger" to the nation. The Espionage Act was constitutional because Congress had the right to protect the nation.

Other kinds of speech that are not protected by the First Amendment are

- **defamation**: false words that damage a person's good name, character, or reputation
- **slander**: spoken defamatory speech
- **libel**: written defamatory speech
- **"fighting words"**: speech that is so insulting that it would cause a person to hit another
- **student speech**: two types of student speech within schools
  - indecent or vulgar speech
  - speech in school newspapers, plays and musicals, and similar school-related and school-supported activities

People who are the object of **defamation** may sue in civil court for money damages. However, in various rulings, the Supreme Court has limited the right of public figures to sue. The Court's concern is that such lawsuits might keep people from criticizing government officials.

The Supreme Court has also ruled that school officials may censor **student speech**. Students may not say or do anything in school that school officials consider improper. In other words, school officials may determine what students may or may not discuss in school newspapers or express in other school activities.

stop and think

Do you agree or disagree with the limits on the protection of student speech? Discuss the question with a partner. Make a T-chart to list pros and cons of the issue. Then write a persuasive essay giving reasons to agree and disagree with the limits on student speech. Conclude your essay with your personal opinion.

Supreme Court Case Extension

A year after passing the Espionage Act, Congress passed the Sedition Act, outlawing speech that was critical of the government or showed disrespect for the flag. Justice Oliver Wendell Holmes wrote in his opinion that just as people were not free to yell "Fire!" in a crowded theater and cause a panic when there was no fire, so during war they were not free to endanger the nation by urging resistance to the draft. However, by late 1919, Holmes had second thoughts, writing that only the imminent danger of harm or intent to harm should be the standards in limiting free speech.

Extension

While some people in 1919 were dismayed by the ruling in *Schenck* v. *United States*, more activity that now seems contrary to the First Amendment was yet to come. More than 4,000 bewildered immigrants suspected of subversive activity were arrested during the infamous Palmer raids during the 1919–1920 winter. Of the raid, even the *Washington Post* later wrote, "There was no time to waste on hairsplitting over infringement of liberty."

Extensions

1 Have students investigate other situations in which free speech was limited, such as during the Sedition Act in the late 1700s and during the Civil War, when Lincoln shut down newspapers that opposed his policies. Ask them to use graphic organizers to compare and contrast the situations and present their findings to the class.

2 Divide the class into five groups, assigning each group one of the five unprotected categories of speech. Ask the groups to find at least one real-life example to illustrate that kind of speech. If possible, they should find a Supreme Court case, using library resources or the Internet.

Stop and Think

Students' T-charts and essays will vary but should take a stand for or against limiting the protection of student speech and give reasons for the position.

Freedom of the Press

A free press is an important tool in a democracy. It offers a place for people to voice their views about government. A free press enables reporters to investigate and report on government and business wrongdoing.

Freedom of the press means that there is no prior restraint on what is published. **Prior restraint** forbids the expressing of ideas before they are expressed. Doing this is censorship. How can something be forbidden before it occurs? The government could make up a list of what may or may not be expressed, either in writing or speaking. However, the Constitution forbids prior restraint.

The ban on prior restraint, however, is not complete. The Supreme Court has ruled that prior restraint is allowed in wartime. It is also permitted if the publication (printed or spoken) is obscene, meaning vulgar, or encourages violence. Student speech comes under the Court's test of prior restraint.

Free Press Issues

One of the biggest issues facing a free press is confidentiality, or secrecy, of sources. Many people will talk to reporters only if their names are kept secret. One of the most famous confidential sources was Deep Throat, the source for information about President Richard Nixon and the Watergate scandal. Mark Felt, the deputy director of the FBI during Watergate, revealed himself to be Deep Throat in 2005. You can understand why he did not want his name known in 1972.

Sometimes reporters are called to testify before grand juries that want to know the sources of stories the reporters wrote or researched. Reporters usually refuse to testify. They claim First Amendment protection. They fear that if they reveal their sources, no one will talk to them in the future.

The Supreme Court has ruled that reporters have no such right. The First Amendment does not protect a reporter's refusal to testify. The Court suggested a remedy, however. If reporters want special protection, then **shield laws** need to be passed. Some 30 states have passed laws to shield reporters and their sources. However, Congress has not passed a federal shield law.

Judith Miller, a *New York Times* reporter, was jailed for 85 days in 2005 for refusing to reveal a source.

Picturing Government

The photograph on page 244 shows journalist Judith Miller speaking to reporters after being held in contempt of court in 2004. The following year, she was sentenced to serve up to four months in prison for refusing to testify before a grand jury. Miller, who was implicated in the leak of a CIA operative's name, would not give the name of her sources. After nearly three months in prison, Miller agreed to testify, because her source, the vice president's chief of staff, gave her permission to do so. The case highlights the need for a federal shield law for reporters, according to the publisher and chair of the New York Times Company, her employer.

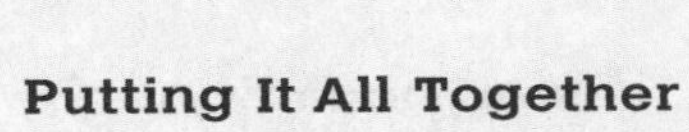

The First Amendment also applies to the electronic media. In 1952, the Supreme Court extended First Amendment protection to movies. Radio and television stations use the public airwaves, and are licensed by the federal government. In general, radio and television stations may not broadcast indecent programs. Cable is a paid service and has many more choices for viewers. Choice is an important difference when the Supreme Court considers cases.

The Telecommunications Act of 1996 replaced many of the regulations about radio and television in place since 1934. The act also attempted to regulate cable and the Internet. However, the Supreme Court struck down some parts of the law. The Court ruled that the Internet was protected by the First Amendment.

These decisions do not mean that Congress can do nothing. Congress can attempt to limit content on the Internet and cable in the future. However, any new laws must address the specific issues that the justices found unconstitutional.

Commercial Speech

Commercial speech is speech for business purposes. Advertising is an example of commercial speech. Until the 1970s, commercial speech was not considered protected speech. However, a series of Supreme Court rulings beginning in 1975 changed this view. It has struck down state or federal laws that banned

- listing prescription drug prices in ads
- listing liquor prices in ads
- radio and television ads for casinos

However, federal and state governments may ban certain kinds of advertising. False and misleading ads, and ads for illegal goods or services are banned. For reasons of public health and safety, for example, ads for cigarettes have been banned from radio and television.

Putting It All Together

Review the definitions you wrote in Thinking on Your Own. Write a paragraph to explain freedom of speech and a paragraph to explain freedom of the press. Share your work with a partner. Ask how you might improve your paragraphs to make them clearer to the reader.

Putting It All Together

Students' paragraphs on freedom of speech and freedom of the press will vary but should reflect lesson content.

Extension

Have students work in four small groups. Assign each group one of the following categories: Internet and online computer services, telephones, radio and television, cable networks. Ask each group to use library resources or the Internet to find out more about the Telecommunications Act of 1996 and the applications of the act to their topic. Host a panel discussion on the act as it applies to free speech.

Lesson Summary

The First Amendment guarantees freedom of assembly and of petition.

Lesson Objective

Students will learn about the freedom to assemble and the right to petition.

Focus Your Reading Answers

1 Time, place, and manner regulations help ensure public order and safety. They allow traffic to move smoothly and other people to use the streets.

2 Issues in freedom of assembly include the prohibition against assembly on private property. Another question is if the police have a right to end a demonstration that has caused violence.

3 The right of association allows people who support the same ideas to gather with others who share their views, including a wish for social, political, or economic change.

Picturing Government

The two photographs on page 246 show two different demonstrations regarding the war in Iraq. The top photograph, taken in New York City in 2004, shows protestors against the war on the first anniversary of the start of the war. The bottom photograph, taken in Atlanta before the war began, shows supporters of the war. Both groups were subject to time, place, and manner regulations.

LESSON 4

Freedom of Assembly and Petition

Thinking on Your Own

The authors of the Bill of Rights believed the right to hold and attend public meetings was essential to democratic government. Do you agree? Create a bulleted list of reasons in your notebook to support your opinion.

focus your reading

What is the reason for time, place, and manner regulations?

What issues are involved in freedom of assembly?

What is the right of association?

words to know

content neutral

Freedom of assembly and the right to petition allows people to gather together in private and in public places. The right of people to make their views known to public officials is also guaranteed. People may write petitions, letters, and ads to government officials. They may also lobby lawmakers and take part in marches, parades, and demonstrations. The right to assemble is one of the reasons people can form political parties, interest groups, and professional associations.

During the war in Iraq, demonstrations were held by those who were against the war (top) and those who supported the war (bottom).

Remember the principle of incorporation from Lesson 1. The Fourteenth Amendment applies to all the freedoms explained in Lessons 2 and 3. Because of the Fourteenth Amendment, these freedoms are protected from actions by state and local governments. The Fourteenth Amendment also protects the rights to assemble and petition government.

Freedom of Assembly

The First Amendment guarantees the right to assemble peacefully. However, people cannot just get together in the street and decide to march on city hall. The Supreme Court has allowed limits in order to ensure public order and safety. For example, in 1941, the Court ruled that states and cities

Words to Know

Discuss the vocabulary term with students.

Content neutral means that the content of a demonstration or protest cannot be regulated in the time, place, and manner rules. *Content neutral* ensures that the rules are applied equally to all.

may require a permit for a demonstration, march, or parade. The purpose, however, cannot be to limit freedom of assembly. The permit is meant to control traffic flow and allow others to use the streets.

Regulations for protests and parades are known as time, place, and manner regulations. Rules may set the when, where, and how the protest may be carried out. For example, a permit might state that the march must begin at 10 A.M. and end by 1 P.M.; marchers must assemble at 12th Street and must walk east on Maple Street to city hall; there can be no bullhorns.

Time, place, and manner regulations must be specific and applied evenly to all groups. However, the content of a protest or demonstration may not be regulated. The rules regulating assemblies must be **content neutral**.

In 1977, the National Socialist Party, a white supremacist group, was allowed to march in Skokie, IL, a predominantly Jewish community.

Freedom of Assembly Issues

The Supreme Court has ruled that freedom of assembly does not extend to private property. For example, a group may not take over a shopping mall to hold a demonstration. A shopping mall is not like a public street with stores. Shopping malls are businesses owned by companies. However, the Court has upheld the right of peaceful petition in shopping malls. Individuals may approach shoppers to sign petitions.

Public property is property that people usually think of as places to demonstrate. These include streets, sidewalks, parks, and public buildings. The Supreme Court has upheld the right to assemble in public places. However, issues still arise about how to apply the freedom of assembly. Two questions in particular have come before the Court. Does the Constitution require the police to

Picketing is the walking back and forth of striking workers at a business. If the picketing is peaceful, it is protected. If it incites violence, it is not.

stop and think

How have the courts limited the right of assembly? List these limits in your notebook and work with a partner to decide whether you agree or disagree with each. As you read about the freedom of association, think about whether that right should also have limits. Explain your opinion in a one-sentence statement.

Picturing Government

The 1977 photograph at the right of page 247 shows a group of American Neo-Nazis responding to a court order prohibiting the group from marching in Skokie, Illinois. Skokie is a community with a large Jewish population in which one of every six Jews was a Holocaust survivor or directly related to a survivor. Frank Collin, shown speaking at left, was not only the head of the National Socialist Party of America, but also the son of a Jewish Holocaust survivor. The case was a costly victory for the American Civil Liberties Union, whose attorney, David Goldberger, was a Jew defending the rights of Nazis against his fellow Jews. About 30,000 ACLU members left the group over the case, and after winning the case, the Neo-Nazis decided not to march in Skokie after all. The freedom of speech case highlighted the need to defend that right, even when the speech is unpleasant.

Picturing Government

The photograph at the bottom left of page 247 is of striking workers at the Fairmont Hotel in San Francisco. In 2004, hotel owners locked out more than 4,000 employees at several hotels. The dispute spread not only to other cities in the United States, but also to Australia, since the hotels were global corporations. Hotel employees working in expensive hotels were among the lowest-paid groups.

Extension

What should be the limits to free speech? Have students use library resources or the Internet to find out about current instances of hate speech on high school or college campuses. Have a panel discussion on the rights of students to unlimited freedom of speech after high school limitations have been removed.

Stop and Think

Students' opinions on the limits to the rights of assembly will vary but should be expressed in one sentence.

Civil Liberties: Constitutional Freedoms 247

Supreme Court Case Extension

Gregory v. *City of Chicago* was, according to Chief Justice Earl Warren, who wrote the opinion of the Court, a "simple case." The Court's logic rested on the fact that the demonstrators were peaceful, but the bystanders from the mayor's neighborhood were not. Gregory and the others had been charged with disorderly conduct. Citing a 1961 case, *Garner* v. *Louisiana*, the Court indicated that had the demonstrators been charged with resisting arrest, the conviction would have stood. However, they had been charged with a crime they did not commit and for which the Court could not convict them. In a concurrent opinion, Justice Black took issue with the original wording of the law and the implication that police officers had the right to determine what was likely a "diversion tending to a breach of the peace."

Landmark Supreme Court Case: Freedom of Assembly

***Gregory* v. *City of Chicago* (1969):** Dick Gregory, an African-American entertainer and activist, organized a march in Chicago. The march protested segregation in Chicago schools. The protesters had a permit and police protection as they marched five miles from city hall to the mayor's house. There, they marched in front of the house. About 1,000 people gathered to watch. After a while, the crowd began to throw rocks and eggs. They also shouted insults at the marchers. The police feared a riot. They ordered the protesters to end the demonstration and leave. The protesters refused. The police arrested them. Gregory and several others were convicted of disorderly conduct.

Gregory and the other protesters appealed. The Court sided with them. The protesters were peacefully exercising their First Amendment right. Because the protesters acted peacefully, they could not be charged with disorderly conduct. It was the crowd that had become disorderly.

allow a demonstration to continue if it has caused violence? When can the police order an end to a demonstration? The ruling in *Gregory* v. *City of Chicago* helped to answer these questions.

Freedom of Association

Freedom of assembly grants, or allows, a right of association. People may gather with others who share their views, interests, and concerns. These concerns may include working to create political, economic, and social change.

Organizations such as the American Medical Association routinely hold meetings for their members.

The right goes back to a Supreme Court ruling in 1958. The state of Alabama demanded that the Alabama chapter of the National Association for the Advancement of Colored People (NAACP) turn over its membership list. The NAACP refused and was fined. It appealed and the Supreme Court ruled in its favor. The Court said that association with others who support the same ideas is a guaranteed right.

Putting It All Together

Why is freedom of assembly important in a democracy? Use the information from the lists you created to write a paragraph to answer the question.

248 Chapter 13

Putting It All Together
Students' paragraphs will vary but should explain why freedom of assembly is important in a democracy.

Picturing Government

The photograph on page 248 shows the 2005 annual meeting of the American Medical Association's House of Delegates in Chicago. This policy-making and legislative body meets each year to hear, discuss, and debate reports and resolutions related to health care.

LESSON 5

Rights of the Accused

Thinking on Your Own

What happens when a police officer arrests a suspect? Think of an arrest that you have watched on a television program or movie or one that you imagine. Answer the question by writing a bulleted list in your notebook.

focus your reading

List the rights a person has at the time of arrest.

What rights protect a person who is on trial?

What does the Constitution say about punishment?

words to know

due process
search warrant
probable cause
exclusionary rule
good faith exception
self-incrimination
bail
preventive detention
double jeopardy
capital punishment

Due process is guaranteed by both the Fifth and Fourteenth Amendments. The Fifth Amendment states that the government may not take from any person "life, liberty, or property, without due process of law."

The Fourteenth Amendment picks up these words. It extends due process to state governments. In its decisions, the Supreme Court has applied each of the guarantees discussed in this lesson to the states.

What exactly is due process? The best way to define **due process** is that the government must act fairly and obey the rules of law. Due process is especially important to people in the criminal justice system.

Rights at the Time of Arrest

Because of the Fourth Amendment, police cannot just go into a home or business and search it. They must have a **search warrant** issued by a judge. A police officer must swear under oath that there is probable cause. **Probable cause** means the reasonable possibility that evidence of a crime or criminal is in the place. However, the Supreme Court ruled that the police

Lesson Summary

The Fifth and Fourteenth Amendments guarantee due process at all stages of the criminal justice process. An accused person has the right to protection against unreasonable search and seizure, to remain silent, to an attorney, and to protection against excessive bail. During a trial, the accused has the right to a speedy and public trial by a jury of peers and the right to protection against double jeopardy, along with the right to question witnesses. People are also protected against cruel and unusual punishment.

Lesson Objective

Students will learn about the rights of the accused that are guaranteed by the Constitution.

Focus Your Reading Answers

1 At time of arrest, a person has the right to protection against unreasonable search and seizure, to remain silent, to an attorney, and to protection against excessive bail.

2 A person on trial has the right to a speedy and public trial by a jury of peers and the right to protection against double jeopardy, as well as the right to question witnesses.

3 Punishment cannot be cruel or unusual.

Words to Know

Discuss each of the vocabulary terms with students.

Due process requires that the government act fairly and obey the rules of law. *Due process* is guaranteed by the Fifth and Fourteenth Amendments.

A *search warrant* is a document issued by a judge that allows police to search a home or business. A *search warrant* is not needed if police see someone breaking the law. *Probable cause* is the reasonable possibility that evidence of a crime or criminal is in a home or business. To get a *search warrant*, a police officer must swear that there is *probable cause*.

The *exclusionary rule* means that evidence obtained through an illegal search cannot be used in a trial. The Supreme Court developed the *exclusionary rule* in 1914. The *good faith exception* to that rule covers cases in which police acted in good faith that their warrant was correct, when it was not. The *good faith exception* came about because of a 1984 trial.

Chart Extension

Divide the class into four groups, assigning each one of the following amendments: Fourth, Fifth, Sixth, Eighth. Ask the students in the group to become knowledgeable about the provisions of their amendment as it applies to the rights of the accused. After students have learned their amendment's provisions, play a Jeopardy-style game with the students, using the five stages as categories.

Extensions

1 Invite students to use library resources or the Internet to find the historical background for the inclusion of the need for a search warrant before conducting a search at a home or business. Allow time for them to share their findings with the class.

2 In the 1996 case *Whren* v. *United States*, the Court ruled that police could seize illegal drugs in a vehicle that was stopped for a traffic violation. In 2001, the Court ruled in *Atwater* v. *City of Lago Vista* that a driver of a car in which children were not wearing seat belts could be arrested. The Court did not feel that either of these cases violated protections against unreasonable search and seizure. Summarize these cases for students and have them debate the issue.

Constitutional Protections for the Accused

Stage of the Criminal Justice System	Section of the Constitution	Protection
Gathering Evidence	Fourth Amendment	Protection against "unreasonable search and seizure"
Arrest and Questioning	Fifth Amendment Sixth Amendment	Right to remain silent Right to have an attorney
Jailing Before Trial	Eighth Amendment	Protection against "excessive bail"
Trial	Sixth Amendment Fifth Amendment Article III, Section 2, and the Sixth Amendment Sixth Amendment	Right to a "speedy and public trial" Protection against "double jeopardy" Trial by jury Right to question witnesses
Punishment	Eighth Amendment	Protection against "cruel and unusual punishment"

do not need a warrant if they see someone in the act of breaking the law. They can search and arrest a person at the scene of a crime.

What if the police conduct an illegal search? Can the evidence be used in a trial? In a 1914 ruling, the Supreme Court developed the **exclusionary rule** for such cases. The general answer is "no." However, as the Court continues to hear illegal search-and-seizure appeals, it continues to work on the exclusionary rule. For example, in a 1984 case, the Court developed the **good faith exception**. The police had asked for and received a search warrant based on probable cause. The warrant was later found to be incorrect. The Court upheld the conviction. It said the police had acted in good faith in believing that their warrant was correct.

The Supreme Court has found that students on school property do not have the same Fourth Amendment protections.

Words to Know, continued

Giving testimony against oneself is called *self-incrimination*. The Fifth Amendment is a guard against *self-incrimination*. Money that a defendant deposits with the court as a promise to appear for trial is called *bail*. The Eighth Amendment doesn't prohibit *bail* but states that it is not to be excessive. *Preventive detention* occurs if a person may commit another crime. A judge may call for *preventive detention* instead of *bail*. Being tried twice for the same crime is called *double jeopardy*. The Fifth Amendment protects against *double jeopardy*. *Capital punishment* is also known as the death penalty. The Supreme Court has ruled that *capital punishment* may be used only in cases of murder.

Landmark Supreme Court Case: Student Searches

New Jersey v. *T.L.O.* **(1985):** A student was suspended and tried in juvenile court for having marijuana. The marijuana was found when the assistant principal searched her purse. He thought she had been smoking cigarettes in the restroom. He found the cigarettes as well as the marijuana.

The Supreme Court ruled that school officials do not need a search warrant or probable cause. However, school officials must have a reasonable belief that the search will find that the student has broken school rules. In later drug testing cases, the Court has ruled in favor of drug testing. No probable cause is needed to test students who want to take part in extracurricular activities.

The Fifth and Sixth Amendments offer protections to people suspected of or arrested for crimes. The Fifth Amendment guarantees that they do not have to incriminate themselves. **Self-incrimination** means giving testimony against oneself. A person does not have to help the police prove his or her guilt. The Miranda rule, which is read to suspects and those being arrested, states: "You have the right to remain silent. Anything you say may be used against you in a court of law." The Fifth Amendment also protects people from being pressured, tortured, or beaten into confessing.

The Miranda rule also states that the person "has the right to have an attorney present during questioning." Because of two other rulings, an arrested person must be represented by an attorney. If the person cannot afford an attorney, the court must appoint one. This is the result of *Escobedo* v. *Illinois* and *Gideon* v. *Wainwright*.

The Eighth Amendment does not state that everyone arrested for a crime must be allowed bail. **Bail** is money that a defendant deposits with the court as a promise to appear for trial on the appointed day. The judge in the case sets the amount of bail. The Eighth Amendment says only that the amount may not be "excessive." If it is feared that a person may commit another crime, a judge may decide not to set bail. This is called **preventive detention**. The Supreme Court has ruled that this is legal.

stop and think

Review the bulleted list you wrote for Thinking on Your Own. Did the police officer involved follow the law? If not, what should the officer have done? Add or remove items from your list. Share your answers with a partner.

Supreme Court Case Extension

The case *New Jersey* v. *T.L.O.* began when a teacher found two girls smoking in the school restroom in violation of school policy. Sent to the principal's office, one of them admitted to smoking. The second girl, identified as T.L.O., denied any wrongdoing, which was when the assistant principal opened her purse and removed a pack of cigarettes. Noticing cigarette papers in the purse, the man searched the purse more carefully and found evidence that T.L.O. was selling marijuana at school. In handing down its decision, the Supreme Court reversed the decision of the New Jersey Supreme Court.

Stop and Think

Students' lists and their interpretations of them will vary.

Picturing Government

The photograph at the top left of page 252 shows a lawyer consulting with a client before trial. *Gideon* v. *Wainwright* established the right of the accused to counsel, overturning a 1942 Supreme Court decision. Those accused also must be given a speedy trial by jury.

Civics Today Extension

Youth courts fall under the auspices of the National Youth Court Center, which is at the American Probation and Parole Association. The National Youth Court Center sponsors the world's largest service event, an annual National Youth Service Day. In 2005, some 70 youth courts received small grants to take part in the day. Projects ranged from painting address numbers on street curbs so that people could readily be found and helped in an emergency, to cleaning up trash for the elderly, to creating magnets to inform the community about legal resources for youths.

Rights Related to Trial

The Sixth Amendment provides two protections once a person is arrested for a crime. The first is a guarantee of a "speedy, public trial." The government must bring an accused person to trial quickly. Today, the public part of the guarantee often involves media coverage. Local crimes often lead off the nightly television news and make front-page headlines. The courts have to balance the public's and media's desire for news with the defendant's right to a fair trial. The Supreme Court has ruled that the media has no special right to cover a trial.

People accused of a crime are guaranteed a lawyer.

The second protection is the right to confront witnesses during the trial. The attorney for a defendant has the right to question anyone who testifies against the defendant.

The Sixth Amendment also reinforces an earlier section of the Constitution, Article III, Section 2. This guarantees a person's right to a trial by jury.

Civics Today

Youth Court

Many local courts are overburdened by criminal cases. One solution for juvenile crimes is youth court, also called peer, teen, or student court. Youth court is only for first-time offenders under the age of nineteen. They must be accused of minor crimes only, such as trespassing and truancy.

In about half of youth courts, everyone involved is a teenager: the judge, jury, lawyers, and the bailiff, who swears in witnesses. Volunteers from seventh to twelfth grade take part in the program. The jury foreperson, judge, bailiff, defense attorneys, and prosecutors receive ten hours of training for their roles. They serve for a year and take turns at the different court jobs. In many youth courts, former defendants must be jurors at least once.

Most hearings take less than an hour. Jurors determine sentences. Sentences usually involve community service, writing a letter of apology, taking a victim-awareness class, and touring the local jail.

More than 1,000 youth courts have been set up. They hear more than 100,000 cases a year. Youth courts have impressive records. Students who go through youth court are more likely to stay out of trouble than students who go through the regular juvenile justice system.

Extension

Have students find out where the nearest youth court is held. If possible, have students attend a meeting or interview a student involved with youth court.

The Fifth Amendment protects a person from **double jeopardy**—being tried twice for the same crime. There are some limits to this protection, however. Suppose a jury cannot agree on a verdict. The defendant may be tried for the crime again. Sometimes a crime is both a federal offense and a state offense. A person may be tried for the crime in both a federal and a state court. A crime may include several acts. For example, a person counterfeits CDs and sells them. The person can be charged and tried for both counterfeiting and selling fake goods.

Punishment

The Eighth Amendment prohibits "cruel and unusual punishment." Most Eighth Amendment cases that reach the Supreme Court involve **capital punishment**. This is another term for the death penalty. The death penalty is a heavily debated topic. Many human rights advocates say that it violates human rights. They point to the high numbers of minorities on death row. They also note the number of people who have later been found innocent of the crime of which they were convicted. However, supporters of the death penalty say that it keeps others from committing murders. It can also provide some end to the grief of victims' families.

Capital punishment remains a topic of much discussion in the United States.

Since the 1970s, the Supreme Court has made several important rulings related to the death penalty. The death penalty may be used only if the crime is murder. The penalty must be used fairly. It cannot be used more for one type of defendant than for others.

Recent Court rulings have refused to allow the death penalty for the mentally retarded and those under eighteen. The Court also decided that juries, not judges, must decide on whether to sentence a convicted killer to death.

Putting It All Together

Work with a partner. Imagine that you are reporters for the local television station. You get a call that the police are going to raid an illegal betting operation. You go along on the raid. Then you follow what happens until the end of the trial. Write a summary for your audience when the trial is over. Explain the action the police took before the raid, the arrest, the bail hearing, and the trial.

Picturing Government

The photograph on page 253 shows people in Austin, Texas, demonstrating against the death penalty. The Supreme Court reinstated the death penalty in 1976. In 2003, Texas led the nation in executions, with 24 people executed. The United States is one of 75 nations that retain the death penalty. Nearly one-half of the nations of the world have abolished it in law or practice. Over the past decade, an average of more than three countries annually have abolished the death penalty.

Putting It All Together

Students' summaries will vary but should reflect an understanding of the lesson content.

Extension

Divide the class into two groups, affirmative and negative, to debate the question of whether the death penalty should be abolished. Review proper debate format with students. If desired, have a school librarian come to class to explain to students how to find more information on the topic.

Civil Liberties: Constitutional Freedoms 253

Participate in Government

Suggest that students working in small groups devise scenarios illustrating the different categories of people who require green cards. Have each group role-play what a person in each category must do to obtain a green card and the various ways that people can legally immigrate.

Participate in Government

Apply for a Green Card

A green card is officially known as a Permanent Resident Card. It is an official form of identification. It shows that a person is a lawful permanent resident (LPR) of the United States. The person is living and working here legally. In order to get a job in the United States, a person must show proof of citizenship or a green card.

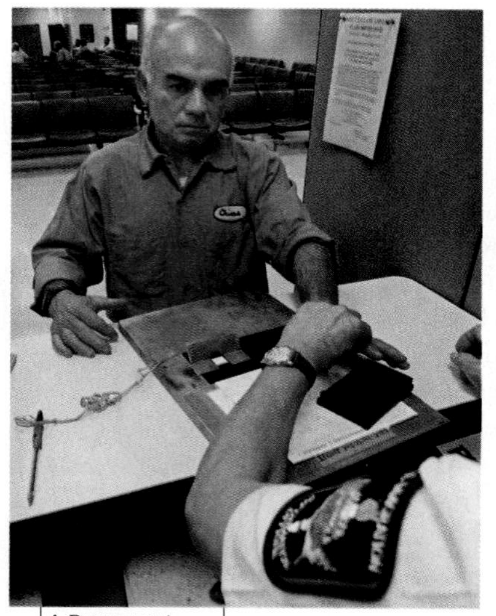

A Permanent Resident Card must be renewed every ten years

A green card is usually issued for two or ten years. A two-year card gives a person conditional permanent resident status. Certain conditions must be met before the two years are over. Then the person may apply for a Permanent Resident Card. Permanent cards expire at the end of ten years and must be renewed.

The U.S. Citizenship and Immigration Services Web site is a great tool for people wishing to become LPRs. The site provides information on how to apply. Among the ways are immigration through a family member or employment. Among those eligible are husbands or wives, unmarried children, married children, brothers and sisters, and parents of U.S. citizens or LPRs already living in the United States.

There are also special classes for refugees and asylum seekers. Refugees are people who have fled their countries because of war or famine. Asylum seekers fled because they feared jail or murder for their political views.

To Find Out More About Applying for a Green Card:

- Check the U.S. Citizenship and Immigration Services Web site (USCIS) for forms, fees, and addresses of CIS office.

Research Resources

Below is a list of reference books and Web sites that relate to the issues covered in this chapter. Students may wish to use these to further their research on ideas in the preceding lessons. Web site addresses may change over time. Use keyword searching on a major search engine to locate sites.

Reference Books:

Patricia Hinchey. *Student Rights: A Reference Handbook*. ABC-CLIO, 2001.

Waldo E. Martin, Jr., and Patricia Sullivan. *Civil Rights in the United States*. Macmillan Reference USA, 2000.

Christopher Waldrep. *The Constitution and the Nation: A Revolution in Rights, 1937–2002*. P. Lang, 2003.

Web Sites:

The Legal Information Institute offers an overview of civil rights as well as links to cases and amendments.

The U.S. Constitution site offers interesting information on things that people believe are in the Constitution but are not.

The American Civil Liberties Union is often in the courtroom attempting to preserve rights guaranteed by the Constitution. Their site offers summaries and analyses of cases.

Skill Builder

Identify Point of View

A person's point of view is shaped by his or her family, religion, education and reading, friends, personal experiences and time period.

For example, consider probable cause and the searching of bags. Should people's bags be searched before they get on an airplane? Before the 1980s, the answer would have been "no." Then airplane hijackings began and that point of view changed.

It is not always easy to determine point of view. To help you identify point of view, follow these steps:

1. Identify the author or the speaker. Learn about the person's background. If the person belongs to an organization, try to find out if the group supports conservative or liberal causes.
2. Identify the argument or issue. Find the main idea and supporting details of the piece of writing or speech.
3. Identify the facts and other information used to support the argument. Distinguish facts from opinions.
4. Examine the kinds of words and phrases that the author or speaker uses. Do some words and phrases seem more favorable to one side of the issue or the other?
5. State the person's viewpoint in your own words.

Use the following excerpt to answer the questions.

> I consider the foundation of the Constitution as laid on this ground: That "all powers not delegated to the United States, by the Constitution, nor prohibited by it to the States, are reserved to the States, or to the people."
>
> —Thomas Jefferson, Secretary of State, February 1791.

1 What do you know about the writer?

2 What point or argument is he making? What information does he use?

3 Write a sentence stating the writer's point of view about the powers of Congress.

Skill Builder

1 The writer is Thomas Jefferson, then secretary of state, and later president.

2 The foundation of the Constitution is that powers belong to the states or to the people, unless the Constitution specifically gives it to the United States or denies it to the states. To go beyond that boundary is to take too much power. He quotes the Constitution.

3 The powers of Congress are bounded by the power delegated to the national government and to the states.

Classroom Discussion

Discuss with students some of the broader topics covered in this chapter.

- How have civil rights expanded or been restricted over the past century?
- How can the separation of church and state be maintained in schools while still being fair to all groups wishing to express their faith?
- Are the distinctions made over the rights of high school students versus adults fair?

Recommended Reading

Below is a list of books that relate to the issues covered in this chapter. The numbers in parentheses indicate the related Thematic Strands of the National Council for the Social Studies (NCSS).

Phillis Engelbert, ed. *American Civil Rights Biographies.* Dimensions, 1999. (VI, X)

Tom Head. *Freedom of Religion.* Facts on File, 2005. (VI, X)

Andrea C. Nakaya, ed. *Civil Rights and War (Examining Issues Through Political Cartoons).* Greenhaven Press, 2005. (VI, X)

Related Transparencies

T-18 Three-Column Chart

Key Blacklines

Biography—Rosa Parks

CD Extension

Encourage students to use the reading comprehension, vocabulary reinforcement, and other activities on the student CD.

Getting Focused

After students have made their lists, challenge them to think of how each amendment might apply to each group pictured in the photographs on page 256. Make a four-column chart of their ideas and use them as a checklist as students read through the chapter. Add to the list as more examples come to light.

Chapter 14 CIVIL RIGHTS: EQUAL JUSTICE

Getting Focused

Skim this chapter to predict what you will be learning.

- **Read the lesson titles and subheadings.**
- **Look at the illustrations and read the captions.**
- **Review the vocabulary words and terms.**

Civil rights are the rights of everyone to equal protection of the laws. Discrimination based on race, religion, gender, or ethnic origin is against the law. The Fifth and Fourteenth Amendments protect us from discrimination by government or by any other group or individual.

What are the Fifth and Fourteenth Amendments about? Write down as much as you can remember about both amendments. Then check your ideas against the amendments.

Women's rights (top left), civil rights (top right), Native American rights (bottom left), and rights of those with disabilities (bottom right) have all been the focus of demonstrations.

Pre-Reading Discussion

1 Bring to class and discuss with students any recent news stories about immigration and nonresident aliens in your area. Challenge students to begin thinking about the problems and possible solutions to illegal immigration, in light of increasing security concerns after 9/11.

2 Have students identify any teams or programs within the school that target a special population, such as sports teams for young women. How do they feel about coed teams in football or soccer? What advantages and disadvantages do they see in separate teams for men and women?

LESSON 1

Equal Protection Under the Law

Thinking on Your Own

What does the term "civil rights movement" mean to you? Write a paragraph in your notebook to explain what the civil rights movement was and who was involved.

focus your reading

What tests do courts apply to decide if a law is discriminatory?

List the groups that have had to fight for their civil rights.

words to know

discrimination

rational basis test

strict scrutiny

fundamental rights

intermediate scrutiny

segregation

Equal protection under the law is guaranteed by the Fourteenth Amendment. The amendment declares that a state may not "deny to any person within its jurisdiction the equal protection of the law." Jurisdiction means authority or rule. Equal protection is also guaranteed under the due process clause of the Fifth Amendment.

Why is the guarantee of equal protection needed? The nation has a long history of discrimination against various groups. **Discrimination** is the unfair treatment of people. Discrimination may be based on race, gender, ethnic origin, age, mental or physical disability, or religion.

Classifications and Judicial Tests

Not all different treatment is discriminatory. Governments may pass laws based on distinctions among groups. This means that governments may set up classifications that recognize differences among groups. For example, a state government may classify students at its state university as in-state and out-of-state. The state government may then charge out-of-state students more to attend the state university.

Lesson Summary

The Fifth and Fourteenth Amendments guarantee equal protection under the law. Discrimination has existed against various groups, based on ethnic origin, age, gender, race, religion, or physical or mental disability. To judge laws for discrimination, the Supreme Court uses several tests. One is the rational basis test, which looks for a link between the classification and an acceptable purpose of the government. A second test is strict scrutiny, which is used in cases involving fundamental rights as they apply to race or national origin. Intermediate scrutiny applies to cases of possible discrimination against women. This governs any law based on the notion that women are weak or inferior to men. Groups that have sought equal rights include African Americans, women, Hispanics, Native Americans, those with physical and mental disabilities, and gays and lesbians.

Lesson Objective

Students will learn about the battles of various groups for equality under the law and the tests that the Supreme Court uses in determining if a law is discriminatory.

Picturing Government

The photograph montage on page 256 shows the four different marches for justice. At the top left, women take part in a march on the first Women's Equality Day, August 26, 1971. Representative Bella Abzug of New York was one of the women who persuaded Congress to set aside the day commemorating passage of the Twentieth Amendment. The photograph at the top right shows the 1963 March on Washington for Jobs and Freedom. Demonstrators marched from the Washington Monument to the Lincoln Memorial, where several leaders, including Dr. Martin Luther King, Jr., spoke. The bottom left photo shows a group of Native Americans protesting past government treatment in Cleveland, Ohio, in 1973. At the bottom right, a group of disabled people are shown in a 2002 march on Washington to lobby for better allocation of Medicaid funds. The group, American Disabled for Attendant Programs Today (ADAPT), called for help so that the disabled could live at home. They cited the 1998 Supreme Court case *Olmstead* v. *L.C.*, which affirmed a person's right to live in the community.

Focus Your Reading Answers

1 To decide if a law is discriminatory, courts apply the tests of rational basis, strict scrutiny, and intermediate scrutiny.

2 The following groups have had to fight to gain their civil rights: African Americans, Hispanics, Native Americans, women, those with physical and mental disabilities, and gays and lesbians.

Picturing Government

The photograph on page 258 shows an older worker in a general store. In 2003, the workforce included some five million Americans sixty-five and older, who made up 3.4 percent of the United States labor force. About 16–18 percent of men in that age group work, compared to 8–10 percent of women. Employers have come to value older employees for their experience and work ethic.

Stop and Think

Students' charts should list the following three tests: rational basis, strict scrutiny, and intermediate scrutiny. Their summaries of the facts will vary.

The laws of the United States prohibit age discrimination.

In its rulings, the Supreme Court has developed three tests to determine if a law is discriminatory. The basic test is the **rational basis test**. Is there a reasonable relationship between the classification and an acceptable government purpose? For example, the states can set the legal drinking age at twenty-one. It is assumed that people under twenty-one are not mature enough to drink responsibly. To refuse alcohol to all blue-eyed people regardless of age is not a reasonable law. There is no relationship between eye color and responsible drinking. The rational basis test is applied to laws dealing with age, disability, income, and similar categories.

The second test is called **strict scrutiny**. This test is applied to laws based on race or national origin. Courts ask if the classification meets a "compelling public interest." They also ask if there is no other way to achieve that goal. For example, the Supreme Court has upheld affirmative action laws based on race. The Court recognizes the need to make up for years of discrimination against African Americans. It has also determined that affirmative action laws are required to achieve this goal.

In addition, the Supreme Court uses the strict scrutiny test for cases involving **fundamental rights**. These include the Bill of Rights, the right to vote, and the right to travel freely between states.

Possible discrimination against women comes under **intermediate scrutiny**. This lies between rational basis and strict scrutiny. The Supreme Court has thrown out any law based on the idea that women are weak or inferior to men. For example, the Court ruled that the states may not keep women from serving on juries. The Court has also upheld laws that seek to correct past injustices against women. The Court has upheld equal athletic programs for men and women under Title IX of the 1972 Education Act. The Court asks if the gender distinction serves an important government objective. The distinction must also be substantially, or largely, related to achieving the goal.

stop and think

The Supreme Court uses three tests to rule about discrimination. Create a T-chart to explain the three rules mentioned in this lesson. In the left column, list the rule. In the right column, list the facts. Work with a partner to complete the chart.

Words to Know

Introduce each of the following vocabulary terms to students.

Explain that *discrimination* is treating some groups of people differently from others. *Discrimination* may be based on gender or age. The *rational basis test* looks for a relationship between the classification of a law and an acceptable government purpose. Setting a minimum age for drinking alcoholic beverages is an example of a *rational basis test.*

The *strict scrutiny* test looks at laws based on race or national origin. The *strict scrutiny* test checks to see that the classification meets a compelling public interest or is the only way to meet a goal.

Rights covered in the Bill of Rights, as well as the right to travel freely between states and the right to vote, are considered *fundamental rights*. The Court uses *strict scrutiny* in cases of *fundamental rights*.

The Fight for Civil Rights

Everyone's civil rights have not always been protected. In 1866, Senator Charles Sumner led a group in Congress who strongly supported passing a civil rights bill. The law, if enacted, would have protected slaves from Southern Black Codes. By the 1870s, **segregation**, or the separation of whites and African Americans, was the law throughout the South. In *Plessy* v. *Ferguson*, the Supreme Court ruled that "separate but equal" was constitutional. It was almost 60 years before the Court overturned this decision. This time, it ruled that separate schools were inherently unequal, in *Brown* v. *Board of Education* in 1954.

The civil rights movement began with African Americans, as early as 1900. The National Association for the Advancement of Colored People was founded in 1909. Its lawyers filed the lawsuit that became the landmark case *Brown* v. *Board of Education*.

The decision in *Brown* was soon followed by the Montgomery bus boycott of 1955–1956. The bus boycott resulted from Rosa Parks's refusal in Alabama to give up her seat on a bus to a white man. In 1957, the governor of Arkansas refused to allow African-American students to enter Little Rock Central High School. President Eisenhower called out federal troops to enforce integration.

By the 1960s, civil rights leaders such as Dr. Martin Luther King, Jr., were leading marches and protests against segregation. Protesters were beaten and jailed. Some were murdered for their work.

By the early 1970s, many other groups were following their lead. Hispanics and Native Americans staged protests against discrimination. Women held marches and lobbied for equal rights and reproductive rights. Those with physical and mental disabilities and their supporters demanded education, jobs, and housing. In the 1980s, gay and lesbian activists were also marching for equal rights.

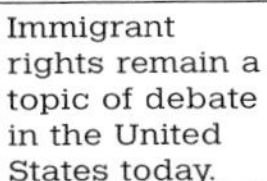

Immigrant rights remain a topic of debate in the United States today.

Putting It All Together

Write a paragraph in your notebook describing the role the Supreme Court plays in guaranteeing equal protection under the law. Does it always ensure that all groups are treated equally?

Picturing Government

The photograph on page 259 shows a demonstration protesting the new Illegal Immigration Reform and Immigrant Responsibility Act, which took effect in 1997. The law included harsh provisions against anyone overstaying the authorized period listed on his or her visa and those attempting to work without proper authorization to do so.

Putting It All Together

Students' paragraphs will vary but should take and support a position on whether the Supreme Court always ensures that all groups receive equal treatment.

Extensions

1 Have students use library resources or the Internet to find current statistics on women enrolled in or practicing in fields once denied them, such as medicine, law, or clergy. Ask them to graph the changes over several decades.

2 Ask students to investigate the provisions of Title IX, as well as the critics of and challenges to that law. Suggest they create graphic organizers that highlight pro/con arguments about the law.

Words to Know, continued

Between the first two tests is *intermediate scrutiny*. *Intermediate scrutiny* covers cases of possible *discrimination* against women. *Segregation* is the separating of African Americans and whites. The decision in *Plessy* v. *Ferguson* upheld the practice of *segregation*.

Civil Rights: Equal Justice 259

Lesson Summary

Congress began passing civil rights acts in 1957, with additional civil rights laws and voting rights laws in 1960, 1964, 1965, 1968, 1970, 1975, and 1982. Laws covered such things as charging poll taxes; denying service to anyone in a public place; and refusing to sell a home to someone for reasons of race, color, gender, national origin, religion, or disability. The government has adopted a policy of affirmative action to counter past discrimination. To fulfill the policy, some schools and employers set up quota systems. Some people believe these are forms of reverse discrimination. Since the 1970s, the Court has overturned laws that are rooted in discrimination against women. The Court uses the Bill of Rights and the Fourteenth Amendment to uphold the right to privacy.

Lesson Objective

Students will learn about the civil rights laws passed at the federal level.

Focus Your Reading Answers

1 Conflict over affirmative action exists because some people believe that it promotes reverse discrimination through a system of quotas.

2 The Supreme Court judges laws based on gender differences by determining if they benefit men while discriminating against women.

3 The right to privacy protects such things as school records, credit information, and medical records.

LESSON 2

Federal Civil Rights Laws

Thinking on Your Own

Before reading the lesson, create a five-column chart in your notebook. Label column one, "What I Know About Civil Rights Laws"; column two, "What I Want to Know About Civil Rights Laws"; column three,"What I Learned About Civil Rights Laws"; column four, "What I Still Want to Know"; and column five, "How I Will Learn This." Fill in the chart as you read.

focus your reading

Why is there conflict over affirmative action?

Explain how the Supreme Court judges laws based on gender differences.

What kinds of things are protected by the right to privacy?

words to know

quota system

reverse discrimination

The civil rights movement pushed Congress to act. In 1957, Congress passed the first civil rights law in many decades. Additional civil rights laws were passed in 1960, 1964, and 1968. Congress also passed a series of important voting rights acts—in 1965, 1970, 1975, and 1982.

The laws touched many parts of U.S. life. To vote in some southern states, people had to pay a poll tax. The tax discriminated against African Americans because many were poor farmers. The poll tax was banned. Employers and labor unions are now barred from discriminating against workers because of race, color, gender, religion, physical disability, or age.

It became a federal crime to deny anyone service in a public place because of race, color, religion, or national origin. Restaurants, hotels, buses, and movie theaters are examples of public places.

A civil rights commemoration in Philadelphia, MS

Homeowners are barred from refusing to sell a house to someone because of race, color, religion, national origin, gender, or disability. Landlords are barred from refusing to rent to someone based on the same categories.

Words to Know

Discuss each of the vocabulary terms with students.

Quota systems involve setting aside a certain number of admissions openings or jobs for women and ethnic groups. The attempts to follow the policy of affirmative action led to *quota systems*. Some people believe that affirmative action discriminates against white males, which is *reverse discrimination*. The case *Regents of the University of California* v. *Bakke* was the first major case dealing with *reverse discrimination*.

Affirmative Action

The civil rights laws made illegal all present and future discrimination. However, past discrimination had left its effects on U.S. society. What could be done about these effects? The federal government adopted a policy of affirmative action to answer this question. Affirmative action gives special consideration to African Americans, members of other ethnic groups, and women for employment and admission to colleges and universities. State and local governments and all federal agencies must follow this policy. All schools that receive federal aid and all employers doing business with the federal government must also follow it.

Affirmative action policies allow colleges and universities to show special consideration when enrolling ethnic groups and women.

The policy was first used in 1965. President Lyndon Johnson signed an executive order to use affirmative action in awarding federal contracts to businesses. Many employers and schools set up **quota systems** to try to fulfill the policy. They set aside a certain number of jobs or admissions openings for ethnic groups and women.

Not everyone was, or is, pleased with the policy. Some people say it is **reverse discrimination**. It discriminates against those who are not members of minority groups or women. The first major challenge to affirmative action occurred in 1978, when the Supreme Court ruled that Allan Bakke, a white male, had been unfairly denied admission to medical school as a result of affirmative action.

Landmark Supreme Court Case: Affirmative Action

***Regents of the University of California* v. *Bakke* (1978):** Allan Bakke, a white male, applied to the medical school of the University of California at Davis. He was denied admission. The school had set aside 16 of its 100 openings for nonwhite students. Bakke claimed reverse discrimination and sued. His lawsuit charged the school with violating the equal protection clause of the Fourteenth Amendment.

The Supreme Court agreed that Bakke had been unfairly denied admission to the medical school. The Court ruled that race may be among the factors used in making affirmative action decisions. However, race may not be the only factor. Strict quota systems are unconstitutional.

Picturing Government

In the photograph on page 260, the governor of Mississippi and others commemorate the 25th anniversary of the passage of the 1964 Civil Rights Act in Philadelphia, Mississippi. In 2005, eighty year-old Edgar Ray Killen, the man responsible for the deaths of the three men whose names are visible on the memorial, was convicted of three counts of manslaughter. The events of the 1964 killings led to the 1988 movie *Mississippi Burning*.

Extension

Ask students to use library resources or the Internet to find more recent examples of court cases or news articles on affirmative action in either the workplace or in education. Suggest that they use a 5Ws chart to summarize their findings. Have them present those findings to the class by using the Student Presentation Builder on the student CD.

Supreme Court Case Extension

Regents of the University of California v. *Bakke* grew out of Allan Bakke's rejection by UC-Davis not once, but twice. Bakke knew that his test scores and grade point average from college exceeded those of the minority students who were admitted in those two years. The Court was split. Four justices believed that a racial quota system violated the 1964 Civil Rights Act. Four justices believed that using race as an admissions criterion was acceptable. Justice Lewis Powell cast the vote ordering Bakke to be admitted to medical school. He also agreed that race could be one factor among many in admitting students. Thus, in finding for Bakke, the Court minimized opposition to equality while maintaining affirmative action.

Stop and Think

Classifications that don't permit discrimination include ethnicity, religion, gender, race, color, age, or physical or mental disability.

Picturing Government

The photograph on page 262 shows a female member of the armed forces. Although women served as nurses, ambulance drivers, and in other auxiliary roles prior to World War II, they were not granted military rank until 1948, with limits set on the top ranks. The Pentagon officially bans women in combat; however, that policy was tested during the war in Iraq. In a suicide bomb attack in June 2005, three female marines were killed and another 11 were wounded. As of that time, 39 female troops had died in Iraq, and three female defense workers were killed there, while six female troops had died in Afghanistan. Because of Iraqi guerrilla tactics, even though women are generally assigned to support units, they still face major risks.

Since the Bakke case, other affirmative action lawsuits have reached the Supreme Court. With each decision, the Court has rethought the policy. By the mid-1990s, the Court had narrowed the use of affirmative action. In a decision in 2004, the Court stated that it hoped that in 25 years, affirmative action would no longer be necessary. However, for the time being, affirmative action still needed to be enforced.

stop and think

Discrimination on the basis of various classifications, or differences, is illegal. What are those differences? Reread the introduction to the lesson. With a partner, make a list of the classifications.

Women's Rights

Gender has often been the basis of laws. The purpose of these laws may have been to protect women. However, the end result was often discriminatory. For example, a law against women working at night kept them from high-paying assembly-line jobs. This law discriminated against women while benefiting men.

However, the Supreme Court did not overturn any laws based on gender until 1971. In *Reed* v. *Reed*, the Court struck down an Idaho law. It gave fathers preference over mothers in handling the estates of their children. The Court ruled the law violated the equal protection clause of the Fourteenth Amendment.

Although women may serve in the armed forces, only men can be drafted.

Why was this law overturned when earlier laws were not? The nation was undergoing vast changes in the 1960s and 1970s. Views about women's roles were changing. As you read in Chapter 12, the Court in general reflects the opinions of the nation.

Since 1971, the Court has overturned a number of gender-based distinctions. For example, girls cannot be barred from joining Little League teams. Membership in men-only clubs and community service groups must be opened to women. Women must be paid the same retirement benefits as men. However, not all gender-based distinctions are unconstitutional. For example, the Court has approved the male-only draft for military service.

Picturing Government

The photograph on page 261 shows a women's lacrosse game. Since the passage of Title IX in 1972, more girls and women have been able to participate in competitive sports. Lacrosse is one of the ten college varsity women's sports most frequently offered. In 1972, colleges averaged a little more than two athletic teams for women. Six years later, when Title IX became mandatory, the number had risen to 5.61 per school. The figure in 2004 was 8.32 women's teams per school, for a total of 8,402 women's teams in the country's NCAA (National College Athletic Association) colleges and universities.

Right to Privacy

Congress has written several laws related to personal privacy. In 1974, it passed the Family Educational Rights and Privacy Act. Among other things, the act gives parents the right to see their children's school files. Students who are eighteen years of age and older may inspect their own files.

In 1996, Congress updated the Fair Credit Reporting Act. This law regulates the collection and distribution of information about people's credit. Using the Internet for browsing and shopping has complicated protecting personal information. Sites now regularly collect information about the people who visit them.

At age eighteen, students are able to review their education files with school counselors.

The Supreme Court has also recognized a person's right to privacy. In various cases, the Court has used the Bill of Rights and the Fourteenth Amendment to support the right to privacy. Decisions in cases about abortion and the sharing of personal information without someone's knowledge have been based on the right to privacy.

Putting It All Together

Fill in the chart that you began at the start of this lesson. Then write a summary of this lesson. Share your summary with a partner. Ask if you covered all the main points. If not, ask what you need to include in a revision. Revise your summary.

Picturing Government

In the photograph on page 263, a guidance counselor discusses academic options with a high school student. Some states supplement the federal law to give students access to their school records before they are eighteen. For example, California allows students who have completed tenth grade or are sixteen and older to see their files. The school must respond within five days to a request to view a school record.

Putting It All Together

Students' summaries will vary but should include all main points in the lesson: affirmative action, women's rights, and the right to privacy.

Extension

Have students choose a field in which women have traditionally been denied a role. Ask them to use library resources or the Internet to find key events and make timelines showing the progress women have made in the field. Post timelines in the room, perhaps on the bulletin board, with illustrations. Allow students to work on these in small groups or pairs.

Lesson Summary

The United States immigration policy has changed several times. The laws were sometimes designed to keep certain ethnic groups from entering the country. A preference system is used, which gives top priority to people with skills most useful to the country. The presence of undocumented aliens continues to be a problem. After 9/11, immigration laws were more strictly enforced. Noncitizens have most of the rights of citizens, but cannot vote or serve on juries. They also do not have freedom of movement. Citizens may be native-born or naturalized. Citizens have the responsibility to take part in the political life of the nation.

Lesson Objective

Students will learn about the rights of citizens and the national policy dealing with immigration and noncitizens.

Focus Your Reading Answers

1 U.S. immigration policy has changed throughout the years. After 1882, limits on immigration began. A quota system was set up determining how many people would be allowed to come from various nations, based on the 1890 census. That act favored those from northern and western Europe. That system, begun in the 1920s, ended in 1965, with totals set for the Eastern and Western Hemispheres and a preference system. The latest rewriting of the system came in 1990, which set a maximum number of immigrants and made a provision for refugees.

LESSON 3

U.S. Citizenship

Thinking on Your Own

Think about what it means to be a citizen of the United States. Write a letter to a friend in your notebook to explain what it means to be a U.S. citizen.

focus your reading

How has U.S. immigration policy changed over the years?

What rights and duties do aliens—or noncitizens—living in the United States have?

What are the responsibilities of citizenship?

words to know

citizen
preference system
undocumented alien
amnesty
resident alien
lawful permanent resident
nonresident alien
refugee
deported

Most of the people who live in the United States are **citizens**. A person is a citizen of the United States either by birth or by naturalization. Naturalization is the process of becoming a citizen. A person who is born in another country, is still a citizen of that country, and lives in the United States is known as an alien, or a noncitizen. Noncitizens must go through naturalization to become U.S. citizens. By the early 2000s, about 12 percent of the U.S. population was born somewhere else. Of these 33 million people, more than 12 million were naturalized citizens.

U.S. Immigration Policy

At some time or another, all American families came from somewhere else. Since 1776, more than 70 million immigrants have come to the United States. Immigrants have made many significant impacts on the country. Cesar Chavez, for example, was the son of Mexican immigrants. He dedicated his life to improving the working conditions of migrant farm workers. Chavez, who died in 1993, was awarded the Presidential Medal of Freedom by President Bill Clinton in 1994. The work he did through the United Farm Workers union dramatically improved the lives of migrant farm workers.

2 Rights and duties of noncitizens living in the United States include nearly all the same rights and duties as citizens have; noncitizens, however, may not vote and generally don't serve on juries. They must notify the Customs and Enforcement Service when they move. They must pay taxes, obey the law, and do nothing to harm the nation.

3 The responsibility of citizenship is to take part in the political life of the country. This includes knowing one's rights, respecting the law, becoming informed voters, campaigning for candidates, working the polls on election days, joining groups that support causes of interest, and expressing opinions on public policy to elected officials.

The policy of the United States toward immigration has changed over time. Before 1882, no limits were placed on immigration. In 1882, Congress passed the Chinese Exclusion Act to ban Chinese people from immigrating to the United States. Another law that was passed that year barred people with mental illness and disabilities, convicts, and the poor from entering the United States.

The Immigration Acts of 1921 and 1924 and the National Origins Act of 1929 set up a quota system for immigrants. Only a certain number of people from each nation were allowed to immigrate. The number depended on how many people from that nation had settled in the United States by 1890. Most people had come from northern and western Europe. Far fewer people had come from southern and eastern Europe. As a result, the quotas for southern and eastern European nations were very small. In addition, people from Asia and Africa were barred from immigrating.

Ellis Island served as the gateway to the United States for thousands of immigrants during the late 1800s and early 1900s.

In 1965, the quota system ended. The Immigration Reform Act of 1965 set the total number of immigrants from the Eastern Hemisphere at 170,000. The total from the Western Hemisphere was set at 120,000. The earlier acts had limited immigration from all places to 165,000. However, the new act set up a **preference system**. People whose skills would be useful to the nation were given top priority. Nuclear scientists, for example, fell into this category. The second group was unmarried adult children of U.S. citizens. Third were husbands, wives, and unmarried children of permanent residents.

Between 1965 and the mid-1980s, **undocumented aliens**, also called undocumented immigrants, came to the nation in ever greater numbers. They entered the country without proper papers such as a passport, visa, or entry permit. To try to stop illegal immigration, Congress passed the Immigration Reform and Control Act of 1986. It had two major parts.

First, the act gave some undocumented aliens the opportunity to become citizens. Without papers, they would never be able to apply for citizenship. An undocumented alien must have entered the country before 1982 and lived here

Picturing Government

The Lewis Hine photograph on page 265 shows a family of Italian immigrants at Ellis Island. Have students interested in photography investigate the work of Hine, whose photojournalism affected child labor and labor safety policies.

Extensions

1 Have students use library resources or the Internet to find examples of other immigrants who have affected the life of the nation. If students have difficulty, suggest some of the scientists who fled Nazi Germany and worked on the nuclear bomb. Allow students to share their findings with the class, perhaps by dramatizing the person's life or giving a news broadcast.

2 Have students use library resources or the Internet to find the top five ethnic groups that came to the United States in several time periods, such as 1850, 1900, 1950, and 2000. Invite them to make charts showing the differences.

Words to Know

Discuss each of the vocabulary terms with students.

A resident of a country is a *citizen*. A *citizen* may be born in the United States. The process of becoming a *citizen* if one is born in another country is called naturalization.

A *preference system* favors people with special skills useful to the nation. Since 1965, the United States has used a *preference system*. A person who enters the country without proper papers is an *undocumented alien*. *Undocumented aliens* are also called undocumented immigrants.

Amnesty is a pardon or forgiveness for a crime, granted by the government. In 1986, the United States offered *amnesty* for some undocumented immigrants. The *amnesty* allowed people a way to become lawful residents.

Immigration laws govern who is admitted to the United States.

continuously. Undocumented aliens who met these conditions could apply for amnesty. **Amnesty** is a pardon, or forgiveness, for a crime granted by the government. With amnesty, many became lawful, temporary residents.

Second, the 1982 act made it a crime to hire undocumented aliens. Now employers are required to make sure that their workers are either citizens or in the nation legally.

In 1990, a new Immigration Act rewrote the quota system. Immigration is now set at 675,000 people a year. The preference system continues in effect. Family members of citizens and of permanent residents make up about one-third of immigrants each year. Another 140,000 places are given to people who have jobs waiting for them here. In addition to the 675,000 immigrants, the 1990 act also allows the nation to admit refugees fleeing war and persecution.

Since the attacks of 9/11, immigration laws are more strongly enforced. Federal government agencies dealing with immigration are now part of the Department of Homeland Security.

stop and think

Create a timeline based on the information about U.S. immigration policy. Share your timeline with a partner.

Rights of Noncitizens (Aliens)

Federal law has several categories of aliens. Undocumented aliens are only one category. A **resident alien**, or a **lawful permanent resident** (LPR), is someone who has moved permanently to the United States. A **nonresident alien** is someone who is in the country only for a short period. Foreign tourists and foreign students are nonresident aliens. A **refugee** is a person fleeing persecution. During the 1990s and early 2000s, the United States admitted refugees from war-torn nations in Africa and eastern Europe.

Lee Shong, a Hmong refugee from Laos, smiles as she arrives at the Sacramento airport in June 2004.

Picturing Government

In the photograph at the top left of page 266, a United States Customs officer checks an airline passenger, using biometrics. The screening uses fingerprinting and photography to document individuals. Part of an initiative from the Department of Homeland Security, the program is called US-Visit. It became mandatory on September 30, 2004, for all foreign nationals arriving in the United States.

Stop and Think

Timelines should include the dates and events from pages 264–266.

Picturing Government

The photograph at the bottom left of page 266 shows the 2004 arrival of Hmong refugees from Laos. More than 200,000 Hmong have left Laos as refugees since 1975. About 90 percent of the Hmong refugees have resettled in the United States as a result of their role during the U.S. war in Laos, part of the Cold War. California, Wisconsin, and Minnesota have the largest number of Hmong immigrants. Hmong have also settled in Canada, France, and Australia.

Words to Know, continued

A *resident alien* is someone who has moved to the United States permanently. Federal laws include *resident alien* as one category of aliens. *Lawful permanent resident* is another term for a *resident alien*. A *lawful permanent resident* is sometimes simply called an LPR. A *nonresident alien* is only in the country for a short time. A tourist is a *nonresident alien*.

Someone fleeing political or religious persecution is a *refugee*. The 1990 Immigration Act makes provisions for anyone who is a *refugee*.

Persons returned to their original country are *deported*. People are generally *deported* after committing serious crimes.

The Supreme Court has ruled a number of times about the rights of aliens. Noncitizens, or aliens, have almost all the same rights as citizens. However, aliens may not vote and usually do not serve on juries. They do not have the same freedom of movement as citizens. Noncitizens must notify the Customs and Enforcement Service when they move within the country. They have no obligation to join the armed forces. Yet around 30,000 were serving in the military in the early 2000s.

Aliens have the same duties as citizens. They must pay taxes and obey the law. They must also do nothing to harm the country. An alien who has committed a serious crime may be **deported**. The person is then returned to his or her country of origin. Illegal entry into the United States is also a reason for deportation. The Supreme Court has ruled that in deportation cases, rights such as the right to a court hearing do not apply. Deportation is a civil matter, not a criminal matter.

Citizenship

Most U.S. citizens are citizens because they were born in the United States. People born in U.S. territories such as Guam, Puerto Rico, and the U.S. Virgin Islands are also U.S. citizens. Children born to immigrants to the United States, including undocumented aliens, are also citizens. Anyone else gains U.S. citizenship through naturalization. Read the feature on page 269 to find out how a person becomes a naturalized citizen.

As part of the naturalization process, applicants must answer questions and take a test.

At one time, being born in the United States was not enough to be a citizen. A person had to be white. In 1857, the Supreme Court ruled that African Americans were not citizens. In *Scott* v. *Sandford*, the Court said that neither free nor enslaved African Americans were citizens.

In 1868, Congress made sure that this argument could never be used again. It approved, and the Northern states ratified, the Fourteenth Amendment. This amendment grants citizenship to "all persons born or naturalized in the United States." It further declares that "no state shall make or enforce any law" that denies the rights of citizenship to anyone.

Picturing Government

In the photograph on page 267, a Mexican worker fills out an amnesty application form at the Immigration and Naturalization Service Center in Houston, Texas, in 1988.

Extension

Have students find out about the latest efforts to secure the U.S. borders, particularly the border with Mexico. You may wish to divide the class into two groups, debating the issue of illegal immigration and undocumented workers or the so-called vigilante groups that patrol the borders.

Extension

Have students use library resources or the Internet to find out about the rates of immigration in your state. Which groups are most populous? What is the rate of immigration and the percentage of native-born to foreign-born in your community?

Citizenship grants rights to those who hold it. These rights are the subject of this chapter. Citizenship also sets up certain responsibilities. Among the duties of responsible citizens are

- to know their legal rights
- to respect the law
- to become informed voters
- to work at the polls on Election Day
- to join groups that work for causes they are interested in
- to write to elected officials to state their views

In other words, responsible citizens take part in the political life of the nation.

Putting It All Together

The oath that new citizens take is one very long sentence. With a partner, paraphrase, or rewrite, the oath so that it is easier to understand. As you write, turn each clause, or new idea, into one or two sentences.

Primary Source

Oath of Affirmation for New Citizens

To become a citizen, a person must meet certain requirements. When a person is judged ready to become a citizen, the person must take the following oath of allegiance:

"I hereby declare, on oath, that I absolutely and entirely renounce and abjure all allegiance and fidelity to any foreign prince, potentate, state, or sovereignty of whom or which I have heretofore been a subject or citizen; that I will support and defend the Constitution and the laws of the United States of America against all enemies, foreign and domestic; that I will bear true faith and allegiance to the same; that I will bear arms on behalf of the United States when required by law; that I will perform noncombatant service in the Armed Forces when required by law; or that I will perform work of national importance under civilian direction when required by law; and that I take this obligation freely without any mental reservation or purpose of evasion: So help me God."

Primary Source Extension

Work with students to help them understand the formal vocabulary of the oath. For example, words such as *abjure* and *potentate* are not used in common, everyday speech. You may wish to pair students and assign them specific terms, then have them teach the rest of the class the meanings. Ask students to imagine the effect repeating such an oath might have on a new citizen.

Putting It All Together

Students' paraphrases will vary but should give each new idea its own sentence.

Participate in Government

Become a Naturalized Citizen

How does a person become a naturalized U.S. citizen? The following lists the steps to naturalization.

1. A person must:
   - be at least eighteen years of age.
   - have entered the nation legally.
   - have lived in the United States for at least five years. (It is three years for husbands and wives of citizens.)
2. A person must
   - file a petition for naturalization.
   - pay an application fee.
   - be interviewed by an immigration official.
   - have two witnesses testify to the person's character.
   - be able to read, write, and speak English. (Anyone over fifty years of age who has lived in the United States for twenty years does not have to meet this requirement.)
   - be of "good moral character."
   - support the Constitution and the United States.
   - know basic information about the history and government of the United States.
   - take the oath of affirmation.

A person must pass a citizenship test to become a U.S. citizen.

A lawful permanent resident must meet the first three items on the list. Then he or she may apply for citizenship. The person files an application and pays a fee. Citizenship and Immigration Services (CIS) runs a background check. CIS is looking for a criminal history. The agency also makes sure the person is not a risk to the nation's security. Next, the person has an interview with CIS and takes the citizenship test. If the application is approved, the person joins other new citizens in a naturalization ceremony.

Participate in Government

If any students in your class have friends or relatives who have become naturalized citizens, invite them to speak to the class about their experiences.

Research Resources

Below is a list of reference books and Web sites that relate to the issues covered in this chapter. Students may wish to use these to further their research on ideas in the preceding lessons. Web site addresses may change over time. Use keyword searching on a major search engine to locate sites.

Reference Books:

Kathryn Cullen-DuPont. *Encyclopedia of Women's History in America*. Facts on File, 2000.

Charles D. Lowry and John F. Marszalek, eds. *The Greenwood Encyclopedia of African American Civil Rights. 2nd ed.* Greenwood Press, 2003.

William Thompson. *Native American Issues: A Reference Handbook*. ABC-CLIO, 2005.

Web Sites:

NativeWeb offers resources for indigenous peoples around the world, with an emphasis on communication and news stories.

The National Women's Hall of Fame maintains a site, which includes biographies of female inductees as well as news and events.

The Library of Congress site African American Odyssey covers both history and civil rights.

Civil Rights: Equal Justice 269

Skill Builder
Students' dialogues will vary but should present arguments for and against having a female president, along with underlined statements of bias.

Recommended Reading

Below is a list of books that relate to the issues covered in this chapter. The numbers in parentheses indicate the related Thematic Strands of the National Council for the Social Studies (NCSS).

Dennis Fradin and Judith Fradin. *The Power of One: Daisy Bates and the Little Rock Nine*. Clarion Books, 2004. (III, IV, VI, X)

Susan Dudley Gold. *Brown v. Board of Education: Separate but Equal?* Benchmark Books, 2004. (VI, X)

Cheryl Harness. *Rabble Rousers: 20 Women Who Made a Difference*. Dutton Children's Books, 2003. (V, VI, X)

Skill Builder

Recognize Bias

Bias is strong feeling for or against a person or issue without facts to support that feeling. Bias is an emotional reaction based on opinion. Another word for bias is *prejudice*.

Usually, bias is against a person or issue, rather than in support of someone or something. An example was the refusal of districts to integrate schools in the 1950s and later. This refusal was based on the bias of whites against African Americans.

Voters can also be biased for or against candidates and government policies. For example, some voters are biased against having a woman as president. Some do not think that a woman could be tough enough. Others do not think that women are smart enough. The fact that women run the governments of other nations does not change their minds. People with a bias may refuse to accept any facts that conflict with their viewpoint.

To determine bias:

1. Identify the issue.
2. Identify the arguments that are made about the issue.
   - Are the arguments based on fact or opinion? Can the arguments be proven to be true or false? If not, then the arguments are based on opinion.
3. Identify the speaker or writer.
   - To what political party or other group does the person belong?
   - What is the viewpoint of this organization on the issue?
   - What else do you know about the person or group?

Complete the following activity.

Two friends are arguing about whether a woman should be elected president. With a partner, take the two sides in the argument. Write a dialogue that presents arguments for and against having a female president. After you are finished, reread the dialogue. Underline any statements that show bias on either side of the argument.

Classroom Discussion

Discuss with students some of the broader topics covered in this chapter.

- How can immigration rules best treat people fairly?
- How can local groups help ensure that no minority groups experience discrimination?
- What efforts could a school make to increase fairness to all people in the school?

UNIT 6 TAKING PART IN GOVERNMENT

- **Join a political party.**
- **Campaign for candidates.**
- **Donate money to a public interest group.**
- **Attend League of Women Voters candidate nights.**
- **Become an informed voter.**
- **Write your member of Congress or your local council member to let him or her know your opinion on issues.**
- **Vote.**

These are just some of the ways that ordinary citizens can take part in government. This unit will explain more about the political party system and voting. You will also learn about influences on public officials and public policy.

Unit Objectives

After studying this unit, students will be able to

- explain the role of both major and independent political parties
- describe the history of the expansion of American voting rights and the ways that candidates are selected
- analyze the work of interest groups, lobbyists, and media on the politics of the United States

Unit 6 focuses on the ways that citizens can participate in government.

Chapter 15, Political Parties, examines the purpose, history, and organization of political parties.

Chapter 16, Elections, Voting, and Voter Behavior, explains the election process, including choosing candidates and financing campaigns, as well as the extension of voting rights and the characteristics of voters.

Chapter 17, Interest Groups, Public Opinion, and Mass Media, explores the role of interest groups and lobbyists. It also focuses on scientific polling and the effect of the mass media on the political scene.

Picturing Government

The photograph on page 271 shows preparations for a Junior Statesmen Foundation conference with presidential hopeful Dennis Kucinich. The foundation is a nonprofit educational corporation. Its group, the Junior State of America (JSA), is the nation's largest student-run organization. A nonpartisan group, it sponsors activities, including summer programs and meetings with members of Congress, to increase political awareness.

Getting Started

Have a student read aloud the title of the unit and the list and paragraph that follow it on page 271. Ask students to brainstorm ideas they already have for ways to take part in government. Ask students to record their ideas in their notebooks. They might also jot down any questions they have about the content of this unit. Encourage them to add answers to those questions as they read Unit 6.

Related Transparencies

T-18 Three-Column Chart

T-20 Concept Web

Key Blacklines

Civics Today—What Do Political Party Chairs Do?

CD Extension

Encourage students to use the reading comprehension, vocabulary reinforcement, and other activities on the student CD.

Getting Focused

Allow students to work in pairs or small groups to create their tables. Then have them share with the class. Correct any misinformation that may be given. Create and post a master list for the class, adding to it as you work through the chapter.

Picturing Government

The left-hand photograph on page 272 shows the Kerry-Edwards team and supporters at the 2004 Democratic National Convention. The photograph on the right is of President George W. Bush entering to speak at the 2004 Republican National Convention.

Chapter 15 POLITICAL PARTIES

Getting Focused

Skim this chapter to predict what you will be learning.

- **Read the lesson titles and subheadings.**
- **Look at the illustrations and read the captions.**
- **Review the vocabulary words and terms.**

Create a table with three columns. Label the first column "Democratic Party." Label the second column "Republican Party." Label the third column "Third Parties." In columns one and two, list the positions each party has taken on major issues that you know about. In column three, list anything you know about a third party or the history of third parties in the United States.

The 2004 Democratic National Convention (left) was held in Boston, MA. The 2004 Republican National Convention (right) was held in New York, NY.

Pre-Reading Discussion

1 Challenge students to discuss what they know political parties do and why we have them at all. Create a word web on the board to record their responses and refer to it during the chapter discussion.

2 Bring to class copies of articles from a recent newspaper or newsmagazine that concern at least one of the political parties. Have students work in groups to read and summarize the articles; then have them share the content with the class.

LESSON 1

Purpose of Political Parties

Thinking on Your Own

Why do you think nations have political parties? What do you think political parties do? Make a list in your notebook of activities that you know political parties carry out.

focus your reading

Describe the functions of the political parties.

What types of party systems exist in different countries?

Who are independent voters?

words to know

political party

multiparty system

coalition

one-party system

Republican, Democratic, Libertarian, Conservative, Green—how many political parties are there in the United States? Most people would say two. A **political party** is an organized group of people who share common values and goals. Members of political parties try to get their candidates elected to office.

The Democratic and Republican Parties are the most powerful. Most people who belong to a party belong to one of them. However, the nation has a number of other political parties. These are known as third parties. Some third parties have played important roles in our nation's electoral history.

How does a person join a political party? All a voter has to do is say, "I am a Republican" or "I am a Democrat." There are no membership dues, though political parties may ask their supporters for contributions. However, no one has to donate money to join a political party.

Voters can register as members of a political party or as independents.

Functions of Political Parties

The Constitution does not mention political parties. George Washington even warned against setting up political parties. However, modern political parties serve five major functions, or roles.

Lesson Summary

The United States has two major political parties, the Democratic Party and the Republican Party. Political parties have five major roles: to nominate candidates for office, to help govern the nation, to educate the public on issues, to serve as the "loyal opposition" to the party in power, and to reduce conflicts. Other countries have multiparty systems, in which there are several major and minor parties, which may form coalitions. A few countries have one-party systems, generally the Communist Party. Some voters are independents, belonging to no organized party. This group has become increasingly important since the 1990s.

Lesson Objective

Students will learn about the functions of political parties and the types of party systems.

Focus Your Reading Answers

1 The functions of political parties include nominating candidates for office, helping to govern the nation, educating the public on issues, serving as the "loyal opposition" to the party in power, and reducing conflicts.

2 In other countries, political party systems may be multiparty systems, in which there are several major and minor parties. These, in turn, may form coalitions. A few countries, generally Communist nations, have one-party systems.

3 Independent voters are those who belong to no organized party. They make up one-third to one-fourth of all registered voters.

Words to Know

Introduce each of the following vocabulary terms to students.

Explain that a *political party* is an organized group of people sharing common values and goals. A major function of a *political party* is to get candidates elected.

In a *multiparty system*, there are several major and minor parties. Most nations have a *multiparty system*.

A *coalition* is a partnership of a major and minor party to form a majority in the legislature of countries with the *multiparty system*. Leaders of a minority party of a *coalition* are appointed to the cabinet.

If the party and the government are the same, the nation has a *one-party system*. Vietnam is an example of a country that has a *one-party system*.

First, political parties nominate candidates for public office. Party officials look for members who will appeal to voters. Candidates must be honest and trustworthy. They must be qualified to do the job if elected. Candidates must also be good campaigners and support the major policies of their political parties.

Senator Dianne Feinstein reads California's roll call at the Democratic National Convention in Boston in 2004.

Second, political parties play a role in governing the nation. Remember that Congress is organized along party lines. So are state legislatures. Like legislators, the president and state governors are elected with the support of a political party. The president and governors depend on legislators elected by their party to get laws written and passed. The president and state governors fill top-level jobs in executive departments with their own party members.

Third, political parties educate the public about issues. Candidates for office mail out brochures describing their positions on issues and send press releases to the media. Candidates take part in debates, give interviews, and speak to groups. Their campaign organizations pay for ads and Web sites. The goal of these activities is to educate and inform the public about a candidate—and his or her party's—views.

Remember that a candidate generally supports the views of his or her party. Parties also serve as reliable labels for candidates. They help voters make up their minds about candidates. For example, the Republican Party claims to be for lower taxes. A candidate who is a Republican is therefore likely to promise tax cuts. A voter who thinks this is important will vote for a Republican candidate.

Debates such as this one between Johnny Byrd, Mel Martinez, and Bill McCollum during the 2004 campaign in Florida help voters understand the positions of each candidate.

Fourth, the political party not in power becomes the "loyal

Picturing Government

The photograph at the top right of page 274 shows Senator Dianne Feinstein of California at the 2004 Democratic National Convention. A member of the Senate since 1992, Feinstein was chosen to read the presidential nomination role call. Feinstein serves on several Senate committees, including Judiciary, Appropriations, and Energy and Natural Resources. Feinstein's political career began in her native San Francisco at the County Board of Supervisors.

Picturing Government

The photograph at the bottom left of page 274 captures a debate among candidates for one of Florida's U.S. Senate seats in the 2004 election. From left to right, Mel Martinez, Johnny Byrd, and Bill McCollum discussed the issues prior to the primary election. Voters chose Martinez, who became the first Cuban-American member of the Senate in 2005. Martinez was one of the 14,000 children who left Cuba under Operation Peter Pan, an endeavor of the Roman Catholic Church during the early 1960s, when tensions with Cuba were high, to rescue children from the Communist regime.

Picturing Government

The photograph on page 273 shows a voter registration drive before an election. However, voter registration can also be done by mail; at the Department of Motor Vehicles or other government offices, such as libraries; at the courthouse or local board of elections office; or in public places such as street fairs and colleges.

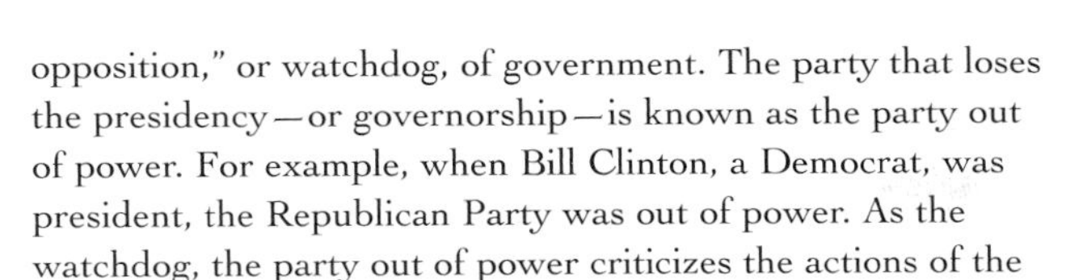

opposition," or watchdog, of government. The party that loses the presidency—or governorship—is known as the party out of power. For example, when Bill Clinton, a Democrat, was president, the Republican Party was out of power. As the watchdog, the party out of power criticizes the actions of the party in power. It also offers alternatives to the president's policies.

Fifth, political parties reduce conflict. The nation is made up of people with many different points of view on issues. Political parties provide ways for people to work together—in and out of government. Political parties also provide for the peaceful transfer of power from one election to the next.

Political parties alone perform the first two roles and the last one. Other groups, such as the media, also educate the public about policy issues. Public interest groups, too, act as watchdogs over government actions. Environmental groups, for example, issue press releases about proposed laws.

stop and think

Review the list of activities you wrote for Thinking on Your Own. Add to or cross out items based on what you just read. Share your list with a partner. Decide which activities relate to the various roles of political parties.

Types of Party Systems

The United States has basically a two-party system. The Republican and Democratic Parties are much more powerful than any third parties. These two have far more money and members than the other parties combined. For example, in 2005, Republicans held 55 of the 100 seats in the U.S. Senate. Democrats held 44 seats, and one senator was an independent. Only about a dozen nations have a two-party system.

Most nations have a multiparty system. In a **multiparty system**, there are several major and minor parties. Each party wins some offices, including seats in the national legislature.

Italy is an example of a nation with a multiparty system.

Stop and Think

Students' lists and revisions will vary.

Picturing Government

A session of Italy's parliament is shown in the photograph on page 275. The parliament is comprised of two houses, the Chamber of Deputies and the upper house, the Senate. Citizens directly elect members of both houses for five-year terms of office. Italy has many political parties.

Extensions

1 Have students use library resources or the Internet to find another nation that has a two-party system. Ask students to create comparison/contrast charts of the two nations' systems and how they function.

2 Invite interested students to find out more about the smaller third parties in the United States, such as the Green Party and the Working Families Party. Have them present to the class issues that concern these parties and attempts they have made in local and national elections.

Extension

Ask students to use library resources or the Internet to find issues in the most recent or upcoming elections at local, state, or national levels. Have them summarize the candidates' positions on major issues and present their findings to the class by using the Student Presentation Builder on the student CD.

Political Parties 275

Ideas to Remember Extension

Review the ideas listed, further explaining difficult vocabulary words. Have students create graphic organizers in their notebooks to help them visualize the five functions of political parties.

Picturing Government

The photograph on page 276 shows Ross Perot, the independent candidate for president in 1992 and 1996. At the left of the photograph is Bill Clinton, who won the elections those years. Perot, a billionaire from his computer businesses, was able to spend vast amounts on his campaigns. In 1992, he received 19 percent of the popular vote, which some saw as a sign that Americans were disillusioned with the two-party system.

Putting It All Together
Students' essays will vary.

ideas to remember

The functions of political parties are

- to nominate candidates for public office.
- to play a role in governing.
- to educate the public on issues.
- to monitor what the other party does.
- to reduce conflict and provide an orderly transfer of power.

Often, a major party must partner with a minor party to put together a majority in the legislature. The partnership is known as a **coalition**. Leaders of the minor party are appointed to the cabinet. Many European nations and emerging democracies have multiparty systems.

A few nations have **one-party systems**. The party and the government are the same. The leaders of the party are the leaders of the government. The only candidates are ones that the party approves. The former Soviet Union was a one-party nation. Today, China, Vietnam, Cuba, and North Korea have one-party systems. Like the former Soviet Union, the Communist Party dominates each.

Ross Perot ran as an independent in the 1992 presidential campaign.

A Word About Independents

Between one-quarter and one-third of all registered voters are independents. They belong to no organized political party. Independents, too, can play a major role in deciding which candidate is elected. Their votes have become increasingly important since the 1990s. The two major parties have about the same number of members. As a result, candidates, especially for president, need to appeal to independents in order to win.

Putting It All Together

What if no one belonged to a political party? Discuss the question with a partner. Make notes as you talk. Then use these notes to write an essay titled "What If No One Belonged to a Political Party?"

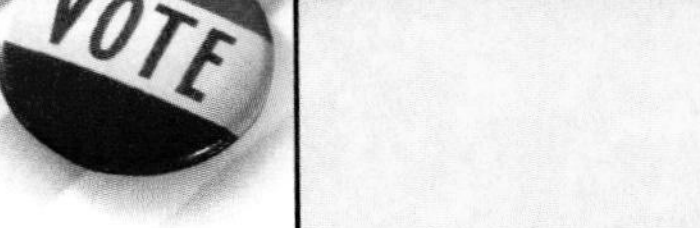

LESSON 2

Beginnings of U.S. Political Parties

Thinking on Your Own

Suppose you were going to start a political party in the United States today. Think about the government policies that are important to you. List five policies in your notebook. Then write a sentence to explain why each policy should be supported.

focus your reading

What were the main issues that divided political parties before the Civil War?

Explain how power has shifted between the major parties since 1932.

Describe the role third parties have in U.S. politics.

words to know

third party

single-issue party

ideological party

splinter party

Political conflict began early in President George Washington's first administration. His secretary of the treasury, Alexander Hamilton, proposed a plan to improve the nation's credit. It included creating a Bank of the United States. Secretary of State Thomas Jefferson and Congressman James Madison were outraged. The Constitution, they argued, did not give Congress the power to set up a bank. A majority in Congress voted for Hamilton's bank, but the issue divided the nation's political leaders. By 1797, two political parties had developed. One was the Federalist Party, and the other was the Democratic-Republican Party.

From Washington to Lincoln

Supporters of Hamilton's policies became the Federalists. They believed in a strong central government and a loose interpretation of the Constitution. The supporters of Jefferson and Madison called themselves Democratic-Republicans. They were strict constructionists, and favored a weak central government.

The Federalists were able to elect John Adams as president in 1796. However, by 1800, the Federalists had lost many

Lesson Summary

Two political parties, Federalist and Democratic-Republican, had developed by 1797. The Federalists elected John Adams as president in 1796. From 1800 until 1828, Jefferson's party, Democratic-Republican, won all the presidential elections. The Democratic-Republican Party is the forerunner of the modern Democratic Party. The modern Republican Party was founded in 1854 and elected Lincoln in 1860. It became the dominant party; the Democrats won only four presidential elections between 1860 and 1932. Only one Republican was elected president between 1932 and 1968. Republicans were in the White House all but four years between 1968 and 1992. After Bill Clinton won the elections of 1992 and 1996, Republicans returned to power. Third parties may be single-issue parties, ideological parties, or splinter parties.

Lesson Objective

Students will learn about the origins of the two-party system in the United States.

Focus Your Reading Answers

1 The main issues dividing political parties before the Civil War were tariffs and the national bank.

2 Since 1932, power has shifted between the two major parties, with Democrats and only one Republican in office between 1932 and 1968, and Republicans and only one Democrat in office from 1968 to 1992. In 2000 the presidency went back to the Republican Party.

3 The role of third parties in U.S. politics is to focus on a single issue, to change society, or to follow a dynamic leader who splinters the party. Third parties are sometimes called "spoilers."

Words to Know

Discuss each of the vocabulary terms with students.

A *third party* is a minor party in the United States. When a group of people believes that the major parties are not dealing with some important issue, a *third party* is born.

A *single-issue party* comes into being to deal with one moral, economic, or social issue. The Free-Soil Party was a *single-issue party.*

An *ideological party* is interested in changing society. The Libertarian Party is an example of an *ideological party*.

When a group breaks off from a major party, it is called a *splinter party*. The Bull Moose Party was a *splinter party* in 1912.

Picturing Government

The handbill shown on page 278 was one Andrew Jackson used to deride John Quincy Adams in the 1828 presidential election. For his second attempt to win the presidency, Jackson mounted the first grassroots presidential campaign in U.S. history. Jackson's supporters, aware of his nickname, Old Hickory, symbolizing his toughness, placed hickory poles around the country. They also sponsored local barbeques, picnics, and parades. Because the candidates agreed on most issues, the campaign relied on personal attacks.

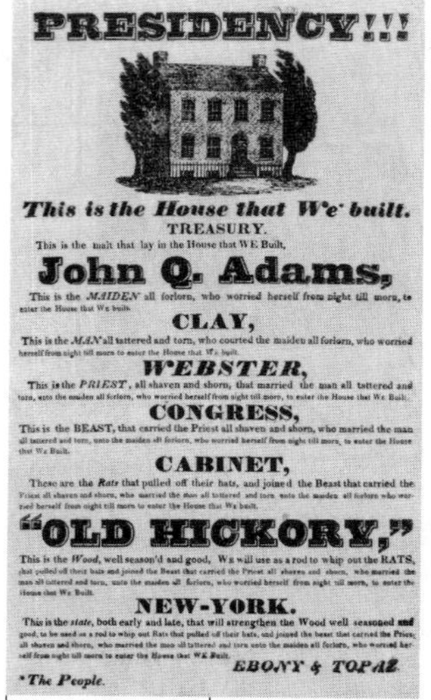

The 1828 race for president was the first to use a nationally organized political party. These efforts allowed Andrew Jackson to defeat John Quincy Adams.

supporters, and Jefferson's party was far stronger. Jefferson was elected president in 1800 and again in 1804. The Democratic-Republican Party won every presidential election until 1828.

By the election of 1828, the Democratic-Republican Party had split into the Democratic Party and the National Republican Party, or Whigs. A national bank and tariffs divided the Democratic-Republican Party along regional lines. Tariffs are taxes on goods brought into the country. In general, northern members of the party favored the national bank and tariffs. Western and southern members were against tariffs and the national bank. In time, the issue of slavery would also split the nation politically.

The modern Democratic Party traces its history back to Jefferson's Democratic-Republican Party. From 1828 until the 1850s, the Democratic and Whig Parties were the two major parties. However, the Whigs were able to elect only two presidents.

By the 1850s, slavery dominated U.S. politics. The Whig Party had collapsed. Several smaller parties tried to appeal to former Whigs and anti-slavery Democrats. Among them was the Free Soil Party. It wanted to ban slavery from the new territories to protect white workers.

The modern Republican Party was founded in 1854. It was the most successful of the new parties and quickly picked up supporters. By 1860, its candidate, Abraham Lincoln, won the presidency.

stop and think

Make a two-column list in your notebook. Title one column "Before the Civil War" and list the issues that divided political parties during that era. Title the second column "After the Civil War." As you read the rest of the lesson, list the major issues that divided parties during that time period.

Modern Political Parties

After the Civil War, the Republican Party was the dominant party. It was the party that saved the Union and ended slavery. It also supported high tariffs and free homesteads in the West.

Stop and Think

Students' lists of issues may include the following:

Before the Civil War: tariffs, national bank, slavery

After the Civil War: role of government, economic policies, social policy

Extensions

1 You may wish to have students set up a sequence chart or other type of graphic organizer to track the name changes of the two major parties. The name changes can be confusing, and the graphic organizer will give students a visual to track them. Suggest that students include dates on their charts.

2 Have students interested in economics investigate the current role of tariffs, particularly in light of trade agreements in North and South America. Allow time for students to share their findings with the class.

278 Chapter 15

President Franklin Roosevelt addressing Congress in 1935

In the northern states, businessmen, farmers, and many laborers voted Republican. So did most African Americans in states that allowed them to vote. The Democratic Party was strongest in the South and Midwest. Between 1860 and 1932, the Democrats won only four presidential elections.

One of those presidents, Woodrow Wilson, won because the Republican Party split in the 1912 election. Former president Theodore Roosevelt and his supporters left the Republican Party over the party's choice of presidential candidate, President William Howard Taft. They founded the Progressive Party, also known as the Bull Moose Party. As a result, Roosevelt and Taft divided the Republican vote. Democratic candidate Woodrow Wilson was able to win.

A shift in power occurred in the 1932 election. The nation was in the depths of the Great Depression. The policies of Republican president Herbert Hoover were not working. Voters elected Democrat Franklin D. Roosevelt. During President Roosevelt's New Deal era, the Democrats supported labor unions, price supports for farmers, and Social Security. Between 1932 and 1968, only one Republican was elected president, Dwight Eisenhower, a World War II general and hero.

The power shifted again between 1968 and 1992. Republicans held the White House for 20 of those 24 years. Voters turned to Democrat Jimmy Carter in 1976 after the crimes of the Nixon presidency. Carter failed to win reelection against Republican Ronald Reagan in 1980. Reagan was the most conservative president since the early 1920s. He won the votes of Democrats unhappy with their party's social policies, as well as the votes of traditional Republicans. By the late 1980s, more and more southerners were voting Republican.

Then Democrat Bill Clinton won the 1992 and 1996 elections. A southerner, he was able to pick up support in the South. He also appealed to moderates in both parties. In addition, a third-party candidate, Ross Perot, may have taken some votes away from the Republican candidate, President George H. W. Bush.

President Ronald Reagan was sworn into office in 1981 and became one of the most conservative presidents since the early years of the twentieth century.

Picturing Government

The photograph at the top of page 279 shows President Franklin Roosevelt in 1935, stating to Congress his belief that the country needed a program for jobs, not simply relief. The second phase of the New Deal began in 1935. This phase included the establishment of the Works Project Administration and the National Youth Administration. Both provided jobs for young people.

Extension

Jimmy Carter and Bill Clinton were the only two Democratic presidents between 1968 and 2008. Have interested students do biographical studies of the two men, pointing out similarities and differences, as well as suggesting how they may have appealed to voters.

Picturing Government

In the photograph at the bottom right of page 279, President Ronald Reagan smiles before making his 1987 State of the Union address, while his vice president, George H. W. Bush, and Speaker of the House Jim Wright look on. The first professional actor to become president, Reagan was dubbed "the Great Communicator." He had worked as a radio sportscaster and a spokesperson for General Electric, along with starring in movies for nearly three decades. Reagan, who had been a Democrat, switched parties during his presidency of the Screen Actors Guild. From 1967 until 1975, Reagan was governor of California. With the economy in bad shape in 1980, Reagan took 44 states' Electoral College votes, though he gained only 51percent of the popular vote. In 1984, he won 59 percent of the popular vote and the largest electoral vote in history, with every state except Minnesota and the District of Columbia voting for him.

A contested election in 2000 put a Republican back in the White House. George W. Bush defeated Al Gore after the U.S. Supreme Court ruled against counting contested ballots in Florida.

Third Parties

While U.S. politics is dominated by two major parties, third parties also play a role. **Third parties** are also called minor parties. A third party develops when a group of people believes that the major parties are not dealing with some important issue.

There are three types of third parties. The **single-issue party** arises to deal with a single social, economic, or moral issue. The Free Soil Party was a single-issue party.

An **ideological party** wants to change society rather than solve a single problem. The Socialist, Socialist Worker, Socialist Labor, and Communist Parties want to do away with private ownership. They want the government to control all business. The Libertarian Party, on the other hand, wants to do away with most government control. Ideological parties win few votes, but they tend to last for a long time.

A **splinter party** breaks off from a major party. Splinter parties are often based on a politician's personal popularity. When the candidate fails to win office, the party collapses. As in the 1912 election, splinter parties can make a difference in an election. For this reason, they are sometimes called "spoilers." They spoil the outcome for one group.

It is possible that the 2000 election could have turned out differently without a third-party candidate. The Green Party candidate, Ralph Nader, ran on a platform of protection for the environment, health care for everyone, campaign finance reform, and similar policies. He won 2.8 million votes, or 2.7 percent of the total cast. Most experts believe that without Nader, most of these votes would have gone to the Democrat, Al Gore.

Picturing Government

The Bull Moose Party was, in effect, Theodore Roosevelt himself, as the photograph on page 280 demonstrates. The official name of the party was Progressive, but the nickname was from Roosevelt's claim that he was as "strong as a bull moose." Roosevelt, who, after serving out President William McKinley's term and being elected in 1904, had handpicked his friend William Howard Taft as his successor, fretted that Taft was not carrying out Progressive policy.

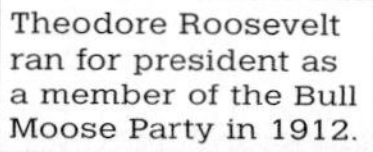
Theodore Roosevelt ran for president as a member of the Bull Moose Party in 1912.

Putting It All Together

With a partner, create a timeline of major political parties in the United States. On your timeline, indicate which parties dominated time periods before the Civil War and since the Civil War.

Putting It All Together

Students' timelines may show the following eras:

1796: Federalist

1800–1828: Democratic-Republican

1828–1850: Whig

1850s: Whig, Democrat, Free Soilers, Republican

1860–1932: Republicans dominated

1932–1968: Democrats dominated

1968–2008: Republicans dominated, with Carter and Clinton the Democrat exceptions

LESSON 3

Organization of Parties

Thinking on Your Own

Do you belong to a social group or club? What are the titles of the officers of the clubs? What does each officer do? Write a paragraph in your notebook to explain how a club is set up.

focus your reading

What does each part of the national party do?

How is the state party organized?

Summarize the different organizations of local parties.

words to know

primary election
national convention
platform
national committee
state central committee
county committee
precinct
ward

As you just read, anyone can join any political party, or choose not to join a party. In some states, a person must declare a political party to vote in a primary election. **Primary elections** choose the candidates from each party who will run in the general election. A voter does not have to belong to a party to vote in a general election.

Political parties are loosely joined groups of people with similar views on issues. Many people do nothing more than vote for their party's candidates. Others actively work for their party, especially at the local level. Working for a political party is one way to influence what government does.

The National Party

Every four years, Americans watch as the national parties carry out one of their most important duties. The parties hold their **national conventions**. The conventions have only two tasks. They nominate the party's presidential and vice-presidential candidates, and they write the party's platform. A **platform** states the party's position on various issues. It is a promise of what the party will do if elected. For example, the platform may state that the party will reform the nation's health-care system.

Words to Know

Discuss each of the vocabulary terms with students.

Primary elections are elections that are held before the general election to narrow the field of candidates.

The *national convention* is a gathering of party members to nominate the presidential and vice-presidential candidates and to write the party's platform. Parties hold a *national convention* every four years. The *platform* is a statement of the party's position on different issues. A *platform* is a promise of what the party will do if elected.

The *national committee* is responsible for running the party between conventions. The national chairperson runs the *national committee* on a day-to-day basis.

Continued on next page

Lesson Summary

The primary election is used to determine each party's candidate for the general presidential election. That person is formally nominated at national conventions, at which the party's platform is written. Between these four-year conventions, a national committee runs the party. The chairperson of that committee runs the party organization on a daily basis. The parties each have campaign committees for congressional races as well. At the state level, a state central committee runs the party. The state party tries to get candidates elected at statewide levels. There are also county committees and precincts, the smallest units of elective government. Precincts, which are headed by captains, are combined into wards. In some places in the country, local political parties are organized into township or district committees.

Lesson Objective

Students will learn about the way that political parties are organized.

Focus Your Reading Answers

1 Each part of the national party attempts to get its candidate elected.

2 The state party is organized by a state central committee. The state party chair, who is elected or chosen by party convention, runs the party. The job of state parties is to get candidates elected at statewide levels.

3 The organizations of local parties include county committees, precincts, and wards. Local political parties may also be organized into township or district committees.

Picturing Government

The photograph on page 282 shows a ticket for the 1936 Democratic National Convention in Philadelphia. At that convention, the rules were changed from requiring a two-thirds majority to nominate a presidential candidate to requiring a simple majority. Franklin Roosevelt rode on his New Deal successes, while his Republican challenger, Alf Landon, charged Roosevelt with violating the Constitution. An inaccurate telephone poll led to predictions of Landon's win, but Roosevelt took 61 percent of the popular vote and all Electoral College state votes except Maine and Vermont.

During the 1936 presidential campaign, the Democratic Party provided convention attendees with tickets and a party handbook that explained the party's position.

Between conventions, the national party is run by the **national committee**. This committee is headed by the national chairperson. The president selects the national chair for his or her party, and the committee approves the choice. The national committee of the party out of power picks its own chair. The job of the chairperson is to run the party organization on a day-to-day basis.

The national committee is made up of a man and a woman from each state. They are often large donors to the party or important politicians. The national committee handles disagreements among different groups within the party over the party's positions on issues. The national committee also raises money for campaigns. Another task, especially for the party out of power, is getting media coverage. The party wants to keep reminding the public what they are doing and what the opposing party is not doing.

stop and think

Draw a diagram to show how national parties are set up. Leave enough space to list what each part does. Work with a partner to create and fill in your diagram. Then as you read, create a similar diagram for state parties.

Each national party also has a Senate campaign committee and a House of Representatives campaign committee. These congressional campaign committees raise money for House and Senate races. They also recruit candidates to run for office. The chairs and members of the committees are elected by fellow senators or members of the House.

The State Party

State law and a party's own rules determine how political parties are organized on the state level. A **state central committee** runs the party at the state level. Committee members are usually elected from local parties and usually

Stop and Think

Students' diagrams will vary but should reflect information from the lesson.

Words to Know, continued

The *state central committee* runs the party at the state level. The *state central committee* tries to get candidates elected to statewide offices.

The *county committee* is a smaller part of the state committee. The chair of a *county committee* may be a powerful person who recommends people for jobs in state executive departments.

A *precinct*, which is made up of 300–600 people, is the smallest unit of elective government. A *precinct* in a large city may be a single apartment building.

Precincts combine to make a *ward*. A *ward* leader tries to coordinate the work of *precinct* captains.

elect the party state chair. However, in some states, a state party convention chooses the state chair.

The state party has several duties. The major effort of the state party is to get statewide candidates elected to state government and to Congress. It raises campaign funds to support statewide candidates. Some of the funds may also be given to county and local candidates.

Many areas require that campaign workers remain at least 100 feet from a polling place.

The Local Party

Each county within a state has a **county committee**. Local parties elect its members. A county chair runs the committee. In some states, the county chairs are very powerful. Candidates running for office in a state need their support. The county chairs may actually choose which candidates the party will back. County chairs also recommend people for appointment to judgeships and jobs in state executive departments.

There are several different local party structures. The **precinct** is the smallest unit of elective government. Everyone in a precinct votes at the same polling place. A voting precinct contains from 300 to 600 people. In a very large city, a single apartment building may be a precinct.

The precinct may also be the smallest unit of the local political parties. In that case, each precinct has a volunteer precinct captain for each political party. The job of the precinct captain is to organize party members to work in election campaigns. One of the tasks is to get members out to vote. Several precincts are combined into **wards**. Ward leaders coordinate the work of precinct captains, especially during election campaigns. Some cities also have political clubs. They focus on a certain section of a city or on electing a particular candidate.

Picturing Government

The photograph on page 283 shows a group of George W. Bush's supporters at a rally prior to the 2004 election. The presidential campaign that year more than tripled the cost of the campaign from just four years earlier; the two major candidates for the 2004 presidency, each personally wealthy, spent a total of more than $600 million on television and radio advertising alone.

Extensions

1 Have students use the Internet to view images from the most recent national conventions. Ask them to identify ways that each party projects an image of itself. For example, each party generally sticks with a red, white, and blue color scheme, appealing to prospective voters with those "patriotic" colors.

2 Ask students to find out who the national chairperson of each major party is. Challenge them to find out that person's background, political experience, and qualifications for the position, and then write a mock résumé for that person.

3 Have students use the Internet to check Web sites of state and local officials. Ask them to identify the issues currently being discussed and to take a position on one of them, and then write a short paper explaining the issue.

Picturing Government

The computer screen shown on page 284 depicts Carlos Manzano, president of the McManus Democratic Association. Born in Colombia, Manzano has served in a number of positions in New York City, including managing the New York City Board of Elections' poll site unit.

Putting It All Together

Students' flowcharts will vary.

Reading for Understanding

1 The system works because of something that was not in the Constitution.

2 The alternative would be to elect someone from a different party.

3 He is describing the voting process.

Political clubs often support local candidates and promote issues of community importance.

In some areas of the country, there are no precincts. Instead, cities, towns, townships, and villages are divided into districts for voting. The local political parties in those areas are organized into district or township committees.

Putting It All Together

Suppose a person wants to become active in a local political party. Where should the person start? How far could the person go in the party? Create a flowchart that shows a person's progress through different levels of a political party, ending at the national level. Work with a partner to be sure you do not skip a step.

Primary Source

Passing Judgment on a Party's Policies

In the following excerpt, President John F. Kennedy describes how the party system works. He was speaking to national and state Democratic committees at the White House in 1963.

"Our Founding Fathers did not realize that the basic fact which has made our system work was outside the Constitution. And that was the development of political parties in this country so that the American people would have the means of placing responsibility on one group, that group would have a chance to carry out its program, and the American people would have an opportunity to indicate their dissatisfaction by going to an alternative."

—President John F. Kennedy, 1963

reading for understanding

1. Explain what the president means by "outside the Constitution."
2. What is the "alternative" that President Kennedy mentions?
3. What is the process that President Kennedy is describing?

Join a Political Party—or Not

The two major political parties are the Democratic Party and the Republican Party. There are also a number of minor parties.

When you register to vote, you will be asked how you want to register. Do you want to register as a Republican, a Democrat, an independent, or for some other party? To help you decide, you should do some research and some thinking.

To Find Out More About the Parties:

- Check the Web sites of the national parties.
- Contact your local election board to find out if you can vote in primaries if you are an independent. You can find the phone number in the white pages of the phone book.
- Check the phone book for the number of any minor party you may be interested in learning more about.

To decide how to register, think about the following questions.

- Are you a liberal, conservative, or moderate on public policy issues?
- Do you believe in a strict or loose interpretation of the Constitution?
- Can independents vote in primaries in your state?

Democrats tend to be loose constructionists and liberal. The party supports civil rights, women's rights, and government aid for health care, education, housing, and the environment. Republicans tend to be strict constructionists and conservative. The party supports tax cuts and less government aid to individuals, local communities, and the states. Independents may hold more liberal views on some issues and more conservative views on others.

Remember to register when you turn eighteen!

Participate in Government

1 Invite a local politician from each of the major parties to come to the class and speak about his or her experiences.

2 If possible, get a copy of a ballot and show students how ballots are marked in your area.

Research Resources

Below is a list of reference books and Web sites that relate to the issues covered in this chapter. Students may wish to use these to further their research on ideas in the preceding lessons. Web site addresses may change over time. Use keyword searching on a major search engine to locate sites.

Reference Books:

George Thomas Kurian. *The Encyclopedia of the Democratic Party.* Sharpe Reference, 1997.

George Thomas Kurian. *The Encyclopedia of the Republican Party.* Sharpe Reference, 1997.

Robert North Roberts. *Encyclopedia of Presidential Campaigns, Slogans, Issues, and Platforms.* Greenwood Press, 2004.

Web Sites:

The Rock the Vote site aims at young voters and includes a link to register to vote. It also recommends films, promotes social activism, and sells items such as shirts, hats, and buttons.

The official site of the Democratic Party includes information on the party, plus national, local, and community news.

The Republican National Committee's site offers a link for voter registration and provides party information and history.

Skill Builder

Bring to class recent newsmagazine or newspaper ads about candidates. Have students working together in small groups analyze the ads for the various types of propaganda devices mentioned in the Skill Builder.

1 Students' ads will vary.

2 Students' paragraphs will vary.

Classroom Discussion

Discuss with students some of the broader topics covered in this chapter.

- How can political parties better serve the interests of the American people?
- What are the advantages and disadvantages of a two-party system?
- In what ways could third parties become more successful in the United States?
- How can political organizations better reach out to young people?

Skill Builder

Recognize Propaganda

Propaganda is the spreading of information, beliefs, and ideas to influence people for or against an issue or person. Propaganda does not always tell the whole truth. It is usually biased.

Advertising is a form of propaganda. Advertisers may exaggerate claims about their products. Candidates for public office also use propaganda to get people to vote for them. There are seven major propaganda techniques that are used in political campaigns.

- **Card stacking**: The candidate gives only the positive side of his or her record. This is the most popular technique.
- **Labeling**: A candidate pins an unflattering name on an opponent. In 2004, John Kerry was labeled a "flip-flopper."
- **Glittering generality**: The candidate speaks in broad terms about what he or she will do to solve problems. Richard Nixon promised "peace with honor" in the Vietnam War but never said how he would achieve this.
- **Plain folks**: Although worth millions of dollars, a candidate acts like an ordinary citizen.
- **Testimonial**: Movie actors, singers, and other famous people may publicly support a candidate. People who admire the celebrity may vote for the candidate.
- **Transfer**: A candidate uses a patriotic symbol, such as the American eagle, on ads. The hope is that voters will associate the candidate with patriotism and vote for him or her.
- **Bandwagon**: A candidate urges voters to vote for him or her because "everyone else is."

To analyze propaganda, look for these techniques in campaign ads, brochures, and Web sites.

Complete the following activities.

1 With a partner, design an ad that uses one of the techniques.

2 Think of a recent political campaign. Write a paragraph and explain any examples of propaganda that you remember.

Recommended Reading

Below is a list of books that relate to the issues covered in this chapter. The numbers in parentheses indicate the related Thematic Strands of the National Council for the Social Studies (NCSS).

Bruce Fish and Becky Fish. *The History of the Democratic Party*. Chelsea House Publications, 2000. (VI, X)

Elaine Landua. *Friendly Foes: A Look at Political Parties*. Lerner Publishing Group, 2003. (VI, X)

Norma Jean Lutz. *The History of the Republican Party*. Chelsea House Publications, 2000. (VI, X)

Chapter

16 ELECTIONS, VOTING, AND VOTER BEHAVIOR

Getting Focused

Skim this chapter to predict what you will be learning.

- **Read the lesson titles and subheadings.**
- **Look at the illustrations and read the captions.**
- **Examine the tables.**
- **Review the vocabulary words and terms.**

Every four years, voters elect a president. Every two years, they elect members of the U.S. House of Representatives. Elections that occur between presidential elections are known as off-year elections. Voters also elect their U.S. senators, their state's governor, members of the state legislature, their mayor, members of the local school board, and more. In a democracy such as ours, all levels of government are freely elected.

Choose a recent election. It could be for a local, state, or federal office. Make a bulleted list with facts about the election, such as candidates, issues, the winners, and so on.

The democratic process allows citizens to participate in government through voting, political party activities, and electoral campaigns.

Pre-Reading Discussion

1 Ask students to recall what they can about the previous presidential election. Who were the major candidates and what were the issues? If the students could have voted in the election, for whom would they have cast their ballot? Why?

2 Focus on a recent school election, such as for student council. Have students identify characteristics of the election, such as posters, buttons, and campaign speeches. Tell students to keep these elements in mind as they study the national process to note similarities and differences.

Related Transparencies

T-18 Three-Column Chart

T-19 Venn Diagram

T-20 Concept Web

Key Blacklines

Civics Today—Asian and Pacific Islander American Vote

CD Extension

Encourage students to use the reading comprehension, vocabulary reinforcement, and other activities on the student CD.

Getting Focused

Students' choices of elections and facts will vary. Challenge students to create a bulletin board about a recent or upcoming election with the material they have collected.

Picturing Government

The photograph on page 287 shows a young girl at a campaign rally for John Kerry in the presidential election of 2004. Stress to students that young people can participate in the election process even if they cannot vote.

Lesson Summary

Candidates may have their names placed on ballots in four ways: caucus, convention, direct primary, and petition. The caucus was the earliest method but was discontinued after people complained that caucuses were undemocratic. Instead, parties developed the nominating convention. Nominating conventions are used for choosing candidates for state, county, and local offices as well as in presidential elections. Most states now use direct primary elections to determine candidates. Petitions must be signed and filed with the board of elections, with the number of signatures required dependent on the office.

Lesson Objective

Students will learn about the various ways that candidates are nominated for office.

Focus Your Reading Answers

1 A caucus is a meeting of party leaders to determine who will run for office. A nominating convention is a public meeting of party members to decide the candidates; it is considered more democratic.

2 The different kinds of primaries include direct primary elections, which include closed primaries and open primaries, proportional representation primaries, winner-take-all primaries, and preference primaries.

3 The petition is an example of direct democracy in that people must get signatures on a request to run for office.

4 Major parties nominate presidential candidates through national conventions. Candidates are chosen prior to the convention through primary races.

LESSON 1

Nominating Candidates

Thinking on Your Own

Suppose you want to run for class president. You are going to self-announce your candidacy. This is a way that people let others know they want to be elected to a certain office. Write a press release in your notebook announcing your candidacy. In it, explain why you are running and what issues you think are important.

To **nominate** a candidate means to select a candidate to run for office. There are four ways that candidates have their names placed on ballots. They are the (1) caucus, (2) convention, (3) direct primary, and (4) petition. Which one a person uses depends on the office he or she is seeking. A candidate for town council may get on the ballot by petition. A presidential nominee from a major party is chosen at a national nominating convention.

focus your reading

Explain the difference between a caucus and a nominating convention.

What are the different kinds of primaries?

How is the petition an example of direct democracy?

Describe how the major parties nominate presidential candidates.

words to know

- nominate
- nominating convention
- party bosses
- general election
- direct primary election
- closed primary
- open primary
- petition
- proportional representation primary
- winner-take-all primary
- preference primary

Ross Perot self-announced his candidacy for president in both the 1992 and 1996 elections.

Caucus and Nominating Conventions

The earliest method for choosing candidates was the caucus. Party leaders met and decided who would run for office. By the 1820s, however, voters were complaining that caucuses were undemocratic. As a result, parties developed the nominating convention.

A **nominating convention** is a public meeting of party members to choose candidates for office. By 1832, the major parties were using nominating

Words to Know

Introduce each of the following vocabulary terms to students.

Explain that to *nominate* is to select a candidate to run for office. Party leaders no longer are the ones who *nominate* the candidates. A public meeting of party members to choose candidates for office is a *nominating convention*. The *nominating convention* also seems undemocratic to many.

Party leaders are known as *party bosses*. Candidates whom the *party bosses* favored ran in the elections.

A *general election* determines who will hold office. The *general election* is held in the fall.

In a *direct primary election*, voters choose who will run for the party. Most states today use the *direct primary election*. A *closed primary* is limited to the registered members of political parties. During a *closed primary*, party members may vote only for candidates from their own party. Any registered voter may vote in an *open primary*. Nearly half of the states use an *open primary*.

conventions to choose presidential candidates. By the 1840s, nominating conventions were also used for state, county, and local offices. Party members in the precinct or district elected delegates to a county convention. At the county convention, the delegates chose candidates to run for county offices. The delegates also elected delegates to the state convention. This convention chose candidates for statewide offices.

Conventions soon became as undemocratic as the old-style caucus. In many areas, party leaders known as **party bosses** chose the delegates. They, in turn, made sure the bosses' candidates were chosen to run in elections. In the early 1900s, primary elections replaced conventions in many areas.

The Iowa Caucus takes place around the state.

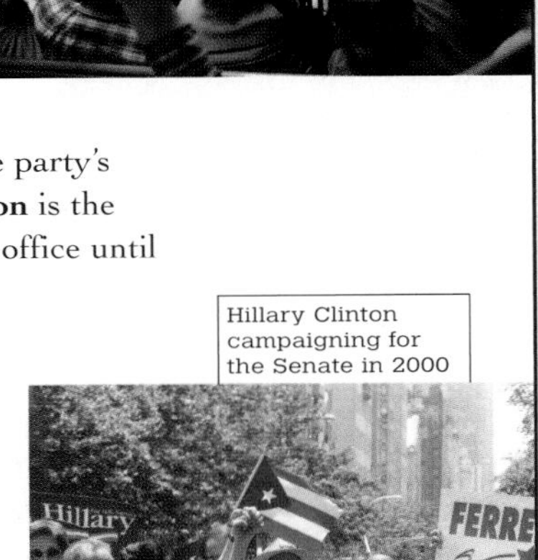

Caucuses and conventions did not stop. Both are still used in a number of states. However, there are changes. In a modern caucus, party leaders do not make the choices. Instead, members of a political party meet in their districts or precincts on caucus day. They discuss the qualifications of the candidates and then vote. Whoever wins the most votes becomes the party's candidate in the general election. The **general election** is the election in the fall that determines who will hold the office until the next general election.

Primary Elections

Today, most states use **direct primary elections** to select party candidates. In these elections, several candidates from the same party campaign against one another. Voters cast their ballots on primary election day. The person with the most votes will run against candidates for that office from other parties.

Hillary Clinton campaigning for the Senate in 2000

There are two types of direct primary. The **closed primary** is limited to registered members of political parties. Each party has its own ballot. Republicans may vote only for Republican candidates. Democrats may vote only for Democrats. New Jersey uses the closed primary.

Words to Know, continued

A paper stating that a person wants to run for office is a *petition*. The candidate must get signatures on his or her *petition*.

When each candidate is awarded delegates in proportion to the percentage of votes cast, this is called a *proportional representation primary*. The Democratic Party uses a *proportional representation primary* system. In a *winner-take-all primary*, the candidate who gets the most votes gets all the delegates. The Republicans use a *winner-take-all primary*. When voters indicate which candidate they prefer, the state uses a *preference primary*. The result of a *preference primary* is advisory only, not binding.

Picturing Government

In the photograph in the center of page 289, a caucus in Iowa is shown. Because it conducts the first caucus in the election cycle, Iowa traditionally has been an important state in the process of choosing a presidential nominee.

Picturing Government

The photograph at the bottom of page 289 shows Hillary Clinton, later a member of the United States Senate, campaigning in 2000 as part of a parade on Puerto Rican Day in the Bronx, New York. Clinton's run for the Senate drew fire from those who pointed out that she had not lived in New York prior to purchasing a home in Westchester in 1999. During her first term in the Senate, Clinton served on the Senate Armed Services Committee; the Senate Committee on Environment and Public Works; the Senate Committee on Health, Education, Labor & Pensions; and the Senate Special Committee on Aging.

Stop and Think

Students' concept webs will vary but may include caucus, convention, direct primary, and petition.

Picturing Government

The photograph on page 290 shows a Seattle voter signing a petition while a representative of the League of Education Voters looks on. A grassroots, statewide organization, the League of Education Voters focuses on improving public schools in the state of Washington.

Extension

Have students use library resources or the Internet to find out more about the most recent national conventions for presidential elections. Challenge them to discover how the conventions run, encouraging them to see the dramatic structure of the event, leading to the climax of the candidate's acceptance speech.

In an **open primary**, any registered voter may vote for any candidate. This means that independents may vote. However, the voter must choose which party he or she wants to vote in. A voter may not vote for a Republican for mayor and a Democrat for governor. Texas is one of the 23 states that use the open primary.

stop and think

Create a concept web to show how candidates are selected. Label the large circle "Nominating Candidates." Then add smaller circles and connect them with lines to the large circle. In each circle, write one way that a candidate is nominated. Share your web with a partner. Add one detail to each circle.

Petition

The petition is another way for a candidate to get on the ballot. A **petition** is a paper that states that a person wishes to run for a particular office, such as town mayor. A certain number of voters must sign the petition and it must be filed with the board of elections. The voters must live in the area that will be served by the candidate if elected. The number of signatures needed varies, based on the office. A person running for governor needs more signatures than a person who wants to be a city council member.

Petitions are one means of putting a candidate's name on the ballot.

Nominating Presidential Candidates

Nomination for president is somewhat different from nominations for other offices. Presidential candidates have to compete for delegates to the national convention. The 2004 Republican convention had 2,520 delegates. The Democratic convention had 4,348. The national committee of each party gives each state committee a certain number of delegates. The voters decide who those delegates will be and whom they will support. In presidential primaries, voters do not vote for the candidates. Voters cast their ballots for delegates who support the candidates.

Most states use presidential primaries to choose delegates. However, Iowa uses the caucus system. About one-quarter of the states hold conventions.

Picturing Government

The photograph on page 288 shows Ross Perot in 1992 after he re-entered the campaign for the presidency in October. Perot dropped out of the running as a Reform Party candidate from July until October 1992. Even though that cost him supporters, he still gained nearly one-fifth of the popular vote in that election.

There are three kinds of presidential primary: (1) proportional, (2) winner-take-all, and (3) preference. Each state has its own laws for setting up its primary. Remember that depending on the state, the primary may be open or closed. In some states, each candidate is awarded delegates in proportion to the number of votes cast. For example, if Candidate A gets 70 percent of the votes, then 70 percent of the delegates will represent Candidate A at the convention. This is known as a **proportional representation primary**. The Democratic Party uses this type of primary. In the **winner-take-all primary**, which is used by the Republican Party in most states, the candidate who gets the most votes gets all the delegates.

Franklin Roosevelt, in 1932, was the first presidential candidate to address a party convention.

A few states use a **preference primary**. Voters do not vote for delegates. Instead, they vote to show which candidate they prefer. Party conventions later choose the delegates. The number of delegates for each candidate is based on the number of votes each receives. However, most preference primaries are only advisory—the party is not bound by the results of the primary. Most award their delegates on the basis of winner-take-all.

Putting It All Together

Suppose your school held nominating conventions for student council president. Which type of primary do you think would be the most fair to candidates? Remember that each type of presidential primary may be open or closed. Discuss the question with a partner. Make notes as you talk. Then write a paragraph to explain which type of primary you think is most fair. Be sure to explain your reasons.

Picturing Government

In the photograph on page 291, then-governor of New York Franklin Roosevelt makes his acceptance speech after receiving the nomination at the Democratic National Convention in July 1932. Eager to demonstrate his fitness for the task, Roosevelt, though paralyzed by polio, made history by accepting the honor in person. The airplane made it possible for the Roosevelt family to fly from Albany to Chicago. In the earliest days of the nation, candidates may not have known of their selection for a week. After receiving notification, the candidate made an acceptance speech. Even though communication and transportation had advanced since the horse-and-buggy days, candidates continued the tradition.

Putting It All Together

Students' choices and reasons for them will vary but should be supported.

Extension

Invite students to use library resources or the Internet to find out more about party bosses such as Mark Hanna, William Tweed, or Huey Long. Ask them to find out where each person wielded power and for what party, as well as the results of their work on behalf of that party. Have them present their findings to the class by using the Student Presentation Builder on the student CD.

Lesson Summary

Federal elections, as well as many state and local elections, are held on the first Tuesday after the first Monday in November. As a result of problems voters had in 2000, Congress passed the Help America Vote Act in 2002. Elections are financed through public money and private donations. The Federal Election Commission oversees campaign finance laws. Contributions are restricted to try to prevent people or corporations from buying influence. Candidates have managed to find ways to avoid limits of the 2002 Bipartisan Campaign Reform Act. The president and vice president are elected by members of the Electoral College in December; the votes are counted in January.

Lesson Objective

Students will learn about the ways in which elections are regulated and financed, focusing specifically on presidential elections.

Focus Your Reading Answers

1 Elections are regulated at the state and federal levels.

2 Candidates may finance their campaigns through private donations and public contributions. Federal funds are available, but because of limits, many candidates refuse to take them.

3 Soft-money contributions are limited by the Bipartisan Campaign Reform Act of 2002.

4 The Electoral College elects the president and vice president, based on the vote in each state.

LESSON 2

Elections and Election Campaigns

Thinking on Your Own

Think about a recent political campaign in your community, state, or in the nation. Perhaps the mayor or governor was running for office. Perhaps it was the year when members of the U.S. House of Representatives were being elected. In your notebook, list five things that you remember about the candidates and the campaign.

focus your reading

What levels of government regulate elections?

What are the different ways that candidates may finance their campaigns?

Describe how the use of soft money is limited.

How are the president and vice president elected?

words to know

political action committee

hard money

soft money

popular vote

electoral vote

The right to vote freely is basic to democracy. Citizens exercise this right on Election Day. For candidates, that day is the end of their campaign for public office. Depending on the office, the campaign may have lasted as long as two years and cost millions of dollars.

Regulating Elections

Most elections in the United States choose state or local officials. As a result, most laws that govern elections are state laws—not federal laws. However, federal laws regulate federal elections. These laws, in turn, impact state election laws. For example, Congress has the power to set the date for the election of members of Congress. This date is the first Tuesday following the first Monday in November. As a convenience and a cost saver, many state and local elections are held on the same day.

Polling places can be in schools, firehouses, libraries, or other community buildings.

In 2002, Congress passed the Help America Vote Act. It requires changes in how states carry out elections. This law

Words to Know

Discuss each of the vocabulary terms with students.

A *political action committee*, or PAC, is a political organization formed by a special-interest group.

Money that candidates raise and spend themselves is called *hard money*. Regulations govern the use of *hard money*.

Money raised and spent for party-building activities is called *soft money*. Registering voters could be financed by *soft money*.

The number of votes that citizens cast is called the *popular vote*. Newscasters track the *popular vote* on election nights. The *electoral vote* is the number of votes each state has in the Electoral College, along with three votes for the District of Columbia. Each state's *electoral vote* is calculated by adding each state's two senators and the number of representatives in the House.

was passed as a result of the ballot and voter registration problems in the 2000 presidential election. Among the sections of the law, all states must upgrade their voting machines by 2006. Poll workers must be better trained to deal with voter registration problems on Election Day. Voter registration files must be computerized.

Financing Elections

Campaigns for local and state offices tend to begin during the year the election will be held. In recent years, presidential races have begun as early as two years before the election. Even races for Congress start as much as one year early. Long campaigns require a great deal of money to rent offices, pay campaign workers, and run ads on television and radio and in newspapers. Campaigns also finance Web sites.

Howard Dean's 2004 campaign for president was the first to use the Internet for soliciting campaign contributions.

Where does the money come from? Contributions come from private donors and from public money. In 1971, the Presidential Election Campaign Fund Act set up public funding for presidential campaigns. Taxpayers may check off a box on their income tax form to direct $3 of their tax to the fund. In 1975, Congress set up the Federal Election Commission (FEC) to oversee campaign finance law. Campaigns must report donations to the FEC.

Candidates may use the money for primary and caucus campaigns. The money may also be used by the national parties to help pay for their national convention. Presidential candidates may also apply for funds for the general election campaign. The federal fund matches campaign contributions dollar for dollar. In a recent campaign, this amounted to $76 million for each of the major party candidates. However, if a candidate accepts the federal money, he or she may not spend money over this amount. If the candidate does not accept the funds, he or she may spend as much money as he or she wishes.

Campaign money can lead to abuses. Donors of large amounts often expect favors in return for their money. As a result, Congress has passed a number of campaign finance laws. The table on page 294 shows the limits for contributions to candidates in federal elections.

Picturing Government

The photograph on page 293 shows Howard Dean campaigning during the 2004 presidential election. The physician and former governor of Vermont galvanized a grassroots, Internet-based support system unprecedented in political history, but lost the Democratic nomination to John Kerry. However, in 2005, Dean became chair of the Democratic National Committee.

Picturing Government

The photograph on page 292 shows a polling place in Santa Monica, California. The multilingual sign indicates the diverse community served by that polling place. Suggest that students check their local polling places to see if they are bilingual or multilingual facilities, or what plans are in place for citizens whose first language is not English.

Extension

The Federal Election Commission, an independent regulatory agency, has three broad duties: overseeing of the public funding of presidential elections, disclosing campaign finance information, and enforcing the law. Challenge students to use indexes to magazines or newspapers to find examples of each of the three functions in action in a recent presidential election.

Table Extension

Numerous Web sites track campaign contributions. Have students use one of the sites to check contributions in the latest presidential campaign. What groups or individuals gave the most significant amounts of money? How do students feel those contributions may have influenced the candidates and their agendas?

Cartoon Extension

Have students identify the weapons in the cartoon on page 294. (a sword and a slingshot) Tell students the story of David and Goliath from the Hebrew Bible. David, a young, untrained shepherd, goes against the enemy's giant, Goliath, with merely a slingshot and a few pebbles. He kills Goliath. The cartoon alludes to the physical inequality between a giant, representing unregulated campaign funding, and the person who is a hero for the morally right course of action, the reformer.

Limits on Giving to Campaigns for Federal Office

Primary Election	General Election	Political Action Committee	National Party
No more than $2,000 to a single candidate	No more than $2,000 to a single candidate	No more than $5,000 to one PAC in a year	No more than $95,000 during two years between congressional elections

There are also other restrictions. Corporations and labor unions may not give money directly to candidates. However, their political action committees may. A **political action committee** (PAC) is a political organization formed by special-interest groups such as companies and labor and professional organizations. The American Medical Association (AMA) and the National Rifle Association (NRA) are examples of special-interest groups. Each has a PAC.

PACs may not give more than $5,000 to a single candidate in an election or a total of $10,000 to a candidate for a primary and a general election. PACs set up by professional groups get their money from donations by their members. If the PAC is set up by a corporation, the corporation's employees donate the money.

Hard Money and Soft Money

Donors and candidates found a way around the campaign finance laws. The laws regulated **hard money**. This is money raised and spent by the candidates for Congress and the White House themselves. However, the laws said nothing about **soft money**. This is money raised and spent for party-building activities. These include registering voters and get-out-the-vote activities on Election Day.

By the 1990s, the two major parties were raising millions of dollars in soft money. There were no laws to govern how much soft money could be raised. Although soft money was supposed to be used only for party building, the parties found ways to use the money to help their candidates.

Extension

PACs change and new ones begin. PACs concentrate on location, party, or gender/age/race issues. Have students check online for a PAC that interests them. Ask them to report to the class on what the PAC does and supports.

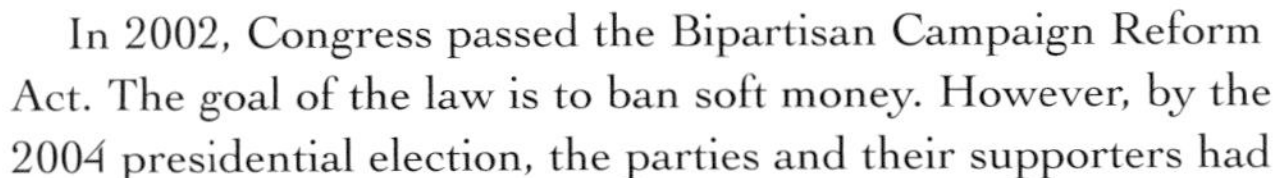

In 2002, Congress passed the Bipartisan Campaign Reform Act. The goal of the law is to ban soft money. However, by the 2004 presidential election, the parties and their supporters had found a way around the new law. Donors were setting up Section 527 organizations to raise and spend money to support their party's candidates. A Section 527 organization is similar to a PAC, except it is not regulated by the FEC. Instead, it is governed by the Internal Revenue Code.

stop and think

Create a flowchart to show the causes and effects of trying to regulate campaign financing. Work with a partner. Then discuss whether limits should be placed on how much money is spent by presidential candidates. Summarize your point of view in a paragraph.

Presidential Elections

From studying the Constitution, you know that voters do not elect the president and vice president. Voters choose electors who meet in December as the Electoral College. They choose the president and vice president. On the Monday after the second Wednesday in December, the electors in each state meet in their state capitols to vote. The votes are sent to Congress. On January 6, the Senate and the House count the votes in a joint session. The candidate who has the majority of the electors' votes is declared president.

January 6 is the date when a joint session of Congress meets to officially count the electoral votes in a presidential election.

Of course, by then the nation already knows the outcome. On election night, newscasters keep a running count of both the popular vote and the electoral vote. The **popular vote** is the number of votes cast by citizens. The **electoral vote** is the number of votes that the states and the District of Columbia have in the Electoral College. Each state's electoral vote is the sum of its two senators plus the number of its members in the House. The District of Columbia gets three electoral votes.

Stop and Think

Students' flowcharts and paragraphs will vary but may include information on the Presidential Election Campaign Fund Act, the Federal Election Commission, regulations on PACs, and the Bipartisan Campaign Reform Act.

Picturing Government

In the photograph on page 295, Vice President Dick Cheney and House Speaker Dennis Hastert look on while electoral votes from the 2004 presidential election are certified. Both houses of Congress were called into separate meetings to consider the electoral votes after Representative Stephanie Tubbs Jones, a Democrat from Ohio, submitted an objection. This was only the second time since 1877 that such a consideration was needed.

Extension

The need for and effectiveness of the Electoral College has long been a subject for debate, renewed at least once in every presidential election. Since its founding, there have been more than 700 attempts to revise the way the electors function. Have students find out what the main arguments are and summarize them in a graphic organizer.

In all, there are 538 electoral votes. To become president, a candidate must get 270 votes. Sometimes, a candidate may win a huge number of electoral votes. For example, in 1980, Ronald Reagan defeated President Jimmy Carter by 489 votes to 49. Elections may also be much closer. In the 2000 election, George W. Bush won 271 votes to 266 for Al Gore. In the popular vote, Gore won 500,000 more votes. However, it is the electoral vote that counts in the election for president, not the popular vote.

Putting It All Together

How is a presidential election similar to and different from other elections? Discuss this question with a partner. Take notes as you talk. Then create a Venn diagram to show the differences and similarities. Refer to the notes you made in the Thinking on Your Own activity at the start of the lesson for ideas.

Antonio Gonzalez (1957–)

Antonio Gonzalez is president of the Southwest Voter Registration Education Project (SVREP). It was founded in 1974 and is the largest and oldest nonpartisan Latino voter participation organization in the nation. SVREP is based in Los Angeles but works with Latino communities across the country.

Gonzalez joined SVREP in 1984. He had graduated from the University of Texas at San Antonio and done graduate work at the University of California at Berkeley. His family was not rich. His father emigrated from Mexico and loaded trucks for a living.

Gonzalez began as a community organizer for SVREP. He put together voter participation activities. By the time he became president of the organization in 1994, there were five million Latinos registered to vote. In ten years, Gonzalez's efforts have almost doubled the number. SVREP ran hundreds of voter-registration and get-out-the-vote campaigns in 14 states to achieve this goal.

It is not just presidential elections that motivate Gonzalez and SVREP. They work to get Latinos involved and voting in local and statewide elections. Gonzalez believes that Latinos must participate in politics. Otherwise, they will not be able to solve the problems of their communities. SVREP's slogan is "Your Vote Is Your Voice."

Putting It All Together

Students' Venn diagrams will vary but may suggest that presidential elections occur every four years, while several other offices have elections more or less frequently; federal monies are available to presidential candidates; laws regulating contributions have been passed.

People in the News Extension

In 2005, *Time* magazine named Antonio Gonzalez one of the "25 most influential Hispanics in America." In the 2004 election, 81.5 percent of registered Hispanic voters cast ballots. Gonzalez administers a $4 million budget, based largely on grants from corporations and foundations. SVREP used more than 10,000 volunteers and 700 paid staff members for the voter registration campaigns in the 2004 election. Gonzales deals with local as well as national concerns. Since 2002, he has helped California voters approve new school bonds worth more than $30 billion. SVREP has trained more than 50,000 leaders in more than 400 communities through its various programs.

LESSON 3

Voting Rights and Voting Laws

Thinking on Your Own

Create an outline of this lesson in your notebook to help you study the information. Look at the subheadings and the vocabulary words. Be sure to include information from the table. Fill in the outline as you read the lesson.

focus your reading

What groups have benefited from the expansion of the right to vote?

What laws have been needed to expand voting rights for African Americans?

words to know

suffragists

grandfather clause

literacy test

poll tax

The right to vote is guaranteed to all U.S. citizens today. However, this was not always the case. African Americans were not even considered citizens until 1868. Women were not allowed to vote until 1920. Native Americans were not granted citizenship until 1924.

As you read in Lesson 2, states set most election laws. State laws also govern voter qualifications. However, the Constitution has set limits on what states can do. The table on page 298 shows how these limits developed.

The History of Voting Rights

During the early years of the United States, states had religious and property requirements for voting. The religious qualification was left over from the many colonies that wanted to live according to their religion. For that reason, a man had to be a member of the church to be able to vote. By 1810, religion was no longer a requirement for voting in any state. However, the property qualification continued until the mid-1800s. Only men who owned property and paid taxes on it could vote. As the population grew, fewer men owned land. They made their living as shopkeepers and factory workers. As a result, the property requirement was also eliminated.

Lesson Summary

Restrictions of religion and property ownership on voting gave way early in the history of the nation. However, the battle for women, African Americans, and Native Americans to vote lasted until the 1960s. Native Americans were not considered citizens until 1924. Efforts in the South to prevent African-American men from voting after passage of the Fifteenth Amendment included grandfather clauses in state constitutions, poll taxes, and literacy tests. Voting Rights Acts in 1965, 1970, 1975, and 1982 have expanded opportunities for African Americans to vote and hold office. In 1971, the Twenty-sixth Amendment lowered the voting age to eighteen.

Lesson Objective

Students will learn about the extension of voting rights to all Americans.

Focus Your Reading Answers

1 The expansion of the right to vote has benefited African Americans, Native Americans, and women, as well as those eighteen to twenty-one years old.

2 To expand voting rights for African Americans, the Fifteenth Amendment and Civil Rights Act of 1964 were required.

Words to Know

Discuss each of the vocabulary terms with students.

Suffragists were people who campaigned for women's right to vote. *Suffragists* worked another 50 years after African-American males gained the right to vote.

A *grandfather clause* originally referred to the clause in some Southern states' constitutions stating that only men whose grandfathers were free to vote before 1867 could vote without passing a *literacy test* or paying a *poll tax*. The *grandfather clause* was a way to keep African Americans from voting. A *literacy test* required some voters in the South to explain a complicated section of the Constitution. The Voting Rights Act of 1965 abolished the use of the *literacy test*. A *poll tax* was a fee to vote. The *poll tax* was just high enough to exclude poor farmers from voting.

By the mid-1800s, all white male citizens could vote. However, women could not vote. In the 1840s, suffragists began to campaign for the vote for women. **Suffragists** are people who supported the right to vote, especially for women. As tensions grew over slavery in the 1850s, suffragists put aside their own fight to work for an end to slavery. When the

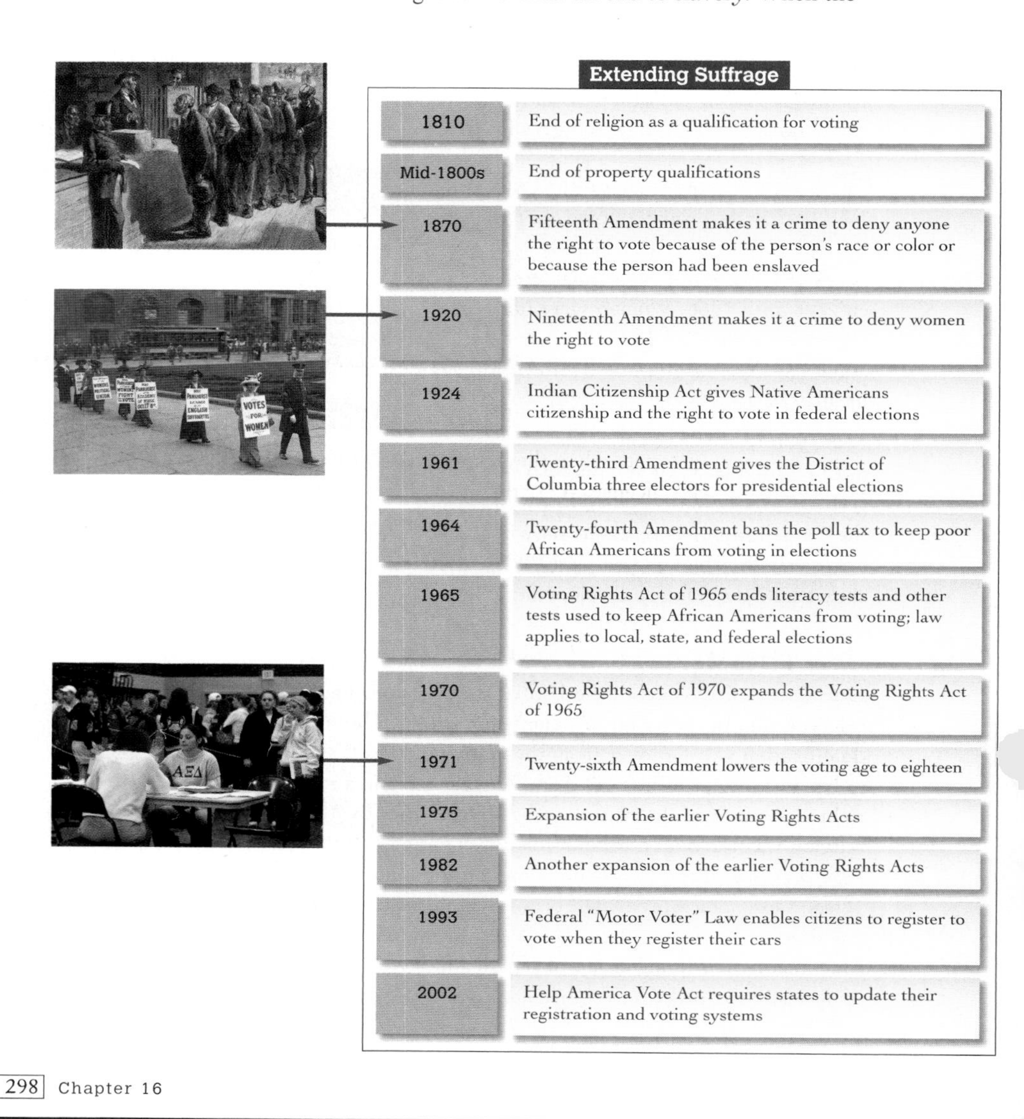

Extending Suffrage

Year	Change
1810	End of religion as a qualification for voting
Mid-1800s	End of property qualifications
1870	Fifteenth Amendment makes it a crime to deny anyone the right to vote because of the person's race or color or because the person had been enslaved
1920	Nineteenth Amendment makes it a crime to deny women the right to vote
1924	Indian Citizenship Act gives Native Americans citizenship and the right to vote in federal elections
1961	Twenty-third Amendment gives the District of Columbia three electors for presidential elections
1964	Twenty-fourth Amendment bans the poll tax to keep poor African Americans from voting in elections
1965	Voting Rights Act of 1965 ends literacy tests and other tests used to keep African Americans from voting; law applies to local, state, and federal elections
1970	Voting Rights Act of 1970 expands the Voting Rights Act of 1965
1971	Twenty-sixth Amendment lowers the voting age to eighteen
1975	Expansion of the earlier Voting Rights Acts
1982	Another expansion of the earlier Voting Rights Acts
1993	Federal "Motor Voter" Law enables citizens to register to vote when they register their cars
2002	Help America Vote Act requires states to update their registration and voting systems

Picturing Government

The top image on page 298 shows African-American freedmen voting in Richmond, Virginia, in 1871.

In the middle photograph, suffragettes, also called suffragists, march in Brooklyn in 1920. They are advertising a speech by the noted British suffragette Emmeline Pankhurst. American suffragette Alice Paul adopted many of Pankhurst's strategies to win the vote for women; like Pankhurst, Paul spent time in jail and called attention to the cause with hunger strikes.

The photograph at the bottom shows voters in New Hampshire on Election Day 2004. Many of the new voters were college students at the University of New Hampshire.

Extension

Have students select a figure in the fight for civil rights for African Americans, women, or Native Americans. Ask them to present a biographical sketch of that person, perhaps by coming to class in character and costume, explaining that person's efforts on behalf of full civil rights.

Table Extensions

1 Have students work in pairs to make flash cards with the information about the progress in extending suffrage. Have them quiz each other to achieve mastery of the material before a test or quiz.

2 Invite interested students to use library resources or the Internet to find out the background of the Twenty-sixth Amendment. Ask them what significance 1971 had on the pressure to lower the voting age to eighteen. What arguments were used?

Civil War was over, women expected to get the right to vote along with African Americans. However, the Fifteenth Amendment made it a federal crime to deny the vote to any *citizen* because of race, color, or enslavement. The word *citizen* was understood to mean "men."

Women campaigned for another 50 years to get the vote. They did not succeed until 1920. The Nineteenth Amendment guaranteed women the right to vote.

During the 1960s, Congress passed major laws to end voting discrimination against African Americans.

The final expansion of voting rights was the Twenty-sixth Amendment in 1971. It lowered the voting age from twenty-one to eighteen for all local, state, and federal elections.

Congress has also passed other voting laws that affect the states. The "Motor Voter" Law of 1993 allows people to register to vote when they apply for a driver's license. After the problems with the 2000 presidential election, Congress passed the Help America Vote Act of 2002.

stop and think

How has the right to vote been expanded to different groups during the history of the United States? List each group that has gained the right to vote. Use the text and the table to make your list. Review your list with a partner. Add any groups you missed.

qualifications to vote

To vote, a person must be

- a native-born or naturalized citizen.
- at least eighteen years old.
- a resident of the state in which he or she wishes to vote. Residency requirements vary from state to state. It is typically 15 to 30 days.
- registered to vote. The exception is North Dakota.

Voting Rights Laws

The goal of the Fifteenth Amendment was to expand voting rights to African-American men. However, Southern lawmakers found ways to keep them from voting. Some states added a **grandfather clause** to their state constitution. Only men whose grandfathers had been free to vote before 1867 could vote. Because most African Americans had been enslaved, their grandfathers could not have voted. The U.S. Supreme Court ruled the grandfather clause unconstitutional in 1915.

Stop and Think

Students' tables should incorporate information from the table on page 298.

Qualifications to Vote Extension

Review the ideas listed, further explaining difficult vocabulary words. Have students create graphic organizers in their notebooks to help them visualize the four qualifications to vote.

Extension

One of the provisions of the Help America Vote Act mandated the replacing of voting machines operated by lever and punch card. Have students use library resources or the Internet to find out the controversy over these machines in the 2000 election that led to this mandate.

Picturing Government

In the photograph on page 300, African Americans take an oath during a voter registration drive in Mississippi in 1966. After the passage of the Civil Rights Act of 1964 and the Voting Rights Act of 1965, many voter registration drives were conducted in the South, where whites had used a number of techniques to prevent African Americans from voting.

Putting It All Together

Students' summaries will vary. You may wish to use the summary on page 297 as a guideline.

During the 1960s, voter registration drives were held throughout the South.

The Voting Rights Act of 1965 outlawed the literacy test. Before 1965, whites as well as African Americans could be asked to pass a **literacy test**. However, whites could pass by writing their names. African Americans had to explain some point of law such as a section of the U.S. Constitution.

The **poll tax** was a fee of a few dollars that a person had to pay in order to vote. For poor farmers, this was a lot of money. The Twenty-fourth Amendment outlawed the poll tax.

By the 1960s, the civil rights movement was awakening Americans to the evils of segregation and racial discrimination. Congress reacted with major civil rights laws. One of them was the Voting Rights Act of 1965. This act was renewed and expanded in 1970, 1975, and 1982. Over the years, the laws have called for

- the federal government to register voters in districts where fewer than 50 percent of African Americans were registered or voted in the 1964 election.
- the federal government to register voters in districts with a history of discrimination against African-American voters.
- federal examiners to ensure that all votes are counted.
- federal approval for any change in voting laws or practices in areas with a history of discrimination.
- an end to the creation of election districts that lessen the influence of African Americans or other minority groups.
- ballots to be printed in the native languages of Hispanics, Native Americans, Asian Americans, and Alaskan natives in areas with more than 10,000 non–native English speakers.

By the late 1990s, more than 13,000 elected officials in the nation were African Americans. Between 1960 and the 1990s, the percentage of African-American registered voters doubled to 60 percent.

Putting It All Together

Write a summary of this lesson. Use the outline that you wrote in the Thinking on Your Own activity to help you. Share your summary with a partner. Revise your summary if needed.

300 Chapter 16

LESSON 4 # Voter Behavior

Thinking on Your Own

Nonvoting is a big problem in the United States. Why do you think citizens do not vote in elections? Write a bulleted list in your notebook to explain your opinions.

In a recent presidential election, only 51.2 percent of registered voters cast their ballot. In a recent election for the U.S. House of Representatives, only 33.9 percent of registered voters voted. Why do some citizens vote in every election and some never vote? How do voters decide for whom to vote?

focus your reading

What factors influence how a person votes?

What is the profile of a regular voter?

Explain the reasons people give for not voting.

words to know

generalization

straight-ticket voting

political efficacy

Influences on Voting Decisions

Influences on How a Person Votes

Personal Characteristics
- Age
- Ethnic Background
- Income
- Occupation
- Education
- Gender
- Religion
- Geography

Group Associations
- Family
- Friends
- Co-Workers

Political Factors
- Party Identification
- Candidates
- Issues

There are three broad categories that influence voters. One category includes personal characteristics of the vote. The second is groups such as family. The third involves party identification and the particular election. The table at the left lists each category. In real-life decisions, the categories interact. Personal characteristics and group associations combine. Together, they influence how a person views the candidates and issues.

"Let's try voting for the greater of the two evils this time and see what happens."

The following descriptions are **generalizations**. They show how voters in general are influenced. They may or may not apply to any single person.

Elections, Voting, and Voter Behavior 301

Lesson Summary

Voters are influenced by personal characteristics, family, and party identification, as well as by the issues of a particular election. Generalizations can be made about who votes and why, as well as which party they are likely to support. In the past 40 years, fewer people have voted for a straight party ticket. The major factor determining whether a person votes is political efficacy.

Lesson Objective

Students will learn about the behavior and characteristics of voters.

Focus Your Reading Answers

1 Factors influencing how a person votes include personal characteristics, groups such as family, party identification, and the particular election.

2 A regular voter tends to be a college graduate with a higher income and who is over forty-five, with more women than men voting. Married people vote more often than single people. So do those who have lived in a place for a long time and those who regularly attend religious services.

3 Nonvoters may believe that there is little hope for change or improvement, regardless of who wins an election. Others see no need for change. They may not believe that they can influence government by voting.

Words to Know

Discuss each of the following vocabulary terms with students.

A *generalization* is a statement that applies to people or situations in general, but may not apply to every or any person. One example of a *generalization* is that women tend to vote more than men.

Straight-ticket voting occurs when a voter selects one party's candidates only. Over the past 40 years, *straight-ticket voting* has declined.

Political efficacy is the sense that by voting, a person can influence government. *Political efficacy* is the factor that outweighs the others in determining if a person will vote.

Picturing Government

In the photograph on page 302, then-governor of California Gray Davis is shown at a 2003 no-recall rally. Davis was criticized for his handling of California's fiscal affairs, but voters had reelected him just the previous November for a second term. Despite his efforts and those of his supporters, voters recalled Davis and replaced him with movie star Arnold Schwarzenegger. Gray was the second governor in U.S. history ever to be recalled.

Extension

Challenge students to conduct polls to determine how their community mirrors the generalizations given in the lesson. Have them work in small groups to devise questionnaires that are not invasive or offensive. Then have them conduct polls at their places of worship, at home, with sports teams, and so on. Have them tabulate the results to see if they are typical and explain why they are or are not.

Former California governor Gray Davis at a Democratic campaign rally

In general, younger voters tend to vote Democratic. For most elections between 1960 and 2000, voters under thirty voted for Democratic candidates. African Americans have generally voted Democratic since the New Deal in the 1930s. Before that, they generally voted Republican, because Lincoln had been a Republican. Historically, immigrant groups have voted Democratic. However, since the mid-1990s, Latinos are voting Republican in larger numbers.

Voters who make higher incomes—$100,000 or more—tend to vote Republican. Doctors, lawyers, and business executives tend to vote Republican. This fits with the incomes of these jobs. A large number of college graduates tend to vote Republican. High school graduates tend to vote Democratic. Women tend to vote based on issues. More women vote for candidates who support abortion rights and health-care coverage, and who are against war. Based on these issues, slightly more women vote Democratic.

Protestants tend to vote Republican. Catholics and Jews tend to vote Democratic. In general, this matches the support that ethnic groups give the two parties. More immigrants are Catholic than Protestant.

Since the 1970s, southerners and westerners have been voting more heavily for Republicans. The Northeast and Midwest are generally more Democratic. Voters still tend to vote Democratic in large cities. Voters in small cities, the suburbs, and rural areas tend to vote Republican.

Most voters support the policies of one or the other of the major parties. As a result, they naturally tend to vote for that party's candidates. This is known as **straight-ticket voting**. In the last 40 years, candidates and issues have become more and more important to voters. They can cause voters to jump to the other party.

stop and think

Write profiles of the typical Democratic voter and the typical Republican voter. Work with a partner. Then discuss what could make a typical voter support a candidate from the other party.

302 Chapter 16

Stop and Think

Students' descriptions will vary but should incorporate information from the lesson, particularly page 302.

Cartoon Extension

Voter behavior is one of the areas that politicians and analysts try to understand. While many voters are registered members of a political party, voting decisions are often made at the last minute. Ask students what issues they think influence voter behavior, specifically what may change a voter's decision about whom to vote for in an upcoming election.

Voters and Nonvoters

The regular voter is the voter who votes in most, if not all, elections. Regular voters share certain characteristics. They tend to be college graduates with higher incomes and over forty-five. Those sixty-four and older have the highest rate of voting. More women than men vote regularly.

Married people are more likely to vote than single people. People who have lived in the same place for a long time are more likely to vote than those who move around. People who attend religious services regularly are also more likely to vote.

Millions of citizens, however, fail to vote in each election. They skip local, statewide, and national elections. In a recent presidential election, 100 million people—about one-half of the eligible population—did not vote. Why? Around the world, people fight and die for the freedom to vote. Why do millions of Americans give up their vote at every election?

Some people move right before an election and do not meet the residency requirement. Some people just never get around to registering. Others do not vote because they believe that little will change regardless of which party is in power. Some do not vote because they are happy with the current government and see no reason to take the time to vote.

Others do not vote because many nonvoters lack a sense of political efficacy. **Political efficacy** is the idea that a person can influence government by voting. Those who have a sense of political efficacy are more likely to vote.

Political scientists describe the average nonvoter as male, under thirty-five, single, and with a low level of education. Nonvoters generally work at unskilled jobs. However, there is one factor that outweighs all others in determining whether a person will vote. That factor is a sense of political efficacy.

Putting It All Together

Create a T-chart. Label one column "Voter." Label the other column "Nonvoter." Work with a partner to complete the T-chart and fill in information about each group. How can people develop a sense of political efficacy? Write a statement describing one thing a person could do to feel that his or her voice will be heard.

Picturing Government

The banner shown on page 303 is from the 2000 election but is timeless. Remind students of the importance of voting. Encourage students to register to vote if they are eligible.

Putting It All Together

Students' T-charts will vary but should be based on lesson content. Statements on political efficacy will vary.

Extension

Have students use library resources or the Internet to find the rate of voter participation in at least ten other nations. Have them make charts or graphs showing the results.

Participate in Government

Have students brainstorm areas of interests and list them on a sheet of paper. Then have them form groups based on at least one shared interest. Have them use the Internet or local sources to find groups that represent that interest, such as Greenpeace or the Sierra Club. Have them report to the class on the group's local activities.

Participate in Government

Join an Interest Group

An interest group is a group of people with common concerns who join together to influence government policy. There are different kinds of interest groups. Some accept members based on their shared economic interests or work. The Farm Bureau was organized for farmers. The American Dental Association accepts only dentists. Actors Equity accepts only actors.

However, there are some interest groups that anyone can join. These are the interest groups for special causes, such as the Audubon Society. People who want to protect birds join the society. National organizations like the Audubon Society often have state chapters that sponsor programs for members.

Not all interest groups are national. Some are local. The Sourlands Planning Council, for example, works to preserve the Sourland Mountains in central New Jersey. Local groups like this one are often nonprofit volunteer organizations. These groups have either no paid staff or a part-time paid director. The work is done by volunteers. To join, people pay small yearly dues. To get money to run programs, members hold fund-raisers like raffles.

These organizations are generally nonprofits. They pay no taxes to federal, state, and local government. Contributions to them are tax deductible. A taxpayer may claim any money donated to them as deductions on his or her income tax.

Joining interest groups that work to improve life is a good way to use free time. It gives people a good feeling to know they have helped others.

To Find Out About National, State, or Local Interest Groups:

- Check the local paper for news of meetings of groups.
- Check the Web for groups that deal with issues that interest you. See if they have state or local chapters.

Research Resources

Below is a list of reference books and Web sites that relate to the issues covered in this chapter. Students may wish to use these to further their research on ideas in the preceding lessons. Web site addresses may change over time. Use keyword searching on a major search engine to locate sites.

Reference Books:

Elizabeth Frost-Knappman. *Women's Suffrage in America*. Facts on File, 2004.

Arthur Meier. *Running for President: The Candidates and Their Images*. Mason Crest Publishers, 2005.

Arthur M. Schlesinger, ed. *History of American Presidential Elections 1789–2001*. Chelsea House Publications, 2001.

Web Sites:

The League of Women Voters offers information on current issues, as well as local links, on their Web site.

The Justice Department site offers information on various civil rights laws.

The Documents Center at the University of Michigan provides links to information on caucuses, political parties, primaries, the 2004 elections, and so forth.

Skill Builder

Interpret Political Cartoons

The goal of a political cartoonist is to make people think about an issue. A political cartoonist has a point of view. He or she may be for or against the issue and wants readers to agree with that point of view. The bias is usually easy to see.

Political cartoonists use symbols and caricatures to make their point. A symbol is a person or object that stands for something else. The usual symbol for the Democratic Party is a donkey. An elephant stands for the Republican Party.

A caricature is an exaggerated detail about a person. For example, cartoonists often exaggerate physical features of presidents. For a man in his seventies, President Ronald Reagan had a lot of hair. Cartoonists drew him with even more hair.

To analyze political cartoons:

1. Identify the topic of the cartoon and any figures.
2. Read any labels.
3. Identify what is happening in the cartoon.
4. Identify the point of view of the cartoonist.

Complete the following activities.

1 Who are the figures in the cartoon?

2 What does the text tell you about the topic?

3 What are the people doing in the cartoon?

4 What message is the cartoon sending?

Skill Builder

1 The figures in the cartoon are a candidate for election and voters.

2 The message is that the candidate will say anything to get elected.

3 They are listening to the candidate.

4 The cartoon sends the message that candidates try to appeal to all voters by using general statements that most people would agree with.

Recommended Reading

Below is a list of books that relate to the issues covered in this chapter. The numbers in parentheses indicate the related Thematic Strands of the National Council for the Social Studies (NCSS).

Deanne Durrett. *Right to Vote.* Facts on File, 2005. (VI, X)

Suzanne Levert. *The Electoral College.* Franklin Watts, 2005. (VI, X)

Ann Rossi. *Created Equal: Women Campaign for the Right to Vote, 1840–1920.* National Geographic Society, 2005. (VI, X)

Classroom Discussion

Discuss with students some of the broader topics covered in this chapter.

- How can elections be made fair for all?
- How can more people be encouraged to vote and take part in the political process?
- Should the United States have additional parties?
- How can campaign reform be successful?

Related Transparencies

T-18 Three-Column chart

T-19 Venn Diagram

T-20 Concept Web

Key Blacklines

Biography—George Gallup

CD Extension

Encourage students to use the reading comprehension, vocabulary reinforcement, and other activities on the student CD.

Getting Focused

Create a master list of questions that students would like answered. Then, as they are related to chapter content, either provide answers or invite students to research further.

Pre-Reading Discussion

1 Ask students to summarize the last news story related to politics that they read, watched, or heard. In the center of a concept web, write "Politics Now," adding their thoughts to get an overview of the current political climate.

2 Use the word *web* to discuss ways that students receive political news and how they evaluate what they hear.

Chapter 17 INTEREST GROUPS, PUBLIC OPINION, AND MASS MEDIA

Getting Focused

Skim this chapter to predict what you will be learning.

- **Read the lesson titles and subheadings.**
- **Look at the illustrations and read the captions.**
- **Review the vocabulary words and terms.**

After skimming the chapter, work with a partner to answer the following questions: What is this chapter about? What questions does this chapter answer? What questions do I still have about this chapter?

Mass media has a significant impact on public opinion.

Picturing Government

The photograph on page 306 is of news anchor Dan Rather rehearsing his final broadcast for *CBS Evening News,* in March 2005, after 24 years of television journalism. Rather resigned following a report questioning George W. Bush's service in the National Guard; the report's information was never proven. Rather had taken the position at CBS following the legendary Walter Cronkite, who retired in 1981. Rather was at the network's news program longer than any news anchor in history. He continued working for the network on *60 Minutes*, as well as on other news assignments. It was a transitional period for news anchors; NBC's *Nightly News* anchor Tom Brokaw, sixty-four, also announced his retirement in 2004. Peter Jennings, ABC's *World News Tonight* anchor, died of lung cancer at sixty-seven in August 2005.

LESSON 1

Interest Groups

Thinking on Your Own

Suppose you want to get your local government to turn an empty lot in your neighborhood into a playground. How could an interest group, made up of like-minded neighbors, help you accomplish this?

focus your reading

Explain how interest groups apply pressure to government.

What is the goal of economic interest groups?

Describe some special causes that interest groups support.

What is the difference between a public-interest group and other types of interest groups?

words to know

special interest

labor union

public-interest group

The American Association of Retired Persons (AARP), the National Rifle Association, the National Association of Manufacturers, and the American Medical Association are among the thousands of interest groups in the United States. An interest group is a group of people with common concerns who join together to influence government policy. This may sound like a political party. However, there are important differences between interest groups and political parties.

Political parties nominate candidates for public office. Interest groups do not nominate candidates. However, they often work for or against candidates during elections. For example, an interest group that favors public transportation may back, or support, candidates who will vote in favor of more money for railroads. Interest groups generally focus on one or just a few issues. Political parties work for solutions across a range of issues.

Organization of Interest Groups

Professional administrators manage most interest groups. Membership depends on the group. Unions are made up of union members. Professional groups are made up of doctors, lawyers, or accountants, for example. Other types of interest groups consist of people who share a common concern about civil rights, the environment, women's rights, or another issue.

Lesson Summary

Interest groups influence public policy on a particular issue. They are not the same as political parties. Interest groups can wield great power by raising funds during campaigns. Interest groups pressure government officials by testifying at hearings, advertising, writing letters, and demonstrating. Economic interest groups include business and trade groups, labor unions, farm-related groups, and professional associations. Public-interest groups work for public policies to benefit most or all Americans.

Lesson Objective

Students will learn about the workings of interest groups in political life.

Focus Your Reading Answers

1 Interest groups apply pressure to government by contributing to campaigns, giving testimony at hearings, advertising, writing letters to lawmakers, and demonstrating in front of the legislature.

2 The goal of economic interest groups is to affect government regulations and tax policies that have a bearing on how they do business and how much money they can earn.

3 Interest groups support special causes such as civil rights, the environment, women's rights, or different religious groups.

4 The major difference between a public-interest group and other interest groups is that a public-interest group works for the good of most or all Americans, not just one small group.

Words to Know

Introduce each of the following vocabulary terms to students.

Another term for interest groups is *special interests*. *Special interests* help to raise money for the candidates and issues they support.

A *labor union* is an organization that represents people working in the same industry or job. A *labor union* may be independent or part of a larger group such as the AFL-CIO.

A *public-interest group* works for public policies representing most or all Americans. People do not need to be part of a *public-interest group* to gain benefits from its actions.

Picturing Government

The photograph on page 308 shows a farmers' "tractorcade" protest in the nation's capital in 1977. Farmers wanted a revision of the 1977 Farm Bill, which didn't guarantee high enough farm prices for small farms, but encouraged large-scale farming. The protest was an effort of the American Agriculture Movement. Almost 3,000 farmers and their tractors arrived in Washington, D.C., to protest.

Stop and Think

Students' answers will vary.

Farmers protested high farm prices in Washington, D.C., during 1977.

Interest groups can be very powerful. Political Action Committees (PACs) and Section 527 groups of large national organizations raise millions of dollars during elections. These political arms of interest groups raise money for the campaign. These groups then expect the candidate, if elected, to support and vote in their favor on laws. A candidate may claim that his or her opponent is the "tool of special interests." Interest groups are the **special interests** that politicians sometimes complain about. In reality, few candidates today are elected without the support of at least some interest groups.

In addition to contributing to election campaigns, interest groups pressure government officials in other ways. Members testify at government hearings for or against proposed laws. Groups take out ads in newspapers and on television, cable, and radio to let officials know their views. Members write letters to their lawmakers. Sometimes they demonstrate in front of the legislature.

stop and think

You are still working to turn the empty lot into a playground. As you read, decide which kind of interest group described in this lesson would best be able to help you accomplish this goal. Write your answer in your notebook.

Economic Interest Groups

There are four categories of economic interest groups: (1) business and trade groups, (2) labor unions, (3) farm-related groups, and (4) professional associations. These groups are concerned about government policies that affect how they do business and how much money they earn. They lobby for and against government regulations and tax policies.

Each type of interest group may have a different view of the same public policy. As a result, groups sometimes clash. For example, the insurance industry wants Congress to rewrite a federal law about malpractice cases. These are lawsuits against doctors for the way they treated patients. The insurance trade group wants Congress to put a cap, or limit, on damages awarded in these lawsuits. Trial lawyers oppose the cap because they earn money on such cases. Both interest groups lobby Congress to protect their own interests.

Extensions

1 Have students skim the lesson looking for the names of specific interest groups. Ask students to find one that interests them, or to find a related interest group using library resources or the Internet . Ask them to find out the group's goals and history, as well as ways that young people can volunteer to help. Have them present their findings to the class by using the Student Presentation Builder on the student CD.

2 Invite students to create posters based on one of the four categories of economic interest groups. Have them design their posters to include basic information, but also to attract attention through color and bold, attractive design.

A trade group, or trade association, is made up of companies in the same industry. For example, the National Restaurant Association is made up of people who work in the restaurant business. Business groups such as the Chamber of Commerce include many different kinds of companies.

Labor unions represent people who work in the same job or the same industry. The AFL-CIO is the umbrella group made up of over 50 separate unions. These unions include the Retail Clerks International Union and the American Federation of State, County, and Municipal Employees. There are also independent unions such as the Fraternal Order of Police and the International Longshore and Warehouse Union. Issues that concern union members include the minimum wage, Social Security, tax credits for day care, and similar economic and social policies.

United Farm Workers president Arturo Rodriguez negotiated a pledge with Lucky stores that gave workers the right to organize.

Farm groups include the American Farm Bureau and the National Farmers Union (NFU). The Farm Bureau represents the interests of large farm owners. The NFU represents small farmers. In addition, producers of certain commodities are also organized into interest groups. Groups such as the American Meat Institute lobby state and federal government for regulations that favor their product over others.

Professional groups are groups such as the American Medical Association for doctors and the American Bar Association for lawyers. There are also much smaller groups, such as the National Science Teachers Association. Professional groups deal mostly with regulations related to their profession. For example, state bar associations determine how many hours of continuing education lawyers in their state must take each year. However, professional groups also lobby government about issues of importance to them.

Picturing Government

In the photograph on page 309, Arturo Rodriguez, the president of the United Farm Workers of America, (UFW), raises his fist in a victory salute. The union had just won the right to operate in farms that Lucky/American stores purchase from. Rodriguez is the second president of the UFW. After the death of his father-in-law, the legendary Cesar Chavez, in 1993, Rodriguez assumed the presidency. In the first year after Chavez's death, Rodriguez recruited some 10,000 new farm workers to become associate union members. A native Texan and a graduate of University of Michigan Ann Arbor with a master's degree in social work, Rodriguez first became active during the historic 1969 grape boycott.

Extension

Ask students to choose any two of the economic interest groups in the lesson and to make Venn diagrams showing how they are alike and how they are different. Remind students that even within the same categories, there will be differences. They may choose two groups in two different categories, or they may focus on differences and similarities within one category. Have students explain their Venn diagrams to a partner.

Picturing Government

The three photographs on page 310 showcase three different interest groups. At the top, volunteers working with the Sierra Club pull tires out of the mud flats of San Francisco Bay during low tide. The American Legion color guard marches in a Fourth of July parade in the center photograph. The bottom photograph shows the National Organization for Women (NOW) marching in Washington, D.C., in 2004, carrying the original 1978 NOW banner.

Putting It All Together

Students' three-column charts and choices of interest group will vary.

Interest Groups for Special Causes

In addition to economic interest groups, there are hundreds of other groups. Some are organized around environmental issues. These include the Sierra Club, the Audubon Society, and the National Wildlife Federation. Others, such as the National Women's Political Caucus and the National Organization for Women, support women's rights. Some support the civil rights of different groups, such as the National Association for the Advancement of Colored People and the Mexican American Legal Defense Fund. There is also the Children's Defense Fund.

Some issues create groups on both sides. Abortion and gun control are two such issues. The National Right-to-Life Committee protests abortion. The National Abortion and Reproductive Rights Action League supports a woman's right to choose it. Handgun Control, Inc., supports background checks on gun purchasers. The National Rifle Association opposes them.

The Sierra Club (top), the American Legion (center), and the National Organization for Women (bottom) are all interest groups that lobby the government to promote their causes.

Public-Interest Groups

A **public-interest group** works for public policies that will benefit all or most Americans. Whether people belong to the public-interest group does not matter to these organizations. The groups work for Americans in general, rather than just for their members. Common Cause is an example. It works for openness and fairness in the political system.

Putting It All Together

Create a table to organize information about interest groups. Make three columns, titled "Type of Group," "Purpose," and "Example." Which kind of interest group did you decide could best help you with your playground plan? Discuss your answer with a partner and include it in your notebook.

LESSON 2

Influencing Public Policy

Thinking on Your Own

Interest groups try to influence public policy. Do you know of others who try to do this? How do they work?

focus your reading

Who are lobbyists?

Describe how lobbyists work.

Why have Congress and state legislatures passed laws to regulate lobbyists?

words to know

lobbying

You just read about some ways that interest groups try to influence government. However, the most successful way is by lobbying lawmakers. **Lobbying** is making direct contact with lawmakers, their staffs, and government officials for the purpose of influencing the passage of laws and regulations.

Lobbyists are the people who work to sway public officials toward a particular opinion. Lobbyists get that name from the days when they would wait in the lobbies of Congress to speak to members of the House of Representatives or senators. Successful lobbyists are paid hundreds of thousands of dollars a year for their work. This means that interest groups with large numbers of members or members who are wealthy have the most influence. These organizations can afford to hire the best lobbyists.

Who Lobbyists Are

Some lobbyists set up their own businesses in Washington, D.C. Interest groups hire them on contract to work for them. Other lobbyists are employees of large organizations such as the major labor unions or the Chamber of Commerce. Lobbyists are not limited to trying to influence Congress. Interest groups also use lobbyists to persuade state lawmakers and officials to support their side of issues.

"WHO SAYS THE AMERICAN PEOPLE AREN'T SAVING ENOUGH?"

Lesson Summary

Lobbyists try to sway public officials toward a particular opinion. They once waited in the lobbies of Congress to speak to various legislators. Interest groups hire lobbyists. These may be former government employees who understand how government works from the inside. Lobbyists may also be public relations experts, lawyers, or former reporters. More than 14,000 lobbyists are registered with the federal government. Lobbyists give government officials information about issues and may testify before committees or write reports or legislation. About half of all bills have been written in part by lobbyists. Lobbyists also use mass media outlets to deliver their messages.

Lesson Objective

Students will learn about the work of lobbyists in influencing public policy.

Focus Your Reading Answers

1 Lobbyists are people working to sway public officials toward a particular opinion.

2 Lobbyists work through personal meetings with legislators or public officials to present their arguments. Lobbyists also raise money for candidates. They give government officials information about issues and may testify before committees or write reports or legislation.

3 Congress and state legislatures have passed laws to regulate lobbyists because of past abuses of power and instances of bribery and false testimony.

Words to Know

Discuss the vocabulary term with students.

Making direct contact with lawmakers, their staffs, and government officials to influence passage of legislation is called *lobbying*. Organizations and special interests spend money for experts in *lobbying*.

Lobbyists are often former government employees. They may have worked for executive departments or been senators or members of the House. These people know from the inside how government works. They have friends in agencies and among lawmakers. This closeness between lobbyists and officials can cause concerns about favoritism. As a result, federal law bars members of Congress from becoming lobbyists for at least one year after leaving Congress.

Public relations experts also work as lobbyists. An important job of lobbyists involves public relations. Sometimes lobbyists are lawyers or former reporters. Lobbyists work to make sure that the public images of, or ideas about, the groups they represent are favorable.

stop and think

What advantages do groups that can afford to hire lobbyists have over ordinary citizens? Discuss this question with a partner and write an answer in your notebook.

How Lobbyists Work

Lobbying is a huge industry. In a recent year, more than 14,000 lobbyists were registered with the federal government. By one estimate, more than two dozen groups work to protect Alaska's environment. On the other side, oil companies and their allies work to expand drilling in Alaska. Lobbyists represent all these groups.

Lobbyists use a variety of methods. First, they try to meet with lawmakers or public officials to tell their side of the issues. Lobbyists may make appointments to see lawmakers or officials in their offices. If the lobbyist knows a person well enough, the lobbyist may entertain the person at lunch or dinner. The federal government and state governments set limits on the amount and type of gifts that government officials may take from lobbyists.

The chairmen and CEOs of SBC, Inc.; AT&T; MCI, Inc.; and Nextel testify before Congress.

As you read in Chapter 16, PACs and Section 527 groups raise money for candidates. A campaign contribution does not mean the person will vote the way the interest group wants. However, it probably means the lobbyist for the group will get an appointment with the official.

Stop and Think

Students' ideas will vary but may suggest that groups that hire lobbyists have an advantage over ordinary citizens because lobbyists can be in physical proximity to the people they wish to influence and have an organization and money backing their efforts.

Picturing Government

In the photograph on page 312, chief executive officers (CEOs) of major United States communications companies testify before Congress. The House Committee on Energy and Commerce held hearings on "Competition in the Communications Marketplace" in March 2005. In addition to the six CEOs of communications companies, others who gave testimony included university professors and lobbyists.

Cartoon Extension

The cartoon on page 311 depicts a group of lobbyists all fighting to save a program or issue. Point out the briefcase in the foreground with "K Street" on it. Tell students that K Street, just blocks north of the White House, has traditionally been a street of corporate offices and trade associations where lobbyists would try to wield influence.

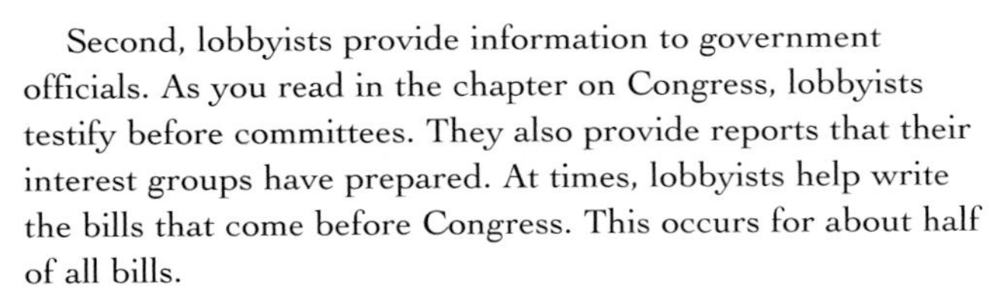

Second, lobbyists provide information to government officials. As you read in the chapter on Congress, lobbyists testify before committees. They also provide reports that their interest groups have prepared. At times, lobbyists help write the bills that come before Congress. This occurs for about half of all bills.

Third, lobbyists also use the members of the organizations that hire them. They ask members to write letters and e-mails to lawmakers in support of or against bills.

Fourth, lobbyists use the media to get their message to the public. They provide information for magazine and newspaper articles favorable to their side. They recruit well-spoken supporters to appear on television and cable news shows.

Regulating Lobbying

In the past, lobbyists and public officials were guilty of abusing their power. Officials took bribes from lobbyists. Lobbyists gave false testimony before committees. However, Congress and many states have moved to end these abuses.

In 1995, Congress passed the Lobbying Disclosure Act. It strengthened earlier regulations. All lobbyists and organizations that work to influence Congress must register with the federal government. They must list their clients and explain all their lobbying activities. Each lobbyist and group must file these reports twice a year.

A meeting of Florida lobbyists

Putting It All Together

Create a two-column chart. In the left column, list the methods lobbyists use to influence government. In the right column, evaluate these methods. Do they strengthen or weaken a democratic government? Then write a paragraph that summarizes your chart.

Picturing Government

The photograph on page 313 shows a group of lobbyists meeting in an office to discuss plans. Many former members of Congress have become lobbyists after leaving Capitol Hill. Between 1995 and 2004, nearly 300 former members of Congress registered as lobbyists, despite regulations prohibiting the lobbying of former colleagues for one year after leaving office. In addition to retaining political influence, lobbyists are better paid than members of Congress.

Putting It All Together

Students' charts and paragraphs will vary, but in the left column, they may include the following ideas:

personal meetings

raising money

giving information about issues

testifying before committees

writing reports

writing legislation

communicating through mass media

Extension

Ask students to use the Internet to find at least one former member of Congress who has become a lobbyist. Then ask them to write a brief position paper on whether this person's access to Congress should be limited.

Lesson Summary

The ideas and opinions of a significant number of Americans about political and government issues make up public opinion. Politicians learn of public opinion through written or oral comments, voting patterns, and opinion polls. Political socialization is the process of shaping attitudes and ideas about government. Factors important in this process include family, school, peer groups, social characteristics, mass media, events, and opinion leaders. Politicians track public opinion through personal contact, election results, and the media, as well as through interest groups and scientific polls.

Lesson Objective

Students will learn about the ways that political opinions are formed and studied.

Focus Your Reading Answers

1 A person's attitudes about government and political issues may be influenced by family, school, peer groups, social characteristics, mass media, events, and opinion leaders.

2 Politicians measure public opinion through scientific polls.

3 The process of scientific polling involves choosing a universe, selecting a random sample, writing questions, conducting the poll, and analyzing the data.

LESSON 3

Forming and Measuring Public Opinion

Thinking on Your Own

The news media often reports the results of public opinion polls. You have your own opinions about public issues. Why do you take those positions and not others? Do other people influence your opinions? If so, who? What do you know about public opinion polls and polling? Write three statements in your notebook about public opinion polls and polling.

focus your reading

What influences a person's attitudes about government and political issues?

Explain how politicians measure public opinion.

Describe the process of scientific polling.

words to know

public opinion
political socialization
midterm election
scientific poll
universe
sample
random sample
margin of error

What is public opinion? **Public opinion** is the ideas and attitudes that a significant number—or large amount—of Americans have about government and political issues. The phrase "significant number" is important. There is no single public agreement in this country about any political issue. This helps to explain why there is a need for political parties.

Even within the two major parties, however, members hold different opinions about issues. Some Republicans do not believe that the federal government should set education standards. However, the No Child Left Behind Act does exactly that. It was proposed by a Republican president, George W. Bush, and supported by a majority of Republican members of Congress.

Public opinion reflects what most people who express their opinions believe. This is why the phrase "significant number" is important. Politicians look for consensus, or a general agreement, on an issue by a large number of people.

Words to Know

Discuss each of the vocabulary terms with students.

The ideas and opinions that a significant number of people have about political or government issues are called *public opinion*. *Public opinion* can be expressed in spoken or written form.

The shaping of a person's attitudes and ideas about government is called *political socialization*. Factors that influence *political socialization* include family, peer groups, and schools.

The *midterm election* occurs between presidential elections. The results of a *midterm election* tell politicians about *public opinion*.

How do politicians determine public opinion? To be considered part of public opinion, a person must express his or her views. This expression can be spoken or written. It can also be expressed by marching in a protest and by voting. The outcomes of elections tell politicians whether voters support certain policies or not. Even before elections, opinion polls can tell politicians much about how the public thinks.

ideas to remember

Factors influencing political attitudes:

- family
- schools
- peer groups
- social characteristics: age, gender, income level, ethnic group, region of the country
- mass media
- opinion leaders: the president, Congress, interest groups
- events

How Attitudes About Government Are Shaped

What a person thinks about government is shaped by many factors. The Ideas to Remember box lists the major factors that influence political attitudes. These factors are similar to the ones that influence voting behavior. The process of shaping one's ideas and attitudes about government is called **political socialization**.

The first and possibly most important factor is family. Parents' views about government and their political party, if any, greatly influence people. More than two-thirds of adults belong to the same political party as their parents.

The second influence is school. Schools teach basic civic values. Children learn to say the Pledge of Allegiance. Courses teach about the nation's political system. U.S. history courses teach about the clash of ideas and the resulting compromises. These experiences and knowledge help to shape people's ideas about what government should do.

Cartoon Extension

Point out the folded flag that the woman in the cartoon on page 315 is clutching as she listens to the evening news in 2005. Have students identify the cartoon's allusions: folded flags, which are often given to next of kin when a military person is killed; peace activist Cindy Sheehan, who camped at the President George W. Bush's Crawford, Texas, property asking to talk to the vacationing president about the war in Iraq; Lance Armstrong, Texas native and winner of the Tour de France for the seventh consecutive time in 2005; and President Bush, who was bicycling during that vacation and did not meet with Sheehan.

Ideas to Remember Extension

Review the ideas listed, further explaining difficult vocabulary words. Have students create graphic organizers in their notebooks to help them visualize the seven factors influencing political attitudes.

Words to Know, continued

A *scientific poll* follows certain rules for establishing the accuracy of the poll. One way to measure *public opinion* is by taking a *scientific poll*. The group of people to be studied is the *universe* of the poll. A *universe* might be all the residents of a major city between certain ages. A *sample* is a small group of a *universe*. The usual size of a *sample* is about 1,500 people. A *random sample* means that everyone in the *universe* has a chance to be selected. The *random sample* does not target certain groups. The percentage measuring the poll's accuracy is known as the *margin of error*. The *margin of error* is expressed in percentage points.

Picturing Government

Former director of the Federal Emergency Management Agency (FEMA) Michael Brown is shown in the photograph on page 316. At the time of Hurricane Katrina, in 2005, which devastated the Gulf Coast and the city of New Orleans, Brown was the director of FEMA. Although Brown resigned on September 12, 2005, he remained on the FEMA payroll for another month. While Brown accepted some blame for the federal government's slow response, he also faulted New Orleans's mayor and Louisiana's governor.

Public opinion after Hurricane Katrina in 2005 led to the resignation of FEMA director Michael Brown.

A peer group is a person's circle of friends. Friends tend to have similar views. Constant contact among friends reinforces those views. There is no one with a different opinion to challenge those views.

Some members of the public are more concerned about some issues than others. These issues, therefore, have a greater influence on their political views. For example, a voter in his or her sixties will be more interested in laws affecting Social Security than a thirty-year-old.

The mass media is any form of communication that reaches a large number of people. Television, cable, blogs, radio, newspapers, magazines, CDs, movies, videos, and books are the major media. They both reflect public opinion and help to shape it. The aftermath of Hurricane Katrina in 2005 is an example. The media showed hours of video and printed pages of stories and photos about the lack of federal response for the victims in New Orleans. The public responded with food, water, money, and clothes for the victims. It also turned sharply against the Bush administration. The media then reported this shift.

The media, especially television networks, covers the president's activities daily. He or she uses this coverage to promote policies and programs. This is a major help to the president and his or her party in shaping public opinion. Other federal officials, as well as state and local officials, also use the media to get their ideas out. Personal contact and mailings to constituents—members of an elected official's district—are other ways they get their views in front of the public.

Events also shape the public's view of the proper role of government. Before the Great Depression, the federal government had a limited role in people's lives. However, the suffering of people during the Depression changed many people's views. They came to believe that only the federal government had the resources to help pull the nation out of the Depression. During the civil rights movement, many

Extensions

1 Choose a current controversial issue in the news, or have students select one on their own. Ask them to use library resources or the Internet to find the major opinions of both Republicans and Democrats on the issue. Have them look for dissenting opinions from each party. Ask them to create a table or other graphic organizer to summarize what they learned.

2 Invite students to write a letter to a member of Congress or a state legislator expressing their opinion on one of the issues identified. Review with students the proper salutation and form for such a letter.

stop and think

Draw a table with three columns. Label the first column "Factors Influencing Political Attitudes." Label column two "Explanation." Label column three "Example." Work with a partner to fill in the details for each column.

Americans turned to the federal government to force states and communities to end discrimination. However, times change and with them, people's views. Public opinion swung the other way in the 1980s. As President Ronald Reagan said, "Government is not the solution to our problem. Government *is* the problem."

Measuring Public Opinion

Politicians monitor public opinion in a number of ways. Their staffs read their mail and e-mail to learn what constituents think about issues. Members of Congress make regular trips home to talk with their constituents. The president often announces a new program by visiting the state that will benefit from it. At these stops, he or she meets with local and state officials. Sometimes ordinary citizens are invited to meet with him or her. State and local officials also meet both formally and informally with voters. All of these methods are known as personal contact.

The results of elections also tell politicians about public opinion. The election held between presidential elections is called a **midterm election**. In the midterm election of 1998, voters increased the number of Democrats in the House of Representatives. This was considered a message to Republicans. Since the 1950s, voters in midterm elections had never increased the number of House members from the president's party.

The media both shapes public opinion and reports it. Politicians read papers and watch television news just like voters. They can easily see if their political message is getting out to people. Politicians also listen to interest groups. However, they are aware that interest groups represent only a portion of the public. They do not speak for the general public, only for their members.

Stop and Think

Students' three-column tables will vary but should reflect the information on pages 315–316.

Extensions

1 Ask students to check the Internet or another source to find out how each party fared in the most recent midterm elections. Did many seats in Congress change parties? Have them show their findings in a chart or graph. Interested students may wish to track midterm elections over a decade and graph the changes.

2 Ask students to view two different newscasts on the Web, in a newspaper, or on television. Have them track a national or international story of interest to them. Ask them to look for differences in the accounts. You may wish to suggest they select a national and local media outlet or a mainstream and public broadcasting source for greater contrast.

Picturing Government

In the photograph on page 318, a woman votes in California in 2003 using a punch card machine. California was one of several states that sued following the 2000 election, claiming that the controversy over hanging chads caused a disproportionate number of votes by minorities (who often vote Democrat) to be discounted.

Scientific Polling

A better way to read public opinion is scientific polling. A **scientific poll** asks voters for their opinions about candidates, issues, and government policies. However, pollsters do not just ask any voter any question. The word *scientific* is important.

Many voter polls take place outside polling places after voters have cast their ballots.

First, pollsters choose a **universe**. This is the group of people the pollster wants to study. It may be all voters in New York City or all voters in New York City between ages twenty-five and fifty. Second, pollsters select a **sample**. This is a small group of the universe. Usually, pollsters question about 1,500 people to determine how the general public feels about an issue. The sample is called a **random sample**. Everyone in the universe has an equal chance of being selected.

The third step is writing the questions to ask voters. This is a very important step because the questions must be carefully worded. They cannot lead people to give a certain answer. Suppose the question was "Would you vote to give aid to developing nations?" Most people would answer "yes." Suppose the question was "Would you vote to give aid to developing nations if it meant raising taxes?" The answer then is not so easy to answer. It is a better question, however. It will show how strong or weak support is for aid to developing nations.

The fourth step is conducting the poll. Most interviews today are done over the telephone. They can last from three to 15 minutes, depending on the number of questions. If the questions are too long, the person being interviewed may become confused. Too many choices for the answer may also be confusing. These are all problems that pollsters recognize. However, telephone polls are relatively inexpensive and a fast way to test issues and candidates.

Extension

Following the vote-counting controversy in the 2000 election, a federal law later mandated that all states replace their punch card or lever voting systems no later than 2006. Interested students may wish to find out more about this controversy, using library resources or the Internet.

ideas to remember

Scientific polling includes the following steps:

- choose the universe for the poll
- select the sample
- write valid questions
- conduct interviews
- analyze the results

The final step is analyzing all the data from interviews. The answers are fed into computers. Pollsters analyze the results and report their findings. They always indicate the **margin of error**. This percentage is a measure of the poll's accuracy. Suppose the results are accurate "plus or minus 3 percentage points." This means that 3 percent more or 3 percent fewer people in the poll universe may agree with a statement.

Putting It All Together

In your notebook, write a summary paragraph about public opinion. It should 1) define public opinion, 2) explain how opinions are formed, and 3) describe how public opinions are measured. Share your paragraph with a partner.

Putting It All Together

Students' paragraphs will vary. You may wish to use the lesson summary on page 314 as a guide.

Reading for Understanding

1 The challenger will pick up enough of the undecided votes to win.

2 If the voter has gone that far in the election cycle and is still undecided, that person will probably want a change.

3 Answers will vary.

Primary Source

What Polls Say About the Undecided Voter

Reports of opinion polls generally focus on which candidate is leading. However, there is also the category of undecided voters. These are the people who have not made up their minds about whom to vote for. Larry Hugick, chairman of Princeton Survey Research Associates, addressed the importance of undecided voters in the following excerpt from a news article.

reading for understanding

1. What will probably happen if the final poll shows a tight race with a large number of undecided voters?
2. Explain what is meant by "gone that far."
3. Do you agree with Mr. Hugick's reasoning about why undecideds vote for the challenger?

"Mr. Hugick's favorite last-minute indicator concerns the lingering undecided voters. . . . [I]f the final poll [before the election] is 48 percent to 48 percent, with 4 percent undecided, it is probable that the [challenger] will pick up enough of that vote to come out on top. . . .

"'What it seems is that if you are undecided at the very end, you are more likely just trying to figure out if you want the guy to stay in office. If you have gone that far, you probably really want a change.'"

—Robert Strauss, "As Far as Political Polls, N.J. Owns the Pole Position," *The New York Times*, October 31, 2004.

Ideas to Remember Extension

Review the ideas listed, further explaining difficult vocabulary words. Have students create graphic organizers in their notebooks to help them visualize the five steps of scientific polling.

Lesson Summary

The media is an important influence on politics in the United States. The media, by deciding what stories to broadcast, helps to influence the public agenda. It also influences the outcomes of presidential elections through televised debates, advertisements, and time devoted to each candidate. C-SPAN broadcasts the daily workings of Congress; most members of Congress have a press secretary to communicate their activities. The media also covers major trials, particularly in the Supreme Court.

Lesson Objective

Students will learn about the effect of mass media on political life.

Focus Your Reading Answers

1 The media influences the public's view of issues by helping to set the public agenda and by covering presidential elections, congressional activities, and the Supreme Court.

2 The media has become so important in presidential elections because media coverage can be used to make an impact on voters. Television ads and debates put forth the candidates' ideas and personal style. Television also pays the most attention to front-runners.

3 The media interacts with Congress and the Supreme Court through press secretaries and reporters, as well as through C-SPAN coverage.

LESSON 4

Mass Media

Thinking on Your Own

Review the definition of *mass media* in the Glossary. How many forms of mass media have you used in the past week? Make a list in your notebook.

focus your reading

How does the media influence the public's view of issues?

Why has the media become so important in presidential elections?

Describe how the media interacts with Congress and the Supreme Court.

words to know

public agenda

The media, or mass media, is an important influence on U.S. politics. Most Americans get their news about government and political issues from television, newspapers, radio, and magazines. Since the 2004 election, the Internet has grown in importance as a source of information.

You have read about some of the ways that the media influences political socialization and public opinion. The media also influences the public agenda and presidential elections. The media covers the activities of Congress and the decisions of the Supreme Court.

The Media's Influence on the Public Agenda

The **public agenda** is a list of societal problems that both political leaders and the general public agree need government attention. Over the years, these issues have included health care for the elderly and the poor, civil rights for African Americans, and protection of women's rights. The federal government responded with Medicare and Medicaid to provide health care. The Civil Rights Act of 1964 and the Voting Rights Act of 1965 ended racial discrimination. Women's rights are protected through Title IX and other laws, regulations, and Court rulings. Each time, the media puts these issues before the public.

Words to Know

Discuss the vocabulary term with students.

A list of societal problems requiring governmental attention is the *public agenda*. Protecting women's rights and health care for the elderly are examples of the *public agenda*.

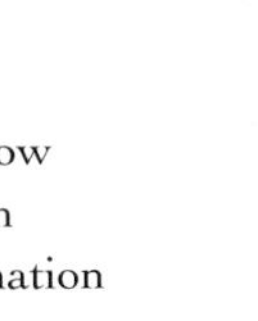

The media's choice of what to show and what not to show helps set the public agenda. When the media focuses on an issue, people begin to think about it. People absorb information through the perspective of their own bias—conservative, liberal, or moderate. The media usually does not make people think about issues in a certain way. However, the media does get people to think and talk about issues.

Sometimes this results in shifts in people's attitudes and values. Television, cable television, and video and photos posted on the Web can have a great impact on people. Even before the time of cable and bloggers, television coverage of the war in Vietnam caused a shift in attitude in the country from prowar to antiwar. This shift affected the 1968 presidential election. Democratic president Lyndon Johnson chose not to run for reelection. Republican candidate Richard Nixon won. One reason was Nixon's campaign promise to get the United States out of Vietnam. Political leaders pay attention to what the media is saying.

The Media's Influence on Presidential Elections

Presidents use the media to explain and promote their policies and programs to the American public. Reporters are assigned to cover the president. The media also plays a role in who becomes president.

A good example is the 1960 presidential election. Vice President Richard Nixon had the advantage of being vice president. John Kennedy was a senator from Massachusetts. The 1960 election was the first presidential election that included televised debates. Nixon sweated heavily under the hot lights and looked nervous. Kennedy looked confident and at ease. Those who listened to the debate on radio thought Nixon won. Those who watched it on television believed Kennedy won. Kennedy went on to win the election. Many thought it was because of his performance in the debates.

The 1960 presidential debate

Picturing Government

The photograph on page 321 shows the first televised presidential debate, between John F. Kennedy, at left, and Richard M. Nixon, at right. The moderator for the debate, Frank McGee, is shown between the contenders; he was an NBC news correspondent. The October 1960 debate was key in giving Kennedy the victory.

Extension

Have students choose a recent historic event and determine how the media shaped America's understanding of it. For example, how did news coverage shape public perception after 9/11? Encourage students to share their findings with the class, using video clips if possible, or creating storyboards to explain the effect of media on the topic.

Bill Clinton campaigning on television in 1991

There are three ways that television shapes presidential elections. First, little-known candidates can make an impact on voters. Second, candidates' television ads reach more people than ads in newspapers. Third, television networks put more resources into covering the front-runners in primaries.

Bill Clinton's campaign for president in 1992 is a good example of how television can influence elections. In 1988, Governor Bill Clinton of Arkansas had delivered a speech at the Democratic National Convention. He used this speech to begin building name recognition around the nation and won the election.

stop and think

Choose two current events that represent how the media impacts people's decisions or choices. Write a two-line newspaper headline for each event. Then explain how the media influenced the event.

The Media and Congress and the Supreme Court

Most media coverage for members of Congress is done in their home state or district. Most also have a press secretary whose job it is to get news coverage of the member's activities.

C-SPAN broadcasts daily from the houses of Congress.

Back in Washington, most work of Congress is done in committee meetings and hearings. Some hearings get news coverage because of the topic of the hearings. Since 1986, C-SPAN has broadcast the daily sessions of the House of Representatives and the Senate.

Some state and local courts allow cameras to broadcast trials. The federal court system does not. However, reporters attend daily sessions and report what happened. The media also reports on the hearings that take place before the Supreme Court and then on the Court's decisions.

Putting It All Together

Create a concept web to show the groups with which the media interacts. Draw a large circle in the center of a sheet of paper. Label the circle "The Media." Draw smaller circles for each group with which the media interacts.

Picturing Government

Then-governor of Arkansas Bill Clinton is shown in the photograph at the top of page 322, playing a saxophone at a fund-raiser in 1991. Clinton, a jazz fan, has continued his interest in music. Along with trumpeter Wynton Marsalis, Clinton is part of an effort to save the historic Apollo Theater in Harlem. Clinton has also praised jazz for bringing together white people and black people in a time when they did not find other common ground, and suggested jazz as a tool for freedom.

Stop and Think

Students' choices of events and subsequent headlines will vary but should reflect the influence of media impact.

Picturing Government

The photograph at the bottom of page 322 shows the adoption of the first article of impeachment against President Bill Clinton in 1998. Major television networks may suspend regular programming to cover events of national importance, such as the Watergate trials, the Clarence Thomas hearings, or the Clinton impeachment proceedings.

Putting It All Together

Students' concept webs will vary but may include the president, Congress, and the courts.

Analyze Public Opinion Polls

Polls measure the public's opinion about an issue at a point in time. They are a snapshot of what Americans think. Not every American can be asked the questions. As a result, scientific sampling is used to find a representative group of people.

It is important to know the following information about any poll you hear or read about:

1. when the poll was taken
2. who was asked the questions
3. how large the sample was
4. what the margin of error is
5. what the questions were

Newspaper articles about poll data should provide this information. A long article about an important issue may have a separate box titled something like "How the Poll Was Conducted." It should tell you items 1 through 4. The article may also reprint some of the most important questions. If the article is brief, look for the same information in the body of the article.

The national poll was conducted by Research Polls, Inc., from Friday night through Monday night. The telephone poll reached 1,251 adults. The responses of racial, ethnic, or gender groups were not separated out. The margin of sampling error is plus or minus 3 percentage points.

Knowing when a poll was taken is important. It tells you how fresh the issue was in people's minds. Before an election, pollsters conduct polls right up to two or three days before the election. They hope to find out if any last-minute events have changed voters' minds.

To Be an Informed Poll Reader:

- Read the complete news article to find out how the poll was conducted.
- Check the Web site of the polling organization or the newspaper or television news program to find out more about the poll.

Participate in Government

Have students identify a current issue and a poll about it, using library resources or the Internet. Ask them to follow the steps listed in the box and to identify the five information items listed in the second paragraph. Allow students a day to role-play as reporters to present their findings to the class.

Research Resources

Below is a list of reference books and Web sites that relate to the issues covered in this chapter. Students may wish to use these to further their research on ideas in the preceding lessons. Web site addresses may change over time. Use keyword searching on a major search engine to locate sites.

Reference Books:

Paul S. Herrnson, ed. *The Interest Group Connection: Electioneering, Lobbying, and Policymaking in Washington*. CQ Press, 2005.

Kelle S. Sisung, ed. *Special Interest Group Profiles for Students*. Thomson Gale, 1999.

Web Sites:

The Public Broadcasting Service site (PBS) has many links to politics and mass media.

The Web site for the Center for Lobbying in the Public Interest offers sections on strategies, resources, the law, and rationale for lobbying.

The Polling Report site reports nonpartisan, independent tracking of American public opinion on current issues and elections past and to come, with a current ongoing poll on its home page.

Skill Builder

1 (a) $147 million
(b) $42 million

2 yes

3 Very, Somewhat, Not Too, Not At All

Recommended Reading

Below is a list of books that relate to the issues covered in this chapter. The numbers in parentheses indicate the related Thematic Strands of the National Council for the Social Studies (NCSS).

Alison Cooper. *Media Power? (Viewpoints).* Sea to Sea Publications, 2005. (VI, X)

Geoffrey M. Horn. *Political Parties, Interest Groups, and the Media.* World Almanac Library, 2003. (VI, X)

Skill Builder

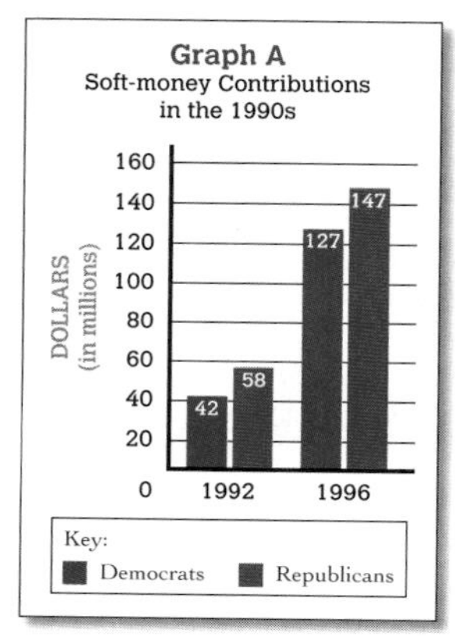

Analyze a Bar Graph

A bar graph shows data about different subjects at the same time. Graph A is the typical bar graph. The quantity, or amount, is listed along the left, or vertical, axis of the graph. The subjects are shown along the bottom, or horizontal, axis. The time period may be given in the title, or along the side or bottom of the graph.

Sometimes, poll data is shown on a different kind of bar graph. The results of a few questions are pulled out of the survey. The question is stated and the results are placed on a horizontal graph. This type of bar graph is used to show percentages of responses. Graphs B and C are examples of this type of graph.

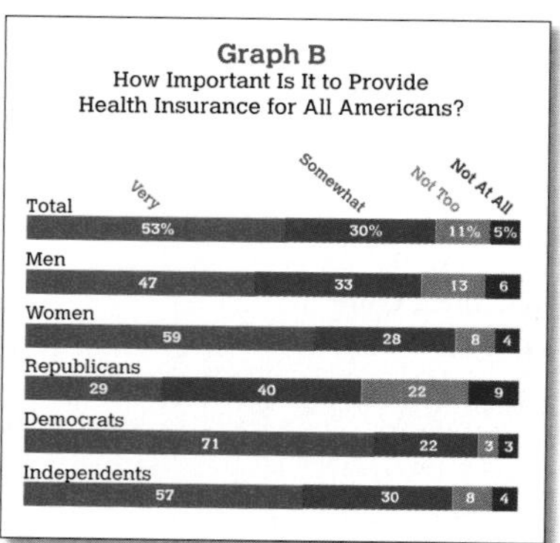

Graph C
Did Candidate A Address Your Concerns in the Debate?

	Yes	No
Total	43%	57%
Men	62	38
Women	30	70
Republicans	78	22
Democrats	28	72
Independents	45	55

To read a bar graph:

1. Read the title of the graph.
2. Examine each axis to learn the subjects.
3. Examine the labels and the data.
4. What can you determine about the relationships between bars?

Complete the following activities.

1 How much soft money was raised (a) by the Republicans in 1996? (b) by the Democrats in 1992?

2 Did more men than women answer "yes" to the question in Graph C?

3 What were the four answers that people could have given to the question in Graph B?

Classroom Discussion

Discuss with students some of the broader topics covered in this chapter.

- How should contributions from interest groups be managed so as not to give these groups unfair advantages over individual citizens?
- How can lobbyists be more effectively regulated?
- What are the drawbacks to the numerous political polls presented in the news media?
- In what ways is the media responsible to the American public?

UNIT 7 PUBLIC POLICY

Public policy is the goals that government sets for itself in order to solve problems. The national government sets public policy for the nation as a whole. The state and local governments set public policy at the state and local levels.

The executive branch of the federal government turns public policy into public programs. Congress passes the laws that set up the programs. These laws lay out the goals and describe what is to be done. The executive departments and agencies are responsible for putting these laws into practice. They create the operations that make the laws work on a day-to-day basis. How is all this paid for? Most money to fund programs comes from taxes.

Picturing Government

The photograph on page 325 shows the Thomas Jefferson Memorial in Washington, D.C. It is constructed of materials from several states: limestone from Indiana for the ceiling, gray marble from Missouri for the pedestal, Danby imperial marble from Vermont for the exterior walls and columns, Georgian white marble for the interior walls, and Tennessee pink marble for the interior floor. Congress passed a joint resolution to form a Thomas Jefferson Memorial Commission in 1934. Ironically, rather than holding a competition for a design honoring the man so dedicated to democracy, the commission unilaterally chose architect John Russell Pope. Controversies, ranging from the expense during the Depression years to the loss of cherry trees, continued to plague the project. Nevertheless, the building opened in 1942 and was dedicated the following year.

Unit Objectives

After studying this unit, students will be able to

- explain how the federal government finances its programs
- describe the domestic policies of the United States
- analyze the goals of United States foreign policy

Unit 7 focuses on public policy.

Chapter 18, Financing Government Policies, examines the federal budget and other financial instruments.

Chapter 19, Domestic Policy: Education, Housing, Transportation, and Security, explores the key federal policies in education, housing, transportation, and security.

Chapter 20, Foreign Policy and National Defense, explains the goals and tools of foreign policy.

Getting Started

Have a student read aloud the title of the unit and the two paragraphs that follow it on page 325. Ask students to create K-W-L charts for the unit. Encourage them to add to the chart as they read Unit 7. During the study of the unit, be sure to have students check their progress.

Chapter

18 FINANCING GOVERNMENT POLICIES

Related Transparencies

T-11 Types of Taxes Collected by the Federal Government

T-18 Three-Column Chart

T-20 Concept Web

Key Blacklines

Biography—Ben Bernanke

CD Extension

Encourage students to use the reading comprehension, vocabulary reinforcement, and other activities on the student CD.

Getting Focused

Poll the class to see which government programs they believe should receive more or less funding. Then select a program and divide the class into two groups based on whether they oppose or are in favor of more funding for that program. Have the groups prepare a debate or symposium and present it in class.

Getting Focused

Skim this chapter to predict what you will be learning.

- **Read the lesson titles and subheadings.**
- **Look at the illustrations and read the captions.**
- **Examine the map, table, and graphs.**
- **Review the vocabulary words and terms.**

Taxes pay for government programs, such as defense and Social Security. Make a list of all the government programs that you know about. Then indicate which program you believe should receive more or less tax support by placing a plus (+) or a minus (-) beside each.

Policies related to federal taxation and spending are decided by lawmakers in Washington, D.C.

Pre-Reading Discussion

1 Discuss with students how big a role they feel the federal government should have in the economy. For example, should the government raise and lower interest rates or impose tariffs?

2 Ask students to identify four areas they feel should be most important in the federal budget. First, you may wish to have them brainstorm some of the areas that the federal government does in fact support, such as highways and libraries.

LESSON 1

Taxing and Borrowing

Thinking on Your Own

Make two lists from the Words to Know for this lesson. In one list, include the words you already know. In the other, list those you do not know. Then use each word that you know in a sentence. Write the sentence in your notebook.

focus your reading

What types of taxes can the federal government collect?

Why does the federal government borrow money?

words to know

taxes
progressive tax
exemption
dependents
payroll tax
protective tariff
tax credit
regressive tax
deficit
surplus
national debt

Taxes are payments by individuals and businesses to support the activities of government. The power of the federal government to tax comes from Article I, Section 8, of the Constitution and from the Sixteenth Amendment. Article I states that the government may levy and collect "Taxes, Duties, Imposts, and Excises to pay the Debts and provide for the common Defence and general Welfare." In 1895, the United States Supreme Court ruled that Congress could not tax incomes. The Sixteenth Amendment, ratified in 1913, gave Congress that power. In a recent year, the federal government collected almost $1.8 billion in taxes. This was about $6,690 per person.

Types of Taxes

Congress decides what to tax and what the tax rates should be. The first pie graph on page 329 shows how much money each tax raises. The second pie graph shows how the government spends the money.

Residents in a Manhattan post office rush to file their tax returns before the midnight deadline on April 15.

Lesson Summary

The Constitution gives the federal government the right to tax businesses and people. Congress decides the tax rates and what is taxed. Since 1913, people and businesses have paid a progressive income tax based on their ability to pay. Tax credits may be used to lower taxes. Everyone is taxed at the same rate for social insurance taxes, which are regressive. The government has generally run a deficit each year and borrows money to keep funding programs. This creates a national debt of trillions of dollars.

Lesson Objective

Students will learn about the government's policies on taxing and borrowing.

Focus Your Reading Answers

1 The federal government can collect income taxes from corporations and individuals, social insurance tax, excise taxes, customs duties, estate taxes, and gift taxes.

2 The federal government borrows money when it needs to spend more than it collects in taxes and other revenue sources.

Words to Know

Introduce each of the following vocabulary terms to students.

Explain that *taxes* are the payments that people and businesses make to support the government's activities. The right to levy *taxes* comes from the Constitution. Tax based on a person's or business's ability to pay is called a *progressive tax*. The income tax is an example of a *progressive tax*.

An *exemption* is given for a person depending on the person being taxed for food, clothing, and shelter. Children are the major *exemptions*. Another term for *exemptions* is *dependents*. Regulations determine the maximum age of most *dependents*.

Tax collected to pay for major social programs is a *payroll tax*. Both employees and employers must contribute to a *payroll tax*.

A *protective tariff* is a high customs duty placed on goods coming into the United States. A *protective tariff* is designed to protect businesses.

Picturing Government

The photograph on page 326 shows several key structures on the National Mall at night. In the background is the Capitol Building. At the center is the Washington Monument. In 1833, a group of private citizens formed the Washington National Monument Society. The idea of an Egyptian obelisk won favor at an 1836 design competition. The official dedication occurred in 1885. The Lincoln Memorial is at the far left. A classical Greek design was chosen to honor the president who wanted to defend democracy. The words of two speeches are inscribed on the walls: the Gettysburg Address and the Second Inaugural Address.

Table Extension

Ask students to use the table on page 328 to answer the following questions.

- What are some examples of items subject to excise taxes? (gasoline, tires, cigarettes, liquor, airlines, and long-distance telephone calls)
- Which tax helps to pay for Medicare and unemployment? (social insurance tax)
- What is another term for customs duties? (tariffs)

Income taxes are **progressive taxes**. They are based on a person's or business's ability to pay. The president of a corporation pays at a higher rate of taxation than a teacher. Current rates for the personal income tax range from 10 to 35 percent.

Types of Taxes Collected by the Federal Government

Tax	Definition	Explanation
Individual income tax	Tax on a person's income minus exemptions and deductions	An **exemption** is for a person who depends on the person being taxed for food, clothing, and shelter. Children are the main exemptions. Exemptions are also called **dependents**. Deductions include interest on mortgage payments and state and local taxes that a person pays.
Corporate income tax	Tax on a corporation's income minus expenses and deductions	Expenses and deductions are the cost of doing business.
Social insurance taxes	Taxes collected from employees and employers to pay for major social programs; also known as **payroll taxes** and social insurance taxes	The major social programs are Social Security, Medicare, and the unemployment compensation program. The taxes are taken from a worker's pay. The employer pays a similar amount.
Excise taxes	Taxes on the manufacture, transportation, sale, or use of goods and performance of services	Examples of goods and services that are taxed are gasoline, tires, cigarettes, liquor, airlines, and long-distance telephone calls.
Customs duties	Taxes on goods brought into the country for sale; also called tariffs	Customs duties are used to raise money for the government. They can also be used to protect U.S. businesses. For example, a high duty is placed on imported shoes or grain. This raises the price to U.S. buyers. High customs duties are also called **protective tariffs**.
Estate tax	Tax on the property and wealth over $1.5 million of a person who dies	The tax applies to less than 3–5 percent of estates. The tax does not apply to estates left by spouses to each other.
Gift tax	Tax on gifts above $11,000 to any one person given in any one year	This tax is meant to keep people from getting around the estate tax. Before this tax, they could give away all their money and property so there was nothing left to tax when they died.

Words to Know, continued

A *tax credit* can be used to lower *taxes*. Day care is an example of a *tax credit*.

When everyone pays the same rate, the tax is called a *regressive tax*. The social insurance tax is an example of a *regressive tax*.

When more money is spent than collected, a *deficit* occurs. The federal government has run a *deficit* in most years since the 1950s. A *surplus* occurs when more money is collected than spent. The government ran a *surplus* during some of the Clinton years.

The *national debt* is the sum of all the money that the United States has borrowed. By 2005, the *national debt* was nearly eight trillion dollars.

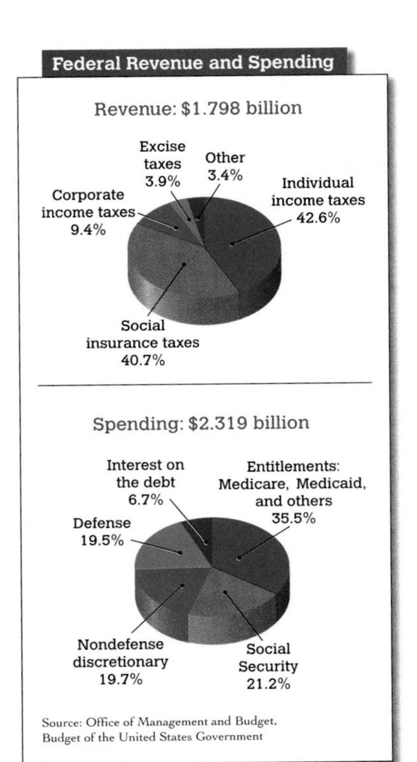

Many individuals and companies can use **tax credits** to lower their taxes. For example, families can receive a tax credit to help pay for day care. There are also tax credits for businesses. For example, companies that hire and retrain workers receive a tax credit.

Social insurance taxes are **regressive taxes**. Everyone is taxed at the same rate. However, the taxes take more out of the paychecks of lower-wage earners. Suppose one worker earns $200 a week. Another worker earns $2,000 a week. They both pay $50 in social insurance taxes. The worker who earns $200 loses a larger portion of his or her salary in taxes.

Social insurance taxes go into special trust accounts in the Treasury. Money is taken out of the accounts to pay Social Security, Medicare, and unemployment compensation benefits as needed. The other taxes go into the general fund to pay for government services.

stop and think

Play "What Am I?" with a partner. Write a definition for each type of tax. Use information from the text as well as the table. End each definition with the question "What am I?" Take turns giving definitions and asking the question.

Federal Borrowing

Most taxes are used to raise money to pay for government services. However, in most years since the 1950s, the federal government has run a deficit. A **deficit** occurs when the amount of money spent is more than the amount of money collected. In the years 1998–2001, there was a **surplus**. More money was collected than the government spent. Beginning in 2002, tax cuts and the war in Iraq created a yearly deficit.

Graph Extension

Ask students to use the graphs on page 329 to answer the following questions.

- What percentage of revenue comes through social insurance taxes and individual income taxes? (83.3 percent)
- What portion of federal spending currently goes toward interest on the debt? (6.7 percent)
- What proportion of expenditures on entitlements and Social Security is NOT covered by social insurance taxes? (16 percent)

Picturing Government

In the photograph on page 327, people at a Manhattan post office on April 15 are preparing their individual income tax forms before the midnight deadline. The government assesses penalties for late filing; it also offers an installment plan for those who cannot pay what they owe and the option to extend the deadline. Another plan is to pay taxes quarterly. The Internal Revenue Service (IRS) will compute tax returns for those who do not file.

Extension

Have students find out about the history of the Sixteenth Amendment, ratified in 1913, which permitted the government to tax personal income. Ask them to look at American history to find why this particular time in history seemed to be the right time to pass this amendment. Try to help them understand that the great wealth of men like Rockefeller and Carnegie had to have played a role. Encourage them to do research using library resources or the Internet. Have them present their findings to the class by using the Student Presentation Builder on the student CD.

Stop and Think

Students should use the definitions from the table on page 328 to form the clues for their questions.

Graph Extension

Ask students to use the graph on page 330 to answer the following questions.

- In what year did the government last have a surplus? (2001)
- When did the deficit begin to decrease? (2004)
- What is the total amount of change in the federal budget from greatest surplus to greatest deficit? (540 billion dollars)

Putting It All Together

Students' charts will vary.

List of taxes in the first column should include:
individual income taxes, corporate income taxes, social insurance tax, excise taxes, customs duties, estate taxes, and gift taxes.

Possible second column explanation:
The government sells treasury notes and bonds to investors, promising to pay them back with interest.

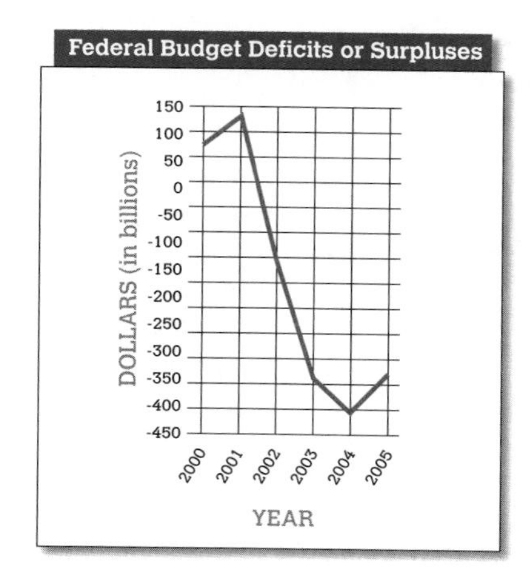

What happens when the government spends more than it takes in? It borrows money just as individuals, families, and businesses do. However, the government does not borrow from banks or credit unions. The Treasury Department sells treasury notes and bonds to investors. These papers promise that the government will pay back the money. Like other debtors, the government must pay interest on the money it borrows.

The result of all this borrowing is the **national debt**. By 2005, the national debt was more than $7.9 trillion. People don't agree about the national debt. Some people are concerned about the size of the debt. They fear that it will make it harder for Americans in the future to have a good life. Others believe that the national debt is good for the economy. They argue that using borrowed money for investment, such as infrastructure projects, has a positive effect on the economy.

Putting It All Together

Make a two-column chart in your notebook. Title one column "Taxes" and the other "Debt." In the first column, list the types of taxes the government imposes. In the second column, explain how the government borrows money and goes into debt.

LESSON 2

The Federal Budget

Thinking on Your Own

A government, like many individuals and families, has a budget. It lists the amount it can spend for various items or purposes. In your notebook, make a list of the items that you would include in the federal government's budget. Compare your list with that of a friend.

focus your reading

What is the difference between controllable and uncontrollable spending?

What is the president's role in developing the budget?

How does Congress interact with the president in making the budget?

words to know

appropriate
controllables
uncontrollables
entitlement
discretionary spending
continuing resolution

Each year the federal government creates a budget for itself. The budget describes how the federal government will "provide for the general welfare" of the nation. Article I, Section 9, Clause 7, of the Constitution gives Congress the power to appropriate money. **Appropriate** means to set aside money for certain uses. In 1921, Congress passed the Budget and Accounting Act. This law directs the president to begin the budget-making process.

Each February, the president sends Congress a proposed budget. This budget is more than just numbers. It lays out what the president considers to be important policies and proposes amounts of money to pay for them. Without money, policies cannot be carried out. However, there are limits to what the president can propose.

Controllable and Uncontrollable Spending

The president and Congress have control over about only 30 percent of the yearly budget. This 30 percent is known as **controllables**. The other 70 percent is called uncontrollables. **Uncontrollables** are spending that is required by laws or by earlier obligations. Payment of interest on the national debt is

Lesson Summary

Congress has the power to appropriate money. About 30 percent of the budget is controllable; the remainder is spent on earlier obligations or spending required by law. The budget process takes about 18 months. The departments and agencies submit budgets in February of the year before they will take effect. Budget requests go to the president. One year after the president begins, the budget package is sent to Congress. Budget committees draft concurrent resolutions on the budget in May and in September. Appropriations committees review the budget and hear testimony. There are 13 separate bills that must be approved by October 1. If they are not all approved, Congress will pass a continuing resolution.

Lesson Objective

Students will learn about the way that the federal budget is created.

Focus Your Reading Answers

1 The president and Congress have power over controllable spending. Uncontrollable spending is required by previous obligations or laws.

2 The president sends a proposed budget to Congress in February of the year the budget is to take effect.

3 Congress reviews the president's requests and does its own analysis of the budget. It also sets binding limits on spending. Congress then votes on a total of 13 appropriations bills or passes a continuing resolution if agreement cannot be reached.

Words to Know

Discuss each of the vocabulary terms with students.

To set aside money for certain uses is to *appropriate*. According to the Constitution, the power to *appropriate* money rests in Congress.

The part of the budget that the president and Congress have control over is *controllables*. Only 30 percent of the federal budget involves *controllables*. *Uncontrollables* involve the spending required by law or previous obligations. Paying the interest on the national debt and payments for Social Security are *uncontrollables*. An *entitlement* is a payment of social insurance. Medicare is an example of an *entitlement*.

Discretionary spending is the controllable part of the budget. Deciding how to allocate *discretionary spending* is what makes the budget process challenging.

If the budget isn't fully passed in time, Congress passes a *continuing resolution*. The *continuing resolution* allows the agencies to continue operating at the rate for the previous budget.

Picturing Government

The photograph on page 332 shows Senator Edward Kennedy and two wounded veterans from the war in Iraq taking part in a news conference. Kennedy was seeking ways to help returning veterans and their families. More than 15,000 U.S. citizens were wounded between March 2003, when the war in Iraq began, and October 2005. In addition to obvious physical wounds, many soldiers suffer psychological problems such as post-traumatic stress disorder (PTSD). The Department of Veterans Affairs (VA) has suffered from budget cuts, yet more than 250,000 veterans were treated for PTSD in 2004. An additional 60,000 new cases were projected in 2006. The VA also highlighted a $1.7 billion need by 2007 to cover the gap in funding for mental health care.

Stop and Think

Students' responses will vary but may suggest that the first two photographs depict uncontrollable spending, while the last photograph shows controllable spending.

Senator Edward Kennedy (D-Massachusetts) holds a press conference to discuss veterans' benefits.

an uncontrollable expense. So are payments for Social Security, federal workers' pensions, veterans' benefits, Medicare, and Medicaid. These are also known as **entitlements**.

Examine the second pie graph on page 329. In a recent year, 56.7 percent of the budget went to entitlements. Another 6.7 percent paid interest on the debt. That left 36.6 percent for all other spending. Subtract spending for the Defense Department. About 17.1 percent was left. In dollars, that was about 400 million for controllable, or **discretionary spending**. On top of that, Congress borrowed another $500 billion.

That is a lot of money. However, consider how it has to be divided. It must fund the work of the other 14 executive departments. It also supports more than 150 independent agencies, government corporations, and commissions, as well as Congress and the president. That is why the budget process is long and difficult.

stop and think

Examine the photographs in this lesson with a partner. Decide whether the photographs show controllable or uncontrollable spending. Write a sentence or two to explain why you think each photograph is one or the other.

The President's Role in Budget-making

The budget process takes about 18 months. It starts in February of the year before the budget will go into effect. For example, the budget process for October 2007 through September 2008 began in February 2006. The federal government's budget year runs from October of one year through September of the next year.

The executive departments, independent agencies, and regulatory commissions work out their budgets. These are sent to the Office of Management and Budget (OMB) in the Executive Office of the President (EOP). The OMB reviews each budget request. Often, the OMB holds hearings with the heads of the various groups. These officials must justify their budget requests.

Extensions

1 Have students use library resources or the Internet to find out what percentages of the current federal budget are controllable and uncontrollable spending. Challenge them to find out how the percentages have changed over two or three presidential administrations. Do the allocations reflect party priorities?

2 Invite students to choose an executive department or independent agency or commission. Ask them to find out the current budget figures for that group and how it compares with others. Students may wish to graph the information.

The Director of the OMB and the Council of Economic Advisers (CEA) then take the budget to the president. They advise him or her on how the individual budgets do or do not match his or her policy agenda, or plans. They also discuss how the requests may affect the deficit, borrowing, and taxes.

The president must sign budget bills into law.

After this meeting, the budget requests are returned to the various groups. They must then revise their requests. Usually, the revised budgets are lower than what the groups first wanted.

The final budgets from the executive branch are put together in one budget package. This package is then delivered to Congress by the first Monday in February of the year the budget will go into effect.

Congress's Role in Budget-making

When a budget arrives in Congress, it is sent to the Senate and the House Budget Committees. Each committee reviews the budget with the help of the Congressional Budget Office (CBO). Congress set up the CBO in 1974 to get independent advice. Because of the CBO, Congress does not have to rely on the president's data. The CBO does its own analysis of the budget.

The House and the Senate Budget Committees draft a concurrent resolution on the budget. It estimates the total revenue and spending for the budget year. Both houses must pass the resolution by May 15. In September, the two budget committees draft a second resolution. This one sets binding, or required, limits on spending. Federal departments, agencies, and commissions may not spend above these limits.

In the meantime, the House and the Senate Appropriations Committees and their subcommittees review the president's budget. They ask officials from executive departments and

Picturing Government

In the photograph on page 333, President George W. Bush signs a 2003 tax break into law. The Congressional Budget Office (CBO) found that the tax benefits packages since 2001 actually increased the tax burden on the middle class while offering relief to the top 20 percent of earners. The top 1 percent of wage earners received a 20 percent drop in the effective federal tax rate. Tax rates for the poorest taxpayers dropped 16 percent, while taxes on the middle 20 percent of taxpayers fell 9.3 percent.

Extension

The Office of Management and Budget (OMB) also controls the expenditures permitted on government credit cards. After Hurricane Katrina struck in 2005, the maximum amount on those cards was raised for a few months to deliver needed relief supplies. After the recovery was well under way, the limits were again lowered to prevent abuse and fraud. The OMB has strict guidelines about the use of government credit cards.

Extension

The Congressional Budget Office makes its analyses available on its Web site. The supplements to the federal budgets that have been enacted between 2000 and 2005 dealt most often with the following categories: defense, response to terrorism, and national disaster relief.

Picturing Government

The photograph on page 334 shows the Mars Exploration Rover (MER), one of two robot geologists that landed on Mars in January 2004. The robots are part of the quest to learn more about water on Mars by studying its rocks and soil.

Putting It All Together

Students' charts will vary. Possible response:

October–January: Various groups create their own budget proposals. These go to the OMB, which holds hearings. The budget goes to the president, then is returned to agencies.

February–February: Budget is worked on in Executive Branch.

February: The president submits the budget package to Congress. The Senate and the House Budget Committees review the budget with the CBO.

May: Congress drafts concurrent resolutions.

September: Congress drafts concurrent resolutions with binding limits on spending. Congressional appropriations committees review the budget, hear testimony, and write 13 separate bills.

Bills are approved by October 1, when the new fiscal year begins.

agencies to testify about their budget numbers. Outside experts, including lobbyists, also testify. These committees write the actual bills that appropriate funds for government activities.

In all, Congress votes on 13 appropriations bills each year. The business of the government is broken down into 13 areas. As you learned in Chapter 7, if one house makes changes in a bill, the bill must go to a conference committee. Committee members try to resolve the differences. Then both the Senate and the House must vote again on the bill.

Some federal funds are allocated for space research, such as for the Mars Exploration Rovers.

The deadline for passing the budget is October 1. The new budget year begins on October 1. However, all 13 bills are not always approved by then. If a bill is not passed, the agencies funded by the bill will have no money. They would have to shut down. To keep this from happening, Congress passes a **continuing resolution**. When the president signs it, agencies can continue to operate. However, they receive their funding at the same rate as the previous budget. When the appropriations bill is passed, the agencies will get the money in the new budget.

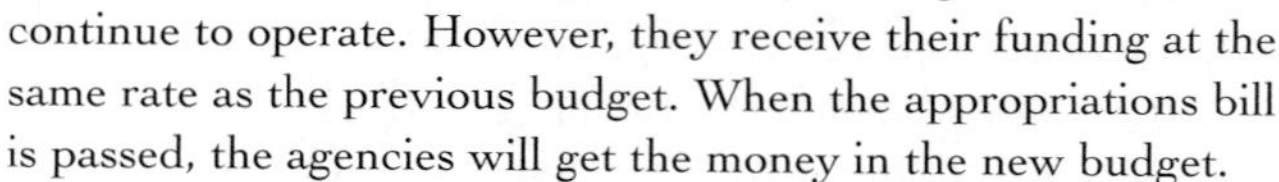

In reality, the budget is not necessarily the final amount of money the government receives. Emergencies may occur during the year. The president must then ask Congress for more money. For example, the war in Iraq required additional budget requests each year. In 2005, billions of dollars were added to the budget to help victims of Hurricane Katrina and Hurricane Rita.

Putting It All Together

Create a chart to show the budget-making process. Label each step. Share your chart with a partner. Discuss the chart to be sure that each label is clear.

LESSON 3

Managing the Economy

Thinking on Your Own

Turn each of the subheadings in this lesson into questions in your notebook. As you read, write the answers to the questions.

focus your reading

What is monetary policy?

How does the Federal Reserve regulate the economy?

words to know

fiscal policy

monetary policy

Federal Reserve System

nonpartisan

discount rate

reserve requirement

The first pie graph on page 329 shows where government revenue comes from. The second pie graph shows where it goes. The "wheres" indicate what the president and Congress think are the nation's most important issues. These issues become the basis for public policy.

One issue that the nation always faces is economic growth. For various reasons, the nation's economy goes through good times and bad times. In good times, most people have jobs. They are able to borrow money at low or moderate interest rates. In bad times, unemployment is high and so are interest rates. Should the government try to influence the economy to improve? Most Americans answer "yes" to this question. However, there is less agreement on how the government should do this.

Fiscal Policy

Fiscal policy uses government spending and taxing to influence the economy. The biggest tool of fiscal policy is the federal budget. It determines how much the government will take in and how much it will spend.

During the Great Depression, President Franklin Roosevelt used the federal budget to speed up the economy. He persuaded Congress to add millions of dollars to the budget. This money provided loans to businesses and farmers. It also created relief

Lesson Summary

The federal government determines a fiscal policy through the budget. It influences the economy through government spending and taxes. Presidents have used taxes to create programs and jobs for the poor and unemployed. They have also cut taxes to try to create jobs. In both cases, the national debt has increased. In 1999, President Clinton cut the deficit to zero and the budget balanced. However, by 2003, the balanced budgets ended due to tax cuts and the fight against terrorism. The Federal Reserve System controls the national monetary policy, which is the control of the supply of money in the economy and the cost of borrowing. These factors influence the economy. The Fed has 12 districts with a main Federal Reserve Bank and branches. The president selects the members of the Fed's Board of Governors, who serve for 14-year terms. The Fed influences monetary policy in three ways.

Lesson Objective

Students will learn about the ways that the government manages the economy.

Words to Know

Discuss each of the vocabulary terms with students.

Fiscal policy is the use of taxing and government spending to influence the economy. The federal budget is the biggest tool of *fiscal policy*. Controlling the supply of money in the economy and the cost of borrowing money is a *monetary policy*. Neither Congress nor the president controls *monetary policy*.

The *Federal Reserve System* is "the bankers' banks" that control *monetary policy*. The *Federal Reserve System* includes 12 Federal Reserve Districts and a Board of Governors.

To be free to act independently of political pressure is to be *nonpartisan*. The Fed is a *nonpartisan* system.

The interest rate that member banks pay on loans from the Fed is called the *discount rate*. The Fed can raise or lower the *discount rate* to control the *monetary policy*. The *reserve requirement* is the sum that member banks must deposit in the main Federal Reserve banks. Raising or lowering the *reserve requirement* is another way the Fed controls *monetary policy*.

Focus Your Reading Answers

1 Monetary policy controls the supply of money in the economy and the cost of borrowing to influence the economy.

2 The Federal Reserve regulates the economy by adjusting the discount rate, adjusting the reserve requirement of member banks, and buying and selling government securities.

Picturing Government

The 1933 photograph on page 336 shows young men in a Civilian Conservation Corps (CCC) camp in California. Corps members planted an estimated three billion trees between 1933 and 1942, when the program ended. One of the goals for the program was to use unemployed men from major urban areas to fight declining timber resources and growing soil erosion. The Emergency Conservation Work Act, signed into law during the Hundred Days of Franklin Roosevelt's first term, mobilized more than three million young men into a peacetime army. The first inductee entered the CCC only 37 days after FDR's inauguration, a testament to the unusual cooperation among all agencies and branches of the federal government. More than 2,650 camps operated in all states by the end of 1935. The program also included Hawaii and Alaska, which were not yet states, Puerto Rico, and the Virgin Islands. Members of the CCC were offered educational programs; an estimated 40,000 young men were taught to read and write.

Stop and Think

Students' charts will vary. Possible response:

Column 1, Fiscal Policy: budget

Column 2, Monetary Policy: The Federal Reserve adjusts the discount rate, adjusts the reserve requirement of member banks, and buys and sells government securities.

The Civilian Conservation Corps was one means used by the federal government to stimulate the economy during the Great Depression.

programs and jobs for the poor and unemployed. The economy improved, but the national debt grew as well.

Starting in the 1980s, Republican presidents and Congress used a different strategy. They did not use tax money to create jobs. Instead, they cut taxes. They wanted taxpayers to keep more of their income. They thought if taxpayers had more money, they would spend more. This would create jobs and improve the economy. The result was reduced government programs and an increasing national debt.

The solution appeared to be careful spending combined with deficit reduction. This enabled President Bill Clinton to cut the yearly deficit to zero in 1999. The result was a balanced budget. However, the cost of wars in Afghanistan and Iraq, fighting terrorism, and tax cuts ended balanced budgets by 2003.

stop and think

Make a two-column chart in your notebook. Title one column "Fiscal Policy" and the other "Monetary Policy." Then list the fiscal policy tools that officials can use to influence the economy. As you read, list the monetary policy tools available to them.

Monetary Policy and the Federal Reserve

Monetary policy controls the supply of money in the economy and the cost of borrowing to influence the economy. Neither the president nor Congress controls monetary policy. The **Federal Reserve System**, or Fed, controls monetary policy.

The Federal Reserve System is "the bankers' banks." The nation is divided into 12 Federal Reserve Districts. There is a main Federal Reserve Bank and branches in each district. A Board of Governors oversees the Fed. These seven economists or bankers are chosen by the president and confirmed by the Senate. They serve for 14 years. The chairperson of the Board of Governors is chosen by the president and serves a four-year term. However, the Fed is **nonpartisan**—meaning that its Board acts independently of political pressure from either the president or Congress.

The Fed controls the nation's monetary policy in three

Extensions

1 Invite students to use library resources or the Internet to compare and contrast the fiscal policy of Franklin Roosevelt and his predecessor, Herbert Hoover. Ask them to use a chart or other graphic organizer to show how the men were alike and different in their fiscal policies.

2 Ask students to find out more about the role of the Chairman of the Federal Reserve Board. In 2005, President Bush appointed Ben Bernanke to succeed long-term chair Alan Greenspan, who retired in January 2006. Ask students to find out what ways the two men differ or agree on monetary policy.

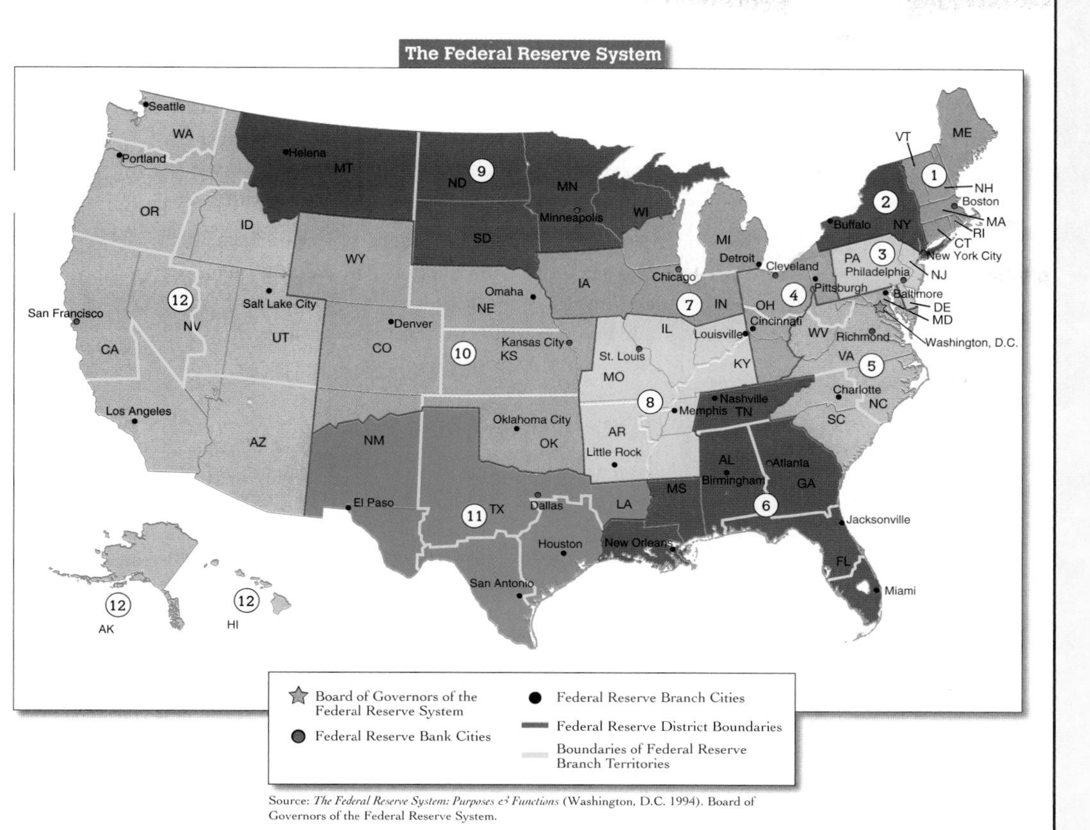

Source: *The Federal Reserve System: Purposes & Functions* (Washington, D.C. 1994). Board of Governors of the Federal Reserve System.

ways. First, the Fed may raise or lower the **discount rate**. This is an interest rate. Member banks pay this rate on loans from the Fed. A lower discount rate costs member banks less to borrow the money. They, in turn, charge their customers lower interest rates on loans. This helps economic growth. The higher the discount rate, the less member banks borrow. The result is less money to lend customers. The economy slows down.

The Federal Reserve Bank in Washington, D.C.

Second, the Fed may raise or lower the reserve requirement of member banks. The **reserve requirement** is the amount of money that member banks must keep in the main Federal Reserve banks. The reserve is a percentage of the money

Map Extension

Ask students to use the map on page 337 to answer the following questions.

- Which states are in district 1 of the Federal Reserve System? (Maine, New Hampshire, Vermont, Massachusetts, Rhode Island, and Connecticut)
- People in Wyoming who want to go to a Federal Reserve branch city might go to what cities and states? (Salt Lake City, Utah, or Denver, Colorado)
- In what direction does the numbering of the Federal Reserve Districts go? (from east to west)

Picturing Government

The photograph on page 337 shows the Federal Reserve Bank in Washington, D.C. The bank, a modernized example of the Beaux-Arts style, was dedicated in 1937. The architect, Paul Philippe Cret, had already designed several well-known buildings, including two bridges and the Folger Library in Washington, D.C., and the Rodin Museum and Federal Reserve Bank of Philadelphia.

Extension

Have students locate the nearest Federal Reserve Bank offices in the district in which they live. Ask them to find out who heads the bank and that person's credentials.

deposited in the member banks by customers. If the reserve rate is low, member banks can lend more to customers. This means there is more money in the economy to produce and buy goods and services. The economy grows. If the reserve rate is increased, member banks have less money to lend.

Third, the Fed may buy and sell government securities such as bonds and T-notes on the open market. By buying them, the Fed puts money into the economy. By selling them, the Fed takes money out. Investors rush in to buy up the securities. The result is less money in the economy.

Putting It All Together

Create a concept map to show how the economy is managed. Draw a large circle and label it "The Economy." Then draw two smaller circles connected to it. Label one "Fiscal Policy." Label the other "Monetary Policy." Share your map with a partner. Ask your partner to check to make sure you have included all the important information.

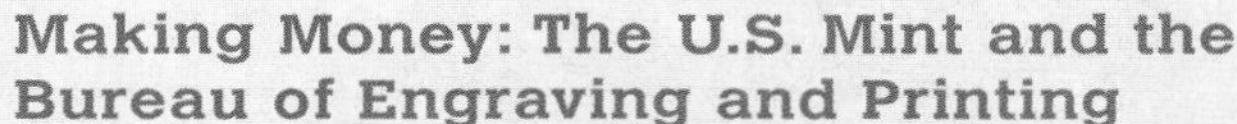

Making Money: The U.S. Mint and the Bureau of Engraving and Printing

If the federal government runs low on money, it cannot just make new money. It must sell bonds and notes to investors. However, the federal government does print and coin new money regularly. Bills and even coins wear out from continuous use. They are also lost, rolling into storm drains and behind seat cushions.

The U.S. Mint produces all the nation's coins. The headquarters of the U.S. Mint is in Washington, D.C. Other plants are located in Philadelphia, Denver, San Francisco, and West Point, New York. The U.S. Mint is also responsible for protecting the nation's gold supply. At Fort Knox, Kentucky, $100 billion of gold is stored under guard by the Mint.

The Bureau of Engraving and Printing (BEP) produces the nation's paper money. It also prints documents for other government departments. These include treasury notes, alien identification cards, and naturalization certificates. The BEP has facilities in Washington, D.C., and Fort Worth, Texas.

Putting It All Together

Students' concept maps will vary but should reflect lesson content.

Civics Today Extension

The Denver Mint makes about 32 million coins daily. It has stamping presses with four dies that can stamp up to 530 coins per minute. In addition to producing coins for circulation, the Philadelphia Mint also manufactures commemorative coins, gold bullion coins, national medals, and uncirculated coins. The Bureau of Engraving and Printing (BEP) began in 1862 in the Treasury Building's basement with two men and four women. Now the bureau employs more than 2,500 people in its two buildings.

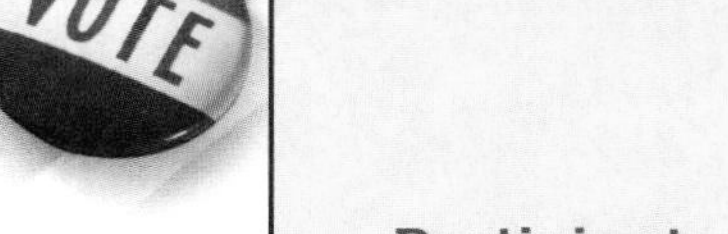

Participate in Government

File Your Income Tax

Once you begin to work, you will need to file a federal tax return each year. You probably will have to file a state tax return, too. Only a couple of states do not have personal income taxes. Depending on your community, you may also have to pay a city income tax.

People known as tax protesters claim that the federal income tax is unconstitutional. They make many different arguments against the federal income tax and refuse to file tax returns. However, the Internal Revenue Service (IRS) prosecutes tax protesters. In every case, the courts have found tax protesters guilty of tax evasion, or failure to pay taxes. Their arguments are not based on the law. They are based on their desire not to pay taxes. As this chapter explains, taxes are used for programs to benefit the "general welfare," or good, of the people.

Federal and state tax returns are due every year on April 15. Both citizens and resident aliens who work in the United States must pay taxes. Tax forms are available online. Taxes may also be filed online. If you are due a refund, you often will receive it faster if you file online.

During the year, file all of your financial records in one place. This makes it easier to find information when it is time to prepare your tax return. File receipts and records in separate envelopes or folders. Then you will not have a mound of paper to sort through.

To File Your Return:

- Gather your records. Get your W-2 form from your employer.
- Fill out the return. Get help from the IRS online or by phone.
- Mail the return or file it online by midnight on April 15.

Participate in Government

Divide the class into small groups. Have them find out what kinds of financial records they need to keep for their income tax. Have them design systems for storing them. You may wish to invite a tax professional to class to talk to students about filing taxes and deductions they can take.

Extension

Discuss with students a quotation from former Supreme Court Justice Oliver Wendell Holmes, "Taxes are what we pay for a civilized society." Ask students to imagine the nation without the benefits that taxes allow. Do they agree or disagree with Holmes?

Research Resources

Below is a list of reference books and Web sites that relate to the issues covered in this chapter. Students may wish to use these to further their research on ideas in the preceding lessons. Web site addresses may change over time. Use keyword searching on a major search engine to locate sites.

Reference Books:

Thomas Carson, ed. *Gale Encyclopedia of U.S. Economic History*. Gale Group, 1999.

C. Eugene Steuerle. *Contemporary U.S. Tax Policy*. Urban Institute Press, 2004.

Bruce Wetterau. *Congressional Quarterly's Desk Reference on the Federal Budget*. Congressional Quarterly, 1998.

Web Sites:

The U.S. Bureau of Engraving and Printing maintains a site. It offers facts about money as well as links and information about the Treasury.

The federal government's Treasury site includes facts about currency and coins, as well as taxes.

The Federal Reserve site is packed with information about the Fed and related institutions.

Skill Builder

1 The graph is about recent Medicaid beneficiaries.

2 Dependent children under twenty-one receive nearly half of the funding.

3 The second-largest percentage goes to adults in families with dependent children.

4 Children, the blind or disabled, elderly, and adults in families with dependent children benefit from Medicaid.

Recommended Reading

Below is a list of books that relate to the issues covered in this chapter. The numbers in parentheses indicate the related Thematic Strands of the National Council for the Social Studies (NCSS).

Melanie Ann Apel. *The Federal Reserve Act: Making the American Banking System Stronger*. Rosen Publishing Group, 2006. (VI, X)

Joann A. Grote. *The Internal Revenue Service (Your Government: How It Works)*. Chelsea House, 2001. (VI, X)

Skill Builder

Analyze a Pie Graph

A pie graph shows parts of a whole. It illustrates how much of the whole each slice, or segment, represents. Usually, pie graphs illustrate percentages. The entire pie is 100 percent.

To Read a Pie Graph:

- Read the title of the graph, so you know what it is about.
- Read the labels for each segment.
- Compare the parts of the circle to find the relation each has with the other.
- Draw conclusions about the information and the relation among the parts.

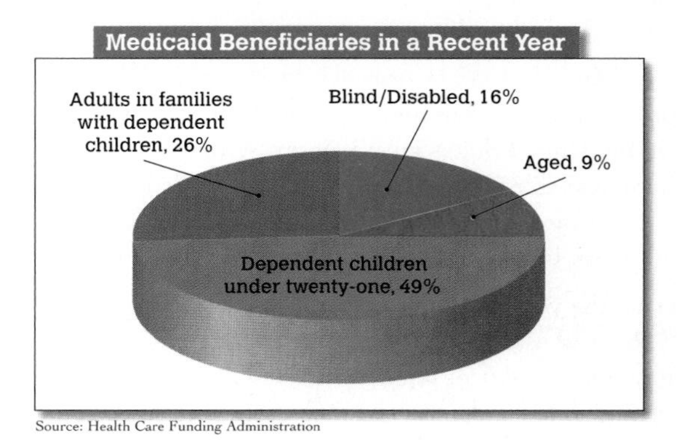

Source: Health Care Funding Administration

Use the pie graph to answer the following questions.

1 What is the graph about?

2 Which group gets the largest percentage of funding?

3 Which group gets the second-largest percentage of funding?

4 Who benefits from Medicaid funding?

Classroom Discussion

Discuss with students some of the broader topics covered in this chapter.

- In what circumstances should the federal government interfere with the economy? Does the involvement contradict the principles of free enterprise?
- How can the government help the economy without running a deficit?
- What are the key arguments for and against tax reform?

Chapter

19 DOMESTIC POLICY: EDUCATION, HOUSING, TRANSPORTATION, AND SECURITY

Getting Focused

Skim this chapter to predict what you will be learning.

- Read the lesson titles and subheadings.
- Look at the illustrations and read the captions.
- Examine the graph.
- Review the vocabulary words and terms.

Domestic policy is policy that relates to government regulations and programs in the United States. Foreign policy relates to U.S. interactions with other nations. Social Security, Head Start, and running veterans' hospitals are examples of domestic policy. So are fining companies for polluting the air and screening passengers' bags in airports. What other domestic programs do you know of? List at least five.

President George W. Bush signed an appropriations bill for Hurricane Katrina relief in September 2005. Domestic policy is one of the responsibilities of the president.

Pre-Reading Discussion

1 Have students share their lists of domestic programs. Try to group them into the appropriate agencies. Ask students what limits, if any, should be placed on federal assistance.

2 Discuss with students how federal programs are funded, reminding them of the information they have just read on the budget. Should all departments be equally funded from the controllable spending?

Related Transparencies

T-18 Three-Column Chart

T-19 Venn Diagram

Key Blacklines

Primary Source—How Government Agencies Work Together

CD Extension

Encourage students to use the reading comprehension, vocabulary reinforcement, and other activities on the student CD.

Getting Focused

Allow time for students to share their lists and explain any items not familiar to the class as a whole. Challenge students as they read the chapter to identify the correct department that oversees each program.

Picturing Government

In the photograph on page 341, President George W. Bush signs a $10.5 billion relief package for those affected by Hurricane Katrina in 2005. Congress passed a much larger bill that included $2,000 debit cards for families. Initially, about 10,000 workers filed with the Labor Department for unemployment benefits, with more filings expected.

Lesson Summary

The federal government promotes U.S. businesses at home and around the world. One way to do this is by regulating the cost of imports through tariffs. The trade agreement among the United States, Mexico, and Canada is known as the North American Free Trade Agreement (NAFTA). A similar agreement with nations in Central America is known as the CAFTA. The government offers three types of subsidies to businesses: tax credits, loans at low interest rates, and free information. The Commerce Department began in 1913. Antitrust laws try to prevent or break up monopolies in order to restore competition within an industry. Regulatory laws also govern businesses. In the 1970s, the federal government began deregulating some industries. Unions led the battle for safe working conditions and better wages for workers.

Lesson Objective

Students will learn about the efforts of the federal government to regulate and promote business.

Focus Your Reading Answers

1 The federal government promotes U.S. businesses by a free trade stance and by offering subsidies to businesses. Three types of subsidies are tax credits, low-interest loans, and free information.

2 The federal government regulates U.S. businesses by passing antitrust and regulatory laws.

3 The federal government and labor unions have often had an adversarial relationship. The government has tried to prevent abuses. Labor unions object to tariffs, regulations, and to controls about when unions can strike.

LESSON 1

Business and Labor

Thinking on Your Own

In your notebook, write a paragraph that includes as many of the Words to Know as you can. As you encounter these words in your reading, check to see if you used them correctly.

focus your reading

Explain how the federal government promotes U.S. businesses.

How does the federal government regulate U.S. businesses?

Describe the relationship between the federal government and labor.

words to know

- domestic policy
- mixed market economy
- free trade
- trust
- monopoly
- deregulate
- bargain collectively
- union shop

Promoting U.S. businesses at home and abroad is one of the tasks of the federal government. Also, the federal government has another role in relation to business. Since the late 1800s, the federal government has actively regulated business activities. The result is a **mixed market economy**. The economy is based on the private ownership of goods and services. However, the government both promotes and regulates the workings of private enterprise.

Promoting Business

At various times in the nation's history, the government has supported either free trade or protectionism. **Free trade** means low tariffs, or customs duties, on goods brought into the country for sale. At other times, the government has used high tariffs to keep imports out. High tariffs protect U.S. businesses. Tariffs used to protect U.S. businesses are known as protective tariffs.

In recent years, the United States has placed fewer restrictions on imports from other countries. In 1994, Canada, the United States, and Mexico joined in the North American Free Trade Agreement (NAFTA). Barriers to trade among the three partners will end over a period of 15 years. In 2005, President George W. Bush signed into law the Central

342 Chapter 19

Words to Know

Introduce each of the following vocabulary terms to students.

Domestic policy relates to government regulations and programs in the United States. Social Security is an example of *domestic policy*.

A *mixed market economy* is one in which the government plays a role in regulating business activities. Private ownership is still part of a *mixed market economy*.

Low tariffs on imported goods mean *free trade*. The United States has set up several *free trade* agreements with other nations.

A *trust* combines several corporations into a single business. In the late 1880s, the goal of a *trust* was to end competition in an industry. When one company controls all or most of an industry, a *monopoly* results. Antitrust laws attempt to prevent a *monopoly* from forming.

American Free Trade Agreement (CAFTA). It is similar to the NAFTA and focuses on trade with Central American nations.

The federal government provides three major types of subsidies, or financial supports, to businesses. The first is tax credits. Like families, businesses are given tax credits in exchange for certain activities. For example, businesses may subtract the cost of training workers under the Welfare to Work Program.

The federal government also offers loans to businesses at low interest rates. Small businesses, especially minority- and women-owned businesses, greatly benefit from this service.

stop and think

Make a three-column chart in your notebook. Title one column "Promoting Business," another "Regulating Business," and the third "Protecting Workers." List three ways that the government promotes business. As you read ahead, include three items in each of the other two columns.

Small businesses and giant corporations also benefit from the third major way the government supports businesses. The government provides masses of information free to companies. Otherwise, they would need to pay for this research. This is a major job of the Department of Commerce, which supports the interests of U.S. businesses.

Workers assemble circuit boards at a manufacturing facility in Nevada.

The Small Business Administration (SBA) is an independent agency of the executive branch. It aids small businesses in direct ways. It offers help with all areas of starting and running small businesses. All this aid is free.

Regulating Business

The Commerce Department was not set up until 1913. However, the federal government's power to regulate commerce, or business, rests in the Constitution. Article I, Section 8, Clause 3, is known as the Commerce Clause. It says that Congress shall have the power "to regulate commerce with foreign nations, and among the several states . . . ."

In the United States, the Industrial Revolution began in the early 1800s. By the 1880s, a few giant companies controlled major areas of the economy. **Trusts** combined several corporations into a single business. The purpose was to end

Extension

Divide the class into two groups, assigning each group either the NAFTA or the CAFTA. Ask students to find and read recent articles in newsmagazines or on the Internet and to present a panel discussion on the advantages and disadvantages of free trade agreements in the Americas.

Picturing Government

The photograph on page 343 shows women putting circuit boards and other computer devices together. While this particular photograph was taken in the United States, many such jobs have been outsourced to countries where labor is more cheaply available.

Words to Know, continued

To remove regulations from an industry is to *deregulate* it. The federal government began to *deregulate* some industries in the 1970s.

To *bargain collectively* is to negotiate a contract between a company and a union. The Wagner Act of 1935 guarantees the right to *bargain collectively*.

A *union shop* is one in which nonunion members may be hired, but are then required to join the union. The *union shop* is not like a closed shop, which hires only people who are already union members.

Stop and Think

Students' charts will vary. Possible response:

Column 1: Promoting Business

1 free trade agreements

2 subsidies

3 loans

Column 2: Regulating Business

1 antitrust laws

2 regulatory laws

3 deregulation

Column 3: Protecting Workers

1 laws regulating hours, working conditions, and wages

2 Wagner Act gives right to bargain collectively.

3 National Labor Relations Board supervises union elections and hears complaints.

Picturing Government

The photograph by Jacob Riis on page 344 shows a crowded tailors' shop in New York City's Lower East Side. Workers received 45 cents per dozen pairs of knee pants. Riis, a native of Denmark who came to the United States in 1870 at age twenty-one, used both words and film to document the miseries of tenement life and child labor. He and Theodore Roosevelt, then head of the New York Police Board of Commissioners, were friends; Roosevelt often accompanied Riis to the slums.

Poor working conditions, such as in this tailors' shop in New York City, led to regulations for businesses during the late 1800s.

competition in an industry. As a result, they could set any prices they wanted for their goods and services. They could also drive out of business suppliers who would not sell to them cheaply. They paid their workers poorly and did nothing to make their factories, mines, and railroads safe for workers.

In an effort to end these abuses, Congress passed the Interstate Commerce Act in 1887. It was the first law regulating businesses. It set limits on what railroads could charge to carry freight. Other antitrust laws were the Sherman Antitrust Act in 1890 and the Clayton Antitrust Act in 1914. The Antitrust Division was set up in the Justice Department to enforce antitrust laws. Antitrust laws have three goals. The first is to prevent monopolies from occurring. A **monopoly** is the control of an industry or most of an industry by one company. The second is to break up any monopolies that do exist. The third is to restore competition in the industry.

In addition to antitrust laws, there are other kinds of laws that affect how businesses operate and what they can and cannot do. These are regulatory laws. Since the 1930s, Congress has passed many laws regulating businesses. For example, cars must have airbags. A television or cable company may not own all the television or cable stations in a city. Prescription drugs cannot be sold unless they are approved by the Food and Drug Administration. The Security and Exchange Commission licenses and oversees stockbrokers.

However, regulating business is not popular with all Americans. Some believe that it raises the price of goods and services. Others claim that it hinders competition. Every industry has its own concerns. Carmakers want fuel efficiency standards relaxed. Manufacturers want clean air and water laws weakened.

Beginning in the 1970s, the federal government began to **deregulate** some industries. A number of regulations were removed from the banking, television and cable, airline, railroad, and trucking industries. Deregulation has worked better in some industries than in others. For example, since

Extension

1 Invite students interested in entrepreneurship to use library resources or the Internet to find out more about the Small Business Administration (SBA). Ask them to suppose they are starting a small business. What help could the SBA offer them? Have them present their findings to the class by using the Student Presentation Builder on the student CD.

2 Invite students with an interest in visual arts to prepare for the class an exhibit of photographs taken by muckrakers such as Lewis Hine and Jacob Riis, as well as of other noted photographers such as *Life*'s Margaret Bourke-White. You may then wish to have students write about the photographs and what they think the effect of them would be.

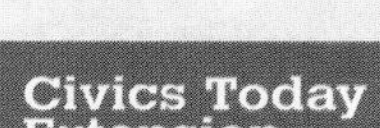

the airlines were deregulated in 1978, several of the large airlines have declared bankruptcy. They have cut jobs and services in order to keep flying. Some airlines have gone out of business. The result is cheaper fares in cities with several airlines. However, a number of cities have lost all airline service or have very limited service. Fares in these cities remain as high or higher than they were when several airlines served them.

Labor

Today, laws protect workers. Laws regulate working hours, ensure safe working conditions, and set the minimum wage. This was not always the case. In the late 1800s, government supported business owners, not workers. The courts even used the Sherman Antitrust Act against labor unions. The Supreme Court ruled that unions were an attempt to limit the activities of businesses.

Workers organized into local unions as early as the 1790s. By the 1860s, national unions were struggling to survive.

Civics Today Extension

The Consumer Product Safety Commission (CPSC) Web site regularly updates lists of product recalls. The CPSC also offers an e-mail subscription to recall lists. The Web site includes data on product-related injuries as well. Consumers can report products they feel are unsafe through a letter, phone call, fax, or e-mail.

Civics Today

Consumer Protection

One regulatory agency that directly affects Americans daily is the Consumer Product Safety Commission (CPSC). It is an independent regulatory commission. The CPSC was set up in 1972 to protect consumers from dangerous products. Some 15,000 consumer products are under the CPSC's review. Its employees investigate injuries caused by products such as power tools, cribs, and microwaves.

In the 30 years since CPSC began, the injury and death rate from consumer product accidents has gone down 30 percent. The CPSC sets required product-safety standards. If products do not meet these standards, the CPSC orders their recall.

People can find free and low-cost information about consumer concerns from the Consumer Information Center (CIC). Each year the CIC publishes a free "Consumer Action Handbook." The handbook offers information about how to solve consumer complaints and where to file complaints. Among the CIC's most popular publications are ones on how to save money, how to protect against identity theft, and how to choose the best wireless telephone service. To help consumers find what they need, the CIC publishes a free catalog of publications.

A demonstration by the CPSC about the dangers of window blind drawstrings.

Extension

Have students work together in small groups to research one of the industries that has been deregulated. Ask them to find out the effects of the deregulation on consumers, workers, and owners or shareholders. Allow time for students to present their findings to the class. Then discuss whether deregulation is a good idea.

Picturing Government

In the 1993 photograph on page 346, protestors try to prevent passage of the North American Free Trade Agreement. The Amalgamated Clothing and Textile Workers Union (ACTWU) sponsored the protest. The ACTWU merged in 1995 with the International Ladies Garment Workers' Union to form UNITE, the Union of Needletrades, Industrial and Textile Workers, which has a membership of more than 300,000. The cruel irony is that more than ten years after the passage of the NAFTA, manufacturing jobs have left not only the United States, but also Mexico. Cheaper labor can now be had in Indonesia, China, and Vietnam, where nearly 500,000 of the 750,000 factory jobs created by the NAFTA had gone. In the United States, more than three million manufacturing jobs have been lost, and more than 500,000 workers have been helped by the Department of Labor's program for those affected by the NAFTA.

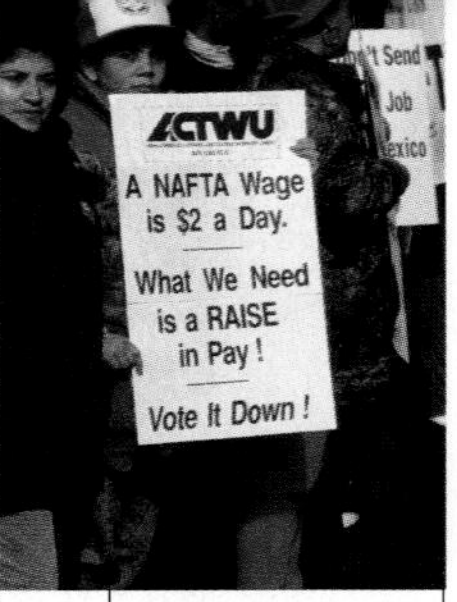

Unions organized against the NAFTA during the 1990s.

However, business owners refused to recognize unions. Unions wanted to negotiate contracts with business owners. Employers did not want to guarantee wages or spend money on making workplaces safer.

By the early 1900s, Americans' views of business and labor were changing. Congress and the Supreme Court reflected these changing views. Journalists known as muckrakers were exposing how badly companies treated their workers.

The result was new laws and new Court rulings. Congress set up the Department of Labor in 1913 to aid workers. The Clayton Antitrust Act of 1914 states that unions are not conspiracies, or plots, to limit business activities. In 1935, Congress passed the Wagner Act. It guarantees workers the right to organize unions in workplaces and to **bargain collectively**. This means to negotiate a contract between a union and a company.

The act also set up the National Labor Relations Board (NLRB). When a group of workers wants to start a union in their workplace, the NLRB oversees the election. A majority of workers have to vote to join the union before one can be started. The NLRB also hears complaints about supposed unfair labor practices by employers.

By the late 1940s, some Americans thought that labor unions had too much power. In 1947, Congress passed the Taft-Hartley Act. The Taft-Hartley Act set up a 60-day cooling-off period before a union could strike. The union had to notify the company that it would strike. The idea was that during this time, the union and the company could reach an agreement. It ended the closed shop, but allowed the **union shop**. Only union members can be hired in a closed shop. Nonunion members may be hired in a union shop. However, they must then join the union.

Putting It All Together

How does the federal government interact with business and labor? Write a summary paragraph to answer this question. Use the lists you made in the Stop and Think activity. Exchange your paragraph with a partner. Ask your partner if your paragraph includes all the main points of the lesson. If not, which ones did you miss?

Putting It All Together

Students' paragraphs will vary but should reflect lesson content.

LESSON 2

Agriculture, the Environment, and Energy Resources

Thinking on Your Own

The environment includes the air, water, land, trees, plants, animals—the natural world around us. Environmentalists believe that every generation has a responsibility to take care of the environment for the next generation. What do you think about this belief? What if it means higher prices for things like gasoline, cars, and food? Write a paragraph in your notebook to explain your answer.

focus your reading

Explain why the federal government became involved in farm policy during the 1930s.

Why were environmental laws passed?

Describe some of the issues involved in energy policy.

words to know

global warming

Since the early 1800s, the United States has more than doubled its territory. As the nation expanded, so did the role of the federal government. The Agriculture Department was set up in 1862 to help farmers. Congress set up the Environmental Protection Agency in 1970. It was created because of concern about the environment. The Energy Department was set up in 1977 because of the oil shortages of the mid-1970s. With each new department or agency, the federal government took on a new policy-making role.

Modern Farm Policies

The original purpose of the Agriculture Department was to help farmers become better farmers. Department agents showed them new equipment and new ways to farm. By the 1920s, farmers were producing more than the nation needed. They could not sell the surplus overseas, because foreign nations had little money to pay for imports after World War I. The result was declining prices for U.S. farm goods.

Employees of the Department of Agriculture helped farmers develop new ways of farming.

Words to Know

Discuss the following vocabulary term with students.

The warming of Earth's surface is known as *global warming*. Producing less carbon dioxide is the only way to stop *global warming*.

Lesson Summary

The Agriculture Department began in 1862, with helping farmers as the goal. During the Great Depression, this help was crucial. The 1996 Federal Agricultural Improvement and Reform Act ended many of the programs, although the Commodity Credit Corporation still aids farmers. The Environmental Protection Agency started in 1970. Congress passed acts protecting water, air, and endangered species. Congress set up the Energy Department in 1977 following an oil embargo. Efforts to reduce carbon dioxide emissions that occur from burning fossil fuels have been largely unsuccessful.

Lesson Objective

Students will learn about the federal agencies that regulate agriculture, the environment, and energy.

Focus Your Reading Answers

1 The federal government became involved in farm policy during the 1930s to help farmers who were struggling during the Depression.

2 Environmental laws were passed to prevent businesses, farms, and communities from harming the water, air, and land, along with several threatened or endangered species.

3 Some of the issues involved in energy policy include global warming, reduction of carbon dioxide emissions, and creation of a national energy policy.

Picturing Government

The photograph on page 348 shows surplus grain going to an African food relief program. The food was donated by USAID. In the first three years of the new millennium, the largest amounts of food aid went to North Korea (4.2 million tons total), Ethiopia (4.0 million tons), Bangladesh (1.4 million tons), and Afghanistan (1.1 million tons). Countries in sub-Saharan Africa and in Asia have received more than 60 percent of the total amount of food aid over the past decade and longer. In 2002, the United States contributed 64.9 percent of food aid; the European Union was next, with 13.8 percent. Japan and Canada, considered among the largest donors, contributed 3.2 and 1.7 percent, respectively.

The United States provides food relief to many African nations.

By the time of the Great Depression, thousands of farmers had lost their land. Like other Americans in need, farmers appealed to the government for help. By the early 1930s, Americans had realized that they had no control over a worldwide economic depression. In the 1932 election, they rejected President Herbert Hoover and elected Franklin Roosevelt.

Roosevelt began a series of actions to aid all Americans. For farmers, he used the principle of supply and demand. Farmers were paid to produce less than they had in the past. As a result, the supply of certain farm goods, such as corn, wheat, and hogs, was limited. This raised the price that farmers could charge for these products.

Since the 1930s, the federal government has continued to aid farmers. In 1996, though, Congress passed the Federal Agricultural Improvement and Reform Act to end many of the earlier programs. The Commodity Credit Corporation (CCC), however, continues to aid farmers in many ways. The CCC helps farmers find markets and makes it easier to sell farm goods overseas. It provides research on prices and the best time to sell. The CCC also buys farm products for food assistance programs in the United States and overseas. This includes food for school lunch programs, the armed forces, veterans' hospitals, and correctional institutions.

stop and think

In your notebook, make a list of federal government policies that have helped agriculture. As you read ahead, list other policies that show how the role of the federal government has expanded in recent years.

Picturing Government

The photograph on page 347 shows an early group of U.S. Department of Agriculture employees. The department currently includes seven divisions: Food Safety; Natural Resources and Environment; Rural Development; Food, Nutrition, and Consumer Services; Marketing and Regulatory Programs; Farm and Foreign Agricultural Services; and Research, Education, and Economics. Divide the class into seven groups to investigate the role and work of each division. Have students use library resources or the Internet to find out more.

The Environment

The CCC also oversees conservation programs through the Natural Resources Conservation Service. These programs include overseeing the national forest system and soil conservation districts. Their goal is to protect, or conserve, the environment.

Before the 1950s, the federal government was not involved in environmental policy. In the 1950s, Americans began to see the damage caused to the environment by businesses, communities, and farms. Factories released pollution into the air from smokestacks. Communities disposed of sewage in rivers and lakes. Farmers let chemical fertilizers and pesticides run off into streams and rivers. The air over cities was unhealthy to breathe. Sources of drinking water were unsafe.

The bald eagle is protected by the Endangered Species Act of 1973.

By the 1960s, groups had organized and were lobbying for environmental laws. In 1970, Congress passed the first Clean Air Act and the Water Quality Improvement Act. The Endangered Species Act of 1973 requires the federal government to protect the animals, birds, and other wildlife, including plants that are on the list of endangered species.

In 1970, Congress set up the Environmental Protection Agency (EPA). Its mission is to make sure that environmental laws are obeyed. Since 1970, Congress has passed additional environmental protection laws. The EPA then writes regulations to enforce these laws. For example, in 2000, the EPA set standards for clean exhaust from buses and heavy trucks.

Superfund Environmental Protection Agency workers clean a site near Houston, Texas.

Not everyone agrees with environmental protection policies. Many of these environmental regulations require costly changes in how companies, communities, and farmers do business. The result is often a debate over the strictness of new environmental laws and regulations.

Picturing Government

The American bald eagle is shown on page 349. When adopted as the national emblem in 1782, the bald eagle numbered between 25,000 and 75,000 in what would become the contiguous 48 states. Almost 200 years later, in 1973, when Congress passed the Endangered Species Act, the bald eagle was listed as endangered or threatened in most of those states. The population of bald eagles had dropped to fewer than 450 nesting pairs in the lower 48 states by the 1960s due to the effects of the pesticide DDT. By 1999, such progress had been made that the U.S. Fish and Wildlife Service suggested removing the bird from the endangered and threatened species list.

Picturing Government

In the photograph at the bottom of page 349, workers are cleaning up a site where oil leaked from an oil well. The EPA provides Superfund grants to states to help with spills.

Extension

The Commodity Credit Corporation (CCC) began in 1933 and was transferred to the Department of Agriculture six years later. The CCC helps to develop new markets, both domestic and foreign, and marketing facilities. It also coordinates the sale of agricultural commodities to foreign governments and the donation of farm goods to relief efforts. Within the United States, the raw materials are generally first converted to food, then distributed to charitable institutions, summer camps, school lunch programs, and so on. Grain also may be requisitioned for starving migratory birds or other wildlife.

Stop and Think

Students' lists will vary but may include limiting the supply of farm goods and passing the Federal Agricultural Improvement and Reform Act.

Picturing Government

In the photograph on page 350, cars line up to buy gasoline during the 1973 oil crisis. Customers in early 1973 had experienced brownouts and rising prices for fuels. The situation worsened in October when the Organization of Arab Petroleum Exporting Countries (OPEC) issued an oil embargo against nations that were allies of Israel, an act of retaliation for the Yom Kippur War. That year, the crisis was highlighted by President Richard Nixon's decision not to turn on the lights on the national Christmas tree. Gasoline prices jumped 70 percent within a year.

Putting It All Together

Students' revisions will vary.

Energy Resources

Global warming cuts across environmental and energy issues. **Global warming** is the warming of Earth's surface. It is occurring because of growing levels of carbon dioxide and other greenhouse gases in the atmosphere. Carbon dioxide is produced when fossil fuels—coal, oil, and natural gas—are burned. The carbon dioxide acts like insulation. It collects in Earth's atmosphere and traps the energy from the sun under the atmosphere. This extra heat warms Earth. The only way to stop global warming is to produce less carbon dioxide.

However, developing nations and the United States rarely support efforts to reduce carbon dioxide. Developing nations claim that such changes will cost too much money. U.S. politicians have argued that such efforts will put too much of a cost burden on businesses. Environmentalists in the United States continue to lobby politicians to pass laws to cut carbon dioxide. They want tougher clean air regulations and more money to research other energy sources.

During the 1970s, long lines at gas stations were the result of oil crises.

In 1973 and 1974, Arab nations refused to sell oil to the United States. The United States had decided to support Israel against its Arab neighbors. The Department of Energy was created in 1977. Since then, various presidents and Congresses have tried to shape a national energy policy. But, competing groups and political beliefs make shaping a national energy policy difficult. During the 1980s, policy-makers urged energy conservation. People bought smaller, more fuel-efficient cars. A national highway bill set the speed limit on interstate highways at 55 miles per hour. During the 1990s, small cars gave way to less fuel-efficient sport utility vehicles (SUVs). The speed limit was raised to 65 miles per hour.

Putting It All Together

Review the paragraph you wrote at the beginning of the lesson. Do you still agree with what you said? If not, revise your paragraph. If you still agree, write another paragraph to explain why. Share your writing with a partner. Discuss your viewpoints and try to reach an agreement about the environment.

LESSON 3

Health and Social Service Programs

Thinking on Your Own

Should the federal government provide benefits to the elderly, widows or widowers and dependent children, and those with disabilities? Or should people save enough to take care of themselves and their families? In your notebook, write your opinion using what you already know.

focus your reading

What are the social insurance programs?

List and describe the major public assistance programs.

How does the federal government promote public health?

Describe the benefits provided to veterans by the Department of Veterans Affairs.

words to know

social welfare program

entitlement program

public assistance program

The federal government's social welfare programs began during the Great Depression. **Social welfare programs** provide benefits to individuals, especially those in need. During the Great Depression, many people lost everything they had. Parents went without food so their children could eat. State and local governments and private charities did what they could. However, the problems were too great and too widespread. Only the federal government had the power to help so many people across so many states.

Franklin Roosevelt was elected president in 1932 on his promise to end the Depression and help people. He pushed programs through Congress that created jobs and aided farmers. He also proposed a program to pay benefits to retired people, widows and their children, and people with disabilities. It was the first of many social welfare programs that Congress has passed since 1935.

Social Insurance Programs

Roosevelt's proposal was the basis of the Social Security and unemployment insurance programs. Social Security is an entitlement program. **Entitlement programs** must be funded

Words to Know

Discuss each of the vocabulary terms with students.

A *social welfare program* provides benefits to individuals, especially those in need. The Great Depression was the beginning of government-sponsored *social welfare programs*.

An *entitlement program* is funded every year, and people are entitled to the benefits. Social Security is an example of an *entitlement program*.

A *public assistance program* pays benefits to people who do not contribute to it. Medicaid is an example of a *public assistance program*.

Lesson Summary

Social welfare programs began during the Great Depression. Social Security, unemployment insurance, and Medicare are entitlement programs. Public assistance programs include Medicaid, food stamps, Supplemental Security Insurance, and Temporary Assistance to Needy Families. The Department of Health and Human Services is in charge of programs relating to general public health. The Department of Veterans Affairs includes both health and human services for veterans.

Lesson Objective

Students will learn about the federal departments responsible for health and social service programs.

Focus Your Reading Answers

1 The social insurance programs are Social Security, Medicare, and unemployment insurance.

2 Major public assistance programs include Medicaid, food stamps, Supplemental Security Insurance, and Temporary Assistance to Needy Families.

3 The federal government promotes public health by conducting research, educating the public, directing response to health emergencies, and approving prescription drugs and medical devices.

4 The Department of Veterans Affairs (VA) offers benefits such as health care in VA hospitals and clinics, financial programs, education, training, life insurance, and low-cost home loans.

Picturing Government

The photograph on page 352 shows a line of unemployed people waiting outside an office of the State of California Employment Development Department. The state's unemployment rate has consistently been above the U.S. average. Ask students to use library resources or the Internet to compare their state's percentage of unemployment to the national average.

People wait in line at a California unemployment office.

every year. Workers and employers contribute to the program through payroll taxes. Social Security pays a monthly benefit to retired people, people with disabilities, and widows or widowers of workers and their dependent children. The Social Security Administration is an independent federal agency.

Unemployment insurance is also an entitlement program. However, only employers pay the tax. The money is paid to the federal government, which returns it to the states. Benefits vary from state to state. Workers who are laid off from their jobs apply for weekly payments. The money helps them with basic living expenses until they can find a new job.

Medicare is the third social insurance program. It was set up in 1965. An earlier effort to pass a law to help retirees with medical costs was defeated. However, by the 1960s, health-care costs were rising. They were becoming a burden to many retired people. There was enough pressure to push Congress to pass the new bill.

Medicare pays part of the cost of hospital care for retired people and people with disabilities. It is funded by payroll taxes on workers and employers. Those eligible for Medicare may also pay a small amount for Medicare B. This is insurance coverage for doctors' visits, X-rays, and some other services. Like Social Security and unemployment insurance, Medicare is an entitlement program.

Public Assistance Programs

Public assistance programs are different from social insurance programs. They pay benefits to people who do not contribute to the programs. They are known as "means-tested" programs. People who qualify do not have the means, or money, to pay for them. Taxes pay to fund public assistance programs. The major public assistance programs are Medicaid, food stamps, Supplemental Security Insurance (SSI), and Temporary Assistance to Needy Families (TANF).

Extensions

1 Have interested students use library resources or the Internet to find out more about the New Deal programs created after Franklin Roosevelt took office and the controversies surrounding them, both then and now. Allow time for students to present their findings to the class.

2 Ask students to find out more about Lyndon Johnson's Great Society vision (of which Medicare was a component) and how it compared to the New Deal. Suggest that they use library resources or the Internet, and that they present the results of their findings to the class with a graphic organizer such as a Venn diagram.

Medicaid was signed into law in 1965. It pays hospital, nursing home, and medical costs for those who qualify. States administer the program and pay part of the cost. The federal government, however, provides most of the money. Benefits vary from state to state, but they cannot go below a certain level.

The food stamp program was set up in 1964. It provides debit cards that can be used to buy food. The cards are given to people whose income falls below a certain limit.

Social Security payments assist in the living expenses of people age sixty-five and over.

SSI provides cash payments to people who are elderly, have disabilities, or are blind. To qualify, their income must be below a set level. The program began in 1974. The federal government administers SSI and funds it with tax money.

stop and think

Create a table to compare and contrast social insurance and public assistance programs. Label the columns across the top "Name of Program," "Description," "Who Benefits," "Funding," "Entitlement/Not an Entitlement." Work with a partner. Be sure to give the table a title. Fill in the table. Then write three sentences that make comparisons or contrasts about the information in the table.

TANF is a new program. It was signed into law in 1996 and takes the place of a previous welfare program. TANF is also known as Welfare to Work. It offers two years of job training, child care, and health care in return for an agreement to find work. If a person does not go to work within two years, he or she loses all benefits. The lifetime limit for collecting welfare is five years. The federal government pays for the program, but it is administered by the states.

Public Health

The Department of Health and Human Services also runs programs related to the health of the general public. Four of these agencies are the National Institutes of Health (NIH), the Centers for Disease Control (CDC), the Office of Public Health Preparedness (OPHP), and the Food and Drug Administration (FDA).

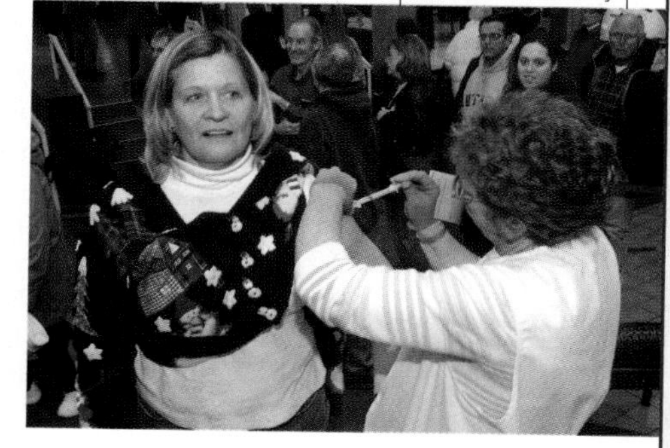

The CDC promotes flu shots as part of its mission to keep Americans healthy.

Picturing Government

The photograph in the center right of page 353 shows elderly people at an Ohio food bank. The percentage of people living in poverty in Ohio rose each year from 2001 to 2003. The state was hit hard by job losses in the manufacturing sector. From 2001 to 2004, the Department of Labor's Trade Adjustment Association certified a loss of more than 32,000 manufacturing jobs, most of which were lost to international trade. Ohio food bank use in 2003 was up 27 percent; 97 percent of households visiting the emergency food banks were living below the federal poverty levels. Have students find the trends and poverty rates for different populations in their state, using library resources or the Internet.

Stop and Think

Students' tables and three sentences will vary.

Picturing Government

In the photograph at the bottom right of page 353, a woman is being vaccinated against the flu. In late 2005, fears of a bird flu pandemic spurred President George W. Bush to push for a multibillion-dollar plan for the early detection, containment, and treatment of an outbreak, as well as for stockpiling antiviral drugs. The World Health Organization had identified 62 deaths due to avian flu by November 2005. The virus had spread to birds in 16 nations. During the twentieth century, three flu pandemics occurred. The most serious, in 1918, caused the deaths of more than 500,000 Americans and between 30 million and 50 million people worldwide. Other outbreaks occurred in 1957 and 1968.

Extension

Ask interested students to use library resources or the Internet to find out about the Influenza Genome Sequencing Project, a project of the National Institute of Allergy and Infectious Diseases. Ask them to discuss the controversies generated by the project after it began in 1995.

The NIH conducts research on health issues and provides grants to other researchers. The CDC educates the public about infectious diseases such as flu and AIDS. It also conducts research on these easily spread diseases. Its mission is to stop their spread. The OPHP was set up after the terrorist attacks of September 11, 2001, because of the nation's concern with terrorism. Its mission is to direct the response to health emergencies, especially bioterrorism. The FDA approves the sale of all prescription drugs and medical devices used in the nation. Companies must conduct thorough tests on their products before the FDA will approve them.

Aid to Veterans

The Department of Veterans Affairs (VA) also carries out health and human service policies. It provides benefits to veterans and their families, including widows, widowers, and dependent children. Supporting veterans is national policy. There is little or no disagreement over this.

The GI Bill was enacted after WWII to help veterans to pay for college after serving in the armed forces.

The VA provides health care for veterans in VA hospitals and clinics. In a recent year, more than five million people were treated through the VA health-care system. The VA also administers several financial programs for veterans. These include cash benefits for veterans who were disabled by injury or disease while in the service. Veterans may also receive education and training benefits. Since 1944, more than 20.4 million veterans have used the GI Bill of Rights and later laws to attend college and acquire other educational training. The VA also offers low-cost home loans and life insurance to veterans.

Putting It All Together

What are the nation's social policies? Do you agree with what the federal government does about social issues? Work with a partner to answer these questions. Identify each social policy mentioned in the lesson and give an opinion.

Picturing Government

In the 1951 photograph, on page 354, men eligible for education benefits under the GI Bill complete paperwork on the final day to register. The GI Bill offered up to $500 per term for college or vocational school for any World War II veteran who had served at least 90 days. Some eight million veterans took advantage of the education vouchers, causing a boom in college enrollment and campus housing. It has been called a Marshall Plan for America. While that original bill expired in 1956, veterans of the Korean and Vietnam Wars were also eligible for subsequent scaled-down GI bills. Currently, the Montgomery GI Bill offers education and job training benefits for military recruits.

Putting It All Together

Students' choices and opinions will vary but should be supported with information from the lesson.

LESSON 4

Education, Housing, Transportation, and Security

Thinking on Your Own

The federal government supports programs for education, housing, transportation, and security. Choose one area. In your notebook, list five programs in your community that you think the federal government does or should support.

Federal aid to education began in the 1860s. Congress passed the Morrill Land Grant Act during the Civil War. Among other things, it offered land to states to build colleges to teach agricultural and mechanical arts. Over 70 land grant colleges have been built. Many state universities, such as Texas A&M, began this way.

Today, the federal government supports education in many ways. It also sets policies for housing, urban development, transportation, and security.

focus your reading

How does the Department of Education impact students and school districts?

Describe the role of the Department of Housing and Urban Development.

How has September 11, 2001, affected the mission of the Department of Transportation?

words to know

equal access
financial aid
school vouchers
charter schools
urban renewal
public housing
mass transit

Federal Aid to Education

Federal aid to elementary and secondary education is a recent development. Historically, support for public schools has been a state and local responsibility. In 1953, Congress created a cabinet-level Department of Health, Education, and Welfare. Federal aid for K–12 students dates from the Elementary and Secondary Education Act passed by Congress in 1965. It provided funds for schools that had students living in poverty.

Lesson Summary

The federal government's involvement with education began with the Morrill Land Grant Act during the Civil War. Until 1953, elementary and secondary education were the responsibilities of state or local governments. In 1965, Congress passed the Elementary and Secondary Education Act, giving funds to schools serving students living in poverty. The Department of Education provides equal access for all students and sets policies on financial aid. Federal aid is dependent on following the No Child Left Behind Act. Parents use school vouchers to send children in low-performing public schools to private schools. Charter schools are public schools that do not have to obey all the rules that most public schools do. Federal involvement in housing began during the Great Depression to help builders and potential homebuyers. Programs to help cities are known as urban renewal programs. Public housing policies are also part of this department's responsibilities. The Department of Transportation exists to ensure a fast and safe transportation system. Mass transit systems and highways are part of its impact. The newest department is Homeland Security, created after the terrorist attacks of September 11, 2001. It is a controversial department because its actions sometimes seem to threaten civil liberties.

Lesson Objective

Students will learn about federal efforts in education, housing, transportation, and security.

Words to Know

Discuss each of the vocabulary terms with students.

Equal access means that schools don't discriminate based on race or gender. *Equal access* is guaranteed by the Department of Education. *School vouchers* are money given to parents of children in low-performing public schools so that they can send their children to private schools. Public schools that do not have to obey all of the rules and regulations of most public schools are *charter schools*. *Charter schools* are typically located in large cities with many underperforming schools. Money for students in financial need to attend college and graduate school is called *financial aid*. Some *financial aid* does not have to be paid back.

Urban renewal is rebuilding of cities. The federal government provides money for *urban renewal*. Low-income housing is called *public housing*. Most money for *public housing* is spent on rent subsidies.

Mass transit is a form of transportation that can move many people at once. Buses, subways, and trains are examples of *mass transit*.

Focus Your Reading Answers

1 The Department of Education impacts students and school districts through its policy of equal access to education for all students. It also sets financial aid policies and monitors testing to qualify for the aid.

2 The Department of Housing and Urban Development assists people in buying or building homes. It also offers programs to help cities rebuild and makes public housing available.

3 September 11, 2001, has affected the mission of the Department of Transportation because the Department of Homeland Security now imposes restrictions on travelers. People can have their belongings searched, must have a photo ID, and can be held for questioning.

Picturing Government

The photograph on page 356 shows a teacher and some of her students. Ask students to use census data to track enrollment in public schools in their state over the past decade. Then have them create graphs that show the changes.

Stop and Think

Students' concept webs will vary but may include collecting national statistics on education, setting financial aid policies, and monitoring testing of students.

The Department of Education, created in 1980, ensures **equal access** to education for all students. It guarantees that schools do not discriminate on the basis of race or gender. The department also collects national statistics on education.

Some student loans are forgiven when people agree to teach in areas that require more teachers.

A major responsibility of the Department of Education is to set policies on **financial aid**. The department gives financial aid to school districts. Federal aid to K–12 schools makes up about 9 percent of state and local budgets for these schools. Since 2001, states have been required to test students in grades three through eight in reading, math, and science. Their federal aid depends on obeying the No Child Left Behind Act.

Two other topics in education are school vouchers and charter schools. **School vouchers** give money to parents of children in low-performing public schools. The parents use the money to send their children to private schools. **Charter schools** are public schools. However, they do not have to obey all the rules and regulations of public schools. They are also free to experiment with different kinds of curricula. Charter schools are typically opened in large cities with many underperforming schools.

The federal government also provides financial aid to college and graduate students. Students receive money based on financial need. Pell Grants do not have to be paid back. There are also Perkins and Stafford Loan programs. They require the payment of interest as well as the original loan amount. The payment period is extended over ten years.

stop and think

Create a concept web for the Department of Education. Draw a large circle in the center of your paper. Label it "Department of Education." Draw and label smaller circles for each activity the department does. Connect these smaller circles with lines to the large circle. Work with a partner.

Aid to Housing and Urban Areas

In a recent year, the budget of the Department of Housing and Urban Development (HUD) was $38 billion. This money was spent on programs such as grants for community planning and development, lead hazard control, public housing, and loan programs for home ownership.

Extensions

1 Have interested students find out if any of the universities or colleges in their state were originally land grant colleges. If not, have them find the nearest one. Ask students to find out about the history of the college, using library resources or the Internet, and share their findings with the class.

2 Ask students to use library resources or the Internet to find out more about Pell Grants, Perkins Loans, and Stafford Loans. How could they help students in the class as they prepare for college costs? What are the eligibility requirements that students should be considering? Have students create a brochure or fact sheet to share with the class or place in the school library.

The federal government has been involved in housing policy since the Great Depression. In 1934, Congress created the Federal Housing Administration (FHA) and passed the National Housing Act in 1937. The purpose of both was to help builders and potential homeowners. The FHA continues to guarantee bank loans to builders and middle- and low-income home buyers. The FHA also runs housing programs for the homeless.

The "urban development" part of the department's title refers to programs to help cities. In the 1950s and 1960s, many large cities in the Northeast and Midwest had become run-down. People who could afford to were moving to the suburbs. Businesses followed. Parts of cities became filled with empty and decaying buildings. The people who were left became poorer and poorer.

The federal government stepped in with money for **urban renewal**, or rebuilding. Issues arose, however, about how the money was used. Often, poor people were forced out of their homes, which were then torn down. Office buildings and apartments for middle-income and wealthy people took their place.

Many housing projects, such as these in Chicago, are being replaced with affordable, low-income housing.

HUD also helps cities through its public housing policies. HUD provides aid to local governments to set up and operate public housing programs. In the beginning, **public housing** took the form of high-rise apartment buildings for low-income families. Problems with crime, drugs, and poor maintenance halted the building of these projects. Low-rise apartment buildings and townhouses are now built in some areas as public housing. The majority of public housing money is spent on rent subsidies. Low-income families pay a part of the rent themselves. A federal grant pays the rest.

Transportation Programs

The mission of the Department of Transportation (DOT) is to ensure "a fast, safe, efficient, accessible, and convenient transportation system that meets our vital national interests and enhances the quality of life of the American people." The DOT does this in a number of ways.

Picturing Government

In the photograph on page 357, Chicago's notorious projects, Cabrini Green, tower over new mixed-income apartments and townhomes being built to replace the low-income housing. Chicago planned to have all 53 of the city's public housing high-rises replaced. Some 40,000 people will be uprooted and given the chance to live in housing that is not substandard, with rent subsidized by the government. People who applied were subject to mandatory drug tests, criminal background checks, and home inspections. Seventy-nine Cabrini Green families were moving to North Town Village, which contains 261 townhomes and condos. All the units sold before they were built, due to the prime location a mile from the most exclusive strip in Chicago.

Extension

Have a local historian visit the class to talk about urban renewal efforts or public housing in your community if appropriate. Have students prepare a list of questions to ask the guest.

Domestic Policy: Education, Housing, Transportation, and Security 357

Picturing Government

The photograph on page 358 shows a crash test done by the insurance Institute for Highway Safety. The institute is a private, nonprofit agency. The federal government's program for testing vehicles is under the Department of Transportation's National Highway Traffic Safety Administration, which establishes safety standards for equipment and vehicles.

The DOT runs labs that test the safety of cars and trucks. It publishes the results of these rollover and crash test studies. These reports keep consumers informed about the safety of cars and trucks they might be thinking of buying.

The Federal Aviation Administration (FAA) sets standards for airline safety. Its mission is to provide the safest, most efficient aerospace system in the world. It also aids in the investigation of airline crashes and issues reports on their causes. The National Transportation Safety Board (NTSB) is an independent federal agency that investigates every aviation accident in the United States. It also investigates significant railroad, highway, marine, and pipeline accidents.

The Department of Transportation conducts tests on vehicles in the United States to ensure consumer safety.

The most direct impact of the DOT comes through federal spending on highways and mass transit. Trains, buses, and subways are **mass transit**. Unlike cars, they transport large numbers of people at one time. The federal government has been aiding state highway building since 1916. The greatest boost to highway construction began in 1956. In that year, Congress passed the Federal-Aid Highway Act. The federal excise tax on gasoline, tires, and similar goods is given to states to build and improve the national highway system. There are 45,000 miles of multi-lane highways that join most of the nation's major cities.

Mass transit, on the other hand, suffers from a lack of funding. A few rapid transit rail lines, like San Francisco's BART (Bay Area Rapid Transit), have been built. However, these projects cost millions of dollars. States and cities look to the federal government for help for at least some of the cost.

Homeland Security

A major change in domestic policy came after September 11, 2001. The terrorist attack on the United States showed how at risk the nation was. As a result, President George W. Bush proposed the creation of a Department of Homeland Security. The mission of the department is to "prevent and deter terrorist attacks against and respond to threats and hazards to the nation." The department ensures safe and secure borders, welcomes lawful immigrants and visitors, and promotes the free flow of commerce.

Extension

Invite students interested in mass transit to find out more about systems in other countries, such as Japan's maglev trains. Have them investigate obstacles to creating such systems in the United States.

The new department combined 22 agencies from existing executive departments. For example, the Secret Service, Coast Guard, airport baggage screeners, and border patrol officers became employees of the new department. The main focus of the department is terrorism. However, it is also responsible for the government's response to natural disasters. Its Federal Emergency Management Agency (FEMA) provides aid after major floods, tornadoes, and hurricanes.

Americans welcomed the new department when it was created. However, disagreements have arisen over how it does its job. Immigration officers have increased arrests of undocumented aliens. Often, these arrests are of people who have lived, worked, and raised families in the United States peacefully for years. Critics claim that these people pose no threat to the country.

Controversies have also arisen over the Patriot Act, which allows the government to search out terrorists without giving them some of the protections of the Bill of Rights. Supporters say it is needed to track down terrorists. Others claim it threatens people's civil liberties. Critics claim the act endangers the freedom of all Americans.

Critics also claim that more money should be spent on securing the nation's harbors. Millions of tons of cargo come through U.S. ports daily. Little of it is inspected. Big cities like New York want more money for security. In a recent budget, New York City received what amounted to $5 a person. Western states like Wyoming received $33 a person.

Like all policy disagreements, these will be solved through the give-and-take of public discussion and elections. Not everyone will be happy with the solutions. However, everyone will have a chance to make his or her ideas known at election time.

Putting It All Together

Imagine you are a member of Congress. There is $100 million to divide among housing, transportation, and homeland security. How much would you give to (1) public housing, (2) highway repairs, (3) mass transit, and (4) improvements to harbor security? Explain in two or three sentences how you decided on the amount given to each program.

Putting It All Together

Students' budget numbers and rationales will vary.

Participate in Government

Obtain a sample census form to show students. Make copies and have students work in small groups to fill out a sample form.

Participate in Government

The Census: Fill It Out and Be Counted

Every ten years, the U.S. Census Bureau counts every American—or tries to. The Constitution requires that a census, or count, of residents be taken every ten years. The first census was in 1790. U.S. marshals went from house to house counting people. They found that the new nation's population was 3.9 million. It is now close to 300 million and growing.

Today, census forms are mailed to every household in the nation. Most forms are "short forms." They contain just a few questions about age, gender, ethnic group, race, and similar topics. One person is supposed to fill out the form for everyone living in the home. About one in six forms is a "long form." It asks a long list of questions. They deal with topics such as disability, income, occupation, number of rooms in the house, value of the home or monthly rent, and number of cars. The long form attempts to get a summary of certain characteristics of the nation's households.

Some people lose their census forms. Others just forget to fill them out. Still other people do not like to give information to the government. To get as accurate a count as possible, the Census Bureau hires people to visit households that have not returned their form.

Why is it important to fill out the census form when it arrives in the mail? Many government programs depend on population information. The census provides data that is used

- for redrawing districts for members of the House of Representatives and for state lawmakers.
- for distributing federal funds for programs such as Medicaid and aid to education.
- for planning where to build schools, roads, and other government facilities.

Be counted—fill out the census form when it comes!

Research Resources

Below is a list of reference books and Web sites that relate to the issues covered in this chapter. Students may wish to use these to further their research on ideas in the preceding lessons. Web site addresses may change over time. Use keyword searching on a major search engine to locate sites.

Reference Books:

Kathleen Hill. *Encyclopedia of Federal Agencies and Commissions.* Facts on File, 2004.

George Thomas Kurian, ed. *A Historical Guide to the U.S. Government.* Oxford University Press, 1998.

Web Sites:

The Web site for the Environmental Protection Agency gives information on topics as diverse as global warming, acid rain, oil spills, and wetlands.

The Department of Homeland Security's Web site offers news and press releases, as well as indicating the current level of threat.

The Web site of the Department of Housing and Human Services has links to states and communities.

Skill Builder

Analyze a Line Graph

A line graph shows information about a topic over a period of time. Usually, the time is shown along the bottom, or horizontal axis, of the graph. The quantity, or amount, is given along the left side, or vertical axis, of the graph. The line or lines on the graph show the ups and downs of the topic. A graph key explains what each line represents.

By reading a line graph, you can determine if there is a trend, or pattern, over time. Understanding you decide how important something is over time. A line graph may show a rising federal deficit.

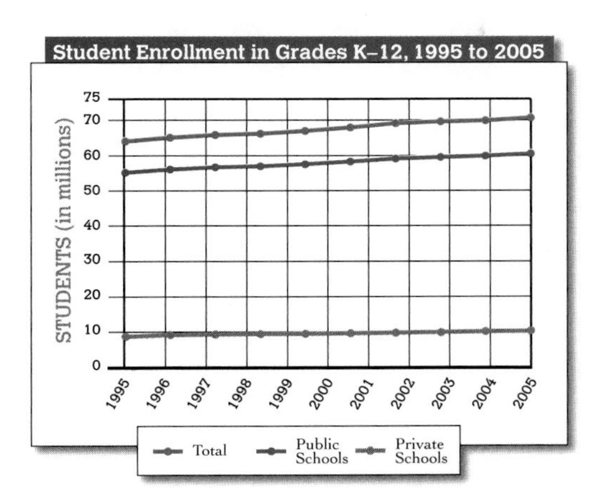

To Read a Line Graph:

- Read the title of the graph to see what it is about.
- Examine the vertical, or side, axis to determine the quantity.
- Examine the horizontal, or bottom, axis to determine the time period.
- Read the key if there is more than one line on the graph.
- Examine the line (or lines) on the graph. Does the line go up or down steadily over time? Does the line zigzag over time?

Study the graph and then answer the following questions.

1. What is the title of the graph?
2. What do the lines represent?
3. Does the number of students ever decrease?
4. Do the numbers move steadily, or do they zigzag?

Skill Builder

1. The title of the graph is Student Enrollment in Grades K–12, 1995 to 2005.
2. The lines represent the total number of students enrolled, in millions.
3. no
4. The numbers move steadily.

Recommended Reading

Below is a list of books that relate to the issues covered in this chapter. The numbers in parentheses indicate the related Thematic Strands of the National Council for the Social Studies (NCSS).

Tristan Boyer Binns. *EPA: The Environmental Protection Agency*. Heinemann, 2002. (VI, X)

Geoffrey M. Horn. *The Cabinet and Federal Agencies*. World Almanac Library, 2003. (VI, X)

Wallace Stephany, Fred Israel. *The Department of Transportation*. Chelsea House Publishers, 1998. (VI, X)

Classroom Discussion

Discuss with students some of the broader topics covered in this chapter.

- What should be the limits of government regulation of businesses?
- How can the United States protect itself from terrorism without denying civil liberties?
- What should be most important, the environment or the rights of corporations?
- Should the federal government continue funding entitlement programs?

Related Transparencies

T-12 U.S. Foreign Policy Alliances and Major Groups Within the United Nations

T-18 Three-Column Chart

T-19 Venn Diagram

T-20 Concept Web

Key Blacklines

Biography—Condoleezza Rice

CD Extension

Encourage students to use the reading comprehension, vocabulary reinforcement, and other activities on the student CD.

Getting Focused

Ask students to share their lists of foreign policy issues. Then challenge them to work in pairs, choosing one issue, and serving as the foreign correspondent on that issue. Have students use the Internet, newsmagazines, and newspapers to continue updating the class on these issues as they read the chapter. Students may also wish to use a bulletin board to post relevant articles.

Chapter 20 FOREIGN POLICY AND NATIONAL DEFENSE

Getting Focused

Skim this chapter to predict what you will be learning.

- **Read the lesson titles and subheadings.**
- **Look at the illustrations and read the captions.**
- **Examine the tables and Time Box.**
- **Review the vocabulary words and terms.**

On many days, foreign policy issues seem to take over the news. The president spends a great deal of time dealing with other nations. List at least four foreign policy issues that you know the current president is dealing with.

The president of the United States is responsible for setting foreign and domestic policy agendas. In this role, the president regularly meets with other world leaders, such as during this meeting of NATO members.

Pre-Reading Discussion

1 The idea of nation-building or spreading democracy has been in the news in recent years. Can democracy be spread through military or humanitarian actions?

2 What should be the goals of U.S. businesses working in other nations? How can these corporations build goodwill and make a profit at the same time?

LESSON 1

U.S. Foreign Policy

Thinking on Your Own

Read the Time Box on page 365. Choose one entry. Write at least three things in your notebook that you already know about that event.

Foreign policy is all the strategies and goals that guide a nation's dealings with other countries. It includes trade treaties like the NAFTA and treaties that limit nuclear weapons. It includes military actions such as peacekeeping as part of the North Atlantic Treaty Organization (NATO). Diplomats such as ambassadors, however, carry on most foreign relations. These people are representatives of the government who deal directly with other nations.

focus your reading

What are the goals of U.S. foreign policy?

Explain how U.S. foreign policy has changed over time.

How has internationalism affected U.S. foreign policy?

words to know

foreign policy

alliances

isolationism

globalization

The Goals of U.S. Foreign Policy

Five basic goals underlie all U.S. foreign policy. Some of these goals, such as national security, date back to the beginning of the United States. Others, such as world peace, are more recent.

National security: The nation's borders and territories must be kept safe from invasion or control by other countries. This is the meaning of national security. The first interest of all U.S. foreign policy is to keep the nation safe.

Trade: The economy of the United States is based on the ability to buy and sell freely in other nations. U.S. businesses buy and sell more than just finished goods such as cars. They buy and sell natural resources, as well as services. In return, U.S. businesses sell their services overseas.

Words to Know

Introduce each of the following vocabulary terms to students.

Explain that *foreign policy* involves all the goals and strategies that guide a nation's dealings with other nations. The United States's *foreign policy* has shifted several times since the nation began.

Partnerships are also called *alliances*. George Washington warned against foreign *alliances*.

Isolationism is the refusal to become involved in world affairs. The United States followed a policy of *isolationism* into the late nineteenth century.

The interaction of people, companies, and governments of different nations is known as *globalization*. Critics of *globalization* believe that working conditions in U.S. trade partner countries should be improved.

Lesson Summary

The strategies and goals guiding a country's dealings with other nations is its foreign policy. Five basic goals underlie U.S. foreign policy: national security, trade, world peace, democracy, and humanitarianism. U.S. foreign policy has changed over time, moving from isolationism to expansion and status as a world power, then back to cycles of isolationism that ended with entrance into world wars. Currently, U.S. military policy focuses on fighting against terrorism. U.S. economic policy focuses on globalization.

Lesson Objective

Students will learn about the goals and history of U.S. foreign policy.

Focus Your Reading Answers

1 The goals of U.S. foreign policy include national security, trade, world peace, democracy, and humanitarianism.

2 Early presidents warned against involvement with other nations. This was followed by a period of isolationism. Late in the nineteenth century, in its search for new markets and cheap raw materials, the U.S. began to annex other areas. The U.S. entered World War I reluctantly, then retreated back into isolation, entering World War II only after Japan attacked the naval base at Pearl Harbor. Following the war, the Cold War lasted for 45 years. When the Cold War ended, the nation focused on globalization and antiterrorist efforts.

3 Internationalism has affected U.S. foreign policy by encouraging involvement in world affairs.

World peace: For much of the twentieth century, the United States acted as the world's peacemaker. After World War I, it tried to get other nations to stop building weapons. During World War II, the United States worked to get other countries to establish the United Nations.

U.S. soldiers served as peacekeepers in Bosnia during the 1990s.

Democracy: The United States is the oldest constitutional democracy in the world. It serves as a model to other nations. The United States also has a long history of helping others fight undemocratic governments. For example, Communist governments in Eastern Europe collapsed in the late 1980s. Many of the new governments received U.S. economic aid and political help to set up democracies.

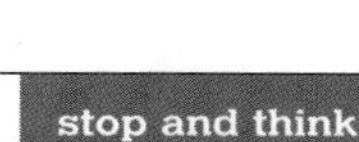

Create a concept map to represent the goals of U.S. foreign policy. Work with a partner. Decide what to label the central circle and the smaller circles for the goals. Add another smaller circle to each goal with an example from the text and from class discussion.

Humanitarianism: This is concern for the welfare of humanity. Both the U.S. government and private citizens respond to world crises. The outpouring of aid to the tsunami victims in South Asia in 2004 is an example.

U.S. officials see world peace, democratic nations, and a concern for humanity as ways to ensure the nation's security.

U.S. Foreign Policy Over Time

President George Washington warned the United States to stay out of foreign **alliances**. He believed that having partnerships with other nations could be dangerous. The next few presidents agreed with Washington. They thought the nation was still too weak to fight another war. As a result, the nation followed a policy based on **isolationism**. It did not become involved in world affairs, particularly those of Europe.

In 1823, President James Monroe warned Europe to stay out of the Americas. This is called the Monroe Doctrine. In truth, the United States was still not powerful enough to defeat European nations. Monroe knew that the United States could rely on Great Britain to help enforce this policy. Great Britain had territories in the Americas and wanted to keep other nations out, too.

Picturing Government

In the photograph on page 364, U.S. soldiers march through a village in Bosnia on a peacekeeping mission in 1996. After a four-year conflict in the Balkan states, NATO imposed a cease-fire, and the United States, along with eleven other nations, sent troops for Operation Joint Endeavor. The group enforced the cease-fire, enforced the move of combatants to their barracks, and enforced the move of weapons to storage sites, as well as supervised the marking of boundaries. It also aided in overseeing the nation's first democratic national elections.

Stop and Think

Students' concept maps will vary. Possible response: national security, such as securing borders with Mexico; trade, such as imports from Canada; world peace, such as efforts to prevent the building of weapons after World War I; democracy, as in efforts leading to the collapse of Communist countries in eastern Europe; and humanitarianism, such as the aid to tsunami victims

Picturing Government

In the photograph on page 362, George W. Bush speaks at a White House ceremony marking the addition of seven new nations to the North Atlantic Treaty Organization (NATO). NATO is open to any European nation willing to meet certain economic, political, and military goals. Member nations are expected to contribute to the security of as well as benefit from the alliance. Nations are invited to join by the North Atlantic Council. NATO assists nations wishing to join through its Membership Action Plan (MAP).

364 Chapter 20

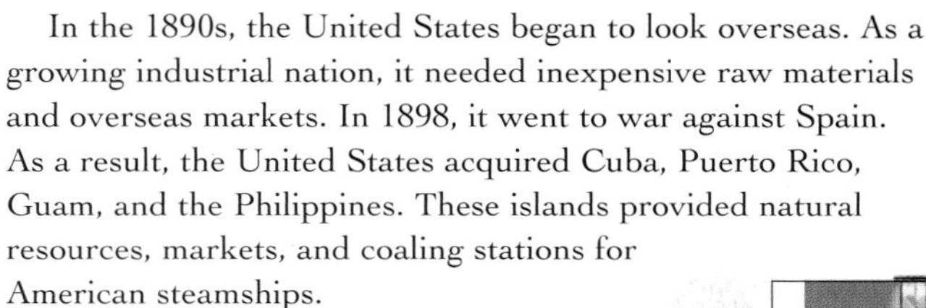

In the 1890s, the United States began to look overseas. As a growing industrial nation, it needed inexpensive raw materials and overseas markets. In 1898, it went to war against Spain. As a result, the United States acquired Cuba, Puerto Rico, Guam, and the Philippines. These islands provided natural resources, markets, and coaling stations for American steamships.

Many Americans did not want to be pulled into World War I. However, by 1917, it looked as though Germany would win. The United States then entered the war. President Woodrow Wilson declared that the United States would make the "world safe for democracy."

World War I resulted in a huge loss of life and was very costly. In the 1920s and 1930s, the United States stopped intervening in the affairs of other nations. It did not want to get caught in the war that seemed to be building in Europe. When Japan bombed U.S. forces at Pearl Harbor in 1941, the United States entered World War II against Japan, Germany, and Italy.

After World War II, the United States remained involved in world affairs and kept its place as a world power. For the next 45 years, it waged a Cold War against the Communist Soviet Union and People's Republic of China. No actual wars were fought against these nations. But each side supported other groups in pro-Communist and anti-Communist conflicts. The Korean and Vietnam Wars were the longest and most costly. During this time, the United States, the Soviet Union, and China also built massive nuclear weapons.

The Cold War thawed somewhat during the 1970s. However, President Ronald Reagan toughened foreign policies toward Communist nations in the 1980s.

Time Box

U.S. Foreign Policy

1789–1823
Isolationism

1823
Monroe Doctrine

1823–1890s
Expansion of the U.S. across the continent

1898–1914
U.S. as a world power

1914–1917
Return to isolationism

1917–1919
World War I

1920s–1930s
Return to isolationism

1939–1945
World War II

1945–1989
Cold War; Korean War; Vietnam War; nuclear weapons

1969–1970s
Détente

1980s
Return to a hard line against the Communist Soviet Union

1989
End of the Cold War

1990s–present
Globalization and fighting terrorism

Time Box Extension

Have students make flash cards and drill each other on the events in the Time Box. Encourage them to add artwork or graphics that will help them link the event and the date in their minds.

Extension

Both Puerto Rico and the United States have been divided on the question of the island becoming the 51st state. Have students use library resources or the Internet to find out more about the issue. Have them list cost/benefits to both nations. Then host a panel discussion or debate about adding Puerto Rico, which is currently a possession, as another state.

Extensions

1 The border patrols along the U.S.-Mexico border have failed to keep illegal immigrants from entering the United States. Challenge students to use library resources or the Internet to find out more about efforts to secure the border and counter efforts to assist those trying to enter the United States to find work. Have them present their findings to the class by using the Student Presentation Builder on the student CD.

2 Ask students to use library resources or the Internet to find out about organizations making efforts for world peace. Suggest they focus on a project linked to a specific group, such as Women in Black or the World Peace Project for Children.

Picturing Government

The photograph on page 366, taken in Moscow in 1988, shows President Mikhail Gorbachev of the Soviet Union (left) shaking hands across the table with U.S. president Ronald Reagan (right). The two men first met in Geneva in late 1985, which was the beginning of a long and ultimately successful attempt to limit nuclear weapons. By December 1989, Reagan's successor, George H.W. Bush, and Gorbachev declared that the Cold War had ended.

Putting It All Together

Students' tables will vary but should reflect the five foreign policy goals listed on pages 363–364 and the information in the Time Box on page 365.

President Ronald Reagan and Soviet president Mikhail Gorbachev shake hands during a meeting in 1988.

Communism collapsed in Russia and Eastern Europe in the late 1980s and early 1990s. Most of the new governments were democratic. In the 1990s, China became more open to private enterprise. However, it remains Communist.

U.S. Foreign Policy Today

U.S. foreign military policy is focused on fighting terrorism. The first terrorist attack on U.S. soil was a bombing of the World Trade Center in New York City in 1993. Between then and 2001, terrorists carried out other attacks on U.S. interests such as the U.S. Navy ship the USS *Cole*. On September 11, 2001, terrorists flew planes into the World Trade Center in New York City and the Pentagon in Washington, D.C.

Since the attacks of September 11, 2001, the federal government has waged a "war on terrorism." President George W. Bush sent troops into Afghanistan looking for the terrorists who were responsible for planning the attack. The United States and European nations help one another track down and arrest terrorists. It is a fight that will go on for many years.

Economic Foreign Policy

U.S. economic foreign policy is focused on globalization. **Globalization** is the interaction among people, companies, and governments of different nations. International trade is one force behind globalization. Another is investment. Technologies such as computers, robots, and the Internet aid globalization. U.S. trade policies aid U.S. companies as they buy and sell in the world market.

Globalization offers jobs and wages to many people who would have none. However, many workers in developing nations work in unsafe and unhealthy factories. Critics of globalization believe the United States should do more to improve conditions in other nations.

Putting It All Together

Work with a partner. Create a table with five columns. Label each column with a foreign policy goal. Then classify the events in the Time Box by goal. You may write an event in more than one column. With a partner, discuss any differences between your tables.

LESSON 2

Shared Powers

Thinking on Your Own

As you skim the lesson, make an outline of it in your notebook. Remember to include the subheadings. Start each section of your outline with the most important information. As you read, fill in the details of the outline.

focus your reading

List three of the outside influences on foreign policy decision-making.

How do the president's roles affect foreign policy?

Who are the president's chief foreign policy advisers?

Explain how the president and Congress interact in making foreign policy.

words to know

economic interest group

human rights group

ambassador

intelligence

hot spot

The president is the chief architect of U.S. foreign policy. The Departments of State and Defense and the Office of National Intelligence, an independent agency, advise the president. Congress also has a role in foreign policy.

Influences on Policy-makers

Like all policy decisions, foreign policy is influenced by outside factors. Both public opinion and interest groups influence foreign policy. In the early 1960s, the public supported the Vietnam War. As the war dragged on and the human and money costs mounted, the public turned against the war. In 1968, President Lyndon Johnson decided not to run for reelection. It seemed certain he would lose. He had become unpopular because of the war. Richard Nixon won the 1968 election because he promised to end U.S. involvement in the conflict.

Groups with an interest in foreign policy include unions and trade and farm associations. Special-interest groups such as human rights organizations also try to influence U.S. foreign policy. Some **economic interest groups** lobby Congress to protect their

Antiwar protesters demonstrated against the Vietnam War in May 1971.

Lesson Summary

Although the president makes U.S. foreign policy, others have influence as well. The Departments of Defense and State and the Office of National Intelligence, along with Congress, also have input. Public opinion and both economic and human rights interest groups also affect foreign policy. The president has both diplomatic and military responsibilities in receiving ambassadors from other nations and acting as commander in chief of the military. Foreign policy advisers brief the president daily. Congress can affect foreign policy through its power to declare war and ratify treaties, as well as through its budget powers. However, the president can negotiate executive agreements, which do not need congressional approval.

Lesson Objective

Students will learn about the power shared among the president, several executive agencies, and Congress in developing foreign policy.

Focus Your Reading Answers

1 Three outside influences on foreign policy decision-making include public opinion, economic interest groups, and human rights groups.

2 The president's power to break off or reestablish diplomatic relations with a country and the president's role as commander in chief of the military both affect foreign policy.

3 The president's chief foreign policy advisers include heads of the Departments of State and Defense.

Focus Your Reading Answers, continued

4 Congress has the power to declare war and to ratify treaties, as well as budget and confirmation powers that can work for or against the president. The president sets the direction for foreign policy, speaks for the nation as the head of state, and has access to classified documents that Congress may not see. The president can approve executive agreements and thus bypass Congress.

members. Others want free trade to make U.S. goods less costly for other nations to buy. Unions and some trade and farm groups want high tariffs to make imports more expensive. **Human rights groups** want U.S. foreign policy to punish nations whose policies violate people's human rights. These groups want the United States to withhold support from the governments that fail to act against human rights abuses. The president and Congress must weigh these competing foreign policy goals.

The President's Foreign Policy Roles

Article 3, Sections 2 and 3, of the U.S. Constitution lists the powers and duties of the president. Among these are diplomatic and military responsibilities. As head of state, the president represents the United States to the rest of the world. The president often takes an active role in world affairs. For example, both Presidents Jimmy Carter and Bill Clinton tried to make peace between Israel and its Arab neighbors.

Israeli prime minister Yitzhak Rabin, President Bill Clinton, and PLO chairman Yasser Arafat in 1993

The president is also chief diplomat for the nation. In this role, the president receives **ambassadors**—official representatives—from other countries. The president can also break off diplomatic relations with other nations. This occurs only over serious disagreements. For example, President Dwight Eisenhower broke off relations with Cuba after the Communists came to power there. On the other hand, President Bill Clinton reestablished diplomatic relations with Vietnam in 1995.

The president is commander in chief of the military. It is the president who decides when and if U.S. troops will be sent into battle zones. Although the president can use the military around the world, Congress must be notified of such a decision.

Foreign Policy Advisers

Foreign policy is about more than terrorism and war. Foreign policy also involves issues such as trade and energy resources. As a result, most executive departments have foreign policy issues. However, the Departments of State and Defense play the major roles in foreign policy decisions.

368 Chapter 20

Picturing Government

The 1971 photograph on page 367 shows a May Day protest against the Vietnam War. The protests began in 1965, just after the United States sent the first combat troops, marines, to Vietnam. The May 1971 protest was an attempt to shut down the federal government by stopping traffic flowing into the District of Columbia. To keep the government functioning, police arrested more than 7,000 people in one day. Without sufficient jail space, prisoners were held at the football practice field of the Washington Redskins.

Picturing Government

The photograph on page 368 shows President Bill Clinton with Israeli prime minister Yitzhak Rabin (left) and Palestinian Liberation Organization chairman Yasser Arafat (right). The two men had just signed a peace accord, which Clinton had helped negotiate. The accord gave Palestinians limited self-government in Jericho and on the Gaza Strip, but further conflict continued. Rabin, Arafat, and Israeli prime minister Shimon Peres received the Nobel Prize in 1994 for ending decades of bloodshed. A Jewish right-wing fanatic assassinated Rabin at a peace rally in Tel Aviv a year later.

Words to Know

Discuss each of the vocabulary terms with students.

An *economic interest group* is a collection of people with an interest in U.S. economic policy. Labor unions and farm associations are two examples of *economic interest groups*.

A *human rights group* is concerned with punishing nations that violate the human rights of their citizens. The interests of a *human rights group* are often opposed to those of an *economic interest group*.

A country's *ambassador* is its official representative to another government. As chief diplomat, the president receives a nation's *ambassador*.

Another word for information about political events is *intelligence*. Experts in the State Department are responsible for analyzing *intelligence*.

A *hot spot* is a region of political tension and violence. The Middle East has often been regarded as a *hot spot*.

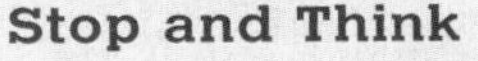

The Department of State runs all diplomatic activities of the government. The secretary of state is an expert in foreign affairs. He or she represents the United States in discussions and negotiations with high-level officials of other nations. The State Department employs thousands of area experts. These people gather and analyze **intelligence**, or information, about political events in different areas of the world.

The secretary of defense is responsible for all branches of the armed forces—army, navy, air force, and marines. The strength of the U.S. military is important in deciding whether to send troops to some world hot spot. A **hot spot** is an area of political tension and violence. The Defense Department also has intelligence experts.

Secretary of State Condoleezza Rice, Defense Secretary Donald Rumsfeld, and President George W. Bush in 2005.

stop and think

List three foreign policy issues. Choose one to write about. State your position on the issue in one sentence. Write three reasons to support your position. Use this information as the basis for a letter to the president. Write your letter. Share it with a partner. Ask your partner if your letter is clear. How could you make it clearer? Also ask your partner to proofread your letter.

Primary Source

The following is from a speech given by a member of the U.S. Agency for International Development in 2005. It states the agency's and the U.S. government's view of the proper role of foreign aid.

"Without trade, there can be no sustained economic growth. Without economic growth, there will be no increase in tax revenues to support improved public services. Without growth and services, there will be no increase in wealth and reduction in poverty. Unless foreign aid contributes to economic growth, it is failing to achieve its primary mission."

—Andrew S. Natsios, Administrator, U.S. Agency for International Development, July 20, 2005

reading for understanding

1. What is needed for economic growth?
2. Explain what is needed to improve public services.
3. Describe what foreign aid must do.

Stop and Think

Students' choices of issues, supporting reasons, and letters will vary. Review with students proper forms of address. See that the letters are mailed or e-mailed.

Picturing Government

In the 2005 photograph on page 369, President George W. Bush, with key advisers Secretary of State Condoleezza Rice and Defense Secretary Donald Rumsfeld behind him, speaks at a press conference from his ranch in Texas. The president reaffirmed his commitment not to withdraw troops serving in the War in Iraq, which was becoming increasingly unpopular after more than 2,000 U.S. deaths.

Reading for Understanding

1 Trade is needed for economic growth.

2 An increase in tax revenues will improve public services.

3 Foreign aid must contribute to economic growth.

Extension

Have students work together in small groups to find out how recent presidents have intervened in world affairs. Suggest that they build on the examples given in the text or research other situations, such as Reagan's challenge to tear down the Berlin Wall.

Primary Source Extension

You may wish to have students make cause-effect graphic organizers or flowcharts using information from the quotation. Students can work in pairs on this.

Picturing Government

The photograph on page 370 shows a June 2005 Senate Foreign Relations Committee hearing on North Korea's nuclear program. After a three-year standoff over the possibility of North Korea developing nuclear weapons, that nation agreed in September 2005 to end the program in exchange for benefits in the areas of energy, security, and economy. Six nations worked to negotiate the treaty, which required North Korea to abandon efforts to produce atomic bombs, dismantle any existing ones, and allow international inspections at its nuclear facilities. Beijing pushed for the agreement after negotiations were at a standstill. The Bush administration softened its language and stopped referring to North Korea as part of an "axis of evil."

Putting It All Together

Students' summaries will vary. You may wish to use the summary on page 367 as a guideline for assessment.

After the attacks of September 11, 2001, a national commission studied the government's intelligence system. The commission determined that a better system might have uncovered the September 11, 2001 plot. As a result, the Office of National Intelligence was created in 2005. This independent agency directs the work of 15 other government agencies that gather intelligence. The mission of the office is to make the 15 agencies work more efficiently and share information.

Congress and the President

Article I, Section 8, of the U.S. Constitution lists the powers of Congress. Declaring war and ratifying treaties relate directly to foreign policy. However, Congress can use its budget and confirmation powers to make foreign policy. It can approve part of or more than what the president asks for foreign aid. It can hold up or refuse to confirm a presidential nominee.

The president, not Congress, sets the direction for foreign policy. The president decides whether to send troops as part of a United Nations peacekeeping mission. Congress approves and funds programs proposed by the president. However, sharp differences can arise. The war in Iraq began with bipartisan support. However, when no weapons of mass destruction were found in Iraq, Democrats began to speak out against the war.

The president has certain advantages over Congress in foreign policy. The president is the head of state and therefore the only person who speaks for the United States in dealings with other nations. The president has the benefit of reports from all the government intelligence agencies. Much of this is classified, or secret. Congress may not be allowed to see all of what the president sees. Therefore, Congress does not have all the information to make decisions about foreign policy.

If the president feels it necessary, Congress can be bypassed. Instead of signing a treaty with a nation, an executive agreement can be issued. Unlike treaties, executive agreements do not have to be approved by Congress.

The Senate Foreign Relations Committee routinely holds hearings on foreign policy issues.

Putting It All Together

Use your outline to write a summary of this lesson. Share your summary with a partner. Revise your summary if needed.

LESSON 3

Tools of Foreign Policy

Thinking on Your Own

Examine the photographs in this lesson. Choose one photograph. Describe the photograph in a paragraph in your notebook. Who is shown? What are they doing? Include any information you already know about the topic.

America's foreign policy is a mix of programs and actions. Military force is one tool, but the United States uses it carefully. The nation has declared war only five times in its history. However, it has frequently sent troops to aid allies, protect the innocent, and preserve freedom.

The goal of U.S. foreign policy is to protect national security by means other than war. Defense and economic agreements combined with foreign aid are two methods. The United States is also a member of the United Nations and other organizations that work to keep world peace.

focus your reading

What is the purpose of the alliances and pacts to which the United States belongs?

What is the goal of foreign aid?

What groups are part of the United Nations?

words to know

internationalism

regional security alliances

Alliances

After World War II, the United States did not return to a policy of isolationism. It adopted **internationalism**. The nation became deeply involved in world affairs. Soon after the war, the United States sent billions of dollars in aid to Europe to rebuild and to fight communism. This aid included food, machines, and weapons. The United States was also a founding member of the United Nations. In addition, the United States entered into **regional security alliances** with nations in different parts of the world.

Lesson Summary

The United States uses military force as a tool of foreign policy. Other tools include defense and economic agreements, along with memberships in organizations such as the United Nations. Since World War II, the United States has followed a policy of internationalism. This involves aid and membership in regional security alliances. During that same time period, foreign aid has become an important part of foreign policy. This may take the form of advisers, loans or grants of money, food, equipment, technology, or seeds. Military aid may also be part of foreign aid. Along with nearly 200 other nations, the United States is part of the United Nations and its agencies. The nation is one of five permanent members of the UN Security Council, and an American heads the World Bank.

Lesson Objective

Students will learn about the various programs and actions that the United States uses in foreign policy.

Focus Your Reading Answers

1 The alliances and pacts to which the United States belongs exist to better the world through aid and the quest for peace.

2 The goal of foreign aid is both humanitarian and economic. The long-term goal is to grow the economies of developing nations.

3 Groups that are part of the United Nations include the Food and Agriculture Organization, the International Monetary Fund, the International Bank for Reconstruction and Development, the World Health Organization, and UNESCO.

Words to Know

Discuss each of the vocabulary terms with students.

Being involved in world affairs is called *internationalism*. The opposite of *internationalism* is isolationism.

Regional security alliances are mutual defense agreements. All countries that sign *regional security alliances* pledge to defend the others from attack.

Table Extension

Ask students to use the table on page 372 to answer the following questions.

- Which treaty was signed first? When? (Rio Pact, 1947)
- Which defense alliance includes New Zealand? (ANZUS)
- What is the difference between NATO and NAFTA? (NATO is a defense alliance; NAFTA is an economic alliance.)

Picturing Government

President Harry Truman is shown in the photograph on page 372. Truman, who had been vice president only five weeks before Franklin Roosevelt died, had little knowledge of foreign policy, because FDR had not included him in policy development meetings. Until being sworn in as president, Truman had no knowledge of the program to develop the atomic bomb. However, Truman presided over several major foreign policy issues during his two terms in office, including dropping the atomic bomb on Japan, setting up the Marshall Plan, proclaiming the Truman Doctrine, and commanding the troops during the Korean War.

The Inter-American Treaty of Reciprocal Assistance—commonly known as the Rio Treaty, or the Rio Pact—was an agreement made in 1947 in Rio de Janeiro among many countries in the Americas. The treaty stated that an attack against one country is to be considered an attack against them all; this was known as the Hemispheric Defense Doctrine. President Truman signed the pact on behalf of the United States.

The following table shows the major U.S. defense alliances. Each alliance commits its members to defend one another. Suppose the Soviet Union had attacked France in the 1950s. All NATO members would have been duty-bound to defend France.

U.S. Foreign Policy Alliances

Defense Alliances	Economic Alliances
North Atlantic Treaty Organization (NATO; United States, Canada, and 17 European nations, 1949)	Organization of American States (OAS, 1948)
Rio Pact (United States, Canada, and 32 Central, Caribbean, and South American nations, 1947)	North American Free Trade Agreement (NAFTA; United States, Canada, Mexico, 1994)
ANZUS (Australia, New Zealand, United States, 1951)	World Trade Organization (WTO, 1996)
Japanese Pact (1951)	Central American Free Trade Agreement (CAFTA: United States and Central American nations, 2005)
Philippines Pact (1951)	
Korean Pact (United States and South Korea, 1953)	

Three of the pacts shown on the table are between the United States and a single nation—Japan, the Philippines, and South Korea. In addition to these three, the United States has defense pacts with 50 other nations. The United States agrees to defend these nations if they are attacked.

The table also shows major economic agreements that the United States has signed. The WTO is an international organization. Its goal is to make trade among nations easier and fairer. It sets trade regulations and settles trade disagreements among nations. The NAFTA and the CAFTA have eased trade between the United States and the nations of North and Central America.

stop and think

Why are defense and trade agreements good foreign policy? Discuss this question with a partner. Draw a T-chart. Label one column "Defense." Label the other column "Economic." List your reasons in the T-chart. Share your T-chart with another pair. Try to come to agreement on the best three reasons for each type of agreement.

Extension

The Rio Pact was the middle component of three defense initiatives in the Western Hemisphere enacted during the 1940s. In March 1945, the Act of Chapultepec set out a security agreement for the duration of the war. Its provisions were similar to those adopted in the 1947 Rio Pact, which was the first postwar pact that the United States entered into. The Organization of American States (OAS), building on the Rio Pact, was formed in 1948 with the signing of the Charter of Bogotá.

Stop and Think

Students' reasons and supporting arguments will vary but should be based on lesson content.

Foreign Aid

Foreign aid is military and economic assistance to friendly nations. The aid may be in the form of money, food, seeds, equipment, technology, and advisers. Money is given either as loans or grants. Grants do not have to be paid back. There is one condition to any grant or loan, however. The money must be used to buy U.S.-made goods.

The United States contributes to the United Nations World Food Programme.

Most economic aid programs are run through the U.S. Agency for International Development (USAID). It is part of the State Department. The goals of economic aid programs are humanitarian and economic. Foreign aid provides developing nations with food, medical care, and educational programs. These fulfill the humanitarian goal of U.S. foreign policy.

Because the developing nations must buy U.S.-made goods, foreign aid helps the U.S. economy. This is a short-term result. However, the long-term purpose is to grow the economies of developing nations. As their economies improve, these nations will be able to buy more U.S. goods over time.

Most military aid programs are run through the Defense Department. In addition to weapons, military aid includes sending military advisers. They help friendly nations train and build up their armed forces.

Foreign aid became an important part of U.S. foreign policy after World War II. For many years, the United States used it to help nations fight communism. Since World War II, the United States has spent more than $500 billion in foreign aid. In the beginning, most of the aid was economic. Between 1948 and 1952, the United States gave $12.5 billion to 16 nations in Western Europe to rebuild.

Military aid is provided by the United States to many countries around the world.

Since the 1950s, much of the aid has been military. Instead of Europe, the aid has flowed to nations in the Middle East, Asia, and Latin America. At first, it was used to support friendly governments from Communist takeovers. Since the 1990s, the aid has been focused on the fight against terrorism. Israel has also received large amounts of foreign aid in its 60-year conflict with its Arab neighbors.

Picturing Government

In the photograph at the top right of page 373, schoolchildren in North Korea in 2002 are eating a lunch supplied through the UN World Food Programme. The United States contributes surplus food to developing nations and the United Nations food programs.

Picturing Government

At the bottom right of page 373, Israeli soldiers man American-made Patriot missiles. The Patriot Missile Air Defense System is used by the United States, Israel, the Netherlands, Japan, Germany, Greece, Saudi Arabia, Egypt, Taiwan, and Kuwait. U.S. forces used the Patriot, an all-weather, all-altitude, long-range defense system, during Operation Desert Storm in 1991.

Extensions

1 Invite students interested in foreign policy to find out why the United States was a founding member of the United Nations, but had refused to join the League of Nations following World War I. Have them use library resources or the Internet to find information. Ask them to make a comparison/contrast chart, such as a Venn diagram, explaining the differences.

2 The World Trade Organization (WTO) has its share of critics. Invite students to present both sides of the argument for the WTO, using library resources or the Internet to support their positions. You may choose to hold a formal debate or simply a class discussion.

Picturing Government

In the photograph on page 374, workers at a cooperative farm in North Korea store maize. North Korea has faced severe food shortages, and the United Nations World Food Programme (WFP) has offered assistance. In 2003, the WFP helped 5.8 million North Koreans escape starvation. The single biggest source of funding comes from more than 60 governments that support the WFP. The opening years of the millennium saw more than 30 food emergencies each year, more than double the average during the 1980s. In 2004, the WFP delivered 5.1 million tons of food to assist 89 million people in these crises. Food is delivered by air, land, and sea; 40 ships travel each day, carrying as much as 50,000 tons of food.

International Organizations

The United States is a founding member of the United Nations (UN). The first session met in 1945. That first session had 50 member nations. Today, the UN has 191 member nations.

The UN Charter is similar to a constitution. It states the purpose of the organization and its rules. The goal of the UN is to maintain friendly relations among nations. The General Assembly is the main body of the UN. It debates issues and makes recommendations to the Security Council. All member nations have a vote in the General Assembly.

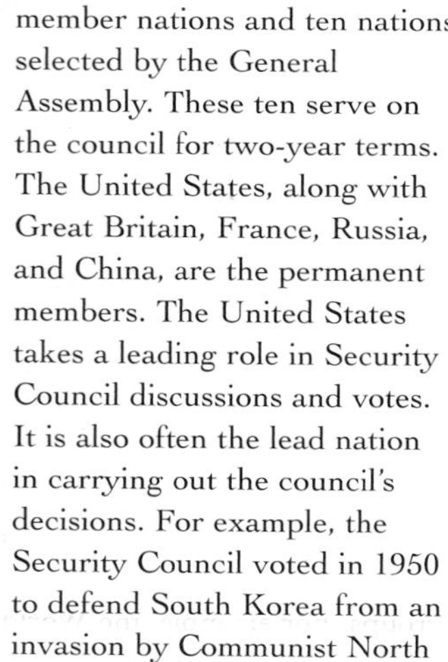

The United Nations Food and Agriculture Organization and the World Food Programme provide assistance to developing nations around the world.

The Security Council is made up of five permanent member nations and ten nations selected by the General Assembly. These ten serve on the council for two-year terms. The United States, along with Great Britain, France, Russia, and China, are the permanent members. The United States takes a leading role in Security Council discussions and votes. It is also often the lead nation in carrying out the council's decisions. For example, the Security Council voted in 1950 to defend South Korea from an invasion by Communist North Korea. The United States provided most of the troops and equipment for the Korean War. The United States also took the lead in the war in Iraq in 2003.

The International Court of Justice (ICJ) is the judicial branch of the UN. The court has 15 judges who serve for nine-year terms. The General Assembly and Security Council select the judges. The court hears cases between member nations and provides legal advice to other groups within the UN.

Extension

Divide the class into small groups, assigning each group one of the following areas of the world: the Middle East, Asia, Latin America, or Europe. Have each group use library resources or the Internet to find out about United States foreign aid, either economic or military, to nations in each region. Have each group report its findings to the class.

Major Groups Within the United Nations

Agency	Purpose
Food and Agriculture Organization (FAO)	Provides assistance to increase food production
International Monetary Fund (IMF)	Promotes international trade
International Bank for Reconstruction and Development (World Bank)	Makes loans to developing nations to • invest in projects • promote trade • repay debts to developed nations
United Nations Educational, Scientific, and Cultural Organization (UNESCO)	Promotes international exchanges of educational, scientific, and cultural information
World Health Organization (WHO)	Provides assistance to developing nations to • set up health services • promote health education, nutrition, and sanitation • fight epidemics

The UN does not have a president or prime minister. A secretary general manages the huge bureaucracy that runs the UN on a day-to-day basis. The secretary general is elected for a five-year term by the General Assembly.

The table on this page lists some important agencies within the United Nations. The United States is often the major supporter in these groups. For example, the World Bank is always headed by an American nominated by the U.S. government.

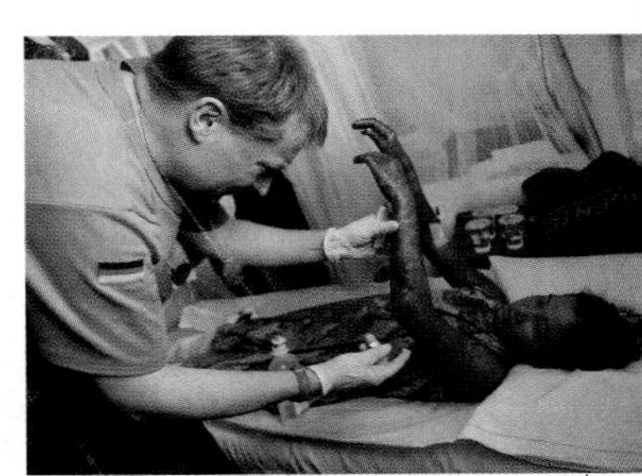

After the tsunami of 2004, the World Health Organization provided medical assistance to those affected by the disaster.

Putting It All Together

Create a concept web to illustrate how the United States puts its foreign policy goals into action. Draw a large circle and label it "U.S. Foreign Policy." Draw smaller circles for each tool it uses. Connect these with lines to the large circle. Add smaller circles and lines with examples. Work with a partner.

Table Extension

Ask students to use the table on page 375 to answer the following questions.

- What is the goal of UNESCO? (to promote international exchanges of educational, scientific, and cultural information)
- Which organization promotes international trade? (the international Monetary Fund)
- How is the World Bank different from the IMF? (The World Bank actually makes loans.)

Picturing Government

In the photograph on page 375, a German Army doctor examines an Indonesian survivor of the 2004 tsunami and earthquake. The World Health Organization worked to prevent outbreaks of malaria, measles, and diarrhea after the disaster. In Aceh, the area near the earthquake's epicenter, there was a lack of safe water, and the water distribution and sanitation systems had been destroyed. Field hospitals were set up to treat the more than 720,000 in Aceh directly affected by the disaster.

Putting It All Together

Students' concept webs will vary but may include the smaller circles of defense alliances, such as NATO, ANZUS, and the Korean Pact; economic alliances, such as the WTO, NAFTA, and OAS; foreign aid, such as USAID; and membership in international organizations, such as the International Court of Justice and the United Nations.

Participate in Government

Have male students create timelines centering around their eighteenth birthdays to mark the time when they must register for Selective Service. Ask female students to do the same for any close relatives or friends nearing that age.

Invite students who know someone who has registered to interview that person about the process and report to the class.

Participate in Government

Register for Selective Service

The Selective Service System (SSS) is the way the United States registers young men for possible service in the army. It is not the same as the draft. A draft actually calls up young men for service. The draft was ended in 1975.

Who must register with the SSS?

- all male U.S. citizens between ages eighteen and twenty-six living in or outside the United States
- all male legal permanent residents between ages eighteen and twenty-six
- all undocumented male aliens between ages eighteen and twenty-six
- all men between ages eighteen and twenty-six who hold U.S. citizenship as well as citizenship in another country. It does not matter whether they live in the United States.

Foreign men who are in the United States on student or visitor visas do not have to register. Neither do men who work for a foreign government in the United States.

Men have from 30 days before to 30 days after their eighteenth birthday to register. A male noncitizen who becomes a resident of the United States must register within 30 days. If the man is older than twenty-six, he does not have to register.

Registration is easy. The SSS Web site has a form that can be submitted online. Post offices have copies of the form. The Federal Student Financial Aid (FAFSA) form has a SSS checkbox. If a student checks this box, the Department of Education sends the necessary information to SSS. Some high schools have SSS registrars who will register male students.

Those who do not register are breaking the law. Failing to register carries a fine of up to $250,000 and five years in jail. In addition, those who do not register cannot get federal student loans and grants. Registering is a condition for U.S. citizenship for men between the ages of eighteen and twenty-six. Only those who register are eligible for federal job training programs and for federal jobs.

Research Resources

Below is a list of reference books and Web sites that relate to the issues covered in this chapter. Students may wish to use these to further their research on ideas in the preceding lessons. Web site addresses may change over time. Use keyword searching on a major search engine to locate sites.

Reference Books:

Alexander DeConde, Richard Dean Burns, and Fredrik Logevall. *Encyclopedia of American Foreign Policy*. Scribner, 2002.

Cynthia Ann Watson. *Nation-building: A Reference Handbook*. ABC-CLIO, 2004.

World at Risk: A Global Issues Sourcebook. CQ Press, 2002.

Web Sites:

The State Department's Web site offers links to international issues and history.

The Council on Foreign Relations is a nonpartisan resource supplying information by region and issues. On its Web site is also a section for educators.

The think tank Foreign Policy in Focus Web site provides articles and reports on foreign policy and international affairs from a progressive viewpoint.

Skill Builder

Problem-solving and Decision-making

Identifying a problem and deciding what to do about it are two important citizenship skills. Government officials need these skills and so do ordinary citizens.

Suppose there is no traffic light within six blocks of the elementary school. Cars speed through stop signs. Children crossing the street on their way to school are in danger. What can citizens do?

First, they have to identify the problem—too many fast-moving cars. Then, they have to study solutions. They decide on one and present it to the city council. The city council agrees. However, the job of the citizens' group is not over. Members have to determine if the solution has fixed the problem.

To help you identify problems and make decisions, follow these steps:

1. Identify the problem.
2. Gather information about the problem.
3. List as many solutions as you can think of.
4. Review the advantages and disadvantages of each solution.
5. Decide on your solution.
6. Put your solution/decision into practice.
7. Review and evaluate your decision after a period of time.

Complete the following activities with a partner.

1 Think of a problem in your community. Go through steps 1 to 5 to reach a possible solution. Then think of a way to evaluate your solution.

2 Write a letter to the mayor about the problem and your solution. State the problem. Then state your solution. Describe how everyone will be able to tell if your solution is working.

Foreign Policy and National Defense 377

Skill Builder

1 Students' choices of problems and the steps they follow will vary.

2 Students' letters will vary. Review with students the proper form of a formal letter. Collect the letters and mail them.

Recommended Reading

Below is a list of books that relate to the issues covered in this chapter. The numbers in parentheses indicate the related Thematic Strands of the National Council for the Social Studies (NCSS).

Karen F. Balkin, ed. *War on Terrorism (Opposing Viewpoints)*. Greenhaven Press, 2004. (VI, X)

Christopher Collier and James Lincoln Collier. *The United States in the Cold War 1945–1989*. Benchmark Books, 2001. (VI, X)

George Edward Stanley. *An Emerging World Power 1900–1929*. World Almanac Library, 2005. (VI, X)

Classroom Discussion

Discuss with students some of the broader topics covered in this chapter.

- How does fighting terrorism involve a different sort of "war" than the United States has fought in the past?
- Should the United States or the United Nations continue to impose sanctions on countries for human rights violations? Are these sanctions effective?
- What are the dangers of regional security alliances?

Unit Objectives

After studying this unit, students will be able to

- describe the workings of state governments
- explain the types and activities of local governments

Unit 8 focuses on the work of state and local governments.

Chapter 21, State Government, examines state constitutions, branches of government, public policy, and finances.

Chapter 22, Local Government, explores the types of local government as well as public services provided by and funding of local government.

Getting Started

Have a student read aloud the title of the unit and the two paragraphs that follow it on page 378. Ask students to create graphic organizers that show the relationship of federal, state, and local government. Have them use appropriate artwork to help them recall the various important ideas. Encourage them to add to the graphic organizer as they read Unit 8.

STATE AND LOCAL GOVERNMENT

State governments are older than the federal government. The Fra used the states as the model for the federal government. As a res there are many similarities between the federal and state governm The states have constitutions and executive, legislative, and judici branches. The federal and state governments have some of the sa powers, such as the power to tax. However, only the states have certain powers, such as the power to set up school districts.

The authority to found local governments comes from state government. Local governments have executive, legislative, and judicial branches. Local governments also have powers similar t the states, such as the power to enforce laws and tax citizens.

Picturing Government

The photograph on page 378 shows the state capitol of Illinois, in Springfield, which was built in the years following the Civil War. The site had been selected as a burial place for Abraham Lincoln; however, Mrs. Lincoln preferred the Oak Ridge Cemetery. The site became the place of Illinois's sixth and final capitol building. In March 1868, ground was broken. Construction materials were delivered by railroad; a new spur was specially constructed to the site. Wooden derricks lifted the limestone blocks. After eight years, the General Assembly moved into the still-unfinished building. The capitol was finally completed in 1888. The building is 361 feet from the ground to the dome, and 405 feet from the ground to the top of the flagstaff.

Chapter

21 STATE GOVERNMENT

Getting Focused

Skim this chapter to predict what you will be learning.

- Read the lesson titles and subheadings.
- Look at the illustrations and read the captions.
- Examine the tables.
- Review the vocabulary words and terms.

State governments have a constitution and executive, legislative, and judicial branches. What do you think the purpose of each of these is for a state? Think about their purposes for the federal government. Then write a sentence to describe the purpose of a constitution and of executive, legislative, and judicial branches in state government.

State governments provide many services to residents, including education, social programs, and recreational areas, such as Jedediah Smith Redwoods State Park in California.

Pre-Reading Discussion

1 Discuss with students how state and national governments each have distinct spheres of authority. Have students identify projects within their state, such as highways, that are funded with federal monies.

2 Ask students to share what they have heard and read about taxes in the state or community. Challenge them to explain how taxes are required to support social programs.

Related Transparencies

T-13 Types of Courts in a State Court System

T-18 Three-Column Chart

T-19 Venn Diagram

T-20 Concept Web

Key Blacklines

Primary Source—State Awards Support Local Recycling Programs

CD Extension

Encourage students to use the reading comprehension, vocabulary reinforcement, and other activities on the student CD.

Getting Focused

Extend the Getting Focused activity by having students find out the key members of each branch of state government for their state. You may wish to divide the class into three groups, assigning each group one of the branches of government, then allowing each group to share their findings with the entire class.

Lesson Summary

Like the national Constitution, state constitutions create the government's three-branch structure; outline the local government structure; describe the powers and duties of the different units of local government; create agencies, boards, and commissions; and identify how money may be raised and spent. State constitutions may not conflict with the federal constitution. Basics of state constitutions are similar to the U.S. Constitution. State constitutions are usually more detailed than the federal Constitution. Amendments come about through state legislatures, constitutional conventions, and voter proposals. State constitutions have become lengthy documents that could be revised.

Lesson Objective

Students will learn about the basics of state constitutions and the process of amending and reforming them.

Focus Your Reading Answers

1 State constitutions are alike in that they create structure for state and local government; describe the powers and duties of each unit of local government; identify ways to raise and spend money; and set up state agencies, boards, and commissions. They are different in the details of each of these areas.

2 State constitutions can be amended in most states by voters. The state legislature may propose an amendment or call a constitutional convention. Voters may also propose amendments in 18 states.

3 There is a need for constitutional reform because most state constitutions are very long with many amendments, some of which are not enforced, and filled with details.

Words to Review

Review each of the previously discussed vocabulary terms with students.

limited government TE p. 40

popular sovereignty TE p. 40

separation of powers TE p. 40

checks and balances TE p. 40

Bill of Rights TE p. 35

judicial review TE p. 40

amendment TE p. 39

ratified TE p. 27

LESSON 1

State Constitutions

Thinking on Your Own

In the United States, states as well as the national government have constitutions. Why are state constitutions necessary in a federal system of government? What would you call a system of government that lacked state constitutions? Discuss this question with a partner and write your answer in your notebook.

focus your reading

Explain how state constitutions are alike and how they are different.

How can state constitutions be amended?

Why is there a need for constitutional reform in the states?

words to review

limited government
popular sovereignty
separation of powers
checks and balances
Bill of Rights
judicial review
amendment
ratified

Every state constitution serves the same purpose for the state that the U.S. Constitution does for the federal government. State constitutions

- create the structure for state government: executive, legislative, and judicial
- create the structure for local government, such as county, parish, city, township, and borough
- describe the powers and duties of each unit of local government
- identify the ways that the state and the local governments may raise and spend money
- set up state agencies, boards, and commissions

State agencies, boards, and commissions are independent. For example, all states have state boards of education. They oversee the schools within the state and make education policy for the state.

The U.S. Constitution is the supreme law of the land. State constitutions and state law may not conflict with the U.S. Constitution. This is a very important fact.

The Basics of State Constitutions

Limited government and **popular sovereignty** are common to both state constitutions and the U.S. Constitution. In other words, the government may not set policy or act if the people do not wish it to do so. The government operates within limits that the people set for it.

Common Characteristics of State Constitutions

State constitutions are based on the principles of

- Limited government
- Popular sovereignty

State constitutions create a system of state government that includes

- Separation of powers
- Checks and balances
- Judicial review

State constitutions describe

- The structure of state government: executive, legislative, and judicial branches
- The structure of local governments
- The powers reserved for each branch of the state government and to local governments
- A Bill of Rights
- The process for changing the state constitution

The Framers also borrowed the three branches of government, **separation of powers**, and **checks and balances** from the state constitutions. The federal and state governments all have executive, legislative, and judicial branches. Each branch has its own powers and duties. The state constitutions set up ways that the three branches check and balance each other's powers.

Each state constitution has a **Bill of Rights**. Most have guarantees similar to the U.S. Bill of Rights. However, a few list additional rights. For example, the right to self-government and to be free from discrimination based on race or gender may be included.

State constitutions, like the U.S. Constitution, describe the process for amending the constitution.

There are two other characteristics that most state constitutions have in common. State constitutions tend to be long and detailed. This is not true of the U.S. Constitution, which gives only a broad outline of what the federal government should be.

stop and think

Create a two-column chart to show the similarities and differences between the U.S. Constitution and state constitutions. Work with a partner to complete your chart.

Table Extension

Suggest that students make flash cards of the information using color coding to help them remember the three categories. They may use colored index cards or markers to code the information. Allow students to work in pairs to quiz each other.

Stop and Think

Students' charts will vary. Possible responses:

Similarities:
limited government, popular sovereignty, separation of powers, checks and balances, Bill of Rights, amendment process spelled out

Differences:
State constitutions tend to be wordy, but the U.S. Constitution is brief; state constitutions go into great detail, but the U.S. Constitution sketches broad outlines; state constitutions create structure of local government, but the U.S. Constitution does not set up structure of state government.

Picturing Government

The photograph on page 379 shows a trail through California's redwood forest. The state has three parks that, together with the Redwood National Park, are jointly administered by the California Department of Parks and Recreation and the National Park Service. The three state parks were created in the 1920s after the lumbering industry had reduced the supply of redwoods. The Redwood National and State Parks (RNSP) are designated as an International Biosphere Reserve and a World Heritage Site. The RNSP include not only old-growth redwood groves but also two large rivers, 37 miles of California coast, and open prairies.

Picturing Government

In the photograph on page 382, then-governor of California Jerry Brown hosts a news conference about the passage of Proposition 13, which cut property taxes in that state by 53 percent. About 65 percent of the voters were in favor of Proposition 13. The measure began a "tax revolt" in other states. However, California has had a series of fiscal crises since the first half of the 1990s. To balance the state budget, lawmakers shifted public service costs back to local government levels, pushing those local units to financial peril as well.

Cartoon Extension

Lead students to recognize the humor in a defendant worried about a future political office in the cartoon on page 382. You may wish to encourage students to use library resources or the Internet to find out more specifics about your state's qualifications for political offices at both the state and local level.

Putting It All Together

Students' additional chart material will vary but should reflect content in the last two subheadings.

Former California governor Jerry Brown (left) during a 1978 news conference discussing Proposition 13—a law that changed property taxes

Amending State Constitutions

Like the U.S. Constitution, state constitutions can be amended. Approved **amendments** are ratified by the voters. Delaware, however, requires the legislature to ratify amendments. There are three basic ways to amend state constitutions.

First, the state legislature may propose an amendment. In most states, an amendment is proposed and voted on in one session of the legislature. In a few states, an amendment must be approved in two different sessions. This gives lawmakers a chance for second thoughts.

Second, a legislature may call a constitutional convention. The voters must approve the need for it. A constitutional convention is usually used to revise the constitution or to write a new one.

Third, the voters may propose amendments in 18 states. Voters must sign a petition asking for the amendment to be placed on the ballot. If the petition drive succeeds, the amendment is voted on at the next general election.

Constitutional Reforms

The first state constitutions were written in the years right after 1776. Only 17 states have proposed and **ratified** new constitutions. This means that the constitutions are all close to or over 100 years old.

Age is not necessarily a problem. The U.S. Constitution is more than 200 years old. However, state constitutions have grown significantly in length. Unlike the U.S. Constitution, state constitutions have acquired many amendments.

"GUILTY? DO YOU REALIZE HOW THAT WOULD LOOK IF I DECIDE TO RUN FOR POLITICAL OFFICE?"

Many constitutions are filled with sections that are no longer enforced. New amendments have taken the place of these old sections. In addition, the constitutions are filled with details such as what subjects should be taught in school.

Putting It All Together

Refer to your chart from the Stop and Think activity. Work with a partner to add information from the last two subheadings in this lesson. Refer to Chapter 3, if necessary, to add information about the U.S. Constitution.

Extensions

1 Ask students to check the local paper, either online or in hard copy, for articles that illustrate separation of powers, checks and balances, or judicial review at the state level. You may wish to divide the class into three groups, assigning each group one of the categories. Lead a class discussion on how state government works in your state.

2 Have students use library resources or the Internet to find out about the system of parish government in Louisiana. Ask students to create charts showing how different units of government in Louisiana compare to and function as more familiar government units in other states.

LESSON 2

Legislative, Executive, and Judicial Branches

Lesson Summary

State governments include legislative, executive, and judicial branches, which work in a system of checks and balances. The legislature holds the power to make laws, to tax, to borrow money, and to spend money. States set their own requirements for who may be elected to the legislature. The state legislature draws the districts based on U.S. Census data; districts must have about the same number of people. Like the federal Congress, state legislatures rely on committees to do the work. Bills are passed in a process similar to the way they are in Congress. The governor is the state's chief executive but shares power with other elected officials such as the lieutenant governor, attorney general, secretary of state, and the state treasurer. Governors have the line item veto in most states and limited judicial power. Every state has its own legal system, but most are based on English law. Laws cannot conflict with the federal Constitution.

Thinking on Your Own

Draw three columns in your notebook. Label them "Federal Legislature," "Federal Executive," and "Federal Judiciary." Then list three facts about the federal government in each column. As you read, think about how the federal and state governments are similar and how they are different.

focus your reading

Describe the organization and duties of state legislatures.

Explain the roles and duties of a state governor.

What are the organization and duties of state court systems?

words to know

unicameral
line item veto
pardon
parole
commute
reprieve
opinions
misdemeanor

Like the federal government, state governments have legislative, executive, and judicial branches. Like the branches of the federal government, they act as checks on each other's power. However, they are different from the federal branches in various ways.

The Legislature

The legislature is the lawmaking body in each state government. In addition to the power to make laws, the legislature has the power to tax, to borrow money, and to spend money. The purpose of the powers of the legislature is to promote the general well-being of the state's citizens.

Nebraska is the only state with just one house in the state legislature. Nebraska's legislature is **unicameral**. The other 49 states have two houses. The lower house is usually called the assembly. The upper house is usually called the senate. Legislatures with two houses are bicameral.

Qualifications for members of state legislatures vary from state to state. In general, a person must be at least twenty-one years old to be elected to the lower house and twenty-five to

Words to Know

Discuss each of the vocabulary terms with students.

A government with only one house is called *unicameral*. Nebraska is the only state with a *unicameral* legislature.

The *line item veto* allows a governor to veto one part of a bill without rejecting the entire bill. The *line item veto* is generally used in budget bills.

A *pardon* is a release from the consequences of a crime. The governor has the privilege of offering a *pardon*. *Parole* is the release of a prisoner before he or she has served the complete sentence. A person generally must serve part of the sentence before being eligible for *parole*. To *commute* a sentence is to lessen it. Governors also can *commute* a sentence. A *reprieve* is a postponement of an execution. Governors may offer a *reprieve* to a person on Death Row. *Opinions* are interpretations of state laws. The state attorney general writes *opinions* of state constitutional law. A *misdemeanor* is a minor crime. A traffic violation is a *misdemeanor*.

Lesson Objective

Students will learn about the three branches of state government.

Focus Your Reading Answers

1 State legislatures are almost all organized into two houses, an assembly and a senate. They make the laws for the state through committee work. They have the power to tax, borrow, and spend money. They draw the legislative districts.

2 The state governor's roles include chief executive, chief administrator, and commander in chief of the state's National Guard. Governors also supervise many agencies, promote the state's economy, propose the state budget and legislation, and may veto legislation or call a special session of the legislature.

3 State court systems are organized in a supreme court, with courts of appeals, trial courts, juvenile courts, municipal courts, magistrate's courts, and justice courts. Their role is to interpret and apply state and local laws.

be elected to the upper house. The person must also live in the district from which he or she is elected. Each state sets its own requirement for how long a person must live in the district before running for office.

State legislative districts are drawn by the state legislatures. Every ten years after the U.S. census, states review their population and redraw districts as needed. In 1964, the Supreme Court ruled that districts must be based on population. Before this, many states drew legislative districts based on area. Now, state legislative districts must have about the same number of people in every district.

Four states hold elections for the state legislators in odd-numbered years. The other 46 states hold them in even-numbered years, when members of the U.S. House of Representatives and the U.S. Senate are also elected. State legislators serve for two- or four-year terms. Most members of state assemblies serve two-year terms. Most senate terms are four years.

At one time, many state legislatures met every other year or for one or two months each year. Today, 44 state legislatures meet every year. The sessions have also become longer. The legislators face many more complex issues than they did in the past. Issues range from how to finance education to whether to tax sales over the Internet. If necessary, state governors may also call the legislatures back into special session. In about two-thirds of the states, legislators themselves may call special sessions.

In about half the states, the leader of the upper house is the lieutenant governor. This position is similar to the vice president of the United States. The senators in these states also choose a president pro tempore. He or she oversees the upper house when the lieutenant governor is absent. In the other half of the states, state senators choose their own presiding officer. This person is also called the president pro tempore.

The presiding officer in the lower house is called the speaker. The majority party in the house chooses the speaker. About 99 percent of all state lawmakers are either Democrats or Republicans. Fewer than 100 are independents or members of minor parties.

Extensions

1 Invite interested students to find out why Nebraska developed a unicameral legislature. How does it function differently from the legislatures of other states?

2 Have students use library resources or the Internet to find the requirements for serving in their state's legislature. Ask them to create a table or graphic organizer showing the requirements. Have them present their findings to the class by using the Student Presentation Builder on the student CD.

Like Congress, state legislatures do much of their work in committees. The presiding officers choose committee chairs and members of all committees. This is different from the way Congress chooses committee members and chairs. However, the way bills are passed is similar. Review the diagram on page 140 to see how a bill becomes a law.

Only members of the legislature may introduce bills, which are then sent to committees to consider. People other than members of the legislature usually write the bills. Interest groups write the majority of bills. The governor's office, state agencies, and local governments also send bills to state legislators to introduce. Only about one-quarter of all bills end up in the governor's office for signature. Like the president, governors may veto a bill. Usually, a two-thirds vote in both houses will override a governor's veto.

stop and think

Review the three-column chart that you made at the beginning of this lesson. Draw a line under the lists for the federal government. Prepare to make new lists for each branch of state government. First make a list of three facts for state legislative branches. As you read ahead, add three facts for each of the remaining two columns.

The Executive Branch

The governor is the chief executive and chief administrator of state government. In the past, the position had limited power. Often, a governor was limited to one term in office, and terms were often only two years. However, since the mid-twentieth century, the position of governor has been greatly strengthened. The reason is the same as the one that caused state legislatures to have longer sessions. States must deal with more issues today than they did even 50 years ago.

The table on page 386 lists basic information about the election and term of office of governors. Governors do not have the same amount of power as the president. Governors share their power with other officers of the executive department. The table on page 387 lists the other major officers and their duties. Generally, states have all four positions. Most states fill them through elections rather than by appointing people.

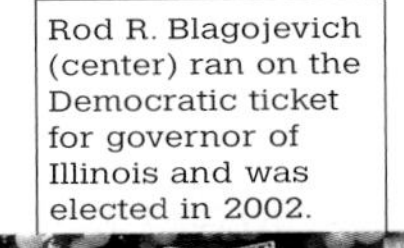

Rod R. Blagojevich (center) ran on the Democratic ticket for governor of Illinois and was elected in 2002.

Stop and Think

Students' choices of facts will vary, but each column should include three facts on the branch of state government.

Picturing Government

The 2002 photograph on page 385 shows a gathering of candidates in Chicago, Illinois, at a "Get Out the Vote" rally. Their efforts resulted in success at the polls for each person. Pictured from left to right are Dick Durbin, U.S. senator; Richard M. Daley, mayor of Chicago; Rod R. Blagojevich, governor of Illinois; Lisa Madigan, state attorney general; and Jesse White, state secretary of state. "Get Out the Vote" is an effort to increase voter turnout, begun by political scientists at Yale University.

Extension

Invite the class to debate the issue of term limits. Some states, such as California, limit terms for both governors and legislators. For an added challenge, ask students to prepare arguments for both sides of the question, then randomly assign teams to affirmative and negative positions.

Table Extension

Ask students to use library resources or the Internet to find out the qualifications for governor in their state. Challenge them to find the same information for three contiguous states, then make a graphic organizer or chart showing how the four states compare.

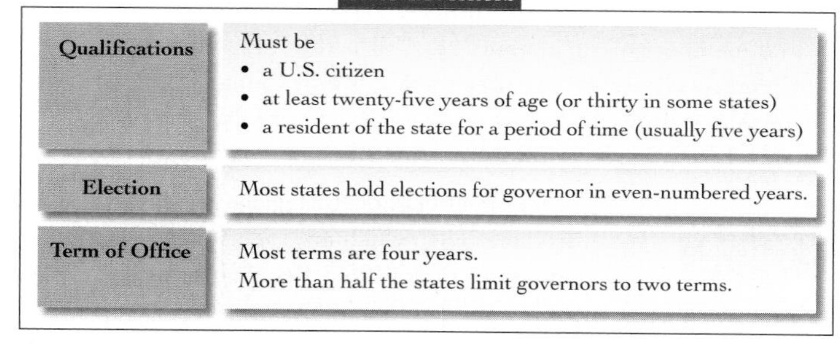

State Governors

Qualifications	Must be • a U.S. citizen • at least twenty-five years of age (or thirty in some states) • a resident of the state for a period of time (usually five years)
Election	Most states hold elections for governor in even-numbered years.
Term of Office	Most terms are four years. More than half the states limit governors to two terms.

Governors have executive, legislative, and judicial powers. As the executives of their states, all governors

- carry out the laws passed by the legislation
- appoint and remove nonelected officials to state government
- supervise the work of the many agencies within the state government
- are commander in chief of the state's National Guard
- promote their state's business and industry

In most states, governors also

- propose the state budget

Governors' legislative powers include

- proposing legislation
- vetoing legislation
- calling a special session of the legislature to deal with an urgent issue

Most governors have the **line item veto**. They may reject part of a bill without rejecting the entire bill. Usually, the line item veto is used only in budget bills. Governors cut out money for programs they want to end. Legislatures may override a line item veto if they can gather enough votes.

Extension

Invite students with an interest in mathematics to do a comparison of their state budget and the federal budget for the most recent data available. What percentage of each was controllable spending? Of that amount, what areas were most heavily funded? Students should make graphs that show the comparisons clearly. If possible, make the graphs into a transparency and have students explain their findings to the class.

386 Chapter 21

Governors have more limited judicial powers. About one-quarter of all state judges are appointed by governors. Most of a governor's judicial powers have to do with people convicted of crimes. Governors may **pardon**, or release, a person from the consequences of a crime. This is different from a parole. A **parole** releases a person from jail without having served a complete sentence. Governors may also grant paroles. In addition, they may **commute**, or lessen, a sentence. They may also grant a **reprieve**, or postponement of an execution.

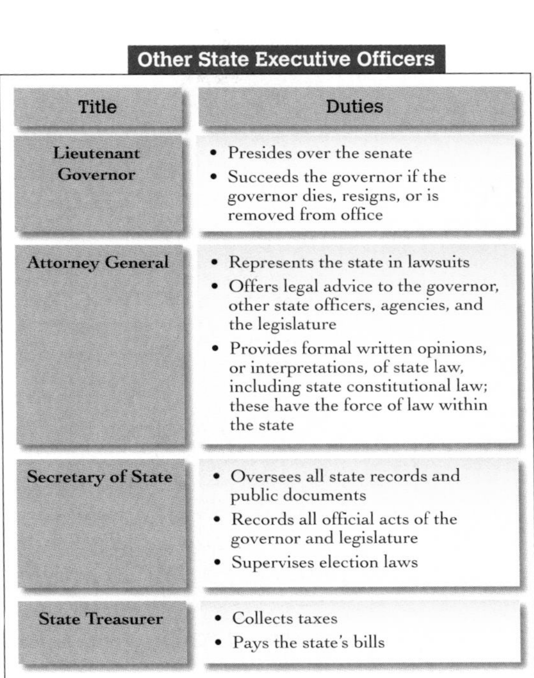

Other State Executive Officers

Title	Duties
Lieutenant Governor	• Presides over the senate • Succeeds the governor if the governor dies, resigns, or is removed from office
Attorney General	• Represents the state in lawsuits • Offers legal advice to the governor, other state officers, agencies, and the legislature • Provides formal written opinions, or interpretations, of state law, including state constitutional law; these have the force of law within the state
Secretary of State	• Oversees all state records and public documents • Records all official acts of the governor and legislature • Supervises election laws
State Treasurer	• Collects taxes • Pays the state's bills

The Judicial System

Each state has its own system of laws. These laws are based on the shared tradition of English law. As a result, the laws are similar. In addition, no state law can conflict with the U.S. Constitution and the law that has developed from it. The purpose of the state court systems is to interpret and apply state and local laws. Courts that hear cases in cities and towns are part of the state court system. The table on page 388 shows the number and types of courts in a typical state court system.

About 75 percent of all state judges are elected. Most of the other judgeships are filled by appointment. Usually the governor selects those judges. However, the legislature appoints judges in two states.

Table Extension

Ask students to use the table on page 387 to answer the following questions.

- Which state executive supervises election laws? (secretary of state)
- Over what body does a lieutenant governor preside? (the state senate)
- What are the duties of the state treasurer? (collect taxes, pay the state's bills)
- Who represents the state in lawsuits? (attorney general)

Extension

The majority of states, as well as the U.S. national government and U.S. military, do enforce the death penalty. In 2004, the death penalty was declared unconstitutional in Kansas and New York. Ask students to use library resources or the Internet to find out the issues surrounding enforcement of the death penalty.

State Government 387

Table Extension

Challenge students to create questions for a "What Am I?" game using the information in the table. Allow students to work in small groups if possible. Then play the game for review before a quiz or test.

Types of Courts in a State Court System

Court	Description
State Supreme Court	• Highest court in a state • Reviews decisions of lower state courts on appeal • Decisions are final unless some issue of U.S. constitutional law is involved. Those cases can be appealed to the U.S. Supreme Court.
Court of Appeals	• Accepts appeals of decisions in lower state courts • Hears arguments by lawyers • Not a trial court • Most decisions are final. Appeals can be brought only on how the law was applied.
General Trial Courts (titles vary by state: district, circuit, county, superior, court of common pleas)	• Hear cases from one or more counties • Divided into criminal and civil courts Criminal court: • Hears cases or accepts guilty pleas from defendants • Sentences guilty defendants Civil court: • Hears cases involving damages, such as a lawsuit over ownership of property or for money for badly done home repairs Most decisions are final. Appeals can be brought only on how the law was applied.
Juvenile Courts	• Hear cases involving those under eighteen • Focus on rehabilitation in sentencing • Depending on crime and circumstances, those under eighteen can be tried in adult court.
Municipal Courts	• Used mostly in large and medium-sized cities • Divided into different types: civil, criminal, traffic, small claims
Magistrate's Courts (also known as police courts)	• Used in cities • Presided over by a judge • Similar to rural justice courts • Hear cases involving **misdemeanors**, or minor crimes, such as traffic violations, vandalism, or shoplifting
Justice Courts	• Similar to city magistrate's courts • Presided over by a justice of the peace • Mostly in smaller towns and rural areas • Hear cases involving misdemeanors

Extension

Invite students to use library resources or the Internet to find current cases facing the state supreme court. Challenge them to write summaries of the cases. During the study of this chapter, track the progress of the cases to see the court in action.

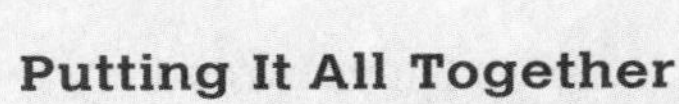

Judges can be removed from office in one of three ways. They can be defeated at reelection time. They can be impeached and tried for illegal or unethical conduct or for incompetence. A state disciplinary board can also investigate judges. The board reports to the state supreme court. Suppose a judge is accused of favoring corporations in civil cases. A civil case involves a disagreement between two or more persons or organizations. No crime has been committed in a civil case. The disciplinary board investigates. The charges are found to be true. The board then recommends that the state supreme court suspend the judge. The state supreme court can also remove a judge.

Putting It All Together

Return to your lists of facts for the legislative, executive, and judiciary branches of government. In your notebook, write a paragraph for each column that summarizes how state and federal governments are similar and how they are different.

Putting It All Together

Students' lists and paragraphs will vary but should reflect lesson content.

Ming Chin (1942–)

Ming Chin's parents were immigrants from China. They settled in Oregon as potato farmers. Chin and his seven brothers and sisters worked on the family farm. A good student, Chin graduated from the University of San Francisco in 1964 with a degree in political science. Three years later, he earned a law degree from the university's law school. Chin later received a bronze star for his service in the Vietnam War.

Chin entered public service when he returned from the war. He served as a deputy district attorney for Alameda County in northern California. In 1973, he moved to private practice and handled civil law cases. However, in 1988, Chin returned to public service. He was appointed Alameda County Superior Court judge. In 1990, the governor appointed Chin to the First District Court of Appeals for the state of California. Chin is a hard worker who takes a great interest in the details of the cases that the court hears.

Bio Facts

- Born 1942.
- Served as captain in U.S. Army, including a year in Vietnam; awarded a Bronze Star.
- First Asian American to serve in a major Oakland law firm and as president of Alameda County Bar Association.
- University of San Francisco Alumnus of the Year, 1988; University of San Francisco Law School Alumnus of the Year, 1993.
- As Presiding Justice of First District Court of Appeal, issued key rulings on environmental issues, surrogate parenting, and admissibility of DNA as evidence in criminal trials.
- Appointed to California Supreme Court, 1996.

Biography Extension

By the age of fourteen, Ming William Chin could drive a combine, jeep, hay baler, and tractor. His parents spoke no English; early on, Chin learned the value of education. Another influence was hearing Dr. Martin Luther King, Jr.'s speech "The Three Dimensions of Life" after meeting King in 1964 at the Democratic National Convention. Chin has a framed copy of that speech in his office.

Lesson Summary

The federal government and state governments sometimes partner to provide services. Both federal and state governments regulate businesses. States also promote business through the governor's attempt to retain or attract businesses or through tax credits.

All states have criminal codes and state police forces to enforce the codes. States also have prison systems, some of which have been outsourced to private companies to be more efficient. States have public education systems, funded mainly through local property taxes. States also offer public health systems and help for the needy. Since the 1980s, states have been passing anti-pollution laws. Most states ask companies to file environmental impact statements before beginning major projects.

Lesson Objective

Students will learn about the states' roles in business, public safety, education, public welfare, and the environment.

Focus Your Reading Answers

1 States regulate business by setting rates for various companies, setting hourly maximums for students working, and licensing professionals. States promote business by offering tax credits or reduced taxes to new businesses and by agencies' or governors' efforts to attract new businesses and keep established ones.

2 The states' role in providing for public safety is to provide a criminal law code, police to enforce the code, and a prison system for those who violate the laws.

LESSON 3

Public Policy at the State Level

Thinking on Your Own

What do you know about public policy at the federal level? What areas of public policy do you think states deal with? In your notebook, make a list of state public policy issues that you believe confront state lawmakers. As you read, check your list against the lesson.

focus your reading

Explain how states both regulate and promote business.

What is the role of the states in providing for public safety?

How do states provide for education and the well-being of their people?

Describe the issues involved in transportation and the environment for the states.

words to know

corrections

outsource

environmental impact statement

Governments put public policy into practice by providing services. Some federal programs are joint activities with states. Medicaid and unemployment insurance are two of these joint programs.

State governments also provide a number of services. Some services are handled directly by the states. Some are handled by their local government unit. Some are activities of both the state and local governments. Education is one example of a joint responsibility.

Regulating and Promoting Business

In the late 1800s, giant corporations were very powerful. They were free to pay workers what they chose and to charge what they wanted for their goods. They could also use dishonest practices to force competitors out of business.

Beginning in the 1880s, the federal government began to regulate big business. States also started to pass laws to limit the actions of businesses. At first, the regulations only

3 States provide for the education and well-being of their people by funding public education and offering higher education systems. They also provide public health and aid for the needy.

4 States are responsible for maintaining a system of roads, as well as licensing car and truck drivers. Setting speed limits, patrolling the highways, and inspecting motor vehicles are also the states' responsibility. Issues in the environment at the state level include conserving land, rivers, and wildlife, as well as making sure that companies pay for cleaning up major chemical spills. States also require companies planning new projects to write an environmental impact statement.

Regulating Businesses

Generally, states regulate most business practices within their borders. The following are just a few of the things states do:

- Set the rates that insurance companies may charge
- Administer licensing exams for doctors, lawyers, and other professionals
- Set rates that public utilities may charge
- Set rules for landlords and renters
- License health-care facilities such as nursing homes and hospitals
- Require accurate advertising and fair sales practices
- Set limits on working hours and jobs for those younger than sixteen years of age
- Protect the right of workers to join unions if they wish

guaranteed competition. However, by the early 1900s, both the federal government and the states began to protect workers and consumers. The box to the left shows just some of the areas in which state governments regulate business.

States must respect each other's civil laws. This requirement is set out in the "full faith and credit" section of the U.S. Constitution, Article IV, Section 1.

Many states have an agency that tries to attract new businesses to the state or to keep businesses. Often, the governor will lead the effort. When he was governor of Arkansas, Bill Clinton went on several trade missions to countries such as South Korea to explain why their businesses should build plants in Arkansas. He also succeeded in getting some large Arkansas companies to remain in the state.

To get companies to build in a state or remain there, they may be offered tax credits and reduced taxes. In the long run, these special tax breaks result in more jobs and more tax revenue for state programs.

Governor Arnold Schwarzenegger (R-California) on an overseas trip promoting the state of California

Providing for Public Safety

Every state has a code, or set, of criminal laws. Actions such as murder, burglary, forgery, robbery, drunk driving, and the sale of illegal drugs are prohibited by state law. Both local police forces and the state police enforce these laws.

Each state has a state police force. Their names vary. In Texas, they are known as Texas Rangers. In California and Florida, they are the highway patrol. In Illinois, they are state

Table Extension

Challenge students to find examples of each of the items in the table in your community. Students may need to use library resources or the Internet to find examples at the state level if no local examples are available. See how many different examples the class can uncover. Consider making a bulletin board with the information.

Picturing Government

In the 2004 photograph on page 391, California governor Arnold Schwarzenegger speaks to a group in Japan. The governor traveled to Japan to promote California agriculture and tourism. He hoped to persuade auto manufacturer Toyota to make the Prius, a hybrid car, in his state.

Words to Know

Discuss each of the vocabulary terms with students.

The *corrections* system is the prison system. More than two million people are held in state *corrections* systems.

Jobs that are *outsourced* have been passed to private companies. States have some of the work of prisons.

An *environmental impact statement* is a report on how a project will affect the environment. States can use the *environmental impact statement* to judge whether the proposed project is a good idea.

Extensions

1 As students read the lesson, have them create Venn diagrams to show responsibilities of the federal and state governments and areas of overlap.

2 Students may be interested in knowing more about insurance rates for teen drivers. Challenge them to find out how their state sets rates based on age, gender, and other factors. Have them present their findings in charts or graphic organizers.

Stop and Think

Students' letters will vary but should include benefits that the state offers to businesses.

Extension

The effectiveness of prison privatization is a topic that students may wish to debate. While fewer than 5 percent of inmates are kept in private prisons, the trend tends to be growing, particularly in the western and southern United States. Ask students to find out if their state offers private contracts for prisons, and if so, why.

The States and Public Safety

The following are some of the responsibilities of states to ensure the safety of their residents:

- Create and enforce a code of laws
- Operate a corrections system
- Fund, build, and maintain a system of roads
- License car and truck drivers
- Set speed limits
- Require safety inspections of motor vehicles
- Police the highways

troopers. The major job of the state police force is to patrol the state's highway system. They can also be called in to investigate crimes. In rural areas, the state police typically act as the local police force.

Each state also has a **corrections**, or prison, system. A state agency such as the Bureau of Corrections runs prisons, prison farms, and juvenile facilities. More than one million people are now incarcerated in state prisons.

Because of the cost, some states have **outsourced** the job to private companies. Instead of the state hiring employees and maintaining the prisons, they hire private companies to do the work. These companies build new prisons at their expense rather than the taxpayers'. They are then paid to run the prisons. The idea is that these companies will be more efficient and save taxpayers' money.

stop and think

Suppose you are the governor of a state. You want to persuade a corporation from another country to locate in your state. In your notebook, write a letter to the corporation's president explaining the services that your state government provides that benefit businesses.

Providing for Education and the Public Welfare

Every state has a system of public education that includes kindergarten through graduate school. Public education from kindergarten through grade 12 is the responsibility of state and local government. School districts are created by the state but run by local governments. The box at the top of page 393 lists many of the ways that states typically oversee K–12 public education.

Funding for K–12 public schools comes from a combination of federal, state, and local governments. The federal government provides about 9 percent of funding for K–12 schools. The amount of state funding varies. Some states fund more than half the cost of the schools. Other states provide much less.

392 Chapter 21

State Education Regulations

States typically regulate the following:

- Number of days in the school year
- Courses that are required to graduate from high school
- Number of years students must go to school
- Grade-level testing, including an exit test from high school
- Content standards and/or frameworks for content and skills
- Minimum teacher salaries
- Teacher qualifications
- Tax rates that districts may charge for education
- The amount of money that districts may borrow

In general, funding for K–12 schools comes from local property taxes. The amount of tax is based on the value of property. Funding for schools has brought about a number of lawsuits. Supporters of schools in big cities have sued their states over the property tax system. Their goal is to make school funding fairer between cities and suburbs. As a result, some property tax systems have been declared unconstitutional by state supreme courts. Texas, for example, had to redesign its system. New Jersey has to provide additional money for 30 urban school districts.

Florida State University is one of many state-funded universities in Florida.

Each state also has a system of public higher education. This includes universities, technical schools, and community colleges. California's higher education system is the largest in the nation. Tuition at these state-supported schools is typically lower for in-state students than for out-of-state students. State funding for these schools has increased greatly and has put an additional strain on state budgets.

In addition to education, states provide for the public welfare. This includes public health and assistance to the needy. Chapter 19 describes the role of the states in Medicaid and Temporary Assistance to Needy Families (TANF). The box to the right lists just a few of the public welfare services of states.

State Public Welfare Services

States typically do the following in the area of public welfare:

- Administer Medicaid
- Administer Temporary Assistance to Needy Families (TANF)
- License doctors and dentists
- Require vaccinations for children
- Operate hospitals and clinics, and oversee group homes for those with mental illness
- Operate facilities for those with developmental disabilities
- License private facilities for those with developmental disabilities
- Regulate the sale of medications
- Enforce antipollution laws
- Inspect workplaces for safety

Table Extension

Invite students to use library resources or the Internet to find out the facts for their state for each of the bulleted items in the table at the top left of page 392. Alternatively, have students work in groups on assigned topics from the list.

Picturing Government

The photograph on page 393 shows a welcome sign at the entrance to Florida State University. The university began as the Florida Institute, a boys' school. After Florida was admitted to the Union, the legislature mandated two schools of higher education for the new state. In 1856, the mayor of Tallahassee offered the land and buildings of the Florida Institute for one of those schools. The mayor who made the offer was Francis Eppes, grandson of Thomas Jefferson. Eppes, who, as president of the Board of Education for the school, shaped it according to Jeffersonian ideals, had spent his early years at Monticello. The year after it opened, the school absorbed the Tallahassee Female Academy and became coeducational. In the 2003-2004 year, the university had nearly 38,000 students and a downtown Tallahassee campus covering 463 acres.

Table Extension

Challenge students to choose an area of public welfare in which they are interested. Ask them to find out more about their state's efforts in that area. Allow time for students to report their findings to the class.

Extension

Ask interested students to investigate their state's system of public higher education. Have them create brochures to distribute to the school library on the various colleges and universities. Ask them to include information on costs and programs offered.

Picturing Government

In the photograph on page 394, an Environmental Protection Agency (EPA) worker takes water samples in Louisiana after Hurricane Katrina caused massive flooding and destruction in 2005. The Louisiana Department of Environmental Quality (DEQ) worked with the EPA to analyze both the floodwater and the water of Lake Pontchartrain. The high level of E. coli bacteria was an initial concern for public health. The DEQ expected the lake to sustain only minimal ecological damage.

Putting It All Together

Students' paragraphs will vary but should reflect lesson content.

Protecting the Environment

States did little to protect the environment until the 1980s. Before that, most environmental laws were federal. In the 1960s, the federal government passed several laws to clean up air and water pollution. The states began passing and enforcing tough antipollution laws in the 1980s.

For example, in most states, a company has to produce an **environmental impact statement** in order to begin a major building project. The statement is really a report. The company must study and report on how its project will affect the environment. In states with this law, federal, state, and local government agencies must also file impact statements before beginning major projects.

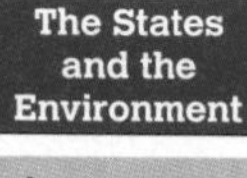

Among state responsibilities for the environment are the following:

- Set limits on air and water pollution
- Regulate the size and placement of roadside billboards
- Set aside public land for conservation and recreation
- Require environmental impact statements
- Regulate certain kinds of land use that harm the environment, such as strip mining

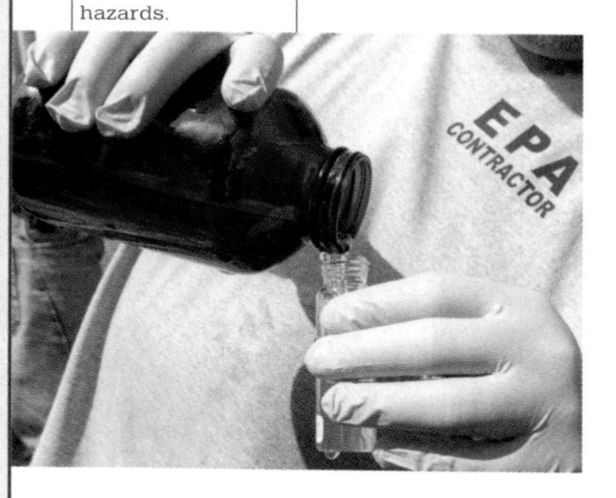

The Environmental Protection Agency is responsible for monitoring pollution and other environmental hazards.

States require companies to pay for cleaning up major chemical spills. In the past, the federal government has helped to pay for the cleanup of long-term polluted areas. The Superfund and Brownfields were two such state programs. Often, the companies that created the problems have moved or are no longer in business. States also have major conservation laws to help save natural resources such as land, rivers, and wildlife.

Putting It All Together

Review the subheadings in this lesson. Then write a paragraph that summarizes the role state governments play in our federal system of government. Share your paragraph with a partner.

LESSON 4

Financing State Government

Thinking on Your Own

Suppose you are on your state budget committee deciding how to spend the state's revenues. What categories do you think are included in a state budget? In other words, what items does a state budget have to fund? In your notebook, make a list of categories.

focus your reading

Explain how the states produce revenue.

Describe how state budgets are developed and passed.

words to know

inheritance tax

progressive

proportional

categorical grant

block grant

States need money to fund all their different programs. Like the federal government, states raise money by taxing residents. States also have other sources of revenue. A major source is the federal government. States may also borrow money.

Sources of Revenue

States have two types of revenue: taxes and non-taxes. Most states have a sales tax. This tax is a percentage of the price of an item. For example, Virginia's general sales tax is 5 percent. A $1.00 pen in Virginia really costs $1.05. The extra 5 cents is sales tax. The general sales tax covers a range of goods, from paper and pens to furniture. Both the tax rate and the range of goods vary from state to state. The sales tax in Illinois is 6.25 percent.

Most states do not tax food goods but do tax paper goods and cleaning supplies.

A second type of sales tax is the excise tax. The federal government collects an excise tax on items such as cigarettes and gasoline. States may also levy excise taxes on the same goods. As a result, anyone who buys gasoline is paying both state and federal excise taxes.

Lesson Summary

States fund programs through taxes. States also receive federal money and may borrow money. The state sales tax is a major source of revenue. Other tax sources include excise taxes, individual and corporate income taxes, estate and inheritance taxes, and licensing fees. Non-tax sources include borrowing, state lotteries, and federal grants, which may be categorical or block. The state budget process is similar to the federal one.

Lesson Objective

Students will learn about the ways that state governments finance their work.

Focus Your Reading Answers

1 States produce revenue through taxes and fees, as well as through borrowing, state lotteries, and federal grants.

2 State budgets are developed through the proposals of the governor, or in a few states, the governor and legislature. State agencies prepare budgets, which are sent to the executive budget office for review. The state agencies rework the final budgets and resubmit them. The governor presents the budget, and the legislature holds hearings and reviews it. Both houses must agree to the budget, which the governor may sign or veto. Should the governor veto or line item veto the bill, it returns to the lawmakers, who may change their requests or try to overturn the governor's veto.

Words to Know

Discuss each of the vocabulary terms with students.

An *inheritance tax* covers money or property that someone inherits. The *inheritance tax* varies from state to state. A *progressive* tax uses different rates for different income levels. People with higher incomes pay higher rates with a *progressive* tax system. A *proportional* tax is a flat tax, affecting everyone at the same rate. In a flat tax system, the poor pay the same rate as the rich.

A *categorical grant* is federal money given for a specific purpose. School lunch programs, for instance, were funded through a *categorical grant*. A *block grant* is given for general purposes, such as homeland security. Fewer guidelines exist for use of a *block grant*.

Table Extension

Have students find out the current rates of taxes for their state. Are there items that are not taxed? Does the state use a progressive or proportional taxing system?

Picturing Government

In the photograph on page 396, customers wait in line to buy lottery tickets for a Powerball jackpot. More than 20 states use lottery proceeds to fund schools. In some cases, however, the state cuts its share of budget funding for education, so that the net gain is less than it appears to be. Using lotteries to fund education has a long tradition in the United States. Both Columbia and Harvard Universities helped fund some of their early construction through the sale of lottery tickets.

Extension

Challenge students to find out how their state uses lottery money. If it is used in educational projects, has it created a reduction in the state budget? Suggest that students write letters to the state lawmakers giving their opinions on linking lotteries and education.

Most states have both an individual income tax and a corporate income tax. The taxes may be progressive or proportional. Income taxes make up about 30 percent of state tax revenue. Sales tax accounts for about 50 percent.

The rest of state tax revenue comes from estate and inheritance taxes and licensing fees. Estate tax is tax on the money and property a person leaves at death. Those who inherit, or get, the money and property may have to pay an **inheritance tax**. The tax rate and the amount that is taxed vary from state to state.

Types of Taxes

- Sales tax is a regressive tax. Sales tax takes a larger percentage of the pay of people with lower incomes. People with lower incomes are affected more than people with higher incomes.
- Income taxes are progressive or proportional.
  - A **progressive** tax uses different rates for different levels of income. People with lower incomes pay a lower rate than people with higher incomes.
  - A **proportional** tax is a flat tax. Everyone is taxed at the same rate. People earning millions of dollars pay the same tax rate as people earning minimum wage.

In addition, states collect fees for driver's licenses, hunting and fishing licenses, and marriage licenses. States also collect fees for registering cars. People may think all these are licensing fees, but they are really taxes.

Non-tax sources of revenue are borrowing, state lotteries, and federal grants. States borrow money by selling bonds to the public. Bonds are investments that repay the amount of the bond, plus interest, by a certain date. States often sell bonds to fund large construction projects such as bridges and highways.

A majority of states have lotteries. Often, states use lottery earnings to fund certain programs. For example, Florida uses its lottery money to support multiple public education programs.

Many states use the lottery as a means of generating revenue for government-sponsored programs.

The federal government returns money to the states through grants. In the past, most grants were **categorical grants**. States received the money for very specific purposes such as to fund school lunch programs. The states had to add money of their own for the programs. In addition, the federal government had very specific guidelines the states had to follow as they managed a grant.

Picturing Government

The photograph on page 395 shows a couple checking out in a store. By 2004, only 12 states taxed groceries at a normal rate. Of the 12, five states provided a low-income credit, leaving only seven states that tax food with no low-income credit. Four states taxed at a reduced rate, while 29 exempted groceries and five states had no sales tax at all. The District of Columbia exempts groceries.

stop and think

Create a table of the revenue sources that states have. List and explain each source. Work with a partner.

Today, most grants are **block grants**. Instead of being given for specific programs, the grants are awarded for more general purposes. For example, block grants are given to states for homeland security and public health. There are fewer guidelines with block grants than there are with categorical grants.

Budget Process

Like the federal government, every state government has a budget. State budgets reflect decisions about public policy. Each state budget answers these questions: Which programs should receive money? How much money should they receive? The answers are based on what the people and the government of the state think are most important.

The budgeting process in the states is similar to the process in the federal government. Each state agency prepares a budget estimate. The executive budget office reviews the estimates. The state agencies make changes and submit their final budgets. The executive budget office then prepares the final budget for the entire state government. The governor presents this to the state legislature.

Nevada governor Kenny Guinn works on the state budget with staff members.

The legislature holds hearings and reviews the budget. When both houses agree on the budget numbers, they pass the state's budget. The governor may either sign or veto the budget. Remember that in some states, the governor may veto just certain line items in the budget.

If the governor signs the budget, it goes into effect. If the governor vetoes all or part of the budget, it goes back to the legislature. Lawmakers either change the budget to agree with what the governor wants, or vote to try to overturn the governor's veto. Once the budget is passed and signed, the governor oversees spending by the state government.

Putting It All Together

Create a diagram to show how a state makes and passes a state budget. Work with a partner. First, list the steps. Then decide how to show them on a diagram. Finally, draw and label the diagram.

Stop and Think

Students' tables will vary but should include lesson content.

Picturing Government

The photograph on page 397 shows the governor of Nevada, Kenny Guinn, working with staff members on the state budget. State grants are increasingly being cut from the federal government's budget. At least 24 states were facing budget deficits in 2006 that totaled around $35 billion. The 2006 federal budget proposal would cut all program grants other than Medicaid to a percentage of the economy that is lower than it was in 2001.

Putting It All Together

Students' diagrams will vary but should include all the steps of the state budget process.

Participate in Government

Have interested students use library resources or the Internet to find out more about the Real ID Act of 2005.

You may also have students find out about additional state requirements for drivers, such as liability insurance. Students may be interested in knowing how much insurance for young drivers will cost. Suggest that they contact several different insurance agencies to find and compare rates.

Participate in Government

Get a Driver's License

To drive legally in the United States, a person must have a valid driver's license. States set the basic requirements for obtaining a driver's license. Generally, a person may apply for a first driver's license at age sixteen. Some states set the age at seventeen. A few states also allow for farm licenses at fifteen.

A person begins the process by applying for a learner's permit. This entitles a person to drive with a licensed driver in the car in the passenger's seat. In addition to this requirement, states may also limit the learner to driving only during daylight hours.

States also may require a student driver to take and pass a driver's education course in school or from a private driving school. A person must also pass a vision test, a test of the state's driving regulations, and a road test. An applicant must also state any disability that might impact driving a car.

In 2005, the U.S. Congress passed the Real ID Act. This act requires that everyone applying for a driver's license show a number of pieces of identification. These are then checked against federal databases. The act is meant to reduce the number of fake driver's licenses. People applying for a new driver's license must show

- a photo identification such as a passport.
- a birth certificate.
- a Social Security card.
- proof of residence such as a phone bill.

To Find Out More About Getting a Driver's License:

- Call your state department of motor vehicles (DMV).
- Check the white pages in the phone book for the nearest DMV.
- Go online to your state's Web site and click on the DMV's page.

Research Resources

Below is a list of reference books and Web sites that relate to the issues covered in this chapter. Students may wish to use these to further their research on ideas in the preceding lessons. Web site addresses may change over time. Use keyword searching on a major search engine to locate sites.

Reference Books:

Jeffrey M. Elliot. *The State and Local Government Political Dictionary*. ABC-CLIO, 1988.

Jack Rimmel Frymier. *Cultures of the States: A Handbook on the Effectiveness of State Governments*. Scarecrow Press, 2003.

Lori L. Smith. *Tapping State Government Information Sources*. Greenwood Press, 2003.

Web Sites:

The National Conference of State Legislatures provides information on a wide variety of issues facing state legislators on its Web site.

The National Governors Association site offers information on issues facing governors, as well as news and information about relations with the federal government.

The Census Bureau makes available information about the states' government on its Web site.

Skill Builder

Read a State Legislative Map

A state's legislative map shows the legislative districts for the state's legislature. The map may show the districts for the upper house, which is typically called the senate. The map may be of districts for the lower house. In most states, the lower house is called the house of representatives.

The state legislative map on this page shows districts for Florida's upper house, the senate. Florida has 40 senate districts and 120 house districts. Unlike U.S. senators, state senators represent only parts of a state. U.S. senators represent all voters in a state, so states are not divided into two U.S. Senate districts.

Florida State Senate Districts

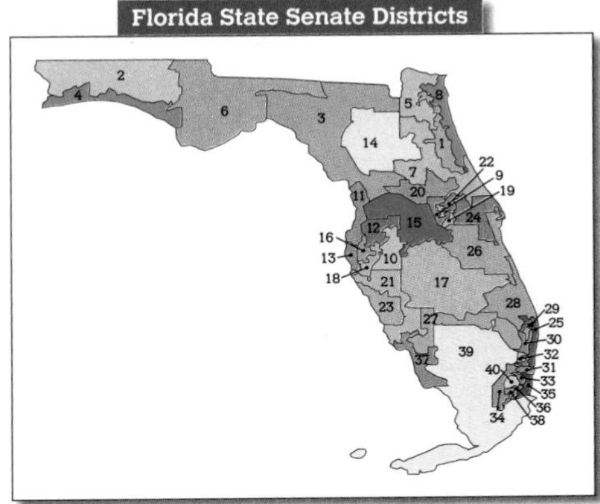

Florida's senate districts do not match its county borders. They are made up of several counties and even cities. The districts for Florida's lower house, or its house of representatives, are also arranged this way.

Answer the following questions about this map.

1 What do the numbers in dark type represent?

2 How are district borders shown on the map?

3 How many senate districts are there at the southern tip of Florida?

4 How many senate districts are there along the eastern coast?

5 Why would there be so many districts in one area and so few in another?

Skill Builder

1 The numbers represent the districts.

2 The district borders are shown by a black line.

3 One

4 13

5 Population determines the size of a district.

Recommended Reading

Below is a list of books that relate to the issues covered in this chapter. The numbers in parentheses indicate the related Thematic Strands of the National Council for the Social Studies (NCSS).

Suzanne Levert. *How States Make Laws.* Benchmark Books, 2003. (VI, X)

Suzanne Levert. *State Government.* Benchmark Books, 2003. (VI, X)

Classroom Discussion

Discuss with students some of the broader topics covered in this chapter.

- Should term limits be mandatory for all governors and lawmakers?
- What are some ways to encourage states to revise and simplify their constitutions?
- How can states offset the decline in federal aid and grants?

Related Transparencies

T-14 Strong-Mayor and Weak-Mayor Systems; Commission Form; Council-Manager Form

T-18 Three-Column Chart

Key Blacklines

Primary Source—Neighborhood Watch

CD Extension

Encourage students to use the reading comprehension, vocabulary reinforcement, and interactive timeline activities on the student CD.

Getting Focused

Review students' answers to the Getting Focused questions, correcting any misconceptions. Have students identify local government officials. If your community publishes a local paper, bring several copies to class. Have students work in groups to compare and contrast the coverage with that of a national paper. Ask them why the coverage might be different.

Chapter 22 LOCAL GOVERNMENT

Getting Focused

Skim this chapter to predict what you will be learning.

- **Read the lesson titles and subheadings.**
- **Look at the illustrations and read the captions.**
- **Examine the diagrams.**
- **Review the vocabulary words and terms.**

What county or parish do you live in? Do you live in a village, city, town, or township? Who is the chief executive of your community? Answer these questions and list as many facts as you can about your local government.

Local governments include cities, towns, villages, parishes, counties, townships, and other forms of locality.

Pre-Reading Discussion

1 Highlight local issues from a recent or upcoming election. Select one, such as a school board election, and discuss with students the issues candidates have identified. Invite students to agree with or to challenge the candidates' arguments.

2 Remind students that local governments take care of daily services such as water and sewage systems and trash pickup. Ask them if they think people could save money by caring for their own needs rather than paying taxes for the government to do so.

LESSON 1

Types of Local Government

Thinking on Your Own

Read the subheadings in this lesson. What would you like to know about each topic? For each subheading, write two questions in your notebook that you would like answered as you study this lesson. After you study the lesson, answer your questions.

focus your reading

What do county governments do?

Explain how towns, townships, and municipalities are the same and how they are different.

What are the possible forms of government in municipalities?

words to know

county
township
town meeting
selectperson
special district
municipality
mayor-council form
strong-mayor system
weak-mayor system
commission form
council-manager form

Local governments are created by the state. They exist only because the state allows them to exist. This is known as a unitary system of government. Unitary government is one in which all government power is held by the state. The state uses its power to set up lesser governments. The state constitution lists the powers that local governments may have. In other words, states have a centralized form of government.

County Government

Imagine that a state is a pyramid. At the top is the state government. Below it are county governments. At the base are towns, townships, special districts, and municipalities, or cities. In most states, the largest territorial and political unit is the **county**. In Louisiana, this government unit is called a parish and in Alaska, a borough. Connecticut and Rhode Island do not have counties.

Counties vary in size and number from state to state. Delaware has three counties. Texas has 254 counties.

Words to Know

Introduce each of the following vocabulary terms to students.

Explain that in most states, a *county* is the largest territorial and political unit. Usually, a *county* has 50,000 or fewer people. A *township* shares duties with the *county*. A *township* may be quite large and include several smaller centers.

Towns have an annual *town meeting* to vote on taxes and spending. The *town meeting* began with the Massachusetts Bay Colony. A town's official is called a *selectperson*. Day-to-day running of the town is left to the town's *selectperson*.

A *special district* is an independent unit of local government dealing with one function. A school district is an example of a *special district*.

A *municipality* is a city. A *municipality* may be as small as 50,000 people.

Lesson Summary

States create local governments. Counties, which can vary in size, number, and population, are the largest territorial and political units. Boards, generally made up of elected officials, usually govern counties. These boards have both executive and legislative powers. Towns and townships are small centers of houses and businesses surrounded by rural areas. A special district is an independent unit of local government that deals with one task. Municipalities use one of three forms of city government: mayor-council, commission, or council-manager.

Lesson Objective

Students will learn about the various forms of local government.

Focus Your Reading Answers

1 County governments include legislative and executive powers. They levy taxes and deal with money matters. They also administer programs and oversee county departments.

2 Towns, townships, and municipalities are the same in that they are units of government smaller than counties. They are different in size and forms of government. Towns and townships often use town meetings and selectpersons to run the local government. Municipalities have several forms of executive and legislative government.

3 Possible forms of municipal government include mayor-council, commission, or council-manager.

Bexar County Courthouse in San Antonio, Texas

The populations of counties also vary greatly. Los Angeles County has nine million people. A typical county has 50,000 or fewer.

A board generally governs counties. In some states, members of the county board are called supervisors. In others states, they are called freeholders. They may also be called commissioners. Generally, people are elected to the boards by the voters, rather than appointed. The typical term of office is four years. A county board may have as few as three or as many as 80 members. The typical board has between five and 15 members.

County boards have both executive and legislative powers. The most important legislative powers are the powers to levy taxes, determine how the money will be used, pay out money, and borrow money.

Using their executive powers, county boards administer programs and oversee county departments. In some states, the members of the county board oversee departments directly. In other states, the voters elect the heads of departments. In this case, the department heads report to the board. Among the departments are the county jail, county school board, county board of elections, county parks and recreation, and county social services such as the county home for the aged and the county hospital.

Some Duties of County Governments

In general, counties have the following jobs:

- Levy and collect county taxes
- Maintain law and order
- Build and maintain the county jail and other correctional facilities
- Build and repair county roads
- Administer elections
- Issue marriage, fishing, and hunting licenses
- Record mortgages and deeds
- Provide for the poor and needy in the county
- Oversee recreational areas and facilities

Towns, Townships, and Special Districts

Towns and townships are more important than counties in New England. In the Midwest, county and town or township governments share duties. The word *town* is used in New England and *town* or *township* in the other areas. The town or **township** includes a small center of houses and businesses and the surrounding rural areas. Townships may be very large and include several centers.

402 Chapter 22

Picturing Government

The photograph on page 402 features the Bexar County Courthouse in San Antonio, Texas. Located on the southern quadrant of historic Plaza de las Islas, the courthouse was being renovated in 2005. In addition to being the site where some 80,000 cases per year are heard, the courthouse also receives one million visitors each year.

Table Extension

Challenge students to create a rap song to help them remember the duties of county governments. Encourage them to find the most basic idea of each point and use that concept in their songs.

Picturing Government

The photograph on page 400 shows the junction of the Sacramento and American Rivers, with a city limit sign posted. First settled by John Sutter in 1849, Sacramento is the oldest incorporated city in, and capital of, the state of California. Sacramento, which is still an important commercial center, was the end point of the state's first railroad, of the Pony Express, and of the first transcontinental railroad.

Words to Know, continued

A *mayor-council form* uses a mayor for executive duties and a council for legislative duties. Most large cities use a *mayor-council form*. A *strong-mayor system* gives the mayor a great deal of power. In a *strong-mayor system*, the mayor may hire and fire high-ranking city officials. A *weak-mayor system* requires the mayor to share executive duties with department heads. The *weak-mayor system* is most often used in smaller cities.

A *commission form* of city government is one with a group of elected officials known as commissioners. In a *commission form* of government, one member is elected by the commissioners to act as mayor. The *council-manager form* separates executive and legislative duties, with a city manager as chief executive. The council makes policy decisions in a *council-manager form* of city government.

MARTA, Atlanta's mass transit system, includes trains and buses.

New England towns are the models of direct democracy. Once a year, citizens of a town meet to vote on tax rates and spending. They also elect town officers at the annual meeting. This yearly **town meeting** dates back to the beginning of the Massachusetts Bay Colony. Between meetings, the town's **selectpersons**, or officials, make decisions and run the government day to day. The selectmen and selectwomen make up the town board.

A **special district** is an independent unit of local government that deals with one function. A school district is a special district. There are 13,522 school districts in the United States and 35,356 other special districts. Compare that with 3,034 county governments, 16,506 towns and townships, and 19,372 municipalities, or city governments. As you can see, there are more special districts than other kinds of local government.

Why are there so many special districts? They are created when no other local government can take care of an issue. Special districts often cross the borders of several counties, towns and townships, or cities. This is often the reason why transportation networks are special districts. Two such districts are Chicago's RTA-Metro and New York's PATH. They each connect a large city and its suburbs. A great variety of special districts exist. Some provide water and sewage services. Others are soil conservation or reforestation districts.

stop and think

Use the statistics on this page to create a bar graph with a partner. Use the lines on a sheet of notebook paper as the sections on your graph. Label your graph "Number of Local Governments in the United States." After your graph is completed, write three sentences about the data on your graph.

City Government

Municipality is another word for a city. Cities vary in size. They can be as small as 50,000 people or as large as Houston, Texas, with almost two million. Regardless of size, cities have one of three forms of government: mayor-council, commission, or council-manager.

About half of all cities use the **mayor-council form**. It is the oldest form and the one that most large cities use. The mayor and the city council are both elected. The mayor has executive power and the city council has legislative power. The typical

Picturing Government

On page 403 is a photograph taken in the Atlanta subway system. The first subway system in the United States opened in Boston in 1897. New York and Philadelphia soon followed. In some cities, subways are combined with above-ground and elevated rail lines. The widespread use of automobiles after World War II led to a pause in the growth of subways. However, as more and more cities try to cope with increasing populations, mass transit systems have again become popular.

Stop and Think

Students' graphs and three-sentence summaries will vary but should reflect the information on pages 401–403 about special districts, country governments, towns and townships, and municipalities.

Extensions

1 Ask students to select a neighboring community with a different form of local government than that of their own. Using library resources or the Internet, have them contrast the two communities. Suggest that they present their findings using a graphic organizer.

2 Invite students to find out about the county departments in their area. They may begin with the list on page 402. Have them work in small groups to find out more about the school board, board of elections, parks and recreation department, and so on. Have them present their findings to the class by using the Student Presentation Builder on the student CD.

3 Encourage students interested in history to find out more about the origins of the town meeting in the Massachusetts Bay Colony. Have them present their findings to the class in the form of a radio drama or documentary.

Diagram Extension

Place students in pairs. Challenge them to explain the information in the diagram to one another. Ask them to focus on explaining why the system on the left creates a stronger mayor. Be sure that each student in the pair explains both sections of the diagram.

city council has ten members. All voters in the city may vote for all council members. They are not elected by district in most cities.

There are two forms of the mayor-council form. One is known as the **strong-mayor system**. The strong-mayor model gives the mayor a great amount of executive power. The strong mayor may

- prepare the city budget.
- veto city council laws and regulations.
- hire and fire department heads and other high-ranking officials of the city government.
- propose legislation and regulations to the council.

The strong-mayor system is often the model used in large cities such as Houston, San Diego, Detroit, and Dallas. The mayor in this system is typically elected for a four-year term.

The other model is called the **weak-mayor system**. It is most often found in smaller cities. The typical term for the mayor in this system is two years. Executive power is shared with department heads and council members. The mayor in this system

- may share budget responsibility with the council, or the council may have budget responsibility.
- may or may not have veto power over council laws.
- shares appointment and firing duties with the council, or the council may have complete power.
- has limited ability to propose legislation to the council.

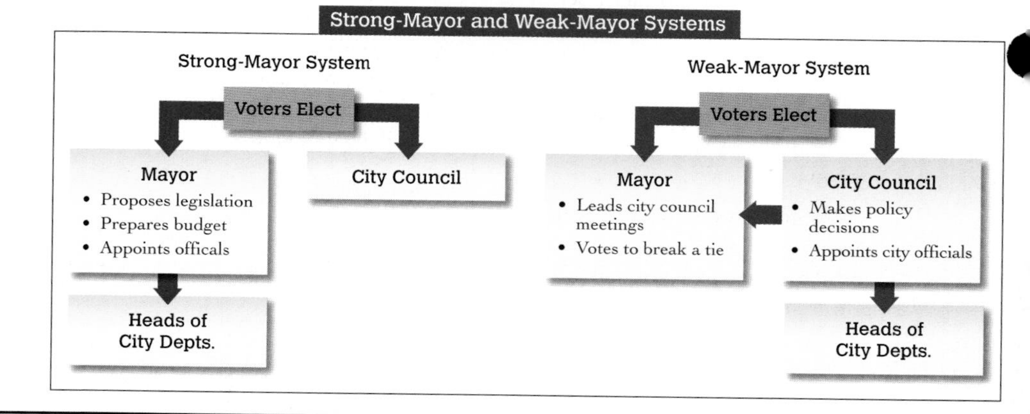

Extension

Divide the class into four groups. Assign each group one of the four major cities listed on this page as using the strong-mayor system, or identify four cities in your state that use the system and assign them instead. Have students use Internet sites for the cities and find out more about the local governments. Ask them to identify recent issues for the mayor, and to compare and contrast their findings as they report to the class. Are there, for example, common issues, such as education or decaying infrastructure, that these cities must address?

The **commission form** of city government is run by a group of elected officials known as commissioners. They have both executive and legislative powers. Most city government commissions have five members. Each member heads a department such as the department of public safety. The members also meet as a group to propose and pass legislation for the city. They make all decisions about public policy. One member is elected by fellow commissioners to act as mayor. He or she leads council meetings and attends ceremonies such as groundbreakings for new buildings.

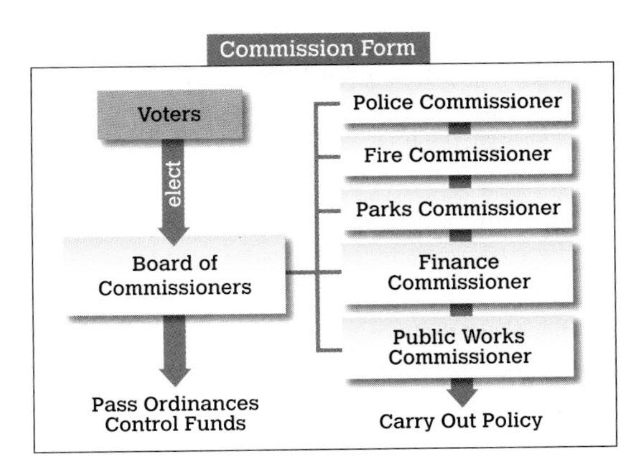

The commission form began in Galveston, Texas, in 1900. Few cities use the commission form today. One problem is the lack of leadership. No single person heads the city government. As a result, there is no one whose job it is to get commissioners to cooperate and compromise. Commissioners may look out for their own departments rather than for the good of the city. This can result in larger budgets than necessary because commissioners try to get as much money as they can for programs for their departments. For these reasons, few cities today have a commission form of government.

The **council-manager form** separates executive and legislative duties. The council makes policy decisions and passes laws and regulations for the city. The council is usually

Diagram Extension

If you live in or near a community that uses the commission form of government, invite students interested in politics or media to attend and videotape the council meeting, after gaining approval to do so. (You may wish to attend and videotape the meeting yourself.) Show the tape to the class and discuss the council meeting.

Extension

Have students meet in small groups to discuss which form of city government seems to them most and least democratic. Have them support their ideas with facts based on the three diagrams on pages 404–406.

Diagram Extension

Discuss with students why they think such a large percentage of cities use the council-manager form of government. Why would that form be most effective for so many cities?

Putting It All Together

Students' charts and decisions about the best form for the city in which they live will vary.

made up of five to nine members. The city manager is the chief executive of the city. However, he or she is not elected by the voters. They elect the council members and the council hires the city manager. The council also has the power to fire the city manager if he or she does not do a good job.

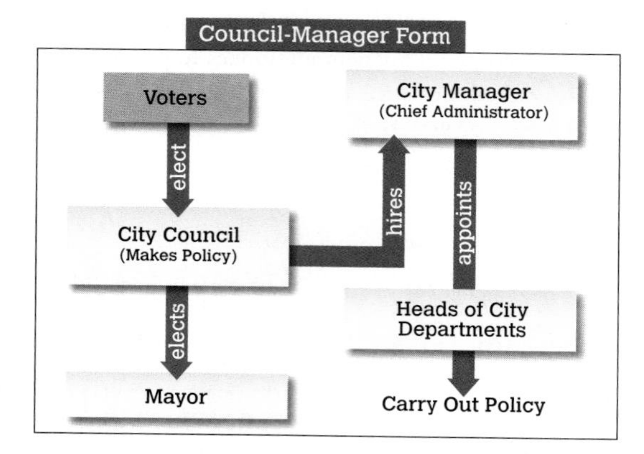

The city manager prepares the budget and sends it to the council for a vote. He or she does not have veto power over decisions of the council. It is part of his or her job to recommend policy to the council.

The city manager also hires and fires city workers. The city manager is a professional administrator. He or she is trained to run a city government on a day-to-day basis. Many city managers have college degrees in public service or municipal management. About 40 percent of cities use the council-manager form.

Putting It All Together

Make a three-column chart in your notebook. Title the columns "Mayor-Council," "Commission," and "Council-Manager." Under each column, include at least one strength and one weakness of that form of government. Then decide which form would be best for the city in which you live.

LESSON 2

Public Services

Thinking on Your Own

Imagine you are founding a community. What kinds of government services would your community need? Think about what you know about the community in which you live. In your notebook, list as many government services as you can for your new community.

focus your reading

Describe the services local governments provide for educational, cultural, and recreational activities.

Explain how zoning laws affect communities.

How do local governments provide for public safety and transportation?

What social services and public health activities do local governments support?

words to know

zoning

metropolitan area

suburb

What services does your local government provide? It can be hard to answer this question. However, knowing how your tax dollars are spent is important. The federal, state, and local governments all contribute to many of the same services. For example, the federal government provides money for schools. That money is passed through the state government to your local school district. Your state also provides money to your school district. The major part of school funding comes from your local community.

Educational, Cultural, and Recreational Services

One of the jobs of local government is to provide education. School districts are local government units called special districts. Local tax revenue pays for the majority of education expenses.

Voters elect a local school board to run the school district. One of its most important decisions is the hiring and firing of the superintendent of schools for the district. This person manages the day-to-day operations of the school district. He or she is responsible to the board.

Lesson Summary

Local governments are responsible to provide education out of local tax revenue through a school board, which is run by a superintendent. Cultural and recreational opportunities are also part of local governments' responsibilities. Local governments regulate land use and construction through zoning laws. They provide for public safety through fire and police protection. Large cities may also provide mass transit options for citizens. Local governments administer social services paid for by federal and state money. They also may manage water supplies, sewage, and sanitation services.

Lesson Objective

Students will learn about the various public services that local communities offer.

Focus Your Reading Answers

1 Local governments provide services such as education, regulated land use through zoning laws, public safety, transportation, social services, and public health.

2 Zoning laws determine how a community grows. The laws restrict areas for businesses and houses, as well as stating the size of building plots required.

3 Local governments provide for public safety with police and fire protections and for transportation through mass transit systems and roads.

4 Local governments provide social services and public health services such as hospitals, homeless shelters, water supplies, and sewage and sanitation services.

Words to Know

Discuss each of the vocabulary terms with students.

Local governments regulate land use and construction through *zoning*. Local boards create plans for the community's growth through *zoning*.

A *metropolitan area* is a large city and its surrounding areas. Many people in a *metropolitan area* use some form of mass transit.

The area surrounding a city is called a *suburb*. Railways and subways help connect the *suburb* to the main city.

Local control is a key part of public education in the United States. Local control means that the local community wants to determine what is taught in its schools. Since the early 2000s, the federal No Child Left Behind Act has raised concerns in many districts. The act requires testing in math, reading, and science in grades three through eight. Local and state governments have to pay for these tests.

Another issue is how local districts raise money to fund schools. Property taxes are the major source of school funding. This leads to great inequality among school districts. Wealthy districts are able to spend more on their schools than poorer districts.

The Duties of School Boards

Typically, school boards have the following duties:

- Hire and fire the superintendent
- Approve the hiring and firing of other school officials including principals and teachers
- Prepare the school district's budget
- Approve the curriculum, programs, and facilities plans
- Set the tax rate to be collected for the district

Laura Bush greets the cast and crew at a theater program for disadvantaged youth in Los Angeles.

In addition to education, local communities also support cultural and recreational activities. Playgrounds, parks, playing fields, pools, and skating rinks are some of the places that local governments fund. Museums and zoos may also be owned and managed by local government. Sometimes counties and cities provide money and tax credits to private companies to build stadiums and arenas in their area.

Zoning

Zoning is the way that local governments regulate land use and construction within their borders. How land is used affects cities, towns, and townships. It can also affect counties and special districts. For example, if a large section of forest is turned into homes, the local school district can suddenly find itself with 500 more students than it had the year before. The local transportation system can suddenly be carrying an extra 1,000 passengers a day. The water and sewage special districts are also affected.

Table Extension

Divide the class into five groups, assigning each group one of the duties listed. Ask each group to come up with at least one question they would like answered about their topic, then to interview the appropriate person or research the topic. Have the groups report their findings to the class.

Picturing Government

In the photograph on page 408, Laura Bush, then First Lady, meets with a group of young actors who have just performed a segment of Shakespeare's *Romeo and Juliet*. In 2003, the Los Angeles Shakespeare Festival/LA's Will Power to Youth won a Coming Up Taller award from the President's Committee on the Arts and Humanities, of which Mrs. Bush is honorary chair. The group consists of between 20 and 30 company members from fourteen to twenty-one years old, who are paid minimum wage to study, adapt, and perform Shakespeare. The group's work includes creating music, set, and costume designs in addition to performance.

Extensions

1 Invite interested students to attend the next open meeting of the local school board. Ask them to serve as reporters for the school radio station or newspaper, or to plan a podcast or blog about current issues facing the school board.

2 Have students profile local organizations devoted to cultural or recreational activities. Compile the reports, which should include the basic five Ws and H, into a brochure and present it to the school library media center. Encourage students to expand the project with a multimedia presentation for the community, uncovering "gems" that may receive little public notice.

Property taxes can be greatly impacted by the decisions made by zoning boards.

Local communities have a set of zoning laws. These describe what can be built in the community, and where. Some areas are reserved for houses only. Some areas are zoned only for businesses. Some are zoned for houses and businesses. The zoning laws also describe the permitted height and width of buildings. These are determined by the size of the plot of land the building will be built on.

To make sure that the zoning laws are obeyed, local governments have zoning boards. Members of zoning boards are usually appointed, not elected. Their job is to plan for growth in their community. They review permits for building. They may approve, reject, or ask for changes to the builder's plans. The zoning board also recommends changes in local zoning laws to the council or commission.

stop and think

Review the services that you have read about in this lesson. List them as headings in your notebook. Under each heading, list two or three examples of this service. As you continue reading, add headings and examples to your list.

Public Safety and Transportation

Two very important services of local governments are fire and police protection. After education, police account for the largest part of the local government budget. Even most small towns have a regular police force.

Large cities have professional, full-time firefighters. Small towns and townships usually have a volunteer fire department. When a fire occurs, volunteers leave their jobs and rush to the fire. Small cities may have a mix of professional and volunteer firefighters.

The United States is a nation of cars. They drive on 45,000 miles of federal highways, four million miles of state highways, and 650,000 miles of local streets. Taxpayers pay for building and repairing all these roads. They also support the nation's mass transit system of railroads, subways, and rapid transit lines. Mass transit is transportation that carries large numbers of people. The fares that people pay to use mass transit also support it.

The "L" train is part of the mass transit system in Chicago, Illinois.

Stop and Think

Students' headings and lists will vary but should include at least two or three examples of services in the various areas mentioned in the lesson.

Picturing Government

At the top left on page 409, the photograph pictures mayors and citizens of New Jersey rallying for property tax cuts in 2003. As a result of their activism, the state enacted a Homestead Rebate Program. Those whose gross income was less than $200,000 were eligible for tax rebates on their principal residence.

Picturing Government

The photograph at the bottom of page 409 shows a passenger train in Chicago. That region's Metra system covers 495 miles in six counties, serving 230 stations. Chicago is an example of what the federal government defines as a Metropolitan Statistical Area (MSA). An MSA has at least one urban center and a population of at least 50,000. The MSA consists of the central county and outlying counties, with many commuters into that central county. Most MSAs offer train service or other mass transit to connect residential and business sections of the metropolitan areas.

Extension

Have students interested in transportation make a map of your community, showing major roads and indicating whether they are the responsibility of national, state, or local government. Suggest they use different-colored pencils or markers for each level of government and create a map legend.

Picturing Government

The photograph on page 410 shows New York City sanitation workers cleaning up after a New Year's Eve celebration in Times Square. New York City's Department of Sanitation is the world's largest. Each day, it collects more than 12,000 tons of institutional and residential refuse and recyclables. Businesses in the city create another 13,000 tons of refuse daily, which is handled by private companies. In 2005, the Department of Sanitation employed nearly 7,000 uniformed workers, and used about 5,700 vehicles, including street sweepers, salt/sand spreaders, and collection trucks.

Many commuters who live in large metropolitan areas such as San Francisco and Chicago depend on mass transit to get around. A **metropolitan area** is a large city and its surrounding area. The surrounding area is called the **suburbs**. Both environmentalists and local governments encourage people to use mass transit instead of their cars. First, mass transit saves gasoline. Second, it pollutes the environment less. Third, fewer cars on the road mean less wear and tear on the roads. This saves taxpayers money. Fourth, mass transit is more efficient. A single subway car can carry up to 100 people at a time.

Social Services and Public Health

The federal and state governments provide money to local governments for certain social services. For example, money to aid those with developmental disabilities may be passed to local governments. Some cities also run their own hospitals. They accept patients with limited means to pay. Cities may also run homeless shelters and help food kitchens feed the hungry. Federal money for housing and for job training is also passed to cities.

Some large cities have their own water supplies. Las Vegas, for example, uses water from the human-made reservoir of Lake Mead. Special water districts are sometimes set up among several local communities to ensure a supply of fresh water.

Local governments also arrange for sewage and sanitation services. Some cities have their own sewage treatment plants. Some communities set up special districts to dispose of sewage. It is important to keep sewage from draining into sources of water such as streams and rivers. Sanitation includes picking up trash and garbage from homes and businesses and keeping the streets clean.

Depending on the community, homeowners and business owners may pay fees for water, sewage disposal, and sanitation services. In other communities, some or all of these may be part of the local taxes. These services all cost money to provide.

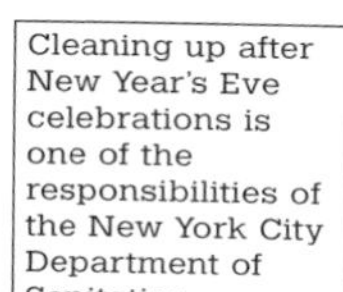
Cleaning up after New Year's Eve celebrations is one of the responsibilities of the New York City Department of Sanitation.

Putting It All Together

Review the list you made for Thinking on Your Own. Compare it to the services mentioned in this lesson. Did you leave out any essential services? If so, add them to your original list.

Putting It All Together
Students' lists will vary but should reflect lesson content.

LESSON 3

Funding Local Government

Thinking on Your Own

What do you remember about types of federal and state taxes? Draw a three-column chart in your notebook. Label the columns "Federal," "State," and "Local." Using what you remember, fill in the first two columns. As you read this lesson, fill in the third column.

focus your reading

Explain why property taxes are a controversial political topic.

What are a local government's revenue sources?

words to know

property tax

tax assessor

assessment

Providing services costs money. Local governments must raise money to provide services. Taxes, fees, and fines are three ways that local governments raise money. They also receive money from the federal and state governments for certain programs.

Property Taxes

A **property tax** is tax on property. The property may be land and buildings or personal property such as jewelry, cars, stocks, and bonds. Usually, local governments tax only land and buildings. Property taxes provide about 75 percent of all local tax revenue. They are an important source of revenue for school districts.

The value of property for tax purposes is decided by a **tax assessor**. He or she makes an **assessment** of property in the community every two or four years. The assessor determines the value of the property. The tax rate is then applied to this value. The result is the amount of tax the owner must pay. Homeowners can dispute this estimate.

There are a number of issues related to property taxes. First, people in school districts with increasing numbers of children pay high taxes to build new schools. People without children or retired people consider this unfair. Second,

Lesson Summary

Taxes, fees, and fines are the three main sources of local government funding. For some programs, local governments also receive state and federal funds. Property taxes, local income, and sales taxes are the ways to raise revenue. Local governments also levy fines for traffic violations and fees for permits and licenses. Sometimes they run local businesses, such as parking garages. They may also borrow money to finance projects.

Lesson Objective

Students will learn about the ways in which local governments are funded.

Focus Your Reading Answers

1 Property taxes are a controversial political topic because some people don't want to pay taxes that support schools if they have no children in those schools. Property taxes are regressive, so those with lower incomes pay a higher portion of their incomes. Property taxes also can create unequal services in communities, because wealthier communities can afford better and more services than can poorer communities.

2 Local government revenue sources include property taxes, income taxes, fees, fines, income from businesses the local government owns, and borrowed funds for moneymaking projects.

Words to Know

Discuss each of the vocabulary terms with students.

A *property tax* is tax on property such as land, buildings, or personal property. The *property tax* is an important source of revenue for school districts.

A *tax assessor* decides the value of property for tax purposes. A homeowner can dispute what a *tax assessor* estimates the tax to be. An *assessment* is a property evaluation for tax purposes. An *assessment* is made every two to four years.

Extension

Ask students to investigate two communities in their state at each end of the wealth spectrum. Have them contrast the schools and services of the two communities. Suggest they present their findings to the class using a graphic organizer.

Property taxes are a continual issue for homeowners.

property taxes are regressive. People with lower incomes pay a higher part of their incomes in property taxes. This also impacts retired people who live on limited incomes.

Third, property taxes can result in unequal services among communities. Wealthy communities can afford more and better services than poorer communities. This is especially true of older, big cities. Their suburbs are much wealthier. In fact, using property taxes to fund schools has been found unconstitutional in some states. The state courts have told local governments to find fairer ways to fund schools.

stop and think

As you read, list each form of revenue that cities have. Decide how a tax or other source of revenue can be fair or unfair in the way it affects people. As you read, rearrange your list of revenues so the most fair is at the top.

Picturing Government

The 1978 photograph at top left shows protesters in Los Angeles supporting Proposition 13, the beginning of state tax revolts. Passed by more than 60 percent of voters that year, after less serious measures had twice before failed, the ballot measure passed as a result of high inflation that caused homeowners to sell because they couldn't afford the taxes on their homes. Some analysts consider the measure a prelude to the Reagan income tax cuts of 1981 and the beginning of the modern conservative, anti-big government movement. Within five years of the passage of Proposition 13, almost 50 percent of the states had passed similar measures to limit the potential of legislators to increase taxes.

Biography

Shirley Clarke Franklin (1945–)

Shirley Franklin took office as mayor of Atlanta, Georgia, in 2002. She was the first African-American woman to lead a major southern city.

The city was facing an $82 million budget deficit. Franklin proposed a 1.5 percent increase in the sales tax and a 50 percent increase in property taxes. She cut 1,000 city jobs. Franklin also cut her own salary by $40,000. The city council agreed to pass the tax increases.

Franklin showed great political courage in raising taxes. People do not like having their taxes raised. However, Franklin was able to convince Atlantans that it had to be done. Under her leadership, the city was on its way to balancing its budget. By 2005, the city had a budget surplus, and city services had improved greatly.

Franklin was born in Philadelphia. She graduated from Howard University in 1968 and earned a master's degree from the University of Pennsylvania. In 1978, she became Atlanta's commissioner of cultural affairs. In 1982, she was appointed the city's chief administrative officer/city manager. To gain the 1996 Summer Olympics for Atlanta, Franklin served as senior vice president of the Atlanta Committee for the Olympic Games. In 2005, she was awarded the John F. Kennedy Profile in Courage Award.

Bio Facts

- Born 1945.
- Became nation's first female chief administrative officer under Mayor Andrew Young.
- Elected first female mayor of Atlanta, 2002, in her first run for public office.
- Reelected in 2005, with more than 90 percent of the vote.
- CEO of a management and consulting firm for community and public affairs.
- Served on the board of the Georgia Regional Transportation Authority.
- Chair of U.S. Conference of Mayors' Women's Caucus.

Biography Extension

In response to growing concerns about water quality in Atlanta, Franklin dubbed herself the Sewer Mayor in 2002 as the city initiated the Clean Water Atlanta (CWA) project. When all projects, which include improvements to the infrastructure and treatment systems of both water and wastewater, are completed, the city will have spent more the $3 billion.The goal of the project is to create within a decade the cleanest urban rivers and streams in the nation.

Other Sources of Revenue

In addition to property taxes, local governments have other ways to raise revenue. A local income tax is paid in addition to federal and state individual income taxes. A local sales tax is usually a low rate. For example, the sales tax in Texas is 6.25 percent. Dallas has a sales tax of 2 percent. Consumers pay both the state and the local sales tax when they make purchases.

Traffic fines and fines for other violations are revenue for local governments. Fees for building permits and licenses also raise revenue. Sometimes a local government will pass a special assessment on homeowners and business owners. For example, homeowners in an area without sidewalks may be assessed if the town decides to put in sidewalks.

Local governments often rely on many sources of revenue, such as fines issued in traffic court.

Local Governments' Sources of Revenues

- Property tax
- Individual income tax
- Sales tax
- Fines
- Fees for certain services
- Special assessments
- Borrowing

Some local governments also run businesses. For example, they may own and operate parking lots and garages. They may provide funding for a stadium and be paid rent from those who use it.

States allow local governments to borrow money by selling bonds. However, states usually regulate the terms of the borrowing. They may set a limit on how much the local government may borrow. Local governments borrow money to build government office buildings, new firehouses, or moneymaking buildings like convention centers and arenas.

Putting It All Together

Without taxes, the government could not provide services. Few people like to pay taxes. Should the government provide all these services or provide fewer services? This is the problem that all lawmakers face. Write a three-paragraph essay to explain your ideas about the kinds of services that government should or should not provide. Share your essay with a partner. Try to come to an agreement.

Table Extension

Invite students to find examples of each source of funding in their own community. Challenge them to make a poster or bulletin board depicting the various sources and their local applications.

Picturing Government

The picture on page 413 shows a California Highway Patrol officer issuing a traffic citation. Assessing such fines is one method used by local and state governments to subsidize revenue. Traffic fines are set by local governments. Encourage students to learn more about the alterative revenue sources in their community.

Putting It All Together

Students' essays will vary.

Participate in Government

Invite students to present the information they find through contacting their local government office in a poster display or brochure. Work with the school's volunteer or community service program to help match students with possible committee assignments.

Participate in Government

Volunteer for a Local Government Commission

Local governments may govern a city of eight million people like New York City. Local governments may also run a 500-person village in New England or a 16,000-person township in Indiana. Regardless of the size, local governments manage many different services for their citizens. Paid employees and elected officials do most of the day-to-day work of local governments. However, communities also have committees made up of volunteers who provide many services.

What kinds of volunteer committees serve communities?

- Planning boards oversee the growth of the communities so that they grow in orderly ways. Too many new buildings and homes can put a strain on schools, water and sewer systems, and other local services.
- Zoning boards recommend whether requests for new buildings should be approved. They also recommend changes to zoning laws.
- Shade tree committees oversee the care and replacing of trees.
- Community parks and recreation committees make sure that parks, playgrounds, and playing fields are maintained. They may also recommend the purchase of new areas for recreation.

Volunteering for local government committees is very important to a community. Volunteers save taxpayers money. They also provide a way for ordinary citizens to have a voice in their community's government.

To Find Out More About How to Join a Committee:

- Contact the local government office in your community.

Research Resources

Below is a list of reference books and Web sites that relate to the issues covered in this chapter. Students may wish to use these to further their research on ideas in the preceding lessons. Web site addresses may change over time. Use keyword searching on a major search engine to locate sites.

Reference Books:

Jeffrey M. Elliot. *The State and Local Government Political Dictionary.* ABC-CLIO, 1988.

Jack Rimmel Frymier. *Cultures of the States: A Handbook on the Effectiveness of State Governments.* Scarecrow Press, 2003.

John William Smith. *The Urban Politics Dictionary.* ABC-CLIO, 1990.

Web Sites:

A meta-site from State and Local Government on the Internet allows searching by state or topic.

The official portal for government information at all levels, FirstGov, includes not only state and local, but also tribal, information access.

Skill Builder

Writing or Speaking Persuasively

Suppose you hear on the news that your community is going to close down an after-school sports program. What do you do? You can complain to your friends, family, and neighbors, or you can complain to the city council. Rather than just complain, you can also persuade the council to keep the program running.

To present a well-organized speech, you have to research your facts and write out your speech. There are certain things you should include in any persuasive speech or piece of writing.

To speak or write persuasively,

- introduce the topic, or main idea, in your first paragraph.
- tell what you want done in the second paragraph.
- in the body of your speech, letter, or essay, develop your ideas about why your position is the right one.
- answer objections about your position in the main part of your speech, letter, or essay.
- restate your main idea in your conclusion, and ask your listeners or readers to take the action that you want.

Practice your speech in front of a mirror. Write out the important points on note cards. You do not need to memorize your speech. However, you need to know it well enough to be able to speak using just your note cards.

Complete the following activity with a partner.

Imagine that an after-school sports program is going to be closed. It serves both boys and girls and provides a variety of sports as well as homework help. The money that had been used for it has been moved to programs for senior citizens.

1 List reasons why the program is important to students.

2 List one objection that the city council might raise about keeping the program open.

3 Use the information from your answers to questions 1 and 2 to write a speech to deliver before the city council. Your speech requests that the after-school program remain open.

Skill Builder

Students' reasons and objections, as well as their written speeches, will vary, but should follow the five bulleted points on this page.

Recommended Reading

Below is a list of books that relate to the issues covered in this chapter. The numbers in parentheses indicate the related Thematic Strands of the National Council for the Social Studies (NCSS).

Eleanor Fremont. *Rudolph W. Giuliani: America's Mayor.* Aladdin, 2002. (VI, X)

Susan W. Thrane. *State Houses: America's 50 Capitol Buildings.* Boston Mills Press, 2005. (VI, X)

Classroom Discussion

Discuss with students some of the broader topics covered in this chapter.

- What can be done to balance the need for state and local services with the public's dislike of taxes?
- How can state and local governments work together most effectively?
- In what ways can young people get involved politically to make a difference at the local level?

Unit Objectives

After studying this unit, students will be able to

- summarize the major political systems of the modern world
- describe the economic systems currently in use

Unit 9 compares modern political and economic systems

Chapter 23, Modern Political Systems, examines democratic and authoritarian systems of government, as well as issues of global security, such as terrorism and nuclear proliferation.

Chapter 24, Modern Economic Systems, explores capitalism, communism, and socialism through the examples of nations that use each system.

Getting Started

Have a student read aloud the title of the unit and the two paragraphs that follow it on page 416. Ask students to preview the unit and jot down any questions they have about its content. Encourage them to add answers to those questions as they read Unit 9.

UNIT 9 COMPARATIVE POLITICAL AND ECONOMIC SYSTEMS

The United States is a representative democracy. Voters elect lawmakers and a president to run the government on a day-to-day basis. There are 192 other nations in the world. Not all 19 are representative democracies. Some have a Communist form of government. Some are run by dictators. Even nations that ar representative democracies have different types of government

The economic systems of nations also vary. In the United States, private businesses are very important to the economy. In many other nations, government has a much stronger say in how businesses are run.

Picturing Government

The photograph on this page shows a building of the European Union in Strasbourg, France. Strasbourg was the seat of the Council of Europe founded after World War II. The Council later became the European Union. The member countries meet in the European Parliament in Brussels, Luxembourg, and Strasbourg. The members of the parliament are elected in their home country. Each location has specific committees and duties.

Chapter

23 MODERN POLITICAL SYSTEMS

Getting Focused

Skim this chapter to predict what you will be learning.

- Read the lesson titles and subheadings.
- Look at the illustrations and read the captions.
- Review the vocabulary words and terms.

If you and your family are native-born Americans, write down the names of three nations. Write one fact about each nation and its government. To help you, think about what you have seen on television or cable news, or what people are talking about. Did you or your family come from another country to the United States? If so, write down as many facts as you can remember about that country and its government.

Japan's prime minister, Yoshiro Mori, meets with U.S. president George W. Bush in the Oval Office.

Pre-Reading Discussion

1 Select a recent world news event that focuses on differences of government systems. Bring copies of a news article to class and be sure that everyone reads the article, and then discuss it.

2 Discuss with students recent movements toward democracy throughout the world. Ask students to evaluate the process of becoming a more free nation.

Related Transparencies

T-18 Three-Column Chart

T-19 Venn Diagram

T-20 Concept Web

Key Blacklines

Biography—Hamid Karzai

CD Extension

Encourage students to use the reading comprehension, vocabulary reinforcement, and other activities on the student CD.

Getting Focused

Ask students to become more knowledgeable about one of the nations they choose to focus on. Tell them that in this chapter they will learn about political systems. They will be responsible for finding out more about the political system of one other nation and for reporting on it to the class. If they choose one of the countries featured in the chapter, encourage them to research the political history of that country for an in-depth picture.

LESSON 1

Democratic Governments

Thinking on Your Own

Many nations in the world today have democratic governments. However, such governments are not all alike. One democratic nation today has a queen. Another has 40 political parties. Some do not have separation of powers. Write a brief paragraph in your notebook explaining how governments so very different can still be democratic.

focus your reading

Explain how the government of Great Britain is organized.

What are the differences between the old Communist government of Russia and its government since 1993?

How is the government of Mexico different from and similar to the government of the United States?

words to know

parliamentary government

command economy

Duma

Democracy is rule by the people. In a representative democracy, voters elect others—representatives—to govern for them. The voters give their representatives the power to make and enforce laws for the community, state, or nation.

A democratic nation has the following characteristics: free elections, political parties, a constitutional government, an independent judiciary, and usually a capitalist, or market, economy. Even with these five characteristics in common, democracies vary in organization.

Britain's Queen Elizabeth II makes a speech during the State Opening of Parliament.

Great Britain

Great Britain is a constitutional monarchy and has a parliamentary government. Queen Elizabeth II is the current British monarch.

A **parliamentary government** is one in which an elected assembly has both legislative and executive powers. In Great Britain, this elected assembly is called Parliament. Its members pass the nation's laws and

Lesson Summary

The five characteristics of a democracy are free elections, political parties, a constitutional government, an independent judiciary, and usually, a capitalist economy. Within that structure, democracies vary. Great Britain, for example, is a constitutional monarchy with a parliamentary government. Russia has also had a federal system of democratic government since the 1990s, following decades of authoritarian Communist rule. Mexico is another example of a democracy with a federal system.

Lesson Objective

Students will learn about several contemporary examples of democratic governments.

Focus Your Reading Answers

1 Great Britain's government is a constitutional monarchy. It has a monarch and an elected assembly, Parliament. Parliament's members select the prime minister, who is the head of the executive branch, and the cabinet. Parliament has two houses, the House of Lords and the House of Commons. Great Britain has a court system for judicial functions, but has no power of judicial review.

2 The Communist government of Russia was authoritarian. Only the Communist Party was allowed; elections were not free. People had few rights and the government controlled the economic system. Since 1993, the government has been under a federal system, with a new constitution guaranteeing the rights of citizens. The Communist Party is only one among 40. The government has executive power and is headed by a president, who is elected for a four-year term. Legislative powers belong to the Duma, the lower house of the Federal Assembly. Members of the Duma are elected. The upper house is the Council of the Federation. There is a court system that has power of judicial review.

3 The government of Mexico is similar to that of the United States in that it is a democracy with a three-branch federal system and a federal district. The president selects top officials, is commander in chief, and recommends legislation. The legislature has two houses. It is different in that the president can serve only one six-year term. Members of the legislature may not run for consecutive terms. The General Congress meets for about a month every year and is considered weak, without much influence on national policy.

418 Chapter 23

ideas to remember

In earlier chapters, many forms of government and terms were discussed.

- A constitutional monarchy is a government that is headed by a king or queen. The monarch's powers are limited by a constitution.
- A bicameral legislature has two houses.
- A standing committee is a permanent committee.
- In an autocracy, a single person holds all the power.
- A federal system divides government powers between the national government and state or provincial governments.
- A dictatorship is a government in which the ruler has absolute power.

choose the prime minister and the cabinet. The prime minister is the leader of the executive branch of government. The cabinet consists of the officials who head the departments of the executive branch. They are all members of Parliament.

Parliament is bicameral. It has an upper house, called the House of Lords, and a lower house, called the House of Commons. The House of Lords is made up of 733 members of the nobility and bishops of the Church of England. The Commons has 646 members who are elected by voters. Each member represents one district.

The House of Lords has limited power over lawmaking. It can delay bills sent to it by the Commons, but it cannot reject bills. The Commons can override a veto by the House of Lords by passing a bill for a second time. The bill then becomes law. The House of Lords may amend bills. However, the Commons may reject the changes by the House of Lords. All money bills must begin in the Commons.

Most bills are introduced by the prime minister or members of the cabinet. Bills are sent to one of ten standing committees. Unlike standing committees in the U.S. Congress, these standing committees do not have particular areas of responsibility. For example, there is no energy committee or homeland security committee. Any committee can review any bill. Committees review bills, hold hearings, and revise bills as needed. The committees then send the bills back to the House of Commons for a vote. Unlike the U.S. Congress, all bills must be reported back to the full house for a vote. They cannot be killed or pigeonholed in committee. The House of Lords has no standing committees.

Picturing Government

In the photograph on page 418, Britain's Queen Elizabeth II reads a message to Parliament. The queen is head of state and meets weekly with the prime minister. Although often referred to as a "figurehead," the queen receives daily summaries of Parliament's proceedings, as well as all cabinet papers and records of meetings of the cabinet. She is also head of the military forces of Britain. In addition, the queen is president or patron of more than 700 organizations and receives about 48,000 visitors at various functions each year.

Ideas to Remember Extension

Review the ideas listed, further explaining difficult vocabulary words. Have students create graphic organizers in their notebooks to help them visualize the six forms of government previously discussed.

Extension

Have students investigate the effect of including bishops of the Church of England as members of the House of Lords. Ask them to note differences created by the lack of separation of church and state between legislative functions in the United States and in Britain. Have them present their findings to the class by using the Student Presentation Builder on the student CD.

Words to Know

Introduce each of the following vocabulary terms to students.

A *parliamentary government* is one in which an elected assembly has both executive and legislative powers. Great Britain has a *parliamentary government*.

A *command economy* is one in which the government controls the economic system and owns all means of production. For most of the twentieth century, the Soviet Union had a *command economy*.

The *Duma* is the lower house of the Federal Assembly in Russia. The *Duma* must approve the prime minister.

Picturing Government

In the photograph on page 417, President George W. Bush meets with Japanese prime minister Yoshiro Mori in 2001 at the White House. A member of Japan's House of Representatives since 1969, Mori was elected by that body in 2000 to be prime minister. He has focused on what he terms the "Rebirth of Japan," seeking rebirth in five areas: education, economy, social security, government, and foreign policy.

Picturing Government

The photograph on page 420 shows Tony Blair, prime minister of Britain, addressing Parliament about Iraq in 2002, building a case for removing Saddam Hussein from power. A lawyer who was elected to the House of Commons in 1983 at age thirty, Blair became leader of the Labour party in 1994, moving that body to a centrist position. Blair has suffered criticism for supporting the United States efforts in Iraq. Nevertheless, he has become the longest-serving Labour prime minister. Students may be interested to know that in college, Blair sang and played bass guitar in a rock band called Ugly Rumours.

Stop and Think

Students' tables and summary statements will vary but should reflect information comparing and contrasting the British and the U.S. governments.

British prime minister Tony Blair answers questions during a session of Parliament in 2002.

There is no required term of office for members of Parliament. This also means that there is no required term of office for the prime minister. However, according to British law, an election must be held at least once every five years. The prime minister generally calls for an election when his or her party seems most likely to win a majority of seats in Parliament.

However, if the prime minister loses the confidence of the Commons, he or she calls for a general election. "Losing the confidence of the Commons" means losing its support for the government's policies. This happens if the Commons votes down some important bill favored by the prime minister.

Great Britain's court system has several levels. County courts hear civil cases. Minor criminal cases are heard in magistrates' courts. Serious criminal cases are heard in Crown Court. There are also appellate courts. The highest appellate court is made up of Law Lords. British courts do not have the power of judicial review.

stop and think

Create a table to compare and contrast the British government with that of the United States. Work with a partner. List the branches of government down the left side of your table. Label the columns "Branches of Government," "British Government," and "U.S. Government." Use Chapters 5 through 12 if you need to review facts on the U.S. government. When you have finished your table, write at least five sentences to compare or contrast the two governments. Share and discuss your statements with another student.

Russia

From 1917 until 1990, the Soviet Union had an authoritarian government. Russia was the largest of the 15 republics that made up the Union of Soviet Socialist Republics, commonly known as the Soviet Union. The officials who headed the government had absolute control over the people. Free elections did not exist. Whoever ran the Communist Party ran the government. The constitution protected the system of government. It did not guarantee the rights of the people.

The government also controlled the economic system. All means of production—land, buildings, factories, and machinery—belonged to the government. This is known as a **command economy**.

Extension

In 2005, Blair was elected to a third term as prime minister. Since World War II ended, the only other person to have done so is Margaret Thatcher. Although Blair is the only leader of the Labour Party to win three elections straight, his margin of victory tumbled significantly. Invite interested students to find out about Blair's and Britain's foreign policy.

In 1985, Mikhail Gorbachev came to power as head of the Communist Party. He began a program of reform that became known as *glasnost*, or openness. He eased some of the limitations on political and economic life. The economic restructuring was known as *perestroika*. He also allowed some freedom of expression and political opposition. By the end of 1991, the Soviet Union collapsed and many of the republics declared their independence.

Mikhail Gorbachev

In 1993, the Russians wrote a new constitution. It set up a federal system with a democratic form of government. The constitution also lists and guarantees a number of rights for the people. Among these are freedom of speech, press, and movement. The Communist Party is now one of 40 political parties in Russia.

The government is divided into executive and legislative branches. Each has its own powers. The executive branch is headed by a president. He or she is elected by the voters for a four-year term. The Russian president also names the prime minister. This official is similar to the U.S. vice president. The Duma must approve the prime minister.

The **Duma** is the lower house of the Federal Assembly. The Duma has 450 members who are elected from districts. The upper house is the Federation Council and has 178 members. Each of Russia's 89 regions elects two members to the Council. Members of both houses serve four-year terms.

The Duma and the Council make laws for the nation. However, the Duma may override Council vetoes. A vote of both houses can also override a presidential veto.

Russia also has a court system of several levels of courts. At the top is the Constitutional Court. It has 19 members who are elected by voters for 12-year terms. This court has the power of judicial review.

Mexico

Mexico's constitution was written in 1917. The Mexican constitution set up the organization and form of the government. It also lists many rights and guarantees for the people, especially the poor.

Picturing Government

The photograph on page 421 shows Mikhail Gorbachev, then head of the Soviet Union, in a 1991 interview outside the Kremlin. For his efforts in reforming the Soviet Union and its satellite nations, Gorbachev received the Nobel Peace Prize in 1990. He worked his way through the Communist Party ranks to become General Secretary, then brought gradual change to the Soviet Union. He left office in 1991, but continues to advocate nonviolent conflict resolution and private ownership. He heads the International Foundation for Socio-Economic and Political Studies, also called the Gorbachev Foundation.

Extension

Vladimir Putin, who became the president of Russia in 2000, announced plans in 2004 to build a new form of nuclear defense. He has often promised to restore Russia's military might. Have interested students find out about Russia's nuclear capabilities and contrast them with those of the United States.

Picturing Government

Vicente Fox, president of Mexico in 2005, is pictured in the photograph on page 422, campaigning for that office in 2000. Fox's election ended the 71-year reign of the Institutional Revolutionary Party. Raised on a ranch in Mexico, he graduated from Harvard University Business School and rose to become the chief executive of Coca-Cola in Mexico. He ran for president on a campaign that stressed the need to improve the economy and end government corruption.

Mexico is a democracy with a federal system. It is made up of 31 states and a federal district. The federal district is Mexico's capital, Mexico City. Each state has a governor, a constitution, a legislature of a single house, and a system of courts. Each state may pass laws for people living within its borders. Each state may also levy and collect taxes. States also receive funding from the federal government.

The federal government has three branches. The executive branch is headed by a president elected for one six-year term. He or she chooses the cabinet members, known as the Council of Ministers. The president is commander in chief and appoints the heads of the armed forces. It is also the responsibility of the president to recommend legislation to the legislature.

Vincente Fox, National Action Party candidate, during the 2000 Mexican presidential election

The legislature is called the Congress of the Union. The upper house is the Chamber of the Senate and the lower house is the Chamber of Representatives. The Senate has 128 members, two from each state and two from the federal district. Senators are elected for six-year terms. The Chamber of Representatives is made up of 500 members who serve for three-year terms. Voters in districts elect 300 deputies. The other 200 are chosen from the many political parties. The number of seats that each party receives is based on the percentage of votes the party received in the national election. Senators and deputies may not run for two terms in a row.

The Congress meets for only four months each year. As a result, the Congress is considered weak. It does not have much influence on national policies.

Mexico has both state and federal court systems. State courts hear cases that deal with state criminal and civil laws. Each state has levels of courts: trial, appeals, and a state supreme court. The federal system has district and circuit courts and a Supreme Court.

Putting It All Together

Create a three-way Venn diagram to show the differences and similarities among the governments of Great Britain, Russia, and Mexico. Work with a partner. When you have finished, write an essay of three paragraphs explaining how these governments are different.

Putting It All Together

Students' diagrams and essays will vary but should reflect lesson content. Diagrams should show comparisons and contrasts among the governments of Great Britain, Russia, and Mexico. Essays should focus only on contrasts.

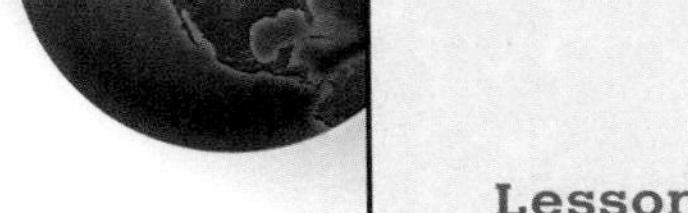

LESSON 2

Authoritarian Governments

Thinking on Your Own

Stalin, Mussolini, and Hitler were twentieth-century dictators. They ruled with absolute power in Russia, Italy, and Germany. What do you know about their leadership methods? In your notebook, write at least two facts about how each of these dictators ruled.

focus your reading

Describe how the Communist Party controls the government of China.

Explain how a junta controls a government.

How do nations shift from authoritarian to democratic?

words to know

theocratic republic

junta

martial law

ethnic groups

The Soviet Union collapsed in 1991. However, it was not the last authoritarian government. A number of these governments still exist today. Only a few are Communist. Today, most authoritarian governments are led by military officers or are civilian governments supported by the military. Many authoritarian governments include the word *republic* in their name. A republic is a representative democracy. Calling itself a republic helps to disguise the authoritarian nature of the government.

There are also a few **monarchies**. Saudi Arabia and Jordan are both headed by monarchs. Jordan, like Great Britain, is a constitutional monarchy. However, in Saudi Arabia, the king is the sole ruler. There is no constitution and the rights of citizens are limited. This is especially true for women.

Iran is a **theocratic republic**. It has a constitution based on a strict interpretation of Islam. Citizens vote for candidates for public office. However, the rights of citizens, especially women, are limited.

Lesson Summary

Most contemporary authoritarian governments are headed or supported by the military rather than being headed by a Communist government, as had been the case in the past. Other forms of authoritarian governments include monarchies and theocratic republics. Juntas have taken control of several Latin American countries. Juntas have also come to power in several Asian nations. Dictatorships are generally run by a single person or a small group. Dictators rule Syria and North Korea.

Lesson Objective

Students will learn about the various forms and examples of authoritarian governments.

Focus Your Reading Answers

1 The Communist Party controls China's government through a constitution that does not grant rights to citizens. The Party's highest officials select the president, whom the National People's Congress merely approves.

2 A junta controls a government by seizing control from elected civilian officials. Its goal is to help wealthy citizens and military officers retain their wealth and power. The junta establishes martial law and suspends the constitution and elections.

3 Nations shift from authoritarian to democratic because they do not benefit citizens. However, the shift is not easy, because groups in power want to keep their power.

Words to Know

Discuss each of the vocabulary terms with students.

A *theocratic republic* is a form of government based on a religious tradition. Iran's constitution, based on Islam, is an example of a *theocratic republic*.

A dictatorship of military officers is called a *junta*. The goal of a *junta* is to end reforms made by civilian governments.

Martial law is another term for military law. *Juntas* often rule by *martial law* rather than by the laws set up in the constitution.

Tribal groups are also known as *ethnic groups*. Fighting in African nations is often between *ethnic groups*.

Picturing Government

The photograph on page 424 shows a busy street in Beijing, China's capital. The city, which has more than 12 million inhabitants, was expanded in 1953 and 1958. It is a special administrative unit, covering some 3,386 square miles. Beijing was first made the capital in the tenth century, and has held that place at various times since. The city contains the so-called Forbidden City, the site of the imperial palace.

People's Republic of China

The largest Communist nation today is the People's Republic of China (PRC). Other Communist governments include Vietnam, Laos, and Cuba.

Communists came to power in China in 1949 under the leadership of Mao Zedong. They had been fighting the non-Communist government since the 1920s. When the Communists took control, they set up a command economy. Mao died in 1976. Since then, Chinese leaders have eased economic controls. Most Chinese still live in poverty. Since the 1980s, the Chinese government has encouraged small businesses and investment by foreign companies. However, the Communists have not eased political controls.

The PRC's constitution does not guarantee rights. Unlike the U.S. Constitution, the PRC's constitution is not the basis of China's law. The Chinese constitution describes how the government is to be set up. It also states the policies the nation is to follow. The current constitution was written in 1982. It sets goals to modernize the nation and to become a world industrial power by the twenty-first century.

The Wangfujing shopping district in Beijing, China

The Chinese constitution describes the duties of the National People's Congress and the State Council. The National People's Congress has about 3,000 deputies. The members are elected by local people's congresses, or assemblies, for five-year terms. The National People's Congress has little power. Its role is to approve policies developed by the Communist Party. The Communist Party is the real power in the PRC. For example, the constitution states that the National People's Congress elects the president of the PRC. In reality, the Communist Party's highest officials, called the politburo, determine who will be president. The National People's Congress just approves this person.

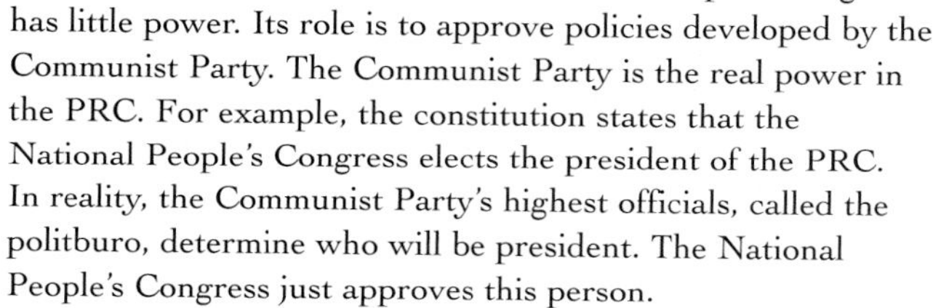

The president nominates the premier, and the National People's Congress approves this person. The premier heads the State Council, which is similar to the cabinet or Council of Ministers in other nations. The State Council manages the bureaucracy in the executive branch of the government.

Extensions

1 Invite interested students to find out about the rights of women in one of the countries mentioned in the lesson. Have them compare those rights with those of women in democratic societies. A number of memoirs of Middle Eastern women have been published recently. Suggest that students read and report on one of these.

2 Challenge interested students to find out more about the governments of China and Taiwan, using library resources or the Internet. Ask them to present the information to the class as a special news report.

The National People's Congress meets once a year for two weeks. The Standing Committee of the Congress deals with legislative business the rest of the year. The Standing Committee as of 2003 had 175 members.

The government of the PRC is unitary. All power flows from the national government to local governments. Local governments could not exist if the national government did not allow them to exist. The PRC has 22 provinces, which are similar to states. There are also five independent regions that are under the control of the Chinese government.

stop and think

Imagine that the Chinese people decided to have a truly republican form of government. What changes would they have to make in their government to become a republic? Discuss the question with a partner. Make a list in your notebook of the changes that would be required.

People protested in favor of free speech and freedom of the press in Tiananmen Square in Beijing, China, in 1989.

The Chinese court system has local courts called the people's courts. They hear both civil and criminal cases. The Supreme People's Court oversees the local courts.

Dictatorships

A dictatorship may be run by a single person or by a small group. Usually, the group consists of military officers. In this case, the dictatorship is called a **junta**.

Over time, various governments in Latin America have been taken over by juntas. For example, in the twentieth century, juntas ruled in Chile, Guatemala, El Salvador, Paraguay, and Peru. Military officers have seized control of governments from elected civilian officials. Usually, the junta is supported by wealthy landowners. The civilian governments are overthrown because they attempt to help the poor. The goal of the juntas is to end reforms by the civilian governments. The military officers and wealthy citizens want to ensure that they will not lose their power and wealth.

Cuban president Fidel Castro

Picturing Government

The photograph at the center right on page 425 shows a lone demonstrator standing before approaching tanks in Tiananmen Square, the largest public square in the world. On June 4, 1989, tanks moved into the square, where demonstrators had been calling for democratic reforms for seven weeks. More than 200 protestors were killed. The protests were held during a visit by Soviet leader Mikhail Gorbachev.

Stop and Think

Lists will vary but may suggest the need for free elections and multiple political parties.

Extension

Have students use library resources or the Internet to investigate the U.S. economic embargo against Cuba. If the embargo is still in effect, have students find out the arguments for and against lifting the embargo.

Picturing Government

Fidel Castro, the dictator of Cuba, is shown in the photograph at the bottom right on page 425. Castro took power in 1959 after prolonged guerrilla warfare; his force of about 800 guerrillas defeated the Cuban army of 30,000. The following year, after Castro had seized U.S. businesses and agricultural estates, the United States broke economic ties with Cuba. Diplomatic ties ended in 1961. The Soviet Union became the chief trade partner and supporter of Cuba, which suffered at the 1991 collapse of the Soviet Union. Some loosening of restrictions has occurred in Cuba; for example, in 1998, Pope John Paul II was permitted to visit the island, which is officially atheistic.

Picturing Government

In the photograph at the top left on page 426, 1991 Nobel Peace Prize winner Aung San Suu Kyi is shown. For protesting the military government of Myanmar, her homeland, Aung San Suu Kyi was placed under house arrest. Offered her freedom if she agreed to leave the country, she refused. Although freed in 1995, she was again placed under house arrest from 2000 to 2002, and again in 2003.

Picturing Government

The photograph at the bottom left on page 426 shows workers in a North Korean factory. A mountainous nation, less than 20 percent of the land in North Korea is arable. Productivity is also hindered because the government collectivized agriculture in the 1950s, and people have little incentive to work hard. North Korea requires on average one million metric tons of food aid annually. Experts estimate that the average person in the cities gets about half of the recommended required daily minimum nutrients. Both urban and country dwellers have become skilled in gathering wild edible plants.

Aung San Suu Kyi won the Nobel Peace Prize in 1991 for resisting the Myanmar junta.

Once in control of the government, the junta usually suspends the constitution. It rules by **martial law**, or military law, not by the guarantees of the constitution. Elections are either eliminated or staged. Only candidates backed by the junta can run for office, or the junta makes sure that opposition candidates lose. Juntas often use kidnappings, torture, and murder to silence opponents. The national legislature may be disbanded. If it is allowed to continue, it can pass only laws the junta approved.

Juntas also occur in other parts of the world. For example, a military junta has been in power in Myanmar since 1962. The last election for a national legislature was held in 1990. However, the junta has never allowed the legislature to meet.

In Syria, a single ruler, Hafez al-Assad, came to power in 1971. The military had seized power in 1963. All political parties except al-Assad's party, the Socialist Ba'ath Party, were banned. Al-Assad ruled with the support of the military until his death in 2000. The military now supports his son Bashar as president.

The North Korean government controls all aspects of business, including this biscuit factory in Hyesan, Korea.

North Korea is also ruled by the son of a previous dictator. In 1953, Kim Il Sung became the leader of North Korea. The Chinese and Soviet Communist governments supported him with foreign aid and weapons. Kim Il Sung introduced a command economy into North Korea and banned all opposition. After his death, his son Kim Jong Il became president. A national legislature, called the Supreme People's Assembly, passes legislation and oversees the judiciary. However, Kim Jong Il really holds all the power himself.

Extension

Have students use library resources or the Internet to find out about the threats of nuclear war from nations that are authoritarian and what free governments are doing to prevent such an attack from occurring. Host a panel discussion on ways to control these dictatorships and juntas.

426 Chapter 23

Governments in Transition

Communist nations collapse because they do not benefit ordinary citizens. Dictatorships work for the group in power, but not for the majority of people. Since the end of the twentieth century, more and more people have fought for democratic governments. The nations of Eastern Europe were quick to end their Communist governments once the Soviet Union collapsed. In some cases, the nations of Eastern Europe forced out their Communist governments even before the Soviet Union collapsed. This occurred in Poland and in the former nation of Czechoslovakia.

Iraqis wait in line to vote during the 2005 elections.

Changing to a democracy is not easy for a nation. Groups in power fight to keep their power. This can be seen in the difficulties in setting up democratic governments in Nigeria, Sudan, and Somalia. Often, in African nations, the fight is not between wealthy landowners and the poor. It is between **ethnic groups**, or tribal groups. One group does not want to share power with another. This was also true in the former nation of Yugoslavia and in the new nation of Bosnia and Herzegovina in eastern Europe. Ethnic and religious groups in these nations fought one another for control.

Ethnic conflict has also caused problems in Iraq since the removal of Saddam Hussein. Backed by the Iraqi military, he seized power in 1979. In 2003, a force of U.S. and British soldiers aided by other nations invaded Iraq. Hussein fled and was later captured. The coalition forces assisted the Iraqis in writing a constitution and setting up a democratic government. However, bitter rivalry still exists between the two major groups in Iraq, the Shiites and the Sunnis. The opposing groups turned the country into a battleground of insurgents.

Putting It All Together

This lesson has presented information about several authoritarian governments. While these governments have much in common, they also are different. Make a two-column list in your notebook. In one column, list what these governments have in common. In the second column, list how each authoritarian government is different from the others.

Picturing Government

The photograph on page 427 shows people lined up to vote in Iraq in 2005. More than 5,000 polling centers opened for the first free election in 50 years. Terrorist groups' threats and acts of violence did not hinder Iraqis, who voted in higher numbers than expected. U.S. forces in Iraq helped ensure safety.

Putting It All Together

Students' charts will vary but should reflect lesson content.

Lesson Summary

One of the major global issues is terrorism, which tries to force change through acts of violence. Four types of terrorist groups are Islamic militants, groups that want to create a Palestinian state, those wanting to create their own nations, and those trying to overthrow governments. The United Nations members have pledged to fight terrorism. Global security is also threatened by regional and civil wars. These wars can draw other nations that are allies into the conflict. The UN and NATO both have peacekeeping forces in places of great conflict. A third danger to global security is nuclear proliferation. Groups work to find peaceful uses for nuclear energy.

Lesson Objective

Students will learn about contemporary concerns related to global security.

Focus Your Reading Answers

1 To end terrorism, nations are sharing information. Members of the United Nations who signed Resolution 137 are cooperating in counterterrorism efforts.

2 Regional wars are most often fought because of border disputes.

3 To end the spread of nuclear weapons, 189 nations have signed a Nuclear Nonproliferation Treaty (NPT). The United Nations tries to enforce the NPT through the International Atomic Energy Agency. South Africa has destroyed its nuclear weapons.

LESSON 3

Issues of Global Security

Thinking on Your Own

What does the phrase "global security" mean to you? Brainstorm what the phrase means with a partner. In your notebook, write whatever ideas come to mind. After you study this lesson, review your list. Add topics to your list. Cross out any topics that apply only to one country.

focus your reading

Describe what is being done to end terrorism.

Why are regional wars fought?

What is being done to end the spread of nuclear weapons?

words to know

terrorism

weapons of mass destruction

civil war

nuclear proliferation

Today, trade, travel, and communications connect the nations of the world more than ever before. Nations are no longer isolated from one another. Together, the global community faces many issues. Some issues, like global warming, threaten the environment. Others, like the movement of factory jobs to poorer nations, are economic issues. Terrorism, regional wars, civil wars, and nuclear weapons are issues of global security. They threaten the safety of all nations.

The world's nations have taken steps to protect their security. In 1945, they founded the United Nations (UN). The goal of the UN is to work for world peace. The United States was one of the original founders. The United States also belongs to regional security associations such as the North Atlantic Treaty Organization (NATO). The goal is to protect the security of member nations through cooperation.

Terrorism

Terrorism is a political strategy that uses violence against people or property to achieve a goal. Often the goal is to force a change in government or society.

428 Chapter 23

Words to Know

Discuss each of the vocabulary terms with students.

Terrorism is a political strategy that uses violence against property or people to force a change in government or society. The attacks on the World Trade Center and Pentagon in 2001 are one example of an act of *terrorism*.

Chemical, biological, and nuclear weapons that can kill large numbers of people are *weapons of mass destruction*. The United States invaded Iraq in 2003 because of the belief that the nation had *weapons of mass destruction*.

A *civil war* takes place when groups within a nation battle for power. The Korean War is an example of a *civil war*.

The spread of nuclear weapons to those nations that do not have nuclear capabilities is called *nuclear proliferation*. Several groups are working to prevent *nuclear proliferation*.

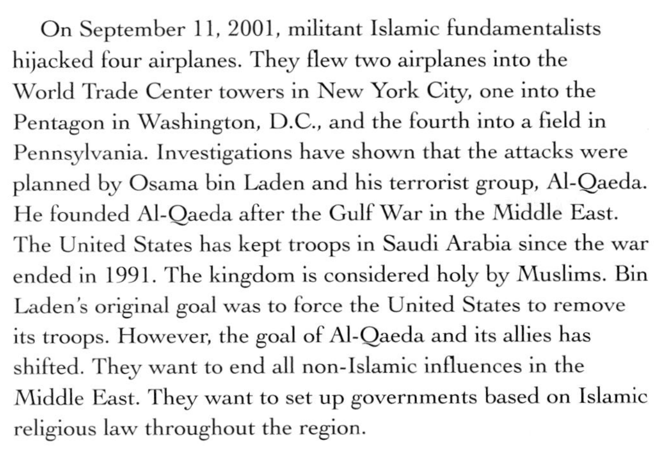

On September 11, 2001, militant Islamic fundamentalists hijacked four airplanes. They flew two airplanes into the World Trade Center towers in New York City, one into the Pentagon in Washington, D.C., and the fourth into a field in Pennsylvania. Investigations have shown that the attacks were planned by Osama bin Laden and his terrorist group, Al-Qaeda. He founded Al-Qaeda after the Gulf War in the Middle East. The United States has kept troops in Saudi Arabia since the war ended in 1991. The kingdom is considered holy by Muslims. Bin Laden's original goal was to force the United States to remove its troops. However, the goal of Al-Qaeda and its allies has shifted. They want to end all non-Islamic influences in the Middle East. They want to set up governments based on Islamic religious law throughout the region.

In 2003, the United States and its allies invaded Iraq. One goal was to remove the dictator Saddam Hussein. The other was to end his program to build **weapons of mass destruction**. These are chemical, biological, and nuclear weapons that can kill large numbers of people. After the invasion, the United States discovered that Iraq had already destroyed its weapons of mass destruction. Many Americans concluded that Iraq had not been a serious threat to our national security.

Police investigate a bombing at a Bali nightclub in 2002.

Once Hussein was overthrown, the United States and its allies also wanted to help the Iraqis set up a democratic government. The invasion and occupation of Iraq led to attacks by insurgents against the American forces and their allies. The insurgency was led by supporters of Saddam Hussein and Islamic fundamentalist fighters. Some of the fighters came from other Islamic nations in the Middle East. The insurgents used roadside bombs and suicide bombers to kill allied troops and Iraqis who worked with them. Many Iraqi citizens disliked their violent methods, but shared the insurgents' goal of getting foreign troops out of Iraq.

There are four types of terrorist organizations. One is made up of Islamic militants who want to end U.S. and European influences in the Middle East. They fought the allies in Iraq

Picturing Government

The photograph on page 429 shows Australian police officers investigating a nightclub in Bali that was bombed in 2002. Almost three years after that attack, which killed 202 people, a second bombing killed nearly 30 people. Jemaah Islamiyah, an extremist group linked to Al-Qaeda, was believed to be responsible for both attacks. The bombings were seen as attempts to undermine religious freedom in Indonesia, which has the largest Muslim population in the world. Other terrorist incidents in Indonesia, both blamed on Jemaah Islamiyah, occurred in Jakarta in 2003 and 2004.

Extensions

1 Divide the class into small groups. Assign each group one area of the globe and have them use library resources or the Internet to find out what regional security alliances exist in that part of the world. Ask them to find out what the group is doing to maintain the security of member nations. Allow time for students to share their findings with the class.

2 Invite interested students to use library resources or the Internet to find out more about the conflict in Iraq. Suggest they make a timeline for the classroom, highlighting key events over at least a decade.

Picturing Government

The photograph on page 430 shows the World Trade Center (WTC) aflame after terrorists flew airplanes into its two towers on September 11, 2001. The WTC included seven buildings on 16 acres. Officially opened in 1973, it was operated by the Port Authority of New York and New Jersey. Both buildings had 110 floors and were, for a brief time, the tallest and largest buildings in the world.

Stop and Think

Students' T-charts will vary but should reflect lesson content.

United Airlines Flight 175 was one of four airplanes used by terrorists during the attacks of September 11, 2001.

and took their campaign of terror to Europe. They bombed trains in Madrid and London and planned similar acts in other nations including the United States. However, counterterrorism agencies in European nations and the United States shared information. This cooperation halted a number of plots.

Another is made up of terrorists such as HAMAS. Their goal is to create a nation for Palestinians. They are Arabs who left their lands when Israel was created in 1948. Israel was set up as a homeland for Jews. Islamic militants want to destroy Israel and take back the land. However, the conflict eased somewhat in late 2005. Israel gave up the West Bank region to Palestinians as part of their future nation.

Other terrorist groups want to create their own nations. For example, Chechnya is a region in Russia. In 1991, it declared itself independent. The Russian government did not recognize its independence. Since then, Chechen rebels and Islamic fundamentalists have attacked several sites in Russian cities, including a theater in Moscow and a school in Beslan. The goal of the rebels is to set up their own government. They want it based on Islamic law.

Terrorists also operate in Latin America. For example, the *Sendero Luminoso*—the Shining Path—fought for many years to overthrow the government of Peru. However, in 1992, the democratically elected president took action against the rebels. He also began a series of reforms to aid the poor. Conflict continued throughout the 1990s. In 2003, the last Shining Path leader was caught.

The United Nations has 19 global and regional treaties relating to terrorism. Many of these date to the 1970s. After the terrorist attacks of September 11, 2001, the UN adopted Resolution 137. All nations that signed the resolution agree to fight terrorism. The UN also set up a Counter-Terrorism Committee. The committee's job is to make sure that UN member nations cooperate in the fight against terrorism.

stop and think

Create a T-chart with the label "Types of Terrorist Groups" in the left column. Label the right column "Examples." Fill in both columns. Share your T-chart with a partner. Discuss what a nation might do to end terrorism within its borders.

Extension

Invite interested students to use library resources or the Internet to find out about the World Trade Center bombings in 1993. How does that event compare to later acts of terrorism in both the United States and in other nations?

Regional Wars and Civil Wars

Regional wars are wars that break out in a particular part of the world. The Arab-Israeli wars of 1948–1949, 1956, 1957, and 1973 are examples of regional wars. So is the Indian-Pakistani war of 1971 over the region of Kashmir. Both nations claim the area. The claims are still not settled. Regional wars often break out over border disputes.

Sudanese refugees wait at a feeding center in Bahai, Chad.

Regional wars threaten global security. Other nations besides the original ones can be drawn into the fighting. Each side has allies that may come to the aid of the nations that are at war. For example, in 1990, Iraq invaded Kuwait. Saddam Hussein wanted Kuwait's rich oil fields. The United States is an ally of Kuwait. It demanded that Iraq withdraw. When it did not, President George H. W. Bush established a coalition, or group, of 13 nations to fight Iraq. Iraq began sending missiles against Israel. However, no Arab allies joined Iraq. Within six weeks, the coalition had invaded and defeated Iraq.

Civil wars can also draw other nations into the fighting. A **civil war** is a war in which groups within a nation battle for power. The Korean War, for example, began when North Korea invaded South Korea in 1950. The United States came to the aid of South Korea. The Chinese Communists supported North Korea. Both China and the United States sent troops, weapons, and other supplies. The war dragged on for three years and ended without a victory for either side. A peace treaty still has not been signed. In the meantime, the United States keeps troops in South Korea as part of the UN's peacekeeping forces.

UN peacekeepers patrol in Bosnia in 1995.

Other regional security associations also send peacekeepers when civil war breaks out. For example, after the collapse of communism in eastern Europe, some nations split apart. Serbia and Montenegro declared independence from Yugoslavia. The Serbian province of Kosovo, however, wanted to unite with Albania. A civil war broke out. NATO sent troops into Kosovo to put down the rebellion. The peacekeepers remain in Kosovo.

Picturing Government

In the photograph at the top right on page 431, women and children wait at a feeding center at a camp for Sudanese refugees in Chad. Nearly two million people have fled their homes in Darfur, Sudan, because of a war that began in 2003. Problems in the camps include water and food shortages as well as ethnic conflicts. The situation has been worsened by one of the most severe droughts in 50 years.

Picturing Government

The 1995 photograph at the bottom right on page 431 shows Dutch United Nations peacekeepers in Bosnia. Although the war officially ended in 1995, tensions in the region were still high a decade later. The United Nations Security Council called for an additional one-year renewal of the European peacekeeping force in 2005. Peacekeeping forces from NATO were replaced by almost 7,000 troops from the European Union in late 2004.

Extension

Invite interested students to select one of the conflicts mentioned in the section "Regional Wars and Civil Wars." Ask them to use library resources or the Internet to find out what has happened in that nation and to report their findings to the class.

Picturing Government

The photograph on page 432 is of the first testing of an atomic bomb, July 16, 1945, in Alamogordo, New Mexico. The code name for the test was Trinity, thought to be a reference to the Hindu trinity of Brahma, Vishnu, and Shiva—the Creator, Preserver, and Destroyer. Robert Oppenheimer, one of the project leaders, was interested in Sanskrit literature, which he'd taught himself to read in the original language. After the successful test, Oppenheimer reportedly paraphrased a quote from the opening of the Hindu book the *Bhagavad-Gita*:

If the radiance of a thousand suns

Were to burst into the sky,

That would be like the splendor of the Mighty One. . . .

I am become Death,

The shatterer of worlds.

A mushroom cloud rises above an atomic bomb test near Alamogordo, New Mexico, in 1945.

Nuclear Proliferation

Nuclear proliferation is the spread of nuclear weapons to nations that do not have nuclear capabilities. It is one of the greatest dangers to global security. The United States was the first nation to develop a nuclear bomb. Today, Russia, China, France, and Great Britain are also known to have nuclear weapons. India, Pakistan, and Israel are suspected of having them. Experts also suspect that Iran and North Korea either have nuclear weapons or are capable of building them. South Africa destroyed its nuclear weapons in 1991.

In 1970, the Nuclear Nonproliferation Treaty (NPT) went into effect. Since then, 189 nations have joined the treaty. India, Pakistan, and Israel have not. North Korea withdrew in 2003. The other nations with nuclear weapons (NWS) have all agreed to the treaty. According to the NPT, NWS will not help nations without nuclear weapons (NNWS) to develop them. NWS also will not sell nuclear weapons to NNWS. NWS agree to their own complete disarmament, or getting rid of nuclear weapons. For their part, NNWS have agreed not to develop or buy nuclear weapons.

The International Atomic Energy Agency (IAEA) was created by the United Nations to make sure that nations obey the NPT. The IAEA helps NNWS carry out programs that use

Extension

Private groups and public charities, as well as national governments, are working to prevent the spread of nuclear weapons. The Nuclear Threat Initiative, begun in 2001 with seed money from media mogul Ted Turner, sponsors programs to assist governments in making peaceful decisions.

nuclear materials for peaceful uses. For example, nuclear material is used to create energy in nuclear power plants. The IAEA also polices member nations to make sure that they do not use their nuclear materials to build weapons.

Nations that want to hide their nuclear programs can refuse to allow IAEA inspections. In the early 2000s, Iran's leaders refused to allow IAEA inspectors to work in Iran. However, the IAEA and the NPT have succeeded in keeping nuclear weapons out of the hands of many nations. Experts believe that without their efforts, 28 nations would have nuclear weapons today.

Putting It All Together

What do you think is the greatest threat to global security? Discuss the question with a partner. Make a table with three columns. Label each column with one of the threats discussed in this lesson. List reasons that explain why each topic is a serious threat to the world. Decide which threat you think is most serious. Write a paragraph to explain your reasoning.

People in the News

Mohamed ElBaradei and the IAEA

Mohamed ElBaradei (1942–) is the head of the International Atomic Energy Agency (IAEA). The IAEA is the UN agency that polices the use of nuclear materials around the world. Dr. ElBaradei is an Egyptian lawyer and diplomat. He was named head of the IAEA in 1997. The IAEA was involved in the search for weapons of mass destruction in Iraq before the U.S.-led invasion in 2003. The IAEA is also part of the discussion about potential nuclear weapons in Iran and North Korea.

In 2005, Dr. ElBaradei and the IAEA were awarded the Nobel Prize for Peace. This important award recognized the work of the IAEA to "prevent nuclear energy from being used for military purposes." The award also praised the IAEA for its efforts "to ensure that nuclear energy for peaceful purposes is used in the safest possible way."

Putting It All Together

Students' tables and paragraphs will vary but should address a serious global threat.

People in the News Extension

- Born in Egypt, 1942.
- Earned a Doctorate of International Law at New York University School of Law, 1974.
- Began diplomatic career in 1964, working on arms issues.
- In charge of International Law Program at the United Nations Institute for Training and Research, 1980.
- Reappointed as Director General of the IAEA for a third term, September 2005.

Extensions

1 The transformation of a region in the Ukraine with 700 nuclear missile warheads is one nuclear nonproliferation project. The Ukraine was the site of the world's third-largest nuclear arsenal. Over a three-year period, officials from the United States, Russia, and the Ukraine worked together to remove the warheads and dismantle the silos that housed them. The area became a field of sunflowers, a productive crop. Challenge students to find out more about efforts of cleaning up nuclear sites from the Cold War.

2 The major task of the IAEA is to protect both people and the environment from exposure to radiation. Thus, the agency has a two-pronged approach: safety and security. Invite students to use library resources or the Internet to find additional examples of the agency's work.

Participate in Government

Ask students to prepare a news brief on their agency, department, or branch of government. Tell them to include answers to the questions *Who, What, Where, Why, When,* and *How*. Have students deliver their reports in newscast fashion to the class, limiting their responses to two minutes or less.

Participate in Government

Use Government Resources

Do you

- want to see if the Secret Service has any job openings?
- need a federal income tax form?
- want to apply for a passport but do not know what documents you need?
- want information about Independence Hall for a report?

The United States government provides all kinds of information and resources—in print and online. In Chapter 19, you read about some of the booklets and reports that the Consumer Information Center publishes.

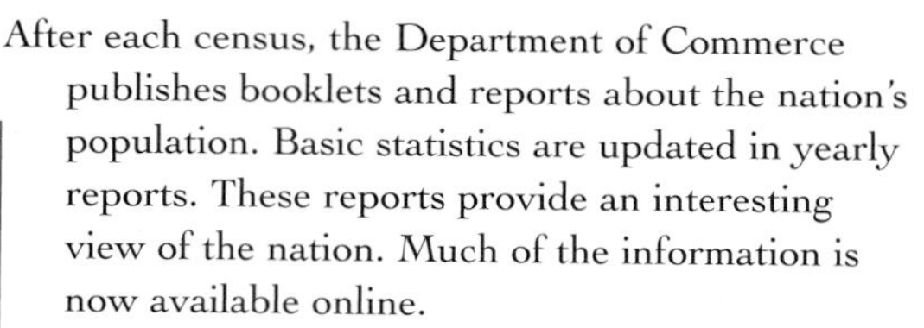

After each census, the Department of Commerce publishes booklets and reports about the nation's population. Basic statistics are updated in yearly reports. These reports provide an interesting view of the nation. Much of the information is now available online.

The National Park Service, the National Archives, the Presidential Libraries, the Library of Congress—all these agencies have sites that offer an abundance of information for students, teachers, and all Americans. Information can be downloaded for free or ordered online to be shipped for a small fee.

The White House, Congress, the Supreme Court, and all the departments of the executive branch have Web sites. These contain the history of each agency, biographies of officials, and the duties and responsibilities of each agency. These sites also post job openings. The Court's Web site contains its decisions.

To Find Out What Resources Are Available from the Federal Government:

- Using a search engine, find the Web site of an agency, department, or branch of government.
- Explore the site to see what is available.

Research Resources

Below is a list of reference books and Web sites that relate to the issues covered in this chapter. Students may wish to use these to further their research on ideas in the preceding lessons. Web site addresses may change over time. Use keyword searching on a major search engine to locate sites.

Reference Books:

Harvey W. Kushner. *Encyclopedia of Terrorism*. Sage Publications, 2003.

C. Neal Tate, ed. *Governments of the World: A Global Guide to Citizens' Rights and Responsibilities*. Macmillan Reference USA/Thomson Gale, 2005.

Web Sites:

The U.S. Department of State monitors and posts human rights practices annually on its Web site.

The Institute for Counter-terrorism, based in Israel, offers articles, case studies, and commentary on its Web site.

The Carnegie Endowment for International Peace site provides news, resources, and analysis.

Skill Builder

Synthesize Information

The author of this textbook consulted many sources in writing the book. He synthesized the information, which means he put together pieces of information into something new. To synthesize means to "bring together separate pieces or parts."

Whenever you buy a CD on the advice of several friends, you synthesize information. One person says you should buy it for this reason. Another friend says you should buy for that reason. You hear it played on the radio and decide you like it. The DJ offers another reason why it is a great CD to own.

Being able to synthesize information is a good skill for school, too. When you write a research report, you have to synthesize information from different sources.

To synthesize information, follow these steps:

1. Choose the sources you will use.
2. Find the main idea and supporting details for the information that you find.
3. Look for links between the information.
4. Put the information together based on those links.

Complete the following activities.

1. Chapter 3 and Lesson 1 of Chapter 21 discuss constitutional government. Chapter 3 talks about the U.S. Constitution, and Chapter 21 describes state constitutions. Work through Steps 2 and 3 to compare the U.S. Constitution to state constitutions. To help you, create a table comparing them. Use information from both chapters to fill in the table.

2. Use the table as the basis for a three- or four-paragraph essay about the similarities between the U.S. Constitution and state constitutions.

Skill Builder

1. Students' tables will vary but should demonstrate comparisons of national and state constitutions.

2. Essays will vary but should be no longer than four paragraphs comparing the U.S. Constitution and state constitutions.

Recommended Reading

Below is a list of books that relate to the issues covered in this chapter. The numbers in parentheses indicate the related Thematic Strands of the National Council for the Social Studies (NCSS).

Glenn Alan Cheney. *Nuclear Proliferation: The Problems and Possibilities.* Franklin Watts, 1999. (VI, X)

Mitch Frank. *Understanding September 11th: Answering Questions About the Attacks on America*. Viking Books, 2002. (VI, X)

Samuel M. Katz. *Jihad: Islamic Fundamentalist Terrorism*. Lerner Publishing Group, 2003. (VI, X)

Classroom Discussion

Discuss with students some of the broader topics covered in this chapter.

- How can free governments extend the benefits of democracy to other nations?
- Could a theocratic republic ever incorporate tolerance for other religions?
- In what ways can individual actions help achieve a more peaceful world?

Related Transparencies

T-15 Map of Developing and Developed Nations

T-17 Map of the World

T-18 Three-Column Chart

T-20 Concept Web

Key Blacklines

Primary Source—New Russian Economy

CD Extension

Encourage students to use the reading comprehension, vocabulary reinforcement, and other activities on the student CD.

Getting Focused

Allow time for students to share examples that support the fact that the United States has a market economy. Challenge students to give additional real-world examples of the other types of economic systems.

Picturing Government

The photograph on page 436 shows a shopping area in Tokyo, Japan. Tokyo, the modern capital of Japan, is the center of that nation's manufacturing, commerce, and culture.

Chapter 24 MODERN ECONOMIC SYSTEMS

Getting Focused

Skim this chapter to predict what you will be learning.

- **Read the lesson titles and subheadings.**
- **Look at the illustrations and read the captions.**
- **Examine the map and tables.**
- **Review the vocabulary words and terms.**

All nations have one of three types of economic systems. In a traditional economy, people barter, or exchange, goods and services. Someone with extra eggs may exchange them with someone with extra wheat. In a command economy, the government tells people what to make, how much to make, and for whom to make goods and services. In a market economy, buyers and sellers decide what to make, how much to make, and for whom.

Which kind of economy do you think the United States has? Give examples to support your answer.

Japan's economy is one of the world's strongest. Tokyo's Jizo Street is a popular destination for shoppers who take advantage of the country's strong economy.

Pre-Reading Discussion

1 Bring to class several examples of business periodicals, such as *BusinessWeek* and the *Wall Street Journal*. Have students work in small groups to browse these works. Challenge them to find one fact about a foreign nation's economy that they did not know. Use the facts as a basis for discussion on the state of current world economics.

2 Ask students to share what they already know about how families in other nations earn their incomes and what goods they might spend their earnings on. Suggest that students consider the examples of Mexico, China, and Russia.

LESSON 1

Capitalist and Mixed Economies

Thinking on Your Own

Many people choose to start their own businesses. Why do you think people want to work for themselves? Make a list in your notebook of reasons why you think people start their own businesses.

Capitalism is based on the market system. Buyers and sellers make their own choices about what to produce, how much to produce, and for whom. The capitalist system is also called the **free enterprise** and the **private enterprise** system.

focus your reading

What are the characteristics of capitalism?

Why is the United States called a mixed economy?

Make a list of some capitalist nations.

words to know

traditional economy
market economy
capitalism
free enterprise
private enterprise
factors of production
capital
entrepreneur
mixed economy

Capitalism

Capitalism has five basic characteristics. First is private ownership. Individuals and private companies own the factors of production. Farmers own their land. Businesses own their factories and machinery. Workers own their labor and sell it to whomever they wish. That is, no one tells workers in a capitalist system for whom to work.

The second characteristic is individual initiative. *Initiative* means the ability to get things done on one's own. Entrepreneurs have a great deal of individual initiative. They are willing to start businesses using just their ideas and whatever capital they can put together. In a capitalist system, everyone has the freedom to start a business. Bill Gates, who started Microsoft, is an example of a very successful entrepreneur.

Lesson Summary

The five characteristics of capitalism include private ownership, individual initiative, competition, profit, and freedom of choice. No pure capitalist systems exist in today's world. The United States and other nations, such as most of those in Europe, have mixed economies. The government regulates private enterprise and takes on responsibility for social policies affecting the economy. Most factors of production are privately owned; however, the government provides funding for some public works.

Lesson Objective

Students will learn about the characteristics of capitalism and mixed economies.

Focus Your Reading Answers

1 The characteristics of capitalism include private ownership, individual initiative, competition, profit, and freedom of choice.

2 The United States is called a mixed economy because the government is involved in setting economic and social policies. Government regulates private enterprise and has funded a safety net of programs for people who need them. Government funding also finances roads and some public corporations, even though most of the factors of production are privately owned.

3 Capitalist nations include Canada, Japan, Singapore, Taiwan, Australia, New Zealand, and most countries in Europe.

Words to Know

Introduce each of the following vocabulary terms to students.

Traditional economies are ones in which people barter, or exchange, goods and services. Many ancient civilizations used a *traditional economy*. In a *market economy*, buyers and sellers decide what to make, how much to make, and for whom.

Capitalism is a market system in which buyers and sellers make choices about what to produce, how much to produce, and for whom. *Capitalism* is the system of most Western nations.

Free enterprise is another term for capitalist economies. *Free enterprise* refers to the fact that governments do not completely control the economy.

Private enterprise is another synonym for *capitalism*. In the *private enterprise* system, everyone has the freedom to start a business.

Table Extension

Ask students to choose a familiar product that they use regularly, such as notebook paper or jeans. Have them explain how each of the factors of production relates to that product.

Picturing Government

The photograph at the center left on page 438 shows a New York business about to close. Although retail sales, payroll, and paid employees increased in the United States between the U.S. census of 1997 and that of 2002 (the latest figures available), the number of retail establishments declined by more than 7,000. Small, independent businesses often cannot compete against national chains. Nevertheless, in 2004, an estimated 580,900 new firms started, compared to 576,200 that closed.

Picturing Government

The photograph at the bottom right of page 438 shows two young entrepreneurs offering lemonade and a wireless hot spot. Lemonade stands have been only one way that children have started businesses. Other typical endeavors have been lawn care, babysitting, pet sitting, and housecleaning. Discuss with students any such endeavors they have begun.

Factors of Production

Every economic system has the following basic resources. They are called the **factors of production**.

- Natural resources: This includes all natural resources found on or in land and in water in rivers, lakes, and ponds. It includes air, soil, iron, coal, and similar resources.
- Labor: Labor is human resources, meaning workers.
- Capital: **Capital** is the means of production. It includes money, factories, and machinery used to produce other goods and services.
- Entrepreneur: An **entrepreneur** organizes the other factors of production in order to produce goods and services. This person risks his or her capital to own and run a business.

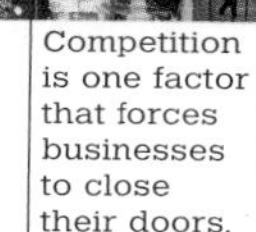

Competition is one factor that forces businesses to close their doors.

Competition is the third characteristic of a capitalist system. Anyone may start a business. As a result, any industry will have a number of businesses competing for buyers of their goods or services. They compete on the basis of high quality, low price, and good service. Businesses try to sell the best quality with the best service at the lowest prices. For example, a number of companies sell computers. The company that sells low-priced computers of good quality and provides good service will take the largest share of the computer market.

The fourth characteristic is profit. Profit is the difference between the amount of money a business takes in and the cost of running the business. An entrepreneur goes into business to make a profit. This is his or her reward for risking capital. However, in a capitalist system, there is also the risk of not making a profit and actually losing all of one's capital. For example, Wang Laboratories was one of the original computer industry giants. It was started by one man, Dr. An Wang. At first, the company made huge profits. Later, when there was more competition, the company went bankrupt.

Businesses of all sizes are often forced to find new and different ways to attract customers.

Words to Know, continued

Resources used in economic systems are called *factors of production*. There are four basic resources known as the *factors of production*.

The means of production are *capital*. *Capital* includes money, factories, and machinery.

An *entrepreneur* is someone willing to risk his or her *capital* to own and run a business. An *entrepreneur* organizes the other *factors of production* to produce services and goods.

A *mixed economy* is one in which the government sets some economic and social policies that affect business, funds some projects, and regulates business. The United States has a *mixed economy*.

stop and think

Create a three-column chart to list the five characteristics of a capitalist society. List the characteristics in one column. In the second column, explain each one. In the third column, give an example of each one. You will need to think up some examples. Work with a partner to create your chart.

Freedom of choice is the fifth characteristic of a capitalist system. Sellers decide for themselves what they will produce and for whom. They also set their own prices for their goods and services. Price is based on the cost of production and what the competition is charging. Workers sell their labor. They choose the jobs they will take and the wages they will accept. If a better job comes along, workers can decide to quit their present job and take the new one. Buyers decide for themselves what they will buy and how much they are willing to spend. The government is not part of these decisions.

A Mixed Economy: The United States

The government is not involved in the capitalist economy. It plays no role in economic decision-making. Today, there are no pure capitalist systems. Instead, nations like the United States have **mixed economies**. Government is involved in setting economic and social policies. Such decisions are not left entirely to individuals.

First, government at the federal, state, and local levels regulates private enterprise. For example, the federal government regulates business activities that affect the environment and public health. Congress has passed clean water and air acts and pure food and drug laws. The executive branch enforces these laws. State and local governments require licenses for certain kinds of businesses such as day care centers.

Delivering mail is one of the responsibilities assumed by the U.S. government.

Second, government has taken on responsibility for many social policies that affect the economy. Since the 1930s, the federal government has provided a safety net of programs for the elderly, the poor, and those with disabilities. These programs include Social Security, Medicare, and Medicaid. State governments participate in Medicaid. They also administer unemployment insurance for laid-off workers.

Stop and Think

Students' charts will vary but should include the five characteristics of capitalism in the lesson, along with explanations and examples.

Picturing Government

In the photograph on page 439, a postal worker delivers the mail to customers' home mailboxes. The United States Postal Service (USPS) delivers more than 212 billion pieces of mail to more than 144 million addresses in the nation, plus Guam, Puerto Rico, American Samoa, and the American Virgin Islands. In 2005, it had more than 700,000 employees. The world's largest postal system, the USPS handles more than 44 percent of all letter and card mail in the world. On average, a letter carrier delivers 2,300 pieces of mail to about 500 addresses daily.

Extension

Invite students to select a product in which they are interested, such as clothing or an iPod. Ask them to track the prices of the item through several stores, as well as online, noting the variations in price. Have them explain the variations in light of freedom of choice in a capitalist system.

Extensions

1 Challenge students to find examples of successful entrepreneurs. The government census data takes special note of minority-owned and women-owned businesses. Ask students to find out about the career of the person and to report to the class. Help them see that an entrepreneur may be a television or movie personality such as Paul Newman or Oprah Winfrey, but that usually an entrepreneur is not involved in the sports or entertainment industries.

2 Alex's Lemonade Stand, begun in 2000 by four-year-old cancer patient Alexandra Scott, is dedicated to raising funds for pediatric cancer research. Within five years, Alex and thousands of others across the nation "fighting childhood cancer one cup at a time" had raised more than $1 million. Although Alex died in 2004, her work goes on. Invite students to find out more about philanthropic work associated with business. For example, some corporations, such as Ben & Jerry's Ice Cream, donate a percentage of profit to worthy causes.

Picturing Government

The photograph on page 440 shows a health center in London, England. In 1946, the British government passed the National Health Service Act, which established a comprehensive health service. Taxes pay the majority of costs for the National Health Service. With few exceptions, the population is covered at no cost. In recent years, advancing medical technology has meant that hospital stays have become more expensive, straining the system.

Putting It All Together

Students' lists will vary but should reflect lesson content.

Third, most of the factors of production are privately owned in a mixed economy. However, government provides funding for some resources, such as roads, highways, and bridges. The federal government also provides funding for public corporations such as the postal service. State and local governments may operate water and power companies. They also run regional transportation systems like bus and subway lines.

Other Nations with Mixed Economies

Most nations in Europe have mixed economies. So do Canada, Japan, Singapore, Taiwan, South Korea, Australia, and New Zealand. However, the nations vary in how much government intervenes in the economy.

England provides socialized medical care for the country's citizens.

For many years, Great Britain had government ownership of large industries such as the railroads. In recent years, the government has been privatizing businesses, or turning ownership over to private companies. Medical care is free. The elderly get government pensions. The fees for public colleges and universities are very low. When the government tried to raise fees in 2005, the public protested.

Japan's government, on the other hand, does not provide much funding for social programs. It does protect Japanese companies from foreign competition, however. High tariffs, or import fees, make goods coming into Japan more costly than Japanese-produced goods.

In recent years, eastern European nations such as Poland and Hungary have privatized many of their businesses. Beginning in the late 1980s, the governments of eastern Europe were no longer controlled by Communists. As a result, these nations have moved toward mixed economies.

Putting It All Together

"In a mixed economy, government becomes involved in private enterprise." Work with a partner to explain this statement. Discuss what you think the statement means. Make a list of the ways that government regulates and also helps businesses.

Extension

Suggest that students interested in business use the federal government's Small Business Administration's Web site to find out more about young entrepreneurs and setting up a business. Have them present their findings to the class by using the Student Presentation Builder on the student CD.

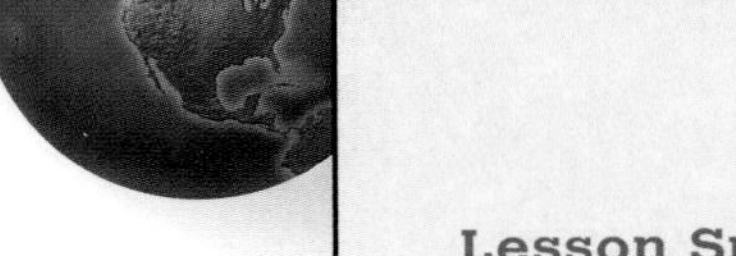

LESSON 2

Socialism and Developing Nations

Thinking on Your Own

Suppose you were part of a committee to develop a plan for the economy of a new nation. Your country is poor, but it has many natural resources. It has few factories, though. There is also a large population of workers, but they have few skills. They are mostly farmers. What would your country need to do to develop its economy? Look at the illustrations in this lesson. Think about the question. In your notebook, write at least five things your country would have to do to improve its economy.

Many of the nations in the Southern Hemisphere are **developing nations**. Their economies are based on farming and the export of natural resources. Many of their citizens live in poverty. These nations were once part of European colonial empires. Latin America's nations gained their independence in the 1800s. African nations did not gain independence until the mid- or late twentieth century. A number of these nations have chosen to develop Socialist economies.

focus your reading

Describe what the characteristics of socialism are.

How are Latin American nations modernizing their economies?

In what ways are African nations improving their economies?

words to know

developing nation

socialism

nationalization

central planning

industrialization

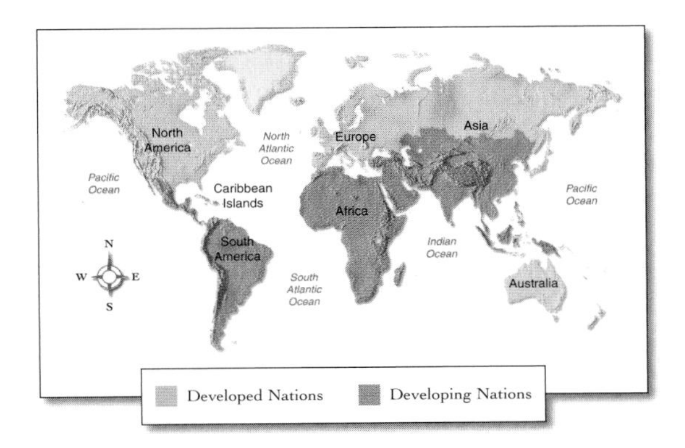

Lesson Summary

In a Socialist system, the government owns the basic means of production and decides how resources will be used. Socialism can be either democratic or authoritarian. The four characteristics of socialism are nationalization, guarantee of public welfare, high taxes, and a centrally planned economy. Many developing nations have chosen socialism for their economic system. Central planning also permits the government to direct capital toward industrializing the nation, which is seen as a means of improving the economy, and thus, of the standard of living for its citizens. This strategy has three problems, however. Agriculture may be overlooked in producing goods to export. Government bureaucracies grow large and unwieldy. Foreign companies are reluctant to invest money in companies that may become nationalized.

Lesson Objective

Students will learn about the economics of socialism, particularly as it applies to developing nations.

Focus Your Reading Answers

1 The characteristics of socialism include nationalization, guarantee of public welfare, high taxes, and a centrally planned economy.

2 Latin American nations are modernizing their economies through industrializing.

3 African nations are improving their economies by nationalizing businesses.

Words to Know

Discuss each of the vocabulary terms with students.

A *developing nation* is one with an economy based mainly on agriculture and the export of natural resources. Generally, a *developing nation* was once a part of a European colonial empire.

An economic system in which the government owns the basic means of production and decides how resources are used is called *socialism*. *Socialism* may be either democratic or authoritarian. When the central government takes over certain major industries, *nationalization* is the result. When *nationalization* occurs in authoritarian countries, the governments do not pay the business owners for their losses.

In economies that practice *central planning*, bureaucrats determine how resources will be used. Nations with strict *central planning* have command economies.

The growth of manufacturing and other industries is called *industrialization*. Most governments believe that *industrialization* will improve the standard of living for their citizens.

Picturing Government

The photograph on page 442 shows a high school classroom in Buenos Aires, Argentina. The nation has one of South America's highest literacy rates. Primary education is free and compulsory. In the nineteenth century, the government funded public education through subsidies. The nation also has a long tradition of higher education; its first university, in Córdoba, was established in 1613.

Socialism

Socialism is an economic system in which the government owns the basic means of production and decides how resources should be used. The government also provides social services such as health care and welfare. The basic principle of socialism is that all members of society should share equally in the benefits of economic activity.

Socialism may be democratic, or it may be authoritarian. For example, Great Britain, France, Sweden, and Germany are democratic nations. Each has Socialist political parties, however. When these parties are voted into national office, they approve programs that distribute more of the nation's resources to poorer citizens. For example, providing free medical care for everyone is a Socialist-supported program.

Like the United States, the Argentinian government provides education for all children.

Socialism has four characteristics: nationalization, guarantee of the public welfare, high taxes, and a centrally planned economy. However, great differences exist among Socialist governments. There are differences in how many of these characteristics are present and how strongly they are followed.

The first characteristic of socialism is **nationalization**. The central government takes over certain industries, such as transportation and steel. These are often the most important companies and have thousands of workers. In a democratic nation such as France, the Socialist government pays the owners of the companies for the loss of their businesses. In authoritarian nations, the government does not pay the owners.

Guarantee of the public welfare is the second characteristic. Socialist governments seek to ensure that the basic needs of all citizens are met. These include free or low-cost medical and dental care; low-cost public housing; free schooling, including a university education; pensions for the retired and those with disabilities; and unemployment payments.

These benefits, however, cost money. As a result, high taxes are a third characteristic of socialism. Taxes are the chief means Socialist governments use to fund benefits. People may pay as much as 50 or 60 percent of their income in taxes. The idea is to even out the distribution of wealth among a nation's citizens.

Extensions

1 Invite students to work in small groups. Ask each group to select a country in Africa or South America not mentioned in the lesson. Have them find out when and how that nation gained independence from a European power. Ask them to investigate the country's economic status and growth, using library resources or the Internet. Allow time for groups to present their findings to the class in a panel discussion on the economic progress of developing nations.

2 Ask students interested in math to use library resources or the Internet to find out about rates of taxation in five countries. Ask that some of the countries be capitalist and some Socialist. Have the students present the information to the class using graphs or charts. Discuss with students the advantages and disadvantages of each system as it relates to taxation.

stop and think

Create a three-column chart to list the four characteristics of socialism. List the characteristics in one column. In the second column, explain each characteristic. In the third column, give an example of each one. Work with a partner to create your chart.

The fourth characteristic is **central planning.** A centrally planned economy is one in which the government decides how resources will be used. In a market economy like the United States, sellers decide what resources they need, how to get what they need, and what to produce. They also decide to whom to sell their goods and services. In a centrally planned economy, government bureaucrats make decisions about what will be produced and for whom. They decide which industries will be able to buy what resources. They also decide how much of any good or service will be produced. A nation with strict central planning has a command economy. Most Socialist nations, however, allow some private companies to operate.

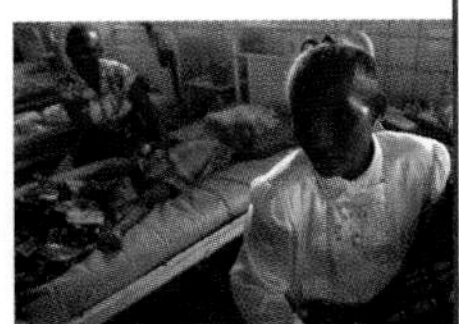

Health care is lacking in many regions of the developing world, such as in Kinshasa, D.R.C.

Developing Economies

The governments of many developing nations have chosen socialism. There are some practical reasons for this.

First, when African nations became independent, they had few locally owned companies. Even in Latin America, foreign investors owned and ran many of the large businesses. Nationalizing foreign businesses puts control of these businesses in local hands. The idea is that their resources can be used to benefit the nation, rather than foreigners.

It does not always work that way. An example is Chile in the early 1970s. Salvador Allende, a Socialist, was elected president in 1970. He nationalized foreign-owned businesses. However, the economy worsened. In 1973, military leaders overthrew him. They set up a dictatorship and welcomed back foreign investors.

Second, a goal of governments in developing nations is to improve the economy. They believe that this, in turn, will raise the standard of living of their citizens. Most governments see industrialization as the way to achieve this. **Industrialization** is the growth of industries such as manufacturing. Central planning enables these governments to direct capital—money and natural and human resources—toward industrialization.

Infrastructure is often lacking in developing countries, including Haiti.

Stop and Think

Students' charts should list the four characteristics of socialism given on pages 442–443. Explanations and examples will vary but should reflect lesson content.

Picturing Government

The photograph at the center right on page 443 shows conditions in what was then Zaire, now the Democratic Republic of Congo, after its leader, Mobutu Sese Seko, fell in 1997. Mobutu had been in charge of the nation for more than 30 years. He intervened in the Rwanda crisis in 1994, permitting refugee camps to be established for those fleeing the civil war in Rwanda. However, Rwanda's Hutu refugees were attacked in Zaire, leading the government to expel all ethnic Tutsis.

Picturing Government

The photograph at the bottom right on page 443 shows a slum, where the houses are made of scraps of corrugated steel, in Haiti's capital, Port-au-Prince. Haiti is both one of the most densely populated and poorest nations of the world. Port-au-Prince has a population of more than 1.5 million, many of whom live in shantytowns, such as the one pictured, outside the city proper. The average annual income in urban Haiti is $300; more than 60 percent of the population lives in rural areas, where more than 80 percent of the people live below the poverty line.

Extension

Have students use library resources or the Internet to find out about the current state of Chile's economy. What effect did the free trade agreement that the nation signed with the United States have on key indicators such as unemployment and gross domestic product?

In Kenya, mechanics receive government training.

Problems of Socialism in Developing Nations

Unfortunately, socialism comes at a cost to developing nations. So many resources may be used to produce goods for export that agriculture is overlooked. Nigeria and other nations have to import food.

Another problem is the growth of government bureaucracies. Central planning requires large numbers of bureaucrats. However, bureaucracy can become so large that it is a drain on the nation's resources. Taxes increase for salaries of the bureaucrats. Decision-making is slowed down.

Nationalization is also an issue. Developing nations need money to industrialize. Foreign companies are unlikely to put money into nations that may nationalize their businesses.

Putting It All Together

Create a concept web about socialism. Label the center circle "Socialism." Label the smaller circles "Advantages" and "Problems." Work with a partner to add details.

Biography

Wangari Maathai (1940—)

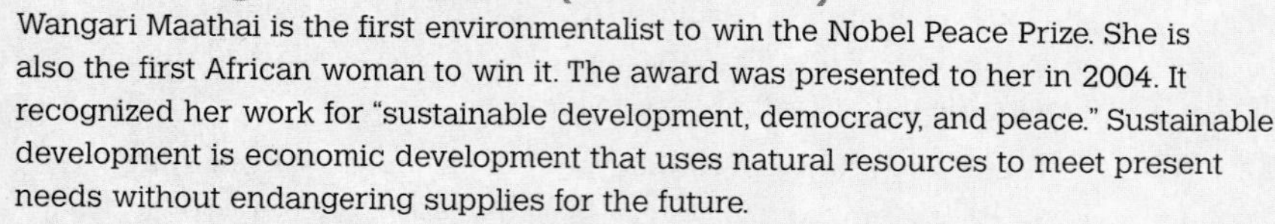

Wangari Maathai is the first environmentalist to win the Nobel Peace Prize. She is also the first African woman to win it. The award was presented to her in 2004. It recognized her work for "sustainable development, democracy, and peace." Sustainable development is economic development that uses natural resources to meet present needs without endangering supplies for the future.

Maathai began her environmental work in 1977 in her native Kenya. In that year, she founded the Green Belt Movement (GBM). Logging and development had stripped the country of its trees. Since 1977, the GBM has planted more than 30 million trees. More than 100,000 people have found work with the GBM, planting and taking care of the trees.

In the 1990s, Maathai and the GBM turned to politics. They opposed the dictatorship of Kenya's president, Daniel arap Moi, who finally banned the GBM. Maathai was beaten and jailed repeatedly over the years. In 2002, Moi was banned from running for office again and a freely elected government took over. Maathai was named Assistant Minister for Environment, Natural Resources, and Wildlife.

Picturing Government

The photograph on page 444, taken in 1973, shows two men in Kenya being trained as mechanics. Most manufacturing in Kenya relates to agricultural products grown there. However, Kenya is also a center for engineering industries, where machinery and motor vehicles are assembled from imported parts.

People in the News Extension

- Born Nyeri, Kenya, 1940.
- Earned biological sciences degree from Mount St. Scholastica College in Atchison, Kansas, 1964.
- Earned Master of Science degree from University of Pittsburgh, 1966.
- Became first woman in East and Central Africa to earn doctorate, University of Nairobi, 1971.
- Chaired Department of Veterinary Anatomy at University of Nairobi, 1976.
- Chaired National Council of Women of Kenya, 1981–1987.
- Elected to Kenya's Parliament with 98 percent of the vote, 2002.
- Appointed by Kenya's president (with whom she is pictured) as Assistant Minister for Environment, Natural Resources, and Wildlife.

Extension

The Green Belt Movement has established more than 6,000 tree nurseries in Kenya. The successful tree-planting campaign has led to other initiatives, including sustainable development, health education, and building skills in areas such as beekeeping, food processing and marketing, and food security. Suggest that students use library resources or the Internet to find out more about the expanded efforts of the Green Belt Movement.

Putting It All Together

Students' concept webs will vary but should include advantages and problems of socialism.

LESSON 3

Communist Systems

Thinking on Your Own

Communist economic systems are another alternative to capitalist or mixed economies. Skim this section and list three characteristics of a Communist system in your notebook. Check the accuracy of your list as you read this lesson.

focus your reading

What are the characteristics of a Communist economy?

Explain what caused the collapse of Soviet communism.

How have the Chinese adapted their economy to capitalism?

words to know

collectivization

commune

In the 1920s, the Communists took over the government of Russia and formed the Soviet Union. They introduced a new form of government and a new economic system. These were based on the ideas of Karl Marx.

Marx was a German philosopher. He believed that there are only two classes—owners and workers. The owners of land, factories, buildings, and the like, are capitalists. According to Marx, they grow rich while their workers suffer. Workers must revolt against the capitalists. They must seize all factors of production and set up a dictatorship of the proletariat. *Proletariat* means "the people." The Russian Revolution of 1917 was the first step. Communists acting in the name of the people overthrew the czar and seized power. They set up a Communist state.

Characteristics of Soviet Communism

Communism has four basic characteristics. First is the role of the Communist Party. The party controls the government. Party leaders make all major political and economic decisions for the nation.

The U.S.S.R. used propaganda posters to promote collective farming.

Lesson Summary

Soviet communism has four characteristics: the Communist Party makes political and economic decisions, the economy is centrally planned, property is collectivized, and the government owns all means of production. Mikhail Gorbachev tried to reform the system but failed. The economic situation worsened. Eastern European satellite countries and the Soviet republics rebelled, leading to the collapse of the nation. Mao Zedong and his followers gained power in China in 1949. Mao instituted a Communist political and economic system, with the goal of modernizing China. After Mao's death, his successor relaxed the central planning and began shifting to a market economy. However, the nation is still politically Communist.

Lesson Objective

Students will learn about the current and former Communist economic systems.

Focus Your Reading Answers

1 The characteristics of a Communist economy are the role of the Communist Party in making decisions, centrally planned economies, collectivization, and government ownership.

2 Soviet communism collapsed because of shortages of consumer goods and food. When eastern European nations rebelled, so did Soviet republics. The Soviet Union collapsed.

3 The Chinese have adapted their economy to capitalism by selling government-owned businesses to entrepreneurs and allowing workers to own and manage their own businesses. Foreign investors and foreign companies are now welcome in China.

Words to Know

Discuss each of the vocabulary terms with students.

The process of taking over privately owned property is called *collectivization*. During the 1930s, *collectivization* occurred in the Soviet Union.

A *commune* is a government-owned agricultural property. Under Mao Zedong, small farms combined to form a *commune*.

Picturing Government

The 1976 poster shown on page 445 is an example of propaganda from the Soviet Union. It was placed on a collective farm in what is now Tajikistan, which received independence in 1991 when the Soviet Union collapsed. The poster celebrates the 25th Congress of the Communist Party in the Soviet Union.

Picturing Government

The 1936 photograph on page 446 shows workers eating lunch in the fields of the collective farm where they worked in the Soviet Union. In the middle of 1929, about five million peasants worked on collective farms. By March 1, 1930, the number had increased to 70 million. Collectivization of farms led to a major decline in the U.S.S.R.'s agricultural output. The dictator Stalin exported grain rather than feed peasants; millions died of starvation.

Stop and Think

Students' lists will vary but may suggest that the government owned all factors of production. Reasons for the collapse of the Soviet Union include food shortages, lack of consumer goods, inflation, slow economic and agricultural growth, unemployment, and failed efforts at reform.

A collective farm in Vilshanka, Soviet Union

Communist nations have centrally planned economies. This is the second characteristic. The national government makes all economic decisions. It decides what will be produced and by whom. It decides which companies and farms will get what resources, including the number of workers.

Government bureaucrats draw up very detailed economic plans. Each farm is given a quota of certain crops and animals to raise. Each factory is given a quota of goods to produce. For example, a factory may have a quota of 500 tractors a month to produce. If the factory falls short, the managers could be punished. Ever-larger numbers of bureaucrats are hired by the government to develop these plans and see that they are carried out.

The third and fourth characteristics, collectivization and government ownership, are related. The government owns all means of production, from trains and buses to housing and stores. **Collectivization** is the process of taking over privately owned property. For example, in the 1930s, the Soviet Union collectivized small farms. The government seized all farms in an area and joined them into a single government-owned collective.

stop and think

How did the Communists in the Soviet Union put Marx's ideas into practice? Discuss the question with a partner and make a list of ideas. As you read further, list reasons for the collapse of communism in the Soviet Union.

Why Communism Collapsed in Russia

From the 1930s through the 1970s, the Soviet economy grew steadily. However, the growth masked a number of problems. For example, there was a lack of goods for ordinary people to buy. Government planners focused on building weapons and machinery. They were not concerned with producing refrigerators, furniture, and stylish clothes.

Extension

Invite students to create timelines of the Soviet Union's progress and collapse, beginning in 1917. Ask them to show the changes in the economy over time, as well as historical events. Post the timelines in the classroom.

Agriculture also suffered under central planning. Farmers in a market economy earn their money by selling their crops. In the Soviet Union, many farmers were paid wages. It did not matter how large their harvests were or if they harvested their crops on time. As a result, there were often food shortages. By the 1980s, the problems were leading to unrest. Both economic growth and productivity had slowed greatly.

Mikhail Gorbachev became head of the Communist Party and the Soviet Union in 1985. He tried to reform the Communist political and economic systems. Central planning was relaxed. The bureaucracy's size was cut. Managers were allowed to make decisions about their factories. Farmers were given land on government-owned farms to grow crops. However, change was difficult. In the end, Gorbachev's efforts were unsuccessful. Shortages worsened. Prices rose for goods that were available. Unemployment also rose.

Long lines in grocery stores were common during the Communist era in Soviet Russia.

At the same time, eastern Europeans were rebelling against their Communist-dominated governments. This led to rebellions among the other Soviet republics. In 1991, the Soviet Union collapsed. The 15 republics became independent nations. A new president of Russia replaced Gorbachev.

Since the early 1990s, Russia has attempted to build a democratic nation and a market economy. It has been difficult. The Russians have no history of democratic government or civil rights and liberties. Before the revolution in 1917, the nation was a monarchy ruled by the czar. Many of the same people who ran the Communist government in the 1980s are still in power. By the early 2000s, the government had strengthened its power over the rights of citizens.

It has not been any easier to improve the economy. The economy of czarist Russia was based on agriculture. The Communists forced the nation to adopt central planning and to industrialize. There is no history of private enterprise. As a result, moving to a market economy has been difficult.

Picturing Government

The 1992 photograph on page 447 shows people waiting in line to buy eggs in the Soviet Union. Food prices sometimes doubled in a day. More than 1,000 basic consumer goods were seldom available by mid-1990. Rationing was common, as was standing in line. A 1990 estimate suggested that 30–40 million hours annually was lost waiting in lines to purchase goods. Prices overall increased 29 percent in 1990, which was a factor in hastening the fall of the Soviet Union.

Extension

Have students use library resources or the Internet to find the most current information on the political and economic situation in Russia and the other former Soviet republics. You may wish to have students work in pairs or small groups, assigning each one of the former Soviet republics. Allow time for students to present their findings to the class, emphasizing the progress toward a market economy and democracy in each nation.

Picturing Government

The photograph on page 448 shows a department store in Beijing, China. Under communism, Beijing has shifted from a cultural and administrative center to a manufacturing and industrial center. Beijing is now second only to Shanghai in total gross value of its industrial output. Agriculture also makes up a large portion of the city's economy, reflecting the Communist belief that all cities need to produce as well as to consume. The city is largely self-sufficient in fruits, fish, vegetables, and poultry.

Shifts in Chinese Communism

Mao Zedong and his Communist followers seized power in China in 1949. Like the Communists in Russia, Mao founded a Communist political and economic system in the People's Republic of China (PRC). Like the Soviet Union, the Chinese economy was based on central planning and government ownership of property. Small farms were combined into large government-owned **communes**. Private enterprise was not allowed. Mao's goal was to modernize China. However, his efforts at raising the standard of living failed.

Beijing has slowly introduced concepts from a market economy.

After Mao's death, Deng Xiaoping became head of the Communist Party and the government in 1977. Deng relaxed much of the central planning put in place by Mao. He and his successors have slowly shifted China to more of a market economy. Many government-owned businesses have been sold to entrepreneurs. Other entrepreneurs are opening their own small businesses. Many businesses are owned and managed by their workers. Foreign companies and foreign investors are welcome to do business in China. China has become an economic giant.

However, political control has not eased. The Communist Party still runs the government and people's rights are limited. No one may oppose the government.

Putting It All Together

Working with a partner, imagine that one of you lived in the Soviet Union and the other in China under Mao. How might central planning have affected each of you as a worker and a consumer? Make a T-chart. Label one side "Soviet Union." Label the other "PRC." Work with a partner to list ideas about how central planning would affect you as a worker or consumer in each of these nations. Discuss how life in the Soviet Union and the PRC is different from life in the United States.

Putting It All Together

Students' T-charts will vary but should reflect life for workers and consumers in the Soviet Union and the PRC under communism.

LESSON 4

Global Economic Issues

Thinking on Your Own

The United States imports goods from many parts of the world. In your notebook, list at least five items you buy that U.S. companies import and sell in the United States.

focus your reading

Explain how technology impacts the interdependence of nations.

How can nations both limit and encourage international trade?

What economic issues does globalization present for developing nations?

words to know

technology

trade barrier

quota

subsidy

free trade

Globalization is the integration of economic activities across national borders. Globalization creates a single world market through the free flow of goods, services, labor, and capital. The globalization of the economy began centuries ago. In the 200s B.C., merchants carried goods along the Silk Road. The trade route stretched from China through the Middle East to the Roman Empire. In the 1400s, European explorers opened trade routes between Asia and Europe. In the 1500s, the Americas joined the international trade network.

Globalization has increased the spread of Western goods around the world.

Since the mid-1800s, the interdependence of economies has increased dramatically. Technology and government policies drive globalization. **Technology**—the use of science in business and industry—includes the ability to move raw materials and goods quickly and cheaply. First, it was the invention of the clipper ship in the mid-1840s. These fast sailing ships sped raw materials and goods around the world. In the late 1800s, even faster

Lesson Summary

Integrating economic activities across national borders is called globalization. Computers have changed the speed with which companies can do business globally. Governments can put up trade barriers such as tariffs, quotas, or subsidies. Regional groups such as the European Union are formed to reduce trade barriers. The World Trade Organization encourages world trade by developing nations, which make up about 126 of the 191 nations of the world. These countries have only 20 percent of the world's resources, but about 80 percent of its people. Problems these nations face include population growth, poor health, civil wars and military rule, and lack of capital combined with a huge debt burden.

Lesson Objective

Students will learn about the current global economic issues, especially as they relate to international trade and developing nations.

Focus Your Reading Answers

1 Technology impacts the interdependence of nations by allowing goods and materials to be moved quickly and cheaply and by sending information quickly and cheaply.

2 Nations can limit and encourage international trade through tariffs, quotas, subsidies, and regional trade organizations.

3 For developing nations, issues related to globalization include rapid population growth, poor health leading to lower life expectancy, civil wars and military rule that limit the amount of economic development possible, and lack of capital along with a huge debt burden.

Words to Know

Discuss each of the vocabulary terms with students.

The use of science in business and industry is known as *technology*. *Technology* includes the abilities to move raw materials and goods quickly, as well as the ability to send information quickly.

A *trade barrier* is any government policy that blocks free world trade. In the Western Hemisphere, nations are trying to remove any *trade barriers*.

A *quota* is a set number of goods allowed into a country during a certain time period. A *quota* will limit foreign-made goods to protect local businesses and jobs from foreign competition. A *subsidy* is a government payment to producers of a good or service to encourage local production. Sometimes nations are fined for using a *subsidy*.

Free trade is trade without barriers. In 1948, the General Agreement on Tariffs and Trade (GATT) was created with the goal of *free trade*.

Picturing Government

A freight train in Alabama carries China Shipping cargo containers in the photograph on page 450. The company, based in Shanghai, began doing business in the United States in 2000 and has since signed contracts with all major railroads in the United States to move goods rapidly.

Extension

Invite students with an interest in art to create a mural or bulletin board showing the development of technology since the mid-1800s. Suggest they consider the murals of artists such as Diego Rivera for inspiration.

steamships replaced clipper ships. Then came railroads, trucks, and airplanes to move goods and passengers within countries and across borders.

Technology also includes the ability to send information quickly. The inventions of the telegraph and telephone made it possible to send information quickly from place to place. Computers and the World Wide Web make it possible to send huge amounts of data cheaply and quickly.

Government Policies and International Trade

All the speed in the world will not expand world trade if government policies block it. There are several ways that governments can put up **trade barriers**.

Some nations use tariffs, or taxes on imports, to make them more costly than locally produced goods. The goal is to protect local businesses and jobs from foreign competition. Governments also use quotas to limit foreign-made goods. A **quota** allows only a certain amount of a good, such as tuna, to be brought into a country during a certain time period.

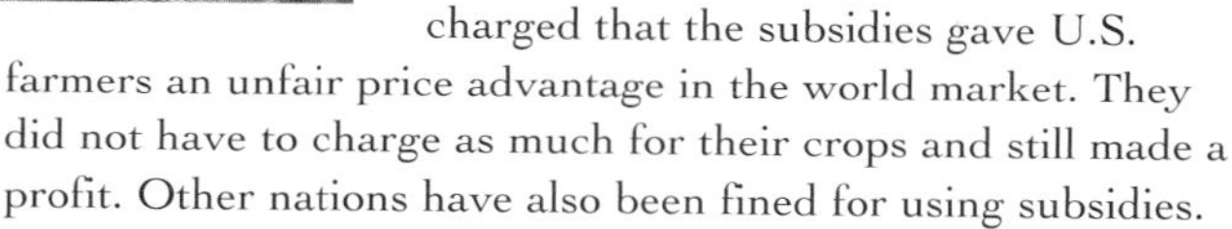

International trade has increased in recent years and allowed a greater flow of goods around the world.

Subsidies are government payments to the producers of a good or service. They encourage local production by increasing the amount of money that the producer receives. However, the European Union (EU) has fined the United States in recent years for its use of subsidies for U.S. farmers. The EU charged that the subsidies gave U.S. farmers an unfair price advantage in the world market. They did not have to charge as much for their crops and still made a profit. Other nations have also been fined for using subsidies.

The European Union is one of the regional organizations that have been formed to promote freer trade. The table on page 451 shows some of the other major groups. Their purpose is to reduce trade barriers among member nations.

Picturing Government

The Coca-Cola sign shown on page 449 is located in the country of Greece. Coca-Cola is one of the many multinational corporations that do business around the world. Coca-Cola has diversified from the main soft drink business, holding a controlling interest in Columbia Pictures for seven years and purchasing Minute Maid, a citrus beverage company.

450 Chapter 24

Major Regional Trade Groups

Common Market for Eastern and Southern Africa (COMESA)
Economic Community of West African States (ECOWAS)
Asia Pacific Economic Cooperation (APEC)
Association of South East Asian Nations (ASEAN)
European Union (EU)
Caribbean Community and Common Market (CARICOM)
Central American Free Trade Agreement (CAFTA)
North American Free Trade Agreement (NAFTA)

In 1948, the United States and 22 other nations created the General Agreement on Tariffs and Trade (GATT). The goals included lowering tariffs and quotas. The goal was **free trade**, or trade without barriers. By 1994, 110 countries were operating under GATT rules. In that year, they agreed to create the World Trade Organization (WTO). It is a permanent agency that enforces trade rules and settles trade disputes. It also encourages world trade by developing nations.

stop and think

Play "What Am I?" with a partner. Write a definition for each term introduced so far in this lesson. End the definition with the question "What am I?" Take turns with a partner asking and answering questions.

Issues for Developing Nations

About 126 of the world's 191 nations are developing nations. Their populations total more than 5 billion. This equals five-sixths of the world's people. However, these nations have only 20 percent of the world's resources.

Developing nations face many problems in improving their economies and the standard of living of their people. Listed here are some of the major problems.

- Population growth

Developing nations tend to have higher rates of population growth than developed nations. This creates a drain on food resources, health care, and education. Some countries have set policies to limit population growth. In an effort to cut population growth, the Chinese government limits families to one child.

Table Extension

Divide the class into eight small groups, assigning each group one of the major regional trade groups listed. Challenge students to use library resources or the Internet to find out more about the trade group. Have them focus on answering the basic questions of a news story (who, what, why, when, where, how), then present the material as a news broadcast.

Stop and Think

You may wish to play a class-wide game of "What Am I?" after students have developed their questions. The game could be used as a review before a quiz or test.

Extension

The World Trade Organization (WTO) has 148 member countries as of 2004. More than 75 percent of those are developing or least-developed nations. The WTO offers those countries special provisions, such as measures to increase their opportunities for trade. Each year, it also pulls together more than 100 technical cooperation missions for those developing countries. Suggest that students use library resources or the Internet to find out more about the World Trade Organization and its critics and defenders.

Picturing Government

The photograph at the top left on page 252 shows a woman and son from Peru waiting in a hospital for treatment for cholera. In 1991, when this photograph was taken, Peru, Colombia, and Ecuador experienced a cholera epidemic. Treatment for the disease is very effective and simple.

Picturing Government

The 1992 photograph at the center left on page 452 shows Somali women at a refugee camp in Baidoa. Somalian refugee camps began in the late 1970s in response to war in the region. By 1990, four of Somalia's 16 regions had refugee camps. A poor nation subject to both flash floods and droughts, Somalia was unable, even with international humanitarian assistance, to care for the refugees properly.

Diseases such as cholera are still of concern in many developing nations, such as Peru.

- Poor health

People in developing nations often suffer from a lack of sanitation, education about good health practices, and medical care. They may live in poverty without enough food to eat and, in many countries, without clean water to drink. As a result, life expectancy is about half of what it is in developed nations. Diseases such as AIDS can infect millions. Polio, which was wiped out in developed nations years ago, has appeared in Africa again.

- Civil wars and military rule

Many of the developing nations are torn by civil wars. Often, military rulers step in and seize power. In the 1970s and 1980s, half of Africa's nations were led by military dictatorships. Many are still ruled by dictators. Instead of using resources to develop the economy, these governments use their resources to support the military. Nations such as Somalia and Sudan are still caught up in civil war. Little economic development can take place when people are not safe.

- Lack of capital and the burden of debt

Generally, developing nations were once part of European or U.S. colonial empires. Their colonial rulers used them as sources of raw materials. They did not invest large amounts of money in developing industry. When these former colonies became independent, they lacked the capital to build industries on their own. As a result, they began to borrow heavily from developed nations.

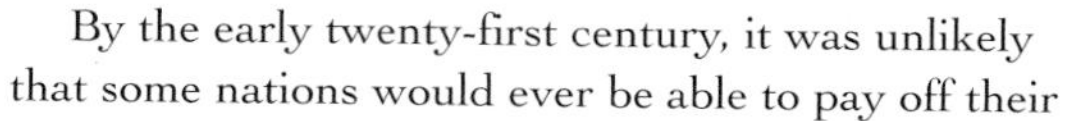

Somali refugees

By the early twenty-first century, it was unlikely that some nations would ever be able to pay off their debts. This made it even harder to grow their economies. In 2005, Prime Minister Tony Blair of Great Britain led developed nations in creating a plan to forgive billions of dollars of debt from the poorest developing nations.

Putting It All Together

With a partner, discuss the economic issues facing developing nations. Choose the one that you think will be the hardest to solve. List at least three reasons for your opinion.

Putting It All Together

Students' choices of the most difficult issue and the reasons they believe that it will be hardest to solve will vary.

Participate in Government

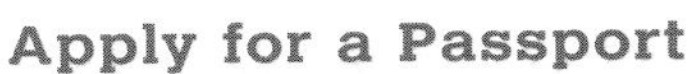

Apply for a Passport

To travel between nations, a person, even an infant, needs a passport. A U.S. citizen needs a U.S. passport. These are available from the passport service of the State Department. There are passport offices in many cities where you can apply for and get a passport. U.S. Post Offices also offer this service.

Passports are valid for ten years. If a person has a valid passport, a renewal can be done online or by mail. However, if a person's passport expired more than 15 years ago, the person must go to a passport office or post office to reapply. If a person has never had a passport or it has been stolen, lost, or damaged, the person must apply in person for a new one.

Children younger than fourteen must apply in person for a passport. Both living parents or guardians must agree to the passport application. Minors between fourteen and seventeen must also appear in person. Parental consent may also be required.

To apply for a passport, a person needs

- a completed but unsigned application form. The person will have to sign the form in front of the passport clerk.
- proof of U.S. citizenship such as the expiring U.S. passport, certified birth certificate, naturalization certificate, or certificate of citizenship.

To Find Out More About Getting a Passport:

- Visit the State Department Web site and look for information on passports.
- Ask your local post office for information.

Participate in Government

1 Have students use the State Department's Web site to find out the specific requirements for passport photographs. Lead a discussion on why the detailed regulations might be in place.

2 Have students interested in math use the Department of State's Web site to find out the number of passports issued in the previous ten years. Ask them to create line or bar graphs to visualize the information.

Research Resources

Below is a list of reference books and Web sites that relate to the issues covered in this chapter. Students may wish to use these to further their research on ideas in the preceding lessons. Web site addresses may change over time. Use keyword searching on a major search engine to locate sites.

Reference Books:

Sarapage McCorkle. *Focus: Economic Systems.* National Council on Economic Education, 2001.

Richard Vietor. *Globalization and Growth: Case Studies in National Economic Strategies*. South-Western College Publishers, 2004.

Web Sites:

The National Council on Economic Education offers lesson materials on economics for all grades on its Web site.

The World Factbook, a Central Intelligence Agency site, provides information about all countries in the world.

Skill Builder

1 Students' sentences will vary but should use the appropriate words listed on the page to show similarities and differences.

2 Students' sentences will vary but should use the appropriate words listed on the page to show similarities and differences.

Recommended Reading

Below is a list of books that relate to the issues covered in this chapter. The numbers in parentheses indicate the related Thematic Strands of the National Council for the Social Studies (NCSS).

Charles W. Carey. *Life Under Soviet Communism*. Greenhaven Press, 2003. (VI, VII, X)

Brendan January. *Globalize It! The Stories of the IMF, the World Bank, the WTO—and Those who Protest*. Twenty-First Century Books, 2003. (VI, VII, IX, X)

Ann Malaspina. *The Chinese Revolution and Mao Zedong in World History*. Enslow Publishers, 2004. (VI, VII, X)

Skill Builder

Make Comparisons and Contrasts

To compare information is to look for how things, people, or events are the same. To contrast information is to look for how things, people, or events are different.

Tables are very useful for comparing and contrasting information. This textbook uses a number of tables to help you see the similarities and differences between and among things related to government. For example, the table on page 34 shows the two competing plans and the compromises that resulted in the U.S. Constitution.

When you talk or write about comparisons and contrasts, there are certain words and phrases that make your meaning clear. They act as signals for your meaning.

Similarities	Differences	
as well as	although	instead
both	even though	on the other hand
in common	but	unlike
in comparison	however	while
like	in contrast	yet
same		
similar		
too		

Complete the following activities using comparison and contrast words to signal similarities and differences.

1 Examine the table on page 34. (a) Write two sentences that compare the two plans with the U.S. Constitution. (b) Write two sentences that contrast the two plans with the U.S. Constitution.

2 Read the sections on capitalism, pages 437–439, and socialism, pages 442–444. (a) Write two sentences that compare capitalism and socialism. (b) Write two sentences that contrast them.

Classroom Discussion

Discuss with students some of the broader topics covered in this chapter.

- How can Western nations assist developing nations to build more secure economies?
- What are the weaknesses of capitalism and how can they be lessened?
- In what ways do regional trade agreements benefit all nations?

Appendix
Supreme Court Cases and Historical Documents

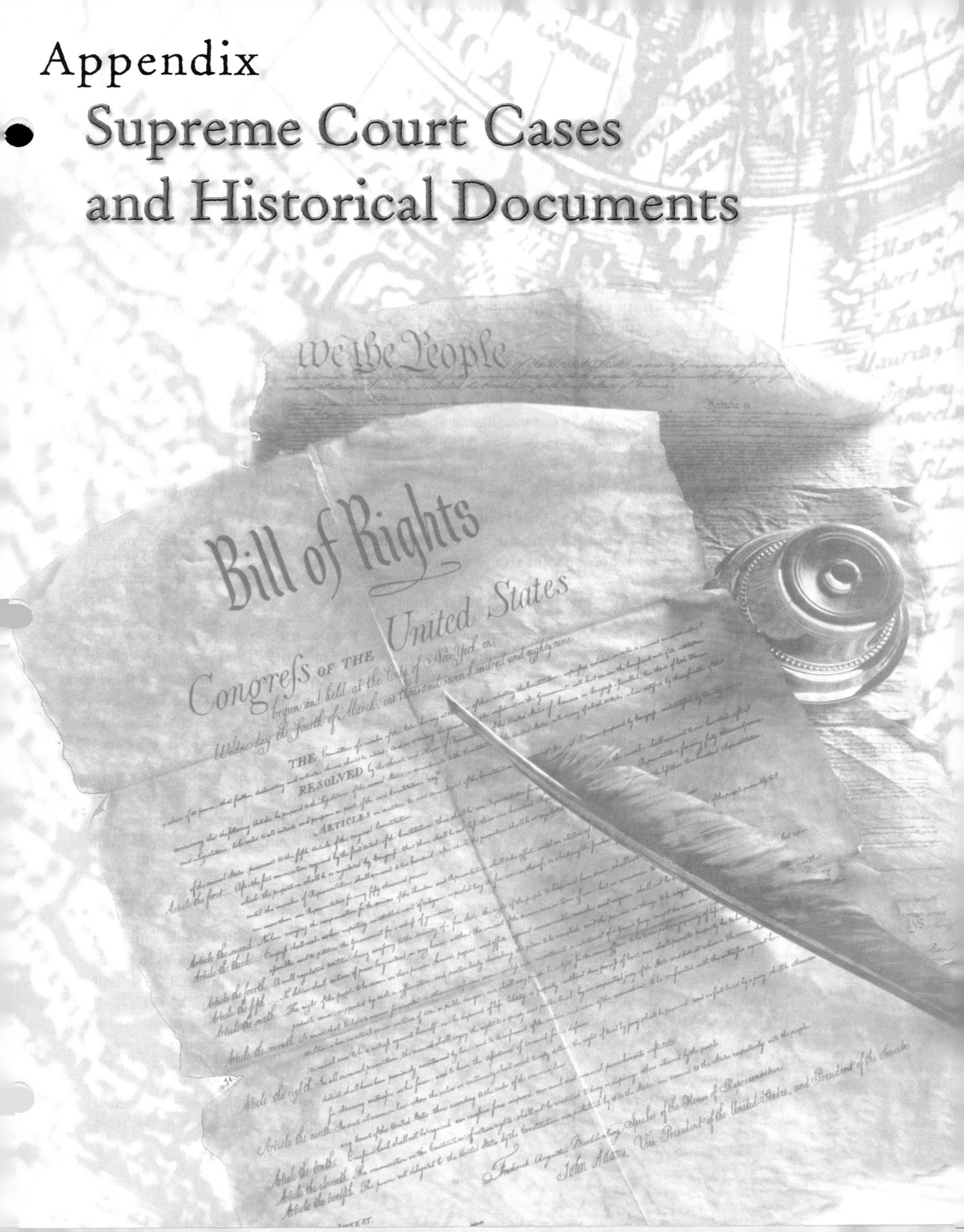

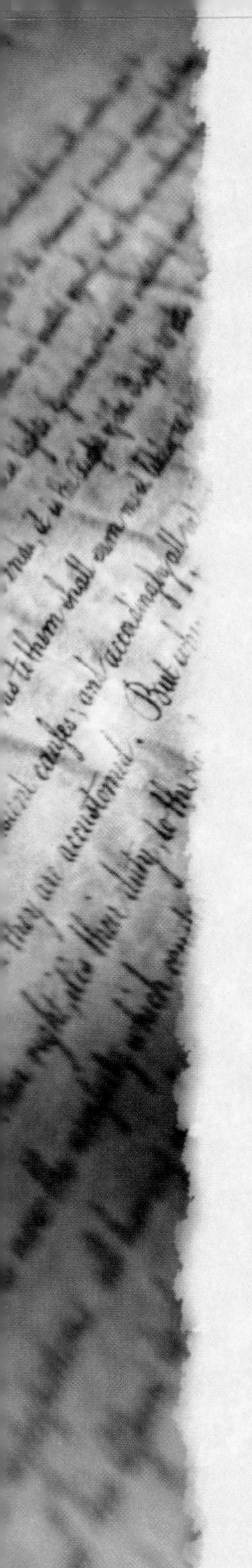

I anticipate with pleasing expectation that retreat in which I promise myself to realize . . . the sweet enjoyment of partaking in the midst of my fellow citizens the benign influence of good laws under a free government—the ever-favorite object of my heart, and the happy rewards, as I trust, of our mutual cares, labors, and dangers.

The Seneca Falls Declaration

July 19–20, 1848

One of the first documents to express the desire for equal rights for women is the Declaration of Sentiments and Resolutions. It was issued in 1848 at the Seneca Falls Convention in Seneca Falls, New York. Lucretia Mott and Elizabeth Cady Stanton led the delegates in adopting a set of resolutions that called for women's suffrage and opportunities for women in employment and education. They formatted these resolutions after the Declaration of Independence.

When, in the course of human events, it becomes necessary for one portion of the family of man to assume among the people of the earth a position different from that which they have hitherto occupied, but one to which the laws of nature and of nature's God entitle them, a decent respect to the opinions of mankind requires that they should declare the causes that impel them to such a course.

We hold these truths to be self-evident: that all men and women are created equal; that they are endowed by their Creator with certain inalienable rights; that among these are life, liberty, and the pursuit of happiness; that to secure these rights governments are instituted, deriving their just powers from the consent of the governed. Whenever any form of government becomes destructive of these ends, it is the right of those who suffer from it to refuse allegiance to it, and to insist upon the institution of a new government, laying its foundation on such principles, and organizing its powers in such form as to them shall seem most likely to effect their safety and happiness. Prudence, indeed, will dictate that governments long established should not be changed for light and transient causes; . . . But when a long train of abuses and usurpations, pursing invariably the same object, evinces a design to reduce them under absolute despotism, it is their duty to throw off such government, and to provide new guards for their future security. . . .

The history of mankind is a history of repeated injuries and usurpations on the part of man toward woman, having in direct object the establishment of an absolute tyranny over her. To prove this, let facts be submitted to a candid word. . . .

Now, in view of the entire disfranchisement of one-half the people of this country, their social and religious degradation—in view of the unjust laws above mentioned, and because women do feel themselves aggrieved, oppressed, and fraudulently deprived of their most sacred rights, we insist that they have immediate admission to all the rights and privileges which belong to them as citizens of these United States. . . .

The Emancipation Proclamation

January 1,1863

On January 1, 1863, President Abraham Lincoln issued the Emancipation Proclamation. This document freed all slaves in states under Confederate control. The Proclamation was a significant step toward the Thirteenth Amendment (1865) that ended slavery in the United States.

Whereas, on the 22nd day of September, in the year of our Lord 1862, a proclamation was issued by the President of the United States, containing, among other things, the following, to wit:

> That on the 1st day of January, in the year of our Lord 1863, all persons held as slaves within any state or designated part of a state, the people whereof shall then be in rebellion against the United States, shall be then, thenceforward, and forever free; and the executive government of the United States, including the military and naval authority thereof, will recognize and maintain the freedom of such persons and will do no act or acts to repress such persons, or any of them, in any efforts that may make for their actual freedom.
>
> That the executive will, on the 1st day January aforesaid, by proclamation, designate the states and parts of states, if any, in which the people thereof, respectively, shall then be in rebellion against the United States; and the fact that any state or the people thereof shall on that day be in good faith represented in the Congress of the United States by members chosen thereto at elections wherein a majority of the qualified voters of such states shall have participated shall, in the absence of strong countervailing testimony, be deemed conclusive evidence that such state and the people thereof are not then in rebellion against the United States.

Now, therefore, I, Abraham Lincoln, President of the United States, by virtue of the power in me vested as commander in chief of the Army and Navy of the United States, in time of actual armed rebellion against the authority and government of the United States, and as a fit and necessary war measure for suppressing said rebellion, do, on this 1st day of January, in the year of our Lord 1863, and in accordance with my purpose so to do, publicly proclaimed for the full period of 100 days from the day first above mentioned, order and designate as the states and parts of states wherein the people thereof, respectively, are this day in rebellion against the United States. . . .

And, by virtue of the power and for the purpose aforesaid, I do order and declare that all persons held as slaves within said designated states and parts of states are, and henceforward shall be, free; and that the executive government of the United States, including the military and naval authorities thereof, will recognize and maintain the freedom of said persons. . .

And upon this act, sincerely believed to be an act of justice, warranted by the Constitution upon military necessity, I invoke the considerate judgment of mankind and the gracious favor of Almighty God.

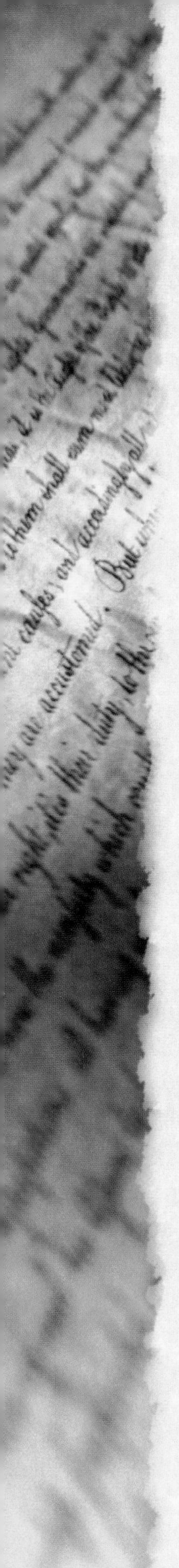

The Gettysburg Address

November 19, 1863

On November 19, 1863, President Abraham Lincoln delivered a short speech at the dedication of a national cemetery on the battlefield of Gettysburg. His simple yet eloquent words expressed his hopes for a nation divided by civil war.

Four score and seven years ago our fathers brought forth on this continent a new nation, conceived in liberty, and dedicated to the proposition that all men are created equal.

Now we are engaged in a great civil war, testing whether that nation, or any nation so conceived and so dedicated, can long endure. We are met on a great battlefield of that war. We have come to dedicate a portion of that field as a final resting place for those who here gave their lives that that nation might live. It is altogether fitting and proper that we should do this.

But, in a larger sense, we can not dedicate—we can not consecrate—we can not hallow—this ground. The brave men, living and dead, who struggled here, have consecrated it far above our poor power to add or detract. The world will little note nor long remember what we say here, but it can never forget what they did here. It is for us, the living, rather, to be dedicated here to the unfinished work which they who fought here have thus far so nobly advanced. It is rather for us to be here dedicated to the great task remaining before us—that from these honored dead we take increased devotion to that cause for which they gave us the last full measure of devotion; that we here highly resolve that these dead shall not have died in vain; that this nation, under God, shall have a new birth of freedom; and that government of the people, by the people, for the people, shall not perish from the earth.

John F. Kennedy's Inaugural Address

January 20, 1961

President Kennedy's Inaugural Address on January 20, 1961, set the tone for his administration. In his address Kennedy stirred the nation by calling for "a grand and global alliance" to fight tyranny, poverty, disease, and war.

We observe today not a victory of party but a celebration of freedom—symbolizing an end as well as a beginning—signifying renewal as well as change. For I have sworn before you and Almighty God the same solemn oath our forebears prescribed nearly a century and three-quarters ago.

The world is very different now. For man holds in his mortal hands the power to abolish all forms of human poverty and all forms of human life. And yet the same revolutionary beliefs for which our forebears fought are still at issue around the globe—the belief that the rights of man come not from the generosity of the state but from the hand of God.

We dare not forget today that we are the heirs of that first revolution. Let the word go forth from this time and place, to friend and foe alike, that the torch has been passed to a new generation of Americans—born in this century, tempered by war, disciplined by a hard and bitter peace, proud of our ancient heritage—and unwilling to witness or permit the slow undoing of those human rights to which this nation has always been committed, and to which we are committed today at home and around the world.

Let every nation know, whether it wishes us well or ill, that we shall pay any price, bear any burden, meet any hardship, support any friend, oppose any foe to assure the survival and the success of liberty.

This much we pledge—and more.

To those old allies whose cultural and spiritual origins we share, we pledge the loyalty of faithful friends. United, there is little we cannot do in a host of cooperative ventures. Divided, there is little we can do. . . .

Let us never negotiate out of fear. But let us never fear to negotiate.

Let both sides explore what problems unite us instead of belaboring those problems which divide us. . . .

Let both sides seek to invoke the wonders of science instead of its terrors. Together let us explore the stars, conquer the deserts, eradicate disease, tap the ocean depths, and encourage the arts and commerce. . . .

And so, my fellow Americans: ask not what your country can do for you—ask what you can do for your country.

My fellow citizens of the world: ask not what America will do for you, but what together we can do for the freedom of man.

Glossary/Index

Glossary terms and locations are shown in **bold type**.

C

F

H

I

O

P

Q

R

W

Y

Z

Acknowledgements

Photo Credits

American Civics and Government Photo Credits
4 ©Associated Press. U.S. Senate; 5 ©JupiterImages Corporation; 7 (tl)©Image Bank/Getty, (tr)©Associated Press, AP, (br)©Associated Press, The Times of Trenton, (bl)©Royalty-Free/CORBIS; 9 ©Comstock Images/Getty/RF; 10 ©Associated Press, AP; 11 ©Hulton-Deutsch Collection/CORBIS; 13 ©Photodisc Green/Getty RF; 15 ©Dennis Degnan/CORBIS; 16 ©Bettmann/CORBIS; 17 ©Bettmann/CORBIS; 18 ©Bettmann/CORBIS; 20 ©Bettmann/CORBIS; 21 ©North Wind Pictures Archives; 22 ©Bettmann/CORBIS; 27 ©Library of Congress; 28 ©CORBIS; 30 ©The Granger Collection, New York; 31 ©Bettmann/CORBIS; 32 ©Bettmann/CORBIS; 35 ©Bettmann/CORBIS; 36 ©Associated Press, AP; 38 ©The McGraw-Hill Companies; 39 ©Bettmann/CORBIS; 42 (r)©Photodisc Blue/Getty, (l)©Photodisc Green, (m)©The McGraw-Hill Companies; 45 ©Associated Press; 47 ©Jason Reed/Reuters/CORBIS; 79 ©CORBIS; 80 ©Getty Images; 81 ©Getty Images; 83 ©Charles E. Rotkin/CORBIS; 85 ©Associated Press; 86 ©Bettmann/CORBIS; 87 ©Bettmann/CORBIS; 88 ©Bettmann/CORBIS; 89 ©Mike Lane, Cagle Cartoons; 91 ©Owen Franken/CORBIS; 92 ©David Butow/CORBIS; 93 ©AP; 94 ©AP; 96 ©AP; 97 ©Hazir Reka/Reuters/CORBIS; 98 ©AP; 99 ©Getty Images; 101 ©Panoramic Images/Getty; 102 ©Mike Theilder/Reuters/CORBIS; 103 ©Associated Press; 104 ©Reuters/CORBIS; 107 ©Bettmann/CORBIS; 108 (t)©Bettmann/CORBIS, (b)©Democratic National Committee; 109 (t)©Larry Downing/Reuters/CORBIS, (b)©Reuters/CORBIS; 110 (b)©Associated Press, (t)©Associated Press; 111 ©Brooks Kraft/CORBIS; 112 ©Associated Press; 113 (t)©Getty Images News, (b)©Associated Press; 114 ©Micah Walter/Reuters/CORBIS; 115 ©Photodisc Red/Getty/RF; 117 ©Associated Press; 118 ©AFP/Getty Images; 119 ©Charles O'Rear/CORBIS; 122 (t)©Bettmann/CORBIS, (b)©Associated Press; 125 ©Kat Wade/San Francisco; 126 ©Wally McNamee/CORBIS; 128 (t)©Associated Press, (b)©Jason Reed/Reuters/CORBIS; 129 ©Associated Press; 130 ©Associated Press; 131 ©Bettmann/CORBIS; 132 ©John Trevor; 133 ©Getty Images News; 134 ©Associated Press; 135 ©www.ca.gov; 137 ©Courtesy of the U.S. Government Printing Office; 139 ©Shaun Heasley/Reuters/CORBIS; 141 ©Associated Press; 143 (t)©Reuters/CORBIS, (b)©AFP/Getty Images; 144 (t)©Micah Walter/GNS/CORBIS, (b)©Getty Images News; 145 ©Associated Press; 146 ©Aaron Horowitz/CORBIS; 147 ©Associated Press; 148 ©Associated Press; 152 ©The McGraw-Hill Companies; 153 ©Hulton Archive/Getty; 154 ©Roger Ressmeyer/CORBIS; 156 (t)©Associated Press, (b)©Wally MaNamee/CORBIS; 157 ©Associated Press; 158 ©CORBIS; 160 ©Associated Press, ©Getty Images News, ©Associated Press, ©CORBIS; 162 ©Photodisc Green/Royalty Free/Getty; 163 (t)©Tim Thompson/CORBIS, (b)©Zack Seckler/CORBIS; 166 ©Reuters/CORBIS; 167 ©Associated Press; 169 ©Reuters/CORBIS; 170 ©Associated Press; 172 ©Associated Press; 173 ©Bettmann/CORBIS; 174 ©Osservatore Romano/Pool/Reuters/CORBIS; 175 (t)©Bettmann/CORBIS, (b)©Brooks Kraft/CORBIS, (m)©AP; 179 ©Associated Press; 180 ©Ralf-Finn Hestoft/CORBIS; 181 ©Bettmann/CORBIS; 182 ©AP; 184 ©Jim Sugar/CORBIS; 188 ©Associated Press; 189 ©Associated Press; 192 ©CORBIS; 193 (t)©Associated Press, (l)©Paul. A. Souders/CORBIS, (r)©Reuters/CORBIS; 194 ©www.osc.gov; 197 ©Bettmann/CORBIS; 198 ©Downing Larry/CORBIS Sygma; 201 ©www.opm.gov; 203 ©Taxi/Getty; 204 ©Rick Friedman/CORBIS; 205 ©Newsday/TMS Reprints; 208 ©Bettmann/CORBIS, ©Brooks Kraft/CORBIS, ©Bettmann/CORBIS; 209 ©www.gpo.gov; 211 ©Royalty-Free/CORBIS; 213 ©Bettmann/CORBIS; 214 ©Stone/Getty Images; 216 ©Reuters/CORBIS; 217 ©CORBIS; 218 (t)©Reuters/CORBIS, (r)©Cartoon Feature Syndicate, (b)©Najlah Feanny/CORBIS; 219 ©Getty Images; 220 ©AP; 221 (l)©www.wickimedia.org, (r)©Alan Schein Photography/CORBIS; 222 (t)©The New Yorker Collection 1992 J.B. Handelsman from cartoonbank.com, (b)©Markowitz Jeffrey/CORBIS Sygma; 224 ©Franklin Delano Roosevelt Library; 226 ©Kim Kulish/CORBIS; 228 ©Associated Press; 229 ©North Wind Picture Archives; 230 ©Ariel Skelley/CORBIS; 232 ©Bettmann/CORBIS; 233 (tl)©Digital Vision/Getty, (bl)©The McGraw-Hill Library, (tr)©The McGraw-Hill Library, (br)©The McGraw-Hill Library; 234 ©Ed Kashi/CORBIS; 235 ©Stone/Getty; 238 ©Digital Vision/Getty; 240 ©The McGraw-Hill Companies; 242 (t)©Bettmann/CORBIS, (b)©Bettmann/CORBIS; 244 ©AP; 246 (t)©Henry Ray Abrams/Reuters/CORBIS, (b)©AP; 247 (t)©Bettmann/CORBIS, (b)©The McGraw-Hill Companies; 248 ©AP; 252 (b)©Daemmrich Bob, (t)©Daemmrich Bob; 253 ©Daemmrich Bob/CORBIS Sygma; 254 ©AP; 256 (tl)©AP, (bl)©Bettmann/CORBIS, (tr)©Flip Schulke/CORBIS, (br)©Reuters/CORBIS; 258 ©Photodisc Red/Getty; 259 ©Najlah Feanny/CORBIS SABA; 260 ©Philip Gould/CORBIS; 261 ©Stone/Getty; 262 ©Aurora/Getty; 263 ©AP; 265 ©Bettmann/CORBIS; 266 (t)©Ramin Talaie/CORBIS, (b)©Christophe Calais/ In Visu/CORBIS; 267 ©AP; 268 ©AP; 269 ©David Butow/CORBIS Saba; 271 ©Barbara Davidson/Dallas Morning News/CORBIS; 272 (l)©Rick Friedman, (r)©Rick Wilking/Reuters/CORBIS; 273 ©Stone/Getty; 274 (t)©AP, (b)©AP; 275 ©Origlia Franco/CORBIS Sygma; 276 ©Wally McNamee/CORBIS; 278 ©Bettmann/CORBIS; 279 (t)©Bettmann/CORBIS, (b)©Bettmann/CORBIS; 280 ©CORBIS; 282 ©Bettmann/CORBIS; 283 ©Reportage/Getty; 284 (t)©www.mcmanudemocrats.com, (b)©Bettmann/CORBIS; 287 ©Brian Snyder/Reuters/CORBIS; 288 ©Robert Maass/CORBIS; 289 (t)©Erich Schlegel/Dallas Morning News/CORBIS, (b)©Ross Frank/CORBIS Sygma; 290 ©AP; 291 ©AP; 292 ©Robert Galbraith/Reuters/CORBIS; 293 ©Kevin P. Casey/CORBIS; 294 ©Jeff Parker; 295 ©AP; 298 (t)©The Granger Collection, (m)©Underwood & Underwood/CORBIS, (b)©AP; 300 ©Bettmann/CORBIS; 301 ©Cartoon Stock; 302 ©Kenneth James/CORBIS; 303 ©AFP/Getty Images; 305 ©www.cartoonstock.com; 306 © AP; 308 ©AP; 309 ©AP; 310 (t)©Bettmann/CORBIS, (m)©Mark E. Gibson/CORBIS, (b)©Katy Winn/CORBIS; 311 ©RJ Matson; 312 ©Michah Walter/Reuters/CORBIS; 313 ©AP; 315 ©Mike Lester; 316 ©Brian Snyder/CORBIS; 318 ©Jim Ruyman/Reuters/CORBIS; 321 ©Bettmann/CORBIS; 322 (t)©Reuters/CORBIS, (b)©AP; 325 ©The McGraw-Hill Companies; 332 ©AP; 333 ©AP; 334 ©Handout/Reuters/CORBIS; 336 ©CORBIS; 337 ©Joseph Sohm/ChromoSohm Inc./CORBIS; 338 (b)©James L. Amos/CORBIS, (t)©AP; 339 ©Photonica/Getty; 341 ©Paul Morse-White House/CNP/CORBIS; 343 ©Jim Sugar/CORBIS; 344 ©Bettmann/CORBIS; 345 ©AP; 346 ©Najlah Feanny/CORBIS Sygma; 347 ©CORBIS; 348 (t)©JA Giordano/CORBIS Saba, (b)©Greg Smith/CORBIS; 349 ©Photodisc Green/Getty; 350 ©Bettmann/CORBIS; 352 ©Joel Stettenheim/CORBIS; 353 (t)©Alison Wright/CORBIS, (b)©AP; 354 ©Bettmann/CORBIS; 356 ©Iconica/Getty; 357 ©Frank Polich/Reuters/CORBIS; 358 ©Tim Wright/CORBIS; 360 ©Getty Images; 362 ©Kevin Lamarque/Reuters/CORBIS; 364 ©AP; 366 ©Bettmann/CORBIS; 367 ©Wally McNamee/CORBIS; 368 ©Reuters/CORBIS; 369 ©AFP Getty Images; 370 ©Getty Images; 372 ©Bettmann/CORBIS; 373 (t)©AP, (b)©Time Life Pictures/Getty Images; 374 ©Handout/Gerald Bourke/Reuters/CORBIS; 375 ©AP; 376 ©Stone; 377 ©Darrell Gulin/CORBIS; 380 ©AP; 383 ©Cartoonstock; 384 ©AP; 385 ©AP; 389 ©AP; 391 ©Getty Images; 393 ©David G. Houser/CORBIS; 394 ©Erich Schlegel/Dallas Morning News/CORBIS; 395 ©Stone; 396 ©AP; 397 ©AP; 399 ©Buddy Mays/CORBIS; 402 ©Richard Cummins/CORBIS; 403 ©Franz-Marc Frei/CORBIS; 408 ©AP; 409 ©AP; 410 ©AP; 412 (t)©Time Life Pictures/Getty Images, (b)©Getty Images; 413 ©Douglas Kirkland/CORBIS; 416 ©K. Hackenberg/zefa/CORBIS; 417 ©Ron Sachs/CNP/CORBIS; 418 ©Reuters/CORBIS; 419 ©Reuters/CORBIS; 420 ©Peter Turnley/CORBIS; 421 ©Victoria Valiterra/Clasos/CORBIS Sygma; 424 ©Liu Liqun/CORBIS; 425 (t)©Bettmann/CORBIS, (b)©Rafael Perez/Reuters/CORBIS; 426 (t)©Reuters/CORBIS, (b)©Gerald Bourke/World Food Programme/Reuters/CORBIS; 427 ©Erik deCatro/Reuters/CORBIS; 428 ©AP; 430 ©Reuters/CORBIS; 431 ©Lynsey Addario/CORBIS, ©AP; 432 ©Bettmann/CORBIS; 433 ©Herwig Prammer/Reuters/CORBIS; 436 ©Tom Wagner/CORBIS Saba; 438 (t)©Gail Mooney/CORBIS, (b)©Jon Feingersh/zefa/CORBIS; 439 ©Henry Diltz/CORBIS; 440 ©Martin Jones; 442 ©Pablo Corral V/CORBIS; 443 (t)©Gilbert Liz/CORBIS Sygma, (b)©Peter Turnley/CORBIS; 444 (t)©Owen Franken/CORBIS, (b)©Radu Sigheti/Reuters/CORBIS; 445 ©Marc Garanger/CORBIS; 446 ©Bettmann/CORBIS; 447 ©Shepard Sherbell/CORBIS Saba; 448 ©Jon Hicks/CORBIS; 449 ©Macduff Everton/CORBIS; 450 ©Owak/Kulla/CORBIS; 452 (t)©Gustavo Gilabert/CORBIS Saba, (b)©David Turnley/CORBIS

Acknowledgements for Primary Sources are found at the bottom of each Primary Source page.

The editor has made every effort to trace ownership of all copyrighted material and to secure the necessary permissions. Should there be a question regarding the use of any material, regret is hereby expressed for such error. Upon notification of any such oversight, proper acknowledgement will be made in future editions.

(t) top, (b) bottom, (m) middle, (l) left, (r) right

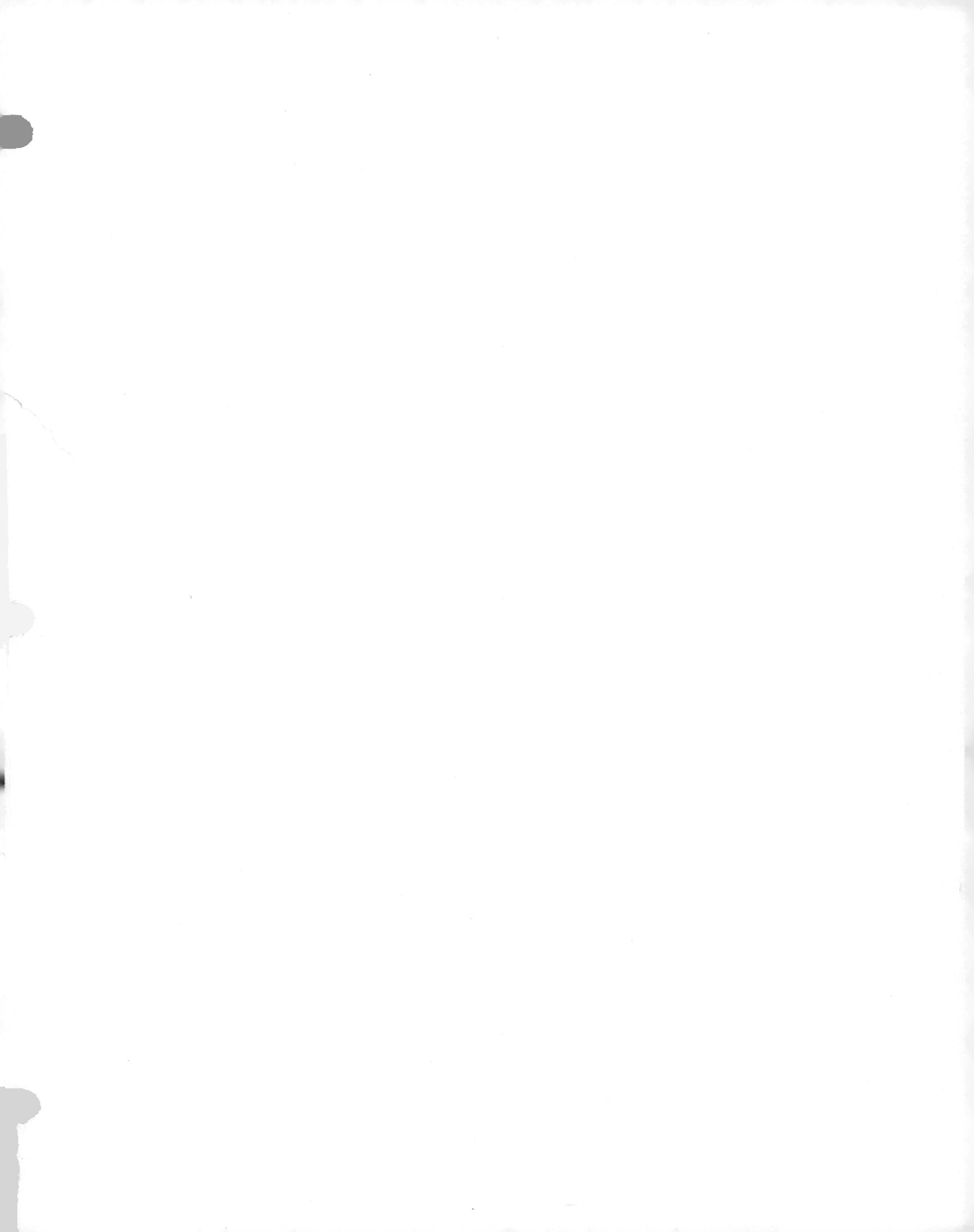